❊ CONQUERED ❊

CIVIL WAR AMERICA

Peter S. Carmichael, Caroline E. Janney,

and Aaron Sheehan-Dean, editors

This landmark series interprets broadly the history and culture

of the Civil War era through the long nineteenth century and beyond.

Drawing on diverse approaches and methods, the series publishes historical

works that explore all aspects of the war, biographies of leading commanders,

and tactical and campaign studies, along with select editions of primary

sources. Together, these books shed new light on an era that remains

central to our understanding of American and world history.

CONQUERED

WHY THE ARMY OF THE TENNESSEE FAILED

Larry J. Daniel

THE UNIVERSITY OF NORTH CAROLINA PRESS

Chapel Hill

Set in Bulmer, Egiziano, and Madrone types
by Tseng Information Systems, Inc.
Manufactured in the United States of America

The University of North Carolina Press has been a
member of the Green Press Initiative since 2003.

Cover illustration: *Battle of Franklin, November 30, 1864*
(Chicago: Kurz & Allison, Art Publishers, 1891)

Library of Congress Cataloging-in-Publication Data
Names: Daniel, Larry J., 1947– author.
Title: Conquered : why the Army of the Tennessee failed / Larry J. Daniel.
Other titles: Civil War America (Series)
Description: Chapel Hill : University of North Carolina Press, [2019] |
Series: Civil War America | Includes bibliographical references and index.
Identifiers: LCCN 2018049280 | ISBN 9781469649504 (cloth : alk. paper) |
ISBN 9781469649511 (ebook)
Subjects: LCSH: Confederate States of America. Army of Tennessee—History. |
United States—History—Civil War, 1861–1865—Campaigns. | United States—
History—Civil War, 1861–1865—Regimental histories.
Classification: LCC E470.5 .D3547 2019 | DDC 973.7/468—dc23
LC record available at https://lccn.loc.gov/2018049280

*For Jennifer
and in memory of departed members of the
Historians of the Civil War Western Theater,
Grady McWhiney, Albert Castel, Nat Hughes,
Wiley Sword, and Michael Ballard*

CONTENTS

FIGURES, MAPS, & TABLES

PREFACE

In 1941, Stanley F. Horn wrote his book *The Army of Tennessee*. It proved to be an excellent introduction, and when I encountered the book as a teen, its subject captivated me. Since Horn used no manuscript material, however, the scope proved limited. In 1967 and 1971, Thomas L. Connelly completed his epic two-volume history of the Army of Tennessee: *Army of the Heartland* and *Autumn of Glory*. Connelly became the father of what, for Civil War historians, is known as western revisionism, elevating the role of the theater in the history of the conflict. So monumental were his works that even to this day they represent the starting point for any serious student of the western Confederacy. Why, then, another book on the Army of Tennessee? Connelly's purpose was to do for the western army what Douglas Southall Freeman had done for Robert E. Lee's Army of Northern Virginia a generation earlier—provide a command-level study. The army is thus viewed from the perspective of a top-down military approach.

Fifty years have come and gone since Connelly's two volumes appeared. It was thus time for a reexamination. Needless to say, many new sources and interpretations have come to light in the ensuing decades. I did not intend this volume to be an extension of Connelly's work; it is designed to view the army as an institution. To further distinguish my work from Connelly's, I avoided a straight narrative approach. I instead partially adapted the topical and narrative approach of Joseph Glatthaar's *General Lee's Army*, which I used as a model. Readers will find that I did not spend an inordinate amount of time rehashing standard battlefield narratives. Since 1971, a half dozen books have been published on the Battle of Shiloh alone, and David Powell recently competed his iconic three-volume study of the Battle of Chickamauga. I thus attempted to insert the latest scholarship and interpretations that have emerged. While I deal with grand strategy and operational movements, my intent was to go beyond the battlefield to examine the army's social history in a war-and-society approach. In order to explore new dimensions and balance the argument—and to keep this book to a single volume—I had to make choices.

The title of the book, *Conquered*, reflects the end of the story. The book itself addresses two questions. First, why did the army come to defeat? Since the Army of Northern Virginia won most of its battles and the Army of Tennessee lost most of its battles, the causes of western Confederate defeat must be distinctive. Connelly's answer was inept leadership and the constant infighting among the generals. He thus saw defeat in terms of personalities rather than competing influences. While personalities unquestionably played a role, many underappreciated factors also affected the Army of Tennessee's ultimate fate. Sectionalism retarded the army's unity. Geographic challenges posed by the region's rivers defied both tactical and political solutions. The army faced diminishing manpower, a declining cavalry corps, and an ill-trained officer corps, especially at the field level. There were also logistical handicaps and a lack of mobility, the destructive political policies of President Jefferson Davis, the intrinsic strategic connection between Mississippi and Tennessee, and Kentucky's feeble response to the Cause.

I do agree with established theory that, for the Confederates, the war was lost on the battlefield. Yet, many cumulative effects of the above handicaps unquestionably weakened and demoralized the army. Defeat in the West cannot thus be seen entirely through the prism of inept generals. If Lee's army came to symbolize what Glatthaar termed "the vitality of the Confederate States," then the Army of Tennessee came to represent the frailty of the Confederacy. Glatthaar concluded that the defeat of the Army of Northern Virginia was not caused by industry, culture, the manpower shortage, or slavery but rather by "intense and sustained Union pressure [that] caused serious fissures in all these areas." The demise of the Army of Tennessee likewise did not come exclusively from internal army factors. Outside influences — Northern policy and leadership and the breakdown of the Southern home front — also played a role.[1]

In light of so many shortcomings, why then did it take the better-equipped, supposedly better-led, and larger Union Army of the Cumberland so long to neutralize its opponent? The answer to that question, beyond inept leadership, which was not confined to the Confederates, is also multidimensional. It revolves around a web of interconnected factors such as the brotherhood of the Confederate soldiery; religious revivals, which not only shielded the men from the stresses of war but also emphasized God's providential blessing over the army; and in the fog of war, a zealous belief that, even as late as 1864, the war was still quite winnable.

If Thomas Connelly was the father of western revisionism, Richard McMurry, more than any historian, developed a succinct western theater thesis that the war stalemated in the East and was decided in the West. The

Confederates lost the military phase of the war, McMurry concluded, and those battles took place in the West. To be sure, there were counterattacks from eastern historians who insisted that the Virginia front was paramount, but the Virginia dominance of Civil War historiography has been seriously challenged.[2]

No manuscript can be completed without the encouragement, advice, and corrections of other scholars. My deep appreciation goes to Steven Woodworth and Timothy Smith for plowing through some of the early chapters of the manuscript and to Richard McMurry for reading a large number of the chapters. They are all veteran authors and friends. Earl Hess graciously sent me the advance galley of his now published book *The Battle of Peachtree Creek* to aid me in my research. Anyone doing research at the Stones River and Chickamauga National Battlefield Parks will encounter Jim Lewis and Jim Ogden, both of whom know their subject better than anyone and are always willing to cooperate. As a member of the Historians of the Civil War Western Theater, I also bounced ideas off several of my colleagues, including Wiley Sword, Dave Powell, and Sam Elliott. My deep appreciation also goes to Bob Jenkins for clarifying some of the North Georgia mysteries.

❖ CONQUERED ❖

❋ **1** ❋

Flawed Foundations
The Provisional Army of Tennessee

The beginning of the Army of Tennessee was the Tennessee state army, the so-called Provisional Army of Tennessee, under the titular leadership of Governor Isham G. Harris. It was the state army that became the genesis of the Confederate army. From its inception, there were cracks in the foundation.

Political clout, slave power, and personal friendship to the governor became the typical gateways to a military commission. Desiring to reach beyond his Democratic base and cultivate the proslavery Whigs, Harris gave the two major general appointments to Democrats, but four of the five brigadier commissions went to Whigs. The appointments of the major generals—Gideon Pillow of Memphis and Samuel R. Anderson of Nashville—did not come as a surprise. Pillow, a two-time vice-presidential aspirant, Mexican War veteran, large slaveholder, and ardent secessionist, had an eight-year association with Harris. He unquestionably had a dark side, being jealous, egotistical, and vengeful. Anderson was the fifty-seven-year-old president of the Bank of Tennessee. He had combat experience, having served as lieutenant colonel of the 1st Tennessee during the Mexican War.[1]

The five brigadiers included Benjamin F. Cheatham, the foul-mouthed, hard-drinking proprietor of the Nashville Race Track; sixty-five-year-old Robert C. Foster, a Franklin attorney, longtime member of the Tennessee General Assembly, and veteran of the Mexican War; forty-one-year-old state attorney general John L. Sneed; an old friend of Pillow's, William R. Caswell of East Tennessee, who, like Sneed, was a captain in the 1st Tennessee cavalry during the Mexican War; and Felix Zollicoffer, a former U.S. senator and Nashville newspaper editor. The Confederate government subsequently granted brigadier commissions to Pillow and Anderson but only reluctantly granted commissions to Cheatham and Zollicoffer.[2]

In his efforts at political inclusiveness, Harris had snubbed West Pointers, granting them only support positions. Daniel Donelson became adjutant general; Bushrod Johnson, chief engineer; John P. McCown, A. P. Stewart, and Melton A. Hayes headed the fledgling artillery corps; and Richard G.

Fain, who had quit the army upon graduation to become a Nashville merchant, became commissary general. Twenty-five-year-old Capt. Moses H. Wright, who had previously served at the Watervliet and St. Louis Arsenals, would lead the Ordnance Bureau. Only McCown and Johnson had any combat experience. McCown had no connection to Harris (he would grow to detest him) and had gone through an embarrassing court-martial incident. Marshall Polk, another West Pointer, commanded a Memphis battery. Five other Tennessee West Pointers — John Adams, Henry Davidson, William H. Jackson, James A. Smith, and Lawrence Peck — had not resigned their U.S. commissions at the time of the state army formation. Andrew Jackson III, grandson of Andrew Jackson, joined the Confederate army before the firing on Fort Sumter. Donelson, the most senior of the West Pointers, had served in the Regular Army only six months before resigning his commission.[3]

Several of Harris's appointments went to civilians with little or no military background. Forty-nine-year-old Vernon K. Stevenson, founder of the Nashville & Chattanooga Railroad, became quartermaster general. The job dealt with contracts and finances, so the appointment seemed reasonable. There may have been another reason: Stevenson was widely rumored to be a possible Democratic candidate for governor in the fall, and Harris may have wished to clear the field for his second run. Also in the Quartermaster Department was George W. Cunningham, a forty-year-old Warren County merchant. Dr. Benjamin W. Avent, a highly respected forty-eight-year-old Murfreesboro physician, was tapped as the army's medical director. William H. Carroll, the Nashville postmaster general and son of a former governor, became inspector general. Those who knew him dismissed him as a stupid drunkard who could be easily controlled.[4]

Politics and position influenced the top appointments, but Tennessee simply lacked the military tradition of Virginia. Of the West Pointers in the state army, only two would distinguish themselves in the Army of Tennessee — Johnson and Stewart. Perhaps even more serious was the fact that there was an even greater dearth of professionally trained officers at the level of colonel. Of the 135 men who would rise to the rank of colonel in Tennessee, excluding Andrew Jackson III, none had attended West Point and only four had graduated from private military academies. In comparison, sixteen West Pointers served as Virginia colonels, fifty-seven from the Virginia Military Institute, two from the U.S. Naval Academy, and seven from private military academies. Even the Virginia Military Institute graduates living in Tennessee proved to be a remarkably undistinguished lot. Eight of the Tennessee colonels had backgrounds in the militia, which were worth little, and nineteen had combat experience in the Mexican or Seminole War. Wealth and prominence served as the basis for the appointments of most of the Tennessee colonels—there were nine physicians and forty lawyers.[5]

The provisional army was also logistically handicapped. Initially, the state arsenal housed only 8,761 arms, almost all old flintlocks. Practically speaking, the entire lot proved worthless, at least until the arms could be altered to percussion. In late April 1861, Louisiana governor Thomas O. Moore shipped to Memphis 3,000 arms and 300,000 rounds of ammunition, all from the captured U.S. arsenal at Baton Rouge. The governors of Mississippi and Arkansas also offered sixteen old field guns. Additional boxes of ammunition arrived from Baton Rouge, followed by two carloads of small arms from Richmond, Virginia. In May, the Confederate secretary of war, LeRoy Walker, released 4,000 muskets to Tennessee, but there were strings attached; they could only be issued to regiments joining the Confederate service. Already three such regiments had been transferred to Virginia. Harris pleaded with Walker to relax the policy but to no avail. Pillow subsequently stopped 3,000 flintlock muskets passing through Memphis on the way to Mobile, Alabama. The general's alarmist language convinced Walker to issue 1,200 of the lot to Tennessee troops. By state count, there were 5,000 percussion muskets in Memphis and 3,000 in Nashville by May 12. Authorities encouraged volunteers to show up with hunting rifles and shotguns. Although the press boasted that 75,000 such firearms existed, officials estimated that only 4,000 could be gathered. Pillow claimed that he could put 25,000 men in the field if he could only arm them.[6]

The men were trained in camps of instruction, such as Camp Brown at Union City and Camp Trousdale in Middle Tennessee, four miles from the Kentucky border. Small until drills occurred, but camp social life seemed to be the order of the day. James Hall, writing from Camp Brown, told his wife, "We see ladies and little girls in camp every day, who come to see the soldiers." "H," also at Union City, described it thus: "We are having a gay time of it here. We are visited every day by the ladies of the neighborhood, and also by the ladies of Jackson, Tennessee." U. G. Owens wrote similarly: "Several big dances every night, great excitement all the time, amusement of every kind on earth you could think of. Great many ladies visit us from the country dance etc." At Camp Trousdale, John Goodner declared, "We have a great many lady visitors here every day from all of the towns around the adjoining counties."[7]

The soldiers, itching for a fight, remained mystified why, for months, nothing happened. The bugler of the 154th Tennessee, camped at Randolph, was told to practice the call for a general alarm. Through a misunderstanding, he sounded the alarm in camp. Rumors quickly spread that enemy gunboats were approaching. "The camp was in a blaze of excitement and the soldiers panted for the opportunity to display their valor." Writing from Camp Trousdale, Matthew Buchanan candidly remarked, "I wish we had the thing over & had arms and orders to pitch into the Yankees."[8]

William H. Russell, a war correspondent for the *London Times*, viewed some of the fortifications along the Mississippi River during the summer. While some regiments, such as the 154th Tennessee, had uniforms and firm discipline, others were ill clad and simply lay around camp. The officers, mostly lawyers, merchants, and planters, were entirely ignorant of drill. Russell noticed that the men awkwardly handled their muskets; indeed, many carried only sticks. When one of the heavy artillery pieces was test-fired, it leaped off the carriage, leaving Russell to believe that it was safer being near the target than on the gun crew. When 800 men lined up for inspection, Pillow offered a brief speech on courage. A staff officer shouted, "Boys, three cheers for General Pillow." One wag shouted back, "Who cares for General Pillow?"[9]

Discipline continued to be a problem. In Polk's Tennessee Battery, a man by the name of Holman kept skipping roll call. The captain warned him several times but to no avail. When he missed again, Holman was ordered to mark time for an hour. "He seemed surly," Captain Polk told his wife. "I ordered my guard to charge bayonets. One of them hesitated. I sprang up saber in hand, not drawn, told him that this was no child's play we were engaged in and ordered him to bring down his gun. He obeyed; I then told Holman to mark time, which he did. The men of Douglas' regiment [9th Tennessee] collected outside my sentinels & I saw trouble was brewing. Merely wishing to make an example I had intended to let the man off as soon as he obeyed[;] but seeing them and hearing their remarks I determined he should mark his sixty minutes or die." Polk's officers and men stood by him while he remained seated with pistol concealed, fully intending to shoot the first man who crossed his line. A colonel and several captains came up and dispersed the mob. The men grumbled loudly about the captain, some of them claiming that he treated them "like they were negroes." Cheatham threatened to call out the entire brigade if the 9th continued its rebellion.[10]

It did not take long for sickness, mostly measles and diarrhea, to ravage the camps. The lack of preparedness and supplies became apparent. A report in the *Tennessee Baptist* criticized the makeshift arrangement of a Nashville hospital. The cots were so jammed together that it proved almost impossible to walk between them. The reporter wondered if generals or colonels would be allowed to lie unattended in such filth. One patient noted: "There were several of us together, and all the bunks being occupied, we had to sleep on the floor by the stove. There were 250 men in that room, their bunks all arranged in rows. A chill ran over me at seeing so many pale faces by gas-light."[11]

In the early days of its formation, the Army of Tennessee was thus crippled in leadership, preparedness, and discipline. The lack of professional officers and noncommissioned officers resulted in inadequately trained troops, looser organization, and lax administration, all of which resulted in a less pronounced discipline. The army would eventually emerge from these baked-in flaws, but it would take time.[12]

The Influence of Sectionalism

The army soon grew beyond the original Tennessee core. Richard McMurry recognized that the Army of Tennessee was more western than the Army of Northern Virginia was eastern. In late 1862 (based on battalions, batteries, and regiments), Robert E. Lee's army counted 61.6 percent of its men from eastern states, 19.5 percent from central states (Georgia and Florida), and 17.6 percent from western states. The lack of an eastern presence, specifically Virginians, robbed the Army of Tennessee of the "mythical aura" of Virginia, and thus affected morale, argued McMurry. When categorizing is done by the actual number of infantry present, however, rather than the number of units (which varied widely), the difference is even more stark. In March 1863, the state-by-state breakdown of the Army of Tennessee's infantry was as follows: western, 90 percent; central, 6 percent; and eastern, 4 percent.[13]

A "more western" army, though on the surface more homogeneous, did not equate to more harmonious. The western theater, that expanse between the Appalachians and the Mississippi River, was divided into three major sections—the Upper South, the Lower South, and the Highlands. Precisely why soldiers had trouble identifying with troops from other sections was complicated. According to a Nashville paper, it was partially grounded in the "petty bigotry and partisan vindictiveness" of politics. Mark Weitz claimed that the South was dominated by localism. Different regions meant different geography and climate, which meant different crops (cotton versus food production), which in turn meant different means of subsistence, which resulted in variant lifestyles and cultures.[14] Sectionalism, especially between the Upper South and Lower South, was grounded in antebellum society and the population distribution of slavery.

Lower South states, the so-called cotton states, had been among the original seven seceding states, whereas Upper South states had shown a more conservative reluctance toward secession. A perception, untrue to be sure, emerged that Lower Southerners represented the cotton aristocracy, while

TABLE 1. *Population distribution of slavery in the South*

State	Slaves	Whites	% of slave owners	% of slaves to population
Tennessee	275,719	834,082	25	25
Arkansas	11,115	324,335	20	3
Mississippi	436,631	354,674	45	55
Alabama	435,080	529,121	35	45

Upper Southerners were undisciplined, knife-toting backwoodsmen, less loyal to the Cause. To be sure, the Upper South was far from a cavalier, planter society. Political differences per se in the Army of Tennessee did not revolve around party politics but rather commitment to secession. Tennessee and Kentucky had supported the moderate Constitutional Union Party in the 1860 election. Lower South troops thus cast a suspicious eye on the latecomers to secession.

The question of the commitment of Upper South soldiers came into play at the fall of Fort Donelson in February 1862. Some 10 percent of the Southern captives, 1,640, took the oath of allegiance shortly after arriving in the North. The overwhelming majority of these came from the Upper South. Indeed, the majority came from four regiments: the 18th Tennessee, with 529; the 30th Tennessee, 651; the 51st Tennessee, 138; and the 15th Arkansas, 167. This is compared to thirty-one who took the oath from eight different Mississippi and Alabama regiments combined. The Northern commission concluded, "The prisoners of war from Tennessee appeared to be true and earnest in their desire to become loyal citizens." Surprisingly, the Tennessee prisoners did not originate from the loyalist eastern section but rather from Middle and West Tennessee. The incident raised the question of the commitment of Upper South troops. Indeed, a Baton Rouge paper began to question whether Tennessee was inclined to pull its own weight.[15]

The internal tension between the Upper South and the Lower South became evident at Corinth, Mississippi, in the spring of 1862. "I thought my Mobile Army was a *Mob*, but it is far superior to Polk's and [Albert Sidney] Johnston's as the one in Pensacola was to ours," Braxton Bragg remarked to his wife. The lack of compatibility extended to the troops. Col. Andrew Blythe begged to get his Mississippi regiment out of a Tennessee brigade, or "this Irish association," as he labeled it. The members of the 11th Louisiana also chafed at being "lashed on the tail of a Tennessee rabble — for those with whom we are placed are little better."[16]

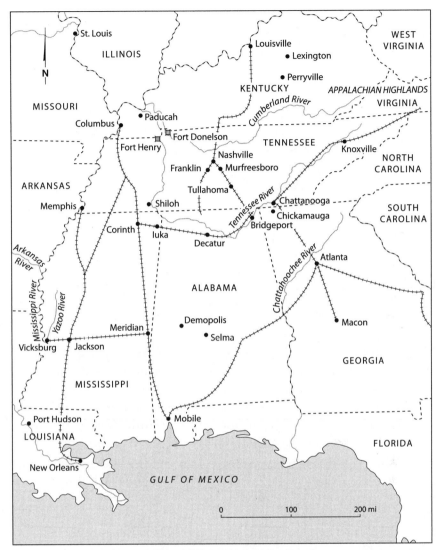

Map 1. The western theater

Such condescending comments might be dismissed as early state pride snobbishness that would soon disappear, but such was not the case. So deep was the sectional divide that negative remarks continued throughout 1863. During the Kentucky Campaign, a member of the 7th Mississippi observed that in Tennessee the "people are different." He later added that everyone in Tennessee appeared to be "a Union man." In January 1863, J. Morgan Smith of the 32nd Alabama pointedly commented, "I hate the state [Tennes-

TABLE 2.

State-by-state breakdown of troops in the Army of Tennessee

State	Number of troops
Western	
Arkansas	3,720
Tennessee	10,317
Louisiana	1,111
Kentucky	985
Alabama	5,773
Mississippi	4,009
Central	
Georgia	923
Florida	910
Eastern	
North Carolina	700
South Carolina	660

see], the institutions and the people and really feel as if I am fighting for the Yankee side when I raise my arm in defense of Tennessee soil." He further wrote of "alienation between the troops of the Gulf and the Border States that may grow into something serious." Kentuckians reciprocated, noting that they were no longer fighting for their state but rather for "a handful of Alabama and Mississippi cotton planters." One contemporary observer noted that the brigades of the Army of Tennessee had been organized by state in order to create a sense of esprit and local pride. Yet, the organization had the opposite effect, dividing the army into cliques that produced "feelings of bitterness, envy, malice, and hatred." The animosity between the Tennesseans and Mississippians was particularly noticeable, the observer claimed, while a similar feeling existed between the Arkansans and Alabamians. Nurse Kate Cummings noticed: "We have a number of Louisianans [in the hospital]. . . . Like all from that state they are very clannish."[17]

The problem of the existing sectional divide was exacerbated by President Davis, who devised a policy of dividing territory into departments, each with its own mission and commander. Although department lines changed many times during the war, in the West they initially fell into Department No. 2 (Upper South) and Department No. 1 (Lower South). After July 1862, Department No. 1 and the Alabama–West Florida Department were merged with Department No. 2 to form the huge Western Department. This merger included Lt. Gen. John C. Pemberton's Department of Mississippi and East Louisiana. While the departments gave a semblance of structure, they also broadly conformed to the existing sectional and cultural divides of the West.[18]

These departmental/sectional divides formed the genesis of many of the cliques and factions that developed in the Army of Tennessee. When Braxton Bragg assumed army command in the summer of 1862, his primary support bloc came from the Department No. 1/Lower South region. Several of the pro-Bragg generals—Patton Anderson and Jones Withers in the infantry and Joseph Wheeler in the cavalry—began their association with him while serving in the Army of Pensacola. Likewise, the anti-Bragg bloc found its base largely in Department No. 2/Upper South generals—Benjamin Cheatham, John McCown, and Nathan Bedford Forrest of Tennessee, Patrick Cleburne of Arkansas, and John C. Breckinridge and William Preston of Kentucky. There were, of course, nuances and crossovers—Daniel Adams, Randall Gibson, and Leonidas Polk, all Louisianans, fell into the anti faction.

The Highland influence in the army, though not extensive, proved to be yet another factor in the sectional divide. By January 1864, the army counted at least a dozen infantry regiments from the Appalachian region—one from Alabama, seven from Tennessee, and four from Georgia. These troops had their own unique culture and war aims. McCown, an East Tennessean, once blurted that the Confederacy was nothing more than "a damned stinking cotton oligarchy, gotten up for the benefit of Isham G. Harris and Jeff Davis and their damned corrupt cliques." The less-than-enthusiastic support of the Highlanders revealed that many agreed with that sentiment. Keith S. Hebert's study of Bartow County, Georgia, an upper central county, revealed three subregions. Of the 940 men from the county who enlisted in 1861, 89 percent came from the two planter regions. The Appalachian hill country portion gave only 15 percent. Fannin County, an isolated mountain region near the Tennessee border, offered little support for the Confederacy. Hebert concluded that the mountain regions either opposed the Confederacy or were ambivalent.[19]

While troops from the Upper and Lower South had a pique with one another, they united in their disdain of the mountain people. They saw them as dirty, Union-supporting, and unbelievably low-class people, and the women were ugly to boot. As the army passed through East Tennessee, Alabamian James Searcy noted that "the people look fit only for the rocks." The women he denounced as "still worse, such people as you would suppose traitors to be made of." A member of the 48th Tennessee, on a foraging expedition in October 1863, expressed dismay at the poverty he witnessed in the East Tennessee mountains. "They are some of the poorest people in this country that I ever saw anywhere. I stop at places just to see how they live. Some places there are no chairs others only one or two broken ones and other furniture in proportion. The children (of which there are generally plenty) are often very ragged and dirty, and taking it altogether they are the most degraded ignorant people I ever met with. It is true indeed that one-half of the world does not know how the other lives."[20]

Todd Groce's study of the mountain Rebels of East Tennessee revealed a culture that exhibited a tenuous commitment to Southern independence. After the January 1862 Confederate defeat at Mill Springs, Kentucky, Southern recruitment declined. Ultimately, no more than 25,000 East Tennesseans served in the Confederate army, representing only 13.4 percent of the population, and 20 percent of them were conscripts. With desertion a constant problem, many East Tennessee units were transferred to Deep South commands to remove the issue of proximity. Even West and Middle Tennesseans often viewed their eastern brothers with disdain, such as when the 29th Tennessee (mountaineers) joined Preston Smith's Tennessee brigade.[21]

Four Georgia regiments in the Army of Tennessee originated from the "up country," as Mark Weitz labeled the mountainous region—the 30th, 34th, 39th, and 40th. The up country held a limited identification with the midstate Plantation Belt and the coastal Rice Belt. These regiments proved "more independent and locally oriented." Indeed, the twenty-one up-country counties identified more with East Tennessee than they did with their own state.[22]

To be sure, the glues that initially held the army together—liberty, evangelical religion, the fear of Northern domination, and racial superiority—outweighed the army's sectional divide and formed unity, if not nationalism. Sectionalism nonetheless explained many of the army's internal attitudes, intra-army political cliques, and war aims. These divides were not always subtle. In the fall of 1863, Bragg broke up the old single-state brigades and divisions, particularly singling out Tennessee and Kentucky troops. He did so purely for intra-army political reasons, namely to disperse the anti-Bragg factions, but a comment by Sgt. James I. Brewer of the 34th Mississippi proved enlightening: "This change is made, I think, to keep down so much dissention, which between some of our troops is most as great as between Yankee and Confederate. Our division will hereafter be mixed and composed of men from all states. This is a good idea and should have been done long sense." E. H. Rennolds added, "This [division breakup] is done to mix troops of different States and prevent State prejudice, it is said." Sectionalism thus retarded the meshing of the army and resulted in intra-army cliques and divided attitudes.[23]

The Geographical Dilemma

Connelly claimed that the sheer geographic size of the West presented a dilemma; territory had to be held and bridges guarded. He may actually have underestimated the problem by limiting his definition of the West to the "heartland," which he defined as Tennessee, north central Alabama, north central Georgia, and northeast Mississippi. Yet, the army was inextricably linked to the events that took place in the entire western theater. Historians have differed over which area was of more importance—Mississippi or Tennessee—but the Army of Tennessee was unquestionably affected by both. The operational area of the western theater could thus be defined as Tennessee, Mississippi, Alabama, one-fourth of Louisiana, and the top one-third of Georgia. The area included not less than 175,000 square miles, the equivalent size of modern-day Germany, Belgium, and Switzerland combined![24]

The sheer expanse of the western theater was less the problem, however, than the rivers that penetrated it. Although much has been written about the importance of the railroads in the Civil War, during the first two years of the war in the West it was the rivers that proved determinative. The Mississippi, Tennessee, and Cumberland Rivers were avenues directly piercing the heart of the West. Precisely how to stop the Union navy thus became a primary political and strategic issue. Indeed, it became a tricky, if not unsolvable, tactical problem.[25]

In July 1861, Davis assigned Maj. Gen. Leonidas Polk, the president's former West Point roommate, to command Department No. 2, which included the river counties in Arkansas, Mississippi, and Louisiana and all of western Tennessee. In the fall, Polk committed the first major blunder in the West: without orders, but claiming "plenary powers," he violated Kentucky neutrality and captured Columbus on September 3. It is not difficult to understand his rationale. The Mississippi River was the obvious invasion route. Visually, the town, atop its 150-foot high cliffs, appeared impregnable—the "Gibraltar of the South," as it was known. Interestingly, the most powerful batteries were near the base of the cliff, not on the summit. Indeed, an ordnance officer predicted that if the Federal ironclads passed at night, Confederate gunners would not hit one shot in 100.[26]

The issue was not whether Kentucky would ultimately come into the Confederate column; the state was already drifting toward the North. Eventually, the Federals would probably have violated neutrality anyway. Indeed, President Abraham Lincoln was already shipping arms to the state and openly organizing recruiting camps. By violating neutrality, the Southerners had unwittingly opened a 400-mile front that they were unprepared to defend. Davis attempted to walk back the action, but eventually he acquiesced. Columbus also created a tactical dilemma. Union general Henry W. Halleck and his army commander, the unimpressive (to date) Ulysses S. Grant, believed that Columbus had such powerful river batteries that it could only be taken from the eastern land side. That approach proved almost impassable due to mud. The generals thus began eyeing a more vulnerable target—Fort Henry on the Tennessee River.[27]

Following the falls of Forts Henry and Donelson, to be discussed in chapter 2, Gen. P. G. T. Beauregard, a Louisiana general who spoke French better than English and was one of the war's early heroes, arrived in the West. Commanding between the Mississippi and Tennessee Rivers, he saw Columbus for the trap that it was and ordered Polk to withdraw. Polk, according to Beauregard, was "totally adverse to its abandonment." He had spent the previous five months building the fortifications and wrote his daughter, "I felt in leaving it as if I were leaving home." He attempted to haggle and requested 5,000 troops to garrison the town, but Beauregard refused.[28]

Columbus underscored the opposite modes of warfare advocated by Beauregard and Polk. Polk believed in massive fortifications, while Beauregard pressed for small garrisons, leaving a mobile army. At Fort Pillow, on the Mississippi River north of Memphis, works had been constructed for 15,000 to 20,000 troops, whereas Beauregard had an inner line of 3,000 in mind. In the event of an emergency, the relief army could come to the garrison's defense—if, of course, the army was not already engaged and could break away. The same argument—static defense versus mobility—was going on a year later at Vicksburg, Mississippi, between Gens. John C. Pemberton and Joseph E. Johnston. Johnston complained that the Vicksburg defenses were "very extensive, but slight—the usual defect of Confederate engineering." Davis issued no formal policy beyond the general understanding that the rivers were to be held as long as possible.[29]

Island No. 10, half in Tennessee and half in Missouri, was arguably a stronger defensive position than Columbus, yet there were problems. Pillow estimated that the garrison at the island and downriver at New Madrid, Missouri, would require 11,000 men. In essence, he desired a "mini-Columbus." The land was low and subject to flooding, and sickness became rampant. Laborers mounted sixty-four guns, but half were light twenty-four- and thirty-two-pounders, unable to penetrate the armor of the Federal ironclads. Some officers began to raise serious doubts that the ironclads could be stopped. Col. Marshal Walker of the 40th Tennessee, a West Pointer, openly stated that the ironclads could pass the batteries any dark and stormy night. Officials ultimately reduced the 7,000-man garrison to 5,500, a third of them sick. Brig. Gen. William Mackall assumed command of what he termed "that internal trap." Eventually, the ironclads did pass the batteries, just as Walker had predicted, and took the island in reverse. The garrison surrendered on April 8, 1862, but not before 1,000 of the defenders escaped on rafts across Reelfoot Lake.[30]

The administration's view on static versus mobile defense would remain unchanged through mid-1863. Perhaps Davis's only real alternative was to marginally defend the rivers and contest the Union army as it advanced inland, but from his perspective, and realistically speaking, the thought of only perfunctorily defending the rivers proved unacceptable. The administration's quasi policy of an all-out river defense led to a succession of mass captures—Fort Donelson, Island No. 10, Arkansas Post, Port Hudson, and Vicksburg—totaling 10 divisions and 62,000 prisoners.

Thus was the western army founded—with a largely unprofessional officer corps, a sectional divide that was structurally built into the early organization, and a largely unsolvable strategic/political dilemma posed by the defense of the rivers. These handicaps helped shape the army's identity and would ultimately contribute to an army conquered.

❋2❋

Losing the Bowl
Savior of the West?

On September 14, 1861, Gen. Albert Sidney Johnston, the newly appointed commander of an expanded Department No. 2, arrived in Nashville. A Mississippi artilleryman described him thus: "He is medium sized portly gentleman of about forty-five & upwards [fifty-eight] & dresses in citizens clothes & slouched hat & upon first site would not impress a stranger very favorably as to be anything more than an ordinary man. Such is the commander of the western Division of the confederate Army." If the cannoneer was unimpressed, several western historians have been strangely bedazzled by the Kentuckian.[1]

In his defense, Johnston's prewar accomplishments surpassed those of Joseph E. Johnston, Beauregard, and Bragg. A graduate of West Point, where he had become friends with Davis, Johnston fought in the Black Hawk War, commanded the elite 2nd U.S. Cavalry, fought Comanches, served in the Texas war for independence and the Mexican War, led an expedition against the Mormons in 1837, and at the commencement of the war commanded the Pacific Department, with headquarters in San Francisco. He held significant sway in the old army, perhaps second only to Robert E. Lee. Efforts to dismiss him as a grief-stricken widower and failure who drifted from job to job ring hollow. By reputation and accomplishments, Albert Sidney Johnston appeared formidable.[2]

Upon his arrival, Johnston faced an immediate decision. Since Polk's Corps was already in Columbus, he either had to withdraw Polk or advance his center into Kentucky. Believing that Kentuckians would rally to the Cause, Johnston chose the latter. His motivation, according to William Freehling, may not have been entirely strategic in nature. As a native Kentuckian, Johnston saw his state as Southern, and he proved unable to get beyond his "cultural conditioning." Kentucky's tepid response to the Confederacy forecast trouble. The Army of Tennessee needed the Bluegrass State to supply as many men as Tennessee—not just an infantry brigade, as it subsequently did, but a division or two. Western Confederates had to offset the massive raw manpower of Ohio, which gave more troops to the

14

Union than the states of Kentucky, Tennessee, Arkansas, and Mississippi combined gave to the Confederacy. The failure of Kentucky's response (71 percent of military-age men sat the war out) particularly damaged the Army of Tennessee. Beyond neglecting to volunteer, Kentuckians also did nothing to disrupt or harass the Federal advance into their state; they became "fatally indifferent."[3]

By January 1862, Johnston's 400-mile-long cordon defense was held by 57,500 troops: 22,000 at Columbus under Polk; 5,000 at Forts Henry and Donelson at the convergence of the Tennessee and Cumberland Rivers; 24,500 at Bowling Green under William J. Hardee; and 6,000 in East Tennessee under George Crittenden. The Confederate line thus had length but not depth. Hardee alone faced an estimated 75,000-man Union army under Don Carlos Buell. Johnston's only advantage was unified command, a benefit squandered by his obsession with the center of the line, where he thought the Union offensive would come. This meant that he placed a naïve trust in Polk to take care of the Henry-Donelson sector, a position that could not be lost under any circumstances. Polk ignored his orders and became involved in his own obsession—Columbus.[4]

Grant and other Union generals recognized what Johnston clearly failed to see—the gaping gap between Columbus and Bowling Green. At the center of this gap were the twin river forts of Henry and Donelson, both fortified but lightly defended. Eleven miles separated the forts. Interestingly, the rivers converged to within three miles just into Kentucky, but Tennessee officials downplayed the significance of the entire sector. Grant devised the strategy of a turning movement, a tactic typically employed on a flank and on a single battlefield rather than as a theater movement. In time, he received permission from his superior, Henry W. Halleck, to proceed.[5]

Although Fort Henry on the Tennessee River has long played the role of historical stepsister to Fort Donelson, Grant always viewed Henry as the prime target, since it was the only fortification between Paducah, Kentucky, and Florence, Alabama. Timothy Smith wrote of the "bowl" of the Tennessee River and the "footprint of impact": The loss of Henry would impact virtually all of Tennessee, northern Alabama, and Mississippi. The trestle of the Memphis, Clarksville & Louisville Railroad, the means by which the Confederates utilized interior lines, would be destroyed. Once past Fort Henry, gunboats could not be stopped short of the shoals at Florence. Tennessee officials never grasped its value. The fort, half under water, fell almost effortlessly to Union ironclads on February 6, 1862. The Confederate garrison escaped to Fort Donelson. Three Union timberclads steamed ahead, arriving at Florence on the eighth. Adding to the embarrassment, hundreds of civilians waved to the boats as they passed. More significant, the Union navy had demonstrated its total dominance of the rivers. Steven Woodworth declared Fort Henry "one of the most decisive battles of the war." The center of Johnston's line had been torn open.[6]

Johnston and Beauregard met for the first time at Bowling Green on February 5; the meeting did not go well. It quickly became clear that Johnston had developed no strategy but rather what Connelly termed "a medley of vague ideas." They butted heads on strategy—Beauregard wanted to concentrate at Fort Donelson and use the Cumberland River as a shield. He claimed in postwar years that Buell never had a pontoon train, which, though true, Beauregard could not have known at the time. What the Louisiana general failed to mention, but which Johnston clearly understood, was that a concentration at Donelson meant that Buell could simply march unopposed into Nashville. Another dangerous dilemma confronted Johnston: if the gunboats passed the heavy guns at Fort Donelson, they could be in Nashville before Hardee's Corps could withdraw to the Tennessee capital. Hardee would then have to march eastward to cross, probably at Gainesboro.[7]

Johnston began evacuating Bowling Green on February 7 and also planned for a withdrawal from Columbus. Realizing that Fort Donelson would be next on the Union hit list, Johnston reinforced the position with 15,000 men, retaining only 14,000 at Bowling Green. Davis, finally admitting the error of his territorial defense strategy, ordered a Napoleonic concentration. General Bragg, leading over 7,700 troops, came up from Pensacola and Mobile. The War Department also ordered Gen. Mansfield Lovell in New Orleans to board 5,000 men onto railroad cars for the trip north. Interestingly, Johnston wanted four of the Louisiana regiments to go to Memphis and one to Iuka, Mississippi. It was Lovell who convinced him that Corinth was the strategic concentration point. Four Virginia regiments were also dispatched under John Floyd, the former governor of Virginia. The government hurriedly sent 3,600 arms, including 1,200 newly imported Enfield rifles. The concentration was actually not as draconian as some historians have portrayed. Troops still remained in Florida and a division-size force in Mobile.[8]

It is clear that Johnston never believed that Fort Donelson could hold out against a naval attack. So then why did he send an additional 15,000 infantry? The general never directly answered the question, so it has been left to historians. Albert Castel and Steven Woodworth believed that the reinforcements were meant to "buy time" for Hardee's Corps to escape to the south bank of the Cumberland River at Nashville. He needed enough infantry at the fort to keep Grant's 27,000-man army at bay to protect the shore batteries. Benjamin Cooling concurred: "He [Johnston] intended Floyd's force at Fort Donelson neither to annihilate the invader nor to be a forlorn hope. Rather, the men he sent to do the job were to act as a delaying force (although he never made that crystal clear to any of his brigadiers)."[9]

Most historians have lined up in their denunciation of Johnston. Although the general did not tactically control the battle, he set up the potential for disaster. He either should have seen Fort Donelson as a holding action only to be maintained for a reasonable amount of time, as McMurry wrote, or he should have brought the garrison strength up to 30,000 or more to fight a decisive battle. He chose a disastrous middle course by having not enough to win and too many to lose. The coup de grace occurred when Johnston placed in command the two most inept political generals in the West, Floyd and Pillow, rather than sending Hardee or personally proceeding to Fort Donelson. Indeed, there were only two West Pointers in the entire 18,000-man garrison. Johnston would later justify his decision by feebly stating, "They were popular with the volunteers."[10]

A decisive battle could have been fought if Bragg and Lovell's 12,700 troops had been dispatched to Tennessee in late December 1861 or if Kentucky had supplied as many troops as Tennessee, which would have put an additional 10,000 men in the ranks. Even so, as Connelly correctly pointed out, the land battle should not have been fought at the fort but in the eleven-mile sector between Forts Henry and Donelson. Johnston had a week to rush to the scene and prepare for such a battle, but he never left Bowling Green. He clearly had not thought out such a tactic, much less conveyed it to Floyd and Pillow. Nor would reinforcing Donelson with the bulk of Hardee's Corps, as Beauregard later claimed that he suggested, have necessarily worked. Grant could simply delay his attack under the protection of the gunboats at Fort Henry while Buell brushed aside the delaying force, which would leave Johnston caught in a pincer movement, something that Johnston well appreciated.[11]

On the bitterly cold afternoon of February 14, the Union fleet, four ironclads and two timberclads, rounded the bend in the Cumberland River and attacked the fort. Floyd dispatched to Johnston that the gunners would not hold twenty minutes. In a stunning upset, however, the river batteries prevailed, disabling all of the ironclads. Simultaneously, however, Grant's army began encircling the land defenses and cutting the Wynn's Ferry Road, the Confederate line of retreat. Connelly argued that this was the moment for Floyd either to attack or cut his way out. With more Union transports on the way, the odds would get no better; Floyd did nothing. The next day, the fifteenth, the Confederate command launched a hammerblow on the Union right, driving it back a mile. A lone Yankee battery held the Nashville road, but Nathan Bedford Forrest's Tennessee cavalry sabered the cannoneers at their guns. Pillow, leading the attack, now hesitated and stunningly ordered the troops back to their earthworks! Grant, seizing the moment, counter-attacked with his left and center. The vise around the garrison of 18,000 was shut tight; the fort was doomed.

What had gone wrong? First, the standard military axiom of the day stated that a defensive line should form at a right angle to the line of retreat, something the neophyte Floyd failed to do. Second, Pillow apparently got caught up in his own minivictory. Contemporary evidence confirms this view. A battery commander wrote that "the general opinion among the Colonels seemed to be that Genl. Pillow was so elated with the success of the attack, that he abandoned the idea of retreating." Another eyewitness claimed that the gloating general rode about yelling: "Another Manassas defeat! Another Manassas defeat!" In a council meeting on February 14, it was never clearly defined what would happen if a breakthrough occurred—would the army retreat or simply hold the road? Several officers, including Forrest, claimed that there had never been any mention of a retreat. Although Pillow made the tactical decision, Floyd's complete ineptitude would earn him the number one spot in the infamous list of the ten worst generals in the Civil War as compiled by six national historians.[12]

The fort surrendered on February 16. Adding insult to injury, Floyd escaped with his Virginians via steamboat. An irate Forrest cut his way out. The loss of the garrison proved nothing short of stupefying. Johnston himself admitted that the loss was "most disastrous and almost without remedy." The Confederates sustained 1,222 killed and wounded and 14,623 captured; only 2,286 escaped. The prisoners were later exchanged in the fall of 1862, but deducting those dead and disabled from prison life and those who took the oath, it is doubtful that 50 percent ever returned to the ranks. Unfortunately, the men were not on the field of Shiloh in April 1862.[13]

The Southern press went on a tear. Fort Donelson was lost due to the "blunders—perhaps the incompetency—of Gen. Albert Sidney Johnston." The *Richmond Examiner*, realizing the role of Bowling Green in the capture of the fort, declared, "The occupation of Bowling Green was always a mystery to the public." The *New Orleans Delta* did not shy from stating its opinion: "General A. S. Johnston may be a profound strategist, but profound as his strategy may have been . . . it does not seem to have embraced the Tennessee and Cumberland rivers within its scope."[14]

There were also political ramifications. On March 8, the Tennessee congressional delegation, headed by Senator Gustavus A. Henry, called upon the president to remove Johnston from command. Davis defiantly defended his friend by saying, "If Sidney Johnston is not a General the Confederacy has None to give you." Rebuffed, the Tennesseans took their case to Congress. On March 10, a heated debate occurred on the floor of the House. Congressman John Atkins said that he would be remiss if "he failed to bear testimony to the incompetency and gross misconduct which had characterized the army in the West." Kentucky congressman John Moore defended Johnston, but the bellicose Henry Foote of Tennessee quickly inquired "if the gentleman would advocate the continuance of any man in command when the soldiers under him had lost confidence in him?" Davis wrote to Johnston, declaring that his confidence had never wavered. The loss of the forts also shook foreign markets. Confederate British minister James Mason admitted that the loss of Donelson had had an "unfortunate effect" on British public opinion. Some in England believed that the American war would soon be coming to an end, thus flooding their market with cotton and driving down prices.[15]

The Army Coalesces

In a meeting with Beauregard in Nashville on February 14, Johnston stated his plan to withdraw to Stevenson, Alabama, along the line of the Nashville & Chattanooga Railroad. At that point, he did not have a western concentration in mind. Once in Murfreesboro, however, he rethought the issue and instead withdrew to Decatur, Alabama, midway between Corinth, Mississippi, and Chattanooga. Some historians have suggested that this reversal was due to Beauregard's increasing dominance and his near-hysterical dispatches from West Tennessee. When Governor Harris met with Johnston on February 23, he related Beauregard's desire to concentrate the two wings of the army at Corinth. Johnston proclaimed that he was on the verge of making just such a move.

Thus began a postwar battle about who chose Corinth—Beauregard or Johnston? Most historians believe that Corinth was an obvious choice because of its vital rail junction and that both generals independently saw the value of the location. By shifting toward Corinth, however, Johnston had created problems. If Buell moved fast enough, he could interpose his army between Johnston's and Beauregard's forces or unite with Grant before the Confederate juncture was complete. Realizing this possibility, Johnston sent Nathan Bedford Forrest, Wirt Adams, and John Hunt Morgan on raids to burn bridges and otherwise slow Buell. The Army of the Ohio could also march unopposed to Chattanooga. Indeed, its failure to do so was one of the great missed opportunities of the war. Johnston apparently believed that reinforcement had been rushed to Chattanooga and that the city was now secure. In truth, East Tennessee lay ripe for invasion.[16]

By late March, a 40,000-man army had concentrated at Corinth, comprised of Hardee's Corps from Bowling Green, Polk's Corps from Columbus, George Crittenden's Division from eastern Kentucky, and Bragg's Corps from the Gulf Coast. "Imagine you are in the streets of New York or not quite so much crowded & you have a pretty good notion of the amount of soldiers about here, carts mules but instead of pavement mud about ankle deep," wrote a member of the 47th Tennessee. On the twenty-third, Johnston met with Beauregard, Polk, and Hardee. The next day, or so Beauregard later claimed, Johnston committed to striking Grant's army camped at Pittsburg Landing, Tennessee, before Buell's Army of the Ohio, marching from Nashville, could join it. Johnston's son William Preston Johnston claimed that this had been his father's intention all along. An interesting dispatch, however, not published in the *Official Records* but printed in William Preston Johnston's book, showed that as of March 15, the general was considering changing his base from Corinth to Bolivar, Tennessee, thirty-eight miles northwest and on the south bank of the Hatchie River. He remained at Corinth, but he was obviously thinking defensively.[17]

The army had barely enough time to organize, much less train, at the division level. One Rebel thought the officers to be "an inefficient set." He disgustedly wrote that "every jackass you meet sports brass buttons & stripes (I had a mind to throw mine away)." As for the newly christened Army of the Mississippi, the soldier wrote bluntly, "Our army is not organized, & should the Federals attack us now, we would be in a bad fix." Of course, the plan was to attack the Federals and hope that surprise would mitigate inexperience.[18]

By April 2, scouts indicated that the Federals were on the move. With Buell closing in, Beauregard sent a message to Johnston: "Now is the moment to advance and strike the enemy at Pittsburg Landing." Beauregard later claimed that Johnston protested, saying that the army was not ready, but historians have questioned the account. On April 3, Johnston dispatched to Davis that his 40,000 men were marching out to give battle. Davis answered, "I anticipate victory." "I was awakened by the long roll which sounded throughout the whole camp. Everything and everybody was in motion. Drums were beating, trumpets sounding, fifes blowing, bands playing, and men hurraying," James Griffin of the 5th Company Washington Artillery wrote his father. Louisianan Joseph Lyman of the Crescent Regiment took time to hurriedly write his wife: "Good-bye. If I do not write it will be because I am working or fighting or wounded or sick or dead." Lacking sufficient time to cook rations, the men drew five crackers each.[19]

Administrative bungling and vague orders (the generals pointed fingers at each other) caused serious delays. On the first day at the Battle of Shiloh, minutes would count; on the third of April, hours were squandered. Bragg's Corps did not move out until 4:30 P.M., ten and a half hours behind schedule. Perhaps it would have helped if a corps, even a division, had bivouacked at Monterey, a tiny village between Corinth and Pittsburg Landing, although supplying it over the miserable roads would have admittedly been an issue. As Johnston departed on the fourth, an aide heard him utter, "Yes, I believe I have overlooked nothing." In fact, he had overlooked much, including the proper preparation of the roads and a deficiency of maps, not to mention a stockpile of rations and a field hospital set up at Monterey. A drenching rain soon marred the advance. James Rosser described the weather at 3:00 A.M. on April 5: "One of the hardest rains fell I ever saw in life and wound up in a considerable hail." A Tennessean remarked that soldiers sloshed along, "wading, stumbling and plunging through water a foot deep." The attack, planned for the fifth, would not begin until the morning of the sixth. At the last minute, Beauregard lost his nerve and advised canceling the attack. "Gentlemen, we shall attack at daylight tomorrow," Johnston replied as he abruptly terminated the meeting.[20]

The Confederate formation, drawn up by Beauregard but accepted by Johnston, has long raised questions. First, the most prominent military theorists of the day, Clausewitz and Jomini, would not have approved of a frontal attack, even a surprise one, against an enemy of equal size. According to Johnston's tactics, the right wing was to sweep around the Federal army and push the Yankees *away from* Pittsburg Landing and into the Owl Creek backwater. The actual stacked linear formation, however, suggested that the army was simply going to assault head on, pushing the bluecoats *back* to the river. Indeed, Beauregard may have thought as much. Part of the problem lay in the maps. A surviving Rebel scout map in the Tennessee State Archives shows Lick Creek and Owl Creek parallel to each other, which was not correct. As the graycoats advanced, their line would get longer, not remain the same.[21]

Shiloh

The Battle of Shiloh started late — an hour and a half late, to be specific. The blame for the tardiness has historically been placed on Hardee for not having his troops fed and in line. The ultimate culpability, of course, lay with Johnston, who, when the first shots were fired at 4:55 A.M. in Fraley Field, was at his headquarters in the rear sipping coffee and still listening to Beauregard rattle on about why there should be no advance. Due to broken alignments, gaps in the line, and starts and stops, Fraley and Seay Fields were not cleared until 7:00 A.M. So much for the "Alpine avalanche" touted by Beauregard. The second issue was related to Johnston's leadership role. His choice to lead from the front and leave Beauregard in the rear to direct operations has long been debated. Beauregard later criticized Johnston for reducing himself to the role of a corps or division commander, as did historians Connelly and Smith. The recklessness with which Johnston exposed himself (at one point being forty yards beyond his own line) can hardly be excused.[22]

By 10:00 A.M., six Confederate brigades, several of them intermingled, swept past Shiloh Church and renewed the assault against the Federals' second position along the Purdy-Hamburg Road. Fierce fighting took place at the intersection of the Purdy-Hamburg and Pittsburg-Corinth Roads—the famed "crossroads." Johnston was on the right and Beauregard in the rear, organizing stragglers into ad hoc units; no single mind controlled.[23]

Throughout the afternoon, Bragg, commanding in the center, launched 10,000 troops in piecemeal attacks against a Union stronghold termed the "Hornet's Nest." Seven or eight assaults were made against the Sunken Road (so named after the war), a depressed wagon path connecting the Corinth Road with the Eastern Corinth Road. Bragg never advanced more than 3,700 troops at a time against the 4,300 defenders. The result of these piecemeal assaults was not inevitable, but it was predictable; there were 2,400 Rebel casualties, 24 percent of those engaged.[24]

Col. Randall Gibson's Louisiana brigade was shattered in the attacks, and he lost nearly one-third of his men. In a letter to his wife, Elise, Bragg later wrote that Gibson was difficult to get into action. "At last he was put in a hot place and at once retreated with his whole force," Bragg wrote. He concluded, "He is an *arrant coward*." Mary Gorton McBride, Gibson's biographer, has uncovered several issues that may have been at the root of Bragg's vindictiveness. Prior to the war, Gibson had owned an adjoining plantation to the Braggs', which he sold. Whether or not this engendered animosities is not known. What is known is that Gibson and Elise Bragg's brother, Towsy Ellis, who served on Bragg's staff, were friends and classmates at Yale. Gibson succeeded in school, whereas Ellis dropped out. Gibson and Bragg also had variances in their views on secession. Perhaps Bragg was also jealous of Johnston's obvious fondness for Gibson and the colonel's connections with Polk, Beauregard, and Breckinridge. The point is that there could well have been, and probably was, a prewar genesis of Bragg's anger.[25]

At about 3:30 P.M., Brig. Gen. Daniel Ruggles, commanding a division in Bragg's Corps, ordered all available artillery brought to bear on the Hornet's Nest. All or parts of eleven batteries (some fifty-three guns) were eventually assembled. At a range of 500 yards, the guns blasted away for twenty minutes. The Hornet's Nest did succumb, but Maj. Francis Shoup, an artillery officer, never thought that the barrage had much to do with it. The Federals to the east and the west had been pushed back, the position nearly surrounded. The defenders were doomed, and the artillery merely added to the inevitable. At 5:30, about 2,200 Federals surrendered. Prisoners had been gained, but time had been lost—time that may have made the difference between failure and success.[26]

Bragg has been rightly criticized for using brute force rather than finesse against the Hornet's Nest; he never carried the position by frontal assault. The one more culpable, however, was Johnston, who lost sight of his objective. He overcommitted troops to the left and allowed headlong assaults in the center that were totally unnecessary. The Hornet's Nest never had to be reduced, only contained by long-range skirmishing and limited sorties. By committing John Breckinridge's reserve corps in the fight, the Confederates drove the Federals back *onto* Pittsburg Landing rather than *away* from it, as the battle plan had directed.[27]

Beauregard, on Johnston's order, reinforced the left by sending Breckinridge's "Corps," actually only a division. He subsequently received information from aides Numa Augustine and George Brent that the center and right were weak and that the army's flank did not extend to Lick Creek. Beauregard thus redirected two of Breckinridge's three brigades to the right center. About 2:00, Breckinridge—who, with "his right leg thrown around the pommel of the saddle, on which his elbow rested, and with his chin on his hand, was surveying the battle field as calmly as if there had been no bullets whizzing, or shell screaming, around him"—arrived on the Purdy-Hamburg Road south of the Sarah Bell Field. With Johnston not present, his aides— Thomas Jordan, David Urquhart, and William Preston (the "mini generals," as Connelly labeled them)—huddled. Realizing that the battle was slowing down, Jordan said, "I think the reserves should be used." Preston expressed agreement. Jordan rode over to Breckinridge and said, "General Breckinridge, it is General Johnston's order that you advance and turn and take those batteries."[28]

Winfield S. Statham's Brigade, supported by Rutledge's Tennessee battery, attacked Stephen A. Hulbert's troops in the Peach Orchard. John Taylor of the 15th Mississippi wrote that "we made a charge and the enemy was behind a fence and had the advantage of us[.] We did not stand their fire but a few minutes. The mini balls were falling thickly around us." Repulsed several times, the Mississippians and Tennesseans sought cover in the "mule lot," a fenced area on the edge of the field. Breckinridge reported to Johnston that Statham's troops refused to make another charge. Offering his assistance, the army commander rode to the mule lot and shouted, "Men they are stubborn, we're going to have to use the bayonet." At 2:00, Johnston waved forward the brigades of William H. Stephens, Statham, John K. Jackson, and John S. Bowen in what Stacey Allen termed a "massive assault." The Rebels charged in what appeared to be certain victory. When Governor Harris approached Johnston, he was alone, all of his aides having been dispatched. The general suddenly reeled, a bullet having struck his right leg below the knee. At 2:45, Albert Sidney Johnston lay dead.[29]

It has long been debated what role Johnston would have played in the West had he lived. Several historians believe that he might have evolved into the Lee of the West. The salient word is *might*. If John Bell Hood, one of the subsequent commanders of the army, had died of his wound at Chickamauga, many could have made the same argument about him—that he would have become the western Lee. Hood, of course, did live and was a failure as army commander. In the world of real and not counterfactual history, not all generals evolved; such might have been the case with Johnston. The facts are these: in the twenty-two weeks that he commanded in the West, he lost Kentucky and Tennessee; had an entire corps captured at Fort Donelson; and arguably was not on the verge of destroying Grant's army at Shiloh when he was mortally wounded, despite the strategic surprise, no entrenchments to encounter, and the incredible good fortune of having an entire Federal division (Lew Wallace's) thrashing around in the woods all afternoon trying to find the battlefield.[30]

Grant, meanwhile, had been forming a final defensive line, his left anchored on the Tennessee River and extending west for over a mile. The line bristled with artillery—forty-one guns to be exact—and 18,000 infantry, supported by the gunboats *Tyler* and *Lexington*. As the sun began to set, the battle momentarily stalled as the exhausted Rebels regrouped and distributed ammunition. James Chalmers's and Jackson's brigades on the far right made a final assault across the 100-foot-deep Dill Branch Ravine, only to be repulsed. Chalmers's Mississippians probably did not get beyond their own picket line. As Bragg formed other troops to attack, word arrived from Beauregard, now commanding the army, to suspend operations. Urquhart later commented, "At the time the order was given, the plain truth must be told, that our troops at the front, were a thin line of exhausted men, who were making no further headway, and were glad to receive orders to fall back."

Both Bragg and William Preston Johnston would later claim that the victory had been thrown away; some historians have concurred, saying that if only Johnston had lived, he would have driven the victory home. Timothy Smith (correctly, I believe) failed to come to such a conclusion.[31]

Bragg fostered much of the "lost opportunity" mantra in postwar years. Connelly pointed out that his statements stood in stark contrast to what he said at the time. Several staff officers and Bragg's own medical director, J. C. Nott, claimed that when Bragg received the withdrawal order, he expressed neither shock nor objection. When Bragg rode to Beauregard's headquarters that evening, Col. Jacob Thompson, a Beauregard aide, emphatically said that Bragg raised no objections—indeed, the subject was not discussed. In letters to his wife immediately following the battle, Bragg raised none of the issues that he was so vehement about eleven years later when a line had been drawn between the Johnston and Beauregard factions.[32]

Whether or not one final assault would have worked was a nonhistorical question, argued Grady McWhiney, but Beauregard was out of position to make the proper call. Back at Shiloh Church, more than two miles from the front lines, all he could see was the debris of battle and returning Yankee prisoners. Angered by the after-action reports of both Bragg and Polk, Beauregard later defended himself with "a mixture of hindsight, exaggeration, and misrepresentation." McWhiney stated that an aggressive commander would not have used the lateness of the hour as an excuse to cease the battle. By continuing the attack, "the Confederates had everything to gain and little more to lose than they lost the next day."[33]

In the midst of a pouring rain, Forrest prowled the Tennessee River shoreline late that night when his scouts uncovered shocking news of the potential landing of Buell's army. The Tennessean went to Chalmers's headquarters in search of Johnston. "I have been way down along the river-bank, close to the enemy. I could see the lights on the steamboats and hear the orders give in the disembarkation of the troops," he told Chalmers. "They are receiving reinforcements by the thousands and if this army does not move and attack them between this and daylight, and before other reinforcements arrive, it will be whipped like hell before ten o'clock tomorrow." The colonel repeated a similar message to Hardee, but in the darkness, he was never able to locate army headquarters.[34]

Throughout the morning of April 7, the Northerners, obviously reinforced with Buell's army, went on the attack, yet the Rebels fought with amazing cohesiveness. At 3:00, the Confederates, with 1,500 to 2,000 men and twelve to fifteen guns, pieced together a final defensive line at Shiloh Church. The 4:00 sortie of Col. Robert Looney's 38th Tennessee would be

Men of the 5th Company Washington Artillery.
Courtesy of the U.S. Army Military History Institute.

heroically remembered, although the Federals groused that it was glorified only due to Looney's prominence on the postwar Shiloh Battlefield Commission. As the army limped back to Corinth, Forrest, who was gaining quite the reputation, unleashed his troopers on the limited Federal pursuit. At a place called Fallen Timbers, according to a Federal colonel, "a fierce yell filled the air." The colonel and 350 troopers careened into a Yankee cavalry battalion and the 77th Ohio, routing both. Forrest received a painful wound in his hip, but within two months he would be back in the saddle.[35]

The ghastly sight of death on a massive scale staggered the men. Richard Pugh of the Washington Artillery wrote of his "feelings when I saw the first man killed. He was within thirty feet of me . . . and just as he was about to fire the gun [cannon], a ball [bullet] struck him in front of the ear, and he fell backwards expiring without a groan." In the Crescent Regiment, a member witnessed a shell striking one of the drummer boys, "carrying his head off his shoulders."[36]

One lesson Shiloh taught was that tactical "surprises" sometimes did not work and could not offset the advantage of operating on the tactical defensive. Indeed, in the two previous surprise attacks in the western theater —

Wilson's Creek, Missouri, in August 1861, in which the Federals attacked, and Mill Springs, Kentucky, in January 1862, in which the Confederates attacked—the defenders in both instances were victorious. The Federals were certainly surprised at Shiloh, but they quickly rebounded and offered stiff resistance. It took the Rebels three and a half hours to push back William T. Sherman's division to its second position.

The nation gasped at the body count: 13,000 Federals (21 percent) and 10,700 Confederates (27 percent). The gloves had come off. Historian Archer Jones viewed the matter in terms of attrition rates. "Since all of the Confederacy's armies numbered only half of the Union's, to keep the attrition even, the southern forces should lose no more than half the northern. By this measure of the outcome of the Battle of Shiloh, the Rebels had suffered a substantial defeat of attrition." Johnston's mission had been nothing less than revenge for Fort Donelson; he had wanted the elimination, or near elimination, of Grant's entire army. Never again would the Confederates have such an opportunity as at Shiloh. The missteps had not started on April 6 but before the army marched out of Corinth. They started when Johnston accepted Beauregard's grandiose organization (there should have been three corps and not four) and bewildering battle alignment (distributing troops evenly along the line).[37]

A tenacious Federal defense, of course, also had something to do with the Confederate loss. Although defeated on the first day's battle, Grant, unlike George McClellan at the Battle of Antietam, fought a second day. Williamson Murray and Wayne Wei-Siang Hsieh also point to the fact that Grant accepted responsibility and did not blame subordinates for the surprise attack, thus forging professional relationships and avoiding the wretched bickering that developed in the Army of Tennessee. Grant also learned something about the nature of the war. According to Steven Woodworth, the general would no longer view the war as "a limited police action against a clique of insurgent politicians."[38]

The Confederates were ultimately reinforced by Earl Van Dorn's "army" from the Trans-Mississippi, but the Federals were likewise joined by John Pope's 21,000 troops fresh from their victory at Island No. 10. The best the Southerners could have hoped for was a tactical but not total victory that would have boosted morale. Does that mean that the North would have sued for peace? No, but it does mean that time would have been bought and Grant's career would have been finished, perhaps the most significant long-term ramification of all. As for the Confederates, the Fort Henry–Shiloh combination resulted in the loss of the Tennessee bowl.[39]

Rethinking Patriotism

The exhausted troops shuffled into Corinth for several days as a pall settled across the army. The railroad platform overflowed with caskets, and at the Tishomingo Hotel, the wounded lay in every room and in the hallway, emitting a foul stench. Beauregard was in a fiery mood. A Yankee prisoner being interrogated showed him his wounded hand, to which the Louisiana general barked, "It was a pity it was not your damn head." In truth, the emaciated and gaunt general faced tremendous stress. Three combined Union armies under Maj. Gen. Henry W. Halleck, numbering an estimated 90,000 troops, inched toward Corinth. The Army of the Mississippi counted barely 35,000 to contest the juggernaut. Col. William D. Rogers of the 2nd Texas expressed concern: "Two to one we can whip them but if we contend with greater odds the result will be doubtful." If Corinth fell, then Fort Pillow on the Mississippi River would be flanked and Memphis would inevitably fall.[40]

When Van Dorn's Army of the West arrived from Arkansas in late April and early May, it numbered only 13,159 present. A Montgomery correspondent contemptuously branded them Americans, half-breeds, Indians, Mexicans, Irish, and Germans. Other regiments arrived, including the 10th and 19th South Carolina from garrison duty in Charleston. "You must not speak of miseries, etc. of 'Mud Hole' until you have seen Corinth. It is the worst place I have ever been in. . . . Mud-mud everywhere. We eat, drink, and sleep in mud," wrote a member of the 10th. Col. Arthur M. Manigault, commanding the regiment, noted with disgust the lax discipline and slovenly appearance of the army.[41]

Disease ravaged the camp. The primary cause was related to the filthy drinking water, contaminated with limestone and magnesium. "I have often seen a hole about 6 ft. square, ten foot deep and in one corner of the bottom a group of men crouched around a small hole waiting for water to spring, and when it did come up had most probably passed through a nearby sink [latrine]," an officer observed. The sick lay thick from the railroad station to the town square. Van Dorn's troops camped in the hills three or four miles southeast of Corinth, but they suffered as much as those near the depot.[42]

The men wrote home of the wretched conditions. "The water we had to drink was the most abominable stuff that was ever forced down men's throats," wrote a Louisiana soldier. The water appeared bluish in color and had a greasy taste, which some compared to castor oil. The rations of beef were so heavily salted that the men remained constantly thirsty. The troops continued digging wells, but overnight a liquid would emerge resembling "coal tar, dish water, and soap suds mixed." On April 18, Colonel Rogers reported 400 men of his 2nd Texas on the sick roll. A Savannah, Georgia, correspondent noted that "the troops and horses were suffering for water to an extent you cannot imagine."[43]

The scarcity of beef and vegetables also presented problems. Before Shiloh, the army commissary had collected 16,000 head of poor cattle in Calcasieu Parish, Louisiana, on the Texas border. The fall of New Orleans in late April 1862 jeopardized the supply. The commissary issued beef once every ten days rather than five times a week as ordered. Beauregard dispatched agents into north Texas and Arkansas to purchase beef herds, but the Commissary Department in Richmond later commandeered a number of the steers.[44]

A correspondent lamented that in Memphis, only ninety miles distant, an assortment of vegetables could be easily obtained, yet no supply existed for the sick at Corinth. He likewise mentioned that ice could be bought in Memphis at three to five cents per pound, "but not a pound have I seen here." He noticed that with every pint of water there was a half ounce of dirt—"you feel it scrape the throat as it goes down." The health of the army somewhat improved in May when several rains offered a supply of fresh water. The public also responded to Beauregard's appeal for fresh vegetables. Nonetheless, by early June, the army still counted 7,286 present sick and 10,983 absent sick, which was 36 percent of the army.[45]

A crisis of allegiance loomed on the horizon. The one-year enlistments would soon expire, and many in the army, overwhelmed with disease, the horrors of war, and suffering, intended to go home. On April 16, 1862, Congress passed the First Conscription Act, drafting all men ages eighteen to thirty-five. Perhaps more significant, all of the one-year volunteers of conscript age would be retained in service for an additional two years. The fact that the men could pay for substitutes to get out of military service and that owners of twenty slaves would also be exempt helped to define the war as "a rich man's war and a poor man's fight."[46]

The men responded with rage. "We are pressed in for two years more, much against our inclination and wishes & but I suppose we will have to put up with it no matter how much we dislike it," a Mississippi artilleryman wrote. "It is very unjust & I fear will cause many to desert the army who would have been free volunteers for the war. Some regiments speak publically of rebelling & going home when their time expires, whether they will carry their threats into execution is more than we can say but we cannot blame them for resisting any encroachments on their rights, no matter from what quarter."[47]

Letters revealed shock and depression. "We received the mortifying intelligence a few days ago that the regiment was compelled to enlist for two years longer. We were never asked to reenlist again but forced against our will," Josiah Knighton of the 4th Louisiana informed his father. Tennessean James Hall feared that the new law "will cause disturbance in the army. A great many men say they will go home when their time is out. I hope they think better of it." A. H. Mecklin believed that "we are doomed men two years longer." A Mississippian wrote bluntly: "I think that it is treating the volunteers ridiculous. I think if they will snatch all of those cowards from 18 to 35 year old that never left home at all they will have army enough after the twelve month troops are out to carry on the war for years, but no that would be treating [badly] them fellows that was too cowardly to go, too bad." An Arkansan at Corinth nonetheless cheered the law: "I expect it will go against the grain with some of the citizens but that is just what I want ther are a great many about Fayetteville as well as through the country that aught to be in the army, instead of lying around home." Even Beauregard complained that the Conscription Act had nearly demoralized the army. That said, it is clear that but for the act, a significant portion of the western army would have melted away.[48]

The downward slide continued as Island No. 10 surrendered with 4,500 prisoners on April 8, and New Orleans did on the twenty-fifth. James Hall expressed concern: "We have had painful rumors today of the occupation of New Orleans by the enemy and the consequent probable evacuation of Fort Pillow, but they were contradicted. The loss of the Mississippi River would be a serious inconvenience to us, but I have been fearful for some time that we will not be able to hold it. If Memphis falls into the hands of the enemy we will be cut off from communications with home." Sickness, the Conscription Act, and battlefield losses all led to the army's first crisis of faith. "I have seen enough & now am very willing that peace may come & I hope it will come soon," Charles Stewart disclosed to his wife. Josiah Knighton feared that "the Confederacy is gone forever." A. H. Mecklin expressed his utter disgust: "A few leading characters have been the chief instigators of this war. The more I see of this war, the more fully satisfied I am that there is not religion about it."[49]

After two aborted sorties, Beauregard, on May 25, assembled his corps commanders to discuss an evacuation. Hardee believed that the town should be immediately evacuated, before Halleck could bring up his heavy guns. The decision was made to withdraw south to Tupelo. A bit of chicanery was used. As arriving trains pulled into the depot on the twenty-ninth, engineers blew their whistles and the troops cheered, giving the impression that reinforcements had arrived. It worked. The Federals became convinced of a massive buildup and of an imminent attack. By the time they figured out the ruse, the Rebel army had vanished. While the retreat was masterfully executed, there were losses. When Confederate cavalry burned the Cypress Creek Bridge near Chewalla, seven trains with sixty-three cars of the Memphis & Charleston had to be torched. Despite hugely exaggerated Northern accounts, Beauregard insisted that only 200 stragglers and deserters were lost.[50]

The bluecoats frankly did not know where the Southerners had gone. A lieutenant ventured a guess: "I am inclined to believe that they have retreated to the swamps and lowlands of Florida, where they will have for their companions snakes and alligators, which they consider more acceptable than the everlastin' yankees." Despite false reports of 12,000–15,000 prisoners (one dispatch claimed that the entire 13th Louisiana had been captured), the Northern press realized the gravity of what had occurred. "He [Beauregard] had but fifty-seven pieces of artillery in his entrenchments, and was so distrustful of his weakness as to resort to the dodge of putting up sham guns, made of wood. With all this in our favor he beat us back at almost every point where we met him during the advance and finally slipped through our fingers like an eel," a paper editorialized. The *Chicago Tribune* labeled the evacuation "one of the most masterly pieces of strategy that has ever been displayed during this war."[51]

The army would live to fight another day, yet as the troops trudged fifty miles southward, they carried with them a sinking depression. Kentucky gone, then Tennessee, now northern Mississippi—where would it all stop?

❋ 3 ❋

High Tide
Bragg Takes Command

Corinth was now in enemy hands, and despite Beauregard's self-congratulation on his stealthy retreat, Davis was livid. In June, Col. William Preston Johnston departed to Tupelo, described by one soldier as "a small dirty looking town." He had orders to inspect the army and have Beauregard answer some very specific and pointed questions, not the least of which was about the purpose of the retreat. The colonel found Beauregard "secluded and inaccessible," and the general immediately inquired of Johnston "to what end [his] mission to him tended." The army chieftain, in a defensive mode, made it clear that "if any shadow of doubt rested in the mind of the Executive as to the propriety of the movement in retreat he would ask for a court of inquiry." As for his part, Beauregard boldly proclaimed the movement "a brilliant victory." The combined Confederate armies equaled 45,000 troops to oppose, according to the most reliable intelligence, 85,000–90,000 Federals. In retreating to Tupelo, Beauregard had hoped that Halleck would follow with a portion of his army so that the offensive could be taken against a smaller force.

Johnston found the troops camped on both sides of the so-called Tupelo Swamp, on a series of wooded ridges. The most common shelters were flies, ten men to a fly. The men cooked in small squads, most of the brigades having brick-faced bake ovens. Some regiments used small company ovens. Wells eighteen to twenty feet deep produced clear and ample water. A more rigid system of inspection enhanced discipline, and properly located latrines and kitchen pits reduced disease. Morale improved and returning convalescents helped fill the ranks. As for the retreat, Johnston concluded that Corinth had proved to be such an unhealthy campsite that it was unfortunate that Beauregard had not withdrawn a month earlier.[1]

Beauregard suffered from his chronic throat ailment and jaundice while at Tupelo, and he approached physical exhaustion. Taking the advice of his doctors, he decided to take a four-month leave of absence at the Blandon Springs spa north of Mobile. Bragg would temporarily command in his absence. Beauregard never requested permission from the president, however, and Davis almost accidentally found out about the general's planned departure. The chief executive, who had never liked the egotistical, anti-administration general, immediately called a cabinet meeting, declared that Beauregard had abandoned his post, and promptly sacked him, giving Bragg command. The troops reacted positively. "General Bragg has been put in command of the Western Department and Beauregard superseded and now we have the right man in the right place. General Bragg is the most energetic and daring General we have and you will hear before long of something being done," Surgeon Terry Carlisle wrote. Many believed that Bragg instilled much-needed strict discipline. "I am glad Bragg is in command. I therefore look for stirring times soon," an artilleryman wrote. Knox Miller, in the cavalry, noted that "since Gen. Bragg has taken command, our own branch of the service has gained more reputation than it has during the rest of the war."[2]

Bragg inherited an army in the midst of crisis. Long retreats and the subsequent conscript law had soured many of the men. "There are many and one in our army who would rather Lincoln would conquer, than that the war would last six months longer," confessed Thomas Davidson of the 19th Louisiana. "Our troops will all fight well and bravely but they are tired of war and would like to quit, which they would do if they could. I refer only to a portion of our troops but a large one."[3]

The army began experiencing its first serious wave of desertions. On May 28, 2,798 infantrymen were listed as absent without leave in the Army of the Mississippi. Many went home on sick leave and simply never returned. Others left based on their contention that their original time of enlistment had ended and they could legally leave, the draft law notwithstanding. "The desertions are principally from Tennessee Regiments—on our march from Corinth there was one Tenn. Reg. lost one hundred men by desertion out of the small number of two hundred and thirty—In our State [Mississippi] there are many that have gone home on sick furloughs that have not returned," Charles Roberts informed his wife. William Mott was "sorry to say that Tennesseans are the only ones that are leaving in that disgraceful manner." A staff officer in the 18th Louisiana noted the desertion of practically an entire company of Irish: "None of them going over to the enemy but merely attempting to make their way home under the plea that their time was out last April." A Texas Ranger believed that some deserters simply joined to get the bounty, and then "some morning finds them on their way back home. Such men are worthless."[4]

Bragg initially addressed the issue of morale with tighter discipline. The army began training as a cohesive unit. "We are drilling very hard, the disiplian of the army is very good indeed. I say 'this more now then it ever has been since the war commenced,'" thought George Blakemore of the 23rd Tennessee. Writing to his wife on July 15, Clement Watson remarked, "General Bragg is one of the most active Generals we have, and there is no doubt that he will improve (I think) every opportunity thrown in his way to win success for our arms and independence for our country." A member of Thomas Stanford's Mississippi battery noted: "There has been a great improvement in regard to discipline and drill. Three hours every day (except Sunday) each regiment, battalion and battery is required to drill upon the field. Discipline is rigid, army movements are kept close, and Gen. Bragg is fast bringing this volunteer army to approximate the standard of regulars." A cavalryman also saw improvement: "Since Gen. Bragg has taken command, our own branch of the service has gained more reputation than it has during the rest of the war." The cases of syphilis, which could be attributable to lax discipline, remained relatively level—179 cases in June 1862 and 120 in July. Not until active campaigning did the number drop—thirty-five cases in September and October combined.[5]

Desertions nonetheless continued, with Tennessee departures getting out of hand. For the week ending June 2, 1862, 100 desertions occurred in the 22nd Tennessee, 81 in the 13th Tennessee, 77 in the 12th Tennessee, 6 in the 47th Tennessee, and 37 in Smith P. Bankhead's Battery. Eight desertions occurred in the 12th Tennessee in the week ending June 12, and eighteen in the 24th Tennessee in the week ending July 5. Desertions were dealt with sternly, and punishments could be brutal. While at Tupelo, two men from the 23rd Tennessee—Dave Brewer, about sixty, and Rube Franklin, about forty-five—were strung up by their hands and lashed, after which their heads were shaved. A man by the name of Reddon of the 24th Mississippi received thirty lashes, was branded on his hip with the letter *D*, and then had his head shaved. A soldier in the 7th Arkansas received thirty-eight lashes while strapped to a wagon wheel.[6]

When traditional punishments, horrid though they were, failed to curb desertions, Bragg did not hesitate to up the ante. Exactly how many executions occurred at Tupelo is not known—only a half dozen can be documented—but the troops expressed shock. Melville Baille and Polk Childress, both in the 21st Tennessee, deserted, protesting that their legal obligations had concluded and they were free to leave. Captured and returned, they met their fate on June 30. Perception became greater than the reality. "Every day or two there is a man shot for some offense," Lt. Augustus Davis of the 7th Mississippi wrote, although he admitted that "I have seen no one shot yet, but there are plenty of them shot." The rumor spread widely that Bragg had a soldier executed for killing a chicken, when in reality the man met a firing squad for shooting in camp in violation of orders and accidentally killing a black man.[7]

Many of the troops turned on Bragg. "Gen'l Bragg is trying to get the army under strict discipline—he is not much liked by the boys on account of having several men shot for being absent without leave and desertion," artilleryman John Magee entered in his diary. Lt. Col. Camille de Polignac wrote on June 11, "There is a great deal of dissatisfaction amongst some of the Regt [18th Louisiana] and companies about Gen. Bragg's sternness. . . . He is unpopular. . . . Gen. Br. is a good officer, and wants reform in the army, but I am afraid he undertakes too many changes at once, and does not possess the discriminating qualities required to carry out such a task." An Atlanta correspondent reported in July, "Bragg is growing somewhat unpopular, owing to his rigid and almost tyrannical system of discipline." Brig. Gen. William Preston, brother-in-law to Albert Sidney Johnston, failed to connect with Bragg from the outset. Writing to William Preston Johnston on June 14, he said, "Bragg is a stern & imperious soldier and is endeavoring by excessive severity to establish discipline, but the men are indignant, and I fear trouble." Some nonetheless believed that the change was long overdue. Writing to his wife, engineer Samuel H. Lockett remarked, "We are going to have no more playing soldier in Genl Bragg's army and I hope we will soon see a very beneficial change."[8]

Beauregard had hoped that Halleck would follow his army to Tupelo, but the Northern general failed to bite. Halleck did not wish to continue stretching his supply line and dealing with what he termed "the swamps of Mississippi." He determined to turn Vicksburg over to the combined fleets of David Farragut, who was moving up the Mississippi River from New Orleans, and Charles Davis, who was moving downriver from Memphis. He retained Grant's army—reinforced with a division from Buell's army—a total of 43,000 men, and Pope's army of 18,000 at Corinth, while Buell's remaining four divisions, 25,000 men, marched due east along the Memphis & Charleston Railroad to Chattanooga. Ormsby Mitchell's 6,400-man Union division held Huntsville, Alabama, allowing the Federals to already control 100 miles of the railroad.[9]

The Kentucky Campaign

It is not difficult to understand why Bragg ultimately chose to concentrate at Chattanooga. Maj. Gen. Edmund Kirby Smith, commanding the Department of East Tennessee, was being overrun. He had two divisions: Carter Stevenson's Division, with 9,000 troops, to oppose a Federal division at

Cumberland Gap estimated at 10,000, and Harry Heth's Division of 6,000 to oppose Buell's approaching army at Chattanooga. Smith pleaded for reinforcements, reminding Bragg of the obvious: Chattanooga was the gateway to Georgia and the Confederate industrial complex. On June 24, the army commander admitted that the loss of the city would be a disaster. On the twenty-sixth, Bragg dispatched John McCown's small division of 3,000 troops to Chattanooga, which arrived July 3–6. Bragg detested McCown, and his troops were from Van Dorn's army anyway.[10]

Historians have declared Bragg's railroad maneuver to Chattanooga a stroke of genius. Sending McCown's Division would be a test of the feasibility of a larger railroad movement. Bragg's wife, Elise, may also have influenced the decision. The general clearly desired to take the offensive and saw the benefit of getting in Buell's rear. In truth, the maneuver was not a stroke of genius or Elise's influence nor was McCown's move a test case for the railroads. Indeed, there is not a shred of evidence to suggest that Bragg ever thought of it as such. The general's plan from the outset had been to attack Corinth, but the war was shifting east; Bragg belatedly rode the rails with it. The army began the 776-mile trip via Mobile and Montgomery on July 23. Colonel Johnston had written about the obviousness of the maneuver on the fifteenth, and Smith wrote similarly on the twentieth; Smith even offered to serve as Bragg's subordinate. The cavalry, artillery, and wagons went cross-country to Rome, Georgia, and thence to Chattanooga. Though Bragg has probably been given more credit than he deserved, the maneuver clearly changed the course of the war in the West.[11]

None of this could have been possible without Buell's methodical movement and the increasingly notorious Nathan Bedford Forrest, recently promoted to brigadier. Buell abandoned the Memphis & Charleston as a supply line and relied instead on the Nashville & Chattanooga Railroad, using Stevenson, Alabama, as his supply base. On July 13, Forrest, with 1,000 troopers, bagged the garrison at Murfreesboro, some 1,400 troops and 4 guns, and destroyed the Stones River Bridge. The incident bought Bragg an additional two weeks, and Buell had to make large detachments to guard his rear.[12]

The question has been raised as to whether Smith's pleas for help were actually a manipulation to get rid of the defense of Chattanooga so that his troops could independently march into Kentucky. Historian Lawrence Hewitt came to such a conclusion. Smith, according to Hewitt, had clearly decided to invade Kentucky by July 14. By the seventeenth, he was transferring troops *away* from Chattanooga and *toward* Cumberland Gap. By the twenty-seventh, Bragg still had no intention of invading Kentucky. Indeed, had he known about the limits of his jurisdiction *before* he got to Chattanooga, he "undoubtedly would have attacked Corinth." The lack of a unified command would prove to be the greatest flaw of the campaign.[13]

Bragg had to secure Vicksburg, northern Mississippi, and Port Hudson, Louisiana, before departing Tupelo. Most of Van Dorn's army deployed at Holly Springs, although five of his Arkansas regiments went to Port Hudson and a half dozen regiments were remounted and converted once again into cavalry. Fifteen or so newly organized regiments (mostly from Mississippi) arrived from camps of instruction, comprised of new levies who had volunteered to avoid the onus of being conscripted. A half dozen regiments reported to Vicksburg from the Gulf Coast and the former New Orleans garrison. In September 1862, 14,000 Fort Donelson and Island No. 10 exchangees arrived, 8,000 of whom went to the emerging Mississippi army. Breckinridge's Division was also retained in the state. Bragg divided the forces into two commands: the District of Mississippi, with 14,000 troops under Van Dorn, and the District of the Tennessee, with 11,000 troops under Sterling Price. Van Dorn was charged with the protection of Vicksburg and Price of northern Mississippi, specifically to keep Grant's and William S. Rosecrans's armies from operating against Bragg.[14]

The myth that Kentucky was a sleeping giant of secessionism primed to be awakened had long captivated the Confederates. Albert Sidney Johnston had fallen for it back in the fall of 1861, and now, a year later, the siren call sounded once again. Only the presence of a Confederate army, assured the Kentucky raider John Hunt Morgan, was needed for Southern sympathizers to rise en masse. In truth, the overwhelming majority of Kentuckians sat the war out.

Smith, reinforced with two brigades (Preston Smith's and Patrick Cleburne's) of 3,000 troops from Bragg's army, would invest the Union garrison at Cumberland Gap. Once the garrison had been neutralized, Smith would return and cooperate with Bragg in a move on Buell's army, after which the combined armies would march into Kentucky. It has generally been concluded by historians that Smith never intended to cooperate (Earl Hess referred to it as Smith's "scheme"). No sooner had he reached Cumberland Gap than the East Tennessee commander notified Bragg that it would take a month-long siege to pry the well-supplied Yankees out of the gap. He suggested covering the gap and proceeding directly to Lexington, Kentucky. Bragg, himself smitten with the thought of a Kentucky offensive, acquiesced, although he warned Smith not to move north until he could be supported. Did Smith subsequently scheme and manipulate, or was he dragged along by developing circumstances? The evidence points to the former.[15]

Was the Kentucky Campaign doomed from the outset? No, but the possibility of success became increasingly diminished. Bragg reorganized his infantry while in Chattanooga, placing his two corps under Hardee and Polk. The army commander did everything in his power to be rid of Polk, but the president sustained his friend. When tactical differences arose, Davis refused to get involved. He philosophically believed that his generals should work in consensus. Operational plans remained confused, although Davis clearly saw the campaign not as a raid but an invasion with the political goal of reinstalling Confederate Kentucky governor Richard Hawes. Humphrey Marshall, commanding 3,000 troops, pledged to push through Pound Gap by August 15 and move toward Cincinnati while Smith marched on Lexington and Bragg on Louisville. Once Kentucky was in the Confederate column, Marshall intended to draft all eligible men. Bragg, on the other hand, saw the campaign as a raid, in which Kentuckians, to the tune of 50,000, would rise up.[16]

The Army of the Mississippi crossed the Tennessee River at Chattanooga on August 28, marching northeast to Pikeville. The ascent up Walden's Ridge proved horrid. "The road up the mountainside was narrow and tortuous, besides being blocked by a continuous line of wagons all the way up," wrote William L. Trask. "We were obliged to make our way around and through them and sometimes over them, thus rendering our ascent the more difficult, slow and tiresome. There was no water and we suffered intensely for it. After resting till 10:00 P.M., we again moved forward and at 2 A.M., after marching twelve miles we halted, very much fatigued and worn out. Haven't seen a drop of water since leaving the foot of the Ridge." Two Kentucky civilians took note of Bragg's transportation: "They had country wagons, in which they could not haul a very heavy load." Another commented that the vehicles were "light two-horse wagons, though frequently drawn by four or six mules. Some were with covers, others with none, or mere sheets thrown over them." He regarded the discipline of the troops as "very strict," and he noticed that all of the officers appeared actively engaged. To one Kentuckian, however, the Southerners appeared "ragged, greasy, and dirty and some barefoot. . . . They surrounded our wells like the locusts of Egypt and struggled with each other for the water as if perishing with thirst, and they thronged our kitchen doors and windows, begging for bread like hungry wolves."[17]

By September 3, Cheatham's Division had arrived at Sparta. From there, Bragg probably intended to go directly to Lexington via Albany. Discovering that Buell remained huddled in Nashville, however, he decided to cut the Federal line of communications to Louisville. To his credit, Bragg totally outmaneuvered Buell. Fearful that the Confederates would swing back and attack Nashville from the north, the Northern general remained focused on the Tennessee capital. He thus kept his army dispersed on a line running north to south. The door to Kentucky was left wide open and Bragg walked in—by way of not Bowling Green but Glasgow.[18]

Smith, meanwhile, marched into southwest Kentucky. Leaving Heth's Division at Barboursville, he advanced with Cleburne's and Thomas Churchill's divisions, 6,000 troops, and John Scott's cavalry brigade of 850 troopers. On August 30, he encountered a Union division on high ground south of Richmond, Kentucky. In a stunning Confederate victory, Smith routed the Federals, inflicting 5,353 casualties, mostly prisoners, while losing only 451. An entire Yankee division had been virtually destroyed by a force of equal size in open battle. It had been Smith's victory, but the rising star turned out to be Patrick Cleburne, who had seen the weakness in the Union center and ordered a counterattack. A bullet struck him in the mouth, smashing two teeth and causing much bleeding, but the Irishman's reputation as a hard charger was on the ascent.[19]

Meanwhile, Bragg's 28,000 troops dodged Buell's 40,000 and marched twenty miles north from Glasgow to Munfordville, which was garrisoned by 4,000 bluecoats under Col. John T. Wilder. Buell could simply not fathom such a maneuver. In later testimony he argued that Bragg moving north of Glasgow would result in a loss of communications with Tennessee and place Smith in a vulnerable position. Munfordville was simply "not essential to Bragg's army," and Buell continued to concentrate on Nashville. Wilder, who had been given orders to hold at all hazards, was doomed. The garrison surrendered on September 16, but not before Brigadier General Chalmers launched a foolish and unauthorized failed attack, in which he lost 288 men.[20]

Though Chalmers's defeat had been small, it nonetheless represented the first engagement under Bragg's leadership. If Bragg had not taken Munfordville, he would have emerged from the campaign with no victories. Nonetheless, concentrating on Munfordville rather than linking up with Smith earned him historical censure. "Bragg would have to pay a heavy price for the satisfaction to be gained in overpowering the garrison," Connelly wrote, since the "all-important junction with Kirby Smith would be delayed." By spending three days at Munfordville, hoping that Buell would attack, Bragg sacrificed the offensive. Connelly criticized what he termed the "Munfordville Myth"—that Bragg had blocked Buell's approach to Louisville. Buell could have taken a half dozen approaches. Bragg should have ignored Munfordville and rushed to Bardstown for the linkup with Smith. Hewitt, on the other hand, argued that if Smith had "concentrated at nearby Shelbyville [nineteen miles northwest of Bardstown], as Bragg expected them to be, the two Confederate armies would then have been in position for a simultaneous advance on Louisville. But, contrary to Bragg's instructions, Kirby Smith dallied in eastern Kentucky, and Bragg was compelled to allow Buell to reach Louisville without a fight." McWhiney concurred. When Bragg was at Munfordville, Smith's forces were 100 miles away, dispersed from Lexington to Cumberland Gap. Smith wanted to link up not at Bardstown but at Lexington. The evidence seems clear, believed McWhiney, that Smith expected Bragg to defeat Buell on his own. He promised to return Bragg's two brigades, but the next day he changed his mind.[21]

Matters appeared grim. First, Kentuckians were not flooding to the Confederate banner. Bragg estimated that 2,500 joined, far from the 50,000 expected. The ability of the Union to raise raw manpower, on the other hand, proved stunning. By the time Buell arrived in Louisville, an entire new corps had been recruited, placing Buell's strength at 75,000! True, many of them were new levies, as opposed to Bragg's veterans, but the numbers were stark even so. Second, Smith's apparent willingness to leave Bragg out on a limb meant that a merger of forces was becoming less likely. In truth, the campaign was falling apart. As early as September 27, Bragg considered retiring from Kentucky. At this point, according to Kenneth Noe, Bragg became overwhelmed with depression and indecision. The general drifted into agitation and mood swings. He inwardly began searching for scapegoats.[22]

On September 28, Bragg headed for Danville to connect with Governor Hawes. From there, he planned a side trip to Smith's headquarters in Lexington, where he would finally be able to exert unified command. For once, good news arrived. The Federal division at Cumberland Gap had retreated out of operational range; Stevenson's Division and Cleburne's and Preston Smith's brigades were on their way to Shelbyville. Bragg seemed to regain his aggressive spirit, and even news of the capture of the 3rd Georgia Cavalry at New Haven on the twenty-ninth failed to dampen his spirit. On a beautiful October 1, Bragg arrived at Lexington and conferred with Edmund Kirby Smith at the Phoenix Hotel. Colonel Brent of the army staff jotted in his diary: "It is generally believed that he [Bragg] will take command of all the forces in Kentucky. I hope so. There must be unity of command or failure will attend us."[23]

On October 2, Bragg received intelligence that the Federals in Louisville were converging in force on Frankfort. He immediately ordered Preston Smith's and Cleburne's brigades to withdraw from Shelbyville and march toward Frankfort. Edmund Kirby Smith's army would attack from the front,

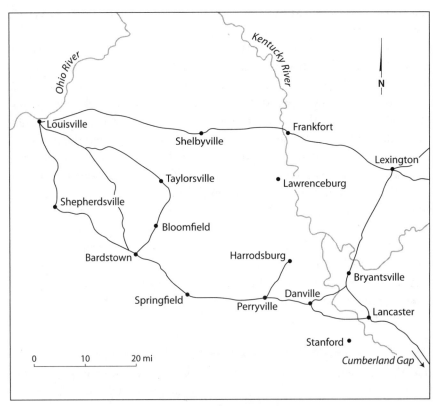

Map 2. Central Kentucky, 1862

while Bragg's army, under Polk's command, would assail the enemy flank and rear via Bloomfield. Bragg did not know, due to poor intelligence, that the enemy advanced over a sixty-mile front. At 3:30 P.M. on the third, Bragg and Hawes departed by train to Frankfort. By 8:00 P.M., the army commander realized that the column moving on Frankfort (two divisions) was a feint, but the enemy continued toward the state capital. He did not know that a much larger separate column closed in on Polk at Bardstown.[24]

Meanwhile, at Bardstown, Polk knew what Bragg did not yet know: three Federal corps were converging on his position. Obviously he could not move north via Bloomfield as ordered when the Federals had that road blocked. In the so-called Bardstown Council of October 3, Polk took a vote of his generals as to whether to obey Bragg's order. Perhaps it was a mere formality and the general simply sought support for a decision he had already made. At any rate, he suggested a retreat to Danville. Only Patton Anderson questioned the advisability of the move, stating that Smith might be in trouble if Polk failed to support him. At 3:00 P.M., a vote ensued and the army retreated. It was the correct decision.[25]

Not all historians agreed. McWhiney noted that the three Federal corps were still twenty miles from Bardstown and a day's march from one another. If Polk had followed Bragg's order and marched to Frankfort, he would not "have necessarily exposed the Confederate flank to attack." Alexander McCook's corps at Taylorsville counted only 10,000 bluecoats, while Polk had 20,000 infantry. Polk and Smith could then have crushed the two Federal divisions at Frankfort. The proverbial devil is in the details. This theory assumes that the two Federal divisions would have sat passively as Rebel strength built up in their front; they could always have fallen back on Louisville. McCook could have stalled Polk long enough for the balance of Buell's army to catch up. At least one of Polk's four divisions would have to have guarded the rear as the main column marched the forty-two miles to Frankfort. Would the Federals have concentrated and mauled that division? Buell's army could also have marched directly to Bryantsville, cutting off Bragg's line of communications. There were simply too many risks involved; Polk got it right.[26]

The Battle of Perryville and Retreat

In early October, Buell caught the Southerners badly scattered. His 58,000 troops converged on Polk's Corps and Cheatham's Division of Hardee's Corps, 16,000 total, arrayed on the eastern edge of Chaplin's Creek west of Perryville. Wrongly believing that Buell was concentrating on either Shelbyville or Frankfort, Bragg maintained Heth's (6,000), McCown's (3,000), and Withers's (6,200) divisions at Salvisa. Stevenson's Division (9,000) held Versailles, and Marshall's Division (3,000) Lexington. Morgan's 1,500 troopers screened Lexington. By October 6, Bragg still had not heard from Hardee or Polk and continued his plan to attack the Federals marching on Smith. Polk received orders to attack the column in his front and then move north where the main battle would be fought, or so Bragg thought. Polk, of course, did not know how many Yankees fronted him, but he knew there was at least a corps. He considered it imprudent to attack an enemy of unknown size. As at Bardstown, he called a council of war and took a vote. He would later argue that he considered Bragg's order to be not peremptory but rather a suggestion. For the second time, the generals decided to disobey a direct order. Polk took up a defensive position on the east bank of Chaplin's River. A stunned Bragg arrived in early afternoon to find that no attack had been ordered.[27]

Historians once again criticized Polk, stating that an attack on the Union center would have worked. Brent, who was actually on the scene, saw what they did not: "General Polk's line was weak, his right if outflanked by the enemy would have cut us off from Harrodsburg and General Smith." James Lee McDonough and Noe, the two most recent Perryville historians and with whom I am inclined to agree, supported Polk. "An attack under such circumstances was a flirtation with disaster," concluded McDonough. Noe wrote that Polk "made the best decision possible." Hess believed that Polk should have obeyed in this instance, but he admitted that a few more hours of fighting would not have made a difference.[28]

Bragg inspected Polk's line and immediately found his right "in the air." The army commander realized the threats on the Springfield Pike and Mackville Road but remained oblivious that another Union corps approached on the Lebanon Pike, guarded only by Joseph Wheeler's Brigade. At noon, Rebel artillery opened fire, and at 2:00 P.M., Cheatham's Division, on the far right, attacked. A half hour later, Hardee's Corps advanced, driving back two Union brigades on the Mackville Pike. Daniel Adams's Brigade, on the far left, swung around the Union flank, only to be checked by Phil Sheridan's artillery. By late afternoon, the Federal 1st Corps had been routed, but the attack sputtered to a halt. Bragg had won a tactical victory, but he now realized his perilous position. During the night he withdrew. Buell sustained 4,211 casualties; Bragg, 3,396. Some 900 Confederate wounded remained in Perryville. Only Northern ineptitude and something called an "acoustic shadow" that blocked the sound of battle at Buell's headquarters saved Bragg's army from annihilation.[29]

Bragg and Smith finally united at Bryantsville; discussions took on a somber tone. Word had arrived of Van Dorn's defeat at Corinth. Intelligence indicated additional Union reinforcements were on the way. To Simon Buckner, the army commander appeared "overwhelmed, didn't know what to do." Only four days' rations remained. On October 13, Bragg began his withdrawal to Cumberland Gap. The retreat along the Old Wilderness Trail resulted in near-starvation conditions. The Army of the Mississippi escaped, but the fifty-five-day campaign had been a cumulative failure. It could have been much worse. If Buell had sent a heavy detachment to capture Chattanooga when Bragg initially marched north, it would, concluded Stoker, "have laid the foundation for the destruction of Bragg's army." Buell also failed to vigorously pursue the retreating Confederates. The only positive result of the campaign was that the Federals had abandoned northern Alabama and Middle Tennessee south of Nashville. On October 14, Brent took pen in hand and wrote, "Kentucky is now surrendered and will prove a heavy blow, but politically it will be one obstacle removed in the settlement of affairs."[30]

The News Reaches Richmond

News of the Battle of Perryville and Bragg's subsequent retreat into Tennessee was slow to arrive in Richmond. Based on initial Union press accounts and a spike in the price of gold in the North, it was widely believed that the battle had been a significant Southern victory. "If Gen. Bragg has been as signally victorious as we hope and believe he has, it will have been, probably the most important event of the war," declared the *Richmond Dispatch*. "It will throw the whole state of Kentucky into the arms of the Confederacy, and will free Tennessee, and eventually Mississippi. It will give new life and vision to our Cause."[31]

John Jones in the War Department did not know exactly what to believe. Good reports continued to arrive in the capital of a great victory in Kentucky, with the enemy losing 25,000 men. On October 17, 1862, Jones cautiously wrote in his journal, "Western accounts are generally exaggerated." The next day a telegram arrived from Knoxville. A wounded officer arrived and confirmed a great victory with 10,000 prisoners. "We shall have our positive news," Jones believed. On the nineteenth, however, Robert Kean, another bureaucrat in the War Department, made a notation: "Bragg is retreating in Kentucky. No official news of the Battle of Perryville at the Department yet." The next day, nearly two weeks after the battle, news remained "very vague." Reports of a victory continued to filter in, yet the army had retreated forty miles and was even then retiring through Cumberland Gap. "Still nothing definite from Kentucky more than the retreat of Bragg," Jones noted on the twenty-first. The truth became transparent the next day when Bragg's Perryville report arrived in the capital. The press continued to put on a positive face, but a disgusted Jones jotted, "Thus Kentucky is given up for the moment!"[32]

Other Richmond administrators quietly expressed their frustration. Jeremy Gilmer, at the Engineer Bureau, explained to his wife that the Kentucky Campaign "is pronounced here a magnificent failure — big show and no result — a march up the hill and down again, and his troops, like the army in Flanders, no doubt 'swore terribly.'" Colonel Johnston, his office across the hallway from the president's, expressed to his wife, "I think Bragg in Kentucky a signal failure." Even the president admitted, "The results in Kentucky have been to me a bitter disappointment."[33]

The Richmond press corps, the "dogs of detraction," as Bragg referred to them, went on a tear. The *Whig* denounced the campaign as "simply a fizzle" and "a brilliant blunder and a magnificent failure." The *Dispatch* credited Bragg with being a good disciplinarian, "but he seems to have been greatly deficient in some other qualities which constitute a great commander." John M. McDaniel at the *Examiner* unleashed in an editorial: "Of genius, military or civil, he [Bragg] has none. Even in judgment and sagacity, for large affairs he is notoriously deficient. As commander-in-chief[,] he is worse than inexperienced, for he has grown old and hardened." The column ungraciously concluded by declaring that the general had "an iron heart, an iron hand, and a wooden head." George Bagby, a gossip columnist writing from Richmond for the *Charleston Daily Mercury*, viciously attacked Bragg's capacity, coming close to questioning his prewar reputation and courage, although he later retracted his insinuations.[34]

With the army safely in Knoxville, Davis summoned Bragg to the capital. Leaving Polk in command, the general departed on October 24. He arrived in remarkably high spirits, all the more curious since everyone suspected that he would be removed from command. He and the president engaged in daily marathon closed-door sessions, lasting from 10:00 to 4:00. On the twenty-seventh, the general stole away to visit his brother Thomas, a member of the president's cabinet. Thomas found him "well & in good spirits," and he was assured that the president had been entirely satisfied with the Kentucky Campaign. John Jones, catching wind of the turning tide, wrote, "Gen. Bragg is here, but will not probably be deprived of his command." George Bagby filed a news report on November 1: "The president has been invisible since last Saturday [October 25]. Up to yesterday he was closeted all the time with Bragg, who returns to his command with the supporting smiles of the Executive."[35]

Davis later explained his support of Bragg by claiming that there was no one to replace him. Lee could not be spared; Joseph E. Johnston, Lee's predecessor, was still recuperating from a wound; and Beauregard had been tested and found wanting. Davis saw Bragg as a good administrator who knew the army, and it would take too much time to assimilate a replacement at any rate. The president also thought Bragg's enemies doubled as those of the administration. He saw their carping as nothing more than an attempt to get at him. Expressions of confidence notwithstanding, the chief executive remained uncertain. Many unsettling rumors emerged that Bragg had lost the confidence of his officers. Davis thus invited Smith, Polk, and Hardee to Richmond. Since he had already determined to sustain Bragg, it seems clear that he was seeking their cooperation. He even offered them lieutenant general commissions, more of a pitiful bribe than a measure of performance.[36]

Smith, suffering from a head cold, arrived on November 3. He had become so depressed over the recent campaign that he seriously considered resigning and thought of going into the ministry once again. Believing himself unworthy of the priesthood, he abandoned the idea. Prior to Smith's arrival,

Davis had written him that Bragg had "uniformly spoken of you in the most complimentary terms, and does not seem to imagine your dissatisfaction." Unimpressed, the East Tennessee commander strongly suggested that Bragg be replaced with Joseph E. Johnston. On Smith's return trip, in an awkward moment, he accidentally met Bragg at the Knoxville train station. Although Smith expected a "stormy meeting," Bragg spoke quite kindly and complimentarily. "I was astonished but believe he is honest & means well," Smith related to his new bride. If Bragg had not bought Smith's loyalty, he at least bought his silence. Thereafter, he never spoke of the Kentucky Campaign.[37]

Precisely when Polk arrived in Richmond is not known, but the forever snooping Bagby saw him on November 10 — "for what purpose we can only conjecture." How the subsequent conversation went can be garnered from an account left by Polk's son. The general considered the late campaign a failure and he suggested Johnston as a replacement. If Smith kept silent on his return, Polk had no such compulsion. Davis was not unsympathetic to his old friend. "I could make good use of him [Bragg] *here* in Richmond," he told Polk, perhaps in Samuel Cooper's position as Confederate adjutant general and inspector general. He even conceded that another general "might excite more enthusiasm, but as all have their defects I have not seen how to make change with advantage."[38]

Hardee, appearing above the fray, begged off the trip. He nonetheless expressed his frank opinion to Col. William Preston Johnston, suspecting, perhaps hoping, that it would be shared with the president. Bragg's enemies had "just grounds for attacking him," he wrote, but finding a successor would be problematic. "Bragg has proven a failure, it is true, but . . . have we any body who will do better[?] I confess this has been a strong reason in restraining me from speaking out boldly in reference to the failure in Kentucky."[39]

Joseph E. Johnston

Gen. Joseph E. Johnston had been severely wounded at Seven Pines on May 31, 1862. His recovery proved slow and painful, but by early November, just as the western crisis came to a head, he was seen walking the streets of Richmond and on horseback. Although far from totally recovered, the general reported for duty on November 12. During his recuperation, Lee's fame had grown and it became apparent that Johnston would not resume his former position as head of the Army of Northern Virginia. Thereafter, the displaced general held a bias against Lee.[40]

Johnston reported to the War Department on November 12. At that time, Secretary of War George W. Randolph notified the Virginian that he had been assigned to the newly formed "Western Department," comprising Smith's department in East Tennessee, Bragg's in Middle Tennessee, John C. Pemberton's in Mississippi, and the Mobile defenses. Noticeably left off the list was the Trans-Mississippi Department, led by Lt. Gen. Theophilus Holmes. Johnston proposed that the forces west of the Mississippi River be united with those under Pemberton. Randolph smiled and read a letter he had written to Holmes instructing that precise movement, but the president countermanded it. The secretary resigned several days later and was replaced by James Seddon. Precisely why Davis created this new command has long been debated. Some have suggested that the president made a genuine attempt to put aside personal prejudices and bring order to the West. As for his part, Johnston never grasped the concept. He wanted command of not a department but an army, specifically the Army of Northern Virginia. He remained highly suspicious of Davis's intention, believing that this was an attempt to place him on the shelf. Indeed, Johnston's wife saw him as being set up as a scapegoat in the event of a disaster.[41]

Well intentioned or not, the concept was doomed to failure. First, it was based on the premise that the Federal army held two primary objectives—Richmond and the Mississippi River. Johnston wanted to know which was more important—Tennessee or Mississippi? Davis refused to answer the question (he believed that both could be held), but it would become clear as time went on that he favored Mississippi. Davis saw the central South—the Nashville, Chattanooga, and Atlanta corridor—as simply a food-producing region. Second, there was the issue of limited authority. Johnston would not be in command of troops directly, only of coordination of troops. Department heads would continue to report directly to Richmond. If one of them proved uncooperative (as Pemberton did), Johnston would not even have the latest intelligence.[42]

Johnston also disagreed with matching Tennessee with Mississippi. He believed that Pemberton's department should be linked with the Trans-Mississippi, especially given that Grant's Federal army and the Tennessee River stood between Pemberton and Bragg. Johnston believed that Holmes had more than 50,000 troops near Little Rock, with no significant Federal force in the state. Pemberton, on the other hand, had only 23,000, plus 6,000 cavalry (mostly irregulars) and the Vicksburg garrison of 6,000. By uniting Holmes and Pemberton, Johnston would have a force of 70,000 to oppose Grant's 43,000. But his figures were faulty. After deducting garrisons and Indians, Holmes actually had a force of barely 16,000 to face 30,000 Yankees at Springfield, Missouri, and 12,000–15,000 at Helena, Arkansas. The most Holmes ever considered sending across the river was Benjamin

McCulloch's 6,000-man Arkansas division. Davis never pressed the issue, fearing the subsequent loss of territory, desertions, and the political ramifications—Arkansas governor Henry Rector had already threatened to pull out of the Confederacy. Pemberton actually faced an army of 50,000 but believed it to be 60,000.[43]

Other issues remained. The immense size of the department made it difficult to timely transport reinforcements over a single rail line. With his troops scattered over 300 miles from Vicksburg, Holmes claimed that they could not arrive in less than a month. Trumping all of these concerns, however, was Johnston's own defeatist attitude. Upon his arrival at Chattanooga, the Virginian wrote, "Nobody ever assumed command under more unfavorable circumstances."[44]

Both politically and tactically, the Confederates had squandered the Kentucky Campaign. What Bragg had intended to be an invasion turned into a raid. Perhaps Southerners simply overexpected, anticipating an army of Kentuckians to rise up as a permanent occupying force. The failed venture left bitter feelings. Edward Brown of the 45th Alabama took pen in hand and bluntly told his wife, "As far as I am concerned, it [Kentucky] may go to the Yankees." Attention now turned back to Tennessee.[45]

❋ 4 ❋

The Officer Corps
The Bragg Influence

In June 1862, Braxton Bragg became the army's third commander. Hardly in better health than his predecessor, he had long suffered from chronic migraines, dysentery, diarrhea, rheumatism, boils, and depression. The blue mass and calomel he took for his liver problem may have led to mercury poisoning. Noe thought his mood swings were possibly the result of narcissistic personality disorder. While this cannot be proved, it is undisputable that Bragg possessed an obsessive desire to define his enemies. A West Point graduate of the class of '37, he had earned a well-deserved reputation in the old army for being argumentative and outspoken to the point of indiscretion. Gen. Richard Taylor once visited the army in Chattanooga and had dinner with Bragg and numerous staff officers. Taylor inquired about a division commander with the army and sat stunned as Bragg said, "General —— [Samuel Jones?] is an old woman, utterly worthless." Taylor wrote, "Such a declaration, privately made, would have been serious, but publically, and certainly to be repeated, it was astonishing." Despite the criticism, those who knew Bragg insisted that his reputation for being a cruel man was patently unwarranted.[1]

Until recently, historians have concluded that Bragg negatively affected the culture of the army's officer corps. His "perversely cantankerous personality" and lack of "imaginative aggressiveness," such as that demonstrated by Lee, resulted in the "war's most woeful army." A who's who of western historians—Castel, McWhiney, Connelly, and McMurry—have lined up in agreement. There is much contemporary evidence that supports their conclusion. Bragg developed an early reputation as a stern disciplinarian. His grim affect caused a soldier to describe him as "a very stern looking old man with gray hair," who appeared "very restless." Opinionated and lacking in charm, he desired people to get to the point in conversation. Many men feared approaching him because he could be so sharp in his sarcasm. Even Bragg's older brother John wrote of his Achilles' heel—"his impulsive and sanguine temper." Brig. Gen. E. P. Alexander of Lee's army never saw Bragg as "a clear and cool thinker, at all." Others described him as "muddle headed." It was whispered that he could not understand a map and that "it was a spectacle to see him wrestle with one, with one finger painfully holding down his own position." A courier once delivered a dispatch to the general, which said that Bragg has a "wild abstracted look and pays little attention to what is passing around him, his mind seems to be in a continual strain."[2]

William Mackall, the army chief of staff during the last half of 1863, described him thus: "He is as much influenced by his enemies as by his friends, and does not know how to control the one or preserve the other. He is very earnest at his work, his whole soul is in it, but his manner is repulsive and he has no social life. He is easily flattered and fond of seeing reverence for his position." He concluded: "If he don't want news to be true, he will listen to nothing. 'It can't be so,' is his reasoning, and if it is proven true, he is not prepared to meet it." His failures as both a strategist and tactician have also been criticized. His near-suicidal frontal assaults at Shiloh, failure during the Kentucky Campaign, strategic loss at Stones River, outmaneuvering in the Tullahoma Campaign, failure to follow up his sole victory at Chickamauga, and disastrous rout at Missionary Ridge have all been a part of the standard litany of criticism.[3]

Recent historians, especially Earl Hess, have counterattacked and challenged preconceptions about the general. Bragg showed flashes of tenderness and what McDonough described as attempts at clumsy humor. The army commander privately wept at the prospect of leaving behind his Stones River wounded. For friendship, he turned to his wife and confidant—Elise. Hess documented the deep love and emotional support he received from his consort. On November 14, 1863, the general invited fourteen ladies to his headquarters, perhaps "because he was isolated from friendly discourse and missed his wife's company."[4]

While the infighting in the army was notorious, Colonel Urquhart, Bragg's aide and friend, wrote of several supportive generals—Joseph Wheeler, Jones Withers, Patton Anderson, John C. Brown, John K. Jackson, William Bate, and E. C. Walthall. In July 1864, Wheeler added to the list A. P. Stewart, Carter Stevenson, W. H. T. Walker, and James Holtzclaw. Letters of support also came from Daniel Donelson, James Chalmers, and Preston Smith. Arthur Manigault became an outspoken Bragg supporter. Indeed, more brigadiers and major generals supported Bragg than opposed him. Unfortunately, his enemies detested him.[5]

It is true that Bragg lacked inspirational leadership, but Brig. Gen. William Preston's statement that "no cheer salutes him as he passes" was untrue. The Louisiana brigade loudly cheered him as he encouraged them forward into the Round Forest at Stones River. After Chickamauga, a Georgian noted,

"Genl. Bragg rode down the lines today and was cheered long and hard." Bragg never put on airs. Indeed, on the field he did not wear a uniform, only gray pants tucked into his boots and a loose hunting shirt, and had no rank showing but a sword and a kepi.[6]

Bragg's skills as a strategist and tactician have also undergone revisionism. Donald Stoker believed that the general's plan after Fort Donelson to mass in the center and then go on the offensive was "the most coherent strategic plan by any Confederate leader during the course of the war." Archer Jones praised Bragg's strategic turning movement in the summer of 1862. Woodworth concluded that Bragg was "an excellent strategist, organizer, administrator, and disciplinarian" but "an average tactician."[7]

Hess saw Bragg's soiled reputation as partially redeemable. He viewed the general's piecemeal frontal assaults at Shiloh as a "common failing" among generals at the time. Bragg showed a "good deal of tactical aggressiveness at Perryville," and although he did not deal well with the problems that confronted him, the campaign "could have resulted far more disastrously than it did." Hess praised Bragg's subsequent move to Middle Tennessee. The first day's battle at Stones River proved "one of the best day's fighting for the Army of Tennessee." His failure to fight at Tullahoma was due to a lack of support from his corps commanders. The second day's assault at Chickamauga is widely criticized by historians, but Hess saw it "as good as any that could have been devised." The inner squabbling that paralyzed the command structure fell largely to Davis's refusal to resolve the issue. After Missionary Ridge, the general was "relieved" to be removed from command. In his aggressiveness, Bragg was not Lee, but "he was half a Lee."[8]

The pendulum had clearly swung too far and needed adjustment; Bragg was a complex personality who exhibited flashes of greatness. That said, multiple mistakes simply cannot be expunged from the record: The repeated frontal assaults at Shiloh, given the Confederate overall plan, were inexcusable. The Federal Army of the Ohio should have been defeated *before* Bragg marched into Kentucky, and he did not deal well with the changing scenarios during the campaign. Despite having been at Murfreesboro for six weeks, he overlooked the most strategic geographic feature on the Stones River battlefield—McFadden's Hill, a hill subsequently occupied by the Federals that proved pivotal. The subsequent assault plan on December 31 was actually Polk's; Bragg had wanted to attack up the center. It is true that Bragg did not have the support of his corps commanders at Tullahoma, but he waited until the eleventh hour to present his questionable flanking maneuver. At McLemore's Cove, Bragg should have arrived on the scene hours earlier and taken personal command. His brute-force plan of attack on September 20 at

TABLE 3. *Estimates of Union and Confederate casualties*

Location	Union casualties	Confederate casualties
Munfordville	4,148	714
Perryville	4,241	3,396
Stones River	12,906	11,739
Tullahoma Campaign	570	2,500 (est.)
Chickamauga	16,170	18,454
Chattanooga Campaign	5,824	8,000 (est.)
Total	43,859	44,803

Chickamauga very likely would have been hurled back but for the cooperation of the Federals. At Missionary Ridge, the mistakes proved too many to count. His organizational skills, long lauded by historians, were not as imaginative as portrayed; his persistence in maintaining the battery-brigade structure could certainly be criticized. While many of his virtues and statistical achievements can result in academic points, in war there is only one issue: Did he win? Hess concluded that "public opinion was indeed Bragg's worst enemy." I believe that Bragg was his own worst enemy.[9]

Bragg's influence can be viewed as mixed. The army's deepest penetration of enemy territory and greatest tactical wins (Perryville, December 31 at Stones River, and Chickamauga) came under his command, in part due to his close-order assaults and preference for the tactical offensive. Some of the army's greatest setbacks also occurred on his watch—the Tullahoma and Chattanooga Campaigns. His aggressive tactics proved costly, inflicting 43,859 Union casualties but sustaining 44,805.

Bragg's Lieutenants

Perhaps Bragg's dark side would not have been so pronounced had he not had such unruly and backstabbing subordinates. Such was the case with Leonidas Polk. Upon his graduation from West Point in 1827, Polk quit the army and entered the Episcopal priesthood. He was never a deep theologian or well versed in church law, and his subsequent rise to bishop of Louisiana came more through his wealth and influence. A roommate and personal friend of Jefferson Davis's at the academy, Polk was awarded a major general's commission from the president at the beginning of the war. He promptly bungled the issue of Kentucky neutrality. Bragg first met him at Corinth in the spring of 1862; he was unimpressed.[10]

Never willing to challenge Southern culture or his own personal opulence as a bishop, Polk had no difficulty challenging Bragg. Although the two officers never meshed from the outset, after Perryville, Polk became part of a clique that openly undercut the army commander. The tragedy of the bishop is that he could have been either the army's pastor and healer or its prophet, speaking truth to power. He was neither, choosing instead to be the army's conniver. He did so primarily through his clandestine letters to Davis. Although the troops loved him, those on the inside saw his true nature. Taylor Beatty saw Polk as "a slow coach—one who cannot be depended on." Dr. David Yandell wrote pointedly: "Genl Polk threatened wonders. He was positively ferocious. But he can't be relied on. . . . He is great at talk, but he is monstrous uncertain. I saw enough of the old grey beard at Shiloh & Perryville to cause me to place no great confidence in him. He will prevaricate. He did say that he was going to do this and going to do that, but the old man forgets; [unless he is] transferred to house duties we will all go to the Devil out here."[11]

Bragg's brother John, though not in the army, seemed to have Polk's number. He rejoiced when the corps commander transferred to Mississippi. "He has always been a nuisance in the Army & always will be. His dream has been, by every sort of insinuation and intrigue, to get command of the Army of Tennessee. . . . The truth is, he ought to have been arrested a dozen times long ago. I sincerely trust this may be the last of him. Let him go back to preaching—his piety is sadly out of repair & requires all of his care." In fairness, the image of Polk as an officer who reveled in disobeying orders has been overplayed. The two most notorious examples occurred in the Kentucky Campaign—both instances proved justified. The bishop on occasion could also be a fair tactician: he suggested the left sweep at the Battle of Stones River (instead of Bragg's proposed attack on the center), he rejected Bragg's ill-planned flank movement at Tullahoma, and he proposed a concentration on Thomas Crittenden's corps before Chickamauga. His counsel to retreat at Stones River and Tullahoma proved correct. Nonetheless, the bishop's mistakes at Columbus, Kentucky, and Chickamauga proved too monumental to be dismissed.[12]

Hardee was a better soldier. A cavalryman described him thus: "Genl. Hardee is a fine looking old gentleman apparently about forty-eight years old. He is about six foot high—of heavy build and thus incline to corpulency. He has gray hair, forehead tolerably high but not broad and a little receding—mile large eyes—tolerably large nose thick lips—upper teeth protruding a little—wore a heavy mustache & thick gray beard on his chin. His mustachios partially conceal his lips & teeth & he is altogether a fine looking man especially at a short distance from him." Joseph E. Johnston never grew close to him. He related to St. John Liddell that Hardee "likes the show of war, but dislikes its labors and responsibilities. I believe he was not intended by nature to be a great leader."[13]

Despite being in the thick of army intrigue, Hardee unfortunately became distracted by what Cleburne called "running with women." By 1862, he had been a widower for eight years, but according to a correspondent, "he has been in love a dozen times since." Indeed, the reporter personally knew two women who were "dying after him." In early 1863, he began courting Miss Alice Reading, sister of John Hunt Morgan's wife. Their frequent trysts became an open secret and the press falsely reported that the two had become engaged. By April 1863, he was seeing another woman, twenty-eight-year-old Mrs. Sue Williamson, a wealthy Huntsville widow. At least two witnesses saw her, along with some other ladies from Huntsville, staying at his headquarters, and on at least one occasion he stole away and visited her in Huntsville. How serious the relationship was is not known, but Sue left her daughter an interesting family heirloom—Hardee's sash. Mrs. Rowena Webster at the Beechwood Plantation noted that Hardee once called upon a servant there, but the woman had gone back to the North to be with her husband. His active social life led to rumors that "it is difficult to locate him."[14]

A top command change occurred in July 1863 when Hardee was transferred to Mississippi. On July 13, Davis rode up to a home in Richmond serving as the headquarters of forty-two-year-old Maj. Gen. Daniel H. Hill, a West Pointer, veteran of the Mexican War, and former North Carolina math professor, now commanding the defenses of Richmond, Petersburg, and the Department of North Carolina. Davis told him, "Rosecrans is about to advance upon Bragg; I have found it necessary to detail Hardee to defend Mississippi and Alabama. His corps is without a commander. I wish you to command it." "I cannot do that," Hill answered, "as Stewart outranks me." "I can cure that," said Davis, "by making you a lieutenant general. Your papers will be ready tomorrow. When can you start?" "In twenty-four hours," he answered.[15]

Beauregard, of course, would have been a better choice, but that proved unacceptable to Davis. Several issues made Hill's selection unfortunate, not the least of which was his health. He had a slightly bent spine, which caused him almost constant back pain, especially when the weather turned cold. He also suffered from dysentery, piles, and chills that resulted in rigors. Complicating the matter was his abrasive personality, which was described as "harsh, abrupt, [and] often insulting in the effort to be sarcastic." Hill himself admitted that he was an odd sort: "I am so unlike other folks that you could not understand my feelings if I tried to explain them for a week," he confided to his wife. Still, "Old D. H." remained popular with his troops.[16]

The story behind his western transfer really had to do with Lee, who considered Hill a competent division commander and nothing more. Hill had criticized Lee in both the Seven Days and Maryland Campaigns in his after-action reports. He vehemently opposed the Gettysburg Campaign, believing that after Chancellorsville, a corps from the Army of Northern Virginia should have been sent to Mississippi. When Lee began his offensive, he desired the return of some of the four brigades he had sent to North Carolina, but Hill refused. In searching for a third corps commander, Lee overlooked Hill and selected A. P. Hill (no relation), a slight that nearly caused Daniel H. Hill to resign. His constant negative harping led Lee to label him a "croaker." Interestingly, Hill had served under Bragg as a lieutenant in his battery in 1845 at Corpus Christi. Their first reunion did not go well. Hill found the general silent, gloomy, and reserved. "He had grown prematurely old since I saw him last, and showed much nervousness." They would become bitter enemies.[17]

Command Turnovers

Early in his command, Bragg took on the issue of what he termed "dead weight generals." When the War Department asked for names of precisely whom he had in mind, he gladly complied: Major Generals Crittenden, McCown, and Cheatham and Brig. Gens. James Trapier—a West Pointer whose debut in the Farmington engagement proved abysmal—and Richard Hawes, the provisional governor of Kentucky, a nominal position. Although he did not specifically name Polk, he pointedly left his name off the list of qualified major generals. Bragg grew weary of "incumbrances [who] would be better out of the way." He stubbornly resisted two practices—seniority, which he considered "fraught with danger," and the so-called State Rule, which said that a brigade predominately from one state should have a brigadier from that state. Bragg tried, usually unsuccessfully, to sweep house— "I do not hesitate to assert that a fourth of our efficiency is lost for want of suitable brigade and division commanders."[18]

Following the Kentucky Campaign, Bragg desired the promotion of six infantry colonels to brigadier ("in order of merit"). First was Roger W. "Old Flintlock" Hanson, a thirty-five-year-old former Kentucky lawyer and politician with experience in the Mexican War. Speaking in a deep guttural voice, he was generally good-natured, but if pushed he could exhibit a volatile temper. Next came thirty-one-year-old former Mississippi lawyer Edward C.

Walthall, an officer with no prewar experience and who began the war as a lieutenant. Forty-three-year-old Zachariah Deas, a wealthy Mobile cotton broker who had served in the Mexican War, had been badly wounded at Shiloh. Col. Arthur M. Manigault (pronounced "manny-go"), an opinionated and wealthy thirty-seven-year-old South Carolina planter, appeared on the list. Thomas Hunt, colonel of the 9th Kentucky, uncle to John Hunt Morgan, and a former Lexington, Kentucky, merchant, was also chosen. Lucius Polk had little to recommend him beyond family connections—he was Leonidas Polk's nephew and President James K. Polk's cousin. A prewar farmer, he began the war as a private. All received commissions except Hunt and Manigault, the latter's denial due to an anti-administration letter that someone had given to the press without his permission. Brent approved of all of the promotions except for Hanson's and Polk's.[19]

S. A. M. Wood, recuperating from his Perryville wound at his home in Florence, Alabama, was temporarily replaced by Preston Smith. Bragg pushed for Smith's promotion to brigadier, but in a letter to the president he mentioned that Beauregard had given Smith command of a brigade at Shiloh. It was the wrong thing to say. Davis endorsed the letter: "What authority had he for this?" Jones in the War Department wrote: "Col. Smith will not be appointed." Several other brigadiers remained on the injured or sick list, including William Carroll and Lucius Walker, neither of whom Bragg considered to be "safe men." Carroll, under indictment for alcoholism and incompetency, resigned and moved to Canada. Walker, constantly sick, received a transfer to Arkansas, where he was later killed in a duel with Gen. John S. Marmaduke. William Bate and John C. Brown were still recovering from wounds. In the cavalry, both John A. Wharton and Morgan received brigadier commissions, but Hardee was unsuccessful in his attempt to win the Kentuckian a major general's commission. "I do not wish to give all my boys all of their sugar plums at once," Davis remarked.[20]

The departure of Simon Buckner to command at Mobile left a vacancy for a major general. Bragg recommended two—Daniel Donelson and Patrick Cleburne. The Donelson suggestion came as no surprise—he was West Point and held seniority. Cleburne, on the other hand, was ranked by seven other brigadiers, but he nonetheless got selected. The story later emerged that Davis was hesitant about the Irishman, but Hardee lobbied strongly for him. Davis later related the story of a cadet he had known at West Point, a bugler by the name of Willis, who led the band. Willis had a protégé by the name of Barnes, whom he considered nearly as good as himself: "Barnes can't be beat. Barnes is the *best* bugler in the U.S. *I* made Barnes." The president was obviously making a comparison to Hardee, and the corps commander got the message. In retelling the story, Hardee smiled and said, "Yes, I made Cleburne." The Irishman was described as "very quiet, has little to say, and any one to see him and not know him would take him much sooner for a private than a Major Gen'l."[21]

When Edmund Kirby Smith transferred to the Trans-Mississippi, Donelson assumed department command in East Tennessee, although he died of chronic diarrhea in April 1863. Receiving command of his Tennessee brigade was Lt. Col. Marcus J. Wright, who skipped over the grade of colonel to become a brigadier. Wright was a favorite of Bragg's, Cheatham's, and Harris's, and they all lobbied for him. Col. John H. Savage of the 16th Tennessee, who had expected to get tapped, erupted in anger. A letter Harris wrote to Donelson became public, in which the governor said that "he had his foot on Savage's neck and he should never be promoted." Savage submitted his resignation in disgust.[22]

The reservoir of trained professional officers became increasingly depleted as general and line officers were killed or incapacitated in what became a war of attrition. Most of the early generals had a college or West Point background or combat and/or militia experience. By 1863, casualties had cut heavily into this stratum.

Two brigadiers fell at Stones River—Hanson and James E. Rains. Bragg attempted to have Hanson replaced with Brigadier General Wright, who had been sick, missed the battle, and was then searching for a command. The move was purely political—placing a pro-Bragg man in command of the Orphan Brigade, the general's staunchest opposition. The appointment did not hold up in Richmond, but as previously stated, Wright received Donelson's Brigade. Brig. Gen. William Helm, a Kentuckian, had been out for an extended period due to hemorrhoids and a horsing accident in which he broke his leg. When he reported for duty in February 1863, he was tapped for the Kentucky brigade. William Bate replaced Rains. The Tennessean had been badly wounded in the leg at Shiloh; doctors had wanted to amputate it, but he held them back with a revolver. Still on crutches, he had been stationed at Bridgeport until he was reassigned to field duty in March.[23]

McCown had been placed on trial and suspended after Stones River; his career with the army was finished. His division departed for Mississippi in the spring of 1863, and a new division formed from the Tennessee troops in Breckinridge's Division that did not go to Mississippi, some of Cleburne's regiments, Henry D. Clayton's newly arrived brigade from Mobile, and a scattering of McCown's former regiments. Many lobbied for A. P. Stewart's promotion. The press had reported that at Stones River, "Old Straight" stood only a few paces behind the firing line, "smoking his pipe as leisurely as if reading his copy of the *Rebel* by a campfire." War Department approval dragged until June 3, when the promotion at last came through. Col. Otho Strahl received promotion to brigadier and was assigned Stewart's old brigade. The thirty-one-year-old Ohio-born officer had no prewar military background, but the *Chattanooga Daily Rebel* pronounced him "popular and efficient." Leonidas Polk considered the brigade one of the best drilled in his corps.[24]

When Brigadier General Chalmers transferred to Mississippi to command cavalry, Patton Anderson received his brigade. "It contains many of my old Mississippi acquaintances and friends," he wrote his wife. Two additional brigadiers who missed the battle at Stones River—Preston Smith due to a lobbying mission in Richmond and Zachariah Deas for reasons unknown—resumed their brigade commands in January 1863. Brig. Gen. John C. Brown, wounded at Perryville, also reported in January, although still on crutches. His handicap did not prevent the widower from courting Miss Mary Armstrong of McMinnville within days of his arrival. In August, Manigault at last received his brigadier's commission.[25]

Following the Battle of Stones River, a sick Jones Withers temporarily recuperated in Mobile. Patton Anderson assumed command of the division and shortly thereafter wrote his wife: "Gen. Bragg intimated that it was to be a permanent thing, though I do not desire it or expect it really. . . . I do not calculate on a Major Generalship for the reasons that there are already as many as there are Divisions for them to command." Manigault believed that the division began to lose its edge in drill and discipline and that Anderson "had much to do with its deterioration."[26]

By summer, the enfeebled Withers requested to be relieved. The command did not go to Anderson, however, but to the abrasive thirty-five-year-old Maj. Gen. Thomas Hindman, who happened to be on detached duty in Richmond at the time. Following Shiloh, Hindman had been sent to Arkansas, where he did a creditable job despite his draconian methods, which had cost him goodwill. "Genl. Hindman, of Arkansas fame, assumes the command tomorrow [August 17]," wrote Lt. Col. Irvine Walker. "We know nothing of genl. H. as a Division commander. There I can't say whether I will like the change. His Arkansas career, however, does not presupposes us in his favor." Walthall wrote that Hindman "is said to have worn out in Arks." Manigault would grow to detest Hindman. "He had the reputation of being a desperate fighter, good disciplinarian, but a scheming, maneuvering, political general, with whom it was dangerous to come into contact. Morally, he stood deservedly low in the opinion of the officers in the Army, but he was certainly a man of talent, and the cunningest most slippery intriguer that I ever met."[27]

The men were not quiet in their opinions of some of the generals. "We are under the striked dissipling that I ever saw. General Claybourne [Cleburne] is our drill officer and the titest one you ever saw," grumbled a Texan. When it came to drill, believed a Tennessean, "General Stewart seems to me to get unreasonable. I see no good to be derived from it. We are learning nothing and as to hardening us we are hard enough now." He later added, "Volunteers drill better, and learn more, to be drilled two hours at a time." Manigault evoked a visceral response from some men: "The troops have no confidence in him. The officers have none, he is altogether a weak man," wrote an Alabamian. Lt. John Davidson concurred: "Old Manigault is a great tyrant." Cheatham ordered his division to have a brigade drill twice a week, but Strahl drilled his brigade three times a week for two hours at a time. A soldier thought him to be "over doing the thing." A visiting British officer was displeased with some of the political generals he saw and saw still others as "good fighters but illiterate and somewhat addicted to liquor."[28]

Field and Line Officers

Filling the positions of field and line officers in many respects proved more difficult than filling those of the general staff. With the passage of the Conscription Act in the spring of 1862, the men were allowed to elect or reelect their officers. "I don't like some of the new officers, but can stand what the company can," T. A. Taylor of the 4th Tennessee wrote. A study of the 19th Tennessee revealed a significant turnover. Of the thirty-nine officers remaining after Shiloh, nine resigned and seventeen failed to be reelected. Seven more received promotions and six remained in their current positions. Nineteen privates received commissions. Beauregard believed that the elections "worked disastrously in the army." An inspector wrote that many of the newly elected officers were "grossly incompetent and unable to pass examination." Indeed, some regiments inched toward "disorganization and anarchy."[29]

By late 1862, 57.4 percent of all traceable infantry colonels in the Army of Tennessee had no prewar formal training. At Stones River, seven infantry colonels were killed and seventeen wounded. Five of the seven had some prewar experience, but only three of their replacements did. At Chickamauga, five more colonels with prewar combat experience were killed. During the battle, 28.5 percent of all infantry regiments were led no longer by colonels but by lower-grade field officers. Casualties increasingly thinned the ranks of experienced personnel.[30]

Bragg, and for that matter the men themselves, did not necessarily see this as an evil. At Stones River, the infantry lost 25 captains and 83 lieutenants killed, 667 captains and lieutenants wounded, and 33 captured. In replacing these casualties, Bragg made it clear that consideration should not be given to seniority; noncommissioned officers and those who had distinguished themselves in battle should also receive consideration. Col. George St. Leger Grenfell, a visiting British soldier of fortune, observed that in the Army of Tennessee the only way an officer could win influence over his men was to show courage and aggressiveness in battle. "They [troops] hold a man in great esteem who in action sets them as example of contempt of danger."[31]

While audacity had its place, examining boards held throughout the spring of 1863 made certain that knowledge of tactics and command also played a role. All officers, current and potential, had to appear before the brigade examining board. A Tennessean wrote on April 13, 1863, "The examination [of officers] I predict will not be as they were at Corinth last spring—a humbug." Col. Newton Davis of the 24th Alabama remarked to his wife: "I expect I have examined fifty officers for promotions since the first of March. It is [a] very responsible duty and I shall be glad when I get rid of it." Lt. Col. Francis A. Reynolds of the 39th North Carolina had all field and company officers drill the regiment, saying that "in case of a fight there is no telling whose hands the Regt. will fall."[32]

Unquestionably, some officers were advanced beyond their ability—at least in the eyes of some. Alex Spence of the 1st Arkansas Mounted Rifles (dismounted) believed that some of the officers in his regiment had "*no horse sense.*" "I assure you we have a very poor set of Field Officers," he related to a friend. "To tell you the truth we have no commanders. . . . If he [Lt. Col. James A. Williamson] had justice he would be put in an asylum." Frank Batchelor of the Texas Rangers concluded that "there are many now commanding Regiments whose only fitness is derived from books—while mine has been taken from the fields & *practice.*" Daniel Miller of the 19th Tennessee expressed disgust with his officers: "[Isaiah] Huffmaster is a consummate fool and a big headed Dutch scoundrel. None of the elite of the company like him at all and looks upon him with contempt. [Lt. William B.] Wiley you know as the best of fellows but his knowledge of military tactics is quite limited. [Lt. William] Etter is not with us—how he will do is yet to be tested. Colonel [Bariah F.] Moore is a pretty good officer, but a man devoid of all principles, he treats men like slaves. Our Major [Rufus A. Jarni-

THE OFFICER CORPS

gan] is an ignorant bragidocio, but I must quit my complaints." A member of the 19th Louisiana bitterly complained about his colonel, Wesley P. Winans, for severely punishing men who took too long from drill practice to answer nature. "A great many men have Dierhear and they have to suffer — some do their business occasionally in their clothes."[33]

The dearth of trained officers at the outset of the war meant that the army was not dominated by career officers and the Old Army culture, which was not altogether negative. Bragg preferred quality over seniority. As the war progressed, experience made up for the loss of the initial pool of educated, if not professionally trained, officers, but turnover through casualties became an ever-increasing problem. Development and retention of qualified officers thus became one more factor that led to ultimate defeat.[34]

✼ 5 ✼

The Army Staff

Little has been noted about the army staff—the men who functioned behind the scene. Like the generals, they proved to be a mixed lot, often engaging in bickering and mistrust. Due to Bragg, each saw his own role in a limited capacity, confined to his own department. Thus, no big picture emerged, no one looked to the future, and potential battle scenarios were not planned or logistically plotted.

Factional Rifts

When Bragg assumed army command, his staff comprised two blocs—the Beauregard faction, which included some of Beauregard's former staff, notably chief of staff Col. Thomas Jordan, and the Pensacola faction, carry-overs from Bragg's corps staff. This organization was done for continuity and experience, but personal loyalty also played a role. Unfortunately, the two factions soon began to undercut each other.

Although desiring to return to Beauregard's staff, Jordan felt honor bound to stay on; it proved to be a mistake. He became convinced that there was an effort afoot "to get rid of your [Beauregard's] staff after you left," he wrote the former army commander in August 1862. "The fact is, there was a hard-working party in the Army of the Mississippi engaged in underrating you—men in various ways connected with the Army of Pensacola. These are the men to be watched, tracked, and, in due time, uncovered. . . . These fellows, I have my eye on them—are toadeaters, sycophants, who think they do service to another high officer [Bragg] by intimating detraction of you, and some of them are staff officers." Jordan also grumbled about the Beauregard staff officers who were retained, denouncing them as "objects of incessant petty jealousy—so much that I should not remain a little while longer." Disgruntled and stricken with rheumatism, the colonel requested a transfer.[1]

Administering the army proved to be an enormous task, requiring (by December 1862) thirty-two or more officers on the army staff and many clerks. With the two escort companies added, the entourage appeared sizable. In January 1863, the escort companies and accompanying headquarter wagons required 187 horses and 26 mules. A surgeon from Lee's army saw Bragg's staff in September 1863 and wrote in his diary, "His [Bragg's] staff and escort very large . . . quite different from the Gen'ls of the Army of Northern Virginia." Unofficially, Bragg's military family could be divided into three groups—administrative, personal, and logistical. The officers would prove to be a mixture of professional (34 percent) and nonprofessional (64 percent) men of varying talents, with an average age of thirty-four years, who kept the army functioning but too often lacked innovative vision.[2]

Throughout the Kentucky Campaign, Bragg served as his own chief of staff. He left his clerks in Chattanooga, an indication that he saw Jordan as essentially an adjutant general. The Confederacy had no army regulations regarding the position—at least not until 1864. Back at Corinth, Bragg had been closely involved with issues related to organization and supply, matters that ordinarily would have fallen to a chief of staff. He revealed an aptitude for administrative detail and it seemed to fit his controlling and pedantic personality. "I do not average four hours rest in twenty-four," he wrote his wife. Constantly weighted down by paperwork best left to an administrator, he needed a chief of staff. In November 1862, Brig. Gen. Johnson K. Duncan, the thirty-five-year-old West Pointer who had formerly commanded the Mississippi River forts at New Orleans, was appointed. He had typhoid fever at the time, a fact known to Bragg, who nonetheless requested him. Duncan died within weeks.[3]

Bragg next turned to Brigadier General Mackall, then stationed in Mobile. The two officers had long been associates, having been West Point classmates and friends in the Mexican War. He also listed Assistant Adj. Gen. Jasper S. Whiting in Richmond as a possible replacement for Duncan. Mackall would eventually come, but for months Richmond authorities vacillated. Meanwhile, Colonel Brent doubled in the role of chief of staff (he was never officially appointed to the role) and assistant adjutant general. The combination proved an unfortunate arrangement. Ever since the departure of Jordan, the positions of chief of staff and assistant adjutant general had overlapped and never been clearly differentiated. "Court Martial orders and records float about in endless prolixity," Brent wrote. The chief of staff in essence became a glorified office worker, and his authority in no way represented an extension of the general.

Unlike Jordan, who desired to be the gatekeeper to Bragg, Brent was satisfied with administrative minutiae—routine orders, reports, and records. This inevitably placed more office work on Bragg. His staff, afraid that he was not receiving sufficient food, sent his meals to his tent and urged him to eat at his desk. Newspaper correspondent Peter Alexander believed that

Bragg stayed at his desk too much. What the general saw as devotion to duty others saw as "unsocial habits." Alexander believed that he should have gotten out and mingled and visited the hospitals. Yet Bragg, as Mackall would later observe, seemed incapable of rising above a near obsession with office details in order to address larger issues.[4]

Brent, like Jordan, had also come to the West with Beauregard. Not being a part of the Pensacola clique, he had trepidations about coming on the army staff in the fall of 1862. "Gen. Bragg is said to be difficult to please. He told me he was exacting 'but tried to be just.'" A graduate of the University of Virginia, the forty-one-year-old former attorney, member of the Virginia senate, and signer of the ordinance of secession, though not a military man, was clearly bright and accomplished. The general respected him, but Brent's daily journal revealed that the army commander never truly confided in him. Nor was the Virginian beyond silently questioning some of Bragg's strategic decisions. He attended general staff meetings but apparently only as a silent observer. Throughout most of his tenure, Brent's title would be assistant adjutant general.[5]

Like Bragg, his staff rarely enjoyed a day of relaxation. In December 1862, young Willie Bryant became a clerk in Brent's office. "My situation is much better and more pleasant than the rest of the clerks of my age, five of them are in my clerk's room by themselves, while I am in the office with Col. Brent, [Jason] Fairbanks, and another very clever gentleman just arrived, where I can know and see all that is going on, and am continually coming into contact with all the 'Biggest Bugs!'" The work proved demanding (9:00 A.M. to 10:00 P.M. daily)—"I hardly have time to think," he wrote. By summer 1863, ten clerks labored in the adjutant general's office and they appeared to be developing factions. Bryant considered three of them "avowed enemies," three "aliens," two "friendly," and one an "ally."[6] Mackall arrived in April 1863 and attempted to assume the same role as Jordan, that of staff coordinator and gatekeeper to the army commander. When Bragg continued his micromanaging, Mackall turned on him. The army commander, he insisted, would issue nonsensical orders for the next day yet cancel them by morning. Brent, who had been away three months on sick leave, returned in August. He watched as Bragg continued to decline and vacillate.[7]

Mackall proved unpopular with his own staff. Willie Bryant thought him to be "a strict, arbitrary old cuss, and had his head full of theories on the business of the AAG office." The new chief of staff made changes to staff duties, "which are unpleasant to all, and a parcel of d——d absurdities, and plays the devil." The clerk later described Mackall as a "stern, maneuvering, tyrannical old cuss, and he has caused much dissatisfaction among Gen-

THE ARMY STAFF

eral Bragg's staff, and Col. Brent and some others have left in consequence, and if he continues in his course almost all others will do the same." When Mackall differed on an opinion, he frequently answered, "I can't think as you do." Liddell observed that it was "only a waste of time to continue the conversation."[8]

Thirty-seven-year-old Lt. Col. George C. Garner also served as an assistant adjutant general. Unlike Brent, Garner was both Regular Army *and* a member of the original Pensacola staff. Beyond that, he issued orders for Department No. 2; Brent did so for the army in the field. Garner transferred to another department in 1863. In January of that year, a former clerk on Bragg's Pensacola staff, twenty-four-year-old Capt. Kinloch Falconer, was promoted to major and assigned to the adjutant general's department. An 1860 graduate of the University of Mississippi, he practiced law in Holly Springs and also worked with his father at the local newspaper. In 1878, he would become Mississippi secretary of state, only to die shortly thereafter of yellow fever.[9]

Initially holding the post of inspector general was thirty-five-year-old Brig. Gen. James E. Slaughter. An attendee of the Virginia Military Institute, Slaughter had served in the Mexican War and remained in the Regular Army until 1861. He saw brief duty on Bragg's Pensacola staff and later received assignment to Beauregard's staff. Jordan never cared for him, probably because he wrote several pro-Bragg newspaper articles. "He [Slaughter] means well but has neither the education nor natural ability for the important place he holds," wrote the Virginian. By November 1862, Slaughter was in Mobile with such a severe case of laryngitis (it would last a year) that he had to be transferred to the warmer climate of Texas. Taking his place would be thirty-two-year-old Lt. Col. William K. Beard, a prewar Tallahassee commission merchant, formerly of the 1st Florida, whom Bragg had known back in Pensacola. Among others serving on the inspector general's staff was Lt. Col. A. J. Hays.[10]

Lt. Col. Harvey W. Walter, although officially in the assistant adjutant general's office, performed the duties of judge advocate and on occasion was assigned to gather in absentees. A native of Ohio, the forty-four-year-old former attorney from Holly Springs, Mississippi, had risen to prominence and wealth before the war. He would die in 1878 of yellow fever. Also spending much of his time on court duty was forty-year-old Col. Alexander McKinstrey, a former Mobile alderman and judge. Col. William P. Jones, assistant inspector general, served on the army staff from 1862 to 1865. Born in 1833, he attended West Point for only one year before joining the army for a five-year stint. After the present war, he, like several other members of Bragg's staff, joined Maximilian's army in Mexico. He returned to the United States in 1867 and practiced law in Pensacola.[11]

The Personal Staff

One historian has made a distinction between the general staff and "the general's staff." The latter comprised Bragg's personal staff, those who actually rode with him on the battlefield and in many ways became his inner circle. The personal staff could be divided into three groups: aides-de-camp, volunteer military aides, and volunteer civilian aides.[12]

Indications are that the staff officer closest to Bragg was his "confidential aide and warm friend," thirty-two-year-old Colonel Urquhart. Son of a wealthy, Scotland-born New Orleans businessman, Urquhart was educated in Europe. A wealthy sugar planter and New Orleans commission merchant, he knew Bragg before the war. The colonel attended private conferences with the generals and was described as Bragg's "private secretary." In March 1863, when Bragg sent a battery of captured guns from the Battle of Stones River to Beauregard in Charleston, he sent Urquhart to personally deliver them. Described as good-natured and genial, Urquhart would write several articles for *Battles and Leaders* in postwar years, always discreetly avoiding any gossip, unlike Charles Quintard, who would write a "tell all" book after the war. Urquhart related pleasant evenings around the campfire with Bragg, in which the general shared stories with the staff about his Mexican War days and his associations with Buell, George Thomas, and William T. Sherman. After the war, he became president of Citizens and Savings Bank of New Orleans. When he was arrested for misappropriation of funds in 1880, a jury found him innocent, believing his offenses to be technical in nature and never rising to the level of embezzlement. Shortly thereafter, he and his family moved to France. He died at his summer cottage in Saratoga, New York, in July 1900.[13]

Twenty-nine-year-old former Yale attorney Lt. Col. Josiah Stoddard Johnston came on the army staff as a volunteer aide in the spring of 1862—a carryover from Beauregard's staff. His father was half brother to Albert Sidney Johnston, making him first cousin to William Preston Johnston. Living in Kentucky at the commencement of the war, he also had ties to Breckinridge. Under the circumstances, it would appear logical that he would have fallen into the anti-Bragg camp, but throughout his nearly one-year tenure, he became one of the general's most ardent supporters. Throughout early 1863, however, he watched as Bragg increasingly attacked Breckinridge. In July, he had seen enough and submitted his resignation. "Gen. Bragg always treated me with great confidence and kindness that I should not remain where I

THE ARMY STAFF

differed with him in a matter so nearly affecting him," he wrote. In postwar years, he would become adjutant general of Kentucky and prominent in the newspaper business, eventually becoming associate editor of the Louisville *Courier-Journal*.[14]

Two aides-de-camp, both dating back to the Pensacola days, served on the army staff—Lt. Towson Ellis and Lt. Francis S. Parker Jr. Thirty-two-year-old Ellis, a Yale attendee and wealthy plantation owner, was Bragg's brother-in-law. Although known to his family as "Towsy," Bragg referred to him as "Mr. Ellis." Ellis's sisters attempted to get high-level gossip from him, but to no avail; he proved tight lipped even to family. Maj. Lemuel P. Conner, a thirty-five-year-old Yale attendee, also served as an aide. He possessed large cotton holdings in Mississippi and owned 282 slaves in 1860. Conner served as a levee inspector before the war when Bragg was on the Levee Board.[15]

Just before the Battle of Stones River, Colonel Grenfell, an English officer and soldier of fortune, reported to army headquarters and requested an assignment. He had been on Morgan's staff but apparently became miffed when the Kentuckian gave a brigade command to someone else. Bragg made him a volunteer aide. A colorful and quite outspoken character, he had served in Tangiers, South America, the Crimea, and India. He conspicuously dressed in an English staff blue coat and wore a red cavalry cap. Bragg had good relations with Grenfell, but in the spring of 1863, he made him Wheeler's cavalry inspector.[16]

The volunteer civilian staff included Governor Harris, who probably had more access to the various cliques within the army than any other person. He was with Albert Sidney Johnston when he bled to death at Shiloh and, more than anyone else, defended Bragg when Joseph E. Johnston came to inspect the army after Murfreesboro. The governor "has been one of us, and has shared all our privations and dangers," Bragg would write. Following the Battle of Chickamauga, a Georgian noted that he had seen Harris "riding around the battle line[.] He seemed to be as much interested as any of the Genls. He is a keen eyed fellow."[17]

The General Staff

The general staff kept the army functioning. The oldest and arguably most qualified member was sixty-four-year-old Lt. Col. Hypolite Oladowski, chief of ordnance. A native of Poland, he ran away from home at sixteen to join the Russian army, where he rose to the grade of captain. During the Polish rebellion of 1830, he returned to his native land and joined the insurrection, serving first as an artillery officer and later as aide to the king of

Poland. Captured and sentenced to life in Siberia, he escaped with the help of a Polish woman who exchanged clothes with him in prison. The fugitive immigrated to the United States, where he became an ordnance sergeant in the U.S. Army. The beginning of the war found him at the Baton Rouge Arsenal. Bragg immediately placed him on his staff, referring to him as "a veteran of many European campaigns." Although he spoke very broken English, Oladowski had the reputation of being a marvelous, but highly opinionated, conversationalist. A bachelor and Catholic, he was never known to live in any one place too long, and he continued his eccentricities after the war, living for a year on a Pacific island. He also became a mercenary, fighting in Maximilian's army in Mexico for two years. Ultimately, he returned to the United States, where Bragg got him employment making improvements in Mobile Bay. He settled in Columbus, Georgia, during the waning days of his life, dying in 1878. His body was interred at Magnolia Cemetery in Mobile.[18]

For slightly over two months (March 30–July 1862), Lt. Col. Eugene E. McLean served as chief quartermaster under Albert Sidney Johnston. Born in Washington, D.C., in 1821, McLean received his appointment to West Point from the state of Maryland. Following the evacuation of Corinth, a court of inquiry investigated the Quartermaster Department. Although McLean was completely exonerated, Bragg subsequently replaced him.[19]

The weak link in the logistical staff was Lt. Col. Lawrence "Larry" W. O'Bannon of the Quartermaster Department. On paper he appeared to be an appropriate choice, having served as chief quartermaster of the 3rd U.S. Infantry in Texas with fifteen years' experience. The *Chattanooga Daily Rebel* praised him as a "West Point man" with a "fine reputation." The responsibilities of the army quartermaster proved demanding—taking care of clothing, shoes, forage for the animals, wagon transportation, and rail transportation—and O'Bannon was simply in over his head. Jordan sarcastically wrote that in peacetime O'Bannon might capably hold down "a two-company post on the Texas frontier." Bragg desired to replace him after the Kentucky Campaign, but he retained him until the end of 1862. Unfortunately, O'Bannon's successor, Lt. Col. M. B. McMicken, a thirty-five-year-old unmarried former Mississippi lawyer and alcoholic, proved equally incompetent. In Richmond, Quartermaster General Alexander Lawton described him as not "having an orderly brain. He carried most of his official papers in his hat, made no adequate records of the officers under him, and did not know what duty and where he had assigned many of them." His subsequent handling of the transportation of the wounded after the Battle of Chickamauga proved disastrous.[20]

Maj. John J. Walker served in the capacity of chief commissary—the all-important position responsible for feeding the army. The forty-eight-year-old West Pointer hailed from the prestigious Walker family of Huntsville, Alabama. His late father served in the U.S. Senate, and his brother, LeRoy Walker, was the first Confederate secretary of war. In 1845, John moved to Mobile to practice law. In 1850, he became the customs collector and later a cotton broker. Walker served on Bragg's Pensacola staff, holding his position as chief commissary through 1863. When Walker traveled to Richmond in the spring of 1863, Bragg wrote his wife, "He has instructions to return as soon as possible, as he has become a necessity to me officially and socially." Bragg admitted that after the war it would be "difficult to sunder the ties." After the war, Walker returned to Mobile, where he later became vice-president of the Mobile & Ohio Railroad. He died in 1884 and was interred at Magnolia Cemetery. In June 1863, Walker transferred to Alabama and was replaced by forty-five-year-old Maj. Giles M. Hillyer, a former lawyer and editor of the *Natchez Courier*. The *Chattanooga Daily Rebel* noted, "We are pleased to learn that there has been a decided improvement in the condition of the [Army of Tennessee] commissary department, which was needed."[21]

Twenty-eight-year-old Lt. Col. James Hallonquist served as chief of artillery. A West Point graduate, he served in the 4th U.S. Artillery, spending much of his time as an artillery inspector at Fort Monroe, Virginia. After commanding a battery in the bombardment of Fort Sumter, he transferred to Pensacola, where he held several positions, distinguishing himself in the attempted capture of Fort Pickens, where he fought in hand-to-hand combat. Although he adequately handled administrative matters, he showed no aptitude for tactical or organizational innovation. Shortly after the war he became a mercenary, joining Maximilian's army in Mexico. His postwar engineering business failed, and he eventually became a school principal in a small South Carolina town. Financial reversals and alcoholism led him to commit suicide in 1883 at the age of forty-nine.[22]

Overseeing the engineer corps was acting chief of engineers Capt. Salvanus W. Steele. A graduate of the University of Virginia, he had ten years of civil and topographical engineer experience before the war. On February 9, 1863, Maj. Stephen W. Presstman was appointed the new chief engineer of the Army of Tennessee. A railroad engineer in civilian life, he had married into a prominent Alexandria, Virginia, family. As a captain in the 17th Virginia, he had received a serious wound in the First Manassas Campaign and thereafter had served routine engineering stints. He transferred to the West at Beauregard's request. Several engineers surpassed him in technical skills, but there was plenty of work to go around, and most of the officers worked independently.[23]

The thirty-three-year-old medical director, Dr. Andrew Jackson Foard of Georgia, had seen over seven years' service in the Regular Army, mostly in Texas posts. Yet another member of Bragg's Pensacola staff, he became army medical director until after the Battle of Stones River. Thereafter, Joseph E. Johnston made him theater medical director — in essence a hospital inspector for three armies. It proved to be an unfortunate decision for the Army of Tennessee. Foard's postwar medical endeavors proved unsuccessful and he died in 1868, apparently of tuberculosis.[24]

A latecomer to the army staff was a forty-year-old alcoholic, Col. Benjamin Hill, formerly of the 35th Tennessee. He became the army's top policeman, in the role of provost marshal, during the late summer of 1863. Known as Old Ben Hill to his men, he had been severely wounded at the Battle of Richmond, Kentucky. He had formerly been in the mercantile business in McMinnville and had served as a state senator. He returned to McMinnville after the war, but exposure had taken its toll and he lived in ill health until his death in 1880.[25]

Historians have leveled two criticisms against the army staff. First, they proved to be an undistinguished lot. By December 1862, the staff had only two West Pointers (Walker and Hallonquist) and five officers with Regular Army experience (O'Bannon, Oladowski, Garner, Jones, and Foard). Clearly there was a dearth of talent compared to Lee's staff, which by the end of 1862 had at least six West Point and Virginia Military Institute graduates. Bragg's staff thus became a microcosm of the leadership shortage facing the Army of Tennessee as a whole. It must be stated, however, that historians have also criticized Lee's staff early in the war for being inexperienced and untrained, though they note that the staff evolved. The same could be said of the Army of Tennessee's staff under Joseph E. Johnston.[26]

The other and perhaps more significant criticism lay in the fact that the staff members became mired in their own separate areas, and there was no one to give Bragg a larger picture of the battlefield. The staff's role in preparing for the retreat from Kentucky and later for the Battle of Murfreesboro proved minimal to nonexistent. Too often, the staff vision was day to day. Perhaps such a concept was simply too modern for the Civil War, but Bragg's compulsiveness when it came to control also played a role in the slow evolution of the army staff.[27]

❊ 6 ❊

The Stones River Campaign
Neck-and-Neck Race for Murfreesboro

In his brief trip to Richmond, Bragg had been supported by the president. Maj. John J. Walker, the army's chief commissary, wrote, "I find the General in fine health and spirits and confident of holding this country." The troops nonetheless remained disheartened. An unidentified officer wrote a letter that subsequently appeared in the *Chattanooga Daily Rebel*: "Great dissatisfaction was felt among the officers of Bragg's army at the falling back and many of them literally wept when the order was given." Alabamian John Crittenden was not sure whether anything was accomplished, but he feared that "the Kentuckians will be discouraged by our leaving the State."[1]

The troops remained in a near-starving condition. "It is a sad parcel of soldiers here [in Knoxville], who are now naked and barefooted. We have had a snow. The ground is covered about ten inches. The unkindest cut of all was that we had to throw away our knapsacks and all our clothes at Sparta, Tennessee on the 8th of September, and consequently we are now naked, dirty, filthy, and lousy," Crittenden wrote. Capt. S. H. Dent described the despair: "Men and horses are very much fatigued and worn down." A correspondent revealed shocking news: "I saw one regiment today of 450 men, and only 220 of them had shoes—the remainder had not a shoe or covering to their feet. This regiment is not an isolated one—nearly every regiment in Bragg's army is destitute of clothing and shoes in the same ratio." To John Marshall of the 41st Mississippi, the troops appeared "nearly lousy as hogs. They look like old government mules."[2]

On November 2, the present-for-duty strength totaled a stunningly low 26,156: 22,945 infantry, 1,504 artillery, and 1,707 cavalry. "Our armies here [in Knoxville] are gradually, but certainly, melting away, whilst we are getting no re-enforcements. No recruits, and cannot see a source from Which they are to come," reported Bragg. Some regiments counted barely 100 privates. The Conscription Act had been in effect for seven months, yet not a single man had reported. The War Department advised that the Kentuckians of conscript age who had followed the army out of the state be drafted, thereby adding several companies. Bragg also saw to it that all men on detached service with staffs be returned to duty. "Some regiments have become skeletons by them," Brent groused. About 1,500 convalescents at Chattanooga, who never made it to Kentucky, were forwarded to Knoxville. A composite list of all deserters from the last eight months was compiled. Those absent without leave were pardoned if they returned immediately to their regiments.[3]

As long as Bragg remained in East Tennessee, he remained in Edmund Kirby Smith's department and operating without a base of supplies. Brent expressed his frustration over the maddening dilemma on November 4: "He [Bragg] has protested to the War Office against the position in which he has been placed. Gen. Smith can mar or defeat his whole plan." Bragg took the opportunity to quickly reorganize the army. Fourteen regiments were consolidated into seven, several of them in Cheatham's hard-hit division. No longer would there be a "left wing" and "right wing" but two corps commanded by Polk and Hardee. With the return of McCown's Division from Smith, which was requested but not yet a certainty, and the arrival of Breckinridge's Division at Murfreesboro, the army would have five divisions. Hereafter, it would bear the name it would forever have throughout history—the Army of Tennessee. "I hope that I will be more proud to claim to be one of this new Army than of the old A. M. [Army of the Mississippi]," Irvine Walker frankly expressed.[4]

We do not know precisely who devised the strategy of a Middle Tennessee invasion, but Governor Harris had been in direct contact with Secretary of War Randolph at the War Department about such a plan. Throughout late September and early October, Harris had become convinced (apparently based on "soft" intelligence) that the Federal garrison at Nashville had been reduced to 3,000–5,000 troops and could be retaken—preferably by Sterling Price's two divisions of 16,800. The governor seemed to ignore the fact that a Federal army under Grant stood between Price and the Tennessee capital. The Southern defeat at the Battle of Corinth in early October had ended any consideration of an offensive from Mississippi. The governor nonetheless continued to plead for action, despite the fact that by early October, intelligence indicated that at least 11,000 Federals were in Nashville.[5]

On September 29, Harris pleaded with the War Department for Breckinridge's 5,000-man division (including 2,000 recently exchanged Fort Donelson prisoners) to be sent to Middle Tennessee. The request was initially denied, and the division continued its journey from Mississippi to Knoxville. Along the way, there was trouble from an unlikely source—the Orphan Brigade. The brigade's men had volunteered under a special arrangement with Buckner: if they furnished their own arms (and they did), they could enlist for one year. Their time was now nearly up, and the troops claimed that they were not liable to the conscript law. Matters grew worse; two companies in the 5th Kentucky stacked arms and refused to obey orders. Two weeks later, the mutiny spread to the 6th Kentucky. Breckinridge became irate. He summoned the Orphans and had the brigade form a square. He raked the men of the 5th and was only slightly milder with those of the 6th, giving the mutineers fifteen minutes to return to duty or suffer the consequences; they complied. The troops then continued to Knoxville.[6]

Breckinridge believed the occupation of Middle Tennessee to be imperative and feared that the Federals would get there first. "It is a neck and neck race for Murfreesboro and Nashville," he wrote on October 18. "I do not think Buell will follow Bragg across the desert [mountains]. They will push all their forces into Tennessee by the other route. We must be ready to meet them." He was partially correct. Buell did not follow Bragg into East Tennessee but shifted to Nashville. Rosecrans had no design to go farther. First, he knew well that Bragg would fill the vacuum in Middle Tennessee—"he cannot live elsewhere." He believed that Breckinridge's Division was only an outpost for recruiting and food supplies and that Bragg's main army would come no farther than Tullahoma. Nonetheless, he would be perfectly content if the entire Rebel army came to the outskirts of Nashville, and he admitted as much to his brother. "If we can make the enemy wear himself out by marches and then fight them near our base and far from his own he runs to risk of annihilation." In 1865, he testified, "Every mile those rebels traveled toward us . . . was an advantage and to them a disadvantage."[7]

Brent described the mood at army headquarters on November 4: "The troops he [Bragg] directly commands, did not exceed 30,000, and yet he is ordered to move." Bragg realized that he could not sustain his army in East Tennessee, and the unoccupied region south of Nashville was an obvious choice. The move to Middle Tennessee began the first week in November. If the general had any real thoughts of attacking Nashville, he quickly abandoned them.[8]

At Bridgeport, the destroyed Howe Turn Bridge was under construction. The troops were thus ferried across the Tennessee River on two small steamboats, and some were then reloaded onto the lice-ridden boxcars of the Nashville & Chattanooga for the final leg into Murfreesboro. Due to a lack of cars, half of the infantry had to walk, many of them barefoot.[9]

Convinced that Bragg could not succeed without Smith's help, Davis ordered the East Tennessee commander to leave a sufficient force in the area and proceed with reinforcements of his choosing to Middle Tennessee. He was given the discretion to accompany them or not. The plan, Smith explained to his wife on November 8, was to occupy as much of Middle Tennessee "as the Yankeys will *let us*." He showed little eagerness to comply and confided his suspicions that the Confederates would soon be "skeedadling back across the Cumberlands before winter." Smith proceeded with McCown's and Carter Stevenson's divisions and John Pegram's cavalry brigade—13,500 in all—leaving a division and some scattered troops in East Tennessee.[10]

In consultation with his generals, Bragg advanced Polk's Corps (15,500) to Murfreesboro on November 18. By November 20, Smith's Corps (11,000) had been deployed at Manchester and Hardee's Corps (12,000) at Eagleville on the Nashville and Shelbyville Pike, with a brigade at Triune. The 32nd Mississippi guarded the Nashville & Chattanooga Railroad between Normandy and Fosterville, and Jackson's Brigade (1,000) guarded Bridgeport. Wheeler's 6,000 troopers screened the army. Brent was not pleased: "It is a triangular position with the apex at Murfreesboro. Manchester is two marches from Murfreesboro. Polk's Corps is exposed." On November 28, he wrote in his diary: "Our position is not very secure. If the enemy has a superior force we must fall back. Dark, gloomy, commenced snowing at night." On December 5, Bragg ordered Hardee to Eagleville and Smith to Readyville. "This makes our base a nearly straight line," wrote Brent. The next day he added: "Our line is not safe. The enemy might mass on either flank before center and other flank can close up." Although Bragg estimated the Army of the Cumberland at 65,000, he remained confident that he could beat Rosecrans "in the open field" and that he would "spare no effort to draw him out."[11]

Meanwhile, in early December, Morgan's scouts brought intelligence of an isolated Federal brigade on the Cumberland River at Hartsville, Tennessee. Bragg quickly devised a plan. On December 6, he created a diversion by sending two of Cheatham's brigades the fifteen miles from Murfreesboro to LaVergne. Under cover of darkness, Morgan set out with a total of 2,140 men, mostly Kentuckians, and pounced the next day on the unsuspecting garrison. The Yankees behaved badly, many fleeing without firing a shot. Morgan killed and wounded 262 and captured 1,834, with a loss of 139. When word got back to the Army of Tennessee, there was great celebration. "There is a joyous night in camp," noted a Tennessean. "Every mouth is full of Hosannas to the heroic Morgan."[12]

Davis Comes West

Johnston arrived in Chattanooga, the theater headquarters, on December 4. The *Chattanooga Daily Rebel* asserted that his presence "will have a most exhilarating effect on the army." The paper described him as being five feet, ten inches tall, 160 pounds, quiet, and dignified. Rumors spread that Bragg would be reassigned to Vicksburg. The first order of business for the Virginian was to repeat that assistance for Mississippi should come from Holmes. Indeed, he would not weaken the Army of Tennessee unless expressly told to do so.[13]

Troubled by the news of sinking morale in the western command, Davis, despite fever and half blindness, determined to visit Bragg's army. He quietly left Richmond with only two aides (one of them Robert E. Lee's son) and a servant on December 10. The president conferred briefly with Johnston at Chattanooga. At Bridgeport, where the bridge remained down, his coach car had to be transported by ferry on a barge across the Tennessee River and connected to a waiting train. As he arrived on the north bank, the Washington Artillery fired a thirteen-gun salute. The train pulled into the Murfreesboro depot on the night of the twelfth to the sound of bands playing "The Bonnie Blue Flag." Davis was quartered in Oaklands, the lavish home of Dr. and Mrs. Lewis Maney.[14]

The next day, December 13, Davis reviewed Polk's divisions a mile south of town on the Shelbyville Road. He pronounced the troops the best in appearance he had ever seen. "Very gratifying to me, as you may suppose," the bishop boasted to his wife. "Jeff reviewing the troops. First reviewed our brigade [Kentucky], and was well pleased with the 'orphans,'" John Jackman observed. A Texan thought Davis to be a "fine looking old chap; he looks more like a farmer than a president." James Hall expressed a bit of disappointment to his sister: "You could not tell him from any other *old citizen*." Many thought that Davis had come to assume personal command of the army. Intelligence indicated that five enemy divisions were hunkered down in and around Nashville and one each at Bowling Green, Mitchellsville, Gallatin, and Lebanon.[15]

Davis had much on his mind. He needed troops for Pemberton in Mississippi, and he needed them quickly. On December 5, he received a dispatch from Holmes that his reinforcements could not arrive in time; in truth, Holmes never had any intention of sending them. There seemed to be a consensus among Bragg's generals that Rosecrans had settled in for the winter. If an unlikely offensive came, Bragg could simply fall behind the Tennessee River, thus exchanging land for time. On the fifteenth, the president thus overruled both Johnston and Bragg and ordered the transfer of Carter Stevenson's reinforced 9,000-man mountaineer division to Mississippi. The troops would follow Bragg's July 1862 route in reverse. The first two brigades departed on December 18 and arrived within ten days, but the last two brigades and the wagons and artillery required three weeks, a week longer than the 1862 journey. Bragg objected on the grounds that he had already done enough, having dispatched Forrest's Brigade to West Tennessee to strike Grant's communications, forwarding a newly recruited 1,500-man brigade of East Tennesseans, and sending 3,000 captured Kentucky muskets.

Although nearly universally criticized by historians, Davis made the correct decision. It seems likely that serious desertions would have occurred had Holmes sent his Arkansas division. A year later, a Texas division chose to desert en masse rather than cross the Mississippi River. The Battle of Chickasaw Bayou was subsequently fought and won on December 29, largely with troops that were already in Mississippi. Thus, the argument goes, Stevenson's Division helped neither Pemberton nor Bragg. This argument in hindsight neglects the fact that the advanced elements of Stevenson's Division arrived in time (contrary to Johnston's predictions) and would have been available had the battle taken a different turn. Better to transfer Stevenson's Division to Mississippi than to have it possibly returned at some point to Smith in East Tennessee. If Vicksburg was vital, then it had to be reinforced.[16]

Some historians have argued that this was a big *if*. The ultimate issue, according to Stoker, was not Benjamin McCulloch's Division versus Stevenson's Division but Mississippi versus Tennessee. The historian strongly sided with Archer Jones's "western concentration bloc." Concentration in Mississippi proved to be "a glaring mistake," as the "real war was in Tennessee," the "center of gravity." Yet would perfunctorily defending the Mississippi River for a concentration in Tennessee have been politically feasible? In the winter of 1862, these issues remained unsettled.[17]

Bragg soon unleashed both Forrest and Morgan, the former in West Tennessee and the latter deep in Kentucky. Between December 18 and 21, Forrest, with his inexperienced and poorly armed 2,000 troopers, captured 147 prisoners at Lexington, 101 at Carroll Station, and 700 at Trenton and then struck the Mobile & Ohio, bagging 94 at Union City. On the return journey, however, he nearly got surrounded at Parker's Crossroads but fought his way out by famously uttering, "Charge them both ways!" Despite roughing up the troops, the campaign proved a success — 1,439 prisoners compared to a loss of 500. The importance of Morgan's "Christmas Raid," beyond the damage inflicted, was that it kept 38,000 Federal soldiers in rear positions guarding lines of communications, including two of Rosecrans's divisions retained at Gallatin, Tennessee, protecting the vital Big South Tunnel of the Louisville & Nashville Railroad.[18]

Christmas Day, the second away from home for many of the men, turned out to be largely bleak and depressing. In the 13th Tennessee, "Captains, Lieutenants, and Privates was drunk and very troublesome." Irvine Walker took pen in hand. "Christmas has passed and still we are in the field," he wrote to his wife, Orie. "Instead of passing the day as I had once with you. I spent it in the midst of camp and surrounded by camp friends. All of the visions of Turkey, Plum Pudding, mince pies, egg nog, we realized in Pork and rice, the latter being a delicacy, was the delicacy of the dinner, not even a glass of wine to drink a Merry Christmas, and a toast to absent friends." The troops settled in for a quiet winter.[19]

Union Winter Offensive

By transferring Stevenson's Division to Mississippi, Davis made a calculation that Rosecrans would not launch a winter offensive; his gamble failed. The Federals got wind of the departure of Morgan's cavalry to Kentucky and Forrest's cavalry to West Tennessee and of the transfer of Stevenson's Division. Seizing his opportunity, Rosecrans advanced on December 26, 1862. The Army of the Cumberland snaked out of Nashville in three columns, moving southwest and then pivoting southeast toward Murfreesboro. At 9:00 P.M., Wheeler, at the Stewart's Creek telegraph office, sent warning of a general movement. With a winter offensive in the offing, Bragg drew in McCown's Division from Readyville to Murfreesboro.[20]

On December 29, Bragg unleashed Wheeler's cavalry brigade on the Federal right. Within forty-eight hours, the War Child had completely ridden around the Federal army, destroying 500 wagons and capturing 2,100 horses and mules and 700 prisoners. Hailed in the Southern press as a smashing victory, it turned out to be nothing more than another one of Wheeler's exaggerated reports. Indeed, he submitted three reports—the first claiming 100 wagons, the second 200, and the third 500. Federal reports documented about 130 wagons destroyed, and most of the animals and prisoners were later retaken.[21]

One historian claimed that Bragg missed his best opportunity for victory by failing to attack Thomas Crittenden's and George Thomas's corps that crossed Overall Creek on the thirtieth. Although Bragg would certainly have to have employed at least a division (presumably McCown's) to observe the Overall Creek crossings, an attack would have meant that he would have encountered five enemy divisions instead of eight. Due to Wharton's failure to properly inform him, it is not certain if Bragg grasped the significance of the gap. Even so, he would not have acted on it. Still worried about the enemy in his rear via the Lebanon Pike, he remained on the defensive. Bragg has also been criticized for fighting at Murfreesboro. The town had no natural barriers and his line was bisected by Stones River. There were too many roads to defend, and the position could be easily turned by way of Columbia, Shelbyville, or McMinnville. More recently, Earl Hess defied conventional wisdom by defending Bragg's choice. Taking a position close to Nashville "made strategic sense" and revealed "a more daring commander than is generally accepted."[22]

By the night of December 30, Bragg had deployed his army mostly west of Stones River, extending from the Nashville Pike to pass the Franklin Road, with Withers's and McCown's divisions on the front line and Cleburne's and Cheatham's in support. Only Breckinridge's Division remained on the east bank, extending eastward from the river to the Lebanon Pike, with an advanced position on Wayne's Hill. A threat via the Lebanon Pike thus became the tail wagging the dog. Bragg feared the Federals would outflank him and take Murfreesboro from the north or that a Federal column from Gallatin would march down the pike. He had had six weeks to study the terrain, yet he failed to grasp that the most significant terrain feature was McFadden's Hill, north of the railroad on the west bank. McFadden's Hill should have been crowned with artillery (eventually it was, but by the Federals) and been the site of an attack made by Bragg's *right*, thus driving the bluecoats *away* from the railroad and the Nashville Pike. But what if a Federal attack *had* come via the Lebanon Pike? To protect his rear, Bragg could have left Hanson's Brigade on Wayne's Hill and John Jackson's small brigade on the Lebanon Pike, with the sector in between covered by John Pegram's and Wheeler's cavalry brigades. That would mean, of course, that Wheeler would not be off on a raid. There was only one goal—to destroy Rosecrans's army. The Northern war machine could easily replace wagons. It was more important to dominate McFadden's Hill and control the Nashville Pike than to give Wheeler exaggerated headlines.[23]

The night of December 30, Bragg held a council of war. He planned to attack the next day up the Nashville Pike; such an assault would likely have failed. Polk countered with a plan to "turn the enemy's right where we outflanked him"; Bragg agreed. The Confederate left would attack in a grand right wheel, pushing the Federals northeast *toward* the Nashville Pike and railroad in what Grady McWhiney termed a jackknife movement. The weakness of the tactic, he wrote, was that the Federal line would pick up strength "like a snowball" as it fell back, while the Rebel line would unwind "like a ball of string." What if Rosecrans attacked Breckinridge's Division first? This was in fact exactly what he planned to do. The Kentuckian would then be "easy prey."[24]

Standard narratives place the opposing numbers at Stones River at 45,000

Federals versus 38,000 Confederates, near parity of strength. A recent study, however, revealed that Rosecrans so miscalculated his strength after the battle that it is difficult not to conclude that it was intentional. Rosecrans had at least 50,000 men on the field when the attack began, and he received an additional 1,800-man brigade during the battle. Bragg would face an army actually 36 percent larger than his own. When Rosecrans failed to attack on December 30, Bragg went on the offensive. Some have suggested that this was the standard military doctrine of the day. Others believe that Bragg had a penchant for the offensive. The Confederates would be advancing in double-line formation, exactly as they had at Perryville.[25]

Bragg Attacks

At 5:00 A.M. on a cold December 31, McCown's Division moved into the Franklin Road and formed for the attack. At 6:15, the men advanced, crossing the 800 yards of rolling hills and muddy cornfields toward the camps of the enemy. Within seven minutes, contact was made and the forces joined in earnest. Curiously unprepared for the Rebel onslaught, the bluecoats put up minimal resistance and broke to the rear. James Rains's Brigade, on the far left, advancing virtually unopposed, instinctively followed the bluecoats as they fled toward Overall Creek. The brigade veered northwest instead of continuing the wheeling movement and inclining northeast, thus creating a gap. Nonetheless, two enemy brigades had been shattered, with 1,000 prisoners and 9 guns captured. As word arrived back at army headquarters, Bragg answered without changing his expression, "Tell General Hardee to keep at them."[26]

At sunrise, Cleburne's 6,000 veterans, in support of McCown, marched out. For an hour, Cleburne marched unopposed, when his men suddenly began taking casualties. The Irishman realized that McCown's Division, which was supposed to be in his front, had "unaccountably disappeared." McCown's men, of course, had not disappeared but veered off to the northwest, thus creating a gap that Cleburne now filled. Bushrod Johnson's Brigade advanced astride Gresham Lane, with Liddell's Brigade to Johnson's left. Savage fighting resulted—"I thought they would kill us all," recalled an Arkansan. In overrunning two guns of the 5th Indiana Battery, twenty-seven-year-old Col. Albert S. Marks of the 17th Tennessee, a future governor of the state, had his arm so badly mangled that it had to be amputated. Evander McNair's Brigade, eventually continuing the wheeling movement, came up on Liddell's left, lapping around the Federal left and forcing it back.[27]

Although the bluecoats continued to reel under the onslaught, the element of surprise had by now obviously been neutralized, and resistance was becoming increasingly fierce. Bragg had two divisions fully committed, and they had not yet encountered Federal reserves. Nonetheless, by 8:30 A.M., five Federal brigades had been rolled up, with a loss of 1,500 prisoners and 11 guns.[28]

Problems developed elsewhere along the line. At the last minute, Polk, commanding the center, reorganized his forces into ad hoc commands. Although Withers's Division was on the front line and Cheatham's the second line, Polk gave Cheatham the two left brigades in both lines and Withers the two right brigades. It was a prescription for confusion. At 6:00 A.M., the left brigades, John Q. Loomis's and A. J. Vaughn's, should have advanced, but nothing happened. An irritated Bragg sent an order to get moving. The problem was a drunk Cheatham who rode the line of Vaughn's Tennesseans and in the process fell off his horse "as limp and helpless as a bag [of] meal." Cheatham eventually collected himself, and at 7:00, an hour late, the attack began, but only piecemeal.[29]

The Federals (Philip Sheridan's and James Negley's divisions) realigned along the Wilkinson Pike in a thickly wooded morass of cedars and limestone outcroppings that would become known as the Slaughter Pen. To protect his flank, Sheridan ultimately formed an angle east toward McFadden's Lane. The Rebels attempted a series of uncoordinated attacks with Wood's, Johnson's, and Polk's brigades, but all were repulsed. Stewart's Brigade finally dented the line, forcing Sheridan to withdraw at about 10:45.[30]

By afternoon, Hardee's attack on the Federal right had sputtered, the enemy line bending back along the Nashville Pike and the railroad. McCown's assaults were beaten back by a wall of massed artillery and musket fire. Bragg ordered Breckinridge's Division (save Hanson's Brigade) to cross Stones River and attack the Federal position along McFadden's Lane and at the apex—a clump of trees known as the Round Forest. Thinking that he might be attacked along the Lebanon Pike (Pegram had provided faulty intelligence), Breckinridge initially refused. When he finally did respond, he sent brigades one at a time. In late morning, Bragg launched a series of near-suicidal piecemeal attacks with five brigades, all of which were repulsed. Chalmers's, Donelson's, Adams's, Preston's, and Palmer's brigades sustained about 2,200 casualties. "Our dead was left in a solid line great many never moved from a kneeling position," witnessed one of Chalmers's Mississippians.[31]

Adams's Louisiana and Alabama brigade attempted the most serious attack against the Round Forest. At 2:00, Polk rode up, received three cheers, and said: "Why this is the old 13th [Louisiana] ain't it? My old Columbus [Kentucky] boys, my comrades, my countrymen! Now I want to see how sincere you are by taking that battery [F, 1st Ohio] away from those Yankees and turning it over to me. I know you can do it like a flash!" The brigade marched up the Nashville Pike and across the railroad. "Suddenly I came upon a line of our dead, who looked as if they had grounded arms, and laid down in line of battle; the color bearer lay dead with his colors underneath him," John Labouisse wrote. Once at the railroad, he "looked up the road and Great Caesar the Yankees were as thick as bees about 200 yards off." The brigade fell back in chaos under a withering fire.[32]

That night, Bragg believed that he had come close to victory. He sent a dispatch to Richmond: "God has granted us a happy New Year." His men had taken 4,000 prisoners and 31 guns, and intelligence reports indicated that the Yankees were retreating to Nashville. Rosecrans's army in fact went nowhere. Throughout January 1, both armies did little more than stare each other down.

Breckinridge's Assault

On January 2, Bragg, to his dismay, discovered that during the night, Samuel Beatty's Federal division had crossed Stones River and held the high ground on the east bank, from which Polk's right could be enfiladed by artillery. Bragg had three choices: withdraw from the battlefield, drive Beatty's division back, or constrict his line by pulling back along the Wilkinson Pike, with Breckinridge's Division just outside the northern environs of Murfreesboro. He chose to attack. He would occupy the east bank knoll with Breckinridge's Division and enfilade the Union left across the river. Breckinridge immediately protested, recognizing that even if he occupied the east bank knoll, he would be exposed to Union artillery fire at a slightly higher elevation on McFadden's Hill. Even Polk did not agree with the assault, stating that his flank was not threatened by Union artillery. The attack would proceed. Wharton and Pegram would cover the right flank with their cavalry brigades, and Capt. Felix Robertson would buttress the division artillery with an additional ten guns.[33]

The Federals detected the move. Beatty received reinforcements as Rosecrans massed infantry and artillery (a staggering fifty-eight guns) on and around McFadden's Hill. Neither Breckinridge nor his brigadiers favored the attack. Hanson was so irate that he threatened to go to army headquarters and "kill Bragg." To make matters worse, at the last moment, Bragg sent recently arrived Brigadier General Pillow to command Colonel Palmer's Brigade. More confusion reigned as Breckinridge and Robertson quarreled over where to place the artillery. No messages arrived from the cavalry; indeed, Wharton later wrote that he had received no word of the attack.[34]

At 4:00 P.M., a signal gun boomed and the division surged forward, impeded by tangled grass and heavy weeds. By sheer determination, the infantry made it to the knoll, sending Beatty's bluecoats streaming over Stones River. Breckinridge's artillery began unlimbering on the knoll, but Robertson's ten twelve-pounder Napoleons could not be found. The captain, of his own volition, had "altered the plan." He never left the woods in the rear. It made no difference—the division was pulverized by massed artillery fire from across the river. The Federals then launched a massive counterattack resulting in a Rebel rout. "We had to march back a mile through an open corn field and many were so exhausted that they could not go faster than a slow walk," a Tennessean wrote his sister. Preston described the desperation to his wife: "Fresh and murderous vollies poured in from the other side of the river and the line recoiled wildly over the crest of the hill we had just won." But with darkness approaching, the Federal attack sputtered to a halt. Breckinridge had lost a third of his division. The relationship between him and Bragg, not good from the outset, rapidly deteriorated.[35]

With casualties rivaling those at Shiloh and more Federal troops arriving, Bragg had few options but retreat. Hess made a case for Bragg's leadership at Stones River. The general projected a "coherent and viable strategy" and "seized the initiative." This was true; indeed, one must wonder what he could have accomplished with Stevenson's Division, then in Mississippi. In defending Bragg's attack on the Round Forest, Hess blamed Polk and Breckinridge. Contemporary evidence exists, however, that the army commander sat next to Polk during the piecemeal assaults. Hess also believed that Bragg's December 31 attack proved more successful that Stonewall Jackson's famed flank attack at Chancellorsville. In the end, however, Stones River resulted in a strategic Confederate defeat. Northern morale was boosted and, more important, the Emancipation Proclamation went into effect with a Union battlefield victory. Rosecrans became the new rising star in the North. As for Bragg, Stones River was a battle that probably should never have been fought. Coming on the wake of the failed Kentucky Campaign, there would be ramifications.[36]

Army Reactions

Initial reports of a great victory had been believed. Southern casualties were reported to range from 7,000 to 9,000; those of the enemy, 20,000 killed and wounded and 5,000–7,000 captured. "There is no doubt but that the Yankees were badly whipped, having lost in killed and wounded at least five to our one, but also 5,000 prisoners, while our loss in prisoners was comparatively nothing," Frank Carter wrote his wife. Texan J. K. Street concluded that the Rebels had given "the abolitionist invaders one of the worst whippings they ever had!"[37]

Viewing the battle as a victory raised the question of why the army had retreated. Many of the troops understandably pinned the blame on Bragg. Cavalryman J. L. Hammer confided to his wife on January 5: "Bragg is the laughing stock of the whole country. Many of the Tennessee troops will desert, and I can't say they are to blame." Frank Carter corroborated that opinion: "There is no doubt that Gen. Bragg has to a great degree lost the confidence of the army and many think there is no reason for the retreat." Capt. Thomas Patton of the 60th North Carolina told his mother: "The more I think of it, the more shameful our recent retreat appears. I am anxious to see what the public and press think about it." Capt. Irving Buck confided to his sister, "The feeling against Gen. Bragg is very strong with both officers and men."[38]

A sizable minority nonetheless expressed understanding, if not outright support. "We cirtanly whipped them bad but they was reinforced & I think it was a pretty good policy in Bragg to fall back," Alfred W. Bell of the 39th North Carolina explained to his wife. Walker was of a like view: "Bragg deserves praise for doing what he has done. With an army barely 30,000 he defeated, or say checked, Rosecrans with over 65,000[,] more than two to one." Frank Batchelor also gave Bragg the benefit of the doubt: "We are all at a loss to know why Bragg retreated on Sunday, but suppose he had good reasons — that he is a great General none can deny and history will no doubt clear up all mysteries." Isaac Alexander of the 10th South Carolina expressed a similar sentiment: "I must say he is a much abused man and must furthermore say he does not deserve it."[39]

The frayed troops settled into winter quarters at Shelbyville and Tullahoma. At the first moment they had, they wrote letters to assure their loved ones that they had made it through the carnage. "With pleasure I am permitted to drop you A few lins to let you know I am still A liv on top of the ground," Pvt. John Reese of the 60th North Carolina informed his wife. Alabamian Thomas Warrick related: "I can inform you I have seen the Monkey Show at last and I don't Waunt to see it no more. . . . Some [bodies] had their hedes shot off and some their armes and legs. One was in too in the midel. I can tell you I am tired of Ware." Writing with remarkable candor to his wife, Alfred W. Bell admitted: "I must confess that I am not as brave as I thought I was. I never wanted out of a place as bad in my life. . . . I want no more Battles." Not since Shiloh had the army been so shattered. The 8th Tennessee sustained 306 casualties of 474 engaged—64.6 percent. Entire brigades had been decimated—Vaughn's with 46.1 percent casualties; Donelson's, 45.3 percent; and Maney's, 42.2 percent.[40]

In practical terms, the Battle of Stones River had accomplished little beyond checking Rosecrans's advance for the next six months. It was a typical western battle, where each side savaged the other with enormous casualties and then fell back and regrouped to do it all over again. In the infantry and artillery, the heart of the army, Bragg had lost 31.1 percent of his troops. The battle proved the difficulty, the near impossibility, of destroying an enemy army.

Richmond Reaction

On New Year's Eve, it appeared as though a great victory had occurred in the West. Even old enemies were seen shaking hands on the street. True, western dispatches were notoriously inaccurate, but this one had Bragg's signature. More good news arrived the next day in army dispatches released by the War Department: the enemy had been driven six miles, and Wheeler had ridden completely around the Federal army. Southern Associated Press reports claimed that 4,000 prisoners and 31 guns had been taken. On January 3, the headlines offered more good cheer. More dispatches had arrived, confirming the South's success. An editorial in the *Richmond Enquirer* under the headline "The Year Opens Brightly!" assured readers that Murfreesboro had been a great victory. Davis made a speech on the steps of the Executive Mansion on the night of January 4. With the recent victories at Chickasaw Bayou, Fredericksburg, and now Stones River, the president confidently proclaimed, "We are invincible."[41]

No papers were printed on Sunday, January 4, making the news of the fifth somewhat startling: the Army of the Cumberland had not in fact retreated from the battlefield, and heavy Union reinforcements were pouring into Nashville. On January 6, the truth finally came out—remarkably through Northern newspapers: Rosecrans had held the battlefield and the Army of Tennessee was in retreat! No one, of course, trusted the Yankee press, but Bragg had shut down all press releases. He finally allowed the Southern Associated Press to publish an abstract of his dispatches. "We are all down again," Jones told his diary on the sixth. "Bragg has retreated from Murfreesboro. . . . I do not know how to reconcile Bragg's first dispatches." Writing from his Richmond residence, Edwin Ruffin noted on January 7, "The accounts are very meager, & obscure; but it is certain that the movements of both armies have been reversed."[42]

The capital press expressed rage. "General Bragg has certainly retreated

. . . from his victory at Murfreesboro, as he did last fall at Perryville," blasted the *Examiner*. The *Dispatch* echoed the statement: Bragg had become "alarmed at his own success and run away from it." On January 12, Davis delivered his address to Congress. "In the West," he solemnly said, "obstinate battles have been fought with varying fortunes, marked by a frightful carnage on both sides." The state of Tennessee, the Battle of Stones River, the Army of Tennessee — none was ever mentioned. It was as though the chief executive was in a state of shock and simply did not know what to say. William Preston Johnston confided to his wife on the twenty-eighth: "He [Bragg] is not equal to his position but the Prest. is always loth to yield a general to the popular clamor or sacrifice one for failure. He always hopes for better luck the next time."[43]

Correspondent Bagby had plenty to say. The January 1863 edition of the *Southern Literary Messenger* allowed him several column inches to unleash his wrath. After the supposed initial victory, "our joy knew no bounds. . . . The capture of Nashville, the redemption of Middle Tennessee, and hemming in of Grant's army and the transfer of the war to Kentucky, and perhaps to the Ohio, were taken for granted." Then the truth became known. Breckinridge's Division had been shattered, but Bragg nonetheless "claimed a great victory." "One thing is for certain," the journalist concluded. "The campaign in Tennessee has failed. . . . Bragg has been given two fair trials. He has failed in both of them." Unfortunately, Bragg's "friend in Richmond," Davis, retained him. A lone pro-Bragg letter written by "J. S. J." appeared in the pro-administration *Enquirer* on January 23. The letter contained such high-level information that it had to have come from someone at army headquarters. J. S. J. was in fact Lt. Col. Josiah Stoddard Johnston, a Bragg aide. It proved too little, too late; a disgusted public had made up its mind.[44]

In February 1863, Alabama congressman James Pugh introduced a seemingly innocuous resolution in the Confederate Congress thanking Bragg and his officers and men for their heroic conduct in the late battle. The resolution, known as H.R. 4, routinely passed 74–4 on the third reading. Only a portion of the Kentucky delegation, still embittered over the loss of its state, refused to support it. The vote margin and the seemingly routine nature of the resolution belied the deep resentment in the halls of Congress. But for a letter from Joseph E. Johnston supporting the resolution, it might well have failed. The next day, the bellicose Henry Foote, who had supported H.R. 4, took to the House floor and corrected a newspaper report that stated he had commended Bragg's skills. He blurted that he considered Bragg an inferior general and that "he had not one word to take back" of his repeated attacks. He had only supported the resolution because of Johnston's recommendation. Kentucky congressman Robert Breckinridge claimed that were the vote taken again, he, James Christman, and Willis Machen would all change their "yea" votes. Texas congressman Franklin B. Sexton confided in his diary on February 26: "I voted in the affirmative with many misgivings. Did it solely because J. E. J. sent in orders that his [Bragg's] conduct was good & his generalship able. Hodge made a strong appeal against it."[45]

The greater problem came in the Senate, where Kentucky senator Henry C. Burnette demanded that Bragg's after-action report for Stones River be received and fully debated before any vote on the resolution was taken. Pugh warned Bragg of "an organized effort to break you down." Many in the Senate did indeed oppose the general, including Gustavus A. Henry of Tennessee, William L. Yancey of Alabama (who had a son in Bragg's army), Louis Wigfall and William S. Oldham of Texas, William E. Simms of Kentucky, John B. Clark of Missouri, James L. Orr of South Carolina, and Robert W. Johnson and Charles B. Mitchell of Arkansas.[46]

The street talk in Richmond claimed that Bragg had become intolerably unpopular within the Army of Tennessee. On February 15, Robert Kean wrote, "Bragg is said to have lost the confidence of his command completely and Johnston has been called from Pemberton's department to take command in person." Bagby's sleuthing uncovered an interesting, albeit untrue, story that several of Bragg's officers had shown up on the doorstep of the president with a petition signed by a staggering 2,000 of their fellow officers requesting the general's removal.[47]

In order to keep his finger on the political pulse, Bragg dispatched Col. John Sale and Capt. Felix Robertson as lobbyists. They arrived in Richmond on Monday, March 2, but clerks had not yet fully prepared copies of Bragg's Stones River report for members of the Senate nor would they for several days. Sale roamed the halls of Congress in the meantime. He learned that several senators were deeply disturbed by reports of dissatisfaction within the Army of Tennessee. The forthcoming Senate debate would be a "semi-official trial," but Sale was confident that the "croakers and malcontents" would be silenced—"your vindication will be *triumphant*." Bragg's Senate defense team would be Clement C. Clay of Alabama, James Phelan of Mississippi, and Thomas J. Semmes of Louisiana. Bragg's addendum to the original report did not arrive until the end of the Senate session, meaning that the resolution was tabled and subsequently never discussed. Bragg would not receive his thanks.[48]

Bragg's amended report placed much of the blame for the loss on Breckinridge. "It is quite manifest that there are deep quarrels in that army, and that Bragg is cordially hated by a large number of officers," Kean noted. Col.

William Preston Johnston got hold of a copy and expressed disgust: "In a word the report turns the little end of the telescope upon him [Breckinridge], in a very damaging way." Initially the report was kept within congressional circles, but Bagby picked up on certain whisperings. The report was subsequently published in the press. Bragg's denunciation of Breckinridge and Cheatham "raised a storm in Congress. . . . [Senator] Henry says however that Gen. Bragg will not be removed. Others . . . speak with equal confidence of his being retired at an early day and say that is the object of his being ordered to Richmond at this time. . . . I venture to predict his certain removal. His [after-action report] has done the work," William Gale notified Polk on March 27.[49]

An anti-Bragg letter appeared in the *Enquirer* on March 31. Internal information made it clear that it had been composed either by a Breckinridge staff officer or a Breckinridge associate who had been given intimate details about Bragg's personality. The army commander was described as "fidgety" and "often unreasonable and sometimes not altogether dignified." Although he was not a cruel man, many saw him in that light. While few doubted his energy, loyalty, and personal courage, they questioned his capacity "to understand the personnel of our army." Bragg was "invested with the idea of failure," and within the ranks "there is a superstition against him." As for Joseph E. Johnston, "the men love him. They believe him to be a man of genius." The letter, signed "E. P. T.," was a reference to Edwin Porter Thompson, an associate of Breckinridge's and the postwar historian of the Orphan Brigade.[50]

The majority of the Tennessee delegation petitioned Davis to replace Bragg. The scene was oddly reminiscent of one that took place a year earlier, when the same delegation requested the removal of Albert Sidney Johnston. At that time, Davis defended his friend by saying, "If Sidney Johnston is not a general, the Confederacy has none to give you." He made no such claim about Bragg, but he nonetheless declined the delegation's request—"disrespectfully," according to Foote. Not content to let the matter lie, Foote subsequently published an open letter in the *Whig* stating that Bragg must go.[51]

Bragg was not the only problem facing the War Department. Joseph E. Johnston's obstinacy with Davis and Seddon increasingly became a source of irritation. On March 28, Kean wrote: "General Johnston has written another of his brief unsatisfactory, almost captious letters, protesting against Bragg's removal. . . . He never treats the Government with confidence, hardly with respect." On April 16, he added: "He treats the [War] Department as an enemy with whom he holds no communication which he can avoid and against which he only complains and finds fault. He is a *very little man*, has achieved nothing, full of himself, [and] above all other things, eaten up with morbid jealousy of Lee and all his superiors in position, rank, or glory. I apprehend the gravest disasters from his command in the western department. Time will show." Johnston continued his carping in Mississippi. Kean bristled: "This is precisely what I have foretold and expected ever since Johnston went there. He seems more anxious to make a point than to gain a battle, to put the Government in the wrong [than] to defend a state. It is very clear to me that the *Mississippi will be lost*." Time would tell.[52]

7

Confrontation
Intrigue

After the Battle of Stones River, Bragg deployed Polk's Corps with Mc-Cown's Division at Shelbyville and Hardee's, much to his chagrin, at Tullahoma, a town Hardee saw as having no strategic value and being difficult to defend. It could be easily outflanked by way of Manchester, he vainly argued, and once south of the Elk River, a Union cavalry column could cut the pike and railroad at Decherd. As for the village, it had no hotel or saloon and proved to be nothing more than a "little wayside depot, with a few squalid huts, a few framed houses and cottages, and a great many body lice just now," according to Captain Carter.[1]

The army chief assured Davis that he would endeavor to hold the Duck River despite his heavy losses. Intelligence sources claimed that Rosecrans was being heavily reinforced from Kentucky; for once, the information proved correct. South of the Duck River, three gaps cut the Highland Rim—Hoover's, Liberty, and Bell Buckle. Beyond that region lay a forty-mile flat and sandy sector known to the locals as the Barrens or Normandy Hills. This area would give Bragg breathing space while he awaited reinforcements. But Davis had none to send. His only advice came on January 15: "For the present all which seems practicable is to select a strong position and fortifying it to wait for attack." Bragg established headquarters in the two-story stone summer residence of U.S. Supreme Court justice John Catron. A stockade built by the Yankees the previous summer still surrounded the home. A clerk at army headquarters wished that he were "almost anywhere else." The roads remained nearly impassable, and an enemy advance seemed unlikely.[2]

The daily train from Chattanooga creaked into Tullahoma on a wet and gloomy Saturday, January 10, carrying the usual mail dispatches and correspondence and a January 7 edition of the *Chattanooga Daily Rebel*. The paper, which had temporarily suspended its usual vitriolic criticism of Bragg due to premature reports of his Murfreesboro "victory," was once again on a tear. The army commander sat stunned at what he read. The paper asserted that Bragg had lost the confidence of the army as well as of his generals, that a change of command was necessary, and that the recent retreat had been against the advice of his generals. Seeking the counsel of his staff, Bragg asked their candid opinion about whether he should step down. The officers caucused and stunningly concurred that he should indeed step down. Only Brent left an account. Urquhart made mention of the incident in his postwar writings, but he offered no details.[3]

On January 11, the general's unfortunate personality traits, his inability to swallow his anger and outwait his opponents, and his insistence on defining his enemies all became apparent. Bragg suspected that press leaks of internal army statements could only have come from staff officers of the generals. Bragg therefore drafted a letter to his corps and division commanders asking if he had misunderstood their advice to withdraw from Murfreesboro. He also instructed them to question their staff officers about leaks. Against the counsel of his staff, he then asked for one more thing: "I desire you to consult your subordinate commanders and be candid with me. . . . I shall retire without regret if I find that I have lost the good opinion of my generals, upon whom I have ever relied as upon a foundation of rock." Historians have variously explained the query as the crushing stress of command and a pathetic plea for love and understanding. At any rate, the general had placed himself in the hands of a jury of eighteen — two lieutenant generals, three major generals, six brigadiers, and seven colonels. Their verdict would be achingly blunt.[4]

On January 12, a dispatch arrived from Hardee's headquarters. Although hesitant to get involved in army politics last October, he now pounced on the opportunity. In response to the first question, he answered that he had not been present to give advice on the retreat but he had subsequently concurred with the decision. On the question of his generals' opinions, he did not mince words: "I feel that frankness compels me to say that the general officers, whose judgments you have invoked, are unanimous in their opinion that a change of command of this army is necessary. In this opinion I concur." On the issue of staff leaks, he had checked with his officers and had been assured that none had come from his headquarters. It was a lie. Hardee's staff officers were in frequent communication with Theodore O'Hara, a Breckinridge staff officer, who acted as a go-between, leaking information to correspondent Samuel Reid. Another anti-Bragg correspondent, an unknown reporter writing under the pen name "Ora," loitered around Breckinridge's headquarters, almost certainly getting his information from O'Hara. Indeed, the corps commander himself leaked confidences. "Hardee has sent me copies of *the correspondence* to the President — he told me so in confidence. I am delighted that he did so," O'Hara passed on to Breckinridge. "B. B. reminds me of the similie of the 'scorpion begrit by fire.' If he bites himself he is sure to die of his own loathsome venom."[5]

Breckinridge admitted that he had agreed with the decision to retreat. As to the second question, the Kentuckian did not equivocate. The brigade commanders voted no confidence, and, he wrote, "I feel bound to state that I concur." The conclusion should have come as no surprise. Breckinridge blamed Bragg for wrecking his division in the late battle. He also felt that he had been made a scapegoat for the Kentucky Campaign because his division did not arrive in time to participate. He flatly denied that there was any breach of security on his staff. Yet the division commander at the very least had given his tacit approval for O'Hara's passing of information to Reid—it could hardly have been otherwise. Reid articles critical of Bragg continued to appear in the press.[6]

Two of Breckinridge's brigadiers—Gibson and Preston—had long denounced Bragg, the latter writing that he was "too weak to fight" and "too unpopular to run." "Boomerang Bragg," as he called him, had a "heart of ice and a head of wood." Col. Robert P. Trabue, who had replaced Hanson, later stood down from his anti vote. An enraged O'Hara wrote, "*Colonel Trabue has actually gone to Bragg & clingingly, basely backed out of his expression of opinion.*" Shortly thereafter, Trabue traveled to Richmond to lobby for a brigadier's commission. While there, he contracted pneumonia and died on February 13. Pillow also renigged on his earlier position. Brig. Gen. John C. Brown had recovered from his Perryville wound and resumed command of his brigade, leaving Pillow without a command. He coveted McCown's Division (the *Charleston Daily Mercury* openly predicted that he would be tapped for the job), and he clearly had second thoughts about agitating the army chieftain.[7]

Cleburne's response arrived on January 13. Bragg apparently thought that he had the Irishman's support. Urquhart later wrote that Bragg remained on good terms with many of his generals—Cleburne was on Urquhart's list of eight. After consulting with his brigadiers, Cleburne concluded that "they say, with regret, and it has also been my observation, that you do not possess the confidence of the army." The division commander had parsed his words. His answer appeared to avoid any personal commitment; he was merely making an "observation." Bragg may have interpreted his answer as an attempt to distance himself from the majority view. He continued to openly praise the Irishman in public. Ora reported that Bragg requested to be relieved, but he later retracted the article.[8]

With Polk on furlough in Asheville, North Carolina, the circular letter went to the temporary corps commander—Cheatham. The Tennessean judiciously withheld a reply. The delayed response, and perhaps Cleburne's veiled reply, strangely gave Bragg renewed hope. On January 12, Brent took pen in hand: "Dissatisfaction in Polk's Corps does not appear so marked & decided as in Hardee's. It is surmised by some that the great 'hue & cry' was raised by Breckinridge, who by some means seduced Hardee to participate therein." Bragg wrote a dispatch to Davis admitting that there had been some dissatisfaction but "that is all subsiding and confidence and tone are again assuming sway."[9]

The intrigue nonetheless continued. On January 14, Bragg penned a letter to Johnston. Although he admitted that he might have to step down "at least for a time," he believed the situation to be under control. He then went on a tear against an unnamed general but with obvious references to Hardee: "The one who aspires to it [army command] is a good drill-master, but [has] no more skills except that he is gallant. He has no ability to organize and supply an army, and no confidence when approached by an enemy." On the seventeenth, Bragg wrote a lengthy letter to Davis that was hand delivered by Urquhart. Bragg assured the president that the dustup in the army was due "to a temporary feeling of a great part of my Army—mostly new men under new officers—that is all subsiding and confidence and tome are again assuming sway. It had its origin in false reports and rumors circulated by newsmongers that the Enemy was falling back when we withdrew from Murfreesboro."[10]

Breckinridge temporarily journeyed to Knoxville, leaving Preston in command of his division and O'Hara in charge of the division staff. On January 19, O'Hara warned the Kentuckian: "Old Bragg is moving Heaven and Earth to prepare to wage war against you *a war to the knife*." Several days later he wrote, "B. B. is evidently preparing & marshaling all his resources of shallow cunning and foolish chicanery, energized by a rankling hate, to make war upon you & wreck to the utmost his ignoble spite against you." He urged the division commander to return and "give back bone to your Co. (conspirators, I had like to say). Bragg will gain an important advantage over you. . . . Give you Hell in his [after-action] report."[11]

Polk belatedly received a copy of the circular letter in Asheville. He returned to Shelbyville on January 20 and did not respond for ten days. Both the bishop and Cheatham were looking for a way out—the former because he desired to ostensibly rise above the infighting (he preferred covert actions) and the latter because he stood to have charges preferred against him for the drunken incident on the first day at Stones River. Polk thus asked for clarification—was there one question being asked or two? Having been stung by Hardee's responses, Bragg was also looking for a way out of what

Connelly called a "dilemma of his own making." He responded that the letter had been "grossly and intentionally misrepresented" and that from the outset only one question had been asked—that about the retreat. Bragg's response, ludicrous though it was, offered Polk his exit strategy. The bishop therefore never responded to question two, but he promptly and surreptitiously wrote a cowardly letter to Davis behind Bragg's back expressing his negative views.[12]

Had a vote been taken in Polk's Corps, Polk assured Davis that the result would have been the same as in Hardee's. Such may not have been the case. Cheatham unquestionably hated Bragg, yet he remained reticent, hoping to avoid his own controversy. Indeed, McCown railed at Cheatham's hypocrisy, stating that he "said one thing among the officers behind Bragg's back and wrote him a totally different thing." Jones Withers gave Bragg his full support in a January 18 article in the *Mobile Advertiser & Register*. He went on sick leave January 8, but he could have expressed his views in absentia. Although he admitted to his wife that Bragg was "more unpopular than ever," Patton Anderson labored under the false impression that Breckinridge had been drinking during the January 2 assault, and he probably would have supported Bragg. Manigault, who readily admitted the army commander's failings, would nonetheless have sustained him.[13]

Polk's deliberate avoidance of the question of Bragg's leadership left Hardee in a compromising position. Two days after sending in his response, the bishop learned, apparently from gossiping staff officers, that he had come under criticism from Hardee and his staff. The corps commander believed that Polk had intentionally avoided the main question, which concerned the issue of Bragg's continued leadership. William Polk, the bishop's son and postwar biographer, conceded that Hardee and his generals felt that they had been placed "in the unenviable position of mere malcontents." William defended his father, claiming that the "public good" had made the bishop's response "the only course open to him." No amount of postwar spinning could get Polk out of his transparently self-serving actions. More significant, a rift now existed between Hardee and Polk. No one trusted anyone.[14]

The Uncooperative Johnston

Davis simply did not know what to think. Had the army's confidence in Bragg collapsed? Was a cabal developing among the generals? Had the army chieftain become unhinged? Mystified that Bragg had "invited judgment" upon himself, Davis notified Johnston on January 22 to proceed to Tullahoma. Ignoring his doctor's warnings about exhaustion, the theater commander hastened from Mobile, arriving in Chattanooga January 25. From there he proceeded directly to Tullahoma. Johnston was to investigate the leadership crisis in the Army of Tennessee and advise the president. If Bragg's removal became necessary, Davis would approve it.[15]

Johnston arrived at Tullahoma on January 26. On the thirtieth, he took the opportunity to express his frustrations to Wigfall. He considered his present post tantamount to being "laid on the shelf." Refusing to take personal command of either the Army of Tennessee or the Army of Vicksburg, he saw his role as that of inspector general. The distances between Tennessee and Mississippi were simply too great for him to control, yet Davis refused to express his priority. Johnston remained at a loss for ideas. If the Cumberland Mountains were lost, he could not possibly hold East Tennessee. Once in possession there, Rosecrans could move either southeast or east for either Mobile or Richmond. Edmund Kirby Smith had barely enough men to repulse raids, and Pemberton's army was far too small. Johnston had requested 18,000–20,000 men from Arkansas, but none were forthcoming. In short, he adopted the same strategy as Bragg and the only reasonable one available—dig in, harass Union supply lines, rebuild the Army of Tennessee, and let Rosecrans come to him on a battlefield of Johnston's choosing.[16]

In personal conversations, Johnston found both Polk and Hardee to be disgruntled, but he seemed to value Governor Harris's opinion the most. Harris, who floated freely among the army cliques, admitted that the generals lacked confidence in Bragg's leadership, due primarily to the Kentucky Campaign, but the negative feelings appeared to be subsiding. Johnston assured the president that the governor "thinks it is not such evil as would result from the removal of Gen'l Bragg."[17]

Johnston realized the anti-Bragg sentiment of the generals, and it is clear that he simply chose to circumvent them. Indeed, there is no evidence that he interviewed a single division or brigade commander. Johnston proceeded to interview every colonel in the infantry—or at least so the *Chattanooga Daily Rebel* claimed. His conclusion to Davis: "They [troops] are represented by their field officers to be in high spirits & as ready as ever for a fight." Though he admitted that the generals would prefer a commander with "fewer defects," he nonetheless expressed his resounding confidence in Bragg's leadership. Should it become necessary to replace Bragg, however, Johnston was adamant that his successor should be "no one in this army, or engaged in this investigation."[18]

On the face of it, the report appeared correct. Even the *Chattanooga Daily Rebel* conceded that the generals had recently become more favorable to Bragg. Urquhart thought that Johnston's report quieted the bad feeling somewhat, although it failed to restore harmony with the corps commanders. "Seldom did either of them visit headquarters except officially," he noted. The army continued to improve throughout February. William Gale of Polk's staff admitted as much. Having been sustained by both Davis and Johnston, Bragg wrote Mackall on February 14 that the allegations against him were found to be "generally totally unfounded" and that the report completely undercut the "scoundrels who were abusing me." On the twenty-seventh, he wrote Benjamin S. Ewell: "I am very happy to say that all seems to be subsiding into quiet satisfaction. And the only dissatisfaction that ever existed was fomented by a few disappointed Generals who supposed they could cover their own tracks and rise on my downfall. They have failed. . . . An expression of regret, now almost universal, reaches me constantly—but I pay no heed & pursue the even turn of my way."[19]

The administration remained unconvinced. Davis and Seddon had assumed that Johnston would make Tullahoma his permanent headquarters, thus resolving a problem. Seddon even suggested that Bragg could remain the titular head of the army, performing the role of administrator, inspector, and disciplinarian. Johnston rejected the notion out of hand, and even Wigfall's urgings could not budge him. "I am sure you will agree with me," Johnston replied to Davis, "that the part I have borne in this investigation would render it inconsistent with my personal honor to occupy that position." To be sure, Johnston's "personal honor" did not prevent him from coveting an army—just not the Army of Tennessee. He desired to have Lee assume western theater command, leaving an opening for him to return to the command of the Army of Northern Virginia. Seddon gave a sharp reply, disagreeing with the "honor" issue and accusing him of a whitewashed investigation.[20]

Clearly anxious to leave Tullahoma, Johnston remained only two weeks. He reassured Bragg that he had not come to assume command of the army. Indeed, even if asked for his assistance in the future, he would return merely to serve on Bragg's staff, not as commander. Johnston's visit, though it had a temporary calming effect, accomplished little. The issue was not resolved.[21]

Retribution

For a month (February 13–March 17) Johnston remained absent from the Army of Tennessee. During this time, Bragg remained busy—not with the Yankees but with the enemy within. Having been sustained by the government, he now attempted to purge the army of his enemies. Even the normally supportive Hess conceded that Bragg "began to relish the fight with his generals for it released his naturally combative spirit." The general began with low-hanging fruit—McCown. Although the Tennessee general had not been one of the signatories of the January petition, the commanding general nonetheless was determined to be rid of him. He had never considered him competent, but the specific charges against him proved petty—he had occasionally sent details of men to Charleston against regulations. The division commander did not help his own case by openly blathering his disdain for Bragg, Davis, and Harris—comments that got back to army headquarters. Bragg stacked the court with generals considered favorable to him—Cleburne, Withers, Anderson, Marcus Wright, Zachariah Deas, Preston Smith, and Edward C. Walthall. Found guilty and suspended with a loss of six months' pay, McCown saw his career with the army finished. Brig. Gen. A. P. Stewart assumed temporary command of the division.[22]

The army commander quickly turned to the person he saw as the chief instigator—Breckinridge. Writing to Mackall, Bragg noted, "The former [Breckinridge] failed most signally at Murfreesboro, and is very anxious to saddle me with the responsibility, but will be beautifully shown up." In his after-action report, Bragg accused the Kentuckian of belatedly supporting Hardee's December 31 assault, of having a faulty alignment during the January 2 attack, and of making a disorderly retreat. He pointedly left him off the list of generals that were singularly praised. For his part, Breckinridge did not appear to be looking for a fight. In his initial report, he did not openly criticize the army commander nor did he mention his vehement opposition to the January 2 assault. Bragg nonetheless forwarded the report to Richmond on March 11 with an addendum that shredded Breckinridge's veracity. Breckinridge gathered evidence of his own, and the feud smoldered throughout the spring.[23]

Though Bragg could not get his hands on Breckinridge, he was more successful with two of his brigade commanders. Brigadier General Preston was banished to southwestern Virginia to take over Humphrey Marshall's command. On March 1, Col. Randall Gibson, temporarily commanding the Louisiana brigade in Adams's absence, was placed with Pillow on conscript duty. Gibson believed that Bragg intended him to taste the "sweets of Siberian exile for daring to express my honest opinions in the discharge of my duty."[24]

Bragg next went after Cheatham. It proved to be a particularly sensitive time for the Tennessean. In February 1863, both his father and one of his younger sisters had died, and he had been unable to attend either funeral. Bragg accused him of being tardy during the December 31 attack, but eventually, perhaps inevitably, the issue of his drunkenness also came up. Bragg's anger might have been addressed had Polk adequately handled the situation, but the bishop gave Cheatham only a verbal reprimand and actually praised his performance in his after-action report. Since Polk clearly chose to brush over the incident of Cheatham's intemperance, Bragg turned the affair over to Seddon. Cheatham never denied the charges, and soon there was talk of a court of inquiry. Yet the division commander proved to be a more formidable challenger than McCown. He maintained the strong support of the Tennessee congressional delegation, the *Chattanooga Daily Rebel* (which advocated for his promotion), and his own troops. To Bragg's chagrin, the incident went nowhere. On February 13, a Mississippi artilleryman wrote, "He [Cheatham] visited our camps yesterday evening and you never saw such enthusiasm — He is the most popular General in the Army." On March 15, as "Mars Frank" inspected his division, his Tennesseans gave him a rousing three cheers. There could be little question where their devotion lay.[25]

Johnston, in Knoxville on February 17, returned to Chattanooga on the twentieth. He continued to fret over reports of growing Union strength, which included five fresh divisions, two of them reportedly from western and northern Virginia. Confederate estimates notwithstanding, Rosecrans had no intention of advancing, and at any rate, the disparity between the armies was not that great. In March, the Army of Tennessee's present-for-duty strength of 53,000 (including 16,000 cavalry) compared favorably with Rosecrans's movable force of 67,000. As long as Bragg kept his cavalry close in on his flanks, he held odds that would make Lee envious.[26]

When Davis pressed for Bragg's replacement, Johnston predictably objected. There would be insufficient time to find a replacement, and despite the lack of support on the part of certain generals, the troops remained "full of confidence." The president desired that Johnston do the dirty work by deposing Bragg, something which the Virginian adamantly refused to do. Johnston explained to Wigfall on March 4 that to remove Bragg after having investigated him "would not look well" and would appear "mischievous."[27]

Meanwhile, Johnston's primary problem in Middle Tennessee remained the same: How could he keep Rosecrans from advancing the seventy-one miles to his prime target — Chattanooga — while simultaneously drawing supplies from the Columbia-Shelbyville sector, his main food-gathering area? While the theater commander pondered how much more he could squeeze in the way of commissary goods from the Duck River valley, he focused primarily on the army's vulnerable right flank, the area between McMinnville and Jasper. Press reports openly stated that Rosecrans would advance by feinting on Shelbyville while thrusting on McMinnville or Manchester. The army thus remained on the defensive throughout the early spring, with only vague talk of a Confederate subsistence raid into Kentucky. Dispositions remained the same, with Polk's Corps remaining at Shelbyville, Hardee's at Tullahoma, the Kentucky brigade at Manchester, the Arkansas brigade at Wartrace, and a brigade in the rear at Allisonia. Wheeler continued to hold the right and Van Dorn the left at Columbia. A more viable deployment would have been to advance Hardee to Manchester and shift Polk's Corps to Wartrace, with a division remaining at Shelbyville. Wheeler should have guarded the gaps—Liberty, Hoover's, and Dug Hollow—and Morgan's men the far right at McMinnville.[28]

Johnston's angst about Richmond smoldered as his continued requests were ignored. He believed that the administration simply failed to appreciate the importance of holding Tennessee and that to abandon the country beyond the Cumberland Mountains would mean "to give up East Tennessee." The closet reinforcements for Bragg would be in East Tennessee, but that department barely had sufficient troops to guard the major mountain passes and control the Unionists, now estimated at 7,000. Humphrey Marshall had 1,500 worthless cavalry in western Virginia, but they were needed for a beef raid in Kentucky. Disgruntled and feeling ignored, Johnston piddled his time away, admitting to Wigfall, "For more than three months I have been doing next to nothing."[29]

Davis had lost all patience with Johnston. Instead of cooperating and taking command at Tullahoma, Johnston had departed on a time-wasting inspection of the Mobile defenses. Seddon ordered him to get back into the war. He was to immediately return to Tullahoma and take command of the Army of Tennessee. Upon Johnston's arrival, Bragg would report to Richmond for consultation, presumably for reassignment. Hess, however, has suggested that the president very possibly would have returned Bragg, as he did after Perryville, at which time Johnston would return to his theater role.[30]

Johnston arrived at Army of Tennessee headquarters on the night of March 18, but Bragg was not present. The day before, he had accompanied his gravely ill wife, stricken with typhoid fever, to Winchester. Col. William Preston Johnston confirmed that she was "trembling on the brink of the grave." Before Bragg's departure, word had already leaked out among the army staff that he had been recalled to Richmond. Although Bragg returned to Tullahoma on the night of the twenty-first, for all intents and purposes he would be in Winchester for the next two weeks. General Johnston immediately occupied Elise's bedroom in the Catron House. Under the circumstances, he took it upon himself to stay Davis's order. Bragg needed to care for his wife. Besides, there were rumors that Grant might be on the move, perhaps to reinforce Rosecrans, and Johnston needed Bragg in Middle Tennessee. Gossip ran rampant that Bragg's days with the army were numbered. A correspondent with the *Shelbyville Banner* even picked up on a potential run: James Longstreet from Lee's army to command the Army of Tennessee, Polk to command at Mobile, Buckner to return to Tennessee to a yet-unnamed position, and Cheatham to succeed Polk at corps command. Others heard that Bragg would be going to Mobile.[31]

Johnston quickly fell into his comfort zone—that of inspector general. On March 19, he conducted a two-hour review of Hardee's Corps on an open plain near Tullahoma. The artillery could not participate due to insufficient space. A great many spectators crowded onto a nearby hillside, while dirty-faced boys scaled trees and rooftops to get a view. A correspondent observed the long lines of gray uniforms pouring into the field. Most of the battle flags were by now weather worn and bullet torn. Johnston, fitting of his role, sat atop a beautiful black stallion. "It really seemed as if every race of people on the face of the earth was represented by at least a brigade by the different brogues in giving commands," a Mississippian noted. The units charged by in columns of regiments, according to Capt. Henry C. Semple, "uttering yells and cries [as] they ran swiftly by, it was a noble sight." As for Johnston, Taylor Beatty thought him to be "the greatest military chieftain we have." A reporter for the *Rebel* saw him in the midst of the troops, talking freely with the regimental officers.[32]

On the twenty-third, Colonel Johnston arrived in Tullahoma, ostensibly on a fact-finding mission to determine the army's readiness but more likely to take the pulse of the army's high command. That same day, a contest was held for the best-drilled regiment in Breckinridge's Division. The men of the 1st/3rd Florida expressed confidence that they had won the bayonet charge, but the Tennesseans had something up their sleeve. A Floridian wrote: "They got half way across the field yelling as loud as they could when all at once the Drum rapped and they all dropped [as if to avoid a volley] like they were dead[;] even the Col. and his horse both came down. The horse lay as close [to] the ground as he could and the Col. right behind him. They all lay for several minutes before they got up. It beat everything I ever saw in my life and I never did hear such cheering [from spectators] in my life as when they dropped. They got the praise and well they deserve it for they beat anything drilling I ever saw." The contest ultimately pitted the 13th/20th Louisiana of Breckinridge's Division against the 17th Tennessee of Cleburne's Division. "They both drilled splendidly but our Louisiana boys beat them," boasted a New Orleans gunner. The Tennesseans demanded a rematch, claiming that their regiment had been embarrassed by recently arrived conscripts.[33]

On March 28, Gen. Johnston arrived at Shelbyville. Two days later, Polk held a grand review of his corps. Colonel Johnston declared Withers's Division to be the best clothed in the army, and McCown's showed "marks of neglect" in several areas. Although personally believing Bragg to be incompetent, the colonel avoided the central issue of command discord. The day of the colonel's departure, Hardee wrote Colonel Johnston a letter in which he unleashed his opinions about General Johnston. He labeled the Virginian a "decided partisan" of Bragg's, and he also complained that Johnston would not confide in him, implying that their conversations had been kept formal. William Preston Johnston returned to the capital fully believing that there was "nobody competent to the command" of the army.[34]

With Elise recovering, Bragg returned to Tullahoma on the night of April 1, but she relapsed and he returned to Winchester the next day. By this time General Johnston had, according to press reports, been "quite sick" for several days. His illness related to his old Seven Pines wounds of eleven months earlier. Two bullet wounds had left two broken ribs and adhesions between his lung and chest wall. The wounds had flared up again; indeed, they had never really gone into remission. On the tenth, Johnston admitted to Davis that he was unfit for command—"General Bragg is therefore necessary here." Yet Bragg remained in Winchester until the thirteenth, thus leaving the incapacitated Virginian in command. Johnston began a slow recovery. Capt. Daniel Coleman saw him on April 18 on the front porch of the Catron House—"he looked calm and hopeful—Great man." Meanwhile, Elise somewhat recovered, and Bragg returned to Tullahoma.[35]

The review of Hardee's Corps on Friday, April 10, went off without a hitch. A reporter specifically singled out the 13th/20th Louisiana, with its Frenchmen, Germans, Creoles, Dutchmen, and Prussians—"the mixed character" of New Orleans. "The troops did very well—weather was good but ground dusty. A great many spectators, especially ladies—for whom Genl. Hardee has given the entertainment—he has several at his house and this is the second or third time they have come up from Huntsville." Cleburne also had his mind on the fairer sex. He returned from a week's rest in Shelbyville "in a most heavenly mood, which still continues," Irving Buck confided to his sister. With the review scheduled for Friday, "Gen'l C. sent me to S. [Shelbyville] after a load of women."[36]

With Bragg back at Tullahoma and Johnston only marginally involved, it might be suspected that internal squabbling would have once again erupted. On the surface, however, all appeared to be harmonious. Polk spent April 9–11 at Tullahoma visiting Johnston, Bragg, Hardee, and Breckinridge. In a letter to his wife on the eleventh, he made no mention of any tension. Yet, just under the surface, the old animosities remained.[37]

Bragg bided his time. Although unsuccessful in his purge of Cheatham and Breckinridge, he now audaciously turned on Polk! He attempted to place the failure of Perryville on the bishop; indeed, the corps commander had admitted "disobedience to my orders" by not promptly attacking on October 8, 1862. On April 13, Bragg sent a letter to Hardee and the other division commanders present asking them to what extent they had sustained Polk's disobedience. Hardee, smelling a court-martial, refused to answer. He advised Polk that "if you chose to rip up the Kentucky campaign, you can tear Bragg to tatters." It was fortunate that Bragg never got wind of a damning pamphlet written by Capt. R. W. Wooley, a Preston staff officer. The material had actually been compiled by Hardee, Polk, Buckner, and Preston. Considered too volatile, the pamphlet was never published. Polk did, however, offer his after-action report to the *Knoxville Register*. It was, according to a Bragg biographer, "full of self-serving lies and omissions."[38]

On Thursday, April 16, Bragg arrived at Shelbyville for yet another inspection of Polk's Corps. When Bragg made his appearance, an Alabamian described him thus: "He is about my height, dark complextion, hair grey, beard which is also grey, which is about half an inch long. His face looks sad and careworn. I could not avoid a feeling of reverence when he took off his Cap to acknowledge the salute of the Colors of the regiment, although, as you are aware, I am not an admirer of his, by any means." Polk remained unaware of Hardee's letter at the time, for that night he dined with Bragg and his staff as well as Cheatham, Withers, and Stewart. He wrote to his wife that the army commander appeared "highly pleased," indicating that the day had gone well.[39]

Hardee's letter arrived the next day. Polk thanked him for the warning about "what was brewing," admitting that he was not surprised. He fully expected Bragg to place him under arrest. Indeed, he had earlier sardonically written that he "felt it to be quite necessary to watch Tullahoma [Bragg] as Murfreesboro [Rosecrans]." After presenting a lengthy defense of his actions in Kentucky, in essence giving Hardee a heads-up of his defense, Polk concluded that "the time for dealing with this has not yet arrived." Nor would it. As with Cheatham and Breckinridge, the issue went nowhere.[40]

Bragg later justified his move by insincerely informing Davis that he had done so "with deep regret and as mildly as possible" and only because the bishop had first moved on him. "He [Polk] will convince himself that his own views are better, and will follow them without reflecting on the consequences." Bragg admitted that there was no longer any pretense of friendship between him and Polk and Hardee. "Of course it will not be possible . . . for cordial official correspondence to exist again between myself and [the] officers who have openly violated [my] trust."[41]

Months of infighting had taken their toll. Cordiality, much less communication, between Bragg and his corps commanders had all but broken down. Davis could have resolved the issue by ordering Bragg to Richmond when practicable and placing Polk in temporary command until Johnston recovered. A better option would have been to place Beauregard in command and retain Johnston in his present role. Such a thought proved too repugnant to Davis, too unthinkable.

The Decline of the Cavalry
The War Child

After the Battle of Stones River, Bragg banked on his cavalry to thwart or forestall a second Union advance. Brent entered in his journal on January 22, "The policy of our general seems to be to annoy and harass the enemy by throwing our cavalry on his flanks and rear, destroying and cutting off his communications." Given the success of Van Dorn's Holly Springs, Mississippi, raid only weeks earlier, in which the destruction of Grant's depot had forced the Yankees to abandon the overland approach to Vicksburg, the strategy seemed logical. Rosecrans, however, had made sure that his advanced depot at Murfreesboro was secure by constructing an enormous, virtually impregnable fortress. Could Wheeler thus duplicate Van Dorn's success merely by striking at Union rail and river communications, especially considering that to some degree Rosecrans had been supplementing his supplies by living off the land? By February, Rosecrans had stockpiled seventy-five days of rations at Nashville and Murfreesboro.[1]

In January 1863, Bragg promoted Wheeler to major general. Whether deserved or not, the ascent of the twenty-six-year-old was perhaps inevitable. A West Point graduate (barely) of the class of '59, Wheeler spent his first stint at the Cavalry School of Instruction at Carlisle Barracks, Pennsylvania. In late 1860, he was transferred to Fort Craig, New Mexico. It was by fighting Indians on his way to his new post that he earned the sobriquet "Fightin' Joe." Bragg's fondness for him dated back to their time together in the Department of the Gulf; Wheeler reciprocated with total loyalty. During his visit to Richmond in October 1862, Bragg requested a brigadier's commission for him. Davis resisted, calling him a "mere boy," but eventually he relented. At five feet, one half inch, he was described by some as pleasant but by others as aloof and possessing a nervous temperament. One visitor commented that he was a "very little man" who wore a coat "much too big for him." A member of his escort later described him as "a very small man . . . [who] looks like a monkey or a ape." The press gave him several tags—the Little Brigadier, the War Pony, the War Child—but to the people he would remain Fightin' Joe.[2]

Wheeler had become Bragg's protégé in the Pensacola days. "It is frequently charged that Gen. Wheeler is a pet of Gen. Bragg's," noted a correspondent. The cavalryman's exploits before and after Murfreesboro had clearly bedazzled Bragg. Historians have been less impressed. While lauding his professional background, aggressiveness, and successes, they also point to his flaws—a lack of genius, his youth, limited cavalry experience, an inability to analyze intelligence, failure to exercise control over his men, and a penchant for making exaggerated claims in his reports. He sometimes referred to himself as "War Child," revealing his level of egotism. To his credit, he could be scrappy in battle (overly so, thought Bragg) and was eventually wounded five times and had sixteen horses shot from under him. The question of promotion to major general, as always, came down to "As compared to whom?" There was "great dissatisfaction" among Morgan's men that he did not get tapped, but the Kentuckian was neither West Point nor an administrator nor did he possess the skills for such a position. Additionally, Bragg had not forgiven Morgan for his delayed return from his Christmas raid that had kept him away from the Murfreesboro battlefield. Forrest, the most capable and ferocious cavalryman in the west, and Wheeler's senior, also had his limitations. It seems clear that Bragg saw him as a partisan who would not have the temperament for close-in army support, and he never gave him serious consideration. Brent concluded that had Forrest been "educated & cultivated he would have made a higher reputation." As for Forrest, he proudly boasted, "I ain't no graduate of West Point, and never rubbed my back up against any college." Some have surmised that Forrest's propensity to lead from the front disqualified him from major command. At any rate, Bragg could control Wheeler; no one could control Forrest.[3]

By January 20, Bragg had deployed Wheeler and all of his cavalry—Wharton (2,217), Col. James Hagan (1,747), and Abraham Buford (724), some 4,688 horsemen—to the right. When Morgan returned from his raid, his command (2,217) was sent to McMinnville, much to the dismay of the Kentuckian, who lacked the disciplined ego for mundane duties. Forrest (2,340) held the left at Columbia. Within two weeks, the cavalry, apparently due to the failing stock of horses, had declined by nearly 1,500 men. Johnston ordered Col. Philip Roddey's Brigade from North Alabama to north of the Duck River and to Chapel Hill and a division of Pemberton's cavalry to Columbia, but it would take time for them to arrive.[4]

Meanwhile, Bragg unleashed Wheeler on Union shipping with Wharton's Brigade and 800 of Forrest's men. With Rebel raiders once again on the prowl, Union authorities simply suspended all shipping, thus robbing the Georgian of any prizes. The cavalry chief then struck out for Dover, arriving on the bitterly cold afternoon of February 3. Precisely what Wheeler expected to accomplish by attacking the Fort Donelson garrison, beyond proving that his recent promotion had been justified, was anybody's guess. Union gunboats were nearby, and the town could not be held even if taken. Forrest strongly opposed an assault. An attack nonetheless proceeded, with Wharton and Forrest approaching on foot from different directions. Forrest, attempting to exploit a momentary advantage, impetuously ordered a large portion of his command to be mounted and charge on horseback, which was only hurled back with a loss of about 200 men. Wharton achieved only limited success. The assault, the maiden outing for the new major general, had proved to be a total blunder.

After the engagement, Wheeler, Wharton, and Forrest assembled in a farmhouse four miles outside of Dover to compose the after-action report. It quickly became apparent that Wheeler intended to gloss over the embarrassing affair, even placing casualties at 100; they were more in the neighborhood of 300. Forrest, overlooking his own impetuousness in the battle, bounded from his chair and fired a salvo: "General Wheeler, I advised you against this attack, and said all a subordinate officer should have said against it, and nothing you can now say or do will bring back my brave men lying dead and wounded and freezing around that fort tonight." He concluded, "I mean no disrespect to you; you know my feelings of personal friendship for you; you can have my sword if you demand it; but there is one thing that I want you to put in that report to General Bragg—tell him that I will be in my coffin before I will fight again under your command." The cavalry chief replied quietly: "Forrest. I cannot take your saber, and I regret exceedingly your determination. As the commanding officer I take all the blame and responsibility for the failure." Thereafter, Forrest never again served under Wheeler.[5]

The press, initially at least, downplayed the debacle, the *Rebel* calling Confederate losses "exaggerated." The troops knew better: "The expedition was an unfortunate one and although the newspapers and friends of Gen. Wheeler may attempt to smooth the matter over it proves that he has been elevated far above his capacity and over men who are infinitely his superiors." It was a subsequent article in the *Rebel*, written by "Cosmopolite," that blew the story open. Exactly who Cosmopolite was is not known, but he was apparently a Forrest staff officer or a source close to a staff officer. He blasted the War Child for picking a fight merely to "brag about his courage." Southern casualties had been grossly underreported, and the fact that Forrest had strongly opposed the assault was not mentioned in Wheeler's after-action report. The article then became pointed. Wheeler had been promoted "upon the strength of being a West Pointer, and a pet to Gen. Bragg; and Generals

Forrest and Morgan were entirely overlooked and ignored." One more blunder for the young major general "like the foolish Donelson affair" and he would lose all credibility with the public. Wheeler, accustomed to getting nothing but glowing press accounts, must have been stung by the article.[6]

Ultimately, dueling newspapers would take up the Wheeler-Forrest rift. The *Appeal* had been running a series of articles on various generals and it ultimately got around to Wheeler. It accused him of being overcautious, slow, and "Bragg's favorite." Wheeler's case was taken up by his hometown newspaper, the *Augusta Constitutionalist*: "Why is it that the *Memphis Appeal* takes every occasion to cast a slur upon the able commander of the cavalry in the Army of Tennessee? Is it because he ranks General Forrest?"[7]

A Deplorable State of Affairs

Wheeler's Corps, comprised of Wharton's and Morgan's divisions, continued to hold the right of the Duck River line. The entire corps began to show signs of deterioration. Morgan became increasingly diverted by his new wife, Mattie, whom he had summoned to his McMinnville headquarters. Mattie described them as a "love sick couple," and the Kentucky raider admitted on January 13 that although he fully expected to be attacked that day, "still my thoughts were of you & not of war." Col. George St. Leger Grenfell, the brigadier's former adjutant, openly groused that Morgan "would never be the same man he was." Even Bragg was beginning to notice: "I fear Morgan is overcome by too large a command; with a regiment or small brigade he did more and better service than a division." Mrs. Virginia French, who lived in McMinnville, began to observe "quite a bitter feeling" between Morgan's and Wheeler's men. When Buford's small brigade was incorporated into Morgan's Division, she observed that they were "as rough looking troops as any I have ever seen," many of them drunk.[8]

Wheeler himself conceded the deplorable state of affairs. In a scathing general circular to his officers on January 22, 1863, he detailed the problem. Certain regiments had been "rendered worse than useless appendages to the Brigade. Companies muster for duty not more than one-fourth or one-fifth their strength and, even then, are allowed to scatter so as to be of but little use to the command." This "disgraceful state of things" was directly due to the "gross neglect of duty on the part of Regimental and Company Commanders." Unfortunately, the Northern press got hold of the circular and published it under the headline "Wheeler's Cavalry Falling to Pieces."[9]

The cavalry continued to experience a breakdown of discipline and leadership throughout the early spring. On the afternoon of March 4, Col. Alfred A. Russell's Brigade, comprised of the 1st Confederate Cavalry and

4th Alabama Cavalry, covered the Shelbyville-Triune Pike. Remarkably, 400 of his 700 troopers remained unarmed. Russell, a thirty-six-year-old prewar physician, who had the habit of constantly buttoning and unbuttoning his coat while under fire, had outposts established at Rover and three miles to the southeast at Unionville. Robert Minty's hard-charging Yankee brigade suddenly struck, overrunning first the Rover and then the Unionville camp. The Southerners stampeded, and a six-mile chase back to their lines ensued. Barely had Col. W. F. Tucker, commanding a Mississippi brigade on outpost from Shelbyville, received pleas for assistance than Russell's men careened through his lines, Minty in pursuit. The Federals broke off the running fight, claiming fifty-four prisoners. Tucker dismissed Russell's troopers as "only an incumbrance." Bragg expressed his annoyance to Wheeler that "if he [Russell] has carried unarmed men to the front with his guards he is not fit for his position."[10]

On March 9, Bragg further expressed his displeasure. He informed Wheeler that "from the frequency with which the cavalry, especially your old Brigade, is stampeded," he feared "a great demoralization is coming upon them." The cavalry branch remained far disproportionate to the size of the army, and Bragg made it clear that if he had his way he would place "one-half we have now in the infantry." Rather than dealing with the issue of dismounting more units, however, he chose to let the branch shrink from attrition. No longer could recruits avoid frontline duty by volunteering for the cavalry. How could he allow the corps to grow, he asked Wheeler, when it was "in danger of disorganization, want of discipline, and forage inca-pacity"? He also reminded him that "horses are not furnished to ride over infantry with, as Russell's regiment [4th Alabama Cavalry] did a few days ago." An early April inspection of Wharton's troopers produced "unsatis-factory results."[11]

It could be argued that Wheeler was still new in his position and, like all Civil War generals, he needed time to grow into his role. Unfortunately, time would not produce growth. In January 1865, Alfred Roman gave a thorough and damning inspection of the cavalry, particularly singling out its leader. He found Wheeler "wanting in firmness. . . . He is too gentle, too lenient." The troops liked him, but they doubted his ability to get sufficient fight out of them. Roman concluded that Wheeler had clearly been promoted beyond his capability. He was fit only for brigade or division command, and "for the good of the cause, and for his own reputation," he should be removed from command. After two years of leadership, it proved to be a damning conclusion.[12]

Discipline in Morgan's Division also continued to deteriorate. The raider seethed at being subordinate to Wheeler. On March 20, he sensed an opportunity to recapture his glory by challenging a Federal column marching from Murfreesboro to Milton. With 1,000 troopers and two guns, he attacked the rear guard as it returned to Murfreesboro. A mile west of Milton, on Vaught's Hill, he collided with 1,200 well-posted bluecoats and two guns. The engagement continued all afternoon, and although Morgan surrounded the position, he could never take it. At 4:30, having received news of strong Union reinforcements arriving from Murfreesboro, he broke off the fight and withdrew. Morgan had been decidedly whipped, losing 150 men, including two colonels who had been killed. Abandoning his hit-and-run tactics had cost him dearly. His subsequent report to army headquarters, according to Brent, proved "vague and unsatisfactory." After Milton, the Northern press branded Morgan as no longer a soldier but merely a horse stealer and bridge burner. The glory continued to fade.[13]

On April 3, a force of 1,500 Union infantry and cavalry under David Stanley encountered Col. Richard M. Gano's Division of Morgan's cavalry at Snow Hill, north of Liberty. The Rebels were so quickly routed, the incident proved to be an embarrassment. In mid-April, a division-size enemy force under Maj. Gen. J. J. Reynolds pounced on McMinnville. The town was unoccupied except for Morgan (who was visiting Mattie), his forty-man escort, and ninety infantry of the 9th Kentucky guarding commissary stores. The couple escaped, but the town was ransacked. The Yankee expedition rode around at will, eventually gathering up 130 prisoners in the district. "Who is to blame for this ugly business," demanded the *Rebel*. "Here is a cavalry dash upon one of our chief frontier towns . . . and yet not a shot is fired, and the vandals escape with glory, trophies and all! Who is to blame for it?" The general's flight soon became the talk of the army. A family member scolded Mattie for "sticking *too close* to your husband," and even the Union press boldly proclaimed that Delilah had shorn Samson's locks.[14]

Hardee, who admitted that he did not have a close relationship with Morgan, felt as though it were time to step in. "I learn that Morgan's command is in bad condition and growing worse," he wrote General Johnston in early May. It had become common knowledge that the Kentuckian chaffed at being under Wheeler, and his reputation with the public continued to diminish. "Would it not be well for you to send for Morgan and have some talk with him. He likes you and will receive kindly any suggestions you may make to him." The end result was that on May 4, Morgan's 2,400-man division was dispatched to Wayne and Clinton Counties in Kentucky, on the Kentucky-Tennessee line, to graze horses and recruit. It would not be the end of John

Hunt Morgan—not yet—but it would be the end of his direct connection with the Army of Tennessee.[15]

The infantry had nothing but disdain for the mounted branch. A member of the 38th Alabama wrote bluntly that the name "cavalry" was a misnomer—they were really nothing more than mounted infantry who rode for speed but actually fought on foot. In a fight with infantry, "they are invariably whipped." While he did not question their gallantry, he did "deny their usefulness." There was simply too much cavalry. "We have here large numbers of cavalrymen who have outlived their horses and are afoot. They grumble furiously of being put into the infantry service." A Tennessean pronounced the 1st Alabama Cavalry to be "the biggest cowards in the army." Brigadier General Manigault noted that the cavalry, never remarkable for its discipline, always believed itself superior to its counterparts. In 1863, however, that branch lost its prestige "and never afterwards recovered it." Perhaps such a remark from a rival service branch could be dismissed, but even a cavalryman expressed disgust. Robert Bunting of the Texas Rangers admitted that too many troopers proved useless—"poorly mounted, poorly armed, and shamefully poor horsemen, they are often a reproach to this honorable arm of the service and are a loss to the webfoots, where they would be compelled to do good fighting." He noted that the majority of the 2nd Georgia Cavalry did not have side arms, thus making them useless in close-quarter work. When they fire their rifles, "they have no alternative but to get out of the way." Another Ranger concurred: "The most of our Cavalry are Georgians, Tennesseans & Alabamians & as they are poorly armed & indifferent riders we do not estimate them highly."[16]

Col. Basil Duke of Morgan's cavalry conceded the decline but blamed it on the scarcity of horses and the inability to logistically feed them. While Morgan's Division recuperated in Kentucky, the 2nd Kentucky Cavalry remained on picket at Woodbury, Tennessee. The animals received only two or three ears of corn a day. Every blade of grass was eaten, and according to Duke, "the trees were barked by the poor animals as high as they could reach." A fourth of them subsequently died. A member of Thomas Harrison's Brigade, writing from Liberty on May 12, concurred: "All along our front the forges [forage] are consumed. We are here to recruit. In doing this necessary work we are hauling corn forty miles. . . . We some days have ten ears of corn for our horses, and frequently without any." When not on picket duty, the cavalry foraged for corn, frequently being out two days at a time with no luck.[17]

An infantryman at Tullahoma raised a significant question: Why was there so much cavalry? "The fact is, we have always had too much of 'the cavalry.' One infantry is worth five cavalrymen, and costs only one-third the money." Even deducting W. H. "Red" Jackson's Division and Roddey's Brigade, both on loan to the Army of Tennessee, Bragg still had 11,000 troopers available in the spring of 1863. The logistical strain placed upon the quartermaster to feed the animals was beginning to offset its usefulness. At the very least, the most ineffective units, Russell's Brigade and Buford's old brigade, in all 1,500 men, could have been dismounted and placed into the infantry. Nor was there any good reason to remount the 11th Texas Cavalry (dismounted). For several months during the spring and summer of 1863, the men of the 4th Tennessee Cavalry Battalion sat idle in a camp of instruction in Coffee County, Tennessee, awaiting mounts. In late May, a small ad hoc battalion of dismounted cavalrymen was formed into an infantry unit and attached to the 9th Alabama Battalion.[18]

Wheeler, like Morgan, also became absorbed in personal distractions. On February 15, the *Shelbyville Banner* reported that the cavalry chief and his staff were in town "on a slight relaxation of duty." He was still there ten days later, attending a ball. In March he finally got back in the war and, assigned to the right wing, made his headquarters at McMinnville. It did not take long for him to begin socializing with ladies at nightly suppers; he also began calling on Miss Mollie Smith. An article that appeared in the *Mobile Advertiser & Register* in April made a clear reference to the general when it stated, "A dashing young bachelor general is said to be the marked out victim of the aspiring ladies who have 'button on the brain!' and they are sending him the tenderist missives." He partied, socialized, and boasted to Mrs. French that he soon would have a book published on cavalry tactics—all well and good but distractions from the task at hand.[19]

An English visitor, Sir Arthur Fremantle, visited William Martin's Division on outpost beyond Guy's Gap in early June 1863 and witnessed firsthand the experience of picket duty. Martin led the Englishman to the outpost of the 51st Alabama Cavalry. "This Colonel Webb [Lt. Col. James D. Webb] was a lawyer by profession and seemed a capital fellow; and he insisted on riding with us to the videttes in spite of the rain," Fremantle wrote. The pickets were at intervals of 300 to 400 yards, with the 51st covering a front of two miles. Some ninety-seven men remained on line at all times. Webb offered to stir up a little fight to entertain his visitor, but Fremantle declined. The troopers, he noted, had long rifles and revolvers but no sabers, and the horses appeared to be in good condition, given their scant rations and hard duty.[20]

The Confederates faced more than immature leadership, lax discipline, and ineptness. In March 1863 only 1,469 of the armed troopers possessed revolvers. The balance of the weapons included 1,469 carbines, 1,363 percussion smoothbore muskets, 4,649 rifles, and 733 shotguns. In August, a few five-shot London-made Kerr revolvers got through the blockade and made their way into Wheeler's cavalry. For their part, the Texas Rangers remained well armed and equipped. Of the equipment belonging to the 406 men present in March 1863, only three saddles and thirty-two bridles were condemned in an inspection. All the horses, save nine, appeared in good condition.[21]

The Union cavalry was on the ascent. Rosecrans mounted an infantry brigade, Col. John T. Wilder's "Lightning Brigade," in the spring of 1863. Armed with deadly Spencer repeating rifles that could fire seven .52-caliber bullets in succession, the brigade became a deadly and near-unstoppable strike force. The Yankees also armed a number of their cavalry with five-shot Colt revolving rifles. By that summer, Rosecrans had increased his horsemen from a division to a corps. Leaders such as Col. Robert Minty became the equals of Wharton or any officer under Wheeler. At a time when the western Rebel cavalry was clearly losing its edge, its enemy counterparts had evolved into a powerful offensive force. The tactics also changed. The aggressive Minty formulated a strategy whereby flanking dismounted troopers and horse artillery preceded saber charges. This proved to be an improvement over charges and dismounted troopers operating in isolation. Having a long line of dismounted skirmishers followed by cavalry in columns of attack also became a routine tactic.[22]

Van Dorn and Forrest

Following Wheeler's defeat at Dover, Forrest's 2,200-man brigade withdrew to Columbia. On February 20, Jackson's 3,433-man cavalry division arrived from Mississippi, having crossed the Tennessee River at Florence. Both Forrest and Jackson would be under the overall command of Major General Van Dorn. Johnston had previously ordered the division up, without consulting Pemberton, to protect Bragg's right flank. He believed that Grant would not make another offensive move until the spring, at which time the horsemen could be returned. This move left Pemberton blind and his department subject to raids. As for his part, Van Dorn, at least according to a news correspondent at Columbia, may have come to Tennessee expecting to have independent command; it was not to be.[23]

Van Dorn quickly got the lay of the land. On March 5, he moved north with his 5,700 troopers in a reconnaissance-in-force. The Texans of John Whitfield's Brigade had no love for Jackson, their new Tennessee division commander, who appeared to put on airs. Before departing Columbia, they burned him in effigy. As the spearhead of the column approached Thompson Station, on the Tennessee & Alabama Railroad, it suddenly encountered a force of unknown size approaching from the north. Jackson cautiously deployed in the hills south of the station, and inconclusive sparring continued throughout the afternoon. Van Dorn received good news as his column approached. He had encountered only a brigade (John Coburn's) recently arrived from Kentucky, two cavalry regiments and a battery. Word of a long wagon train led Van Dorn to quip, "Wait for the wagons, boys, and we'll all take a ride." In the ensuing engagement, Van Dorn suffered 357 casualties, but the victory was undeniable — 377 Federals killed or wounded and 1,151 captured. A Texan wrote to his mother, "I think he [Van Dorn] is more competent to command Cavalry than Infantry, and both officers and men are beginning to have *some little* confidence in him."[24]

William Nugent of the 28th Mississippi Cavalry remained unconvinced. "I have no great confidence in our little General [Van Dorn]," he wrote on March 24. "He is a Northern born man raised in Kentucky, I do not believe he can manoeuvre a regiment in the field. His staff officers are a drinking, rollicking, set of men, and profane as pirates." Indeed, he did not believe that any of the generals or colonels knew anything about tactics or the management of troops in camp. "The General officers are all the time giving their attention to parties[,] balls etc and neglect their troops. . . . Col. [Peter] Starke remarked the other day that this Cavalry Corps was rapidly going to the Devil." Van Dorn foolishly attacked the 8,000-man Franklin garrison on April 10. The 28th Mississippi Cavalry charged into town, where it came under a storm of musket fire. The regiment lost fifty-two killed and wounded and thirteen captured in an effort that proved as valiant as it did fruitless.[25]

Thus stood the cavalry command as the spring of 1863 drew to a close. Clearly out of his depth, Wheeler longed for the glory of another cavalry raid rather than having to develop long-term planning. Wharton, increasingly frustrated by his lack of promotion, quietly harbored ill feelings and rivalry toward his superior. On May 2, his horse collided head on with a tree, badly bruising the brigadier's left knee and foot and placing him out of commission for over a week. Morgan remained in love and could not get his head in the war. Despite Van Dorn's victory at Thompson Station and Forrest's exploits at Brentwood and in capturing Abel Streight's brigade, the cavalry proved incapable of seriously disrupting Rosecrans's supply lines. There was little esprit de corps, and relations were worsening within the top command. Morgan and Wharton detested Wheeler, Van Dorn distrusted Forrest, and as one historian stated, "Forrest did not get along with anybody."

THE DECLINE OF THE CAVALRY

The Mobile paper noted in early May 1863 that Forrest and Morgan should soon regain their independent status "and bickering between our cavalry leaders will cease."[26]

The relationship between Van Dorn and Forrest had probably been icy from the outset, Forrest seeing the Mississippian as an overrated general and aristocratic dandy, while Van Dorn viewed himself as socially and educationally superior to the former slave trader. On Thursday, April 23, Forrest was summoned to Van Dorn's headquarters to discuss two issues, the most volatile being articles that had appeared in the *Chattanooga Daily Rebel* giving the Tennessean credit for the Thompson Station victory. According to Maj. J. Minnick Williams of Van Dorn's staff, the only eyewitness to the conversation, Van Dorn claimed that the articles had been written by one of Forrest's staff; such may have been the case. One modern writer has surmised that the author was Matt Galloway, Forrest's assistant adjutant general. Forrest nonetheless exploded: "I know nothing of the articles you refer to and I demand from you your authority for this assertion. I shall hold him responsible and make him eat his words, or run my saber through him, and I say to you as well that I will hold you personally responsible if you do not produce the author." Taken aback by the outburst, Van Dorn turned to Major Williams and asked if he knew the author. "I do not, and I think, general, that you have done General Forrest an injustice in the suspicion that the articles originated from his headquarters." Van Dorn quickly backed down and said that he did not believe that Forrest was responsible. According to Williams, the Tennessean uncharacteristically cooled down and the two shook hands. Van Dorn later related that both officers at one point reached for their swords and that he had never "felt so ashamed of myself in my life." The two never met again. On April 23, Forrest received orders to go into northern Alabama to counter the raid of Abel Streight. He captured the 1,600-man brigade twenty-one miles outside of Rome, Georgia. Incredibly, only 600 of Forrest's men were able to keep up. When Streight demanded to know exactly how many men Forrest had, the Tennessean barked: "I've got enough to whip you out of your boots." Streight ordered his men to stack their arms.[27]

Two weeks later, Van Dorn's personal life caught up with him. While his primary headquarters remained at the Cheairs home in Spring Hill, Van Dorn frequently spent time at Dr. George Peters's plantation. While the doctor made his calls, the general took walks and carriage rides with the young and attractive Mrs. Peters. The warnings of his adjutant, Maj. Manning M. Kimmel, that "Mrs. Peters can cause you a lot of trouble" went unheeded; people gossiped. On the evening of May 6, the doctor, having obviously heard the stories, came to Van Dorn's headquarters and shot him in the back of the head. What is now known, through the historical detective work of Arthur B. Carter, was that Van Dorn was not at Spring Hill, as tradition has long stated, but rather at his secondary headquarters, a small cabin near Peters's plantation, when the assassination occurred. In a desperate attempt to salvage his reputation, his staff took his body the six miles back to Spring Hill and concocted the story that long stood in history. While the details were kept secret, the gist of the story got out. Speaking on behalf of most, a Tennessee infantryman wrote, "No person seems to regret his death."[28]

The South could afford to lose Van Dorn, but Forrest was another matter. Upon his return from his brilliant exploit capturing Streight's brigade, he requested the transfer of Lt. Andrew Gould, an artillery officer, for what he saw as cowardice for abandoning his two guns in action at Sand Mountain, this despite the fact that nearly all of Gould's horses had been shot. On June 13, the issue came to a head in the Masonic Building in Columbia. The two officers exchanged heated words. Forrest drew a penknife from his pants pocket, and Gould fumbled for a pistol. In the shuffling that ensued, Forrest stabbed the lieutenant in his lung, and Gould shot the general just above the left hip. When a doctor told Forrest that his wound might be fatal, he barked, "No damned man shall kill me and live!" He got possession of a pistol, and in a rage went storming down the street after the lieutenant. When he found him, he fired a shot, missed, and hit an innocent bystander. It didn't matter; Gould's initial wound proved mortal. One firsthand account has the two hotheaded officers reconciling at Gould's bedside before the lieutenant passed—maybe, maybe not. In a week and a half, Forrest was back in the saddle.[29]

❋ 9 ❋

The Manpower Problem

During the first year of the war, the primary problem in the West lay in the dearth of small arms. By mid-1862, the issue had increasingly shifted to manpower and persisted throughout the balance of the war. The need for raw numbers created a vicious cycle—men's reluctance after 1861 to volunteer led to poor-quality conscripts, which led to the rising rates of desertion that frequently resulted in brutal forms of coercion and increased executions. Undergirding this cycle was the breakdown of the home front economy.

The weekly returns told the story; the Army of Tennessee was hemorrhaging men. "Our armies here [Knoxville] are gradually, but certainly, melting away, whilst we are getting no re-enforcements. No recruits, and cannot see a source from which they are to come," reported Bragg. Some regiments counted barely 100 privates. The Conscription Act had been in effect for seven months, yet not a single man had reported. The War Department advised that the Kentuckians of conscript age who had followed the army out of the state be drafted, thereby adding several companies. Bragg also saw to it that all men on detached service with staffs return to duty. "Some regiments have become skeletons by them," Brent groused. About 1,500 convalescents at Chattanooga, who never made it to Kentucky, were forwarded to Knoxville. Men absent without leave would be granted a pardon if they immediately returned to their regiments.[1]

At the Battle of Stones River, the army lost an additional 10,000 men. Adding to the woes, the War Department reassigned Jackson's and Pegram's brigades in early January 1863, the former's to Bridgeport and the latter's to Kingston, Tennessee, thus removing another 1,000 infantry and 1,200 cavalry. During January, the Confederacy counted 473,000 men in its twelve departments and districts. The number proved deceptive—only 325,000 were available for combat. Bragg's department was credited with 51,000 men, but this included Forrest's and Morgan's brigades, which were likely to be detached. The actual January 20 present-for-duty return for the Army of Tennessee, the best indicator of those actually available for the firing line, revealed 30,165 infantry and artillery and 4,713 cavalry (Wheeler's), totaling 34,878. Noncombatants—teamsters, hospital attendants, orderlies, ordnance and commissary personnel, and so on—added another 7,314 to the roll. This meant that for every six men in the army, one served in a support capacity.[2]

It was the absent category that proved the most troubling—30,136. Indeed, in Polk's Corps there were almost as many absent (15,887) as on the line (17,633). Some 2,200 of those absent had been granted permission by lower-grade officers, a number so high that it enraged Bragg. While sickness and details accounted for many absentees, far too many men of conscript age simply hid out, notably in the notorious haunts of East Tennessee and northern Alabama. The majority of the draft dodgers simply desired to avoid service in either army and remain with their families.[3]

Most of the regiments had been reduced to mere skeletons. The ranks of two South Carolina regiments had, according to a member, become "dreadfully thinned." Consolidation again became necessary—this time twelve regiments into six. The men held decidedly mixed views. A "good deal of dissatisfaction" resulted when the 28th and 34th Alabama consolidated, but, John Crittenden noted, "I think it will wear off in a short time." When the 24th and 29th Mississippi merged, Thomas Newberry of the latter noted, "I don't like it much still I think we can get along." While conceding that the men disliked the consolidations, Lt. Col. Irvine Walker thought it for the best. Ed Carruth observed that the merger of the 7th and 9th Mississippi caused some dissatisfaction, "though it is decidedly best for the army." A side effect of the consolidations was that the surplus officers (the less effective ones) were sent home to round up fresh recruits. "I must say they have done well and our increase is due to them," Walker concluded.[4]

Bragg moved to plug the most notorious siphons. He attempted to stop the policy of allowing sick men to convalesce at home, realizing that far too many of them never returned. The practice nonetheless persisted. He also had mixed success preventing future volunteers from joining the cavalry, stating that too many joined that service merely to roam the countryside as marauders. Dismounted troopers would henceforth be placed in the infantry. Bragg placed all detailed cooks back into the ranks in February 1863, returning (according to him) 2,000 men. Furloughs proved out of the question. "I could not get a furlough if my life depended upon it," Washington Ives complained to his sister. "General Bragg has issued an order prohibiting the granting of furloughs until the emergency is over which will be 100 years from now unless things are better arranged than they have been of late."[5]

A soldier could still hire a replacement, but it had become all but impossible to acquire one. Writing from the camp of the 41st Alabama at Tullahoma, William Jones nonetheless begged his wife, Mary, to see if she could find one. "If you was willing I wood giv your land to some one to take my plase." If no one could be found for a twelve- or six-month enlistment, then "I will give fifteen dollars pur months or I will give the land an ten dollars pur month for the whole time. . . . I never intend to desurt as long as I can ceep from it[.] I drother bee at home than to have all I purses in this world[.] I would give all I have in this world to be clear of this . . . wore [war]." On February 7, he again wrote: "The newse [news] her is a most all lise [lies] the officers will tell anything to cheer us up. . . . I don't see now moure prossects of peese [peace] that they was six months ago is a giten mity tired of the wore. . . . Severl run away . . . a few night a go I fer[fear] that will a heap go."[6]

Bragg also cracked down by establishing a provost guard in April. Every brigade in the army would henceforth have a provost consisting of four noncommissioned officers and thirty privates. Essentially a military police force, the provost prevented straggling on the march, closed down gambling houses and brothels, executed sentences passed by the military court, arrested deserters, guarded prisoners of war, and generally policed the army. By June 1863, the provost of Brown's Brigade guarded nineteen prisoners, almost all deserters awaiting trial, although two had been sentenced to be executed.[7]

The ineffective Confederate Conscript Bureau had provided the Army of Tennessee with virtually no men—to be specific, nineteen between April 1862 and April 1863. "We expected large accessions to the army from the conscription & have been sadly disappointed by the meagre result & poor material—one veteran volunteer soldier is worth 20 of them," observed a cavalryman. Samuel Cooper encouraged Bragg to bypass the Richmond bureau and create his own independent conscript bureau. Bragg placed Pillow in charge, thus ridding himself of an inept general officer but, as matters developed, gaining a fair bureaucrat. The Tennessean asserted himself far more aggressively against Southern shirkers than he ever had against the Yankees. Assigned details of officers and companies of cavalry, he began by sweeping Bedford County, Tennessee (Shelbyville was described as a "Union hole"), where an estimated 1,500 men of conscript age (a virtual brigade by 1863 standards) hid out. Indeed, the Northern press reported that the woods in Bedford and Maury Counties were filled with loyalists attempting to get behind Federal lines. Pillow declared a war on draft dodgers—all well and good, but his overzealous methods quickly caused him to butt heads with the rival Richmond Conscript Bureau, which claimed that he interfered with the regular camps of instruction and that he collared many lawfully exempted men. Bragg nonetheless insisted that within six weeks, Pillow had done ten times the work of the conscript officers.[8]

In late January, the 8th Tennessee Cavalry, one of Forrest's outfits, rode into Marshall County, Mississippi, then moved into Fayetteville, Tennessee, and then went west to Williamson and Maury Counties in Middle Tennessee. The 4th Georgia Cavalry, a new regiment, simultaneously converged on Franklin, Giles, and Lawrence Counties. Forrest brazenly rode into Franklin, Tennessee, rounding up every conscript-eligible man in town. When the men were told to go with Forrest, the county court clerk, named Robinson, asked if he could first go home to make arrangements. Forrest promptly took out his revolver and pistol-whipped him. No further questions were forthcoming, and the men were marched out, according to the Northern press, like so many slaves. By spring, the press was reporting that not a single man of conscript age remained in Coffee and Franklin Counties, yet the "sweeps," or "rakes," as they were called, continued.[9]

Conscripts soon began showing up in camp, but their quality proved problematic. "Pillow's conscripts," as the veterans referred to them, were often met with jeers. Capt. Alfred Fielder of the 12th Tennessee noted on January 28, "There was quite a number of conscripts brought in last night and during the day—quite a stir in town[;] all sorts of excuses are being made by the Conscripts why they should be exempt." An Alabamian observed on February 19, "We hav got ten conscripts in our Company & they have been grunting around the Doctor for a discharge." The next day, 140 conscripts arrived for the 28th /34th Alabama. To John Crittenden, "some looked as if they would liked better to have been at home. The Majority appeared to be men thirty and forty years of age. Several of them were handcuffed and are still under guard." Just how effective such men would be remained to be seen.[10]

Bragg hailed Pillow's efforts, claiming that by mid-April 1863, some 10,000 men had been placed into the ranks, 1,200 from the Chattanooga area alone. "Our regiment [34th Alabama] is now being rapidly filled. Conscripts come in every day," James Mitchell wrote on March 21. While thousands were unquestionably swept into the dragnet, the overall number that actually ended up in the ranks may have been exaggerated. The *Chattanooga Daily Rebel* reported that many potential conscripts turned themselves in to the Federals at Murfreesboro instead of awaiting their fate. Large numbers of East Tennessee refugees fled behind Union lines in Kentucky. Of the ones Pillow actually cornered, even his own records reveal that not one in three ended up serving. By mid-March, an impressive 21,581 men had been enrolled in East Tennessee. Of that number, 1,107 were exempted, 1,254 ran away to the enemy, and another 12,500 promptly deserted or were detailed, thus leaving only 6,720 for actual service.[11]

The army unquestionably grew in number, but many of the accessions were returning absentees, not conscripts. Between January 20 and April 10, 1863, the infantry (the heart of the army) rose from 27,592 to 34,009 — an increase of 6,417. Few volunteered during this time (except to avoid conscription), but thousands of sick, wounded, and stragglers returned to the ranks. Also, a small number of prisoners taken at Perryville, paroled and exchanged, returned to duty. Tennessean William S. Dillon, wounded and captured, was one such who, along with others, had been assigned to Camp Douglas, Illinois. Returned by rail through West Virginia and East Tennessee, they arrived at Shelbyville during April. Some 400 Rebel prisoners captured at Stones River were also exchanged in early April. It is not unreasonable to assume that at least a third of the additions to the infantry came from these sources, not conscription.[12]

Another consideration is that each year turned out a new class of eighteen-year-olds who could be conscripted. Government officials estimated that for the class of 1863, Georgia and Alabama produced about 4,000 eighteen-year-olds each. While no numbers were available for Tennessee, doubtless 4,000 would be a fair estimate. According to a study of the 20th Tennessee, the recruits of 1863 were poorer, more likely to be married, and twenty-eight years old on average, as compared to twenty-six and twenty-four in 1861 and '62. Records revealed that by 1864, 7,052 men in Georgia had bought their way out of the war by paying for a substitute. The records of the 11th Tennessee reveal that thirty-five men joined during 1863. Of those with identified ages, only three were seventeen- or eighteen-year-olds, previously too young for the draft. The average age of all of that year's recruits was twenty-seven. Unfortunately, the regiment had lost twenty-seven through desertion, leaving a net gain of only nine for the year. Only one joined as a substitute, and he deserted within a month.[13]

Since a disproportionate number of the incoming conscripts came from Alabama, several of the regiments from that state filled to huge proportions by March 1863: the 28th/34th Alabama had 895 men; the 26th/39th Alabama, 827 men; and the 22nd/25th Alabama, 795 men. In units from states under Federal occupation and beyond the reach of conscript officers, the regiments remained pathetically small: the 2nd Arkansas had 295; the 8th Arkansas, 260; the 5th Arkansas, 240; the 9th Texas, 298; and the 9th Kentucky, 232. Even the West Tennessee regiments were woefully understrength: the 2nd Tennessee had 280; the 5th Tennessee, 255; the 154th Tennessee, 140; and the 13th Tennessee, 247. An April order directed that all regiments with 400 or more men would no longer remain consolidated but revert to their original organization.[14]

The quality of the incoming conscripts throughout the spring of 1863 remained poor. So pathetic were some of them that E. W. Treadwell thought that they would "do much more good at home making corn and taking care of their families." Capt. John Crittenden offered a further description to his wife on April 15: "Some [conscripts] are lame Some blind Some crippled. Nearly all of them have some kind of disease. some will lie in their tents and stave themselves nearly to death trying to get to hospital. What good will such soldiers do us? They are more in the way than anything else. One came to me the other Day and demanded that I should furnish him better provisions than he was getting. He expected that I Should go to the country and purchase such as he could eat. When one of them gets sick he expects me to Send him off immediately to the hospital, as though I was Surgeon Gen. of the army."[15]

In August 1863, Pillow openly expressed his frustration to the War Department. His conscript officers were successfully rounding up draft dodgers and placing them in the Army of Tennessee only to have them desert — some of them two or three times. "It is useless to send them to Bragg's army," he bluntly wrote. Some 8,000 to 10,000 skulkers continued to hide in the mountains of northern Alabama, where they had armed themselves and banded together. Rooting them out could only be done with great difficulty. His solution: henceforth all mountaineer conscripts should be sent to Lee's army, thus eliminating the proximity to home. Lee, unfortunately, was having similar problems in his own army.[16]

With another 18,000 casualties at Chickamauga, the situation became desperate. Bragg had no other answer to the issue of dwindling numbers than to continue to clamp down on the substitute system and draft dodgers. By the fall of 1863, the entire general staff of the Army of Tennessee, Bragg included, petitioned Cooper, saying that unless the ranks were hurriedly replenished "our cause will be lost." The staff claimed that 150,000 young men in the South had hired substitutes, who more often than not took the money and then deserted. Others sought refuge in the quartermaster or other branches. The venom in the generals' words bespoke their contempt for men who sought "fancy duty which could be performed by women" and for "timid and effeminate men" who endeavored to get favors from congressional friends.[17]

Deserters

Even before shots were fired, there were men who had second thoughts about serving in the army. Of all of the problems that confronted the West in the first two years of the war, however, desertion did not top the list. In retreating from Kentucky, Bragg began to crack down on stragglers. Although they were technically not deserters, it was believed that men intentionally straggled in order to be captured. They then would be sent home, where they would wait to be exchanged. Henceforth, Bragg would not allow returning prisoners to go home; they would remain in camp.[18]

By 1863, the problem of desertion was becoming critical. The natural tendency to protect one's family, homesickness, dissatisfaction, despondency, a lack of connection with the Cause, the harshness of camp life, and the inevitable ponderings of just how many battles one could go through without inevitably being wounded or worse all played a part. In his study of Georgia desertions, Mark Weitz concluded that some soldiers deserted out of fear that other men would take their place at home, while others fretted that the countryside was being overrun by deserters. It was the breakdown of the home economy, however, that unquestionably created the greatest concern. Weitz recounted the stories of several Army of Tennessee deserters who felt that their primary loyalty was to home rather than to the army.[19]

On January 22, sixty-nine Rebel prisoners arrived in Nashville from Murfreesboro. Many claimed to be conscripts who had been forced into the army and were ready to take the oath of allegiance. The 9th Tennessee, a regiment that had suffered heavily from desertions throughout 1862, continued the trend. Between January and May 1863, a dozen more men departed, all privates save for one sergeant. A study of sixty-one deserters of the 19th Tennessee during 1863 revealed that most were poor subsistence mountaineer farmers. As the war progressed, the percentage of head-of-household deserters increased—30.8 percent in 1861, 38.2 percent in 1862, and 51.3 percent in 1863. Records also revealed that the death of a brother caused other brothers in the regiment to desert. In March, Empsey Gregg of the 58th North Carolina took flight, having received a pitiful letter from his wife about his family's suffering. Word of his presence eventually got out in Watauga County, and his congregation, the Cove Creek Baptist Church, called him to task. He admitted his guilt and promised to return, which, in due time, he did. His punishment is not known, but in 1864 he deserted again.[20]

A soldier in the 31st Tennessee considered deserters to be the scourge of the army. He held a special contempt for those who came from his own West Tennessee. "The people of West Tenn. need not suppose that the whole army is acting like that section. At least one-half of the West Tenn. troops have deserted," he bitterly wrote. "This is not the case with any other troops, not even among the troops from Tenn. Now as to these deserters, I have no feeling toward them, but contempt. The day will come, when they will be held up to the gaze of the world, scoffed at, spit upon, and held unworthy to associate with a brave and free people. There is no crime (save treason) that sinks a man lower than that of desertion." He went on to say that many West Tennesseans falsely claimed to their neighbors to have come home on furloughs.[21]

Despite the disdain of many, the constant trickle of deserters continued. By January 1863, seventy-nine men at the "Camp of Paroled Prisoners" at Chattanooga had deserted, with members of the 29th Mississippi leading the list. Pvt. E. W. Treadwell watched nervously—two left from his 19th Alabama on the night of April 2, three from the 22nd Alabama, eight from the 25th Alabama, and one from the sharpshooters. Writing on the fifth, he explained: "I am fearful that deserters will be disastrous to our army. It is now a common saying among the men that they will desert as soon as the foliage are large enough to hide them good. They speak of it as though they are jesting but I fear that many of them will take it two far for a joke." Several days later, he added that deserters were leaving "at a rapid rate. I learn to day that 2 left our Regt. last night and 13 from the 25th [Alabama] most of whom carried their guns and 60 cartridges each." The evil persisted. On Thursday, April 30, seventeen deserters turned themselves in to Federal authorities at Murfreesboro.[22]

Others wrote similarly that spring. Sgt. James Parrott of the 28th Tennessee expressed longingly to his wife on April 12th, "I want to see you all sow bad that I can hardly keep from running away it will be a disgrace besides a punishment of some kind but I intend to come home sometime between this and fall, furlow or not if I can get there." In the camp of the 22nd Alabama at Shelbyville, a despondent William B. Gilliland noted on May 17, "I don't think that this war will last very long for all of the men that I have heard talk a bout it is tired of it now & they are deserting & leaving here every day." Despite war-weariness, most of the men remained. At Shelbyville, Thomas Warrick declared, "I do hope we will be spared to get back home, to see our dear friends and our families—God knows that I am tired of this—but until our liberty is gained I am willing to stay."[23]

T. H. Boles took great delight in relating a story to his wife about an attempted desertion in the 25th Tennessee. The soldier tried to persuade an old wagon driver to take him out of camp in a concealed box. The driver refused and promptly told the colonel of the 25th about the plot. The colonel suggested that the driver agree to take him. Several men spirited the culprit away in a box and nailed it shut. As the wagon passed the guard, it was stopped and searched. Several men took the box and tossed it into a nearby creek, leaving the would-be deserter desperately kicking his way to freedom.

"The 44th and 25th [Tennessee] was ther when the man cum out. He was the meanest lookin man you ever saw," Boles wrote.[24]

In the summer of 1863, as the army retreated from Tullahoma to Chattanooga, the *Montgomery Weekly Advertiser* warned that a number of men were deserting or remaining behind to take the oath of allegiance with the idea that they could then quietly go home and sit the war out. Reports coming out of Nashville told a different story. The men were being promptly arrested and thrown in jail. In due time, they would be given the opportunity to join the Federal army or be sent north to a Federal prison camp.[25]

Desertions nonetheless continued, prompting western newspapers to acknowledge that many Tennesseans had taken flight during Bragg's retreat to Chattanooga. Bushrod Johnson reported having 335 deserters in his brigade in the withdrawal. Alabamian Alex McGowin candidly admitted to his brother that the thought of leaving had passed his mind. "If I should again pass home on the railroad as we did last summer it seems to me as if I could not keep from going home. It is hard to bear the name of deserter. Many have deserted from our regiment but not from our company." One deserter, a lieutenant who went over to the Yankees, claimed to be an assistant topographical engineer on Bragg's staff. In the cavalry, the problem was chronic. On July 10, 1863, Wharton's and Martin's divisions totaled 4,718 troopers. In the three months before that, 414 men had deserted and another 37 had gone missing.[26]

Even the Federals expressed shock at the large number of Rebels coming into their lines. "The Cavalry brought in a good many prisoners during the afternoon. They drop out on purpose to be taken," a Minnesota soldier informed his wife on July 6. "They say that they will not fight anymore for they do not get half enough to eat nor wear. The Tennessee Rebels say that they will not cross the Tennessee River to fight if they have to fight, they will only fight in Tennessee, so they are crossing into our lines by squads and giving themselves up. We take a good many. Two of the boys in Company H brought in ten on the second [of July]."[27]

On July 7, Gen. Philip Sheridan reported: "His [Bragg's] losses from desertion are very numerous among the Tennessee troops and others. Many of the companies have lost as many as 20 men. They are coming in small squads, a number having come in this morning, and I hear of large numbers in the mountains who are making their way home, avoiding our army." That same day, another Federal officer observed: "Hundreds, perhaps thousands of Tennesseans have deserted from the Southern army and are now wandering about in the mountains, endeavoring to get to their homes. They are mostly conscripted men. My command has gathered up hundreds, and the mountains and caves in the vicinity are said to be full of them." Dwight Allen observed: "Three Rebel deserters from Bragg's army came in and gave themselves up this morning. They left a week ago yesterday. They have been in the rebel service two years. General dissatisfaction exists in the army & they say that Bragg will lose all of the Ky., Tenn., & Miss. troops."[28]

Descriptions of the prisoners were not complimentary. Charles Cort described forty Rebels who deserted at Franklin, apparently some of Van Dorn's cavalry: "The men were the dirtiest and raggedest set I ever saw but fat and healthy looking. They was no uniform in their dress. They were Texans and did not seem a bit concerned about being taken. They were laughing and joking with each other." Azra Bartholomew of the 21st Michigan believed the prisoners he saw to be "pitiful looking objects, they having a scarcely a garment on them that they had any wool in it."[29]

"Good riddance" was some Rebels' response: "I am glad of it as they [deserters] were such as do us no good except to eat our bread and bacon." Robert Jamison of the 49th Tennessee admitted to his wife on July 28 that "although many have become disheartened and deserted, I think they are enough left of the true steel to let the enemy know we are still in earnest." Writing to his father on July 14, Capt. Anthony Caldwell of the 5th Tennessee related, "The 5th has grown to be very small, but the more she has to encounter the more valiant she becomes, thus supplying to some extent in gallantry what she has lost in numbers." But there were others, such as John Crittenden, who candidly expressed to his wife on July 9 that he hoped the recent retreat would be the final one. "I hope that it will for I am sick of this war. I think if I ever get home again that I will never leave the place again."[30]

Later that month, Col. Claudius C. Wilson's Brigade was sent to reinforce Bragg. On the railroad trek through its home state, Wilson allowed the 30th Georgia, which had largely been recruited along the railroad from West Point to Atlanta, a furlough. It proved to be a mistake—240 temporarily deserted. Indeed, by the end of the month, his mostly Georgian brigade had lost nearly 500 men! "Out of about 450 men, more than half are absent without leave," a member of the 30th wrote. "Our company has 66 absent without leave. We have only nineteen men here [Hamilton County, Tennessee], four of whom were men who were assigned to the company. The boys will have to pay dearly for their trip; they will not come off as easy as many of them think. I hear it is their right intention to stay till Monday week, but, from what I heard an officer say yesterday, they will be apt to come sooner. Tomorrow is muster day, when the troops will be mustered for payment, and I understand it is the intention of Colonel [Thomas] Mangham to stop their wages and punish them besides. I believe he is the maddest man I ever saw.

He considers his regiment disgraced, it being the only regiment that done so, but probably his passion will cool down before the boys get back." On September 3, Marion Brindley of the 22nd Alabama admitted to his sister that there were "many deserters and many others feeling whipped and ready to desert." He feared that "men in that state of feeling cannot be relied upon for a good fight." While camped near Loudon, Tennessee, the 26th Tennessee sustained a staggering eighty-seven desertions between August 24 and September 2, 1863. An East Tennessee civilian intoned in mid-September that "desertions from Bragg's [army] come in by the dozens." Between August 22 and September 20, the Federals rounded up 750 Rebel deserters.[31]

Fifteen deserters left the 9th Mississippi in a single week during mid-August. "I say let them go for such men are not of any benefit to us at all," thought a member. In early September, the 60th North Carolina sustained a serious bout of desertions—over fifteen in a week. "I hardly blame the poor fellows for a great many of them are barefooted and the marching is terrible on them, although this is a bad excuse for them to walk home," Captain Patton explained to his wife.[32]

On October 8, twenty-four-year-old John Floyd of the 17th Tennessee wrote his friend Mary about the continued problem. Many whom he had looked upon as "firm supporters of our cause" were becoming despondent. He feared that many would be willing to "bear the disgrace of desertion, in preference to staying with us." "But," he concluded, "we have lost nothing as the men we have with us now are reliable." Thomas Bigbee of the 33rd Alabama informed his wife on November 1, "Their has severl of our regt diserted and I recon . . . gon home but I think that is making a bad matter worse for I never could lay in the woods."[33]

Punishments

A variety of punishments awaited deserters. If one returned on his own, the offense might be termed "absent without leave," a lesser offense. If caught by conscript officers, bounty hunters, or local sheriffs, however, the punishment could be brutal, if not lethal. Sgt. Hiram Holt witnessed such punishment in September 1862. The culprit was given thirty-nine lashes with a cowhide and then branded on the forehead with the letter *D*. "He screamed prayed and reared around generally," Holt noted. Even though the sergeant detested deserters, he could not help but feel a moment of compassion when he added, "I felt sorry for him."[34]

In mid-December 1862, a private in the 34th Alabama was executed for a second desertion offense. It is not known if this was the man mentioned in John Crittenden's letter of December 20, when a botched execution took place. The dozen-man execution squad had only six guns loaded, as was customary. The order to fire was given, and the man dropped but was not badly wounded. The reserve squad of four then stepped forward and, at a dozen paces, fired. Again the man was struck but not killed. The original squad was then ordered to reload and fire once again. This time, mercifully, the man fell dead, fourteen bullets having been fired.[35]

Three others received death sentences on December 26 — William Little of the 60th North Carolina, Zachariah Phillips of the 28th Alabama, and Asa Lewis of the 6th Kentucky. The last case turned into a strangely controversial affair. The young boy had been captured by a bounty hunter and returned to the army. At his trial it came out that this was his second offense. He claimed that he had entered the war for twelve months and he did not feel legally bound to be extended under the reorganization law. His parents needed him to bring in a crop. When denied a furlough, he requested an audience before Bragg, who also denied him. He became abusive and was arrested for insubordination. Two days later he escaped, fully intending to return, or so he said. The court sentenced him to death. The officers of the Kentucky brigade took up Lewis's cause, but why they did so, beyond the fact that he was a Kentuckian, is not clear. They simply wanted what they wanted, but in Bragg they had met their match. Breckinridge himself made a personal appeal. When the army commander denied clemency for Lewis, Breckinridge became enraged and declared that this would be murder. Bragg allegedly made some remarks about Kentuckians and their independence. When word leaked out, a near mutiny was sparked in the brigade. On the twenty-sixth, the Orphan Brigade formed in the midst of a driving rain. Breckinridge spoke a few parting words to the condemned. The firing squad unleashed a salvo, and Lewis dropped to his death. It proved to be more than an execution; it was a permanent estrangement between Bragg and his Orphans.[36]

Loyalty to home led Pvt. E. P. Norman of the 28th Alabama to desert. On Christmas Day 1862, he took pen in hand to write his final letter to "My Dear and Affectionate Wife and Little Children." Convicted of desertion, he had been sentenced to death. "I haven't language to tell you my feelings at this time when I think of leaving you and my little children never to meet again on this earth. . . . I am condemned to die and no doubt but this time tomorrow will be sleeping in the cold grave." He expressed bitterness that he had simply been "going home to make some necessary preparations for my little family, while others that left at the same time and not even arrested." The next day, as the guard came to take him, he hurriedly jotted his parting words. "I see we can no more meet on this earth but I want you to meet me in a better world than this." He signed, "So good bye for now for awhile. E. P. Norman."[37]

Deserters faced a sure punishment, but exactly what it was depended on the circumstances and sometimes even on the quirks of Bragg. Thus, Norman was quite right about the inconsistencies of sentencing. Relative leniency could be granted at times, but as Norman discovered, one should not bank his life upon it. In late May, seven men of the 39th Alabama deserted one evening, but two were quickly caught. Their punishment, though painful, was more typical of first-time deserters. They were tied down faceup in the hot sun for four hours and then made to ride a wooded horse for three hours. This process was repeated for six days in a row. Actually, few deserters faced a firing squad, but there were exceptions. Between January 1 and June 8, 1863, the military court sentenced thirty men in the Army of Tennessee to death—twenty-two for desertion, five for cowardice in battle, and three for miscellaneous offenses. Ten of the deserters received pardons, as did an artilleryman who got drunk and fell asleep while on guard. On January 24, Samuel A. Templeton of the 16th Tennessee and Elijah L. Thompson of the 28th Alabama were executed. Yet, based on their military records, the court commuted the death sentences of eight others—four from the 24th Tennessee and four from the 1st Arkansas. The youth of one of the Arkansans proved to be a mitigating factor. The alternative punishment was six months' hard labor. The court had no mercy on February 9, however, when it handed down death sentences to four deserters of the 51st Alabama Cavalry. On the thirteenth, a soldier, name and unit unidentified, faced a firing squad for insubordination and for mortally wounding the officer sent to arrest him. Two other men faced firing squads in February.[38]

A soldier recalled the day three deserters were shot at Shelbyville, the regiment not known, but they were not Tennesseans. Two of the three were mere boys; all refused to be blindfolded. One of the lads held a picture of his mother; the other, a photo of his sister. All three men fell at the first discharge. They were then wrapped in their blankets and buried in unmarked graves. The public nature of the firing squads served as an intimidating object lesson, a point not missed on many. An artilleryman caustically commented that the executions were "said to be a good preventative for the homesick."[39]

A Lieutenant Tucker of the 38th Alabama deserted in September, after having received nine months' pay. He was caught, but due to the amnesty then in effect, he was simply cashiered. The regiment assembled, and the major announced that a deserter would be passing down the line and anyone who wanted to kick him had permission to do so. The major then gave him a brutal kick. "At first he walked very slowly giving them a fine chance at him. But they hurt him so badly, that he began to beg them not to 'kick hard' but this only raised the yell of indignation tenfold harder. He then struck a trot and went through in double quick time, to the tune of 'Here's your deserting lieutenant lift him boys.' The privates seemed to enjoy it hugely." The lieutenant then limped back to his quarters, only to discover that he had been conscripted and sent back to the regiment![40]

The executions definitely got the attention of the troops. Tennessean R. H. Richards believed that he would rather "risk his chances in camp" than desert. "Since he has bin in Tullahoma Bragg has Bin in the habit of shooting from one to three men every Friday evening," he added. "Many here are shot for disobeying orders," Augustus Abernathy of the 15th Arkansas wrote on June 5. Although this was perception more than reality, most preferred death on the battlefield to a firing squad. Nonetheless, there were always men willing to take the risk, and the desertions continued. It is doubtful that consistency in sentencing would have changed matters, but the capriciousness of the executions proved brutally unjust. The point seems clear, however, that Bragg, despite his reputation for harshness, attempted to move away from executions even as the problem of desertions increased.[41]

While the troops took no pleasure in the executions, many thought that they "had a good effect on the troops." Pvt. A. G. McLeod thought that "men who . . . desert their country in the hour of trial richly deserve the penalty." Thomas Warrick admitted that it was "mity hard that we have to shot so many of our men for deserting but they [otherwise] would keep doing it." Lt. Col. Irvine Walker regretted that deserters "brought such disgrace upon themselves and their families, but they deserve the death." A private in the 54th Virginia saw matters differently. Those executed had "don nothing wrong. . . . I have often times seen wicked things don but this was the cruels thing I sean."[42]

The most stunning of the executions occurred on a warm May 4, 1864, in Crow Valley, where fourteen men (twelve from the 58th North Carolina and two from the 60th North Carolina) faced a firing squad; it would be the largest single execution in the Army of Tennessee. "I saw them wash and dress themselves for the graves," wrote Chaplain Thomas Davenport. With the division forming a square around them with one side open, the men were marched to their graves to the sound of the "Dead March." As they passed their regiments, they were allowed to give a tearful farewell to their friends. One of the convicted was so wrought up that he begged to be shot at once. At noon, the order was given and the crack of musketry heard. Unfortunately, three of the deserters were not finished off in the first round and had to be shot a second time. The division was then marched passed their coffins. "The private soldiers were all bitterly opposed to the executions of these men," the surgeon of the 60th North Carolina wrote. "I can never, never forget that sad scene; I was heartsick." Another soldier saw it differently: "It is right though and I think the only punishment we can inflict." A correspondent claimed that a total of twenty-two were executed that day. Precisely how many men met their death at the encampment is uncertain, but anecdotally there were at least forty-nine. This number can be compared to only eighteen documented executions during Bragg's year-and-a-half-long tenure.[43]

The army was caught in a vicious circle. Dwindling manpower led to conscription, which resulted in increased desertions, which led to more firing squads. Coercion and violence shaped the thinking of the soldiers. There were no easy choices, and men did not react in predictable ways.

Furloughs and Reenlistments

The desertions, which escalated during the Tullahoma Campaign, reached a critical mass following Missionary Ridge. The chief offending states were Tennessee and Georgia, obviously caused by proximity. "There [are] a great many troops running away from the army[;] Tennesseans and Georgians are the worst of any others," Sgt. John Sparkman observed. Federal officials in Chattanooga tabulated 2,667 prisoners and deserters in January and February 1864. Between December 1863 and April 1864, some 1,365 Georgians took the oath of allegiance in Chattanooga. The bulk of these came from two brigades—Alfred Cummings's in Stevenson's Division, with 551, and Marcellus Stovall's in Stewart's Division, with 547. One study estimated that during the four-month period from January to April 1864, an estimated 2,405 Tennesseans deserted. Some 738 men in Samuel H. Stout's hospitals deserted from January to May 1864. The army could simply not sustain such losses. Johnston declared an amnesty upon his arrival at Dalton, and 649 deserters eventually returned to the ranks—not nearly enough to offset the losses.[44]

At a time when morale was at its lowest ebb, the three-year enlistments expired. Johnston realized that it would take more than his personal charisma to hold the army together. The men could be held under the revised February 1864 conscription law. Some viewed volunteering as a vote of confidence in the Cause, while others were more resigned. "I never intended to be conscripted if I have a chance to volunteer," declared Edward Brown. Sergeant Sparkman reenlisted, but he admitted it was only as a matter of form: "Congress has declared all of us in the army any how."[45]

Most of the men were willing to reenlist, but they needed a chance "to see

TABLE 4. *Confederates received at Chattanooga*

Date	Prisoners captured	Deserters	Total
January 1864	635	1,008	1,643
February 1864	203	821	1,024

the loved ones they have defended." Washington Ives wrote bluntly, "From what I see and hear every day that unless the men are allowed furloughs . . . that at the end of the present term of enlistment, desertions will be very numerous." Hardee initiated a furlough system—one per thirty men, later modified to one per twenty-five men. One officer per company also received a leave, provided all officers were present. "Our company drew for it [furlough] and Ide got it. I expect he will start [home] in a day or two. I was on the sick list and the Capt. Would not let any of the sick draw. May be it will come my turn some time," hoped Grant Taylor of the 40th Alabama. The number of days was based on travel distance but was not to exceed thirty. For every recruit brought back, the furloughed man would receive an extra ten days. John Inglis wrote: "I never saw men so attached to a Genl as our Army is to him [Johnston]. The men are greatly encouraged by the furlough system." Precisely how many men received furloughs is not known, but officially, 3,399 furloughed men returned to the army.[46]

Johnston later altered the rules by saying that in units that reenlisted before March, furloughs would be granted at the rate of one per ten men. Some expressed disgust at the strings attached. "I am provoked with the way I have been treated about a furlough to think that I have been in the service nearly two years & now they don't want to give me a furlough Except I reenlist," Hezekiah Rabb complained to his wife. Edward Brown explained to his wife: "The system of furloughing now in operation [rolling dice] gives me a poor chance. . . . Co. C had another drawing yesterday. We drew six furloughs. Thirty-five was the lowest die that got a furlough. I threw thirty-three. It will now be sixteen days before we have another lottery."[47]

For those with homes far away, furloughs proved problematic. A Mississippian in Stanford's Battery received a furlough, but he could only remain at home three days—"scarcely paid for the trouble in going," remarked a comrade. Those who lived behind enemy lines often encountered harrowing experiences. Capt. Thomas Key went home to Helena, Arkansas. He departed by rail on February 5, going by way of Mobile north to Grenada, where he arrived on the eleventh. Getting across the Mississippi River proved dangerous, but the captain crossed in a skiff on the night of the sixteenth. By the seventeenth, he was home: "It is useless to try to describe the meeting of two hearts that loved like ours," he wrote in his diary. After a two-week stay, constantly hiding from Yankee patrols, he departed on the night of March 3. Bidding farewell to his wife and three small children "so melted my heart and choked my utterance that I could not speak a word." On the twentieth, he was back at Dalton—three days over his limit, but nothing came of it.[48]

With improved morale, entire regiments began to spontaneously re-up for the war. The 154th Tennessee received the honor of being the first. Philip Stephenson of the 5th Arkansas related his experience. The men were roused from their sleep and formed a large gathering around the cabin of Col. John E. Murray. He jumped on a stump and began addressing them, and they volunteered en masse. On the night of January 16, Strahl's Brigade assembled to the music of the brigade band. "Something of the old spirit of '61 seemed to inspire the men as they gazed upon the face of their gallant leader," noted a participant. The next night, the men again gathered and the entire brigade took an oath: "We are the officers and men of Strahl's brigade, do this day resolve to enlist for the war, determined to never lay down our arms, until our homes are rescued from the enemy, and the Confederacy established as one of the nations of the earth." Other regiments got caught up in the reenlistment fervor. In February, Lieutenant Colonel Walker wrote: "I am proud to be able to say that nearly the whole of the 10th and 19th [South Carolina] have re-enlisted for the War. Out of the 500 effective men 443 have gone in for the war however so long it may last, and uncondition-ally." "Reenlisting goes on flowingly. . . . Nearly all of Clayborn's Division have reenlisted," Edward Brown noted.[49]

Most volunteered not simply to avoid the onus of conscription but be-cause they knew that the war would end without them. Too much blood had been sacrificed not to bring the war to its conclusion. George Lea of the 7th Mississippi informed his cousin: "I see the necessity for it and I will[.] it will never do to give up the struggle after contending this far, but I believe this year will close the war anyway." H. M. Lynn informed his wife: "All the Ten-nesseans have re-enlisted. She is still the volunteer state. . . . We will have but little use for conscription among the old troops." Morgan Letterman agreed: "The Tenns. Have all enlisted for the war and are determined to repossess their homes with their lives." The 10th Mississippi formed a line and ad-vanced the colors ten paces. All wishing to reenlist would step forward—the entire regiment advanced. "The old spirit of the beginning of the war seems to be revived in the army," thought a Tennessean.[50]

The enthusiasm failed to stir all. Some of the troops demanded that their regiments be reorganized first, meaning the election of new officers. "Col.

H[ardy] is not so popular as he once was, as was shown by the reenlist-ments in this Regiment. He tried his best to induce the men to reenlist, but with very few exceptions, [they] obstinately refused unless they could have a reorganization—meaning new officers at the head," noted Captain Patton. Others had simply had enough and were ready to go home. Thirty reenlisted in John Crittenden's company, but "the balance still stand that they will be conscripted first." Lt. Roderick Shaw noted the Florida troops' reluctance to get enthused: "They all want furloughs now and reorganization and no consolidation. Poor fools!" The reluctance of the Georgians and Alabamians to reenlist was due to civilians "writing discouraging letters to their friends in the army." Another noted that "all troops from across the Mississippi are rather slow in reenlisting." Grant Taylor wrote bluntly, "I have not reenlisted nor do I intend to do so until I see there is no other choice." Flavel Barber saw that some of the Tennesseans refused to step forward—"I suppose they prefer being conscripted when the time comes." Many of the men saw re-enlistment as a trick. For the officers of the 31st Alabama who refused to re-up, Col. Daniel Hundley held nothing but contempt and believed that they should be reduced in rank or even cashiered. "At a time like the present, we have no need for feint hearts." By March 23, some 17,471 of 22,012 troops in Hardee's Corps had signed for the war—70 percent.[51]

The wave of eager volunteers subsided as the war was protracted. Enlist-ees were mostly conscripts who did not want to be where they were and fre-quently deserted as soon as they could. In the end, western manpower was simply drained. Broadening the draft age, conscripting, and brutally clamp-ing down on desertions proved insufficient. Stewart's Corps's monthly re-port ending September 20, 1864, showed that thirteen had joined by vol-unteering and eighteen deserters had been returned, but thirty-two had deserted, making a net loss of one. By September 1864, the army was perma-nently down by 25,000 men from the previous June. Such depletion could simply not be sustained.[52]

✳ 10 ✳

The Brotherhood

Through shared privations, camp tedium, boredom, amusements, sports, homesickness, pouring rain and searing heat, shanties for quarters, and grief—through it all—the Army of Tennessee, at least at the regiment and brigade levels, formed a bond. A Kentuckian wrote, "I consider the Regiment my home." What kept the men fighting in the midst of battlefield losses, even more than a vague ideology of nationality, was the brotherhood.[1]

Winter Quarters 1863

The weather remained generally raw and disagreeable throughout January 1863, with a couple of inches of snow blanketing the ground. Some of the tents did not arrive until midmonth. Until then, the men had to make do with brush arbors and living in the woods. Hundreds became ill and had to suffer with no protection. "I hardly know how we are to get along," Captain Dent wrote his wife. "I fear we will all get sick if we are exposed much longer." Day after day, the ground remained wet with snow and rain. John Crittenden noted the misery at Shelbyville: "We are now in a bad condition[.] It is raining and everything we have is wet. It is the most disagreeable time I have ever spent." As the shelters slowly arrived, the men began attaching mud-and-stick chimneys at one end. "How unpleasant in a leaky tent wind and rain blowing in the door, chimney smoking, etc.," E. H. Rennolds remarked. Typically, ten to eleven men were jammed in a ten-by-ten-foot wall tent. If fire did not provide sufficient warmth, the men imbibed whiskey. On January 17, Wharton passed out whiskey to the 8th Texas Cavalry, which resulted in a trooper being accidentally shot by a drunk comrade. At Manchester, a soldier in the 6th Kentucky admitted: "All got a little funny. I was drunker than I ever was in my life."[2]

Throughout much of February, the weather remained bitterly cold with intermittent snow, rain, and sleet. Huddled in his tent in Tullahoma, Thomas Bigbee shivered as he scrawled to his wife on the third that it was "so cold I can hardly right." In the camp of the 19th South Carolina, a soldier noted that the men had an "ample number of large and comfortable tents." Pvt.

R. H. Taylor of the 20th Tennessee wrote his parents on February 12, "It makes me think of home to sit in our tent and see the fire burn so bright as ours generally does." Both armies remained mud bound. The Duck River lowlands swelled so badly that communications between Tullahoma and Shelbyville were at times severed. An officer noted that a small stream overflowed to 100 yards across and was deep enough to swim a horse.[3]

Mail deliveries became so infrequent that the men lost touch with the outside world. Rumors, almost always wrong, filled the vacuum. Some heard that a part of Lee's army would be coming to the West. Alfred Bell admitted that he did not even know if the Yankees still occupied Murfreesboro. Charles Roberts heard through the "grapevine telegraph" that a major movement was being planned, but he admitted to being entirely ignorant. "The nearer you are to the army the less chance [you have] of knowing anything," he concluded.[4]

The weather led to extreme boredom, with the men not coming out of their blankets unless absolutely necessary. Sgt. John Sparkman of the 48th Tennessee admitted that there had been so much rain that "half the men lay in bed in order to keep dry and warm." A Tennessean summarized their activity: "No drilling going on. Have nothing to do but cook, sleep, and read papers." One of Polk's soldiers noted on February 18, "No drill, no mail, idleness." Two days later, he added: "Confined to tents all day by rain and bad weather. Read and study. Can't think much. Hard to concentrate in camp." Captain Carter thought that Tullahoma was as "dull as Sunday at a country crossroads." Tennessean Lee Edwards admitted to his mother that he had not had an opportunity to wash his clothes in six weeks—he simply hunkered down. A tragedy broke the routine when an uprooted tree in Swett's Battery came crashing onto a cluster of men, impaling a corporal and badly wounding several others. Cannonading was heard from the direction of Murfreesboro on February 22, but it was apparently nothing more than the Yankees celebrating George Washington's birthday.[5]

And still the rain poured. "We have had a desperate time of it for the last five of six days," John Crittenden wrote his wife on February 20. "It has been raining near all the time. Mud half-shoe deep. The sun shone out yesterday for the first time in a good many days. The wind has been blowing very hard." The reprieve did not last long. On the twenty-sixth, he again took pen in hand: "It commenced raining yesterday morning and has been at it ever since. It rained last night about as hard as I have ever seen it. Nearly every tent this morning has a bold spring of water in it. Water over shoe deep everywhere. I expect it will give us all pneumonia." The next day, Robert Smith saw a camp with a foot of water in the tents. The stench became intolerable, with one Yankee cavalryman later noting that the Rebel camps could be smelled a half mile before arriving at them.[6]

Most of the men did not believe that Rosecrans would attempt a second winter offensive. The pikes remained generally chewed up, and the secondary roads had been reduced to ribbons of mud. Patton Anderson felt "confident" that the bluecoats had been too badly damaged to attempt another advance. Common sense told others, however, that when the Tennessee River began to rise, the army would inevitably be forced to withdraw south. John Crittenden heard the rumor that Bragg intended to draw the Federals away from their base, but he doubted that the ploy would work. Daniel McClean suspected that "we will be here all winter, if we are not run off by the yankees."[7]

Morale varied from soldier to soldier, but most remained remarkably optimistic. Writing to his cousin, W. R. Lacey of the 6th Tennessee related, "Well cousin, our country is in bad situation in such that we could never redeem it but we are in high spirits yet, and still look forward to the day of our redemption, and I think it is not far off." Listening to dispirited Yankee prisoners, Washington Ives became convinced that "the war is going to end soon." Charles Roberts believed that if the fighting went well in the spring, the war would draw to a close. On January 27, Michael Royster predicted that the war would be over by the fall. Many soldiers grounded their beliefs in the so-called Northwest Conspiracy that had been widely reported in the press. According to the reports, efforts were being made in Ohio, Illinois, Indiana, and Iowa to pull out of the Union and form their own confederacy—at least that was the claim. Others heard that France would recognize the Confederacy. Even Polk got caught up in the optimism, writing his wife on February 16, "I do not think it probable that the war will last beyond summer, perhaps not beyond spring." Bets were being placed that peace would come by mid-March or July 4 at the latest. Writing to his wife, Bettie, on February 20, John Crittenden, usually a pessimist about such things, began to think that "there is some prospect of peace." The next day, John Magee wrote that thousands were deserting the Federal army: "The people are beginning to get their eyes open—they see through Lincoln's mask."[8]

Thoughts turned to home and loved ones. "I long dear Maggie for quiet peaceful times again when we can enjoy the pleasures of home," Charles Roberts wrote his wife. "You must write about my little pleasures [children]—I want to know everything about them." John Davidson longed to see his wife: "I do wish to see you today[.] it would be much more agreeable to see & talk to you face to face as in by gon days." To Cellie, his lady friend—and wife after the war—waiting back in Texas, Capt. Knox Miller continued writing lengthy letters punctuated with Shakespearean quotes. R. B. Pittman of the 7th Mississippi wrote to his "Dearest Mary Ann": "Times are dull here[.] all the boys wanting to go home and are tired of the war as well as me myself." Ed Spears wrote that listening to the nightly melodies of the 2nd Kentucky band "puts me in a mind of home & really sometimes I feel sad."[9]

The troops began to take hope as a miserable winter drew to a close. A grand ball held at Shelbyville on February 25 characterized the renewed spirit. In the camp of the 45th Alabama, Joshua Callaway took time to write his wife, "You know my Dear, that I am not a superstitious man, but I can't help trying to believe in the Spring."[10]

Spring

Cloudy skies, harsh cold winds, and light snow kept most of the men in their tents the first week of March 1863. On the night of the seventh, a tornado cut a swath through Shelbyville, taking off the roof of the Baptist church, demolishing several sheds and a number of houses, toppling two railroad cars, and damaging houses for half a mile. The cold and raw day of the tenth caused a great deal of suffering for the horses and mules. The next day, Mississippian Isham Thomas described the misery to his wife: "It rains more than half the time here, some days it rains so much that we can hardly cook anything to eat and we have to lay up in our tents all day, or stand out by the fire in the rain, either is very unpleasant." The engineers had the pontoons over the swollen Elk River removed for fear of losing the boats. "It occurred to me," Brent wrote in his diary on the evening of the fourteenth, "that in the event of any disaster, our position would be most critical." Reports also arrived that the newly completed bridge over the Tennessee River at Bridgeport was beginning to weaken.[11]

A new skillet and frying pan in George Jones's mess keep his spirits intact, yet many were losing stomach for the war. Captain Semple related to his wife on March 6, "It makes me feel sad to think of the losses we have sustained, the hardships we have endured and that we seem to be no nearer to the end of the war than now." Joshua Callaway admitted to "his dear" Dulcinia the true state of affairs: "My Dear, you have no idea how sick I am of this abominable war. You can't form any idea how much I would give to be at home. I have offered one of my fingers for a furlough, and a whole hand for a transfer to some post, and all but my life for peace. Will peace ever be made[?] Alas! I fear not, or if at all I fear it will be a long time first. However, I live in hope." The sheer number of losses began to take a toll on Thomas Bigbee. "I am lonsom now," he admitted. "There is so many of the boys gone that was near to me." James R. Riggs of the 27th Mississippi wrote that he was "getting so tired of war." Alex Morgan of the 19th Louisiana admitted to his wife: "I am very low spirited about the war. I see no prospect whatever of peace."[12]

Capt. Irving Buck did not fret over reports of mounting Union strength — "we will whip them at any odds" — but he much preferred Beauregard or Lee as commander. For Joseph Sams of the 29th North Carolina, war-weariness had clearly crept in. "I hope this war will close this spring or summer then if I live I will come home and stay," he told his wife on March 17. "I do think there has been blood enough spilt for this time. I do hope it will soon close and let us all go home." The food remained generally adequate, although on the twenty-third, the meat ration was cut to a half pound a day. According to a soldier-correspondent of the 32nd Tennessee, the soldiers prayed for turnip greens as much as they did for independence.[13]

Talk of peace spread through the ranks. "All are of the opinion that a few more battles will bring about an end to the war and with it peace," John Crittenden expressed. "Most of the talk now is concerning peace, most of the men think they will soon be home in peace," a Mississippian scribbled in his diary on March 26. A Tennessean attributed many of the rumors to Governor Harris and Cheatham, who had both spread rumors about the peace speculation. Harris even claimed that Polk's Corps would soon be going into West Tennessee. Even though E. H. Rennolds dismissed the talk, he admitted that it had "raised the hopes of some to a high pitch." Another skeptic in Capt. Charles Lumsden's Battery believed that the so-called Northern peace movement had sputtered out: "Officers and men all agree that peace must be the result of hard fighting." Hiram Reynolds of the 7th Mississippi likewise refused to buy into the peace talk: "It looks very dark on our side of the question to me. It seems to me that this is the last year of the war. This war must soon terminate. It cannot last much longer. Our armies have been falling back ever since the war commenced and I see no other indication of them stopping. This will whip us after a while."[14]

The weather took a distinct turn for the better on March 13; an early spring appeared to have settled in. Three days later, William Rogers noted that the sound of chirping birds cheered the men. Alex Spence of the 1st Arkansas took an opportunity to write his wife on the twenty-second: "For several days we have had beautiful weather, ground drying off very fast. The roads are getting very good, and if the Yankees intend advancing, I suppose they will do so in a very few days." Writing from the camp of the 32nd Tennessee, Robert Irwin told his family that "the efficiency of the army has been greatly increased. We have a fine army now."[15]

The warmer weather proved to be a feint. A huge windstorm occurred on the night of March 27, blowing down many of the tents and mud chimneys. Bitterly cold winds continued for the next two days. From 9:00 P.M. to midnight on the thirtieth, three inches of snow fell, blanketing the Middle Tennessee countryside. The snow had melted by midday on the thirty-first, but not before the boys had had their fun. "This morning was celebrated by a 'Snowball Fight.' The 13th and 154th [Tennessee] charged the 11th [Tennessee] and took their encampment—a truce agreed upon peace was made and the three regiments under a leader mounted on a 'lean Sorrell' charged Maney's Brigade took a stand of colors and captured several contrabands," declared Lt. Hirman Moorman of the 13th. The casualties comprised a few blackened eyes and bloodied noses. In the camp of the 33rd Alabama, Thomas Bigbee watched as a snowball fight grew to huge proportions: "Then there came over fore other regiments in line of battle[.] I can tell you it was a pirty sight to see tow or three thousand men in an old fort at one time playing in the snow in regular battle form." Later that night, the Bedford County Courthouse in Shelbyville caught fire, leaving only a charred shell by sunrise.[16]

Back in Tullahoma, the men of Preston's Brigade also engaged in a snowball fight. The 1st/3rd Florida attacked the camp of the 4th Florida, driving the soldiers out. The regiments then combined to attack the 60th North Carolina, which was handily defeated. The attackers then turned on the 20th Tennessee, the regiment having taken up a strong position by a creek. Mebane's Battery joined the 20th, but it proved insufficient. The Tennesseans were driven into their stables but then launched a counterattack, hurling back at the Floridians.[17]

The 5th Tennessee attacked the 48th Tennessee, easily routing the regiment. When the 5th attempted a similar assault on the Irishmen of the 2nd Tennessee, however, the troops got more than they bargained for. "The 5th being outnumbered and rather outgeneraled were driven back some distance but not without a fierce struggle," described John Sparkman. The snow battle lasted two hours, when both sides, exhausted and with little snow remaining to throw, called it quits.[18]

April 1 proved to be "a day suited to its name 'all fool's day' for it certainly has fooled us—it is but the lingering remains of March—windy and cold," assessed Captain Coleman. Captain Lumsden, who commanded an Alabama battery, took the opportunity to trick two of his fellow officers by serving them a cotton-ball biscuit. "I record it as I think it is the first time in my life I ever fooled anybody," he proudly wrote. Four days later, Maj. George Godwin informed "Miss Bettie" that "our Army is in better health,

Snowball fight at Dalton, Georgia, March 22, 1864.
From Battlefields in Dixie Land and Chickamauga National Military Park
(Nashville: Nashville, Chattanooga & St. Louis Railway, 1928).

better spirits, and in every way better prepared to meet the enemy than at any time since I have been connected with the Army of Tennessee."[19]

Spring finally came in earnest, although the nights remained quite cold. With the exception of April 18, when a cold blast threatened to kill the fruit crop, the weather remained beautiful, even balmy, with intermittent spring showers. Coleman recorded on the twenty-seventh that the beautiful weather had done much to cheer the troops. The prospects of active campaigning lifted the spirits of many. "After dark the troops seem to be very cheerful for some cause, they keep a loud yell for an hour or more," noted a Mississippian. The roads had measurably improved, and the men remained confident of victory when the inevitable advance came. Indeed, Robert Jamison was convinced that if Rosecrans did not come soon, Bragg would go after him. James Parrott of the 28th Tennessee happily wrote his wife on the twelfth, "Pepple here is in fine spirits." That same day a Tennessean confidently told his sister, "We could not be better prepared for it [combat] with the forces we have than at present and I say let it come." A Mississippian, writing on April 5, related, "News of peace have all gone away and it remains only for us to fight it out, and in my opinion we are fully able to do that." A member of the 45th Alabama believed his regiment was "ripe for the fight." John

Marshall defiantly wrote: "I had rather fight than to retreat[.] we can whip the devil and his angels."[20]

"We have rumors of a battle in Virginia, also news that Forrest has captured 1800 Yankees near Rome, Ga.," Taylor Beatty wrote on May 5. Subsequent confirmation of Lee's victory at Chancellorsville and Forrest's capture of Abel Streight's brigade electrified the Tennessee army. "It remains to be seen what effect the late battle [Chancellorsville] will have on the Northern mind," Tennessean William Thompson reflected. Bragg addressed his troops in General Order No. 109: "Soldiers of the Army of Tennessee, let us emulate the deeds of the Army of Virginia! Let us make them proud to call us brothers! Let us make the Cumberland and the Ohio as classic as the Rappahannock and the Potomac." A jealous Alabamian wrote on May 10, "The Army of Tennessee is becoming impatient for an opportunity to win more glory." Mississippi defeats quickly tempered the Virginia victory. A Tennessean saw no immediate prospects for a fight—"I think the Yanks are getting tired of it." Concerning the engagement at Port Gibson, John Magee wrote on May 7: "Bad news from Miss. we were whipped and lost many prisoners." Three days later he added, "Wild rumors about our army in Miss." The papers soon confirmed the capture and burning of Jackson and the investment of Vicksburg; Bragg's soldiers began to think the worst. "If Vicksburg falls the yankees will rejoice and our cause will be badly crippled if not lost. God forbid that it should ever fall," a troubled Alabamian wrote on May 24. "If this [siege] is true," surmised James Mitchell, "I lose all hope of a speedy peace." Indeed, if the city fell, he predicted that the war would drag on another three years. On May 29, Captain Coleman recorded: "Greatest anxiety felt about Vicksburg. She still holds out bravely!"[21]

A soldier's life was not all boredom. The men typically entertained themselves with simple pleasures. "The men are all lively. We play marbles, baste ball, etc. everyday. . . . Most everyone seems contented," a soldier noted. Four days later, he wrote that a group of men gathered around the campfire outside his tent and began joyously singing "There Is Glory in My Soul." The Louisiana brigade had a splendid band that played morning and evening. The Kentucky brigade at Manchester entertained 200 townspeople with a play—a farce in which some of the Kentuckians wore women's clothes borrowed from the locals. A mock wedding in the 11th Tennessee provided great fun. There was a phony preacher and two dressed-up soldiers—the "bride and groom," who exchanged vows "for two years or during the war." The married couple received huge applause, and according to a news article, they departed "to parts unknown."[22]

Other diversions included making clamshell rings and having the brigade bands serenade the generals. With the warm weather came the opportunity to take a long overdue bath. So many were in the Duck River on March 16 that George Jones wondered what would happen if the Yankee cavalry suddenly appeared — "we would all be a bad fix." Unfortunately, a slaughterhouse above Shelbyville meant that dead hogs occasionally floated down the Duck, emitting a terrible stench. "But I suppose I might as well bathe in it as to drink it," philosophized Joshua Callaway. Socializing with some of the local women, at least for the officers, included picnics, dances, and church. Capt. James Douglas remarked that "several marriages have occurred and others are spoken of." Lt. Robert Kennedy told his sister that "most of them [ladies] are rather of the cornbread order, but there is one occasionally that possesses some attractions." An Alabamian noticed that when women visited to watch the drills and parades, "who'ever has the most gold lace on his arms, generally sets by the purtiest one."[23]

Reading the latest newspapers occupied the time of many. "We can get papers daily now from Chattanooga, Atlanta, Augusta, Montgomery, and Mobile," noted a Tennessean. An Alabamian complained, however, that he had received only two issues of the *Selma Morning Register* in a month, while another groused about the scarcity of the *Montgomery Weekly Advertiser.* "May be its prest or supprest as the case may be, bekase it don't praze Gineral Bragg like to tother papers that cum to us." Nonetheless, at least three professional correspondents and two dozen soldier-correspondents submitted letters and articles to no fewer than a dozen western newspapers that spring. Surgeon James Brannock complained, however, that it was almost impossible to receive books.[24]

Playing sports remained the most popular pastime. "Many a pleasant hour this fine weather is spent by the boys playing Ball, Prisoners Base, etc.," wrote E. H. Rennolds. He regrettably noted two days later that one young man had his nose broken when accidentally hit in the face with a paddle. William D. Rogers wrote his parents that he would soon "join the Boys in a game of Ball which has become a great amusement here." In April, Manigault had his two South Carolina regiments challenge the Alabama regiments of his brigade to a game of prisoner's base. "The first game the Alabamians took all the South Carolinians prisoners, the second game continued until dark when the South Carolinians were four prisoners ahead," Col. Newton Davis noted. Few participated in the National Day of Prayer in March; "most of the boys are engaged in playing baseball," a Mississippian lamented. Foot racing and cockfighting were also popular.[25]

The Unionville horse race of Saturday, April 14, proved to be the highlight of cavalry entertainment that spring. Maj. Benjamin H. Botts of the

Texas Rangers pitted his sorrel against Col. Thomas Harrison's mare. A huge crowd gathered, placing upward of $25,000 in bets. At the signal, the two riders dashed forward along the 800-yard racetrack. Botts's horse crossed the judge's stand a full thirty yards in the lead.[26]

Going on large-scale rabbit hunts — "running rabbits," as it was called — sparked many men's interest and had the added benefit of supplementing rations. Rufus Daniel of the 6th Arkansas noted one such hunt on March 20, in which ninety-nine rabbits were clubbed to death — "it was fine sport for the boys." An Alabamian wrote about his regiment surrounding a thicket and killing sixty rabbits. Unquestionably, the largest of the hunts occurred in April when scores of men in Liddell's Brigade, then at Wartrace, surrounded a field. Working toward the center while screaming and beating sticks, with dogs barking, men cornered and bludgeoned more than 130 rabbits and 11 partridges.[27]

Catching rabbits and squirrels was one thing, but trapping a robin roost in a cedar brake near Shelbyville took some planning for the men of the 24th Alabama. At night, several privates, including Joel H. Puckett, climbed into a nearby tree. In the darkness, the men on the ground lit torches and began wildly thrashing into the brake. "It beats all," wrote Puckett. "They came into the tree so fast and thick that they would [perch] in our faces, on our heads feet hands and sometimes you can catch them with your mouth. . . . [We caught] in all about 50." The menu that night included robin stew.[28]

When not drilling or playing, the men took time to write home. Robert Jamison apologized to his wife on April 16 for having taken so long to write: "It has been raining for several days until today, and in rainy weather it is almost impossible to do anything unless it is to keep comfortable." Joshua Callaway longed to see his wife, but finding a quiet place proved impossible. "Everybody is in a stew. The boys are all hollowing and singing, a perfect buzz. There was a May party today [May 1] out here somewhere but I don't know where it was. Everybody seems to be lively as May."[29]

Camp life had its miserable side as well. On the night of May 25, the camp of the Cheatham Rifles (B, 11th Tennessee) caught fire, destroying tents, cabins, blankets, and equipment. Lice, or "graybacks," infested the camps as warm weather returned. Thomas Warrick pleaded with his wife not to visit Shelbyville due to the lice infestation — "they are as bad as old red ants." He added: "The Boddy lice would eat up Booth of the children in one knight in spite of all we could do. You don't hav any idea what sort of animals they are." Some men pleaded with their wives not to visit simply because of the lack of accommodations and the crudeness of camp. "There are some fool soldiers who have their wives with them here and although I would not have you here for any amount (that is here in camp) yet I can't help envying those poor fellows their happiness," Callaway admitted.[30]

The illicit pleasure of gambling also thrived. On March 28, Robert Holmes witnessed a footrace on which over $1,000 had been bet. Texan James W. Scurlock assured his brother: "There is few but what gambles in our Company. Gambling and swearing I don't think I will ever do." A strict order came down that no one on sick call could play cards. "Raffling is all the rage," noted an army correspondent.[31]

Training

The infantry began target practice that spring with generally abysmal results. W. C. Tripp told his wife that the 44th Tennessee took shots at a target six feet high and ten feet long at 160 yards. "Heap of the boys mist," he admitted. A member of the 13th Tennessee documented the success of Companies E and I of his regiment. They hit the target seven times in thirty-one tries at 300 yards, fifteen times in thirty-four at 400 yards, and sixteen times in seventy at 500 yards. Other units fared little better. A company in the 12th Tennessee hit a target five times at 400 yards and only twice at 500 yards. At 600 yards, Company C had only a single man get lucky. The practice held by the 4th Tennessee on May 4 was typical: the men, armed with Springfield rifles, were given one shot at 200 yards, two shots at 400 yards, and one shot at 600 yards. In the 29th Mississippi, troops shot at the figure of a man on a board at ranges of 200, 300, 400, and 600 yards, each time firing four shots. "Some of them hit it every time," marveled Thomas Newberry.[32]

The cannoneers held limited target practice due to a dearth of ammunition. The Washington Artillery fired at an eight-by-twelve target from 1,300–1,700 yards but hit only three times in ten. The artillerymen spent the bulk of their time in drills. When it came to hitching up the guns and caissons for action, few batteries could beat the New Orleans gunners; the outfit could be ready to move within nine minutes. Stanford's Battery drilled from four to five hours a day. A contest was held between Scott's Tennessee and Douglas's Texas batteries in May. "I rather think Scott will get the prize as he is a pet with Bragg's army," Douglas disgustedly wrote.[33]

Bragg ordered that one regiment from each brigade and two companies from each regiment be thoroughly trained in the skirmish formation. Some saw the drill as openly training sharpshooters, which in fact was one of the intended purposes. "I like the drill [skirmish] well but I don't know whether I like the mode of fighting," William D. Rogers observed. Mock battles, on the other hand, seemed to delight everyone. Blank cartridges lent a realistic aura to the demonstrations. A sham battle between Breckinridge's and

Cleburne's divisions in late April attracted female spectators from Shelbyville, McMinnville, Huntsville, and Columbia. One of Breckinridge's men declared, "We whipped them powerfully."[34]

The only published manual to emerge from the Army of Tennessee came from thirty-nine-year-old Maj. Calhoun Benham, Cleburne's assistant adjutant general. He seemed a rather unlikely candidate for such a project (he was a prewar attorney), but Cleburne was looking for a compiler not an originator. Most of the instructions in Benham's booklet, *A System of Conducting Musketry Instruction*, came from British regulations. The final publication offered basic information on how to clean and disassemble a musket, how to judge proper shooting distances, and the like.[35]

Consolidation meant that some regiments had to acclimate to drilling with a new outfit. Captain Coleman's battalion merged with the 16th Alabama. When the two units drilled together for the first time, Hardee and Cleburne appeared satisfied, although the captain was not—"I made too many mistakes." One soldier wrote that "the fact of being in Hardee's corps is sufficient proof we have to 'Toe the mark.'"[36]

Col. A. J. Vaughn's consolidated 13th/154th Tennessee lined up for inspection one day in April. Even with forty-seven men on the sick roll, the regiment still counted 470 present for duty, almost all armed with .58 Minié rifles and a few Enfield rifles. Their clothing, though not uniform, was good, but shoes were badly needed. The camp equipage, including eighty-five tents and twenty-three tent flies, appeared in good order, but there was a shortage of axes, spades, and hatchets.[37]

The relentless drilling wore on many of the men. "The Brigade Drill this morning was longer & hotter than usual," complained a Tennessean. "It may be for our own good during the Summer campaign by preparing us for it, but it does seem to be useless and uncalled for, volunteers drill better, and learn more to be drilled two hours at a time than four." In one instance, it was rumored that Colonel Vaughn bet $1,000 that his 13th Tennessee could outdrill Col. Hume Field's 1st Tennessee. On April 14, Brig. Gen. Preston Smith put his Tennessee brigade on a grueling two-hour drill in front of Cheatham and then had them pass in review on the double-quick at charge bayonets. The men "raised a yell equal to a charge on the battlefield," noted E. H. Rennolds. Van Buren Oldham of the 9th Tennessee disgustedly wrote in his journal on May 15: "Nothing to dispel the dull monotony of camp life, besides another day of hard drill. Our captain is very rigid and will depart for no instance [on] a single [iota] from Army regulations." A young Kentucky private explained to his mother how he served as "the marker" in drill. A man holding a red flag marker stood at the end of each wing of the regiment.

The unit aligned on these "markers," and in wheeling movements the flags became the pivot points.[38]

Constant drilling created a renewed esprit, and in the shared hardships and moments of schoolboy fun, the Army of Tennessee was reborn in the spring of 1863. To be sure, problems persisted. Hundreds of reluctant conscripts were entering the ranks, and in quality and patriotism they were not the volunteers of '61. The loss of McCown's and Breckinridge's divisions to Mississippi offset five months of manpower gains. Yet, an Atlanta correspondent visiting on May 31 believed that the army was "well clothed, well fed and in cheerful spirits." Indeed, it would be hard to find men "better looking, better humored, or in better appearance."[39]

In the midst of severe hardship, the brotherhood created a solidarity, but it had its limitations. The bonds rarely extended beyond small units and failed to address the tensions of sectionalism. Nor did comradeship in and of itself sustain army morale in the midst of battlefield defeats and territorial losses. The brotherhood nonetheless served as an outlet from solitude, a support for the shared concerns of family separation, and a diversion from tedium.

The Sway of Religion

Evangelical religion not only addressed the stresses of battle and camp life but also helped to define the war. Southerners saw the Confederacy as having God's favor. This was "not a war of North against South, but one of goodness versus evil, of God versus Satan," concluded Drew Gilpin Faust. Religion thus intersected with patriotism. The Christian soldier would be a good soldier, not simply because he would not fear death but because he "would be obedient and well-disciplined because he would understand the divine origin of earthly duty."[1]

As the Army of Tennessee continued its retreats, it underwent waves of revivalism—with peaks in the spring of 1863 and the winter of 1864—separated by an active campaign and two major battles. The timing of these revivals revealed the state of mind in the army. Many believed that the lack of victories was related to the fact that the soldiers had gone astray; there needed to be a return to piety. The revivals ultimately lifted the spirits of the demoralized, sanctified the Cause, and bonded piety with military success. God's favor would ultimately result in military victory.[2]

The First Wave of Revivalism

In a world surrounded by death, temptation, loneliness, and perceived, if not real, moral evil, some soldiers turned to religion. John Routt urged his wife to "continue to pray for me my sweet wife and for the cause and everyone in it." "I will put my trust in the Lord the only help I no. I want you to pray for me that I may go threw this war safe," John Hudson of the 41st Mississippi advised his wife Sarah. Edward Ward of the 4th Tennessee told his sister that he had begun reading two chapters of the Bible every night, beginning with Genesis. He suggested that she turn to her Bible and "read with me," so that they could have a nightly connection.[3]

Although religion played a role in the lives of thousands of soldiers, army life caused many to stray initially. Characteristic of that attitude was the letter Ward wrote in July 1862: "We in our company 'aint' much on the wash, but we are some on poker so you see Sunday is card playing day with us. . . .

It has been a confounded long time since I have heard a man preach. I really don't think I could stand to hear it, although I would like powerful well to see a church full of people once more."[4]

The frequent indifference to matters of faith continued through 1863. President Davis declared March 27 the National Day of Prayer and Fasting. In the Army of Tennessee, an appalled Mississippian noted that only a few men acknowledged the occasion, adding that "most of the boys are engaged in playing ball & other different games." Sgt. John Sparkman attended a service on that occasion, but as he looked about, he saw others washing clothes, playing ball, and walking about. Seeing killing on a massive scale inevitably caused the numbing of emotions, creating a vacuum that indifference and diverse pleasures quickly filled.[5]

There was a general disregard for religion in the early spring of 1863. "Mentor," a soldier-correspondent at Shelbyville, informed his readers that no drill occurred on Sundays, only inspection and church, but "little else goes on that is holy—cards, marbles, running, jumping, reading." During the winter of 1862–63, the chaplains of the Army of Tennessee considered quitting en masse. Alabamian James B. Mitchell openly admitted to not being a Christian. Thomas Webb of the 24th Tennessee Battalion told his wife on March 2: "I tell you the truth, I don't like to stay here for there is too much devilment carried on for me. A man cannot live well unless he can steal and lie. There is plenty of preaching but it does no good, as I see here a man preaching, and there one swearing and over there is one singing a song to suit himself and right out there is a gang of them playing cards and in fact everything is doing here at one time."[6]

Charles Roberts of Stanford's Battery served on picket duty at a Cumberland Presbyterian church outside Shelbyville on March 9. He described to his wife the disrespect for the sacred surroundings. "If this was a Roman Catholic Church I think they would have to sprinkle holy water over and about the building several times before it would be considered purified," he confessed. "The other night whilst reposing on my blankets . . . I was amused at the scene around me. To my right sat Sergt. [Penn] gnawing a [beef] bone and occasionally varying the [amusement] by taking a bite from a quarter section of corn bread. In front of me a party of four playing [euchre], to the right three playing poker and then two or three smoking and talking. Over the way a small crowd attracted by the fiddler who is scraping some real backwoods tune, and in a corner near the pulpit one of the Company disposing of some pipes by auction. You may judge what a sweet combination of sounds it made."[7]

When the womanizing Van Dorn was killed by a jealous husband, the local Fayetteville, Tennessee, paper could not help but make a comparison between him and the late Stonewall Jackson: "Think of the universal regret paid to the lamented Jackson. The whole country is filled with mourning and tears at his death, while no man expresses even a *regret* at the fate of Van Dorn. Here is the striking difference between sin and righteousness."[8]

In this context, the first wave of revivalism broke out in the spring of 1863. Precisely why this occurred is complicated. The expected short war had now taken on a life of its own. Despite best efforts, the war remained out of control and the death toll mounted. The conflict could go either way. It is not surprising, under the circumstances, that the men turned to the one whom they saw as the ultimate controller of history. What is surprising is that the paradox of war and religion failed to raise serious debate. What became emphasized was the issue of personal godliness: a holy cause could not survive if the army did not purge itself of sinfulness and vulgarity. The revival cleansing addressed the social morality of card playing, drinking, and cursing and urged the men to fill the vacuum with prayer, worship attendance, and Bible reading. The question of whether the Cause was truly righteous was never debated. If the indifferent still outnumbered the converted, and they may have, it mattered not; the issues of life, death, and personal virtue had been brought to the forefront.

Revivalism did not take root immediately, in part due to the scarcity of army chaplains. In Hardee's Corps, four or five brigades lacked a chaplain, and the army as a whole averaged only one per brigade. A Presbyterian minister stated that many entire divisions had not had a sermon preached in months. An Alabamian thought that a preacher could easily have 1,000 in his congregation on Sunday, but there was not a single chaplain in his brigade. Lay preachers stepped in to fill the void but with varying degrees of success. Writing to his mother on March 15, Joshua Callaway revealed: "We had a sermon by Lieut. Coons of the 28th [Alabama]. I don't think we were much blessed by it. He lacks the spirit and power of religion. A very eager and anxious congregation was disappointed." A mid-March revival in the Kentucky brigade, stationed at Manchester, produced limited results. Captain Coleman hoped "as spring comes on that we will have preaching more frequently now. I do not feel right without hearing the word of God preached on the Sabbath."[9]

In late April and early May 1863, with the arrival of a number of visiting civilian ministers ("missionaries," as they were called), revivalism exploded. From privates to generals, the men became captivated. "There has been a general revival going on in this army for the past month and there have been a great many professions of faith. I think some 30 or 40 in this regiment [47th

Tennessee] and a great deal more in others," Assistant Surgeon Andrew J. Harris testified. Lieutenant Davidson told his wife of the revivals on May 10, claiming that many soldiers had "professed faith in Jesus Christ." Captain Coleman noticed an encouraging revival occurring in the 16th Alabama—"I pray that it may result in much good in elevating the morals of our whole Brigade." A thrilled Floridian wrote, "The Spirit of the Lord has come to our Regt. at last." William Estes of the 48th Tennessee recorded in his diary on May 19, "A revival of religion is in our brigade and in two other brigades in our division, many souls have been converted." John Harris was taken aback by the response: "You never in your life saw anything like the revival that is going on in the Army now. Every brigade is having large meetings every night, and I am in hopes it will do much good." Surgeon James Brannock of the 5th Tennessee explained to his wife: "It seems like one perpetual camp meeting. The only difference from the old camp meetings at home is that we don't have women with us, or the chicken fix in usually incident to such occasions. It seems quite strange to see so many men who were a few weeks ago swearing, gambling, cockfighting and now praying and reading their bibles."[10]

The obsession with profanity may sound strange to the modern reader, given the context of the bloodiest war in American history. Yet many in the mid-nineteenth century viewed cursing as a class sin, a practice of the "common" and "ill bred." Evangelical religion never questioned the more substantive issue of the South's "peculiar institution." The problem lay not in evangelical Southerners' literal interpretation of the Bible, according to Woodworth, but their superficial interpretation. Religion became the bedrock of their justification of slavery. Christian slave owners were seen as stewards and missionaries of an institution sanctified by God. The church's mission was viewed as being an agent not of social change but of evangelism and salvation.[11]

The numbers of respondents to the revivalism proved impressive. There were 478 conversions in Cleburne's Division that spring. In two regiments in McCown's Division alone 140 were converted. The revival in the 23rd/25th Tennessee at Tullahoma resulted in 105 conversions. Everyone began to notice a sober attitude throughout the army. "I am glad to say that I see a great improvement in the morals of this whole army. There is much less profanity to be heard than normally," Captain Patton observed. Charles Roberts concurred: "I have no doubt it will be conducive of much good and I am very glad to see it, for there is a great need of something to improve the moral tone of our army." E. H. Rennolds could not help but notice that "a great change has come over the regiment [5th Tennessee]. Gambling and swearing has almost disappeared and a seriousness has settled over all." A chaplain noted that even the most casual observer would not be able to help but notice the marked difference in the soldiers: "Instead of oaths, jests, and background songs, we now have the songs of Zion, prayers and praises to God." Rev. W. T. Bennett of the 12th Tennessee reported the moral climate of his regiment "rapidly changing for the better."[12]

The cavalry regiments were at a distinct disadvantage due to the constant picketing and changing of positions. Chaplain Robert Bunting of the 8th Texas Cavalry began preaching one or two times a week in May with some success. It was the presence of a Presbyterian missionary in July 1863, however, that ignited revivalism. He held nightly meetings for a month, receiving 30 troopers by profession of faith, with another 130 coming under the influence of the revival. Prayers were not always confined to spiritual issues. Dr. Charles Quintard's brother beseeched in open prayer that the Yankees' "moral responsibilities might be awakened by the 'roar of our cannon and the gleam of our bayonets and that the stars and bars might soon wave in triumph through these beleaguered states.'"[13]

The first stage in the religious pilgrimage was the repentance of sin. Those who felt thus convicted would come forward as "mourners," a term referring to the tears sinners often shed as they reflect upon their straying from the path of righteousness. George A. Grammer of Swett's Battery was one such mourner. He wrote in his diary on the night of May 1: "Since October 4, 1862 I have led a life entirely contrary to the principles of our holy religion and to the teachings of God's holy word. . . . By the grace of God I have at last recovered and am arousing from my wickedness. . . . A year spent in wickedness. . . . May God forgive me for that past and give me grace for the future." Michael Royster related to his wife, "Sallie you know that I have never been converted that is feel that my sins were forgiven, but I feel deeply convicted of my sin and I do humbly pray God to pardon them for me and you." Frederick Bradford was pleased to see twenty mourners in a service in his brigade one evening, but he further noted that "none of them were converted." Ed Carruth was moved to see the "strong and tough soldiers humbled in the dust, weeping like infants at the sight of their own sins."[14]

Conviction was frequently followed by profession of faith and baptism. "A great many have professed and many inquiring the way," Sgt. John R. McCreight of the 9th Tennessee noted on May 10. "On last Sunday I stood on the banks of the Duck River amid a large crowd and witnessed the emersion of ten soldiers. They formed a line, took each other by the hand & marched into the River. There were a great many Ladies there to witness the scene. After they came out of the water several of the Ladies came up & extended the right hand of fellowship to them. There are a great many things in camp life that tends to blunten the sympathies and affections of our hearts, but when I witnessed the above scene I could not refrain from shedding tears. On the evening of the same day in the 13 Reg T. V. [Tennessee volunteers] the ordinance of Baptism was administered to several by sprinkling."[15]

The chaplains, local preachers, and visiting army missionaries cooperated in every way and determined, under the present circumstances, to place denominationalism and dogma aside and concentrate on salvation and pastoral topics. Thus, according to one observer, while most of the troops were Baptists and Methodists and the generals Episcopalians, the men were free to express their church preference. At the conclusion of one service, Alfred Fielder noted, a chaplain made an announcement that for those who wished to join a church he would procure "an administrator of the church of their choice to baptize them and give them a certificate of the fact etc. 22 came forward 2 preferred the C. [Cumberland] Presbyterians, 10 the Methodists and 10 the Baptist." Two days later, Fielder remarked that when "the bugle sounded church call, the chaplain called for those who preferred the Missionary Baptist Church to come forward and give their witness, after which ten of whom were taken to the river and immersed. The bugle then sounded for those who preferred the Methodists, at which time six stepped forward and received baptism by pouring." The 7th Mississippi had an old-fashioned Free Will Baptist as a chaplain, but a member admitted that "no strife at all exists between the different sects."[16]

The ongoing work of nurture fell to the lay-led Christian societies. The new converts would often lead the groups in prayer. The members were held accountable for shunning cursing, alcohol use, and cards or any game that was played for money and for attending services faithfully. In the 5th Tennessee, both a Christian association and Sunday school were established, the latter with four classes. Arkansan Rufus Daniel was elated to "see the soldiers manifesting such interest and attaching themselves to this [Liddell's] society." A Christian association formed in the 9th Tennessee to support its members in prayer, allow them to hold each other morally accountable, and visit the sick. On June 2, the Bible Society of the Confederate States of America shipped a huge number of Bibles to the army, averaging 400–500 per brigade or about 100 per regiment, all of which were "gladly received."[17]

Not all men, of course, fell under the spell of the evangelical spirit. Chaplain W. H. Browning conceded that many continued in their "profane, wicked, and rude" ways. A Tennessean recalled that even during the high tide of the revivals, the pious were in the minority. Several men who regularly wrote letters during this period, such as Thomas Warrick and Irvine

Walker, never even mentioned the revivals. The issue for some lay in the style and form of the revivals. There was too much talk of death for some, and the ecumenical spirit and emotionalism did not settle well with others. "I have not attended any of the night meetings, for I have always had a repugnance to this mode of conversion for no sectarian feeling, but to a natural aversion to violent demonstrations of religious feelings," Charles Roberts remarked. Sergeant Holt confided to his wife that while many came under the revival influence, many others continued in their ways of "vulgarity, profanity, and foolishness." Bishop Polk believed the revivals held value beyond their immediate return; religion would help develop a well-disciplined postwar civilization. A similar religious fever erupted in Lee's army that spring, although the tone appears to have been more subdued. As with the Army of Tennessee, many of the eastern troops remained indifferent to the call to revival.[18]

Some frustrated chaplains ungraciously unleashed their wrath upon those not in attendance. "The chaplain added nothing but an uncalled for rebuke for those who did not attend, but did not remain perfectly quiet [in camp] during service," noted a Tennessean on April 19. "He used language which I consider unbecoming a political speaker, still more so a minister. All who I have heard speak of it condemn it." On May 6, he added, "Parson Hearn's remarks in reference to those who come only to ridicule [mock], were unbecoming a minister and entirely uncalled for."[19]

Two visiting preachers appear to have been at the core of the spring revival—Dr. John B. McFerrin of the Methodist Church and Bishop Steven Elliott of the Episcopal Church. McFerrin, who had previously served as an army missionary, arrived that spring and kept a journal of his activities. He preached nightly in Bate's, Johnson's, Polk's, Wood's, and others' brigades, with many mourners and a number of conversions. A Tennessean felt deeply moved after hearing one of McFerrin's sermons: "The word spoken was attended by the witness of the spirit to my heart and I felt that this earth was not my home but that by and by my spirit would be dislodged from this tenement of clay and go to dwell in my father's house above made without hands eternal in the heavens!" On May 16, Captain Fielder wrote of McFerrin's sermon: "The sermon plain and pointed and according to an opinion a most excellent one—There were a number of mourners. Several made an open profession of faith in Christ and joined some of the Baptist some of the Methodist and some of the Presbyterians." After hearing McFerrin on May 20, Captain Coleman noted, "He was broken down from speaking in the open air so much but showed flashes of genius."[20]

The other eminent preacher was Steven Elliott, an Episcopal bishop from Georgia and a religious firebrand of the first order. He believed that the North was totally depraved and that God had ordained the South as an instrument of his chastisement. The present conflict was "as much a moral as a political necessity," and he strongly opposed those who would engage in premature peace talks. He saw slavery as a sacred charge, given a righteous South—"we are elevating them [blacks] in every generation." As for the military misfortunes of the Confederacy, Elliott believed that God "might keep us long in the furnace of affliction, but in the end He would deliver us and justify our trust in Him." He did speak of "our sins," but these were references to personal immoralities. Nowhere did he question the corporate corruptness of an aristocracy that also held down a class of whites. In short, Steven Elliott told people what they wanted to hear—and they listened gladly. On the afternoon of Sunday, May 31, Elliott and Quintard traveled from Shelbyville to Wartrace, where the bishop conducted what probably was the largest service of the spring revival; 3,000 were in attendance according to Elliott, 4,000–5,000 by Quintard's estimate. Those in attendance included Bragg, Polk, Hardee, Withers, Cleburne, and a number of brigadiers. The next day, June 1, Hardee formed Liddell's Brigade in a square and had Elliott address the troops briefly on the "religious aspects" of the war. Elliott demonized the enemy as "lovers of pleasure rather than lovers of God." In one sermon, he espoused that the South was "warring with hordes of unprincipled foreigners, ignorant and brutal men, who, having cast off at home all the restraints of order and of belief, have signalized their march over our devoted country by burning the churches of Christ . . . and by fanning into fury the demonic passions of the ignorant and vile."[21]

Many other visiting missionaries spread throughout the army. "J. M. B.," a Georgia missionary, preached to a portion of Polk's Brigade at Wartrace in late May. He described the scene: "A death-like silence prevailed, the large and interesting audience and at the close of services about seventy persons presented themselves for prayer, five were converted and at the singing and rejoicing surpassed anything I ever witnessed in Georgia."[22]

The revivals crossed the barriers of rank, at least for some. A missionary reported that officers from colonels to captains and lieutenants were all affected. Some of the officers delivered sermons, such as Col. Mark Lowrey of the 32nd Mississippi, a Baptist minister before the war, and Lt. Col. Wiley M. Reed, the provost of Hardee's Corps, who had previously served as a Cumberland Presbyterian minister. The equalitarian nature of the revivals was seen in a confirmation class that came forth one evening at the conclusion of a service—two colonels, one major, one lieutenant, a surgeon, and five privates. A Tennessean nonetheless observed that as "a general thing the gold lace men of our army [officers] do not go to church much."[23]

Yet one officer remained detached—Bragg. He was never seen taking the Lord's Supper and was not known to be affiliated with any church. When Quintard bravely broached him on the subject of his salvation and church membership, the general's response proved surprisingly open: "I have been waiting for twenty years to have someone to say this to me, and I thank you from my heart. Certainly, I shall be confirmed if you will give me the necessary instruction." It was pointedly Bishop Elliott, not Polk, who baptized and confirmed the general at Shelbyville on June 2. "My mind has never been so much at ease and I feel renewed strength for the task before me," the army chieftain would later write.[24]

The men took notice that "the Holy Sabbath is observed now from General Bragg down to all the men." Religion began to break down the barriers between officers and enlisted men. Mississippian R. B. Pittman observed that "the generals and every other officer partakes [in worship] and when the right hand of fellowship is extended to candidates [for church membership] we see officers and men meeting in this token of love, and who could look on and not be moved to exclaim see how these brothers truly love."[25]

The revivals reignited in the summer and early fall. Daniel Kelly related, "I am going to tell you there is a revival of religion going on protracted meetings are now being held threw the entire Army so fare as I notice and souls are being converted to God everywhere." In early June, Dr. Benjamin M. Palmer, famed minister of the First Presbyterian Church in New Orleans, made his way to Shelbyville and the Mississippi brigade. "The preaching often resembles the primitive camp meetings," thought Ed Carruth. As late as September 18, Surgeon George Godwin of the 51st Tennessee noted to "Miss Bettie," "We have preaching or prayer meeting, every time we stop long enough—have had several converts since we started on this march—some have converted while in line of battle."[26]

The spring 1863 revival served as a moral cleansing and spiritual rebirth for the exhausted Army of Tennessee. Coupled with the improved condition of the troops, it clearly assisted in improving morale. On a personal level, it offered hope to the men in the midst of their loneliness and the constant presence of death. Local and state pride may have initially united the troops, but as the war progressed it was the revivals, not inspired leadership or battlefield victories, that bonded the troops and, to the extent that they did, helped cut through the factions and cliques that characterized the army. Yet, there is no evidence that the renewed interest in religion reduced the number of desertions, which continued to plague the army. The nature of the revivals remained personal and pastoral, and the religious contradictions of war and slavery were never discussed. Nor did Bragg's touching conversion, which revealed a rare sensitive side, bring about reconciliation between him and his avowed enemies. The alienation simply proved too deep and the pride too pronounced.

The Second Wave of Revivalism

Although the revival that began in the spring of 1863 never totally abated, the fervor tapered in the midst of active campaigning. And although revivalism had never discontinued, it reignited on a grand scale in February 1864. The timing proved significant since it occurred in the midst of the reenlistments, which would become an extension of the revivals. Those committing "for the war" became the converted. Ceremonies were conducted, with hats removed, hands raised, tears shed, background music offered, and solemn vows given. Religious and military fidelity meshed, and the men responded within the cultural context they understood.[27]

The Dalton revivals began in March. "We have the privilege of going to church every night, when not on duty, at the Methodist Church," Augustus Adamson of the 30th Georgia wrote on the fifth. The previous night, thirteen from the regiment had joined the church. A Mississippian described the scene of several hundred men sitting in a circle on the ground with a preacher in the middle. "It looks quite primeval. There is an absence of all show. No one goes there to be seen. Sober reality is the order of the occasion." Flavel Barber observed that "several of our best young soldiers have manifested a deep interest [in religion]. Indeed, I think there is quite an improvement in point of morals throughout our whole army." "The revival is still going on and producing some good fruits," he continued on April 3. "Desertions have ceased and the soldiers seem better satisfied than they have ever been before." Many men observed the National Day of Prayer on the eighth by abstaining from food, drink, and alcohol until 4:00 P.M. "The revival goes on with unabated zeal and success. There seems to be a powerful awakening and seriousness, more than I have ever seen in the army," a Georgian noted. On April 4, Floridian John Inglis wrote his cousin that there was "quite a revival going on here, and many of our hardy boys are being converted. I wish our whole Army were Christians."[28]

John Crittenden attended preaching on the night of April 3, with 500–600 present. "If we had the right kind of preachers good might be accomplished," he believed. "Some ten or fifteen went up to be prayed for at the conclusion of the Services. Gen. Manigault was present and seemed to manifest considerable feeling in the meeting. We will have preaching again to night if the weather will admit of it. They have prayer meeting nearly every night in our company. Quite a change seems to be coming over the Soldiers. They are not near so wicked as they were a few months back. Boys that have been in the habit of swearing all the time swear scarcely at all." A Tennessean noted on April 3: "The revival is still going on and producing some good fruits. Desertions have ceased and the soldiers seem better than they have ever been before." Not all got into the religious fervor. "Everybody seems to be getting religious but I cannot see why it is. I do know that we all ought to have religion for we do not know when we will be killed," Jacob Weaver wrote his sister.[29]

Tom Stokes of the 10th Texas explained to his sister the transformation taking place. "I have never seen such a spirit as there is now in the army. Religion is the theme. Everywhere, you hear around the campfires the sweet songs of Zion. The spirit pervades the whole army. God is doing a glorious work, and I believe it is but the beautiful prelude to peace." A few days later, he added: "The good work still goes on here. Thirty-one men were baptized at the creek below our brigade yesterday, and I have heard from several other brigades in which the proportion is equally large. . . . There must have been baptized yesterday 150 persons—maybe 200. This revival spirit is not confined to a part only, but pervades the whole army. . . . If this state of things should continue for any considerable length of time, we will have in the Army of Tennessee an army of believers." On April 27, an Alabamian described: "I think I have seen as many as a thousand at one time hear preaching to our Brigade. Hundreds go up to be prayed for and scores are joining the various churches."[30]

The baptisms of Johnston, Hardee, and Hood by Bishop Polk proved to be a highlight of the revival. Hood, due to his amputated leg, could not kneel, but he supported himself on a crutch and bowed his head. His baptism stood as a symbol of a broken South turning to God for salvation. Other generals participated, including Stewart, a Presbyterian, who helped serve Communion, while Colonel Lowrey, a former Baptist minister, preached and gave benedictions. Cleburne frequently attended the services. A Mississippian commented, "Nearly all of our first generals have joined the church."[31]

The religious fervor continued throughout the Atlanta Campaign. Following the Battle of Resaca, Samuel McKittrick believed that "the hand of God appeared to be signally on our side." One soldier found an entire regiment on their knees, asking for forgiveness of their sins and "for success for the Confederate cause." One chaplain reported both holding prayer meetings and preaching in the trenches on several occasions.[32]

The revivals played a vital role in sustaining the army. The soldiers believed that God was on their side and that death in a righteous cause was not to be feared. The Yankees were described as the wicked Moabites who would be "smitten by Israel." "The army is getting away from self-reliance to a dependency upon God," Edward Brown concluded. "They are getting religion & fitting themselves to die, and I believe that they will fight better when the days of battle come." They prayed for God "to buckle on his armor in our defense."[33]

The Middle Tennessee Debacle

The Federals Begin Probing

The Yankees rudely interrupted the Confederate high command's bickering on April 21, 1863, when they suddenly advanced along a broad front on the Rebel right. One column captured and destroyed McMinnville, which Morgan had conveniently left unguarded; another column, estimated at 1,500 cavalry, filed due south down the Woodburg-Manchester Road; and a third force, in brigade strength, advanced directly along the Manchester Pike, probing Hoover's Gap in an effort to reach Beech Grove. The Federals, as matters developed, were on a reconnaissance-in-force. Had Rosecrans made a serious thrust, both Hoover's Gap and Manchester would have been taken. With Manchester captured, the bluecoats would have been in position to advance down the Manchester-Pelham Road, flanking Tullahoma and making it untenable. Hardee could have attacked the Federal flank column via Tullahoma as Johnston had planned, but with Hoover's Gap captured, the Federals could have marched directly into Tullahoma. Although Bragg was obviously caught off guard by Rosecrans's maneuver, the men in the ranks had long anticipated just such a move against Hoover's Gap. Indeed, they expressed surprise that it had taken so long.[1]

Bragg belatedly advanced Hardee's Corps north of the Duck River to the gaps—Liberty, Hoover's, and Bell Buckle—establishing corps headquarters at the Beechwood Plantation at Beech Grove. Martin's and Wharton's cavalry divisions deployed at Fairfield, a "pretty little village." Supplies would come to the railhead at Wartrace, a village with a depot, two taverns, three stores, a blacksmith shop, and about fifteen or so houses. Hoover's Gap, nonetheless, remained unfortified, and Col. Martin Luther Stausel, whose 41st Alabama now picketed the area, wondered why he could not at least have a battery as backup. "We are constantly expecting an attack," he wrote on April 27. Keeping the Yankees off the Highland Rim came with a risk. By late April, the fords of the Duck were becoming near impassable. If the Manchester Pike Bridge and the Schoefner Bridge, five miles west of Wartrace, washed out, Hardee would be stranded north of the Duck. Even if the gaps remained in Rebel hands, they could be bypassed by way of the Woodburg-Manchester Road or McMinnville, something that John-ston clearly understood. In late April, Withers was ordered to post a brigade (Walthall's) at Lewisburg, midway between Columbia and Shelbyville, as an infantry reserve for either location.[2]

Despite these warnings, there was a business-as-usual atmosphere at Hardee's headquarters. On May 18, his eighteen- and twenty-one-year-old daughters, Anna and Sallie, briefly joined him. The staff saw to it that they were properly serenaded, and several officers, including Captain Coleman, made calls. The captain, who considered both ladies "nice and interesting," took Sallie to church. Sallie would not marry for another eight years and, to Hardee's utter delight, her husband would be none other than his former chief of staff Thomas B. Roy.[3]

A dispatch arrived on April 25, warning that Ambrose Burnside's corps would be moving in force into East Tennessee. Bragg, approaching a physi-cal breakdown, nonetheless remained consumed with internal issues. A visitor that spring described him as feeble—"he stoops, and has a sickly, cadaverous, haggard appearance." Increasingly concerned with his emaci-ated appearance and refusal to eat, his staff brought his meals to his desk. On May 1, a staff officer spent three hours with the army commander. "He spoke 'very freely' about the Kentucky Campaign," blaming Polk for his fail-ure to attack at Perryville, according to Captain Beatty. Bragg also claimed that "the council of war at Murfreesboro advised a retreat a full 24 hours be-fore it was made."[4]

The Mississippi Influence

As Bragg continued to rehash bygone campaigns and Johnston struggled to regain his health, matters deteriorated in Mississippi. On the evening of May 9, Johnston received a dispatch from the War Department ordering him to take 3,000 troops and proceed to Jackson, Mississippi. "I shall go im-mediately although unfit for service," he answered. The troops of Matthew Ector's and McNair's brigades of McCown's Division began boarding the boxcars. Taking the morning train on the tenth, the theater commander ar-rived in Jackson on the thirteenth. Frail and exhausted, he went to bed. Grant's army had gotten in the rear of Vicksburg and was on the march in the interior of the state. Jackson fell, and a merger of Johnston's and Pember-ton's forces never took place. It has been argued that if Johnston had left Tullahoma two weeks earlier with a division rather than a brigade, which he had full authority to do, the juncture would have been completed and Jack-son saved. Totally outgeneraled, Pemberton was defeated at Champion Hill on May 16 and at Big Black River on May 17. His army retreated behind the

Vicksburg defenses. Johnston could do little but attempt to gather an army and raise the siege.[5]

Johnston wrote Mackall, Bragg's new chief of staff, on June 7: "Give my regards to the General [Bragg]. Say that if he is tired of Tennessee I shall be happy to exchange with him." Bragg may not have been tired of Tennessee, but he was definitely tired of Johnston. Despite the support of the theater commander, Bragg mumbled to Quintard, "Doctor, he was kept here too long to watch me!" Bragg missed the point. Johnston had not been sent to watch him but to replace him; the general simply refused to cooperate.[6]

Earlier, Johnston had stated that absolutely no troops could be taken from Bragg's army without risking Tennessee. As he now attempted to assemble a piecemeal force at Jackson, he gladly received troops from Bragg. On May 22, President Davis, citing discouraging intelligence from Mississippi, pleaded with Bragg to send troops. Ordinarily the general would have balked, but he now saw an opening. This would be an opportunity to rid himself of his archenemy Breckinridge. The next day he replied that he would immediately return W. H. Jackson's borrowed cavalry division and begin loading three of Breckinridge's four brigades onto the railroad cars.[7]

Realizing that the Orphan Brigade did not relish another summer in the Deep South, Breckinridge received permission to swap it out with a Mississippi brigade. The Kentuckians, believing that this would be construed as them choosing Bragg over their commander, unanimously chose to go. "Where thou goest there we will also go," a member of the 9th Kentucky quoted from the book of Ruth. The Tennesseans in the division—Palmer's Brigade and the 20th Tennessee of Preston's Brigade—would remain. As Breckinridge spoke a few parting words to the 20th, the regiment that bore the flag made from his wife's wedding dress, he briefly lost his composure and broke down. He quickly wheeled about and rode off. A month later, the officers of the 20th sent their former division commander a new horse as a sign of their affection.[8] During May, Bragg thus lost 11,500 troops to Mississippi, and Roddey's Brigade was reassigned to the Florence–Muscle Shoals sector. Partially offsetting these losses were two brigades that arrived that spring. Henry D. Clayton's Alabama brigade, ordered up from Mobile, pulled into the Tullahoma depot on April 21. On May 19, Thomas Churchill's Brigade arrived, composed of Arkansas and Texas troops exchanged from their capture at Arkansas Post; they were not well received. "Who raised the white flag in Arkansas?" the old veterans were heard to yell. "We don't want you here if you can't see a Yank without holding up your shirt to him." Churchill was sent back to the Trans-Mississippi, and James Deshler

TABLE 5. *Troop departures and arrivals*

Units	Strength	Date
Departures		
McNair's Division (2 brigades)	2,789	May 10 and for several days
Roddey's Brigade	1,745	Mid-April
Jackson's Division (cavalry)	3,269	May 23 and for several days
Breckinridge's Division (3 brigades)	5,269	May 23 and for several days
Total	13,072	
Arrivals		
Clayton's Brigade	2,874	April 20
Churchill's Brigade	1,625	May 19
Total	4,499	
Net loss	8,573	

was given command. Rumor circulated that Cleburne was the only division commander who would have them.[9]

The departure of McCown's and Breckinridge's troops left Hardee only Cleburne's Division. A second division was organized under Brig. Gen. A. P. Stewart (his formal promotion to major general came on June 3), composed of four brigades. Stewart and Cleburne swapped Deshler's and Johnson's brigades. Stewart also received Clayton's Brigade, Brown's Brigade (formerly of Breckinridge's Division), and Bate's Brigade, the last of the hodge-podge of regiments from McCown's, Breckinridge's, and Cleburne's divisions.[10]

Historians have criticized Davis for drawing large contingents from the Army of Tennessee to reinforce Mississippi. By the end of May, Bragg's troop strength had been reduced to 37,000 infantry and artillery and 13,800 cavalry, a total of 50,800 present for duty. Yet Rosecrans's army had likewise faced losses for whatever reason—perhaps furloughs. His end-of-May strength stood at about 64,000. Despite all of the shifting of units on both sides, the numbers did not remain that far apart. Indeed, the percentage spread (26 percent) was slightly better than what Bragg had faced at Stones River. The criticism of the administration, from a strictly numerical view, is thus unjustified. The fact that Johnston did nothing with the reinforcements he received was more the issue.[11]

Despite the rumble of troop trains departing for Mississippi, life went on as usual at Shelbyville. On May 12, Bragg, accompanied by Urquhart, Josiah

Stoddard Johnston, and Lt. Francis S. Parker Jr., took the 10:00 A.M. train from Tullahoma, arriving at Shelbyville at 1:00. Another review was held, but something occurred that made this one unusual. Polk dismounted in front of the 4th Tennessee and asked to see the color-bearer. Sgt. Thomas G. Oakley, about twenty years old, stepped forward. At Stones River, he had distinguished himself by advancing the colors ten paces ahead of the regiment under fire. Polk removed his gloves and said, "I must shake hands with you." He then raised his cap to the regiment and said, "I am proud to uncover in the presence of so gallant a man." The Tennesseans gave a resounding cheer.[12]

Hoover's Gap

On June 20, 1863, Bragg wrote Elise that he was "better than I have been for a month." Nine days later and a week into the Tullahoma Campaign, his luck ran out. According to Liddell, Bragg's chronic diarrhea returned, sapping him of all energy. On July 1, Hardee informed Polk, "I deeply regret to see General Bragg in his present enfeebled state of health." Quintard saw him on the second and commented about his obvious frail condition. "Yes, I am utterly broken down," the army commander answered.[13]

During the final week of June, Hardee's Corps occupied the Wartrace sector and Polk's Corps Shelbyville, with the army supply base at Tullahoma. Forrest's cavalry held Spring Hill on the left, Wharton's the center, and Martin's the right. Historians have varied widely in their estimates of the strengths of the opposing forces in the nine-day Tullahoma Campaign. A fair estimate for Bragg was 37,634 infantry and artillery and 9,107 cavalry (Wheeler 5,300 and Forrest 3,807), for a total of 46,741. Rosecrans counted 58,993 infantry and artillery and 9,960 cavalry, totaling 68,953. Even Lee would have had his hands full with such a disparity, and Bragg was no Lee.[14]

On June 5, Hardee broke away from his social life long enough to communicate with Bragg. Whether or not Rosecrans intended to advance, "we should be prepared to meet it." Hardee was clearly opposed to holding Hoover's Gap—it could be easily flanked by way of Bradyville, and if the enemy broke through Liberty Gap they would be between Stewart and Cleburne. "If you wish to dispute the passage of Hoover's Gap, the brigade [Bate's] ought to remain; otherwise it ought to be brought nearer to Wartrace." Hardee understood that the battle was to be fought at Tullahoma, but if elsewhere, "other dispositions should be made." Unfortunately, Bragg's response is not extant, but Hardee's dispatch reveals much. After four months of inactivity and with less than three weeks before active campaigning, Bragg's plans had either not been fully developed or not clearly commu-

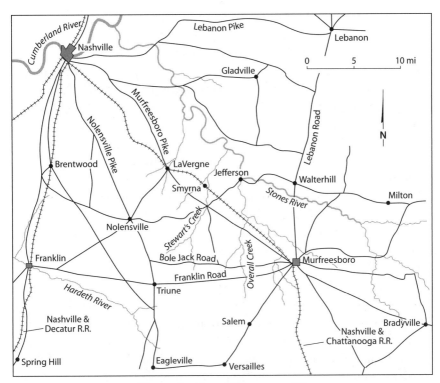

Map 3. Southeast Tennessee, 1863

nicated. Since no changes in deployment were subsequently made, it may be concluded that Bragg desired to hold Hoover's Gap, but to what extent is not known. Hardee made it clear that he was not even certain that Bragg still intended to fight at Tullahoma.[15]

Rosecrans began his advance on June 22 along a broad front, feinting on Bragg's left and making his real thrust on his right center at Hoover's and Liberty Gaps. Both Johnston and Bragg had anticipated such a move since March. Richard Brewer and Julian D. Alford, in their army and marine staff rides of the Tullahoma Campaign, nonetheless insisted that Bragg took the bait hook, line, and sinker. Two times in March and once in April, Rosecrans had conducted strong reconnaissance movements on Bragg's left, and intelligence indicated that Rosecrans would not get far from his communications. Bragg thus became convinced that the feint (8,000 cavalry under David Stanley and 6,700 infantry under Gordon Granger) was the actual movement. He remained "completely fooled and confused," believing that Rosecrans was moving in force through Guy's Gap directly on Shelbyville.[16]

Such a view is traditional—others have stated as much—but there is not a shred of evidence to draw such a conclusion. There are no Bragg dispatches in the *Official Records* or in the Bragg papers during this time frame. Additionally, Brent took sick leave and his diary was blank for this period. What the thinking was at army headquarters is simply not known. The only contemporary document is a letter written on June 25 by "a friend" of the *Mobile Advertiser & Register* who was in Shelbyville—almost certainly a soldier. He wrote, "Yesterday [24th] the Yanks made an advance on the Unionville pike with 8,000 men, consisting of infantry, artillery and cavalry, but it was *merely a reconnaissance with the view of foraging* [italics his]." This letter obviously indicated that Bragg was *not* fooled by the feint.[17]

Historians have criticized Wheeler for deploying a disproportionate number of his troopers on the left, leaving the gaps of the Highland Rim largely unprotected and Bragg in the dark. Martin's Division was indeed shifted from the right to reinforce Forrest's Division at Spring Hill. This move, on June 22, was made under the direct orders of Bragg, who was planning another senseless raid on Rosecrans's rear. David Powell criticized the entire affair as ill conceived. The Federal supply points were "well-garrisoned and likely to be immune to any attack." Additionally, the shift deprived the army right of "an all-important cavalry screen."[18]

On the morning of June 24, in the midst of a drenching rain, Col. John T. Wilder's 1,500-man "Lightning Brigade," armed with Spencer rifles, came charging into four-mile-long Hoover's Gap. To his credit, Bate checked the enemy advance two miles south of the gap, but attempts to dislodge the Federals proved costly. The Southerners lost 146 casualties (twice that of Wilder) of 700 engaged. Who was to blame for the loss of Hoover's Gap? A. P. Stewart's Division covered the sector, but according to "Huntsville," perhaps a Stewart staff officer, in an article in the *Chattanooga Daily Rebel*, "Old Straight" was not at fault. The Tennessean had only been in command of his division for a week. All of the infantry had been withdrawn from the gap *before* his arrival, and he had not been ordered to reoccupy it. Precisely what instructions did Hardee get from army headquarters? The evidence is inconclusive.[19]

Woodworth praised Rosecrans for his "flawless execution" and criticized Bragg for "not keeping more force up at the gaps." He nonetheless acknowledged Bragg's dilemma. If he kept a brigade at all three of the gaps (and another brigade to relieve each of them), he would have insufficient force to contest a flanking maneuver. Additionally, if Rosecrans had moved as slowly from Murfreesboro to the gaps as he had from Nashville to Murfreesboro (only slightly farther), Bragg would have had enough time to react. What had previously taken days, however, on this occasion took only fifteen hours.[20]

Alternatives?

Six miles west of Hoover's Gap lay Liberty Gap, which Rosecrans simultaneously attacked with Richard Johnson's Union division at 1:00 P.M. on June 24. Liddell's Brigade of Cleburne's Division guarded both sides of the gap with the 13th/15th Arkansas and 5th Arkansas, together 540 men, backed by two guns of Swett's Mississippi battery. The Rebels withdrew to a second position at Liberty Church on the Liberty Pike north of Wartrace Creek. At night, they again fell back south of the creek. Both gaps were now in Union hands, but the fighting had been intense and the Yankees had been unable to break out and exploit their gains.[21]

That night, Cleburne dispatched S. A. M. Wood's Brigade to Bell Buckle. On June 25, Col. Daniel Govan's 2nd Arkansas repulsed an enemy sortie. Govan urged Liddell to abandon the position, but he answered: "No, hold on. I must obey the orders, whatever my own views or opinions are, and I will stay there until ordered or forced away." The regiment was nonetheless eventually withdrawn. That night, Cleburne ordered three of Wood's regiments and a section of Semple's Battery forward in support of Liddell.[22]

The issue of the gaps raised serious questions. Why was Liberty Gap occupied by Rebel infantry and Hoover's Gap not? Why was Liddell under the impression that he should hold at all hazards? Ultimately, defense of the gaps made no difference, since Rosecrans simply flanked them with Thomas Crittenden's 21st Corps by marching southeast to Bradyville, beyond the Rebel picket line, and taking Manchester in the rear—precisely as Hardee had predicted nineteen days earlier. The maneuver underscored the weakness of the Highland Rim position. It also pointed to the fact that, as at Murfreesboro, even though Bragg had occupied the terrain for an extended period, he had no clearly developed strategy.

Either through negligence or some grand but poorly communicated design, Bragg had forfeited the gaps. According to Woodworth, however, all was not lost. The Army of the Cumberland was having difficulty "deploying its superior numbers in the narrow gaps." Even if George Thomas's corps broke out, it would still have to negotiate narrow Matt's Hollow. If Hardee could detain Thomas's corps long enough, Bragg might be able to prepare a trap. On June 26, the army commander summoned Polk. He ordered him to take his corps that night up the Murfreesboro Road through Guy's Gap. By dawn of the twenty-seventh, he would be in position to turn east and attack Crittenden's corps in Liberty Gap, while Hardee pressed Thomas in Hoover's Gap. Polk immediately balked at the "heavy cedar growth, and the peculiar topography" and argued that "the position he was about being thrown in [was] nothing short of a man-trap." Bragg nonetheless cut the order.

The attack never came off, because Bragg received word on the afternoon of June 26 that the Federals held the Manchester Pike. He thus aborted his plan. But would it have worked? By comparing projected moves with actual subsequent events, Steven Woodworth concluded that the plan could absolutely have been accomplished. Even with delays in marching, Polk could have been through Guy's Gap and in position to turn east by sunrise of the twenty-seventh. Three miles north of the gap, at Christiana (north of Foster-ville), Polk would have encountered 8,000 Union cavalry and 6,700 infantry commanded by Gordon Granger. Contact would probably not have been made until around 10:00 A.M. According to Woodworth, Polk would probably have left one of his eight brigades at Bell Buckle Gap, which would have deterred Granger, while Confederate cavalry could have held the blue horsemen at bay. This meant that Polk's Corps could have been in position at Liberty Gap by midafternoon. What would it have found? Only two Union brigades. Rosecrans ordered Crittenden to disengage and "swing over to join the concentration for the big push out of Hoover's Gap." Even if Polk had detached another brigade to guard from incursions from Hoover's Gap, he still would have had six brigades to attack two—"the result would almost undoubtedly have been the destruction or rout of the Federals." Such a move would have forced Rosecrans to retreat, and the result would have been "hailed as a great Confederate victory and rightly so." Woodworth concluded that Bragg's plan "had the realistic potential to produce a major victory."[23]

Such a conclusion leaves many unanswered questions. Would Polk have followed through with such an audacious move, a move that he had argued against, or at the last moment, would he simply have ignored Bragg's plan as he had at Perryville under the veil of changed circumstances? Woodworth's conclusion also assumes that Rosecrans was static and could not have changed his plan. Surely his scouts would have detected Polk's column. One of Thomas's divisions could have blocked Hardee's Corps at Hoover's Gap, while Crittenden and three of Thomas's divisions reversed march and attacked Polk. Also, what would have happened if Granger had overwhelmed the hypothetical single brigade at Bell Buckle Gap or mauled the rear of Polk's column as it moved on Liberty Gap? What if Granger had joined Crittenden and Thomas in an assault on Polk? There were too many movable parts to this scheme to conclude precisely what would have occurred. Bragg would discover that plans with too many complexities, such as those at McLemore's Cove in September 1863, could easily collapse. Such may have been the fate of Bragg's Tullahoma plan.[24]

The night of July 26, Bragg ordered the army to fall back and concentrate at Tullahoma. He explained to the War Department that "the line of Shelbyville [was] too long to be held successfully by my force." Such a conclusion could have been determined months earlier. The indefensible length of "the line of Shelbyville" was patently obvious. A division, or reinforced division, could have been kept at Shelbyville to protect the Shelbyville-Columbia food-producing region, reinforced with Forrest's and Wheeler's cavalry. Morgan could have protected the right, rather than galloping on another glory-seeking raid, which in this instance resulted in the capture of his entire command. Placing Polk's entire corps at a position so far from the vital sector—the Tullahoma-Manchester-McMinnville line—resulted in a weakened center and right.[25]

In the early afternoon of June 27, Stanley's cavalry began its drive toward Shelbyville, a scout reporting a Yankee column "as far as the eye could see." Martin's Division gave a stout rearguard defense, but the 1,200 troopers could not hold against 8,000. The Yankee cavalry swept over the earthworks outside of town, routing Martin's men. A fight ensued in town, with the Rebels making their last stand on a hill behind the railroad station. Many fell captive, and the rest stampeded toward the Skull Camp Bridge over Duck River. A number of men, Wheeler included, jumped their horses twenty feet into the river and swam for safety. Wheeler escaped, but at least twenty men drowned or were shot. The Federals claimed 509 prisoners, which may not be an exaggeration—the 51st Alabama Cavalry alone lost 105 men in downtown Shelbyville. Three guns from Wiggins's Battery were also taken.[26]

With Bragg digging in for a stand at Tullahoma, Rosecrans suddenly struck the railroad in his rear. At 8:00 P.M. on June 28, Wilder's brigade, his horses having swum the swollen Elk River, hit Decherd, on the railroad fourteen miles south of Tullahoma. The brigade was met by twenty-six fiercely determined men of the 2nd Tennessee and a local telegraph operator and a railroad engineer who had "nothing better to do" and joined them. Fighting from a stockade and a railroad cut, the defenders held back Wilder's 1,500 Spencer-toting troopers until the bluecoats brought up their artillery and drove them into the woods. The depot and water tank, a local bake shop, and 100 yards of track were destroyed, the latter repaired by the Rebels within three hours. The *Chattanooga Daily Rebel* declared the raid "a farce." The next day, the Southerners occupied Decherd in force.[27]

According to historian Keith Poulter, Bragg was fortunate that Rosecrans had not been more daring. The Northern commander lost sight of the "critical target," the Elk River Bridge at Estill Springs. Had Rosecrans taken Brig. Gen. John Turchin's cavalry division and Wilder's brigade, together some 7,000 horsemen, and used them as a deep, penetrating strike force, the bridge could have been captured and held until supporting infantry arrived. Michael Bradley countered that such a plan was impractical, since the Elk had at least six crossing points over a wide distance: an unnamed ford, Morris Ferry, Bethpage Bridge, the road and railroad bridges at Estill Springs, Rock Creek Ford, and Winchester Springs. As a counter to his counter, however, Confederate dispatches indicated that the heavy rains had made the fords impassable, leaving only Estill Springs (the bridge was actually at Allisonia) and Bethpage Bridge. Wilder did in fact attempt to capture the Allisonia Bridge by riding north of Decherd, but it was too late. From atop a mountain Wilder's horsemen spotted "a considerable force of infantry and cavalry." What they in fact detected was not only Walthall's Brigade, which was guarding the bridge, but also the lead elements of Buckner's Corps from Knoxville, which arrived at an opportune moment. Wilder attempted to break the track to the south at Tantelon and even farther south at Anderson, but three troop trains were spotted at the former and two at the latter; he abandoned the mission and escaped by moving east.[28]

Monday, June 29, dawned warm and cloudy. With the Yankees barely six miles from Tullahoma, the Confederate troops expected an attack. At 7:00 A.M., Lt. Towson Ellis arrived at army headquarters and notified the army chieftain that the enemy was approaching in line of battle on three roads. At 8:00, Polk was ordered to advance his corps to a preselected line. The only thing that came, however, was more heavy rain, which continued on and off throughout the day. The men back at Tullahoma continued strengthening the trenches, even as the ditches were filled "nearly half full of water."[29]

At 9:00 A.M., Polk went to army headquarters, at which time Bragg informed him of Wilder's raid at Decherd the night before. Bragg nonetheless remained committed to a battle at Tullahoma. On the way back to his corps, Polk encountered Hardee, who thought Bragg's decision was ill advised. At 3:00, the corps commanders arrived at army headquarters by appointment. Asked his opinion, Polk said he believed that communications had to be immediately reestablished. Bragg assured him that the railroad track had already been repaired. "How do you propose to maintain them [communications]?" the bishop asked. "By posting cavalry along the line," Bragg answered. Polk was convinced that there was insufficient cavalry to guard both the railroad and the flanks and that the troopers would be driven off within thirty-six hours. The army would then be forced to retreat across the Tennessee River to Huntsville. The men would have to be dispersed in the mountains of northern Alabama to avoid starvation. "That is all very well, but what do you distinctly propose to have done?" Bragg queried. Withdraw toward Chattanooga and without any delay, Polk answered. "Then you propose that we shall retreat?" asked Bragg. "I do," Polk replied, "and that is my counsel." Hardee was not as panicked. He suggested that infantry support the cavalry at various locations along the line. Bragg concurred and ordered that earthworks be thrown up at various vulnerable locations south of Tullahoma. The amazing aspect of the conference was that possible scenarios had not been discussed two months earlier.[30]

As Bragg prepared for battle on the thirtieth, word arrived that a Union column 10,000 strong (the spearhead of Crittenden's corps) was making a wide sweep around his right, in the vicinity of Hillsboro. Clearly rattled, Bragg ordered a withdrawal to Allisonia. Polk was on the road by 7:00 P.M., followed by Hardee on a different road. Bragg arrived at Allisonia at 5:00 A.M. on July 1. If he had remained just one more day at Tullahoma, argued Steven Woodworth, Rosecrans had plans to assault him. "If the Army of Tennessee could not have prevailed in those circumstances, then it might as well have given up and gone home," Woodworth concluded. Bragg nonetheless did right by retreating; he never should have planned a battle at Tullahoma in the first place. Should a stand be made at the Elk River or Cowan? Bragg's lieutenants, afraid of the army chieftain's frail condition, advised Cowan, and it was done. The campaign was effectively over, and Middle Tennessee lost without a major battle.[31]

Earl Hess admitted that it was a mistake to give up so much territory without a fight: "The Army of Tennessee could have taken up a good position at the Elk River." Bragg's failure to do so reflected the fact that he "was losing his power to make hard decisions on his own, relying too much on men who had demonstrated that they did not have his best interests in mind." While true, Bragg cannot escape culpability for his failure to strategize about various scenarios with his lieutenants weeks earlier. In defense of Polk and Hardee, they were handed a plan at the last moment over which they had no ownership. At the Battle of Stones River, Bragg had at least strategized with the corps commanders prior to the battle. At Tullahoma they got no such respect.[32]

The retreat proved grueling. Writing in the company log of Lumsden's Battery on June 30, a scribe noted: "Men and horses completely worn out from fatigue and loss of sleep. Got to Alisonia about 5 P.M. Remained hitched and ready to leave all night. Bragg ordered all wagons to shed 800 pounds to cross the [Cumberland] plateau." Writing the same day, Taylor Beatty noted: "The enemy is still advancing & skirmishing is going on—but the battle can not come off until tomorrow if so early. The ground is very wet and low & artillery will not be of much use to them unless they wait till it dries out." Whether or not Bragg actually intended to make a stand at Cowan is not known. By 4:00 P.M. on July 2, he had ordered a retreat—Polk to Bridgeport and Hardee to Sewanee. The army staff arrived at Southern University (today's University of the South) at 2:00 A.M. on July 3. At 4:00 P.M., Bragg departed and camped that night six miles from the university. The next day, he established army headquarters at Bridgeport. Wharton fought a rearguard action on the morning of July 4. The engagement became so fierce that Clayton's Brigade had to be sent back to end the pursuit. Crossing a pontoon bridge at Shellmound, the army slowly trudged into Chattanooga over the next couple of days. Hundreds were sick, and 1,000 deserted from Polk's Corps along the way. The bishop claimed that recruits picked up along the way meant that the army arrived at its destination with a net gain of 400—a report difficult to believe.[33]

Estimating Confederate casualties during the brief campaign is problematic due to spotty reporting. Casualties can be placed at a minimum of 350, and the Union provost tallied the capture of 1,634 Rebels, with 616 of those being deserters. Bushrod Johnson's Brigade alone sustained 36 casualties and 335 deserters. A fair estimate of losses would likely be in the range of 2,500, as compared to 570 Union casualties.[34]

A pall spread across the army over the loss of Middle Tennessee. Coupled with the surrender of Vicksburg on July 4 and revised reports of what actually occurred at Gettysburg, morale plummeted. "This news [Vicksburg] causes a depression of spirits in the whole army. . . . From Virginia the news is less cheering than at first—we do not claim a victory at Gettysburg and our army is falling back rapidly," an artilleryman wrote. T. H. Bostick of the 4th Tennessee felt "extremely mortified at giving up so much of the state with so little resistance, but all feeling on the subject was absorbed in the greater disaster sustained in the fall of Vicksburg." Lieutenant Colonel Walker lamented to his wife: "Instead of a glorious but hard fought victory we have had an inglorious but necessary Retreat. Bragg will again be censured by the country for failing to do what was impossible—not only for him, but for the greatest general of the age had he been in his place." Isaiah Harlan expressed concern about the political ramifications: "Lincoln has always been determined to prosecute it [war] to the bitter end and I am afraid that a few [more] successes will unit[e] the whole north in in his support." Arch McLaurin of the 7th Mississippi told his sister that there was "a great deal of dissatisfaction in the army here at this time; the most of the Boys think that the Confederacy is gone; I myself think it is a doubtful case." The fall of Vicksburg, thought an Alabamian, proved to be a paralyzing blow: "The future does indeed look dark and gloomy." To a private in the 18th Alabama, it appeared as though the men were "whipt all out of heart they don't put much confidence in the general, Bragg." Realizing the magnitude of the loss, Bragg whispered to Quintard, "This is a great disaster."[35]

❋13❋

Missed Opportunities
All Were Misled

On August 21, 1863, Federal cavalry and artillery opened fire on Chatta-nooga from atop unoccupied Stringer's Ridge. The stunned Rebels with-drew a mile from town, leaving the city in a no-man's-land. That evening, Bragg, still frail and sickly, returned from the Cherokee Springs hospital and established his headquarters at the Reese Brabson Mansion on Fifth Street. Reports had been arriving all day detailing an enemy advance from the east and northeast. Brent took pen in hand: "News has been received of the advance of the enemy on many fronts viz Stevenson, Huntsville, Bridge-port, Jasper, Dunlap, and Pikeville." The most serious concern remained the right wing, where Burnside was clearly maneuvering into East Tennes-see, presumably in a pincer movement with Rosecrans's left, thus separat-ing Buckner at Knoxville from Bragg. After leaving a brigade at Cumberland Gap and another at Saltville, Buckner could muster a movable force of only 7,000–8,000 infantry and cavalry against Burnside's estimated 30,000 (later lowered to 25,000) and Rosecrans's left wing.[1]

The Army of Tennessee remained widely scattered: Cheatham's Divi-sion and Jackson's Brigade were at Chattanooga; Anderson's Brigade, at Bridgeport; Walthall's Brigade, at Atlanta; Hill's Corps, at Tyner's Station and Chickamauga Station; Johnson's Brigade, at Loudon; Wood's Brigade, at Harrison; and Hindman's Division (two brigades), on the west side of Lookout Mountain. The cavalry was even more dispersed: Forrest's Corps was at Kingston; Roddey's Brigade, at Tuscumbia; Wheeler's headquarters, at Gadsden; Wharton's Division, at Rome; and Martin's Division, at Alex-andria, Alabama. The entire force numbered only 33,000 infantry and artil-lery and 11,000 cavalry. Even with Buckner's 7,000, it was no match for the 90,000 Yankees believed to be bearing down on them. Johnston dispatched two of his divisions from Mississippi, something that had previously been discussed and should have already been done.[2]

On August 24, Buckner began concentrating at Loudon to secure a junc-ture with Bragg if necessary. Unfolding events brought only more confusion. "Movements of the enemy are still in nubilous. The river and mountains afford a safe and secure screen [for the enemy]," Brent wrote. Bragg remained fixated on the crossings northeast of Chattanooga, specifically the forty-mile Tennessee River stretch between Harrison's Landing and Blythe's Ferry upriver, the latter at the mouth of the Hiwassee River. Stewart, whose division covered half of the sector, believed that Rosecrans would cross at the mouth of Chickamauga Creek, which was held by a portion of Brown's Brigade, with Bate's Brigade in support. Brig. Gen. Henry Clayton, commanding one of Hill's brigades, guessed Washington as the crossing. Buckner speculated the move would come north of the Hiwassee. Intelligence remained sparse; it was anyone's guess.[3]

In light of subsequent events, Bragg has been criticized for not being more cognizant of his left. In truth, he did precisely the right thing given the information that he had at the time. With only 33,000 infantry and artillery, he could not be strong everywhere. The question now pertained to where he could be weak. If he had gambled on his left and blocked Rosecrans's subsequent crossings, the Northern general could always have turned the upriver feint into the main crossing. Polk's Corps, guarding some of the closer crossings on the left, reported only minor activity. The chance that Rosecrans would break away from his railroad communication and venture into the mountainous terrain of North Georgia seemed remote. Besides, any Union approach south of Chattanooga would have to negotiate Lookout Mountain. The mountain was not just the 2,400-foot northeastern tip towering over Chattanooga but also a narrow plateau that stretched 100 miles from Chattanooga to Gadsden, cut by several gaps; control of the gaps meant control of the mountain. The money was on an upriver crossing.[4]

The morning rain cleared early on Tuesday, August 25. By day's end, Buckner's cavalry was in communication with the two infantry brigades that had marched into Loudon, thirty miles south of Knoxville, where the East Tennessee forces concentrated. Burnside continued his advance on the twenty-sixth. "He [Rosecrans] must be waiting until Burnside's movement is unmasked and then possibly moving by his left effect a juncture with Burnside and cross above here [Chattanooga]," Brent surmised. At 9:00 on August 27, Federal batteries once again shelled Chattanooga; a four-hour barrage resulted in several casualties. Bragg, still convinced of an upriver Federal crossing, loaded Stewart's Division onto the cars of the East Tennessee & Georgia Railroad to proceed ninety miles to Loudon. Bushrod Johnson's Brigade marched to Charleston in order to protect the railroad bridge over the Hiwassee. Henceforth Stewart would report to Buckner.[5]

Polk joined Bragg and Hill in believing that the danger was to the army's right wing. On August 27, he explained to his wife: "We think Rosecrans is moving up the river to make his attempt to cross *above* Chattanooga, but his plans are as yet not developed. He has not crossed at Bridgeport and I think will not, nor at any other place below Chattanooga. He [Rosecrans] will wish to cross where, when he gets over, he will find no mountain obstructing him." Although reports of activity around Bridgeport filtered in, the *Chattanooga Daily Rebel* dismissed them as nothing more than "small parties of cavalry." On the night of the twenty-eighth, scouts reported Rosecrans's headquarters to be at Stevenson, with the bulk of his army between there and Jasper. Brent dismissed it: "Doubtful. Don't think he means to sever himself from Burnside." On the same day, an "old citizen" reported Rosecrans's headquarters to be at Jasper, with his army moving up the Sequatchie Valley.[6]

Officers began to question why Bragg did not attack either Rosecrans's left wing (Crittenden's 21st Corps) or Burnside's army before they united. "If we could cross the river and strike a blow now we could whip them separately," Buckner wrote on August 25. At army headquarters, Brent asked in his journal on the twenty-eighth, "Should not we concentrate and move rapidly on Burnside, even if we give up Chattanooga, and crush him before Rosecrans could come up?"[7]

With Stewart's Division and Buckner's infantry (William Preston's Division) at Loudon, Hill continued to command the thirty-seven-mile sector of the Tennessee River between the mouth of Chickamauga Creek and the mouth of the Hiwassee River. Cleburne's Division guarded Harrison's Landing. Bragg suggested that Hill place a division opposite Harrison and retain Clayton's Brigade at Blythe's Ferry, Liddell's Brigade at Dalton, and "a good force" at Charleston. Polk was ordered to send Hindman's Division, at McFarland's Springs, to the mouth of Chickamauga Creek, near Hill's headquarters. Manigault found Hill to be "very apprehensive" about his position. Only the river separated his pickets from those of the enemy, and they occasionally swam to the middle and conversed with one another. Bragg related to Hill: "It is said to be easy to defend a mountainous country, but mountains hide your foe from you, while they are full of gaps through which he can pounce upon you at any time. A mountain is like the wall of a house full of rat-holes. The rat lies hidden at his hole, ready to pop out when no one is watching. Who can tell what lies behind that wall," he said pointing to the Cumberland Mountains.[8]

At 10:00 A.M. on a bright and cold August 29, the Yankees shelled Chattanooga for an hour, landing thirty-eight shells. At Bragg's headquarters, Brent privately noted: "The position of the enemy and his designs unknown. Hill thinks he [Rosecrans] will try to cross at Harrison." Scouts reported Critten-

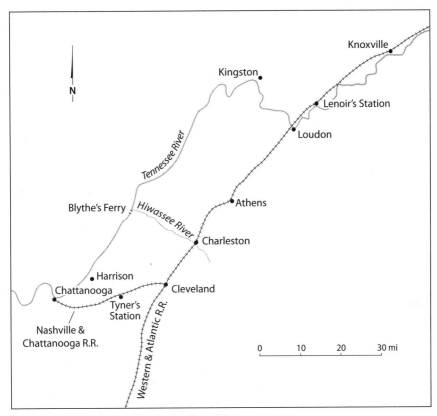

Map 4. East Tennessee, 1863

den's headquarters at Dunlap, his corps and Thomas's inching toward Washington Ferry. One of McCook's divisions remained at Murfreesboro, with the other two positioned between Stevenson and Bridgeport. The report made sense, both substantiating the main Union advance believed to be in the Sequatchie Valley and explaining Union sightings downriver. Even after the Battle of Chickamauga, Bragg continued to insist that Rosecrans's original plan had been "to strike the rear of General Buckner's command, while Burnside occupied him in front." He only changed his plan when Buckner and Stewart withdrew to join up with Bragg.[9]

Additional intelligence arrived that Saturday night that should have raised eyebrows. A Capt. P. H. Rice reported that an enemy brigade had crossed the Tennessee at both Shellmound and below Bridgeport and that Confederate cavalry had fallen back toward Trenton, Georgia. At 1:00 P.M. on the twenty-ninth, William Estes of the 3rd Confederate Cavalry wrote a dispatch, indicating that an enemy cavalry brigade had forded the Tennessee River ten miles below Bridgeport. "The move at Bridgeport is I think a feint. An effort will be made to cross above," thought Brent. The *Chattanooga Daily Rebel*, which obviously had a contact at army headquarters, reported the incident; the paper speculated about a raid between Chattanooga and Dalton. Interestingly, another event mentioned by the paper (but not by Brent) was that 20,000 Yankees were at Bellefonte on August 24, as reported by a civilian who had crossed the river in Alabama.[10]

On the surprisingly cold morning of August 30, Bragg belatedly ordered Buckner's and Stewart's divisions to withdraw and concentrate at Charleston behind the Hiwassee River. Pegram's cavalry would cover the retreat at Lenoir's Station. Before departing, the troopers burned the 900-foot-long East Tennessee & Georgia bridge, thus playing havoc with Burnside's future efforts in joining Rosecrans. Buckner, apparently thinking the order meant the commencement of Bragg's long-awaited offensive, wrote Forrest, "The movement is a general one, and we Tennesseans and Kentuckians will, I think, soon have an opportunity to strike for our homes." In analyzing Bragg's situation, the *Richmond Examiner* would later lament, "O for an hour of [Stonewall] Jackson!" It was not to be. Although Bragg continued to believe that the main Union thrust would occur on his right, a first strike seemed far from his mind. There can be only one logical conclusion—the army commander simply did not know what to do. A slight brush between enemy cavalry and pickets of the 19th Tennessee north of Trenton and west of Lookout Mountain proved to be the only action of the day. Although the force was "probably not large," according to Brent, Bragg nonetheless redirected Wharton's Division, on its way to join Hill, to La Fayette, Georgia. He continued to believe that Rosecrans intended to link up with Burnside and to that end shifted Hindman's Division behind Hill's Corps at Chickamauga Station.[11]

Thus far, Bragg was aware of only Yankee cavalry and small infantry forces on his left wing. At 2:00 A.M. on September 1, the general staff was abruptly awakened to chilling intelligence that would dramatically alter the narrative. I. P. Russell, a citizen of Stevenson, was returning home from a trip via Sand Mountain. From his vantage point, he could clearly see a large Federal force crossing at Caperton's Ferry, thirty-five miles below Chattanooga. Hill later added that the commands were identified as McCook's and Thomas's corps, which had been crossing since the twenty-ninth. If true, Trenton was clearly threatened.[12]

The primary blame for this stunning intelligence failure has been laid at the feet of Wheeler. For six weeks (mid-July to the end of August), he had kept Wharton's Division at Rome, Georgia, and Martin's at Alexandria, Alabama, sixty miles from Stevenson, to forage their jaded mounts and scour the countryside for fresh horses. Bragg himself characterized the cavalry as "much reduced and enfeebled by long service on short rations." A general review of Harrison's Brigade was held on August 5, followed by a barbecue hosted by a large number of ladies from Rome. Yet, an inspection by Mackall on August 28 resulted in a warning to the army commander: "Inspection of Wheeler's cavalry shows it worse than even we thought." The next day, when Wharton's troopers were ordered to Chattanooga, the Texan wrote Hill that his was "really the only division of Wheeler fit for the field," an obvious reference to Martin's command.[13]

The cavalry corps was unquestionably in a wretched condition, but Wheeler had advanced only two regiments (500 men) to watch over ninety miles of the Tennessee River. His actions would attract the censure of modern historians. Equal condemnation should be placed upon Forrest. He had several days to penetrate the Union screen between Harrison's Landing and Blythe's Ferry. Had he done so, Bragg would have discovered only two Yankee cavalry brigades (Minty's and Wilder's) and two infantry brigades (William Hazen's and George D. Wagner's), which had been intentionally creating a ruckus that was nothing more than a feint. If Bragg had crossed the Tennessee during the night of the twenty-seventh or twenty-eighth via several of the eight ferries and fords in Hill's sector, he might well have bagged the two infantry brigades before Crittenden came up in support with his corps.[14]

Division and corps commanders assembled at Bragg's headquarters at noon on September 2. Confirmed intelligence now placed the enemy's main force sixty miles below Chattanooga. Liddell, as junior division commander, spoke first. He suspected that Rosecrans had two corps below Chattanooga and one above. "You don't think Rosecrans so incautious as to take such a step?" Polk asked. "Yes, I feel satisfied that he will for he must have lost all caution after having flanked us so easily out of Middle Tennessee," Liddell imprudently responded, evoking a slight smile on the bishop's face. Hill continued to advocate for an offensive into Middle Tennessee, but Bragg stood to pronounce the idea "absurd." Two days later, Brent noted that although Hill favored the offensive, "he has no specific plan of operations." Bragg also asked for opinions on attacking the two Union corps to the south. Liddell opposed the idea, arguing that they would simply withdraw over the Tennessee River, while Bragg lost Chattanooga to Crittenden's corps. The consensus was to await further developments. Only Wheeler kept silent during the council, and Bragg spoke to him privately. Liddell, who detested the cavalryman, fully believed that the army commander protected him from embarrassing himself with his "vague ideas." The conference, which amounted to nothing, adjourned.[15]

During this period of indecision, Bragg hastily reorganized his army to accommodate the incoming troops. On August 27, W. H. T. Walker's Division began arriving from Mississippi, followed on September 2 by Breckinridge's Division, together 9,000 troops. Bragg could have kept the two on-loan divisions together in a provisional corps, but command would have gone to the senior officer—Breckinridge; it was a nonstarter. Even if he had assigned Buckner's Division to the corps, Breckinridge still would have been senior by four months. The two divisions, if kept together, had to go to either Polk or Hill. In a rather odd fix, Bragg removed Stewart's Division from Hill and gave it to Buckner (the two divisions had been operating together) and gave Walker and Breckinridge to Hill. This meant that Buckner, an officer junior to Breckinridge, now commanded a provisional corps. The two new divisions should more logically have gone to Polk and Buckner's Division to Hill, putting four divisions in one corps and three in the other, thus avoiding an unwieldy three-corps structure. Forrest was also given command over his and Pegram's divisions. Further complicating the matter, Bragg subsequently formed a provisional division, comprised of Liddell's and Walthall's brigades, as Walthall was on provost duty in Atlanta. He also detached Walker's Division from Hill and, along with Liddell's new division, formed a reserve corps under Walker. Liddell was not happy, believing Walker to be a "crack-brained fire-eater, always captious or caviling about something." The resulting four-corps structure was strangely reminiscent of Albert Sidney Johnston's unwieldy and impracticable organization at Shiloh. Polk now had Cheatham and Hindman, Hill had Cleburne and Breckinridge, Buckner was assigned Stewart and Preston, and the reserve corps had Liddell and Walker.[16]

Finally convinced that two-thirds of the Federal army was south of Chattanooga moving on Trenton, Bragg determined to attack Crittenden's corps north of the city. To Buckner, who would lead the attack, he gave a challenge: "The crushing of this corps would give us a great victory and redeem Tennessee. Can you be the instrument to do it?" The problem would be getting the troops across the river fast enough. There were four fords between a point near Charleston and the mouth of the Hiwassee—Anderson's, Knox's, the Old Federal and Georgia Stock Road, and another ford fifteen miles above Charleston. Forrest said that he could use his troopers to help get the infantry across but artillery and wagons would be problematic. A few steamers and flats in the Hiwassee could possibly be used. The assault would presumably be made by Preston's, Stewart's, Cleburne's, Hindman's, and

Walker's divisions. Cleburne, although worried about getting the artillery across, favored the plan, hoping it could be carried out on September 6.[17]

The plan simply coalesced too late. Given that Buckner and Hill had been such strong advocates of an offensive, it seems incredible that a logistical plan had not already been devised. John Wyeth, a Forrest advocate, expressed his disgust in postwar years: "That was the end of it. Burnside was not within five days' march of aid. Crittenden, who could have been surrounded in twenty-four hours with three times his numbers, could not have received assistance within three days. . . . And yet the Confederate general [Bragg], able enough to see the grand opportunities, failed to take hold personally and force them to a successful result." Assuming that all five Southern divisions would have crossed, the odds would have given the Rebels a stunning advantage, with Crittenden's 15,000 infantry pitted against Bragg's 38,000. Wyeth, of course, assumed that Crittenden would have sat passively while a large Confederate force bore down on him, which may not have been the case. He nonetheless made his point.[18]

By September 5, Bragg knew of at least one Federal corps in Will's Valley fourteen miles from Trenton and of a reported Federal column at or near Summerville. Protégé or not, Wheeler's utter failure to block the passes of Sand Mountain and his lack of timely and accurate intelligence clearly grated the army commander. That day he sent a dispatch to the cavalryman, the intent and tone of which could not be missed. Wheeler was ordered to immediately advance into Will's Valley with his entire command and develop the enemy's strength and position at "all hazards." The preemptory order did not reach the Georgian until 1:00 P.M. on the sixth. In consultation with several of his officers, the cavalryman determined to follow the "spirit of the order" but not its literal wording. Wharton could not emerge from the Sand Mountain passes because they had previously been blocked with felled trees. Additionally, enemy pickets at the passes would put up a strong fight. Rome, meanwhile, would be uncovered. Wheeler claimed that he could learn just as much from his scouts atop Lookout Mountain as he could by storming into the valley. He would await further orders. Modern criticism aside, Wheeler for once was right. Indeed, what is often overlooked is that later that afternoon, Martin's troopers were pushed out of Alpine by Stanley's 6,000-man cavalry division, which captured a dozen Rebel prisoners in the process.[19]

Bragg, still unsure whether the turning movement in Will's Valley was a ruse, could no longer wait for verification; he could not take the risk of entrapment. On September 6, he ordered that Chattanooga prepare for evacuation. As at Tullahoma, Bragg had again been duped. He had many legitimate excuses, but the fact remained that Rosecrans had crossed the Tennessee

River completely unmolested, proving that no natural barrier could stop the Army of the Cumberland and that Chattanooga would be surrendered with hardly a shot fired. An opportunity to pounce upon Crittenden's corps with overwhelming numbers had likewise been squandered. Fortunately, Rosecrans remained widely dispersed and subject to being destroyed in detail.

McLemore's Cove

Chattanooga was evacuated on the eighth. Late on September 9, intelligence arrived that a column of Thomas's corps, estimated at 4,000–5,000, was driving in Rebel pickets at Stevens's Gap and was over Lookout Mountain into McLemore's Cove. Bragg immediately saw an opportunity to crush the column (James Negley's division) in a pincer move. At midnight, Hindman's Division (Polk's Corps) was verbally ordered to Davis's Crossroads in McLemore's Cove to attack the enemy's left flank from the north, while Cleburne's Division (Hill's Corps) attacked frontally from the east. There would thus be 15,500 attacking 4,000–5,000. Polk's remaining division (Breckinridge's) and Buckner's Corps deployed at Lee and Gordon's Mill to protect the rear and wagon trains from Crittenden's corps, which would undoubtedly be passing through Chattanooga in pursuit.[20]

McLemore's Cove was a six-to-nine-mile-wide cul-de-sac between Lookout Mountain and a spur called Pigeon Mountain, bisected by the east branch of Chickamauga Creek, with a few cultivated farms and, in places, dense woods. It was a place that would become infamous in the might-have-been history of the Army of Tennessee, along with Shiloh, in the late afternoon on the first day in 1862, and Spring Hill, Tennessee, in 1864. Connelly, in his *Autumn of Glory*, devoted almost as many pages to the incident as he did to the Battle of Stones River. Woodworth referred to it as "one of the most remarkable incidents of the war." The details proved complex — poorly written orders, intricate maneuvers, a supposedly sick general, incomplete intelligence, and vacillating leadership.[21]

When the plan of September 10 went afoul, due in part to Daniel H. Hill's faulty counsel, Bragg canceled Cleburne's approach from Dug Gap and called up Buckner's Corps from Lee and Gordon's Mill. The attack on the eleventh would now be on the Union flank with three divisions — Hindman's, Stewart's, and Preston's — 22,500 versus 5,000. In a confusing turn of events, Cleburne's Division was later again added to the plan. Hindman, disbelieving Bragg's assessment, thought that his army-size force, not Negley's division, was the one actually in jeopardy; he took no action.

What occurred on September 10–11 has been labeled by some historians as near mutiny on the parts of Hill and Hindman, but more likely it was simply confusion and incompetence. An opportunity to capture the enemy division was squandered, and the finger-pointing continued long after the war. Even if the plan had been properly executed, it is probable that a good portion of the Federals would have escaped; they subsequently expedited themselves from the cove with remarkable speed. Connelly and Hal Bridges, Hill's biographer, blamed Bragg for the debacle, but more recent historians, such as Hess, Robertson, and Woodworth, to some degree exonerate the army commander. Bragg's subordinates unquestionably failed him, but given the confusion on September 10, one is left wondering why the army commander did not take the two-hour ride from La Fayette to McLemore's Cove during the early morning hours of the eleventh and personally direct operations.[22]

Good news was on the horizon. Davis, on September 5, approved reinforcements for Bragg—John Bell Hood's and Lafayette McClaws's Divisions of James Longstreet's Corps. Burnside's capture of Knoxville prevented the most direct route, but John Clark's study points to the unreliability of the Virginia and East Tennessee Railroad at any rate, due to burned bridges and a dearth of locomotives. The alternate 950-mile trek went through Raleigh, North Carolina; Columbia, South Carolina; and Augusta, Georgia, to Atlanta, requiring seven to eleven days. Longstreet and five of his brigades would arrive in time to fight in the upcoming battle.[23]

✻ 14 ✻

Great Battle of the West
Chickamauga, the Battle Begins

Before dawn on September 19, Brig. Gen. John Pegram's 1,900-man cavalry brigade rode hard up the Jay's Mill Road from its encampment at Alexander's Bridge. Skirmishing erupted south of Jay's Mill, but the Federals (Dan McCook's brigade, according to prisoners) soon broke off the engagement and withdrew. Pegram's Brigade advanced slightly north and dismounted between the mill and the intersection of the Jay's Mill and Reed's Bridge Roads. A scouting party of the 1st Georgia Cavalry rode northwest up the Reed's Bridge Road for three-fourths of a mile and found nothing. As a precaution, the 10th Confederate Cavalry moved due west into the woods along an old logging trail. Much to the soldiers' surprise, they collided with the skirmish line of another enemy brigade. A cavalry charge was foolishly ordered and easily repulsed.[1]

Forrest, who arrived on the scene, called for reinforcements and determined to fight it out. David Powell believed this to be the first Confederate mistake of the day. "In hindsight it might have been wiser if Forrest had simply screened the Union advance to determine the intent of the enemy," he concluded. There is a counterargument. An enemy of unknown size had obviously overlapped Bragg's right flank a mile and a half to the north. The threat had to be immediately checked, not merely observed. On the other hand, if Forrest had withdrawn down the Jay's Mill Road, he would have constricted the Southern line and perhaps have drawn the Federals closer to Bragg's right. At 8:30 A.M., Wilson's 1,200-man brigade of Walker's Corps arrived and, advancing across the Brotherton Road, struck the Federal brigade (John T. Croxton's of the 14th Corps), but a counterattack drove the Georgians back. At 10:00, a fresh Union brigade (John King's, 14th Corps) charged through the northwest corner of Winfrey Field, striking Wilson in the flank and routing him.[2]

Matthew Ector's Brigade of Walker's Corps arrived on the scene at 9:15 A.M. and was directed by Forrest to the right, along the Reed's Bridge Road. Ector's Brigade, too, encountered an enemy brigade (Ferdinand Van Deveer's, 14th Corps), and after two failed assaults, Ector's troops fell back with heavy casualties—850 out of 1,750, according to a Huntsville news report. At 10:00, two Federal brigades (Van Deveer's and John T. Connell's) attacked Ector, got in his rear, and captured 138 men. As Ector's shattered brigade withdrew, George Dibbrell's cavalry brigade arrived and formed on Ector's right. The Tennessee troopers attempted to flank the enemy but were repulsed with slight casualties.[3]

The Confederates had picked a fight with the advance elements (five brigades) of George Thomas's 14th Corps, which resulted in the routing of both Ector and Wilson. Walker arrived on the scene and immediately ordered up Liddell's 4,000-man division from Alexander's Bridge. At 11:00, Liddell's two brigades swept across the Brotherton Road and routed the unsuspecting Federals, capturing 1,200 prisoners and three batteries. An 11:30 Union counterattack drove Liddell back and recaptured the guns, and by noon all four of Walker's wrecked brigades were essentially out of the fight.[4]

Bragg, at Thedford's Ford, reluctantly realized that his planned southward sweep toward Lee and Gordon's Mill might be falling apart. Three divisions (Preston's, Stewart's, and Johnson's), a half mile east of the La Fayette Road, and Hindman's Corps, opposite the mill—a total of 17,000 troops—had to be kept in position in case the original plan could be salvaged. A tempting one-mile gap existed in the Union center, protected only by Wilder's cavalry and a partial infantry brigade, but Bragg had to know more about the circumstances unfolding on the right. He sent Cheatham's 7,200-man division at Dalton's Ford north to support Walker in a desperate attempt to regain the intiative.[5]

The fight to the north was turning into a monster. Cheatham arrived at 12: 15, and not even having time to form a cohesive line, he committed his brigades piecemeal. The stunned Federals reeled as Cheatham's large division swept through Winfrey and Brock Fields. Eventually, the bluecoats formed a one-mile arc stretching from the Alexander's Bridge Road to the La Fayette Road, passing through the northern edge of Brock Field and curving back around the Brotherton Road. Repeated savage assaults failed to break the Union line. Although both Federal flanks were in the air, Cheatham, swinging northwesterly, simply lacked the strength to go around either. At 1:45, two fresh Union brigades (Horatio Van Cleve's division) arrived on the field, slammed into Marcus J. Wright's flank on Cheatham's left, and captured W. W. Carnes's Tennessee battery.

Cheatham committed his two reserve brigades (Strahl's and Maney's) to replace Preston Smith's and Jackson's. A Tennessean thought that Strahl's men fought at a great disadvantage: "Some old dry fences had taken fire and the wind blew the smoke in the faces of our men completely blinding them."

Strahl was now hit in the flank so hard it prompted a witness to say that he had never seen so many men fall in such a small area. Another Union division (Richard Johnson's) advanced on Maney's Brigade, nearly surrounding it. The Yankees swept around Cheatham's flank, only to be checked by the massed fire of William Turner's, John Scogin's, and Gustave Huwald's batteries. The fierce fighting chewed up Cheatham's Division, which sustained 1,700 casualties, but in the end, it held. Had the division collapsed, the Federals could have gotten in Bragg's rear via Alexander's Bridge or rolled up the entire Confederate right flank.[6]

As a gap developed on Cheatham's right, Bragg called up A. P. Stewart's Division of Buckner's Corps from its reserve position near the Thedford farm. Henry Clayton's 1,446-man Alabama brigade clawed through the thickets to an area near Carnes's abandoned guns, where it smashed into Van Cleve's two brigades. An hour-long exchange ensued, in which Clayton lost 400 men, over half of them from the 18th Alabama. His brigade's ammunition exhausted, Clayton withdrew. John C. Brown's 1,340 Tennesseans replaced the Alabamians, and their charge routed Van Cleve's two brigades and drove them back almost to the La Fayette Road, when Brown was struck by the 75th Indiana in his right flank and almost simultaneously by a Union brigade (John King's) in his left. Brown's men stumbled back through the woods with heavy losses.[7]

Bushrod Johnson's Division extended Stewart's line to the south. At 2:45, Johnson's front line was suddenly struck by a Federal brigade (Hans Heg's) advancing east of the La Fayette Road. Hood, desiring to swing around the southern Federal flank, ordered Johnson to wheel right, but he was already heavily engaged. On his own authority, Hood ordered Jerome Robertson's Texas brigade of Evander M. Law's Division, Army of Northern Virginia, to wheel right of Johnson. One of the Texans was heard to shout to Johnson's men as they passed, "Rise up Tennessee, and see Texas go in." After a brief encounter with Federal artillery and Wilder's Spencer rifles, Robertson's Brigade reeled to the rear. As the brigade returned, a wag shouted, "Rise up Tennessee, and see Texas come out!"[8]

At 4:00, Stewart renewed his assault. William "Fighting Billy" Bate's Brigade on the right swept northwest across the Brotherton Road. By 5:00, 300 of Bate's men, straddling the La Fayette Road, made it to Poe Field east of the road, where they were mauled by twenty concentrated guns. Clayton's and John S. Fulton's brigades advanced 900 yards northeast of the Widow Glenn House. The attack stalled, and by 6:00 the Confederates had still not taken possession of the La Fayette Road, although a portion of James Sheffield's Brigade and others actually crossed the road but withdrew.[9]

Late that afternoon, Liddell attempted to convince Patrick Cleburne, whose division had not yet been engaged, to attack. Harvey Hill eventually gave the order, at which time Liddell said, "General [Cleburne], I hope you will be quick, for a moment now will be worth an hour tomorrow." The Irishman nonetheless "took his time," according to Liddell, taking a half hour to deploy. The three brigades, some 5,380 strong, stretched for a mile. Passing through Liddell's and Cheatham's bloodied and exhausted troops, Cleburne's onslaught routed Johnson's Union division from Winfrey Field and captured 300 prisoners. Due to the darkness and confusion, the Rebels broke off the pursuit, and in Powell's view, the "night attack accomplished nothing of significance."[10]

Connelly's criticism of Bragg on the first day at Chickamauga was twofold. Hood and Buckner should have attacked and "carried both the La Fayette and Dry Valley Roads, and cut off Rosecrans from Chattanooga." Additionally, Hood should have timed his attack to Stewart's, thus taking the Dry Valley Road, cutting off Rosecrans's line of retreat, and "splitting his army in half." Powell, while essentially agreeing, was more nuanced. Both Buckner and Hood were under orders to hold their positions, but Bragg cancelled his "grand advance once the fight around Winfrey Field became significant." Also, the ability to cut the Federal army in half would depend upon the time of day. "By 1 P.M. only five [Union] brigades were south of the breakthrough area and they could have fallen back into Chattanooga Valley simply by moving west from Crawfish Spring, thus avoiding any trap." Nonetheless, Powell and I concur with Connelly's central thought: Bragg, Hood, and Buckner all missed the big opportunity. Woodworth thus declared Rosecrans the winner of day one: "The gap had been closed, the line restored, and disaster staved off."[11]

"Veritan," the army correspondent of the *Memphis Appeal*, was back in Dalton, where he received dispatches from the front. Governor Harris, as usual, served as a kind of information officer, dispersing dispatches and terse official accounts. Reports seemed conflicting—Harris claimed there had been 5,000 prisoners taken in the first day's battle, while Bragg's communiqué to Cooper stated half that many—but it seemed clear that the battle, while unresolved, was tipping in Bragg's favor.[12]

Bragg's plan for September 20 remained essentially the same: turn Rosecrans's left and roll his army south toward McLemore's Cove. During the night of the nineteenth, he decided to divide the army into two wings, with Polk commanding the right and James Longstreet, momentarily expected, the left. Polk would have Cheatham's Division (5,500), Hill's six brigades (9,000), and Walker's Corps (about 4,600), giving him a strike force of

Arrival of Longstreet's troops at Ringgold, Georgia, September 18, 1863.
From Battlefields in Dixie Land and Chickamauga National Military Park
(Nashville: Nashville, Chattanooga & St. Louis Railway, 1928).

nearly 19,000. Longstreet, on the left, would have Buckner's Corps, Hindman's Division, Polk's Corps, and the five brigades of the Army of Northern Virginia. Sensitive to the "needless affront" to Harvey Hill, who was essentially being sidelined, Polk suggested that the army be divided into thirds—Hill on the right, Polk in the center, and Longstreet on the left. An irritated Bragg, still simmering from the McLemore's Cove debacle, would have none of it. Polk was to attack at dawn, en echelon from right to left. The bishop expressed concern that the Federal force at Rossville (Granger's corps) might assault his flank or rear and that he needed more men, but Bragg held to the belief that most of Rosecrans's army remained at Lee and Gordon's Mill.[13]

Longstreet arrived at Catoosa Station, south of Ringgold, at 2:00 P.M. on the nineteenth. No one was there to greet him, a matter that Mackall should have arranged. Longstreet and his aides did not arrive at army headquarters until 11:00 P.M., where they found Bragg asleep in an ambulance. The army commander briefly apprised him of the situation. "Lee's Old Warhorse," commanding the left wing with six divisions, some 23,000 troops, would await Polk's dawn attack on the right and then "take it up promptly." That night, Longstreet slept close to Bragg's headquarters, getting five hours' sleep.[14]

Throughout the night, a series of miscommunications and poorly worded messages occurred. When Polk awakened on the twentieth, it became apparent that Harvey Hill had never been informed that he was to lead an attack at dawn. The bishop-general quickly dispatched two staff officers to find Hill and deliver the attack order. A third staff officer was sent to Hill's two division commanders—Breckinridge and Cleburne—stating that Hill could not be found and that they must immediately attack. Capt. Pollock Lee of the general staff related a tale of finding Polk far in the rear, reading a newspaper and having his breakfast. It was a lie, but Bragg believed it. At 7:25 A.M., Polk found Hill, who gave a litany of reasons why he could not attack—rations were being issued, no reconnaissance had been made of the Federal flank, no cavalry guarded his right flank, the Yankees had been felling trees, and their position appeared too strong to assault. He would need at least an hour. Polk relented and the army waited. A furious Bragg shortly encountered Hill and asked why the dawn attack had been delayed. He answered that this was the first he had heard of it—an overt lie, but Bragg reluctantly acquiesced.[15] Bragg had not learned the lesson of McLemore's Cove. If he desired an attack by the right at 5:30 A.M., he should have been present to see it carried out. Historian Alexander Mendoza also criticized Polk: First, Polk allowed Breckinridge's Division, which had crossed Alexander's Bridge at 10:00 P.M., to bivouac in the rear, more than a mile from the staging position. Second, when Polk sent his 5:30 A.M. dispatch to Hill, he did not order him to attack at dawn but rather "as soon as you are in position." Cheatham's Division was also not in its proper location, still being south of the Brotherton Road behind Stewart. Bragg had no choice but to withdraw the division from the attack and place it in reserve.[16]

The Battle Continues

The temperature plummeted into the thirties on the night of the nineteenth. September 20 began cold and with a dense fog that did not burn off until midmorning. At 9:30 A.M., after a four-hour delay, Harvey Hill finally launched Breckinridge's Division. The center and left brigades—Stovall's and Adams's—encountered light resistance and easily passed the Federal left. The brigades wheeled to the left and advanced south down the La Fayette Road, with Stovall east of the road and Adams to the west. The direct Federal escape route to Chattanooga had been effectively cut off. If Stovall and Adams were to roll up the Federal left, however, they would have to have more men. Historians have criticized Polk for not having Walker's Corps in position to support Breckinridge, but they are incorrect. Polk belatedly brought up Walker's 4,600 or so men (600 more would arrive in the afternoon), but they advanced in line of battle rather than in column, slowing the response. Once they arrived, Walker and Hill, who did not like each other, got into a childish argument about deployment. Polk rode up and witnessed the dispute between Walker and Hill continue. Alexander Mendoza believed that Polk was "more accustomed to creating problems than solving them." In the end, Walker's brigades were parsed out to replace Breckinridge's Division. Govan's Brigade, which relieved Adams's and Stovall's, succeeded in swinging through McDonald Field and momentarily getting in the Federal rear, but Govan's Arkansans in turn were flanked and had to make a precarious withdrawal.[17]

The Federals, in makeshift breastworks along the Brotherton Road, savaged the left half of Brigadier General Helm's Kentucky brigade on the division left. One-third of the brigade fell casualty, including Helm, who was mortally wounded. The rest of the brigade encountered no barricades and routed the Federal line, pursuing it to the La Fayette Road and capturing a section of artillery. At 10:00 A.M., Polk hurled Cleburne's Division into the meat grinder along the Brotherton Road. Woodworth labeled the attack a "fiasco," a "blunder," and a "miserable performance" but placed most of the blame on Polk rather than Cleburne. Orders were confused, and brigades became misaligned and fought alone and unsupported. The division was cut to pieces, losing 1,300 men (27 percent) in an hour and a half. The failed assault nonetheless accomplished one thing—it kept the Union command fixated on its left flank.[18]

By noon, Polk's attacks on the Union left had sputtered out. Robertson placed most of the blame for the failure on Hill for delaying the attack and on Longstreet, who shifted the Confederate left wing 500 yards to the right, where it "pinched out more than six brigades from the [planned] assault and momentarily halted . . . what Bragg had intended to be an army-wide attack." Polk abdicated tactical command to Hill once the offensive began. Polk and Hill "piecemealed Walker's Reserve Corps into oblivion." "How different it [the morning assault] all might have been," Robertson lamented, "if William Walker, whose men were ready at sunrise, had been on the far Confederate right instead of Harvey Hill." Connelly concurred: "Had Polk used these reserves [Walker] well, the Federal left probably would have been smashed." Powell blamed both Polk and Hill. Hill's brigades were stretched over too wide a front. He should have replicated Longstreet's in-depth formation on the left by placing Cheatham and Breckinridge on the front line and Walker and Cleburne on the second line. Such a stacking formation, Powell believed, would have been "devastating."[19]

Action now shifted to the Confederate left wing, where Longstreet had deployed a massive strike force 400 yards east of the La Fayette Road—Stewart's Division on the right, Hood's Corps in the center (Johnson's Division on the front line and Lafayette McLaws's and Evander Law's divisions in rear), and Hindman's Division on the left. William Preston's 4,800-man division remained in reserve near the Thedford and Park farms.

In his impatience to attack, Bragg sent Pollock Lee to Stewart and ordered him to immediately advance. Stewart attempted to explain that he was under orders from Longstreet to hold. Those orders should be ignored, Lee said, as the attack order came directly from Bragg. Longstreet remained in the dark and subsequently sent a message to Bragg stating "that I had probably better make my attack." He stood in awe as Stewart suddenly became engaged. Longstreet believed that Bragg was making the same mistake over and over: committing his divisions piecemeal rather than in a compact formation. By the time Longstreet got the balance of his force (17,000 men) in motion, Stewart had already been repulsed.[20]

At 11:15 A.M., Longstreet unleashed his attack. He deployed eight brigades in columns covering a quarter-mile front, arranged in a 2-1-2-1-2 formation. "The shock power lay not with them [the front line] but with what came behind them, six more Confederate brigades ready to add their weight to the slightest breach in the Federal line," appraised Andrew Haughton. Serious issues nonetheless remained. Mendoza points to the fact that many of Longstreet's brigades had been heavily engaged the day before; Johnson's Division, in the front line, had sustained 30 percent casualties. Additionally, the two brigades from Lee's army (the others had not yet arrived) were, in the words of a Georgian, "in an exhausted state." Massive frontal assaults had been beaten back before at Fredericksburg and Gettysburg.[21]

At this point, luck broke in favor of the Southerners. Due to confused orders and the overfeeding of the Union left, Rosecrans inadvertently opened a quarter-mile gap in the Federal line. Bushrod Johnson's Division barreled into the gap, passing Poe and Brotherton Fields and rushing 100 yards into Dyer Field as the Federal right wing collapsed. Johnson described the scene as "unspeakably grand." Johnson's and Hindman's divisions crushed Davis's Yankee division. Five enemy batteries (twenty-nine guns) lined the woods on the western edge of Dyer Field. The Union artillery at the Battle of Murfreesboro had turned the tide, but today it was not to be, as five Rebel brigades swarmed onto the field. Having lost their infantry support, the Union gunners began to limber up, but not before a staggering seventeen guns were overrun. Hood rode up and told Johnson, "Go ahead and keep ahead of everything."[22]

There were hitches. As Manigault's Brigade, on Hindman's left, neared the Widow Glenn House, the brigade came under the withering fire of Wilder's mounted infantrymen (fighting dismounted), supported by Lilly's Indiana battery. An Alabamian thought that "all the enemies' fire was turned upon the 28th and 34th [Alabama] which we didn't stand long." Robert Trigg's Brigade of Preston's Division came up on Manigault's left but too late to be of assistance. Manigault withdrew 300 yards, having lost 656 men. If Wilder had been allowed to do so, concluded Woodworth, he could have swung north and gotten in Longstreet's rear, causing serious havoc.[23]

By noon, Hindman's Division had routed five enemy brigades. At this point, Longstreet determined to alter Bragg's plan. Rather than turning south, he swung his brigades northward. In order to successfully make this right-turn maneuver, he dispatched Trigg's Brigade (one Virginia and three Florida regiments) to protect Hindman's left flank against Wilder's brigade of horsemen. Wilder had in fact planned to wildly charge into Longstreet's flank and slice it in two, but he was ordered to fall back.[24]

Federal reinforcements were on the way: James Steedman's 3,800-man division of the reserve corps, followed by a 2,200-man brigade. Forrest attempted to intercept them with two of Frank Armstrong's brigades and a collection of artillery—Morton's, Huggins's, and Huwald's batteries and a Napoleon section from Cobb's Battery, thirteen guns in total. The pieces were unlimbered on a ridge 600–800 yards from the highway. The fire proved largely ineffective, with the enemy column detouring to the west and cutting cross-country through the Mullis farm.[25]

The routed Federals eventually made a stand on Snodgrass Hill and a prominence known as Horseshoe Ridge. At 1:30, Johnson's Division attempted to sweep around the right of Horseshoe Ridge. As the division advanced past the Vittetoe cabin, a Tennessean observed, "the ladies of the house came out meeting us, waving their aprons and bonnets. We were almost worn out, but managed to give them a few cheers." Incredibly, a single enemy regiment, the 21st Ohio, armed with Colt revolving rifles, held the sector long enough for Union reinforcements (Steedman's division) to arrive. At 2:30, Joseph Kershaw's Brigade struck hills one, two, and three along the ridge but was driven back.[26]

At 3:00, Longstreet was summoned to Bragg's headquarters, some distance in the rear. Given the rout of the Union right wing, Longstreet believed that Polk should go on the defensive and give him some reinforcements to pursue the Yankees up the Dry Valley Road. Bragg answered that Polk's men were utterly spent and would be of no use. Precisely why Longstreet requested reinforcements when he still had Preston's uncommitted division is not known. Other accounts, clearly more accurate, state that Bragg preferred that Polk resume his attack in order to keep Union reinforcements from the Federals making a final stand on Snodgrass Hill.[27]

Realizing that he was on his own, Longstreet called up his last fresh division—William Preston's. Longstreet, by Robertson's evaluation, had two options—either advance Preston up the Dry Valley Road and outflank Horseshoe Ridge to the west or commit the division to the frontal assaults against the ridge. He did the latter, but successive assaults got nowhere. Although much has been made of the fact that most of the division comprised mountaineers with a high desertion rate, Hindman noted, "I never saw Confederate soldiers fight better." By 7:30 P.M., the Federals broke to the rear, leaving 600–700 prisoners in Preston's hands.[28]

In his after-action report, Wheeler claimed that he had rounded up over 1,000 prisoners and 20 wagons. Assuming the number was correct, although Wheeler typically exaggerated, a large percentage, if not all, of the captured were from the large Crawfish Springs hospital encampment and from other Union hospitals in the rear. Essentially, Wheeler had performed a mop-up operation and had not been a tactical factor in the pursuit. Not once, not twice, but three times, Longstreet requested his assistance in the fight at Horseshoe Ridge. In response, Wheeler sent only the 4th Tennessee Cavalry, which was too little, too late, to be of assistance. Powell blasted the cavalry chief, claiming that his so-called pursuit resulted in only four prisoners. Connelly concurred. A pursuit up the Dry Valley Road and the seizure of McFarland's Gap with dismounted cavalry would have "sealed the route of escape."[29]

Despite what Longstreet and Hill wrote in their postwar accounts, the Confederate top command remained uncertain about Rosecrans's position on the morning of September 21. True, at 5:00 P.M. on the twentieth, Bragg reported to Wheeler that the enemy had been driven back from all parts of the field. Driven back and withdrawn are very different prospects. The high command may not have known exactly where Rosecrans was, but they assumed that he remained nearby. Polk received a report shortly before dawn that Liddell's skirmishers had crossed the La Fayette Road, passed the McDonald farm, and found no enemy in sight. Bragg and Polk remained unconvinced. At 7:00 A.M., the two generals rode to Longstreet's headquarters. Polk wrote his wife that it was 9:00 A.M. before he fully realized the enemy had departed the field.[30]

Once it became known that no enemy was closer than Rossville, Longstreet proposed either a move across the Tennessee River to operate on

Rosecrans's flank or an advance into East Tennessee to attack Burnside. Glenn Robertson declared both of the proposals "fantasies" and "utterly impractical." There was no pontoon train to cross the Tennessee River, and there were not enough troops to protect the beachheads, if any even existed. Longstreet's contingent had arrived with no wagons and was dependent on Bragg for transportation. The army had sustained 2,312 killed, 14,674 wounded, and 1,468 missing—nearly 18,500 casualties, a staggering number even by 1863 standards. Indeed, the battle was surpassed in casualties only by Gettysburg.[31]

The slaughter appeared ghastly. A Texan viewing the battlefield noted, "There was men shot all to pieces, some with their heads busted open; some shot in two and arms and legs shot off, and every where they could be." Washington Ives saw men "swollen as large as oxen and the stench is unbearable." For miles, Joshua Callaway noticed small trees "shot down and large ones shot through and limbs of all sizes shot off, and trees peeled and scarred all over and everything *full* of minnie balls, grape & canister, and the ground literally ploughed up by cannon balls. Well, the woods looked like a corn field after a tremendous wind and hail storm."[32]

Although mostly an empty victory for the Confederates, Chickamauga boosted morale on the heels of the devastating losses at Vicksburg and Gettysburg. Bragg unfortunately kept reporters off the battlefield for over a week and a half, resulting in partial accounts and wild falsehoods, including the capture of 40,000 Federals and the burning of Chattanooga. The battle also gave Bragg his first indisputable victory, although one wonders what the results would have been had Longstreet not ignored the general's orders and attacked on the twentieth. Even having the incredible good fortune of having neither Sherman's Army of the Tennessee nor Burnside's Army of the Ohio on the field, both of which could and should have been present, the Confederates, with large-scale concentration, had been unable to destroy the Army of the Cumberland. As for the Federals, reaction was swift. Two corps under Joseph Hooker were on their way from the Army of the Potomac. Perhaps even more significant, Washington gave the West a new theater commander: Grant.[33]

Cabal

During the thirty-nine-day period between September 22 and October 29, 1863, a cadre of generals plotted what came dangerously close to being a bloodless coup against Bragg. A cabal developed among top generals that nearly left the army command in shambles. From among the participants, no heroes emerged.

On September 22, Bragg turned to the issue of culpability. He asked Polk to explain why he failed to attack at daylight on September 20. When the corps commander had not responded by the twenty-fifth, a clearly irritated Bragg sent a second message, demanding an immediate response. The army commander could no longer control himself. That same day, in a letter to Davis, he went on a tear against the bishop, describing him as "luxurious in his habits, rises late, moves slowly, and always conceives his plan the best — He has proved an injury to us on every field where I have been associated with him." As for Hill, Bragg blamed him for the McLemore's Cove debacle and denounced him as "despondent, dull, slow, and tho' gallant personally, is always in a state of apprehension and upon the most flimsy pretexts makes such reports of the enemy about him as to keep up constant apprehension, and require constant reinforcements — His open and constant croaking would demoralize any command in the world. He does not hesitate at all times and in all places to declare our cause lost." He believed that Buckner, Cleburne, and Hood would make better corps commanders. By the end of the day, Bragg had had enough of Polk's stonewalling and ordered him to report to army headquarters on the morning of the twenty-sixth. Precisely what was said is not known, but Polk later blamed Hill for the delay.[34]

On September 27, Polk met secretly with Longstreet and Hill. A consensus developed that Bragg had to go. Polk once again presumed upon his friendship with Davis, and he also wrote to General Lee. While Polk utterly detested Bragg and encouraged the developing cabal, evidence points to Longstreet being the ringleader. Before coming to Tennessee, he had openly written about the possibility of a swap, with Bragg taking his corps and he the Army of Tennessee. Longstreet wrote Lee, "He [Bragg] is not likely to do a great deal for us." In his letter, he perfunctorily requested that Lee come to the West, knowing full well that it was unlikely. Lee's response proved telling: "I think you [Longstreet] could do better than I could. It was with this view I urged you going." Such flattering words encouraged the ambitious general. Mackall saw through him: "I think Longstreet has done more injury to the general [Bragg] than all the others put together."[35]

Polk also became uncharacteristically aggressive. On September 26, he told Brent, knowing full well that it was likely to get back to Bragg, that the army should have rapidly pursued following Chickamauga and that Hill and Buckner agreed with him. The next day, Polk returned to his more typical clandestine style by writing to Davis: "He [Bragg] is not the man for the Station he fills. . . . He has had as I believe Gen. Rosecranz' army twice at his mercy, and allowed it to escape both times. . . . No troops could be in better spirits, their condition too is good and they chafe at this delay and indecision." The feelings were mutual. On the twenty-seventh, Bragg wrote to Elise, "I shall say candidly to the President that he must relieve Genl Polk or my self."[36]

Bragg suspended Polk on the twenty-eighth. Realizing what a disaster this would be, Urquhart asked Bragg if he would temporarily hold off on the order. Bragg admitted that it would stir controversy but insisted that discipline demanded that he proceed. Colonel Jones of the inspector general's office delivered the order to Polk. The next day, Bragg notified Cooper in Richmond of the suspension of both Polk and Hindman and of the fact that both had been ordered to Atlanta. Davis endorsed the dispatch by stating that Bragg did not have the authority to suspend, only to arrest and prefer charges. Perhaps, as Craig Symonds suggested, this was the president's way to get Bragg to rescind the order. Instead, Bragg had Polk and Hindman arrested. "My personal feelings have been yielded in what I know to be the public good, and I suffer self reproach for having acted earlier," Bragg wrote.[37]

Davis appealed to Bragg's prudence. Considering the troops' affection for Polk, the president hoped for a "lenient course." After all, Polk had not *intentionally* disobeyed an order; in battle, many generals make mistakes. If a court-martial proceeded, there would have to be an investigation—it could get messy. Bragg's enemies would certainly "connect the present action with former estrangement." Perhaps wisdom would dictate that Bragg "overlook the offense." The president failed to directly order him to drop the charge, and his mediation, as usual, proved to no avail.[38]

Meanwhile, Polk sat fuming in Atlanta. Writing to his daughter, he expressed his rage: "I certainly feel a lofty contempt for [Bragg's] puny efforts to inflict injury upon a man who has nursed him for the whole period of his commission with him & has kept him from ruining the cause of the country by the sacrifice of its armies." He later denounced Bragg as a "poor, feeble . . . irresolute man of violent temper. . . . I have contempt for his military capacity and his personal character." He met with many sympathetic supporters, obviously enjoying his victim status.[39]

Davis sent Col. James Chesnut, first cousin to Zachariah Deas, to investigate. Arriving in Atlanta on October 4, he met with Polk, who easily won him over with his charming ways. The colonel thought him "a splendid old fellow" and quickly fell in line with Polk's version of events. That same day, Chesnut proceeded to the Army of Tennessee, where he conferred for ten minutes with Longstreet. It was enough time for the corps commander to plead for Bragg's ouster, and he subsequently sent a letter to Hill and Buckner asking them to do the same.[40]

On the night of October 4, very possibly with Chesnut present, another meeting was held, this one at Buckner's headquarters. Thirteen officers were present: Longstreet, Hill, Buckner, Cleburne, Preston, Archibald Gracie, John Brown, Marcellus Stovall, Lucius Polk, James A. Smith, Bushrod Johnson, Randall Gibson, and Breckinridge (as his son Clifton claimed in 1932). The conspirators ("petitioners," they referred to themselves) were obviously clustered in Buckner's Corps and Cleburne's Division. The petition/scheme was to oust Bragg under the veil of concern for his health. Historians have generally considered Buckner to be the author, but Hill has also been suggested. In postwar years, Hill claimed that Polk suggested the petition but Buckner wrote it.[41]

Breckinridge refused to sign, stating that he had earlier requested a court of inquiry concerning Stones River; he did not wish to have his motives misconstrued. The Kentuckian kept up appearances, hypocritical though they were. On October 4, the day of the meeting, Bragg rode along the line and received a rousing cheer. "As he passed our brigade I noticed Gen. Breckinridge down among the men, with his hat off, whooping as lustily as any private. I am glad to see that they have buried the hatchet," a Georgian wrote. Polk and Hindman remained in Atlanta under arrest. Cheatham also did not sign. With Polk gone, he now commanded the corps; perhaps his silence reflected the desire for permanent command. It should also be noted that one major general (Walker) and fourteen brigadiers either refused to sign or were not asked.[42]

Word of the cabal quickly spread to army headquarters. Brent wrote in his diary on the cold and windy night of the fourth: "Had an unusual amount of work today, an effort being made among the General Officers to have Genl. Bragg relieved from command. Gen. Hill is regarded as prominent in this movement, so also Genl. Buckner." Bragg must have felt stabbed in the back. All three generals he had recommended for corps command had signed the petition, including Cleburne, whom he clearly admired. He expressed "distress and mortification," wrote Mackall. "I do believe he thought himself popular. . . . Bragg has the misfortune of not knowing a friend from a foe, and taking subserviency as evidence of friendship. Buckner was one of the first to sign the petition, and the General was almost ready to quarrel with me the other day because I opposed his superseding one of the best officers by making Buckner a Lieutenant General over his head."[43]

Liddell, who knew about the meeting, may have been the leaker to army headquarters. He had been approached by Lucius Polk to join the plot, but he refused. Davis would never appoint Johnston, he believed, so there was no one better than Bragg. "Anyone would be better," said Polk. To make his point, Liddell answered, "Perhaps Pemberton might be submitted." A stunned Polk said, "Surely not him." Liddell admitted that he went to Bragg with the information in an attempt at reconciliation—or so he claimed. To his utter dismay, Bragg doubled down. "General [Liddell], I want to get rid of all such generals. I have better men now in subordinate stations to fill their places. Let them send in their resignation. I shall accept every one without hesitation."[44]

The next day, October 5, Chesnut telegraphed Davis: "Your immediate presence in this army is urgently requested." Bragg, too, requested the president to come. Although the petition had not yet reached his desk, Davis clearly realized that something of a serious nature was brewing. The next day he boarded a train for Atlanta, arriving on October 8. He desired to make the issue of Polk's arrest go away by simply transferring him to another department. The bishop would have none of it. He desired a trial so that all of the dirty laundry would be aired. That night, Davis telegraphed Breckinridge and Longstreet to tell them to meet him in Atlanta so that they could speak privately on the return trip. As for Bragg, he remained "despondent" throughout the eighth and "blind as a bat to the circumstances surrounding him," according to Mackall.[45]

The president arrived on the ninth, greeted at the depot by thousands of soldiers and civilians. Colonel Johnston described the scene as "truly gratifying." Accompanying the president was Lt. Gen. John C. Pemberton of Vicksburg infamy. Davis told Bragg that, barring prejudices, Pemberton would be assuming command of a corps, presumably Polk's. Mackall was appalled: "There is trouble enough in this army already, and I am afraid this will only increase if he [Davis] puts him [Pemberton] in command here. I would not be much surprised if he relieved Bragg, reinstate Polk, put Longstreet in command, and gave Pemberton his corps." Pemberton discussed the issue with Mackall, who was blunt. "I told him that there was not a division in the army that would be willing to receive him; that I was sorry to be obliged to tell him so unpleasant a truth, but so it was."[46]

Davis reviewed the troops on the morning of October 9; the men received him gladly. "Great deal of enthusiasm among the soldiers," wrote A. J. Neal. Floridian Robert Watson remarked, "As he stopped opposite each Regt. he received 3 cheers and on returning received a regular 'Rebel yell.'" A Texan thought he was "a fine looking old chap; he looks more like a farmer than a president." Col. Robert Bullock of the 7th Florida failed to see anything imposing about him: "He is a very frail looking man." Later that day, the president, along with Longstreet and Buckner, went to the top of Lookout Mountain to view the Federal camps in the valley below.[47]

The rumors continued to swirl at army headquarters. "I heard yester-day [October 9] that Longstreet had signed the petition for the removal of Bragg, and if he has not, at all events he is talking about him in a way to destroy all of his usefulness," Mackall confided to his wife. As for Longstreet's obvious desire for army command, the chief of staff believed that he would be unacceptable to the Army of Tennessee. The soldiers would say, "We don't know him, and we know that Bragg is careful of us, doesn't fight unless he has a good chance." A Mobile correspondent got wind that only two major generals (Buckner and Cleburne) had signed the petition and "that one of those, upon fuller information expressed his regret at doing so." The officer in question had to be Cleburne, but whether the report was true is not known.[48]

On the morning of October 10, Davis rode the lines to the resounding cheers of the troops. Bragg appeared "in a fine mood, evidently thinking he has the President on his side." That evening, Davis called a meeting of the generals at army headquarters. In Bragg's presence, he asked the generals to speak their piece; they did not hesitate. "None flinched or denied his signature or hesitated to state reasons frankly," Captain Buck wrote. The most outspoken were Longstreet and Buckner. Cleburne spoke delicately, but others were not so inclined. In his memoir, Longstreet admitted to being shocked that Davis had posed the question. His tendency was to give an evasive answer, but Davis pressed him. Hill became so blunt that the president cut him off. In an excruciating consensus, the generals concluded that Bragg had lost the confidence of the army and needed to be replaced. "Mr. Davis got more than he came for," a staff officer remembered. Bragg sat dumbfounded, but several weeks later, the president wrote, "My memory is that nothing was unkindly said by any one or received in unkind spirit by Gel Bragg."[49]

Coincidentally, Armand Beauregard, brother of the famed general, arrived that night; he discreetly avoided any contact with the president. Indications are that Bragg met him after the humiliating meeting and before Davis's subsequent announcement. Bragg openly talked about his trials, "having no one to share them." Armand described him as "dejected and nearly despondent." Bragg offered to relinquish command, but if he were retained, he would not tolerate noncompliance with orders. Brent wrote in his journal that evening, "It seems probable that Gen. Bragg will be sustained by the President."[50]

The next day, October 11, Davis conferred with some pro-Bragg generals. Bragg now made his move and requested Hill's removal. On the twelfth, the president toured the Chickamauga battlefield. That night, he was serenaded and made a brief speech, praising Bragg as being "worthy of all confidence."

"The mob shouted, of course, and they would have shouted just as loud if he had told them that their comrade's lives had been uselessly sacrificed and he would send them a better General. Poor man, he is an enigma to himself," Mackall recorded.[51]

There was time for one more debacle. On Davis's last night (October 12), the Southern Associated Press reported that he had made a brief speech praising Bragg — "notwithstanding the shifts of malice that had been hurled at him [Bragg], he had bravely borne it all." Before departing, the president ordered Hill to report to Richmond. The North Carolinian expressed shock and theorized a conspiracy; he had been made the scapegoat for Polk's delinquent September 20 attack. He believed that Polk would return to the army and Pemberton would be given his corps. Hill did not take the dismissal quietly. On October 16, accompanied by Col. Archer Anderson, he proceeded to army headquarters and demanded to know why he had been relieved. Bragg answered that no charges had been preferred against him but that the move had been made for army harmony. He also mentioned the McLemore's Cove incident. Hill claimed that he was being singled out for signing the petition; Bragg did not answer. Hill later transferred to South Carolina, but his career for all intents and purposes was over.[52]

When the president arrived in Atlanta, he was met by Polk, who had read the Associated Press article. Subsequent articles had appeared making it clear that Davis had gone out of his way *not* to make antagonistic statements. The reporter finally confessed that he had not actually heard the speech himself but had been given details by two Bragg staff officers: Colonel McKinstrey and Lieutenant Colonel Walter. Nonetheless, five days after the president's departure, Bragg released a Davis address, which pointedly referred to those who had allowed "selfish aspiration to prevail over a desire for the public good." On October 23, Davis formally exchanged Hardee and Polk. As matters stood, one malcontent would be exchanged for another.[53]

Despite his internal victory, Bragg could not shake his mood swings. Brent jotted on October 21, "Gen. Bragg quite low in spirits." Trouble now erupted in East Tennessee. Bragg stripped Buckner of department command and henceforth viewed him as a division commander. Davis upheld the decision, Buckner's cries notwithstanding. Bragg reminded the president that the general had not only participated "in a mutinous assemblage" but also "was himself mentioned prominently in that meeting as the expected successor." Bragg had successfully dealt with Hill, Polk, and Buckner and in time would deal with Longstreet.[54]

It did not take long for the Richmond press corps to report trouble in the West. Although details were limited, the headlines proved damaging enough: "The Difficulty among the Western Generals," "The Case against General Polk—Who Is to Blame," "The Polk Embroglio," and "General Bragg and His Generals." The *Memphis Appeal* openly took Polk's side and claimed that his removal was due to "some pique or feeling." The bishop's farewell address to his corps was published in numerous papers. The near mutiny was over, but rancor had not been silenced. The man most responsible was Davis—for his failure to address the issue after Stones River.[55]

✸ 15 ✸

The Medical Corps

The medical corps, perhaps the weakest of the services at the start of the war, evolved throughout the conflict. Professionalization and organization nonetheless had their limitations. The pre-antibiotic era left physicians with few options. Mistakes were made and men unquestionably died during the learning curve. Yet, throughout it all, there were remarkable successes. It was these successes that saved lives and kept the army supplied with men.

Spring to Summer 1863

When Bragg retreated from the Murfreesboro battlefield, he left behind 250 sick and 1,423 wounded. Within five months, 640 of the patients had died, and the balance was sent off for exchange. Even before the army limped off the battlefield, the evacuated wounded, thousands of them, began pouring into Chattanooga. One trainload of patients had three cars jerk loose six miles east of Bridgeport, killing seven men. The army's general hospitals, which had beds for 4,000 from Chattanooga to Atlanta, quickly became inundated. Dr. P. F. Thornton at the Newsom Hospital in Chattanooga personally dressed the wounds of 1,500 men within four days. The Academy Hospital filled to capacity and beyond. At the Foard Hospital (the old Crutchfield Hotel), Surgeon Frank Hawthorne noted that all the nurses became "sick or broken down" and that his two assistant surgeons were utterly spent. All usable buildings in Chattanooga were converted into makeshift hospitals. The wounded of Withers's Division occupied the Baptist Female Institute; those of Cheatham's, the Soule Female College; McCown's, the old academy; Cleburne's, the Methodist, Presbyterian, old Presbyterian, and Baptist churches; and Breckinridge's, the city hall, along the Old Liberty Road, and at Dr. January's. A special train transported 500 wounded to Knoxville. One of them, eighteen-year-old Stokley Acuff of the 26th Tennessee, had a ball pass through one of his shoulders and lodge in his thigh. Placed on furlough, his father brought him home in an oxcart. Doctors could never remove the bullet, and the boy spent the rest of his life in pain and unable to work. Another 481 wounded jammed the railcars for the Medical College, Empire, and Gate City Hospitals in Atlanta, 35 percent of them listed as being in serious condition. Fairground Hospitals 1 and 2 received another 800 patients. Seventy of the wounded went as far as Montgomery.[1]

George Lea of the 7th Mississippi, badly wounded at Stones River, recuperated at the Lumpkin Hospital in Rome, Georgia. "My hand and arm is near about well that is the soreness has about left it," he wrote his father on March 3, 1863. "It is still stiff yet. I will always have stiff fingers the bone of my arm was broken and all the leaders of my two small fingers were cut. I suffered a great deal with it but not as much as many others I have seen." Dr. Ira Gunter, at the Fairground Hospital in Atlanta, related to his wife some of the grisly wounds he had seen: "Some have their lower jaw shot all to smash while [others] have their upper jaw mangled. Others have extensive and ugly wounds in the fleshy parts of their system produced by the explosion of shells. Others again have the flesh and bones of their limbs torn all to pieces presenting wounds of a very ghastly nature."[2]

No sooner had the Murfreesboro wounded cleared out than a wave of spring sickness swept over the army—primarily diarrhea and a general ailment referred to as ague, meaning chills and fever. The weekly reports of the sick from Polk's Corps for the weeks ending May 6 and 23, 1863, revealed the depth of the problem: 925 patients in two weekly reports. The camps at Tullahoma had an adequate supply of water, and Hardee was frankly at a loss to explain the number of cases in his corps. In Brown's Brigade, an inspector discovered a want of hygiene. The camps of the 32nd/45th Tennessee had not been properly ditched to permit drainage. Although latrines ("sinks," as they were called) had been dug, the men still frequented a hillside, with the runoff polluting a nearby creek.[3]

The chief culprit of sickness remained diarrhea, of which there were 35,683 cases between January and May 1863. Some complained about the coarse cornmeal that had not been adequately sifted. "When the Diarrhea gets a hold of one it is a hard matter to stop it. I have had it now for about 15 days," wrote John Crittenden on April 23. "As yet I have not found anything that will check it. Sometimes it takes away my appetite so that I cannot eat anything for days. When such is the case I get very weak." A soldier at Shelbyville concluded that "corn bread and fat bacon, day after day, is too much for the stomachs of many of the men, and the result is a prevalence of diarrhea throughout the whole army." The next highest cause of sickness was the category generically listed as "fever." Exposure to the elements played a role. "I had a very bad sore throat a few days ago," a Floridian at Tullahoma wrote his wife, "but it is so windy up here and the weather is so changeable that it is enough to make anybody sick." Sgt. F. Pridmore of the 41st Alabama fell victim to the elements: "I have some fever nearly every evening it is caused I suppose from cold weather continues wet and cold rained all night last night [January 17] and it's raining some this morning there is a great deal of sickness in camp at this time all caused from expouser and cold."[4]

Smallpox was a relatively minor problem, with only 167 cases reported in the first five months of 1863. Nonetheless, an outbreak in December 1862 had caused some desertions, so vaccinations were given. Lieutenant Davidson thought the cure worse than the disease. "My leg is vry painful. It appears I will never get over the effects of vaccination." Sergeant Sparkman noted that there were a number of men at Wartrace who had sore arms from vaccination: "Some are sore for three or four months."[5]

The sick were sent back to the army's general hospitals in the rear. By late 1862, Chattanooga had a capacity of 1,000; Rome, 1,000; Ringgold, 700; Tunnel Hill, 250; Dalton, 500; Catoosa Springs, 800; Atlanta, 1,200; and Cleveland, Tennessee, 600. Some 645 guards were required to prevent desertions. By spring 1863, the makeshift facilities in Chattanooga had transformed into huge laid-out pavilions, or wards, as they were called. The Foard Hospital served as the general receiving facility for the entire army. Under the direction of Dr. G. T. Parsley and two assistant surgeons, the installation was located on a large square near the railroad depot and could accommodate up to 200 patients at a time. It had all the facilities required—bathrooms, laundry, storerooms, apothecary shop, and kitchen. Diseases went to the Newsom Hospital and battle wounds to the Academy and Gilmer Hospitals.[6]

Polk's Chattanooga facilities included the Gilmer and Academy Hospitals. Gilmer comprised five two-story wards, each with a capacity of fifty patients and each with its own pantry and bathroom. "Everything about it was in perfect order," commented Kate Cummings, who visited the facility on May 20. "The bunks had on white comforts, not the least soiled, though they had been in use some time. The view from the upper part of these wards is perfectly entrancing." Dr. Charles E. Mitchell of Charleston led the staff, assisted by four doctors. At the Academy Hospital, formerly the Masonic Female Institute, each of the ten one-story wards, spaced twenty yards apart, had a capacity of twenty-five patients. The attendants slept in nearby tents. The laundry house had boilers built on brick, an ironing room, and a shed for drying clothes in wet weather. Five surgeons managed the facility.[7]

Despite the hospitals' efforts at cleanliness, Cummings reported cases of erysipelas, an acute strep-related skin infection, which spread throughout the hospitals. "The erysipelas, which is infectious, is spreading. Two of the girls in the washhouse had their ears bored, and they have it very badly, taken from washing the clothes, though they are never touched by them, until they are put in a large boiler and well boiled. One of the girls is a perfect sight; her face is so swollen that her eyes are closed, and part of her hair has had to be cut off."[8]

The hospital system eventually grew to twenty-nine facilities in six cities and towns, with six each in Chattanooga and Atlanta. The sprawling Fairground Hospitals 1 and 2 in Atlanta comprised twenty buildings, each designed to accommodate forty patients. Such a capacity proved unmanageable, and the total number was eventually reduced from 800 to 570. The thirty-acre Cherokee Springs Hospital, a tent city with a capacity of 500, received only chronic cases. Unfortunately, the Gate City and Roy Hospitals, located on congested Atlanta streets, were considered unsuitable for the summer months, thus eliminating 900 beds. By the summer of 1863, the bed capacity reached nearly 6,000.[9]

Between January and May 1863, Fairground Hospitals 1 and 2 admitted 3,070 — 585 wounded and 2,485 sick. Of the latter, diarrhea represented 41.6 percent; debility, or a general weakness, 27.9 percent; rheumatism, 12.7 percent; fever, 8.3 percent; pneumonia, 5.3 percent; typhoid, 2.6 percent; and dysentery 1.6 percent. Strict rules regulated daily life, including the changing and washing of clothing, diet, duties of convalescents, and noise level.[10]

The administrative genius behind the department's hospital system was forty-one-year-old Dr. Samuel H. Stout. Although his superintendence of the Chattanooga hospitals had gone well, his initial appointment as department director met with resistance. Indeed, some doctors bluntly asked, "Who in the hell is that fellow Stout?" When asked where he came from, Stout reveled in answering that he had lived "in a hollow beech tree in the back woods of Giles County, Tennessee." He assigned personnel to the various hospitals, dealt tactfully with prickly doctors, kept hospitals supplied with everything from medicines to furnishings, and successfully performed the daily mundane tasks required to keep the huge system functioning. Serving as medical director of the Army of Tennessee was forty-four-year-old Edward A. Flewellen, like several of Bragg's doctors a graduate of the prestigious Jefferson Medical College in Philadelphia. After serving as assistant to Andrew Jackson Foard, the army's first medical director, Flewellen took command on January 8, 1863.[11]

While several of the doctors serving in the general hospitals had graduated from Northern medical schools or from highly regarded Southern schools, some of the surgeons clearly lacked basic qualifications. J. A. Rogers of the 28th Tennessee wrote his father on March 20 that he was serving as the "acting assistant surgeon" of his regiment, although he was only "a first course student." In May, twenty-one physicians in Polk's Corps were reexamined at Shelbyville, and five of them were rejected for "professional incompetency."[12]

On April 12, the Army of Tennessee medical transportation system was updated, allowing one two-horse wagon for the medical officers of each corps, division, and brigade. Two four-horse wagons went to each brigade for medical supplies. One ambulance or two-horse wagon was allotted for every 300 men. Dedicated spring ambulances were a valued commodity—in March 1863, there were only ninety-five in the army. An order was placed with the Dixie Works of Canton, Mississippi, for 150 new ambulances and completed by May 15. Occasionally a highly prized, fully equipped Federal ambulance was taken; twenty-eight were captured during the Stones River Campaign. One of Bragg's doctors noted that it became an easy matter to paint a *C* over the *U* and leave the *S. A.*[13]

Chickamauga

In August 1863, with a potential battle in the offing, Bragg instructed Stout to make arrangements for the removal of the Chattanooga hospitals. It proved to be a hurried affair—150 of the worst cases were left, and limited supplies of medicine, blankets, and furniture, enough for 500 patients, fell into Union hands. Permanently disabled patients were forwarded to Rome. Surgeon D. D. Saunders went to Marietta to prepare the town for an onslaught of patients. Several stores, the courthouse, Masonic Hall, and one of the two hotels could accommodate only 850–900 men. Saunders had his eye on the Georgia Military Institute, which could house an additional 400–450, but Governor Joseph E. Brown, whom Saunders privately considered a demagogue, refused its use. Even a personal plea by Stout did not get him to back down. The director became so infuriated that he indignantly walked out midsentence as the governor went on a tirade against Bragg. In postwar years, the two men developed an amicable relationship and never mentioned the unpleasant incident.[14]

By September, the army's hospital system had grown to an impressive thirty-two facilities in ten Georgia cities. The bed capacity increased to 7,782, with a personnel staff of 53 surgeons, 43 assistant surgeons, 34 contract doctors, 36 stewards, 55 ward masters, 141 matrons, 734 nurses, 220 cooks, and 227 laundresses, for a total of 1,543. Supporting the professional staff were the volunteer hospital and battlefield associations: the Tennessee Relief Association; Georgia Relief Association; Atlanta Executive Aid Committee; Dougherty County Battlefield Relief Association; LaGrange Relief Society; Louisiana Refugee Committee of Columbus, Georgia; Montgomery

Relief Committee; Auburn Relief Committee; and Mobile Hebrew Military Aid Society, the last having a chapter working out of Chattanooga.[15]

Surgeon Saunders estimated that the department required a 10,000-bed capacity for the anticipated upcoming battle—4,000 for the sick, a fairly constant number, and 6,000 for the wounded. As the Federals penetrated farther south, Flewellen concentrated on removing all hospitals north of Resaca. Writing in her journal on September 8, Cummings noted that the hospitals along the Western and Atlantic rail line were being packed up and moved south. At Tunnel Hill, she saw "a number of new hospital buildings; there were so many that they looked like a village. It does seem too bad that they are compelled to leave all of our hard work for the enemy to destroy."[16]

The carnage that finally unfolded along Chickamauga Creek in northern Georgia on September 19–20 eclipsed in scale anything heretofore seen in the western theater, with 14,474 Rebel wounded (more than twice that anticipated) and 2,500 Union wounded who fell into Confederate hands. A couple of large and well-equipped Union hospitals were taken, along with fourteen ambulances, twenty-six hospital tents, and the medical supplies of five regiments. Bragg's army moved north after the defeated Federals fled to Chattanooga, taking with it many of the doctors and ambulances. The medical department proved totally unprepared to care for the massive number of wounded left in the battle's wake.[17]

A train of about 150 commissary wagons and ambulances transported the most seriously wounded from the battlefield, while those who could walk limped in with the help of friends or other wounded. Rosecrans quickly proposed an exchange of wounded, which Bragg accepted, meaning that 1,740 Union patients were paroled and exchanged on the field. On September 29, 300 Yankee ambulances came into the Confederate lines, carrying about 600 Southern wounded. Stout sent an additional thirteen surgeons and assistant surgeons to the army, and their places in the hospitals were filled with civilian contract doctors.[18]

Hindman's field hospitals, located at the Hunt House on Chickamauga Creek at Dalton Ford, were typical. Kate Cummings visited Manigault's brigade hospital shortly after the battle. The 105 litter bearers (four men to a stretcher) had assisted in carrying in the brigade's 426 wounded. They were jammed into the Hunt House and into tents but, in most cases, remained exposed to the elements. "They [surgeons] were out in the rain nearly all morning, trying to make some patients comfortable as possible," Cummings wrote. "They said the rain was pouring down on them [wounded], but it could not be avoided. They informed me that what they had heard of many of the brigade hospitals, the men were in worse plight than theirs." She asked the surgeons what Stout and Flewellen were doing to address the deplorable conditions. They answered sardonically that they were "watching General Bragg look at the army." She later visited Cheatham's division hospital, where she went under a tent fly about 100 feet in length; every man under it had an amputated limb. The surgeons claimed that they were completely out of rations and had nothing but old tent cloth to bind the wounds.[19]

Dr. Carlyle Terry, Hindman's medical director, kept accurate records of his patients. The surgical cases were all treated with chloroform, with most operations taking place in a stable. Only one man got tetanus, but the overall division results proved much better than after the Battle of Shiloh. The case-by-case breakdown, however, revealed that many amputations had fatal results. Typically, loss of blood or the deadly infections of erysipelas and pyaemia were listed as the causes of death.[20]

Eventually, all of the wounded were collected at a place that became known as the Wood Station, or Catoosa Platform, two miles south of Catoosa Station. The railroad bridge had been prematurely burned by Rebel cavalry, thus creating a choke point. The nearest operable railhead was eight miles south. Until the bridge could be repaired, the wounded and sick kept accumulating in what would become the largest single gathering of misery and suffering ever assembled in the western theater. The wood for the trains was stacked on wooden walkways lining the track in the midst of a ten-acre field. As many of the patients as possible were placed on straw underneath the platform to protect them from the elements. The balance lay in an open field, most without any shelter. Fortunately, the nights remained relatively pleasant, and a nearby creek afforded sufficient water. Trains eventually made it through, but on September 26, a full six days after the battle, thirty-five to forty carloads of wounded remained.[21]

Stout eventually got wind of the human disaster from a railroad conductor. He was told that thousands of wounded lay out in an open field in horrid conditions and many of them had not eaten for two days. Stunned at what he heard, he immediately assembled at Marietta a cadre of surgeons, thirty attendants, nurses, and cooks, as well as cooking utensils, food, medicine, and dressings—all that could be spared from the hospitals. He also got permission to take an emergency express train, and within an hour, help was on the way. The railroad bridge was eventually repaired and trains began to run, but the wounded were often bypassed to carry Union prisoners. On the night of September 21, three large trains pulled into Atlanta with 1,630 prisoners but no wounded. Three nights later, another 1,000 prisoners arrived but only 200 wounded. One train had 120 sick but no wounded. Those aboard mostly had coughs, and some confessed that they had recovered, yet they were passed on to Atlanta. "There is evidently a screw loose in the Medical Department, which should be tightened up," wrote an Atlanta correspondent. Stout got into an open war of words with M. B. McMicken, the army chief quartermaster, who frequently refused to furnish transportation.[22]

Removing the wounded by rail to general hospitals proved to be an enormous undertaking. There was a daily train arranged with bunks that could accommodate 200. The mail train, which ran only at night, could take another fifty. Those capable of sitting up could take one of the two daily passenger trains, each of which had a capacity of 125. Stout desired the passenger trains to have at least one passenger car and two boxcars for the exclusive use of the Medical Department, equipped with furniture, water, provisions, and medicine. These sources together totaled only 500, however, far short of the number of spots needed to transport the 1,200–1,500 wounded daily. The only other rail transportation available were the irregular and infrequent troop transport trains, which carried soldiers up from Atlanta. These trains comprised mostly boxcars, which lacked any water and provisions. Sometimes the wounded were placed in cars from which cattle had just been unloaded. An Atlanta correspondent reported wounded sitting on several boxcars for two days before they were moved. Train wrecks between Tunnel Hill and Dalton and south of Cartersville caused further delays, but there were no wounded aboard.[23]

Tensions ran high and a rift developed between Stout and Flewellen. Even writing years later, Stout harbored a grudge. The enormity of the situation "seemed to daze Dr. Flewellen," he wrote. Flewellen made no attempt to inform Stout of the catastrophe taking place, concentrating exclusively on the battlefield and "overlooking the fact that there was a medical director of hospitals in the rear." Flewellen lacked competency for such an undertaking, but there may have been other factors at play. Only a month and a half after the battle, he was relieved due to serious health impairments.[24]

Civilians connected with hospital relief associations arrived at the Wood Station and sent back bleak reports. Agents of the Atlanta Relief Agency arrived at Ringgold at 6:00 A.M. on September 23. The men had great difficulty procuring transportation for themselves and their supplies and medicine. O. H. Jones purchased a horse and rode fourteen miles ahead, where he found a number of field hospitals, all of them in want of nurses and provisions. He saw only two unburied Confederates, but a number of Yankee bodies still lay about, several of them badly burned in the fires that had subsequently broken out. Most of the army surgeons had moved up with the army, and few remained. Jones's party eventually arrived and established the Atlanta Hospital Depot, where all of the supplies were deposited.[25]

"Georgian," a member of one of the relief committees, wrote on September 29 that all of the wounded had been removed to the east bank of Chickamauga Creek, in some cases having to be transported three to four miles. There remained a shortage of wagons to carry the wounded and transport them to the railhead. Once they arrived, there were no trains to take them south—"a crying evil," he denounced. By September 30, an estimated 2,500 of the most dangerously wounded remained in battlefield hospitals. A month later, 500 still remained.[26]

The hell for the wounded often continued in the general hospitals in the rear. "Men, wounded in every shape & form, and others, from the exposure in camp, and the abominable diet they have there, look as though they feel like no one in the world [feels] for them," wrote Theodore Livingston, one of the attendants. "The doctors have a good chance to improve themselves, and they're making good use of it. Every day they perform some operation. As far as I am convinced, I would rather take the Yankee lead in my head, than to suffer as those poor fellows do, and fit subject for young swell head doctors, to experiment on."[27]

Stout's general hospitals could obviously not absorb the tidal wave of wounded pouring in, so many of the patients were forwarded to other departments—Montgomery; Columbus, Georgia; Augusta; and Macon. The slightly more wounded arriving in Atlanta were sent within the department to Griffin and LaGrange. Private families also took a number of the wounded into their homes. Patients who were slightly wounded but unable to recuperate within thirty days (10.5 percent of the total) were furloughed for a month. All other slightly wounded were sent to convalescent camps, where malingerers and "hospital rats" were weeded out. Only 1.4 percent of the total wounded died during the last week and a half of September, a rather remarkable figure given the debacle at the Wood Station and the general lack of preparedness.[28]

Eight to ten days after the battle, 900 wounded and 150 sick were sent 300 miles from Atlanta to Augusta. Little attention had been paid to their wounds, and many lay at the depot for forty to eighty hours before being placed in a hospital. The hospital capacity was soon overwhelmed. Gangrene broke out, undoubtedly from the filthy boxcars, and was probably spread by the attendants who went from patient to patient using the same sponge.[29]

By the end of September, 900 sick and wounded began arriving at Macon, where they were housed at the Blind Academy, the Bibb County

Courthouse, city hall, and the Floyd House. Late the next month, an additional 500 wounded were sent down from Atlanta. Those in a less serious condition went farther south to Americus, Milledgeville, and other points. In Macon, the Aid Committee for the Relief of Wounded of Bragg's Army offered vital assistance in feeding the patients and providing bedding for those flooding the city.[30]

Cummings described in grisly detail the unrelenting pain of many of the wounded even weeks after Chickamauga. A number required amputations, "but the doctors say that their systems are not in a fit state and that they would not stand the shock." By mid-November gangrene swept the Ringgold hospital. "Those whom we thought were almost well are now suffering severely. A wound which a few days ago was not the size of a silver dime is now eight or ten inches in diameter. The surgeons are doing all in their power to stop its progress. . . . It is a most painful disease, and plays sad havoc with the men every way."[31]

In the weeks following Chickamauga, sickness disabled thousands. Robert Watson of the 7th Florida jotted in his diary on September 30: "Nothing to eat but we are all well supplied with lice. Many in the regiment [are] sick from drinking bad water and [eating] poorly cooked food. I think we will all be sick soon if they don't give us more food." On October 7, there were 5,953 sick in the infantry and artillery in camp. Colonel Bullock of the 7th Florida confided to his wife: "The regiment is suffering with dysentery, more than ever before. I have it pretty badly myself."[32]

Justifiable criticism could be leveled at the Army of Tennessee's medical department. No coordinated plan had been formulated for a massive battle such as Chickamauga, and for that both Flewellen *and* Stout bear culpability. Stout's postbattle ad hoc strike team was commendable, but a "making it up as you go along" approach proved too little, too late. Even a reserve medical supply train of a dozen wagons, strategically placed and loaded with hospital tents, blankets, liquor, chloroform, medicine, mess chests, bandages, and spare clothing, would have been of enormous benefit. The Army of the Cumberland had such a reserve train for its infantry with forty-four wagons! There is no evidence that Flewellen even contemplated such a concept. Nor had there been any direct communication with the army's chief quartermaster in advance of the battle to confirm who was in charge of transporting the wounded, a mistake that proved costly. Of Flewellen, Stout, and McMicken, it was Flewellen in the end who shouldered most of the blame. He was the army staff officer in charge, and if no contingency plan existed, if no communication took place, if a void of creativity existed, it must fall to him. It could be argued that no one could have planned for the deluge of casualties that was Chickamauga and that this should not undercut the department's unprecedented achievements. In the end, perhaps the department can only fairly be judged in light of how many men were saved who otherwise would surely have been lost or maimed for life.[33]

Atlanta Campaign

Flewellen resigned at Dalton, Georgia, due to ill health and a refusal to work under the new army commander. Foard thus resumed his former position. Desiring to avoid another Chickamauga-style medical disaster, Stout immediately made plans for the upcoming spring 1864 campaign. Bed capacity was increased to 12,000, and a reserve medical corps was organized. One surgeon per 500 beds would go into the field in the event of an emergency, fully equipped with surgical instruments and supplies. The corps was called out in February when the Federals made a reconnaissance-in-force on Dalton. Although not actually needed, it proved to be a good drill. Within twenty-four hours, doctors from as far away as 300 miles had reported with all of the supplies and medicines needed for several thousand wounded and two days' cooked rations and coffee.[34]

Unresolved problems nonetheless hampered progress, including the issues of patient treatment and transport. A correspondent questioned why no water was made available on the boxcars carrying the sick and wounded, forcing many patients to travel a day and a night without water. Supplies also remained scant. In July 1864, the medical purveyor's office in Atlanta published the standard supply table for a brigade in the Army of Tennessee. It included four dozen roller bandages; one pound of lint; ten yards of muslin; half an ounce of surgeon's silk; four ounces of sponges; half an ounce of line thread; two gallons each of wine, brandy, and whiskey; one pound of candles; two tourniquets; eight ounces of ammonia; eight ounces of *tinctura opii* (laudanum); one dram of morphine; one pound of chloroform; two pounds of cotton bunting; and one lantern.[35]

Each brigade in the field had an infirmary corps that it used as litter bearers. On May 1, Manigault's Brigade of 1,838 counted seventy-one bearers. Each man was equipped with a roll of bandages and tourniquet and every fourth man with two sets of splints. The bearers were trained in the basics of stopping serious bleeding and applying temporary splints. They often had to run 200 yards to help a dying man. Band members typically assisted the surgeons in hospital functions, as no one wanted to take the risk of losing a good musician.[36]

In August 1864, J. H. Erskine, medical director of S. D. Lee's Corps (formerly John Hood's), requested authorization to have a four-horse wagon placed at corps headquarters (in addition to the brigade and division trains) for medical supplies. At Resaca, Anderson's division hospital had been captured and the medical supplies destroyed. Erskine had had to supply Anderson from the reserve supply. Due to critical shortages at Resaca and again when the Macon Railroad was cut, Lee had had to supply chloroform from his personal supply.[37]

In mid-May 1864, Kate Cummings, along with members of several relief associations, planned to board a passenger car in Atlanta. The wounded instead came to them, as they began streaming in from the Resaca battlefield. "O, what a sight we there beheld! No less than three long trains filled, outside and in, with wounded. Fighting behind breastworks, almost all were wounded in the head, face, and hands." Some 700–800 patients unloaded at the depot. Dr. Robert D. Jenkins, who had come with Cummings and her party from Cummings, Georgia, asked the party to come with him. "We were in an immense hall, crowded with wounded, some walking about, others sitting on the floor—all waiting to have their wounds dressed," Cummings described. "Surgeons, ladies, and nurses were scattered all about, so intently employed that they did not seem to notice each other." Cummings dealt with the slightly wounded—those with mangled hands, shot-off fingers, and wounded wrists and one or two with an eye shot out. "The men were laying all over the platform of the depot, preferring to remain there, so as to lie ready for the train which would take them to other places."[38]

In March, the army's hospital system accommodated 7,434 patients and had 4,823 empty beds for an occupancy rate of 61 percent. The numbers drastically changed as the campaign swung into full gear. In July, hospitals in thirteen towns and cities housed 12,386 patients, with an additional 1,290 empty beds—a 91 percent occupancy rate. The support staff consisted of 73 surgeons, 66 assistant surgeons, 36 acting assistant surgeons, 1 sick surgeon, 55 stewards, 60 cooks, 236 hired cooks, 64 detailed ward masters, 4 hired ward masters, 484 detailed male nurses, 614 hired nurses, 49 chief matrons, 44 assistant matrons, 48 ward matrons, 396 laundresses, and 303 hired male attendants, for a total of 2,533 personnel. Available houses, churches, and public buildings in towns throughout Georgia and Alabama (some of them 300 miles from Dalton) had to be appropriated. Soldiers preferred to go to a hospital where there was a surgeon from their own state. Thus, Kentuckians desired to go to Newman or Forsyth, Tennesseans to Griffith, Louisianans to the Academy Hospital in Marietta, Texans to Rome, and Georgians desired the hospital closest to their homes. The Gate City Hospital in Atlanta served as a receiving facility and the one in West Point, Georgia, as a wayside hospital. Compounding the army's already overcrowded hospitals was a bout of summer sickness. In July and August, some 79,709 patients were treated, 63 percent of whom were sick. As always, diarrhea topped the list of diagnoses, with 17 percent. Typhoid and malarial fever represented 11 percent, pneumonia 10 percent, and debilities 5.5 percent.[39]

The records of the Atlanta Fairground Hospitals 1 and 2 revealed that sick patients still outnumbered the wounded. During the height of the campaign, the hospitals received 3,347 patients—38.9 percent wounded and 61.1 percent sick. The failure to properly boil drinking water resulted in diarrhea (32.9 percent) and typhoid fever (14.3 percent). Rheumatism came in third at 9.9 percent. Even during the height of the Atlanta Campaign, during June and July, the percent of gunshot wounds and sickness never surpassed 26 and 38 percent, respectively.[40]

As the army continued to retreat south, hospitals had to be relocated. The citizens of Albany, Georgia, received word that they should prepare to receive 2,500 wounded and sick, the latter experiencing chills, pneumonia, and fevers. The local newspaper editor pleaded with officials not to send them. Any place along the railroad would be preferable to Albany, which was already afflicted with sick civilians. Good water remained scarce and could hardly supply the population of 1,500. As for the Flint River, it was not healthy. Indeed, the editor believed that the general hospitals should not be placed in towns at all but out in the countryside.[41]

Kate Cummings found herself in Americus, Georgia, in early September 1864. An accidental fire on September 1 had destroyed two city blocks. "The Bragg and Foard are the only hospitals here," she wrote on the seventh. "The Bragg is very large, and has a ward about a mile in the country, in a beautiful spot. A large brick college [Female Institute] is its main building. . . . The public square opposite to us is filled with tents, which are full of gangrene cases. One lad suffers so much we can hear him scream for two [city] squares off."[42]

The Army of Tennessee's hospital system, never as sophisticated as its Federal counterpart, nonetheless gave the army what it needed the most—returning soldiers. With less dedication and effort, many more men would have languished and dropped out of the war. Medical personnel were not prepared for the Chickamauga deluge, but lessons were learned. Despite its best efforts, the department could not check the spiraling downward trend.

✳ 16 ✳

Logistics

Even for a moderately sized force such as the Army of Tennessee, thousands of noncombatants were required to work in support positions—as teamsters, hospital attendants, orderlies, staff, provost guards, chaplains, ordnance and commissary personnel, and engineers. On January 20, 1863, one in six men in the army—7,314, to be specific—served in a support position. Additionally, thousands of men and women worked in hospitals, arsenals, textile mills, clothing depots, massive commissary and meat-butchering facilities, railroads, salt mines, medical purveyor depots, storage dumps, and other installations, all in an effort to keep the Army of Tennessee operational. The sheer size and level of sophistication of this logistical system represents one of the untold stories of the war.[1]

The Tennessee Food Supply

The importance of Middle Tennessee as a food-producing region cannot be overstated. In anticipation of the Kentucky Campaign, Bragg had his commissary agents scour the countryside, realizing that anything remaining would be seized by the Federals. Civilians could have held out and sold to speculators at higher prices, but to help the Cause, most sold at government prices. In a four-week period, the agents collected a staggering 80,000–100,000 hogs, 7,000–10,000 beeves, 2.5 million pounds of bacon, 60,000 bushels of wheat, and 8,000–10,000 barrels of flour.[2]

By March 1863, on a daily basis, the Army of Tennessee required 35,000 pounds of pork, 85,500 pounds of meal, 3,500 pounds of rice, 1,400 pounds of soap, 350 gallons of vinegar, 522 gallons of molasses, and 44 bushels of salt. Commissary agents could acquire from counties adjacent to the army all of the meal, vinegar, and soap and half of the pork required, but the balance had to be drawn from the general reserve. For the month of April, that meant a draw of 525,000 pounds of pork, 62,000 pounds of rice, 1,300 bushels of salt, and 50 barrels of molasses. The general reserve was stored in eighteen mostly leased warehouses in Atlanta, where huge stockpiles of boxes, sacks, and barrels were piled high. Indeed, two Georgia mills were hired to produce output exclusively for the Atlanta depot, making duck bags for grain and corn. The reserve included nearly 300,000 pounds of salt beef, 4.7 million pounds of pork and bacon, 2,500 barrels of lard, and 1,700 barrels of flour. An additional 117,000 pounds of beef and 1.1 million pounds of pork and bacon were accumulated in Cartersville, Dalton, Ringgold, and Forsyth, and 3,000 head of cattle awaited shipment in Chattanooga.[3]

Corn was a staple, not just for cornmeal but for feed for horses and mules too. There were probably more than 23,000 animals in the army, each of which required twelve pounds of corn daily, in addition to twelve pounds of forage. The animals could graze and foraging parties could gather corn during the spring and summer, although wagons had to travel upward of forty miles one way. Wheeler's and Hardee's corps claimed the sector east of the Nashville & Chattanooga Railroad, but by April 12, that source had largely played out. By March, Hardee was having to ship in corn from Maury and Giles Counties in Tennessee and from northern Alabama. Van Dorn and Polk's sector, west of the Nashville & Chattanooga, proved more promising. The army quartermaster estimated that supplies would last till May 23, but Polk thought the end of July. On June 7, however, one of Forrest's troopers informed his wife, "The country is all foraged out here about Shelbyville." If all of the army's corn (exclusive of forage) had to be shipped by rail, it would require twenty-six carloads daily—virtually the entire daily rolling stock to Tullahoma! Already, daily shipments of 3,000 bushels of corn were being made by rail, requiring about twelve cars daily.[4]

The shipping problem in northern Alabama underscored the overall logistical complexities. The Athens and Decatur sectors, on either side of the Tennessee River, provided a large source of corn for Bragg's army. On March 3, some 18,000 bushels (about sixty pounds per bushel) awaited transport in these two towns. The logical shipment plan would have been to load the corn on wagons and haul it the thirty-one miles from Huntsville to Winchester, Tennessee. From there it could be placed on cars of the Winchester & Alabama Railroad and taken to Decherd. Wagon transport would require two days, however, with each vehicle averaging one ton, or about thirty-three bushels. To run 18,000 bushels overland would thus take the equivalent of more than 350 wagons and 1,400 mules in constant use. It proved more practical to load the corn on two steamboats leased by the government and ship it to Bridgeport and then Chattanooga—110 miles. The corn was then reloaded on cars of the Nashville & Chattanooga Railroad and hauled to Tullahoma at the rate of 3,000 bushels daily.[5]

The primary transportation problem lay with the Nashville & Chattanooga Railroad, Bragg's sole communication artery. The railroad began the war with twenty-eight locomotives to run the trains and nine for branch, switching, and yard work. The rolling stock comprised 17 passenger cars, 6 baggage cars, 225 boxcars, 31 stockcars, 51 flatcars, 26 coal cars, 16 gravel cars, and 8 camp cars. About 200 of the 300 freight cars went to Mississippi in the spring of 1862. When Huntsville fell, the stock became trapped, leaving the road at least fifty cars short for necessary work.[6]

By December 20, 1862, the railroad trestle at Bridgeport had been repaired, the work done under private contract by professional bridge builders Moore & Marsh and paid for by the government. Moore & Marsh planked the bridge with 50,000 feet of lumber for infantry use. One passenger and two freight trains ran daily to Shelbyville, hauling up to 200 tons. The road was generally in good condition, although the spur connecting Shelbyville and Wartrace was so worn that the train could only go five miles per hour. As the Rebels later withdrew from Middle Tennessee, they removed two and a half miles of railroad iron between Bell Buckle and Wartrace.[7]

It can be estimated that the Army of Tennessee shipped about 204 carloads of pork and cattle and 360 of corn over the Nashville & Chattanooga in April 1863. Based on estimates of 200 tons, probably twenty-six cars shipped daily from Chattanooga, nearly 72 percent of those used for meat and corn. This estimate is not too far off from the railroad tonnage received by the Army of the Cumberland on a daily basis. For the Confederates, this left only 52 tons daily for quartermaster, ordnance, and medical supplies, a third of what the Army of the Cumberland received for an army not hugely larger.[8]

The Atlanta firm of Seago, Kennedy, Palmer & Company supplied the enormous quantity of salt required, which came from the mines in Saltville, Virginia. The daily production of 15,000 bushels required about five freight cars. The distillery of High, Lewis & Company contracted with the Atlanta depot for 3,000 gallons of whiskey a month. The "Government Bakery" at Bridge and Marietta Streets baked flour into hardtack.[9]

The primary problem was the dwindling source of meat. The Atlanta commissary depot proved to be the sole source of salt meat for Lee's army, which required 500,000 pounds per week. Bragg was expected to sustain his army from the field *in addition to* sending beef and pork to Lee! This led Bragg to comment sardonically that but for his "much abused" Kentucky Campaign, "we should now all be in a starving condition." Maj. John Walker, Bragg's chief commissary, raised an alarm. He predicted that by mid-March, the entire Middle Tennessee meat supply would be exhausted, thus making both armies dependent on the Atlanta depot. He placed Georgia pork at a sixty-day supply at one-half pound per man for 350,000 men. In short, the Confederacy was headed for a catastrophe, and the president needed to be advised. Secretary of War James Seddon answered that he was aware of the problem but had no solution other than to drive more cattle out of Kentucky. Commissary officials had their own answer to Bragg's comments. Through December 2, 1862, 100,000 hogs, 15,000 beeves, and 2 million pounds of bacon had been gotten out of Tennessee, with most of the cattle and a large portion of the hogs going to Bragg. In April 1863, the Atlanta depot shipped to the Army of Tennessee 1,010,910 pounds of bacon, 102,055 pounds of beef, and 923 beeves.[10]

For thirty-nine-year-old Maj. John F. Cummings, former owner of a Cincinnati meat-packing company and presently commander of the Atlanta commissary depot, the problem lay elsewhere. Maj. W. W. Guy, assistant commissary of subsistence at Oxford, Alabama, insisted that he could purchase upward of 700 head of cattle and as much corn as riverboats could transport to be shipped on the Coosa River to Rome, Georgia. The wealthy landowners and speculators, however, were holding out for higher prices than the government rates. He further claimed that adequate supplies existed in Montgomery, Lowndes, and Macon Counties but corrupt government agents were buying at one price and personally selling at another (skimming), "at least that is what the population thinks." When Guy purchased 20,000 bushels of corn and several hundred bushels of peas in central Alabama, he was blocked by Buckner's agents, who said that the supplies were earmarked for East Tennessee. There was also a lack of wagons to haul supplies.[11]

Beyond Kentucky, where it was believed 7,000 head could be collected, there were other potential sources of beef. In early May, "Messrs. Yocum & Kerr" were within a week of the Mississippi River with a supply of 5,000 Texas steers. They claimed that they could have them in Demopolis, Alabama, by early July. Additionally, if trading were approved by the Richmond government (one pound of cotton per three pounds of bacon and permission to barter molasses for bacon), an estimated 500,000 to 1 million pounds of bacon could be obtained along the banks of the Cumberland River.[12]

Florida had tens of thousands of semiwild steers, but getting them to market proved a major undertaking. Most were in the region south of Tampa Bay, and herding the beeves to a railhead meant weeks of traversing snake- and mosquito-infested trails. The railroad went to the coast and thence to the Savannah and Charleston garrisons. Herding cattle overland to Albany, Georgia, and thence by rail to Macon and Atlanta proved almost impossible given the marginal forage along the road. Desperate times demanded that attempts nonetheless be made. During August 1863, the Fourth District, headquartered in Madison, shipped between 1,500 and 2,000 head to the Army of Tennessee. During 1863, Florida accounted for 3,564 head for Bragg's army, a third of the state's supply for that year.[13]

Cummings made his own calculations of the efficiency of Walker's agents. He dispatched ten of his own agents into northern Alabama and the counties adjacent to Army of Tennessee operations. Maj. A. B. Banks reported that two months' meat supplies could be acquired in counties on either side of the Nashville & Chattanooga Railroad. Additionally, 1 million pounds of meat could be obtained in Lincoln County and 800,000 pounds from Giles and Maury Counties. An obviously perturbed Bragg responded on March 18: "He [Banks] exhibits such profound ignorance on the subject, and has allowed his mind to become impressed with the statements of men so exaggerated as to satisfy any reasonable man. They are knaves or fools, that I can only answer by simply disclosing my inability to meet his expectations." In June, Walker was replaced by Maj. Giles M. Hillyer, who had served as a commissary officer since 1861.[14]

Another issue lay in the fact that in February 1863, the daily ration was higher than allowed by law. The daily ration for meat was 1.72 pounds of bacon, 1.74 pounds of beef, 1 pound of fresh pork, 1 pound of pickled beef, or 0.75 pounds of salt pork; for bread, 1.74 pounds of cornmeal or 1 pound of flour. Every 100 men also received five pounds of rice, six pounds of sugar, six pounds of molasses, three quarts of vinegar, two pounds of soap, four quarts of salt, and (when ordered) two gallons of whiskey. Richmond commissary officials argued that even if the meat ration were cut, Bragg's army would still be receiving a higher issue than Lee's army. In the spring, the salt pork ration was reduced to a half pound.[15]

Despite the reductions, the letters and diaries make it clear that throughout the spring the men received sufficient, if not monotonous, rations. In March, a Mississippian wrote that he got bacon or pickled beef and cornmeal daily and occasionally a little rice and an extra ration of molasses, salt, and vinegar. The problem was that for weeks on end the men routinely received only fat bacon and cornmeal. "Will you believe me when I tell you I have not seen a biscuit for over a month and such is the case with the larger portion of the army," a soldier revealed. T. B. Settles told his sisters that the men were in good health and spirits, "but not much change in diet." Unfortunately, a late freeze killed off some of the early fruit crop. John R. Hurley of the 39th Alabama insisted, however, that "we get plenty to eat, bacon corn meal and a little flour and yes some peas." William Rogers disclosed that the men received half a pound of bacon, one and a quarter pounds of cornmeal, and occasionally some rice or peas, but not often. Local citizens sold or bartered milk, butter, and eggs but at exorbitant prices.[16]

Although 58th North Carolina member Langston Estes related that "we get tolerable enough," a disgusted Fayette McDonald grumbled that the daily fare was bread with no grease and beef that "could climb a tree. Enough to kill any man." Joel H. Puckett concluded that everyone got enough, except of molasses, flour, and sugar. The grinding monotony of the food continued to be the main complaint. "Day by day the camp kettle is used for no other purpose than to boil beef, and probably twice a month in cooking an old ham. It is bread and beef for morning, at noon, and at night," a Georgian explained. Hog chitterlings were distributed at the Tullahoma slaughterhouse for those men accustomed to eating them; there were always takers. Standing orders prevented the men from hunting. Lieutenant Davidson noted on February 23: "No vegetables until today we got a few Irish potatoes. It is pretty hard any way you take it in the army."[17]

Following the loss of Middle Tennessee, food supplies dwindled again. "Evy thing in the shape of provision is getting scears we ar Onely getting half rashins now and I am afraid they wount hold out long at that," an Alabamian wrote his wife on August 2. As Pvt. A. M. Glazner of the 18th Alabama put it, "O have bin hungry for 10 days all the time get up hungry lay down the same." On August 25, Hillyer reported that the Army of Tennessee was supplied through the thirty-first. Remaining on hand in the Chattanooga depot were 900,000 rations of meat and 1.1 million rations of breadstuffs, 3 million rations of rice and peas, 1.2 million of vinegar, 3 million of soap, 4.5 million of salt, 300,000 of molasses, and 150,000 pounds of sugar. He pronounced the supply of meat after October 1 "gloomy." Lee's army had been on quarter rations of pork for many months by that time, half the rations of Bragg's army.[18]

Bragg's situation would have been dire but for three lower northwestern Georgia counties—Troup, Coweta, and Campbell. In response to a government appeal, these counties sent the Army of Tennessee 2,800 head of cattle in November. Between November 8 and 13, the army received 561 head (perhaps the Georgia beeves), but they averaged a mere 154 pounds. (The Texas cattle received before the fall of Vicksburg had averaged 400 pounds.) Fortunately, the wheat in mid-Georgia was a bumper crop, averaging seventeen bushels an acre.[19]

Arms and Ammunition

The Army of Tennessee required huge amounts of ammunition. The primary supplier was Capt. Moses H. Wright's Atlanta Arsenal, located in a sprawling fifty-acre installation at the racetrack one mile southwest of the city center. From July 1, 1862, to June 30, 1863, the laboratory fabricated 4,164,050 rounds of small-arms ammunition, averaging nearly 12,000 rounds per day, along with 19.5 million percussion caps and 3.75 million pistol caps. The arsenal also turned out 20,000 rounds of fixed-artillery ammunition during that period (fifty-six rounds per day) and 300,000 friction primers.[20]

By January 1863, the Atlanta Arsenal employed 427 hands: the saddle and harness shop, forty-two; the percussion cap factory, fifty-nine; the field artillery laboratory, sixty-one; the small-arms laboratory, ninety-three (mostly boys); the carpenter shop, sixty; the blacksmith and machine shop, forty-six; the armory (musket repair), forty-eight; the tin shop, four; and staff (inspectors, storekeepers, paymasters, etc.), fourteen. The small-arms laboratory continued to grow, with 137 hands in February. By March, an average of 20,370 rounds per day were being fabricated.[21]

Despite the output, supplies strained to keep up with demand. On January 28, 1863, Wright informed Oladowski that he had on hand only 200,000 rounds for the army's cavalry — Enfield, shotgun, buck-and-ball, and navy pistol cartridges. As for ammunition for Maynard, Burnside, and Colt carbines, "I have none. Neither can I make cases or cartridges for them at my laboratory." Other arsenals provided "little or no aid." A 500,000-round order was needed to equip Churchill's Brigade when it arrived in May 1863. The army allotment per man was 140 rounds — 40 in the cartridge boxes and 100 in the wagons. Cheatham's Division, more actively engaged than any other at Perryville, expended thirty-five rounds per man, while Hardee's Corps at Murfreesboro, engaged from morning to late afternoon on the first day's battle, expended forty rounds per man. Polk's Corps at Chickamauga averaged twenty-six rounds per man. The army's total expenditure at the latter amounted to over 1.5 million rounds. Some of the shortfall was made up by 120,000 rounds of ammunition captured at Chickamauga, which sat outside in boxes at Alexander's Bridge for several days for want of wagon transportation. Artillery ammunition also remained in great demand. The field guns in the army were to have 100 rounds on hand at all times. By that standard, there should have been 24,600 rounds available, but the April 1863 count tallied only 18,942 rounds, 16 percent of which were short-range canister. There were only 8,341 rounds of shell and spherical case shot available for the smoothbore guns, an average of eighty-seven per gun, the balance being less effective solid shot. In early September, Oladowski placed an order to Atlanta for an additional 4,180 rounds. Wright was also under pressure to supply .57 and .58 Enfield rifle ammunition (a third of his output) for Charleston, Mobile, East Tennessee, and Mississippi. An irritated Oladowski complained to Richmond that he was not getting his fair share. In response, Wright assured Chief of Ordnance Josiah Gorgas that nearly one-fourth of the entire output of the arsenal (1,125,000 rounds) had gone to Bragg.[22]

By April, Wright had his entire small-arms laboratory focusing on only .57 Enfield and .54 Mississippi rifle rounds, and even so he could not meet the demand. Other arsenals had to fill in the gaps, especially for pistol and carbine rounds. During 1863, some 1,681,000 rounds from other arsenals passed through Atlanta, with 51 percent coming from Augusta, 21 percent from Charleston, 13 percent from Richmond, 4 percent each from Columbus, Georgia, and Selma, and lesser amounts from Montgomery, Macon, and Fayetteville, North Carolina.[23]

Complaints from the field concerning the quality of work were not uncommon. Capt. W. Overton Barret reported that at Murfreesboro nearly all seventy-three six-pounder spherical cases fired by his battery had burst prematurely. The poor quality of the powder, "worthless friction primers," and "entirely worthless" paper fuses also became concerns. Oladowski insisted that the problem lay with the men themselves. He suggested that during the heat of battle, fuses were being cut too short, resulting in premature explosions. The ammunition, he maintained, was "of good quality and well prepared." As for the friction primers, Oladowski had personally observed the fabrication process at the Atlanta Arsenal and he considered it superior. Again, the problem was "more the neglect of artillery officers than their fabrication."[24]

The men complained that some Enfield rifle cartridges were too large, causing the guns to jam after fifteen to twenty rounds. Initially, it was believed that these were manufactured in Atlanta, but subsequent investigation found that they were made at the Selma Arsenal. The problem with the Atlanta cartridges was that they were sometimes not well greased, so the paper absorbed the small amount of lubricant. A deficiency of beeswax resulted in the use of less efficient tallow as a lubricant.[25]

On occasion, Wright sparred with Oladowski. When a shipment of defective ammunition was returned to the arsenal, Wright balked. "I find every ball here to fill every requirement. Some that was overhauled, the sup't., contrary to instructions, failed to have the balls *recast* & are too large for Enfields—but every cartridge for Buck & Ball fitted as well as any could in the world. Suppose that they had been *too large*—why not issue them for *Enfield Musket* Buck & Ball, instead of sending all the way back here, & by the same train, requisitions coming for Enfield musket cartridges."[26]

In March 1863, the infantry of the Army of Tennessee counted 31,811 small arms—37 percent smoothbore percussion muskets and 63 percent rifles of various calibers. An additional 2,166 arms were stored at the Tullahoma depot and 2,040 at the Chattanooga depot. The A. C. Wryly warehouse in Atlanta stored the surplus arms of the Atlanta Arsenal. A March 1863 report revealed 5,497 arms, but that number proved deceptive. Some 2,071 were obsolete flintlocks, 1,217 assorted old shotguns and sporting rifles, 2,086 smoothbore percussion arms, and only 123 assorted rifles. With so many men returning to the ranks that spring, Bragg needed an additional 10,000 arms; by March 17, only 1,450 had arrived. Small arms frequently broke down and had to be sent to the Atlanta Arsenal for repair. During the 1862–63 reporting year, 9,344 muskets and pistols were repaired, or an average of 180 per week. With a sufficient number of mechanics, the number could be increased to 500–600 per week, but getting details of men from the army proved increasingly difficult. Half of the troops possessed no bayonets. The result was a hodgepodge assortment of arms within a brigade. In Stewart's Brigade, for example, the 19th Tennessee had smoothbore muskets; the 24th/31st and 33rd Tennessee, Enfield rifles; the 4th Tennessee, Springfield rifles; and the 5th Tennessee, "refuse muskets." An effort was made to have uniform arms within a regiment. By March 1863, the 1st/48th Tennessee had all Enfields; the 2nd/5th Tennessee, .58 rifles; and the 5th Confederate, .69 smoothbores.[27]

A rented building on Whitehall Street in Atlanta served as the harness and saddle shop. During 1863, the facility fabricated or purchased through private contractors 719 single sets of artillery harnesses, 4,000 cavalry saddles, 4,905 cavalry bridles, and 4,608 saddle blankets. The shops also produced saber belts, holsters, spur straps, and rifle slings. The majority of the saddle blankets came from the Junnis Jordan Company of Eufaula, Alabama.[28]

The artillery captures at the Battle of Stones River looked impressive—thirty guns, four battery wagons, four traveling forges, and twenty-one caissons—yet most of the guns did not remain in the army. A battery of Napoleon guns went to Beauregard at Charleston, ten pieces to Buckner at Mobile, and ten others to East Tennessee to guard bridges. By March 1863, Bragg's armament was badly mismatched, with eighty obsolete six-pounder and twelve-pounder howitzers, sixteen twelve-pounder Napoleons, and twenty-eight rifles of various calibers.[29]

During the spring, Oladowski began taking old six-pounder and twelve-pounder howitzers from the artillery to be recast into more modern, light twelve-pounder Napoleon guns. In March 1863, the army possessed only sixteen of these weapons—twelve cast by Leeds & Company of New Orleans and four captured at Perryville. The primary supplier for the Army of Tennessee was the Augusta Arsenal. The metal design was a recent Austrian invention and was recommended by Confederate diplomat James Mason. The transition proved slow; by April, only five twelve-pounder Napoleons had been received. Six Augusta Napoleons were sent in early June, but the train wrecked and the guns had to be returned to Atlanta for carriage and caisson repair. By September, only fifteen new Napoleon guns had been received.[30]

The ordnance loss during the disastrous Tullahoma Campaign in late June and early July 1863 proved significant. Polk's and Hardee's corps (minus Johnson's Brigade, which filed no report) tallied losses of 2,080 bayonets, 2,407 sets of cartridge and cap boxes, 329,029 rounds of ammunition, 337,468 percussion caps, 1 forge, 1 battery wagon, and 3 field guns. Even worse was the loss of 4,321 small arms, 2,241 of which were from Wheeler's cavalrymen. Ordnance officials admitted that much of the equipment was simply tossed on the roadside.[31]

Quartermaster Stores

Even though it was operating near a railroad, the army possessed 2,276 wagons in March 1863: Polk's Corps had 890; Hardee's Corps, 753; Wheeler's Corps, 284; the District of the Tennessee (northern Alabama), 41; and the general reserve supply, 308. Many of the vehicles wore out from the bad roads and constant usage, leading government officials to contract for 350 new four-horse wagons and 150 spring ambulances. Although the shortage of tire iron caused contractors some delays, by April 20, the order was expected to be completed.[32]

In the first five months of 1863, the Army of Tennessee received 100,000 pairs of shoes. If there was a shortage, insisted one soldier, it was because soldiers traded them. A late March inspection found the army "tolerably well shod." A requisition order was placed for 10,000 pairs, but the Chattanooga depot had only 4,000 pairs in stock, with another 4,000 pairs at the Atlanta Quartermaster Depot. Fremantle saw only a couple of barefoot soldiers when he visited the army in late spring, but the men always seemed to be in need. "I wrote home for clothes but we now have drawn as many clothes as we want but I want some shoes[.] my shoes is all most worn out and I don't expect I can draw any," 39th Alabama soldier John Hurley wrote his sister on April 28. In September, an order was issued in Daniel H. Hill's Corps that no man would be excused from the march for lack of shoes. "Eighteen thousand pairs of shoes have been issued to this corps in the last two months, and still more are asked for. This fact points to abuses on the part of soldiers," the circular pointedly read.[33]

The Atlanta Quartermaster Depot made shoes exclusively for the Army of Tennessee, with forty men turning out about 150 pairs per day. With sixty more laborers and sufficient leather, the machines could make 500 pairs per day. In their eagerness to get out of the army, some overrepresented themselves as shoemakers but were actually only cobblers, and their lack of skills resulted in wasted material. The Columbus Quartermaster Depot, with 120 shoemakers employed, projected its 1863 output to be 100,000 pairs of shoes, but the supply went to Lee's army.[34]

The Columbus depot shipped 20,000 garments to Bragg in September 1862, the material fabricated by the Eagle Manufacturing Company of that city. When the army withdrew from Kentucky, Bragg brought with him enough cotton cloth to make 150,000 garments. The shirts, drawers, pants, and coats that went to Edmund Kirby Smith (90,000) were made in Knoxville and those that went to Bragg (60,000) in Augusta, the latter's depot employing 1,500 women. Smith also brought out of the state 5,000 pairs of shoes, 3,000 blankets, and 2,000 coats.[35]

The Atlanta Quartermaster Depot employed 3,000 persons, only 27 of whom were men. If given the needed materials (225,000 yards of wool, 908,200 yards of cotton, 7,700 gross of buttons, 2,700 pounds of flax thread, and 2,000 dozen spools of cotton thread), the facility could annually turn out 130,000 jackets, 130,000 pairs of pants, 125,000 shirts, and 175,000 pairs of drawers. As of March 26, it had in stock 25,000 jackets, 15,000 pairs of pants, 65,000 shirts, 30,000 pairs of drawers, 2,000 blankets, and 3,800 wool hats.[36]

When Fremantle visited the army, he found the troops well clad — some in gray uniforms, some brown, and almost all with the trademark wool hats of the Army of Tennessee. He observed that even if a regiment were uniformly clothed by the government, it wore mixed colors within a week, the soldiers preferring the course homespun jackets and pants made by their mothers and sisters. Most officers wore a bluish gray coat.[37]

The logistical support required to sustain the Army of Tennessee proved sizable, and it had to come from an industrial region that bordered on antebellum third world. No blueprints for supply administration existed, and spot shortages of food and shoes were never fully resolved. The bureaucracy nonetheless prevailed, more often through reaction than planning.[38]

The Western & Atlantic

When Atlanta became the new supply base for the Army of Tennessee, the sole communication line became the Western & Atlantic Railroad. By September 1863, the road had only thirty-one operational locomotives. Another twelve were being repaired and three had been condemned. Running two passenger trains daily required six engines, and four more were needed for switching and yard work, leaving only twenty-one engines in service. Theoretically, seven freight trains with twelve cars each (a light load) could be sent to Dalton daily, estimating three days to make a trip. Each car could hold 250 bushels of corn, resulting in 26,000 bushels arriving daily. The horses and mules required twelve pounds of corn and a like amount of forage daily, so the trains were able to provide enough corn for daily consumption and even a stockpile. Government officials insisted that the road must have at least 300 cars on hand, so with proper management there should have been more than an adequate supply—at least on paper.[39]

In truth, the men were in desperate straits. Alabamian W. C. Athey wrote his mother on November 12: "I lean that we aire not a going to get any meat onely beeaf seven days and bacon every ten days. . . . That is pretty haird liveing." When no meat was issued, the men received two and a half ounces of sugar. Nearly a week later, Daniel Weaver of the 45th Alabama informed his father of the dire circumstances. "We have not received any bacon since I have been in the fight [Chickamauga] we do not get beef ever day 3 day out of 10 we have not got any beef. They give us rice & sugar in place of beef."[40]

The army's animals were in a near-starving condition. "The loss of horses in this army since the Battle of Chickamauga has already been very heavy, owing to the want of forage and the criminal neglect of quartermasters, teamsters, and artillery drivers," a correspondent noted. "In some instances they have to go from one to four days without a grain of corn, or bundle of fodder." He blamed railroad officials but admitted that the bridges over Chickamauga had been down for several days.[41]

Western & Atlantic officials ramped up shipments. On November 17, for example, sixteen cars of corn were dispatched from Atlanta at 4:00 A.M. and twelve cars at 11:00 A.M., and if another locomotive could be found, another fourteen cars could be sent that night. The next day, fifteen cars of forage went up, and on November 19, eighteen cars of forage at 4:00 A.M. and another eighteen at 11:00 A.M. The supply nonetheless never kept pace with demand. On December 27, Mackall pleaded for more corn for the artillery and cavalry horses, but officials claimed that six of their best locomotives were crippled and three others needed repair. Despite difficulties, supplies of corn continued to get through. Over nine days between March 28 and April 11, 1864, some 153 carloads arrived—thirty-eight of corn, eighty of fodder, and twelve of oats. By May 21, the equivalent of sixty-four cars of forage, perhaps 480 tons, were stockpiled in Atlanta awaiting shipment north.[42]

On January 12, Joseph E. Johnston informed Georgia governor Joseph E. Brown that the railroad was not supplying the army's needs, and he placed officials on notice. An indignant Brown answered that the problem lay with government officials. In the spring of 1862, Albert Sidney Johnston had requested assistance from the Western & Atlantic to supply his army; 8 engines and 200 cars were sent. Brown demanded that at least two engines and fifty cars now be returned. Quartermaster General Alexander Lawton wrote that returning the equipment at this point was simply impossible. Nonetheless, twenty-five boxcars were eventually returned.[43]

A railroad official estimated that the Army of Tennessee needed only fifty to sixty carloads daily (three trains), but the cars obviously could not be devoted exclusively to corn. For three weeks in February, the rolling stock was devoted to troop transport. On March 9, nine cars of horses went up. On the nineteenth, seven cars of horses and mules were dispatched, but five of them (with sixty-four horses) were detained at Kingston for Rowan's Georgia battery. Johnston partially resolved the problem of shipping cattle by having the beeves slaughtered in Atlanta rather than hauled by railroad or on hoof. What used to take five cars thus took two. There was a trade-off: the men detested the quality of the pickled beef. "The rations of beef that we are getting now are very poor indeed," wrote Captain Patton on January 23. "During the cold weather they commenced killing the Beef for this army in Atlanta but this unreasonably warm weather makes it sour and almost uneatable by the time we get it." A Tennessean noted that "the beef we eat is so often killed one day to keep it from dying before the next."[44]

Georgia received its sobriquet "Breadbasket of the Confederacy" for a reason. The tax in kind (a 10 percent government crop impressment for the army) for Georgia in January–February 1864 included 56,078 bushels of sweet potatoes, 972,678 bushels of corn, 118,572 bushels of wheat, 722,903 pounds of rice, 6,892,583 pounds of fodder, 198,196 pounds of cured ham, 19,927 gallons of molasses, 42,479 bushels of peas, and 232,989 pounds of bacon. The problem was not supply but distribution. Major Cummings informed Bragg in January 1864 that he required ten carloads of cornmeal daily from southwest Georgia, but he could get only five.[45]

For the quarter ending in March 1864, in addition to commissary stores, ordnance, and medical supplies, the Quartermaster Department also received and issued at Dalton a large variety of items: 15,170 pounds of hay, 1,001,282 pounds of corn, 15,035 pounds of oats, 121,940 pounds of fodder, 16,208 sacks, 12 feed troughs, 22 horses, 261 mules, 73 four-horse wagons, 31 two-horse wagons, 13 ambulances, 108 wagon sheets, 6,506 pairs of pants, 2,999 pairs of drawers, 104 flannel shirts, 3 pairs of boots, 2,983 jackets, 2,902 shirts, 2,658 hats, 5,183 pairs of shoes, 3,296 pairs of socks, 115 blankets, 96 lead harness, 62 wagon saddles, 133 halter chains, 20 leather harnesses, 224 pounds of sole leather, 24 pounds of harness leather, 70 mule hides, 387 beef hides, 16,208 pounds of beef hide, 134 camp kettles, 190 tin cups, 338 mess pans, 58 buckets, 717 pounds of bar iron, 195 pounds of hoop iron, 2,120 horseshoes, 3,500 mule shoes, 24 horseshoe files, 3 brass drums, 93 saddle blankets, 5 flags, 740 feet of lumber, 4,550 envelopes, 555 steel pens, 124 lead pencils, 30 bottles of red ink, 718 quires of paper, 210 penholders, 192 quartermaster envelopes, 54 bottles of black ink, 108 picks, 90 axes, 75 shovels, 6 hatchets, 3 augers, 56 pounds of rope, 4,580 pounds of salt, 8 kegs of tar, 8 kegs of oil, 1,975 pounds of grease, 342 boxes, 246 pounds of horseshoe nails, 423 pounds of nails, 335 currycombs, 1 bellow, 1 anvil, 206 tents, and 534 tent flies.[46]

With improved train management, Johnston reported in early January that five days' rations for the men and corn for the animals had been stockpiled at Dalton and a three-day supply at Calhoun, twenty miles to the south. He received no supplies on February 1–2, thus reducing the reserve to six days'. Despite all these difficulties, he wrote on January 25 that the daily shipments at Dalton "are now fully equal to the consumption" and barring unforeseen circumstances, a stockpile might even be accumulated.[47]

During the initial phase of the Atlanta Campaign, rations remained scant. William L. Trask wrote: "I have frequently, during the last two weeks, made my breakfast, dinner, and supper on a cold corndodger and a cup of water. Our ration of meat is so small that it doesn't give us a full meal once a day and frequently not that." As the army withdrew toward Atlanta, supplies increased. "Our army is well supplied with good rations. I have plenty of coffee now," Captain Douglas wrote on June 10. Writing to his children on July 8, James Hall noted: "We are doing well in the way of rations. We have plenty of bread and meat, and a little coffee occasionally and a few vegetables." Mississippian James Foster concurred: "The army was never before better fed when in the field. Vegetables are issued once or twice a week and coffee about as often. Rations of tobacco are now issued to the troops."[48]

Post-Chattanooga

The losses sustained at Missionary Ridge left severe ordnance shortages throughout the army. On December 20, 1863, Hardee's and Hindman's corps counted 33,397 effectives with 29,494 arms—short 3,903. The Atlanta Arsenal immediately shipped 1,200 arms. Oladowski appealed to the Selma Arsenal, which had previously sent repaired arms to the Trans-Mississippi. With returning sick (500 arrived the last week in December), the deficit continued to grow. Oladowski requested a shipment of 4,000 arms. By January 25, 1864, an additional 1,400 repaired arms had arrived. As late as March 18, the Atlanta Arsenal shops remained overtaxed. Wright had shipped 2,300 arms to the army, but he could promise only 658 more by April 1.[49]

The artillery had been left in a shattered state. The ninety-six guns atop Missionary Ridge had expended 6,417 rounds, averaging sixty-five rounds per gun. Since the Atlanta Arsenal could manufacture only 125–150 rounds per day, it would require six weeks' line production to replenish the stock. As for leather items, Wright estimated on February 12, 1864, that he could fabricate 500 single sets of artillery harnesses, 500 cavalry sets of equipment, and 2,500 sets of belts, cartridge boxes, and cap boxes by July 1.[50]

Uncovering the truth regarding the shortages proved difficult. On March 7, Hood's Corps submitted shortages in all areas. When Hardee's Corps filed its return in mid-April, however, an investigation reported that the corps was overstocked in all areas, with 1,159 arms, 2,784 cartridge boxes, 761 knapsacks, 3,144 haversacks, and 1,388 canteens. A mid-April internal inspection of three regiments in Reynolds's Brigade revealed problems. The 54th Virginia carried Enfield rifles, but its cartridge boxes were too short for the cartridges. The 63rd Virginia had inferior smoothbore muskets — "locks of most of them too weak to burst a cap first time." The 58th North Carolina carried outdated Austrian rifles, inaccurate at long ranges. Again, the same complaint was submitted about the cartridge boxes — too short for the ammunition.[51]

Supplying the troops with ammunition was a constant problem. On June 19, the men had 1,932,638 rounds in their cartridge boxes and another 1,784,504 rounds in 223 wagons. Railroad cars at Vinings, Georgia, contained 366,000 rounds of ammunition and 1,084 artillery rounds. The Atlanta Arsenal stockpiled 220,000 rounds and Augusta 5,000 rounds. Atlanta continued to manufacture small-arms ammunition at the rate of 30,000 rounds per day.[52]

Adequately supplying the cavalry remained a problem throughout the war. On July 31, 1864, Wheeler's troopers counted 2,562 Enfield rifles, 613 Mississippi rifles, 2,031 Austrian rifles, and 379 .69 smoothbores. Surprisingly, over 1,000 captured Yankee carbines were also in service: 879 Sharps rifles, 184 Burnsides, and 86 miscellaneous carbines. Only half of the men had revolvers: 1,071 Colts, 2,259 navy rifles, and 31 Kerrs. Few sabers (1,302) remained in use by this time. Other items included 7,065 saddles, 492 currycombs, and 893 horse brushes.[53]

All of the batteries needed refitting. On December 14, 1863, the infantry batteries counted only ninety-five guns, eighteen of which were obsolete six-pounders. Several companies lacked a gun or two, and Bledsoe's Missouri and Anderson's Georgia had none. The number of pieces of ammunition in the two corps and artillery reserve averaged 120, 137, and 146, respectively, far short of the recommended 200 rounds. An Augusta Arsenal Napoleon gun in Swett's Battery had to be returned due to flaws, and the rifling in a Tredegar-made three-inch rifle in Oliver's Alabama battery had completely worn away.[54]

By the end of 1863, the foundries at the Augusta, Columbus, and Macon Arsenals had cast fifty-seven, twenty-eight, and thirty-three twelve-pounder Napoleon guns, respectively, with the pieces shipped to the Army of Tennessee, Polk's Army of Mississippi, and the Mobile defenses. The Federals captured at least six of the Macon guns at Missionary Ridge. Macon also turned out eight ten-pounder Parrott rifles. Fresh consignments continued to be rushed to Dalton—in February 1864, two batteries of Augusta Napoleons; in March, a battery of Columbus Napoleons; in April, a battery of Macon Napoleons; and in early May, five Augusta Napoleons. Bellamy's Alabama battery also received a Tredegar three-inch rifle. All of the six-pounders were phased out, and on April 30, the army counted sixty-four Napoleons, thirty-eight twelve-pounder howitzers, six three-inch rifles, ten ten-pounder Parrott rifles, and two Blakely rifles. A gunner in the Washington Artillery loved his new Napoleons—"we would not have exchanged them for Parrott rifles."[55]

Despite large industrial assets, the Army of Tennessee struggled mightily. Severe shortages of meat led to periods of privation, especially following the Kentucky Campaign and the Battle of Chickamauga, which in turn led to depressed morale and increased desertions. In order to protect the prime food-producing area between Shelbyville and Columbia, Tennessee, Bragg wrongly deployed his army following the Battle of Stones River, which in turn led to defeat in the Tullahoma Campaign. Many of the shortages resulted from a deteriorating transportation system. Only five of Longstreet's brigades arrived in time for the Battle of Chickamauga due to a limited rail system. The belated upgrading of the artillery did not come in time for Stones River, where the Union long arm dominated. In addition, the Army of the Cumberland converted to all rifled small arms a full year before the Rebels did. The faltering logistical system thus proved to be yet another nail in the coffin of the Army of Tennessee.

The Road Off the Mountain
Wheeler's Raid

Bragg continued to have mood swings following Chickamauga. "In mind I am greatly harassed and distressed," he confessed to Elise. Indeed, the exchange of their loving, almost playful letters proved to be his only escape from dreadful reality.[1]

Much to Longstreet's chagrin, Bragg rejected his offensive suggestion to move against Burnside on the right or against Bridgeport on the left. Bragg determined instead to besiege Chattanooga. "The enemy are in Chattanooga, strongly fortified and how we are going to get them out I don't see, nor from what I hear, General Bragg has any plan for doing so," one of Longstreet's officers wrote on September 30. The Confederate line ran along the crest of Missionary Ridge, 400–600 feet above Chattanooga Creek. E. P. Alexander's twenty-gun battalion occupied Lookout Mountain, rising 2,200 feet. Pickets stretched along the southern bank of the Tennessee River. An entrenched line in the Chattanooga Valley, extending from the river to the town and Lookout Mountain, completed the investment. Bragg thus occupied the east, south, and west. A Mobile correspondent, upon viewing the situation, concluded that the only way to force the Yankees out was "to dig up to the place, as the enemy did at Vicksburg and Fort Wagner, or to maneuver him out of it."[2]

The Federal supply route south of the Tennessee River, the old Summertown Toll Road, the Memphis & Charleston Railroad, and the river all came together at the foot of Lookout Mountain, where Alexander's guns successfully cut the jugular. The Northerners had three options on the north bank. The Anderson Pike and Haley's Trace, both in wretched condition and subject to cavalry raids, crossed the eastern slope of Walden's Ridge and descended into the Sequatchie Valley. The third path, the Kelly's Ferry Road, was commanded by the west slope of Raccoon Mountain. Supplies slowed to a trickle.[3]

On September 25, Bragg sent Forrest to East Tennessee to verify intelligence that Burnside was advancing. The Tennessean proceeded to Charleston, where he brushed aside enemy cavalry and advanced to within thirty miles of Knoxville. Bragg apparently saw Forrest doing exactly what Morgan had done back in late 1862—getting caught up in his own adventure and riding himself out of the campaign. He went on a tirade: "[Forrest] has allowed himself to be drawn off toward Knoxville in a general rampage, capturing villages and towns that are no use whatever to me. . . . The man is ignorant, and does not know anything of cooperation. He is nothing more than a good raider."[4]

The army commander determined to send Wheeler's cavalry on a raid in Rosecrans's rear in the Sequatchie Valley. He decided to reinforce Wheeler by combining his two cavalry divisions with three of Forrest's four brigades; George C. Dibbrell's would remain at Cleveland. On September 28, Bragg told Forrest to immediately turn the brigades over to Wheeler. Brent saw only folly in the decision: "Coupled with the existing discontents in the Cavalry it will tend . . . to still further impair its usefulness. Forrest, with many objections, however is the best Cavalry commander in the army." Interestingly, David Powell considered Bragg's decision both reasonable and appropriate. Forrest was "not ready to take on such a large command" and was simply not "cut out for conducting standard cavalry operations on behalf of an army." Bragg, of course, would never have chosen Forrest over Wheeler for top command (Powell preferred Wharton or Will Martin). When Forrest's brigades finally joined up with Wheeler three days later at Cotton Port, forty-five miles upriver from Chattanooga, they were badly jaded, poorly armed, and reduced to barely 500 men per brigade.[5]

Forrest predictably went into a rage. When he next encountered Bragg, the army commander extended his hand; Forrest did not return the courtesy. Taken aback, Bragg stepped back and sat down. Forrest grew irate, as witnessed by Dr. J. B. Cowan. The Tennessean claimed that Bragg had been waging a vendetta against him because he "would not fawn over you [Bragg] as others did." Bragg had robbed him of his command back in Kentucky and "gave it to one of your favorites." His words then became menacing: "I have stood by your meanness as long as I intend to. You have played the part of a damned scoundrel, and are a coward, and if you were any part of a man I would slap your jaw and force you to resent it." To threats of arrest Forrest answered, "I dare you to do it, and I say to you that if you ever again try to interfere with me or cross my path it will be at the peril of your life." Forrest then stormed out. "Well, you are in for it now," Cowan said to Forrest. "He'll never say a word about it," said the cavalryman, "and, mark my word, he'll make no action in the matter. I will ask to be relieved and transferred to a different field, and he will not oppose it." He was subsequently ordered to Mississippi.[6]

Leaving a brigade behind, Wheeler quickly reorganized his 4,000 troopers and six guns into three divisions commanded by Wharton, Martin, and Davidson, the latter being Forrest's copped brigades. Brig. Gen. Frank Armstrong begged off the mission due to ill health. The subsequent raid into the Sequatchie Valley would be misreported. There is no doubt that Wheeler created damage, but he again exaggerated the results to the point of fraudulence. His claim of 800–1,500 burned wagons and 3,000 slaughtered mules surpassed even the hyperbole of his December 1862 ride around Rosecrans's army. The earliest report of the raid claimed that 500 wagons were destroyed and 300–400 prisoners were taken. A contemporary eyewitness in the 4th Alabama Cavalry claimed that 500 wagons were captured, 300 of which were burned. An official Southern report later placed the number of wagons at 700. From the outset, Rosecrans claimed 500. The pursuing Federals, two cavalry divisions moving up from Bridgeport, caught up with the rear guard and mauled it, recapturing many of the prisoners, the unburned wagons, and 300 mules, while inflicting 200 or so casualties.[7]

Not only did the exaggerations come under scrutiny, but so did the conduct of the troops. "The facts in regards to Wheeler's circuit of the enemy's rear, are becoming developed," Brent wrote on October 29. Despite the damage inflicted, "it was a disgraceful raid. Plunder and demoralization were manifested. As soon as the train was captured, the men went to plundering. . . . Captured horses and mules were laden with plunder, and when the enemy appeared, the race was on the keep the plunder out of reach." Manigault likewise heard the rumors of blatant drunkenness and looting—yet another indication of the decline of the cavalry, in his view.[8]

Wheeler's luck held out at McMinnville on October 4, when he encountered the cowardly colonel of the 4th Tennessee (U.S.), who surrendered his command without firing a shot. Again the looting commenced—watches, money, rings, overcoats, and in some cases pants, stripped off of prisoners. Even civilians were robbed of all that they had; Wheeler's men were out of control. Two brigades of veteran Yankee cavalry caught up with the raiders at Farmington, inflicting 450 casualties. The gray troopers finally straggled across the Tennessee River at Muscle Shoals, Alabama, on October 9. With casualties and desertions, it is highly likely that Fightin' Joe Wheeler lost 20 percent of his command, prompting Manigault to conclude, "This raid, like many others, did us more harm than the enemy."[9]

While the Federals in Chattanooga were reduced to minimal rations, the Southerners fared little better. By early October, Bragg had nearly 64,000 present for duty, but with noncombatants added, the number swelled to over 70,000. The commissary could not keep pace. Lt. Robert Watson noted on

October 19 that he had had nothing to eat "except a little sour cornbread." Several days later he added, "Drew 1 days rations of cornbread and bacon, just enough for one meal and we eat it up immediately although it is for tomorrow." An Alabamian wrote on the twenty-fifth, "We are living very harde we are barely getting half rashions." The artillery animals began to rapidly fall off for want of long forage and corn. Half of the artillery horses had to be sent to the rear to feed on grass. The weather added to the misery. "Mud ankle deep, almost impossible to keep a fire burning, everything wet and unpleasant, rained all night," a Floridian wrote on the twenty-third. A Mobile correspondent described that "some of our poor fellows have been without food for thirty-six hours, and horses without corn for eight to forty." On November 12, Washington Ives mentioned that the Florida brigade had drawn only one day's ration of beef out of eight—"still you hardly hear a murmur." But the next day, an Alabamian admitted: "There is a grate many men Disertin & going to the yankees their was 32 men went out of one Brigaid yesterday. . . . The Reason they are Disertin so is for the want of something to eat." A New Yorker reported that some nights as many as 150 deserters came in their lines, saying that "they cannot stand the cold nights on the mountain without overcoats and not enough to eat."[10]

Grant, who had replaced Rosecrans, established a supply line via Brown's Ferry on October 27, the so-called cracker line. Federals subsequently occupied Lookout Valley with embarrassing ease. On the morning of the twenty-eighth, Bragg and Longstreet sat atop Lookout Mountain discussing ways to retake Brown's Ferry, when signal officers reported a Yankee column from Bridgeport moving up Lookout Valley, right under the nose of Longstreet's Corps. Bragg demanded that the corps commander do something about it and stormed off. On the nights of the twenty-eighth and twenty-ninth, Longstreet attacked Union forces at Wauhatchie with Micah Jenkins's Division (formerly Hood's). The assault, poorly planned and coordinated, used a single brigade against 12,000 Federals with predictable results. Writing to Davis, Bragg described Longstreet's conduct as "a gross neglect resulting in a most serious disaster." Within a week, the siege had been effectively lifted.[11]

At the end of October, upon the advice of Davis, Bragg sent Longstreet's Corps to retake Knoxville. Wishing to "get rid of him and see what he could do on his own resources," Bragg happily complied. At the time, however, 25,000 men from Sherman's army and 12,000 from the Army of the Potomac were on their way to Chattanooga, so Bragg's decision has been criticized by historians. Longstreet's two divisions, which had most of Wheeler's cavalry, departed in early November. In a swap agreement, Stevenson's small division, recently exchanged from Vicksburg, and Cheatham's Division,

TABLE 6. *Transfers in November 1863*

Losses	Strength
Longstreet's Corps	12,500
Wheeler's Cavalry	5,000 (est.)
Buckner's Division	3,200
Gains	
Stevenson's and Cheatham's divisions	11,000
Pettus's and Moore's brigades	2,500 (est.)
Total net loss	7,200

both already in East Tennessee, were returned to Bragg. On November 22, Buckner's and Cleburne's divisions reinforced Longstreet (Bragg wrongly believed that Sherman would reinforce Burnside), but Cleburne's was subsequently returned. During this time, two brigades (Edmund Pettus's and John C. Moore's) arrived from Demopolis, Alabama. The net result of all of this shuffling was a reduction of 7,200 troops—not the huge loss so often portrayed by historians.[12] Historians have produced widely different figures as to Bragg's strength in November. Thomas L. Livermore's 1900 study of Confederate strength, the most detailed and accurate study, placed the figure at 44,000. His estimate of Union strength, 58,000, represents only those present who fought in the Battle of Missionary Ridge. Adding troops present but not engaged (cavalry, etc.) brings the total Union strength to about 70,000.[13]

Having purged the army of Polk, Hill, and Forrest and having dispatched Longstreet to East Tennessee, Bragg, with Davis's permission, moved to permanently break up the army's cliques, especially the Tennessee and Kentucky factions. Some brigades and divisions became hardly recognizable. Hardee, replacing Polk, received the divisions of Cheatham, Cleburne, Stevenson, and Walker, while Breckinridge got those of Stewart, Bate, and Anderson. Buckner, despite his loud complaints, was removed from corps command, given a small division, and sent to East Tennessee. Bragg presented the reorganization as an attempt to achieve nationalism. "Gov. Harris says that it is the President's orders to break up State divisions, to keep down state prejudices," wrote Rennolds. In truth, Bragg intended to disperse his opposition. Many of the troops despised the restructuring, especially the Tennesseans. "Poor Tenn! The Division that has so long spoken for her can speak for her no more. Who will?" questioned Rennolds. Van Buren Olden

TABLE 7.
Varying measures of the strength of Bragg's army, by finding historian

Historian	Bragg's strength	Rosecrans's strength
Connelly	28,000	80,000
McDonough	32,000–35,000	60,000
William C. Davis	36,000	60,000
Hess	41,500	70,000
Daniel	44,000	70,000

wrote bluntly, "All the men want to get back under Cheatham and Polk." William S. Dillon noted the "dissatisfaction amongst our boys as they do not like Stewart as well as they do Cheatham." On November 13, Rennolds wrote, "All the Divisions are being turned Topsy-turvy by the exchange of Brigades from one another, and soon no one but Gen. Bragg will know anything of the organizations of other troops than those directly around him."[14]

Bragg also broke up Walker's Corps, returning Walker to division command. Liddell had one of his two brigades (Walthall's) removed, reducing the Mississippian once again to brigade command. When asked the reason for the decision, Liddell was told, "Polk complained so much of being deprived of Walthall's Brigade and Walker had annoyed him so greatly, that he had no other course to pursue." Liddell promptly requested a transfer to the Trans-Mississippi—he was denied, at least for now.[15]

The Battles for Chattanooga

Trouble loomed on the horizon. By November 23, Bragg knew that Sherman's reinforcements had arrived in Chattanooga. With Longstreet at Kingston, Bragg feared that a move would be made in his rear at Loudon and Charleston. Hardee advised an immediate retreat. Bragg, however, sent two divisions—Buckner's and Cleburne's—to block the potential Federal move. By noon, most of Buckner's 3,200 men had departed and Cleburne's 5,800 troops were preparing to board, when a sudden dispatch arrived canceling the move. The departed troops would be stopped at Charleston and immediately returned. It seemed as though Grant had not done what Bragg thought he would do.[16]

During the late morning of November 23, Gen. George Thomas began forming a huge attack force of 25,000 bluecoats. His objective was the 800-yard fortified Rebel picket line on and on either side of Orchard Knob. Since Federal movements could be partially seen atop Missionary Ridge, perhaps the position was meant to be a trip wire for a surprise night attack. Some 634 men of the 24th and 28th Alabama regiments held the line. Seeing the mass of bluecoats, Newton Davis of the 24th assumed they were preparing for a review. At 1:50 P.M., thousands of Yankees easily swept over the position, capturing about 175 men.[17]

That evening, Major General Anderson incredibly ordered Manigault's Brigade to retake the Orchard Knob position. Fully understanding the "reckless stupidity" of the order, the South Carolinian rode to division head-quarters, where he found Anderson at supper. He proceeded to explain that his 1,500 men would be attacking 6,000–8,000 Federals heavily supported by artillery, a number Anderson dismissed. Lt. Col. James Barr, division officer of the day, happened to be present and confirmed Manigault's state-ment. Anderson still refused to back down; the attack would proceed. The brigadier rode off fully expecting to ride to his death and have his brigade annihilated. The troops formed for what promised to be a futile and mur-derous assault, when at the last minute, a staff officer rode up and counter-manded the order. Even writing about the incident three years later, Mani-gault seethed with anger.[18]

According to "Sallust," the correspondent of the *Richmond Dispatch*, Bragg had one of two options: he could either defend his communications line on his right or Lookout Mountain on his left—he could not do both. Bragg clearly had to defend the right, so, Sallust reasoned, an enemy attack would come on November 24 on Lookout Mountain. Bragg believed the opposite, that the Federals would feint on his left but attack on his right. Hardee was ordered from the left to the right, taking Gist's division (Walker was on leave) with him. The northern end of Missionary Ridge would be held by the divisions of Stevenson, Gist, and Cheatham. Cleburne's Divi-sion, rapidly moving up from Chickamauga Station, would serve as a re-serve on the right center. Breckinridge held the southern portion of the ridge with the divisions of Anderson, Bate, and Stewart. An ad hoc division, com-manded by Stevenson, would hold Lookout Mountain, leaving Breckinridge an astonishing six miles to cover![19]

The main action on November 24 took place on the left, where Joseph Hooker's three divisions stormed Lookout Mountain in the midst of a heavy fog in what became known as the "Battle above the Clouds." Castel would later term it the "large-scale skirmish among the clouds." The Confeder-ate line curved around the shoulder of the mountain. On the northern end, where the ground became widened and somewhat level, the Rebels con-structed a log-and-stone earthwork 400 yards behind the Craven House. Moore's and Walthall's brigades of 2,700 troops held the line. Walthall's advanced skirmishers held back the Federals for two and a half hours, but requested reinforcements never arrived. Jackson, commanding the ad hoc division, remained at his headquarters and did not bother to investigate. Due to his slowness, the troops branded him with the sobriquet "Mudwall," in derisive contrast to Stonewall Jackson.[20]

At 1:30, Walthall's and Moore's troops fell back in disarray. The retreating Southerners formed along the Summertown Road, where they were reinforced by Pettus's Alabama brigade. Fearful of losing Rossville Gap and endangering his Missionary Ridge line from the south, Bragg ordered Lookout Mountain abandoned. That evening, under the veil of fog, the Confederates evacuated the valley and the gap. The Confederates lost 1,251, including 1,064 captured. Nearly all of the 34th Mississippi fell captive.[21]

At 9:00 P.M., Bragg held a conference with Hardee and Breckinridge. Hardee, afraid both of an attack on his (and the army's) right flank and of the rising waters of Chickamauga Creek, recommended withdrawing four miles east of the ridge to the creek. Breckinridge felt that it was too late to withdraw, and besides, he relished a fight: "I never felt more like fighting than when I saw those people shelling my troops off of Lookout today, and I mean to get even with them." Bragg would later accuse the Kentuckian of being drunk between November 23 and 27, though the accusation was never proved. The army commander agreed that it was too late to withdraw. Hardee related to a Cleburne staff member, "Tell Cleburne we are to fight; that his division will undoubtedly be heavily attacked, and they must do their very best."[22]

Believing the primary Federal attack in the morning would come on the right, Bragg directed Stevenson and Cheatham to move from the left to the right. By daylight, the troops still struggled to get into position. Hardee would command the northern one-third of Missionary Ridge with the divisions of Cleburne, Gist, Stevenson, and Cheatham, while Breckinridge would command the lower two-thirds with the divisions of Anderson, Bate, and Stewart. The 400–600-foot-high ridge appeared deceptively impregnable. There was not a continuous crest but a series of hills, spurs, and deep gullies with no parallel road to shift reinforcements from one side of the mountain to the other. Bragg placed his troops on the topographical crest rather than the military crest, the most direct line of fire. Skirmishers formed at the base of the ridge, meaning that in the event of a reversal, the troops on the crest could not fire for fear of hitting their own men coming up the slope. The artillery was scattered along the extended line in sections and even single-gun crews.[23]

On the morning of November 25, Sherman, as predicted, attacked the

Cleburne's stand at Missionary Ridge.
From Battlefields in Dixie Land and Chickamauga National Military Park
(Nashville: Nashville, Chattanooga & St. Louis Railway, 1928).

Confederate right in the Tunnel Hill sector. Fresh from victories in Mississippi, the men of the Army of the Tennessee doubtless believed that they would crush the Southerners, but they had never encountered Patrick Cleburne. The Rebels repulsed three attacks. In an audacious move, Cleburne, assisted by reinforcements from Alfred Cummings's Brigade, counterattacked. Although initially beaten back twice, Cleburne's attacks down the western slope of the hill eventually routed the Federals. The Irishman's daring and initiative had prevailed.[24]

At 3:00, Grant ordered four of Thomas's Army of the Cumberland divisions to prepare an advance on the works at the foot of Missionary Ridge. The Southerners stared in amazement at the spectacle of tens of thousands of Yankees forming for an attack in the valley below. "The sight was grand and imposing in the extreme," wrote Manigault, who "noticed some nervousness amongst my men as they beheld this grand military spectacle." An astonished Arkansan remembered seeing a line of bluecoats "as far as the eye could see (and we could see for miles)."[25]

As the blue tidal wave moved out, many of the Rebels at the base of the ridge fired a shot or two and fled up the slope. The artillery atop the ridge did little to blunt the attack; indeed, Federal reports indicated few casualties inflicted by artillery. "Oh, what a purty sight it was to see them charge in 3 solid columns across the old field as blue as indigo mud and their arms glittered like new," a Floridian admitted. Confederate artillery on the summit caused the three advancing lines to merge into "one great mass of confused troops. On they came in disorder, at a double-quick, to reach the base of the Ridge," a captain in Moore's Brigade witnessed.[26] The break in the Confederate line occurred simultaneously at several points, although Zachariah Deas's Brigade is usually credited with being the first. Or perhaps it was Tucker's or Reynolds's brigade — there would be much finger-pointing. "After awhile I saw the troops a long way to my left breaking, & the enemy coming over our breastworks. After awhile one of my Staff Officers rode up & told me that he could see the enemy's colors on the crest of the ridge on my left; & riding a few paces, I became convinced of the painful fact and in a few minutes they got possession of some of our Artillery and opened fire on me, enfilading my line with both Artillery and small arms," Deas reported. Tucker wrote similarly: "The brigade was reformed in the works (if they deserve the name) on top of the Ridge. . . . At every point where the enemy could be seen in our front, he was checked or repulsed: but unfortunately the works were so constructed as not to command a view of the front point of a high projecting point about the center of the Brigade. . . . When they suddenly appeared in front of our men at this unexpected point, seized with a panic, they gave way before them . . . until the whole Brigade fell back in disorder." In fifty minutes, the ridge that Bragg had held for over a month was lost. It was the first rout for the Army of Tennessee.[27]

The men of Anderson's Division pleaded their case to the public. In the *Huntsville Daily Confederate*, then being published in Marietta, Georgia, a member of the 34th Alabama said that the "brigades had to deploy in the entrenchments in a single line, pretty much as skirmishers — five to six feet apart, and the enemy came on them in columns, three to five deep, and it was impossible for them to resist so heavy a charge, and they sought safety in flight." A member of the 7th Mississippi wrote that "we were in a single line on the top of the ridge with ditches about knee deep. Here we were ordered to hold our fire as ammunition was scarce. All we would have had to done to shot in that direction to kill Yankees. Still were not allowed to do so." William Chunn of the 40th Georgia noted, "The firing was so terrible that the men could not stand it." James Hall wrote in like manner: "It required more courage to run than to stand still." According to Taylor Beatty, Bragg "exposed himself very much — but uselessly — the men would not rally."[28]

Confederate casualties for the three-day campaign have traditionally been

Confederate prisoners awaiting transport at the
Chattanooga rail depot. The men on the embankment are Federal guards.
Courtesy of the Library of Congress.

placed at 361 killed, 2,160 wounded, and 4,146 missing, a total of 6,667. Between October 20 and December 1, however, Northern records tallied 5,569 prisoners, exclusive of another 573 deserters. If Grant's prisoner number of 5,569 is used, then Confederate casualties totaled at least 8,090, a more realistic figure. Bragg thus sustained an 18 percent loss—not as severe as at Shiloh or Stones River but bad enough. The army also lost 6,175 small arms and a staggering 39 field guns, 28 caissons, 25 limbers, 4 battery wagons, 1 traveling forge, and 2,336 rounds.[29]

The army withdrew on the night of November 25. Bragg and Hardee left at daybreak on the twenty-sixth. The next afternoon the weary troops trudged into Ringgold. On Friday, the twenty-seventh, the wagon train moved out at daybreak, arriving at Dalton in the afternoon. "I saw a mule lie down when the harness was removed, and go as soundly to sleep in two minutes as an infant, and that while hundreds of wagons and thousands of men were marching by within a few paces where it rested," a correspondent reported. A Cincinnati reporter, accompanying Joseph Hooker's pursuing Federal column, noticed the chaos: "All along the road we picked up stragglers, small arms, caissons, limbers, etc. everything, in short, that marks the track of a retreating and demoralized army." Bragg had a stinger in his rear guard, however, in the form of Patrick Cleburne. Having skillfully deployed in the brush in Ringgold Gap and behind Taylor's Ridge, the Irishman prepared to hold "at all costs." The bluecoats were stopped cold, losing about 500 men to Cleburne's 221. Cleburne had once again proved that he was not to be trifled with. A grateful Congress extended its thanks.[30]

Bragg characteristically refused to accept responsibility. He relieved Breckinridge from command, claiming that on the night of the battle, the Kentuckian came into his office "*dead drunk*, and was so in the morning." Bragg called in S. R. Gist and directed him to "put him [Breckinridge] in a wagon and haul him off" if need be, but under no circumstances was Breckinridge to give any orders. Breckinridge's biographer weakly defended him. Whether or not on a four-day drunk, there seems little doubt that on the night of November 25, he was inebriated. Bragg demoted the Kentuckian from corps to division command.[31]

Mackall saw the handwriting on the wall. "I suppose this defeat will raise a storm against Bragg and I think Mr. Davis will send Lee there if he can spare him; if not, I am afraid that he would not like to yield his prejudice in favor of Johnston." Bragg ungraciously blamed the troops. "This disastrous panic is inexplicable," he wrote Johnston. In his official report, he stated: "No satisfactory excuse can possible be given for the shameful conduct of our troops on the left. . . . The position was one which ought to have been held by a line of skirmishers." The statement was absurd. No "line of skirmishers" could have halted the blue tidal wave that swept up Missionary Ridge. According to Hess, "He had naively trusted the topography of Missionary Ridge." Cleburne, in an unusually talkative mood one evening, allowed Captain Key to read his personal diary for the days of November 23–25. "His criticisms on General Bragg and his military mis-management were quite severe," the captain noted.[32]

Back in Richmond, the *Whig* placed the blame less on Bragg ("Doubtless he did the best he could") than on Davis for retaining him in command. Foote launched a congressional investigation, a move designed to embarrass the administration. When the president pointed to the misconduct of the troops, Foote exploded. He countered that the president's own stubborn retention of Bragg had turned the issue. He further accused the chief executive of "gross misconduct in retaining his favourites [Bragg and Pemberton] in office." Incredibly, Davis would move Bragg to Richmond, where he would serve as military advisor, a position more prestigious than substantive.[33]

On November 29, Bragg offered his resignation; Davis quickly accepted. The soldiers had mixed reactions. Artilleryman Neal philosophically wrote: "I am glad he has been relieved not that I want confidence in him or think we have any better general but for this great purpose it is necessary to have unity of action and unbounded confidence in our leader. Bragg has been hunted down by a discontented set of croakers who will in time be ready to cry down Hardee [Bragg's successor]." Rennolds noted, "I think for one we are losing as good an officer as we can ever get, but having lost the confidence of the army it is noble in him to retire and certainly best." Rufus Daniel of the 6th Arkansas noted: "I believe this [Bragg's transfer] will have a bad effect upon our arm[y]. Though the citizens are down on him, yet the soldiers have the utmost confidence in him. Consequently, do not blame him." Frank Carter thought differently: "He has now left us and the confidence of the army has *wonderfully* revived."[34]

Once back at Dalton, Bragg gave a farewell address to the troops. He soon retired with a few of his personal staff—Lieutenant Ellis, Lt. Thomas Butler (Elise's cousin), Lieutenant Parker, and Colonel Urquhart—the Louisiana clique, to Warm Springs, Georgia. There he continued his vitriol against his enemies. He blamed the loss of Lookout Mountain on Carter Stevenson's "utter imbecility" and declared John Jackson "equally unreliable." Cheatham, he heard, "still harps on the injustice done his command at Murfreesboro by my report," Bragg told Liddell. "But what more can be expected of a man whose occupation in Nashville before the war was to keep a drinking saloon and a stallion?" When he heard of subsequent trouble in the Army of Tennessee, he wrote Marcus Wright: "It is now apparent to all, and it is what I desired to establish by the change, that the whole clamor against me was by a few individuals of rank and their immediate partisans, who were actuated by one of two motives, *Ambition and Revenge*." His bitterness would continue long into the postwar years.[35]

The Edge of Collapse

Contrary to popular belief, Davis never offered Hardee command of the Army of Tennessee—only temporary command. Would the president at some point have offered the position to the lone lieutenant general in the army? Probably so, concluded William C. Davis—"he liked Hardee and probably would have risked promoting him to full general for the post, even if it meant slighting his seniors." More to the point, Davis liked the alternatives less. It proved moot, however, for Hardee promptly refused permanent command. He privately confided to Thomas B. Roy that either Johnston or Beauregard would do more to build army command and Johnston held seniority. Perhaps the real reason lay in his self-recognition that he was not the man for the job. Nonetheless, for the next three weeks, he would command. Not all were pleased. "I have seen but one man who thinks Hardee can replace Bragg i.e. is competent to take his place," Alabamian Bolling Hall remarked to his father. B. L. Wyman admitted that Hardee was "not liked by all the men." Mackall wrote to Johnston that even Hardee's best friends "do not pretend to think him more than a good corps commander." An Alabamian thought that Hardee would "make the matter better or worse and I can't tell which it will be."[36]

There may also have been a personal reason that dissuaded him. Hardee had become engaged to twenty-six-year-old Mary F. Lewis of Mobile, twenty-two years his junior, whom he had met in September 1863 while in Demopolis. The decision to wed came quickly. As long as he commanded the army, he could never leave his post—ask Beauregard. "How to get away from the army is the question," he wrote Bishop John J. Beckworth of South Carolina on December 10. "If retained in command I don't see how it [a wedding] is possible." He admitted: "My engagement no longer seems to be a secret. . . . Haven't I won a prize in Miss Mary. She writes me such charming letters, so loving & so affectionate, and expressed in such chaste & elegant language. For her sake I wish I were fifteen years younger." At Hardee's wedding, Cleburne, who served as the best man, met his future fiancée.[37]

Hardee addressed his new command: "I desire to say, in assuming command, that there is no cause for discouragement. The overwhelming numbers of the enemy forced us back from Missionary Ridge, but the army is still in tact and in good health. Our losses were small and will be rapidly replaced. The country is looking to you with painful interest. I feel that we can rely upon you. Only the weak and timid need to be cheered by constant success. The veterans of Shiloh, Perryville, Murfreesboro, and Chickamauga require no such stimulus to sustain their courage and resolution. Let the past take care of itself; we can and we must secure the future."[38]

The words did little to alter the utterly shattered morale. "A great many of the boys are down hearted since the cowardly manner in which some of the troops acted at Missionary ridge," Washington Ives confessed to his mother. George Lea of the 7th Mississippi wrote bluntly: "I can see nothing encouraging of our army here at all. Everything wears a gloomy appearance all are getting very much dissatisfied." Alabamian B. L. Wyman remarked that "a large number are for going back into the 'Union.'" W. A. Stephens had lost all hope: "The lives that is lost in this war now is for no good, I fear." J. B. Mason expressed to "Miss Kenny" on December 2: "This army is worst demoralized now that it ever has bin. . . . Several of our boys [have] gone home in the last week or so . . . [and] there is several others that threatened to go." Cavalryman Joseph Cotton wrote to his wife in a similar vein: "I am sorry to say to you that I am worst out of heart about whipping the yankeys than I have ever been[.] there is lots of our men says there is no use to fite them any more." Pvt. R. B. Ledbetter of the 40th Alabama gloomily wrote: "I think the men of this army intend to run out of every battle not because they are afraid but because they have lost confidence in the cause. . . . I think this confederacy is about played out." Some vowed to stick it out. "We are hungry, cold and starved but I do not intend to give it up as long as I am able to stand," wrote Augustus Abernathy of the 19th/24th Arkansas.[39]

Capt. B. F. Remington, commissary of J. W. Grigsby's cavalry brigade, deserted to the enemy. The Federals did not have to interrogate him; he talked freely. "The army is very much dispirited; in fact I think it is demoralized. In my brigade the privates talk frequently and boldly about going home, numbers are deserting daily. Leading officers think the contest will be ended in May, 1864; that they will be whipped by that time. Rations are very scarce. . . . I consider the Southern Confederacy a complete failure."[40]

Still, winter quarters had to be prepared. "Our shanty is made of nothing but boards. It will do very well in warm weather but when the wind blow as it does now[,] We had almost as well be out of doors. It is now sleeting and everything seems to indicate a great deal of bad weather," John Crittenden told his father. A Tennessean described the layout: "The cabins are built very irregularly and if encampments were extensive enough a person would lose himself in the narrow and tortuous streets. . . . From four to six men occupy each cabin, which contains a chimney, a door closed by an oilcloth, or rather open always, no window, a straw bed, and guns sitting at the center. There is not much variety in architecture; one cabin is just like another." Adding to the misery, according to South Carolina artilleryman J. A. James, the camps became infested with rats.[41]

Rations remained dangerously low. "We have had no bacon or lard since we left Missionary ridge, and still unable to get any," an artilleryman wrote on December 8. A Georgian added, "We air half starved to death we have to live on quarter rashen we draw nothing but corn bread and knott a nuff of that This morning we draw a little peas." A Floridian recorded daily rations as three-quarters of a pound of beef, one pound of flour, and one and a quarter pounds of meal, "with enough salt for seasoning and 2 oz. of sugar every seven days."[42]

In early December 1863, Davis dispatched one of his aides, thirty-five-year-old Col. Joseph Christmas Ives, to inspect the army. Connelly was critical of the selection—Ives had never seen combat and was unfamiliar with the geography of the region. He failed to mention that Ives was a Yale attendee, a West Point graduate, and had served eight years as an engineer in the Regular Army. His only failing was that he was an alcoholic. His subsequent report was not as exaggerated as Connelly claimed. Ives wrote that the army lost about 7,000 men at Chattanooga, which was low by 1,000. On December 7, he noted that the army had 30,000 effectives in the infantry. Stragglers, sick, and slightly wounded were constantly returning (1,000 came in the next day), and by the eighth there were 33,000 in the infantry, 2,500 in the artillery, and 3,500 in the cavalry, all of which was verified in the weekly report. Ives conceded that "considerable despondency and disorder yet exist." His only misstep was claiming that sufficient artillery horses had been procured and that 20,000 surplus arms were in Atlanta.[43]

Hardee acknowledged serious problems. Even though the beef ration had been reduced to three-fourths of a pound, only a two-month supply remained. The Macon Manufacturing Company hurried 50,000 pounds of bacon to Dalton, but the article remained in short supply. The artillery had been wrecked. Five batteries were stripped of their remaining horses and guns and sent to Atlanta to man the field guns in the city's fortifications. By December 14, the two infantry corps counted only ninety-five guns, several of them obsolete six-pounders.[44]

Despite these difficulties, Hardee filed his infamous Christmas Eve letter on the state of the army. There were too many embellishments and half-truths designed to show what a remarkable recovery had occurred under his leadership: The infantry had been mostly rearmed (true), and the troops had received sufficient shoes (untrue; Stewart's Division alone lacked 2,284 pair). The ranks had been increased by 3,666 returning men (true), and with William Quarles's and William Baldwin's borrowed brigades, which Hardee had refused to return to Mississippi, another 4,000 men could be added. The ration was now uniform and full (on paper only). The animal forage was for the first time in excess of the consumption (untrue), and the artillery had been completely refitted (utterly untrue). In Hardee's defense, his statement that the army was "ready to fight," was not a reference to an offensive; he declared that a battle should be avoided for the present. If the enemy advanced in force, he would have no choice but to fall back.[45]

Christmas Eve and Christmas Day revealed a complete breakdown of discipline; many soldiers became drunk. Two companies in the 41st Tennessee, fired up with whiskey, challenged each other to a brawl. Surgeon John Farris expressed disgust. "The Col. Commanding the Brig. was beastly drunk & so was the Col. commanding the Reg't & officer of the day. Some of the guards were drunk. Many men and officers throughout the brigade were the same[.] some of the scenes of yesterday were awful to contemplate. . . . Guards & officers were cursed & abused by drunken officers & privates alike." On Christmas, an Alabamian noted that "the officers of our Division [Cleburne's] generally have been beastly drunk." He concluded: "The army is not under as good condition as when Gen. Bragg commanded it. It is losing its prestige very fast."[46]

Sergeant Sparkman noted the level of alcoholism in his regiment. "Some of the officers of the 35th Tennessee have been drinking too much for a few days and some of them had a fight this morning. Col. [Benjamin] Hill has been on a spree ever since we got to Dalton." He added about a week later, "The Col. of the 35th Tenn. [Hill] and several of the other officers are very often drunk." Correspondent Peter Alexander revealed that drunkenness in the officer corps was becoming rampant, and unless there were reforms, he promised to publish names.[47]

Meanwhile, problems developed in the cavalry; Wheeler and Wharton were at loggerheads. On December 9, Wheeler ordered Wharton's command south of the Coosa River to recuperate. An order subsequently appeared, supposedly from Wheeler, that redirected the command over Lookout Mountain to the Tennessee River, which would have destroyed the horses. Wheeler, who came under much censure, canceled the "order" and did an investigation. He reported that Wharton arrived "in a laughing way" and said that he had "got up a joke" by making a phony order. Wheeler erupted and promptly reported to Johnston that the Texan "forgot that he was an officer and not a frontier political trickster" and that Wharton's ambition had "completely turned his head."[48]

With only four days remaining in 1863, Wheeler created his own trouble. On the prowl in East Tennessee with Allen's and William B. Wade's brigades of Kelly's Division, he encountered a Federal supply train of about 150 wagons guarded by a "few straggling Yankees" at Charleston. Believing it to be easy pickings, he ordered his men dismounted and formed for an attack. At a range of 150 yards, the Rebels suddenly found themselves confronting three lines of blue infantry 2,000 strong and 150 cavalry. After skirmishing for an hour, during which time the wagons escaped, the Federals raised a yell, charged, and easily broke Wheeler's line. The troopers were routed and ran back to the horse holders, most of whom had fled. The result was the loss of 150 prisoners. "So far from being a skillful retreat it was a most shameful and wanton sacrifice of men and horses resulting from the imbecility of the 'War Child,'" Captain Miller angrily wrote. The next day, the division withdrew to Tunnel Hill. It was an appropriate ending to a cursed year.[49]

The Johnston Imprint
Finding a Replacement

Following the Battle of Missionary Ridge, dispatches to the capital proved "unintelligible" and press accounts scant. The secretary of war admitted "he knew nothing." The next day, John Jones in the War Department wrote, "Not a word from Bragg." By December 1, Northern newspaper accounts could no longer be ignored. A disaster had occurred in Tennessee, with Bragg's troops flooding back—not to Ringgold, as first reported, but Dalton! A Richmond correspondent with the Army of Tennessee offered assurances that rumors of a rout were exaggerated, but his words did little to ease jittery nerves.[1]

Davis now grappled with the issue of who would command the army. Clearly Davis wanted Lee sent to the West—at least temporarily. The Virginian turned down the offer, claiming that he would not find "cooperation." Rumors spread throughout the capital. "The appointment of Beauregard to succeed Bragg is not officially announced; and the programme may be changed," Jones wrote. The next day, December 3, he added, "It is doubted whether Beauregard will succeed Bragg." Some heard that Hardee would be given command, not realizing that he had already turned down the position. A reporter heard whisperings that Johnston had been offered the job and turned it down. It would next be offered to Polk, who, it was incorrectly reported, had just arrived in Richmond. The reporter also heard that Davis would be making another trip to the West. A War Department insider noted on the sixth, "Whether Johnston will be trusted with the army is not yet decided."[2]

On December 8, Davis summoned Lee; the general feared the worst. He arrived the next day and went into conference with Davis and Seddon. Congress had by now reconvened, and Foote took to the House floor to go on one of his usual rants, blaming the president for his "gross misconduct in retaining his favorites in office." Furthermore, his trips to the West had never produced any benefits. Davis put more pressure on Lee to accept the position but to no avail. Lee preferred Beauregard, but Johnston was acceptable. Meanwhile, Foote again spoke publicly: "Why is Johnston not now appointed? Why is not Beauregard? The country is tired of the delay and every moment becomes more and more perilous." Davis played his trump card. Representative William Swann of Tennessee, an administration supporter, presented letter after letter showing that it was Johnston, not Davis, who had consistently supported Bragg. This in turn angered Johnston's congressional friends. Just when they thought that they had Davis, he "turned you [John-ston] up as the man who had kept Bragg in command."[3]

The president would never choose Beauregard, and Longstreet had proven to be a failure in independent command. Why then not simply give Johnston the tap? The answer revolved around the loss of Vicksburg, which the president placed squarely on the Virginian's shoulders. He also believed the general to be in cahoots with his political opposition. A War Department insider thought that Johnston had "some very influential supporters and more real popularity in the country than the President has. It [Johnston's removal] would be a first-class disaster." "I did not see Davis but heard that he was blind as an adder with rage & ready to bite himself," Wigfall wrote. Mary Chesnut heard the gossip through her husband, who served on Davis's staff. She wrote that fall that "the president detests Joe Johnston for all the trouble he has given him. And General Joe returns the compliment with compound interest. His hatred of Jeff Davis amounts to a religion. With him it colors all things." Mackall wrote the Virginian on December 9, addressing his letter "Dear Joe": "The people won't stand this nonsense much longer. Mr. D's game now is to pretend that he don't think you a general."[4]

After two weeks of deliberation and under tremendous pressure, Davis finally bowed to the inevitable. At the next cabinet meeting, Seddon submit-ted Johnston's name. Judah P. Benjamin opposed him on the grounds that he lacked aggressiveness; in truth, he had long disliked him. Seddon argued that he should be given another chance, although he conceded his "tenden-cies of defensive strategy and lack of knowledge of the environment." Some supported Hardee, but of course his name was not on the table. Several sup-ported Johnston. Finally, as the meeting dragged on, the cabinet relented to Johnston. Seddon watched as Davis, "with doubt and misgiving to the end," agreed. The chief executive sent a curt order to Johnston directing him to turn the Army of Mississippi over to Polk and proceed to Dalton to assume command of the Army of Tennessee. Armed with Hardee's overly optimistic reports, Davis and Lee desired Johnston to immediately go on the offensive, writing him of the "imperative demand for prompt and vigorous action." A western offensive might forestall an enemy attack on Richmond. As for John-ston, he remained as paranoid as ever.[5]

Malignant Relationship

Exactly who was Joseph E. Johnston? By 1864, his persona as the beau ideal of a general had been firmly fixed in the eyes of soldiers and the public. Reserved and decisive, he was seen as a master strategist, his failings always blamed upon an uncooperative government. Connelly described him as bitter, sarcastic, and uncommunicative, never willing to meet the government halfway. McMurry saw him as a general whose frustrations gave way to mistrust. He was given responsibility but not authority, and he believed that Davis wished him to fail. He was bitterly jealous of Lee in what Glatthaar termed a "one-sided competition." The general was subject to sudden fits of rage. E. P. Alexander related a story in May 1862: Johnston had become annoyed by an unauthorized attack made by John Bell Hood. He rode off in a fury, leaving his staff far behind. As he passed an ambulance, the driver accidently swerved and pinned Johnston's horse to a fence, almost throwing the general. "I don't think I ever saw anyone fly into such a fury in my life," observed Alexander. "God damn you! What do you mean?" Johnston yelled at the driver. Turning to Alexander, he shouted, "Give me a pistol and let me kill that infernal blanketty blank!" Alexander pretended not to have one, and Johnston rode off angrily, arriving at army headquarters a full hour before his staff.[6]

From the outset, commented McMurry, Johnston was hampered by what McMurry termed the general's "malignant relationship" and "borderline paranoia" with Davis. The president would not allow him to take his own personal staff, a move Johnston saw as a slight. He arrived at Dalton on December 28 and established headquarters at the Huff House on Selvidge Street. Lt. Richard Manning, an aide who accompanied the general, snipped that the present army staff "are a poor set and Genl. Johnston can accomplish but little without an efficient staff."[7]

Due to heavy rain and mud, little initially occurred other than conferring with the generals. Johnston subsequently made it clear to Seddon that "the army is now far from being in condition to resume the offensive. It is deficient in numbers, arms, subsistence stores, and field transportation." The generals seemed to know little about the strength and disposition of the enemy, but vaguely estimated their numbers at 80,000, deployed in Chattanooga, Bridgeport, and Stevenson. Johnston's gloomy report thus radically differed from Hardee's promising summary of three days earlier. Manning related his dismal first opinion of the army: "Want of harmony among the officers & dissatisfaction among the men reign supreme throughout our camp. [Matters of organization] all tend to excite alarm & create anxiety — petty jealousies & rivalry among officers of lower grades are rife here, & privates even are partisans."[8]

Walker, who had known Johnston for twenty-five years, expressed elation at his coming. "If I had a bottle of champagne, I would open it on the occasion. For our country's sake I am rejoiced that he has been sent. He is my choice of them all." One person *not* thrilled with Johnston's arrival was Hardee. The two officers had never had a close relationship. Even Brent observed that "between Johnston and Hardee, I think there is a want of harmony." In July 1863, Hardee had written Polk, "Johnston is wanting in all those particulars in which you feared he was deficient." The Georgian could at least now leave for Mobile to get married. The wedding and subsequent honeymoon lasted five weeks. A disgusted Captain Patton wrote that Hardee had the "handsomest house in Dalton fixed up in elegant style for the reception of his bride and his daughter. So much for being a general." Another general definitely *not* happy about the Virginian's arrival was Wheeler, who remained an avowed Bragg supporter. He would privately keep his mentor apprised of affairs.[9]

The men by and large expressed satisfaction with Johnston's appointment. A reporter remarked, "He does business upon the rigid red tape principle, speedily and rather curtly." "We all have more confidence in Johnston than we had in Bragg and the Yankees fear him," a Mississippian believed. Captain Key described the general: "General Johnston is about 50 years of age [57]—is quite gray—and has a spare form, an intelligent face, an and expressive blue eye. He was very polite, raising his cap to me after the introduction." A Texan believed Johnston to be "decidedly a great man. He looks great. I think he is the finest looking man I ever saw. . . . I think that the command of this army could not have fallen into abler hands." He was polite but could be brusque and, according to a correspondent, wore a white, broad-brimmed felt hat. Bragg still had his supporters, however, and not all were thrilled with the general's arrival. When Johnston reviewed Patton Anderson's Division (formerly Hindman's), the reception proved cool. He "never received a single cheer in any Brigade except Vaughn's Tennessee Brigade, and that a very faint one. If Braxton Bragg had made his appearance every hat would have been waved and the air rent with cheers," James Hall observed.[10]

Numerous administrative issues had to be addressed. The Kentucky congressional delegation requested that the Orphan Brigade be mounted and sent on a raid in its home state, the congressmen certain that 20,000 volunteers could be raised. The day had long passed when people believed such hyperbole, and Johnston denied the request. Likewise, when seventy-three men of the 15th Arkansas requested to be transferred to Key's Arkansas battery, the general declined. He told Key that "all of his army would go into cavalry and batteries if it were allowed, and that he would not transfer a soldier drilled in infantry to make a bad cannoneer." A correspondent happened to overhear a colonel in Hindman's Division say that his men desired to be mounted. "Yes, Colonel, doubtless," Johnston replied. "The infantry have the fighting to do, and no one can be spared, and when we have established a peace basis, I am decidedly in favor of allowing every man not only a horse, but a carriage also, if he desires it." Polk asked that all the West Tennessee troops in the Army of Tennessee be sent to his army in Mississippi. Again Johnston declined, noting that as many would be lost to desertion as were recruited. The 1st Florida Cavalry (dismounted) and 4th Florida were consolidated, and the three remaining mounted companies of the 1st Florida Cavalry (dismounted) had their horses removed and the men returned to the parent outfit. Stevenson's mountaineer division was badly maligned by rumors and even by Bragg himself. Johnston exchanged one of the Georgia brigades for that of A. W. Reynolds, yet that brigade had also received bad press.[11]

Davis promoted thirty-two-year-old John Bell Hood of the Army of Northern Virginia to lieutenant general and gave him Hindman's Corps. Hood had commanded a division for nineteen months, had some association with the president, and was not in any way connected with the western army's infighting. Unfortunately, his left arm had been badly mauled at Gettysburg and his right leg so shattered at Chickamauga that it had had to be amputated. He now wore a cork prosthesis and walked on crutches. Nonetheless, Surgeon G. W. Peddy thought he was "the finest looking man I ever saw." Thanks to the detective work of historian Stephen Hood, it has been definitively determined that Hood's painful amputation did not drive him to use laudanum. Indeed, he was treated with only minor doses of morphine, and that only occasionally at night. On Christmas Eve 1863, Hood's love, Sally "Buck" Preston, broke off their relationship. "I hate a man who speaks roughly to those who dare not resent it," she said of him. McMurry insisted that neither his broken relationship nor his amputation in any way changed him; he kept a consistent personality throughout his life. Some historians would later imply that Hood had been sent to Dalton as a spy for the administration, an accusation McMurry labeled "preposterous." William C. Davis suggested that Hood knew the president's anti-Johnston prejudice "and did not hesitate to play to it occasionally."[12]

Hood arrived in Dalton on February 25. Due to his disabilities, he brought a carriage with him from Atlanta, but he soon took to riding a horse with remarkable ease. Johnston gladly received him. They often dined together, and in a letter to Wigfall the army commander remarked, "My greatest comfort since getting here—indeed the only one in a military way—was Hood's arrival." A woman who saw Hood noted, "I like his appearance very much & was surprised to find how well he looked on horseback, although his cork leg is very perceptible & hangs very stiffly, a man follows immediately in his rear with his crutch." In the army he became known as "Old Pegleg." Hindman, who had returned to his former division, did not go quietly, even traveling to Richmond to complain to Davis. "What a poor patriot!" thought Colonel Hundley of the 33rd Alabama. "When, in truth, he was hardly competent to command a Division successfully." Hood had at least won his honors on the battlefield, continued the colonel, "which is more than I can say for a great many of our generals, many of whom seem to have little else to recommend them other than West Point and a fondness for brandy."[13]

Davis also transferred Patton Anderson to Florida. Johnston desired his replacement to be an officer from his former Army of Mississippi—States Rights Gist. Davis instead promoted William Bate. Johnston countered that Bate could be sent to Florida and he could retain Anderson, but the request was denied. One day, Johnston came to Stewart's headquarters, but the general was not present. He had received a telegram from Richmond asking who should command Moore's Brigade. He thought that Col. James T. Holtzclaw was Stewart's selection, but he wished to confirm it. A staff officer assured him that his information was correct. Several days later, Johnston received notification that Col. Alpheus Baker, a stranger to the army, had been given the brigade. "This was my first practical acquaintance with the terms on which Gen. Johnston had to deal with the authorities in control of the government," the staff officer wrote.[14]

Brig. Gen. Henry R. Jackson, commanding a brigade in Walker's Division, took a leave of absence to assist Governor Joseph E. Brown in organizing Georgia state troops. His brigade went to Clement H. Stevens, who received a promotion to brigadier. The forty-three-year-old South Carolinian, formerly in Gist's Brigade, took command in January 1864, although he had not fully recovered from his Chickamauga wound. He did not like his new Georgia command: "My present brigade is a very inferior one. First, because it is a very small one and next because two of the commands, the 66th Geo. Regt. and the 26th Geo. Batt. are of such inferior physical material that they will melt away before the end of one week's march." The troops reciprocated the feeling: "We have the titest Brigadeer Jineral in this world. The boys saies if they ever get in to a fight that they will kill him." When the Yankees finally did kill him, an officer in the brigade wrote, "He took our brigade, the meanest in the army, and made it one of the very best."[15]

Johnston at least got his selections on the army staff. Davis relented and allowed him to retain his former assistant adjutant general — thirty-two-year-old West Point graduate and former college professor Col. Benjamin S. Ewell. He also requested and received Mackall, his old friend, as chief of staff. Mackall immediately recognized Johnston's dilemma: "There has not been one single officer promoted on his [Johnston's] recommendation. They always promote someone agreeable to others," he wrote his wife on January 9. "This is bad and if we don't gain a victory will in the end injure his hold upon the Army. Officers finding he has no influence will soon turn to the Lt. Genls for assistance and parties will spring up."[16]

Changes also occurred in the cavalry. Back in January, Wharton had fallen ill, perhaps due to a ruptured blood vessel in his right lung. Due to continued ill health and his now-open conflicts with Wheeler, the Texan was transferred to the Trans-Mississippi. In his newspaper articles, Robert Bunting blasted Wheeler, "who owes his reputation [more] to newspaper puffs than to genius or merit." Davis was having difficulties with the Texas and Kentucky Senate delegations in approving Wheeler's promotion to major general. He asked for and received Johnston's support, a gesture little appreciated by Wheeler. Captain Miller wondered who would replace Wharton. "I made the acquaintance of Gen. Kelly — a nice prim, boyish looking little fellow, possessing a fine eye and a mouth denoting great decision of character. I like Gen. Humes better the more I see him, but understand that we will probably lose him in a few days — He will probably take command of a Tenn. Brigade, formerly under Gen. Wharton. Gen. Allen, the former Col. of the 1st Ala. Cav., is spoken of as his successor — a gallant man with whom we have been long associated."[17]

In mid-February, Davis dispatched the first of what became a chain of administrative envoys. William N. Browne, born and raised in Ireland and a pro-Southern journalist in Washington, D.C., at the beginning of the war, arrived at Dalton to inspect the army and get a reading on Johnston. He found that the army did have its shortages — bayonets, artillery horses, and rifled shells — but by and large the troops were in good condition. Determining Johnston's plans proved a more vexing matter. The general played his cards close to his vest, "although I gave him many opportunities to speak freely," Browne reported. He concluded that Johnston did not "seem to be sufficiently impressed with the importance of getting ready to strike before the enemy is prepared to assume the offensive." The army commander hinted that he might move into East Tennessee, but he would commit to nothing definite. The corps commanders remained "equally in the dark."[18]

By the first week in March, Davis and Bragg, without conferring with Johnston, envisioned a new western strategy. The Army of Tennessee would invade East Tennessee, cross the Tennessee River at Kingston, and join up with Longstreet's Corps near Maryville, about forty miles from Knoxville. Knoxville would be isolated and Chattanooga threatened. If the enemy refused to offer battle, Johnston would march into Middle Tennessee via Sparta. A move in the rear of Nashville, with the Cumberland River at low ebb, would force the Federals to evacuate. Reinforcements would be sent— 5,000 from Polk and 10,000 from Beauregard—when "you may be able to use them" and "if nothing shall occur to divert them." As a diversion, a large column of cavalry would be sent into West Tennessee. Johnston had to attack Grant in Chattanooga *before* he met Sherman's now-uncommitted army in Jackson and Vicksburg.[19]

The administration's plan, which amounted to a raid into Middle Tennessee without a central supply line, had obvious flaws, which Johnston quickly detected. He could not operate away from a railroad and invest Knoxville; he would exhaust his supplies before the enemy would. Additionally, the Federal army at Chattanooga, 15,000 stronger than at Missionary Ridge, would surely attack him before he would be ready for an offensive. As for the reinforcements, he desired them *before* any battle, not after the fact. In short, his plan remained the same: stay on the defensive, beat the enemy as it advanced, and then go on the offensive. He believed an offensive would be much better through North Alabama. Longstreet also opposed the move— "The President and General Bragg seem bent upon a campaign in Middle Tennessee," he wrote Johnston on March 16. He argued that the Federals in Chattanooga could get to Nashville via railroad much faster than the combined Confederate army could get there.[20]

The issue of competing strategies remained at the core of the problem. Johnston, who did not have to deal with political realities, thought only militarily. He believed that manpower should not be wasted on unimportant territory. Troops must first be concentrated, and then an advance could be attempted. Davis held to his belief that, as McMurry stated, for "psychological, logistical, economic, diplomatic, and military reasons," all parts should be held. McMurry concluded that most southerners concurred with Davis.[21]

On March 11, Brig. Gen. William N. Pendelton, artillery chief of the Army of Northern Virginia, arrived to inspect the long arm and to corroborate Johnston's reasons for not taking the offensive. After several days of inspection, Pendelton filed his report. The horses were thin, but no worse than those in Lee's army. Of the 1,900 horses on hand, 10 percent were unserviceable, and another 445 were required. He found fifteen old six-pounders still in use. Shipments of Napoleon guns, mostly from Augusta, continued to arrive. By the end of April, the armament (exclusive of horse artillery) comprised sixty-four twelve-pounder Napoleons, thirty-eight twelve-pounder howitzers, six three-inch rifles, ten ten-pounder Parrott rifles, and two Blakely rifles.[22]

The War Department denied Johnston's request for Mansfield Lovell as army artillery chief, so he turned to the Virginia army. Indeed, Pendelton had openly lobbied for the promotion of a couple of his Virginia colleagues. Johnston requested E. P. Alexander—Lee's top artilleryman—but again the request was denied. Bragg sent a warning: "Recently some complaints I learn privately have been heard from your artillery officers that they were being sloughed by their juniors in the Army of Northern Virginia." The War Department finally assigned Brig. Gen. Francis A. Shoup, who had led a Louisiana brigade in the Vicksburg Campaign. He arrived at Dalton in late March and Captain Key called on him. He "found him very agreeable and courteous."[23]

In April, yet another envoy arrived—Lt. Col. Arthur H. Cole, inspector general of field transportation. Surprisingly, Cole sided with Johnston on the issue of an offensive. A 250-mile trek through barren East Tennessee would take fifteen to twenty days' rations, requiring 900 additional wagons. As for mules, officials at the Augusta procurement office remarked that an additional 1,000 mules could not be found anywhere in Georgia within two months. The transportation animals remained in a weakened state. Mc-Micken had failed to send the broken-down stock to the rear to recuperate and had thus lost 2,500 animals since January 1. The Augusta office had recently sent 500 horses for the artillery, 100 of which had been diverted for use by clerks and wagon masters, and 306 mules. The Mississippi and Alabama procurement office sent 600 mules earmarked for the pontoon train. Pvt. Linville Sheets, a deserter, told his Union captors, "A large number of new wagons were received by railroad from Atlanta; also a supply of fresh mules." Between November 1, 1863, and mid-April 1864, the Army of Tennessee received 2,701 mules; the Army of the Cumberland received 7,502.[24]

While the administration sent envoys to Dalton, Johnston did the same to Richmond. In April, Col. Benjamin S. Ewell, brother to Lt. Gen. Dick Ewell, arrived in the capital to plead Johnston's case. He explained that the general was not opposed to an offensive, only to the juncture with Longstreet as proposed by the government. An offensive would nonetheless take time— at least until the end of April. The Federals in Chattanooga had 80,000 and had recently been reinforced by James McPherson's 15,000-man corps from Vicksburg. Ewell also pleaded for reinforcements, an issue complicated by the fact that Longstreet had recently been ordered back to Virginia. On April 14, Ewell met with Bragg, who assured him that reinforcements would be forthcoming from Beauregard and Polk once Johnston began the offensive. Bragg asked a pointed question: Would Johnston guarantee an offensive if additional troops arrived? Ewell telegraphed Johnston the question and received a response the same day: It depends. How many Federals would he be confronting? The answer would have proved damaging, but apparently no one in the administration ever saw it.[25]

The president appeared perturbed when he met with Ewell. Intelligence reports wrongly related that three Union corps from Tennessee were now massing against Lee. Johnston's offensive was supposed to prevent such a move. Davis admitted that the need for an offensive no longer existed, but he insisted the Army of Tennessee should nonetheless try. The reinforcements from Beauregard were now going to Lee, and Polk had too few to be of much assistance. The chief executive did dispatch a brigade from Mobile to Dalton and ordered the exchange of one of Johnston's undermanned brigades with a larger one from the coast. While not a complete failure, Ewell's mission was a disappointment.[26]

Mackall expressed dismay. "I am afraid Mr. Davis cannot make up his mind to treat Johnston fairly. . . . In every thing he seems disposed while professing to assist, to thwart him." In late April, he heard a report that several anti-Johnston articles had appeared in the press, written by a member of the cabinet at the behest of the president. "Did you ever hear of a man's allowing his hatred to carry him so far," Mackall asked, "putting an Army in Joe's hands & then trying to destroy the confidence of the people in the Genl[?]" Lieutenant Manning referred to the administration as "the enemy at Richmond," which he regarded "as the most dangerous that this army & its General have" and which was busy "criticizing—blaming—abusing & undermining."[27]

It did not help that Hood wrote directly to Davis, Bragg, and Seddon, telling his own version of affairs. Indeed, it seems likely that Richmond authorities, either directly or with a wink, encouraged him to do so. On April 3, Hood assured Bragg of his anxiousness to advance and concluded with a sentence which belied his true intent: "You know I am fond of large engagements and hope you will not forget me [for army command?]." His most damaging letter was written on April 13: "I . . . am sorry to inform you that I have done all in my power to induce General Johnston to accept the proposition you made to move forward. He will not consent, as he desires the troops to be sent here and it is left to him as to what use should be made of them." Expressing his deep regret, "as my heart was fixed upon our going to the front," Hood also indicated that he had been in private discussions with Hardee. Hood concluded, "He [Davis] has directed us thus far, and in him I have unbounded confidence." Were these the words of a romantic, a true believer, a young warrior enamored by the president's attention, or were they a cynical calculation to win army command?[28]

Meanwhile, Johnston had his five engineer companies (the 3rd Engineers) and two pioneer companies hard at work. Two of the engineer companies and John R. Oliver's and Gillip's pioneer companies began laying 1,600 feet of corduroy on the Dalton and Resaca Road and the Sugar Valley Road for the event of a retreat. An inspector reported that a 500-man detail under the supervision of an engineer would have to be put to work on the latter. "I do not think a large army can possibly get through on this route without a large loss of wagons," he noted. He further recommended that a pontoon bridge be constructed at Resaca. Work was also begun on damming Mill Creek at the gap in order to create an artificial lake. Johnston also had to construct a large pontoon train to cross the Tennessee River in the event of an offensive. Engineer companies C, D, and G were sent to Atlanta to make the boats. The train required 135 wagons, each drawn by four mules, to haul the eighty or so boats, planking, and the required tools and rope. Supplying the mules proved difficult, but by late March, the animals had been collected in Mississippi and were on the way.[29]

Restoring Discipline

On Saturday, January 16, only nineteen days after Johnston arrived at Dalton, an incident occurred in Cleburne's Division at Tunnel Hill that turned ugly. A small group of soldiers in the 33rd Alabama of Lowrey's Brigade began what they almost lightheartedly called a "reenlisting serenade." The men marched with a piece of beef as a banner and tin cups and plates as band instruments. Their terms for reenlisting were a thirty-day furlough, better beef, and a sack of flour for every man. Several hundred joined in the procession. At some point, the half-jovial nature dissolved, the crowd swelled to 2,000, and the aura became that of a mob. They swept over camps, "over guard lines, and in defiance of officers hooping and hallowing," according to an Alabamian. "They visited the quarters of several Brigadiers and demanded more rations," and rumors abounded that division headquarters was next. The men were finally dispersed and returned to camp; guard details arrested several of the instigators.

Trouble continued to stir. On the night of January 18, rumors circulated that the men would go to Dalton and confront Johnston himself; the guards were doubled. That night, a loud commotion came from the camp of the 16th Alabama, also from Lowrey's Brigade. The "raiders," as they became known, knocked down a sentinel and attacked the adjutant of the 16th, striking him in the head with a rock and nearly killing him. "They did not succeed in collecting enough men to carry out their intentions, but common talk now is that the thing is not done with," Edward Brown related to his wife. "Some of those engaged in the raid have been arrested and others swear they shall be released. On Monday night a whole division was posted between us and Dalton and lay on their arms all night to intercept the raiders if they attempt to go to Dalton." While Brown did not approve of their methods, he admitted: "We are in a bad fix. The men are *hungry* and I am afraid they cannot be restrained."

Discipline neared a breakdown and drunkenness became rampant. "Tom Scott, the regimental quartermaster [45th Alabama], has been on another drunken spree the last four or five days," Brown wrote in disgust. "He drinks, curses, pukes and wallows around, but that is a small matter to be endured. At home such things might be a little shocking to sensibilities trained to decency; but it is alright in the Confederate States Army; it is rather a matter of recommendation for promotion than a cause of rebuke."[30]

Sheer monotony and frustration led some men into trouble. About 300–400 troops in Strahl's Brigade became enraged when they saw stocks and barrel shirts in use in Jackson's Brigade. In their fury, they demolished these tools of punishments, but four men were captured in the process. New stocks were erected, and rumors spread that the captives were to be placed in them. A near riot erupted among Strahl's men, but cooler heads prevailed and the captives were released. On the night of February 11, Charles Roberts wrote, some of Strahl's men began making noise "just out of pure mischief and love of Excitement. . . . I know the boys don't mean any harm but tired of the monotony of camp are willing to undertake anything that will give variety."[31]

Johnston had to get control of his army and fast. On December 30, 1863, he held a review of Hindman's Corps; it was not an encouraging picture. "One of the Arkansas Volunteers," as he signed his name in the *Appeal*, related how at least a fourth of Govan's Brigade was nearly barefoot and thinly clad. As for rations, there were twenty-four-hour periods when the men received nothing but bread and not enough of that. Archie Livingston told his sister: "It is almost impossible to believe that men would remain in service under circumstances so trying. Rations are drawn to a mite so scanty that it appears inadequate for a rightful sustenance." Blankets, socks, and overcoats were in dire need. A correspondent also noticed the wretched condition of the artillery horses. One battery commander reported that each of his horses had only thirteen pounds of corn over a three-day period rather than the allotted thirty-nine pounds. Disease spread among the animals in Rowan's Battery; eighteen horses died within three weeks. Capt. Ruel Anderson lost nearly all of his battery's horses. After a review of a corps in February 1864, the Napoleon gun teams could not haul the pieces up a small hill. Johnston informed the president that at least 400 fresh artillery horses were required, but he later raised the number to 600.[32]

"The rations question is the most important," evaluated an Alabamian. "We are not getting now but corn meal, very poor beef & salt, and there in quantities insufficient. I try to become content as I believe it is the best the country can do for us, but a great many complain heavily." He related going down to the butcher pen and viewing some dead steers. "I found that the men carried away everything except the excrement. Some took the tripe, some the heads, some the feet, some skinned the tails that were left to the skins & I even saw men washing the guts to make what are generally called chitlings. I saw one instance in which a cow had been killed the day before & a fetus nearly mature had been thrown aside & that day some men viscerated it & carried it away to eat. When I looked at these things I thought the Confederacy was well nigh 'gone up.' "[33]

Since the beef ration had been reduced to three-fourths of a pound, Johnston desired to have the rice ration doubled. The rice came from the South Carolina coast, however, and transportation shortages made the requisition impossible to fill. To offer some variety, he ordered cured bacon and ham in lieu of beef, as well as sugar, coffee, and flour in place of cornmeal, and the men received tobacco and whiskey twice a week. Shortages nonetheless continued. "We have coffee and good tender Beef once for dinner — ditto for breakfast and no supper — sometimes biscuits sometimes corn and rice bread — we have a fritter of rice and corn meal with molasses for desert [sic]." When Capt. Samuel McKittrick ate with the colonel of the 16th South Carolina, he sat down to a piece of cornbread and a glass of water. "Officers live as hard as privates," he wrote.[34]

Shoes were also a pressing issue. Some 4,200 pairs arrived in January, but the next month Johnston requisitioned 13,300 more, claiming that many of the men were barefoot. "The Fifth Regiment [Tennessee?] will soon be unfit for duty for the want of shoes. The Eighth Regiment will soon be unfit for the same cause; and, indeed, when shoes are supplied the men will be unable to wear them for a long while, such is the horrible condition of their feet from long exposure," he reported. The 59th Alabama claimed 180 shoeless and another 150 with only pieces of shoes. When Sallie Champion visited the army, she was told that socks were a luxury item; Cleburne related that he had not worn a pair in five months. "Most of the men are going barefooted on the frozen ground," an Arkansan observed. "My shoes are in threads. It is strange to see the wealthiest men in Arkansas without enough clothes to cover their nakedness, but that's what I see every day." The issue appears to have been largely resolved by the spring. On March 7, for example, Stevenson's Division, which had been short 2,284 pairs, now required only 137 pairs.[35]

Johnston tightened discipline by instituting strict regulations. The new orders included three hours of drill daily (except Sunday) and roll call five times a day. The men had to turn out in full gear; anyone not present received ten days' extra duty. No more would soldiers be allowed to enter private homes and beg for food, and inspections occurred weekly. Many groused. "I do not like Johnston's course much thus far," Captain Patton wrote on January 17. The general "issued a very ridiculous order trying to make everything very strict and in accordance with Army Regulations." Others, including Edward Brown, saw the benefit. "General Johnston has lately issued a whole batch of orders to the army which if strictly enforced will keep good discipline in the army."[36]

Johnston also shut down the business of camp followers and Dalton brothels. A staff officer wrote: "Complaints are daily made to me of the number of lewd women in this town and on the outskirts of the army. They are said to be impregnating this whole command and the commissariat has been frequently robbed, with a view of supporting these disreputable characters." Captain Key remarked that "rumor says that almost half of the women in the vicinity of the army, married and unmarried, are lost to all virtue." An Alabamian wrote that the only women he had seen for months were those "too poor to get away from the army and some few who seem to be quartered with officers of low repute in morals." Johnston ordered that all of the women unable to give proof of respectability would be transported to other areas. In the future, only sutlers would be allowed within the lines.[37]

Hardee had initiated a furlough system, but Johnston greatly enlarged it; there were strings attached. There would be more furloughs for units that reenlisted for the war. Wrote John Inglis: "I never saw men so attached to a Genl [Johnston] as our Army is to him. The men are greatly encouraged by the furlough system." Others expressed disgust: "I am provoked with the way I have been treated about a furlough to think that I have been in the service nearly two years & now they don't want to give me a furlough Except I reenlist." A lottery system determined who got a furlough. "Co. C had another drawing yesterday [March 19]. We drew six furloughs. Thirty-five was the lowest die that got a furlough. I drew thirty-three. It will now be sixteen days before we have another lottery." How many men ultimately drew a furlough is not known, but officially 3,399 furloughed men returned to the army.[38]

The general reduced transportation to the lowest possible limit. Manigault's Brigade of nearly 2,000 men, for example, counted eighteen wagons (six baggage, five ammunition, one small-arms, four cooking-utensil, one entrenching-tool, and one forage), seven ambulances, and a forge. The division train, besides transporting baggage, comprised a forge, a wheelwright shop, a reserve medical wagon, a portable butcher shop, and an ambulance. The ammunition in the two infantry corps took up 223 wagons (hauling an average of 8,600 rounds each), requiring nearly 900 mules.[39]

Miserable weather continued throughout February. "We are living very hard though the soldiers are resigned to their fate," Neal Hensley of the 32nd Mississippi informed his brother on the fourteenth. "They are willing to endure all of the privations of camp life a while longer for the sake of liberty. The old troops are not nearly as whipped as the citizens at home." Three nights later, with an inch of ice on the ground, a fire consumed four buildings in Dalton, including the commissary depot and Confederate printing office.[40]

The Tennesseans had long desired to be once again grouped into Cheatham's Division; in February, Johnston approved it. The response proved electric. A large crowd marched to Cheatham for a response; overwhelmed with emotion, he could barely speak. Finally, he took a gold piece out of his pocket, tossed it in the air, and said, "Boys, you are as good as that!" The crowd, with an accompanying band, then marched to army headquarters. Cheatham went in, brought out a hatless Johnston, patted him on his bald head, and said, "Boys, this is Old Joe."[41]

The dearth of artillery horses was a serious problem. Sixty-four teams proved incapable of drawing their guns, and another forty-eight teams had to be sent south to Kingston to graze and recuperate. Some 130 wagons had to be pulled out of service to carry the pontoon train then under construction in Atlanta, but Polk promised to offset the loss with 120 wagons from Mississippi. As it then stood, the army had insufficient transportation to carry no more than three days' supply of food and forage. Of the 5,442 cavalry with the army, only 2,300 had effective horses. Two-thirds of the animals had to be sent south of Rome to graze. But these matters had to wait; the Yankees were on the move.[42]

Sherman on the Move

Sherman's army of 35,000 ventured out of Vicksburg and marched through Jackson and on to Meridian, where it arrived on February 14. Richmond authorities calculated that Sherman would take a sharp turn to the southeast and attack Mobile from the north. Polk's Army of Mississippi, even with assistance from Mobile and S. D. Lee's cavalry, could muster barely 14,000. The only other source of reinforcements was the Army of Tennessee. The War Department ordered Johnston to dispatch Cheatham's and Cleburne's divisions of Hardee's Corps to Demopolis, Alabama.[43]

Johnston balked. To do any good, he would have to send 24,000 men, requiring a month to transport. Meanwhile, Federal forces in Chattanooga would surely advance on Dalton. He could not possibly hold them back with half his infantry gone. The next day, Davis sent a direct order: send the troops. To make certain, Davis sent a duplicate order to Hardee. Johnston relented—he had no other choice. Hardee's 16,000 infantry began loading onto the cars for Demopolis. By February 21, however, Sherman's army had withdrawn. Sherman's problem was not Johnston but Forrest. A 7,000-man column under Sooy Smith was to link up with Sherman at Meridian, but along the way, Forrest's 2,500 cavalry defeated it. The next day, Hardee's Corps, whose van had reached Montgomery, was ordered back to Dalton.[44]

On the night of February 22, the long roll sounded at Dalton. "Created quite a stir & now late as it is . . . all is noise and uproar," Colonel Davis wrote. The next morning, Federal forces suddenly appeared at Ringgold. Johnston believed his prediction had come true. Skirmishers were driven in on the twenty-fourth, and the next day, four Federal divisions began probing the Dalton defenses. Having previously returned Baldwin's and Quarles's brigades to Polk (2,700 troops), Johnston was thus short two and a half divisions, with half of his artillery at Kingston.

The Yankees opened with a fierce artillery barrage, which Captain Patton described as "the hottest and most accurate shelling that I have ever experienced." Brig. Gen. A. W. Reynolds brought up his brigade to extend the left. As the bluecoats advanced, Reynolds "rode forward and ordered a charge and this line entirely routed them. I never felt so glorious in my life. . . . I am proud of my brave boys," he wrote his sister. Johnston recognized the movement for what it was—a reconnaissance-in-force. That night, an enemy brigade reportedly seized Dug Gap to the southwest of Dalton. Hiram B. Granbury's Brigade retook it, but the vulnerability of the gap did not go unnoticed—at least not by the Federals.[45]

The Emergence of Nationalism

From the outset of the war, Confederates were connected by what Gary Gallagher termed "shared cultural values." It was not until the end of the second year of the war, however, that a strong national identity began to coalesce. The catalyst proved to be Lee and the Army of Northern Virginia, which, according to Gallagher, became a "highly visible symbol of Confederate nationalism" that rallied the South. Lee represented the model soldier, and his army's victories offset the depressing chain of defeats in the West. It was Lee and his troops who ultimately won the hearts and minds of Southerners.[46]

Well enough for easterners, but did that translate to the West? While westerners were aware of and rejoiced in Lee's victories, they often viewed themselves as the proverbial stepchild, with the "favored son" status residing in the Army of Northern Virginia. English visitor Arthur Fremantle visited the Army of Tennessee in mid-1863 and noticed a tension when it came to the other army: "This one claims to have harder fighting than the Virginia army, and to have opposed the best troops and the best generals in the North." In October 1863, the *Mobile Advertiser & Register* grumbled that an impression had arisen in the West that the government "tends to magnify the importance of Virginia, Richmond and Gen. Lee's army" and "diminish the interest of the central-South, and the Southwestern portions of the Confederacy."[47]

While a vague nationalism had existed in the Army of Tennessee from the outset, its growth was retarded by sectionalism (discussed in chapter 1), the western army's greater distance from Richmond, and the lack of a vast connecting rail system. If an ideological core existed, it appears to have been rooted in slavery. When Longstreet's Corps arrived in North Georgia, the easterners recognized a clear difference between their own war aims and their western brothers'. Capt. Charles M. Blackford wrote: "The people down in these states are not as much enlisted in principle as we are in Virginia. They regard it as a war to protect their property in slaves, and when they are lost, take no further interest in it. In Virginia we are fighting for the right to govern ourselves in our own way and to perpetuate our own customs and institutions among our own people without outside interference."[48]

As for Lee's army being a model for nationalism, Longstreet's men failed to sense even a collegial connection with westerners. When the corps was later transferred to East Tennessee, Maj. Frank Huger was frankly glad to be done with the Army of Tennessee. He considered the western cavalry no comparison to Lee's, and the army as a whole seemed a full year behind the Army of Northern Virginia in organization. Besides, he concluded, "they ain't very partial to us in this Army and they wouldn't care if we didn't come off first best." "If the armys of the West were worth a goober we would soon have peace on our terms," concluded another one of Longstreet's men.[49]

Revivals and the brotherhood promoted patriotism and a belief in Confederate invincibility, but these did not necessarily equate to nationalism. There was a great deal of intra-army finger-pointing following Missionary Ridge; the army remained broken and divided. A Confederate national consciousness did not emerge in the Army of Tennessee until Johnston's arrival. It was grounded in the reenlistments of the three-year troops, drills on a massive scale, and an unbounded confidence in their new commanding general.

The reenlistments of the three-year volunteers not only rejuvenated the army but also allowed the men a definable moment to cast a vote for the national Cause. Although many regiments claimed to be the first to reenlist, the 154th Tennessee received the publicity and honor. Cheatham's Division began what the press termed "the Re-Enlistment Race," yet William D. Pickett, an engineer officer on Hardee's staff, believed that "the movement appeared spontaneous." Philip Stephenson of the 5th Arkansas described the scene in his regiment: "Most of the men had been aroused, suddenly, and had forgotten self entirely. Therefore, there was hardly a fully dressed man. Almost all were bareheaded, barefooted, and in their shirt-sleeves!" The men formed a large congregation around the cabin of Col. John E. Murray. "Colonel Murray had almost gone to bed, for it was after 10 o'clock, but he *felt* in an instant, what the uproar was about, and, catching the unbounded enthusiasm of the moment, sprang from his couch, was up on the stump in a trice, addressing the men!"[50]

On the night of January 16, Strahl's Brigade assembled to the "sweet music" of the brigade band. "Something of the old spirit of '61 seemed to inspire the men as they gazed upon the face of their gallant leader," noted a participant. The next night, the entire brigade took an oath: "We are the officers and men of Strahl's brigade, do this day resolve to enlist for the war; determined to never lay down our arms, until our homes are rescued from the enemy, and the Confederacy established as one of the nations of the earth."[51]

Further instilling army unanimity was Johnston's adoption of a uniform battle flag. Flags had never been uniform in the Army of Tennessee; at Shiloh there were at least six different types in use. Johnston adopted the same design that he had used when he commanded the Army of Northern Virginia. Unlike the Virginia flag, however, the western banner would have no border surrounding it. Cleburne's Division subsequently petitioned to retain its distinctive blue flag, which was granted, but, with this single exception, a standard had been adopted.[52]

Johnston also instituted drills on a mass scale, including sham battles. These exercises enabled the men to see beyond their own brigades or divisions, asserted Jason Phillips. They imbued the soldiers with pride and enhanced the "culture of invincibility." They also offered a needed sense of nationality. "Men had for months seen only their closest comrades now saw Alabamians, Carolinians, Georgians, Floridians, Kentuckians, Tennesseans, Texans, and more. The entire South seemed gathered for imminent victory."[53]

A sham battle on March 31 met all expectations, with Cleburne's and Bate's divisions posing as the enemy and Cheatham's and Walker's divisions as the Confederates. The "Yankees" came onto the field with bands playing "Yankee Doodle" and "Hail Columbia," while the Rebel bands played "Dixie" and "The Bonnie Blue Flag." "Everything fixed like a real battle was to be fought. Only the cannon and small arms were loaded with paper instead of bullets but the stir, noise & smoke, and everything looked like a real battle," a soldier observed. John Crittenden thought it was the "grandest affair I ever witnessed. . . . The Yankees made the attack. They marched up with banners flying to the tune of Yankee Doodle. As soon as the Confederates charged them they fled apparently in the wildest confusion. Five rounds to the man was expended." Capt. George Harper pronounced it a "magnificent sight. The spectators alone numbered thousands if not more." J. T. Kern wrote his mother back in Mississippi: "I wish you could see the Gray Jackets out on the drill field in [a] sham fight as I saw them a few days ago & hear their shouts, it would make your heart rejoice & you would say at once, 'such men are invincible.' "[54]

If Lee was the catalyst for nationalism in the East, Johnston, who had commanded both the Army of Northern Virginia *and* the Army of Tennessee, served as the bridge connecting East and West. For once, the army was united under the one whom they saw as the Lee of the West. The sheer physical difference between the emaciated and sickly Bragg and what Glatthaar termed the "imperial air" of Johnston was obvious. James Riggs of the 27th Mississippi observed that "every body seems to think the army is in better spirits now than they have been in some previous." James Brannock believed that "a new spirit seems to have been infused into the army since Genl. Jo Johnston took command." Thomas Hampton glanced upon an army two ranks deep in three lines that stretched for three miles, pronouncing it "a beautiful Army in good trim & high spirits."[55]

Thanks to mass drills, sham battles, and the reenlistments of the three-year troops, which, for the most part, were a genuine expression of commitment to the Cause, the men began to see beyond their own regiments and brigades. Johnston rejuvenated the army and instilled a sense of nationalism. Unfortunately, the army would also take on Johnston's image to become a defensive and maneuvering army.

✳ 19 ✳

Cleburne, Blacks, and the Politics of Race

In the military operational area of the western theater, in which I have included Tennessee, Mississippi, Alabama, one-fourth of Louisiana, and the top third of Georgia, there lived 2 million whites and 1.4 million blacks. While the majority of the white families in this sector did not own slaves, all had an investment in the peculiar institution. The Southern economy was rooted in slavery. It also offered a social class to which many whites aspired. While the institution was deeply imbedded in the Southern consciousness, the ideology espoused by the Democrats did not always silence a resentment that festered among many poor whites in the West. In 1859, the John Brown Raid led to fears of a slave insurrection. Whites responded by raising dozens of militia companies—Memphis alone raised a battalion. While on the surface whites appeared paternalistic toward blacks, an incident arose in the Army of Tennessee that would prove that paternalism went only so far.[1]

"My Love to the Negroes"

Lincoln's Emancipation Proclamation actually offered hope—at least that is how the western Confederate press saw it. Numerous articles in the *Memphis Appeal* and the *Chattanooga Daily Rebel*, all copied from Northern papers, conveyed an adverse Northern reaction, some papers even suggesting that emancipation was a Rebel plot. Other articles claimed that the unpopularity of the act would cause Lincoln to modify or withdraw the proclamation altogether. Robert Bunting of the Texas Rangers, who regularly wrote articles for readers in Houston, could not help but gloat. "Great and growing dissatisfaction seems to pervade the Northern army, as will be seen by the resignations, removal, and dismissal of their Generals," he wrote on February 2, 1863. "The proclamation of Lincoln, which is the crowning infamy of all his diabolical schemes for our ruin, seems to have had its results, and the work will go until those results will bring great benefits upon our cause." The *Rebel* editorialized that "the nigger crusade of our day will be regarded by future generations as the most stupendous humbug . . . and the chant about

266

the 'poor Africans' will be numbered among the laughable farces for the contemplation of ages after us."[2]

Word soon spread about blacks being recruited into the Northern ranks. Indeed, during 1863-64, 20,000 Tennessee blacks served in the Federal army—by Confederate standards a virtual corps! Isaac Afflex, a Texas Ranger, voiced his opinion on March 25, 1863: "They are raising negro regiments every where, and I expect that we will have to fight some of them at Tullahoma, if we ever come into contact with any of them, we intend to hoist the black flag and give no quarter." When talking with some of the prisoners captured at Thompson Station, Lt. William B. Richmond of Polk's staff made an interesting observation: the boys from Indiana and Ohio were "as cordial haters of the abolitionists as the warmest fire-eaters," but the troops from Michigan and Wisconsin are "unadulterated negro worshippers—they are literally Yankees and that covers the case."[3]

Hundreds of blacks worked in the Army of Tennessee as personal body servants—the Texas Rangers alone had sixty. According to Freehling, Confederates made a distinction between body servants and the mass of slaves. Many of the soldiers described them in a fatherly and caring manner. George Lea wrote his father in November 1862 about Kemp, his personal body servant: "You wish me to say something about Kemp. He is in good health and fat. You wished him sent home if there was any danger of the Yanks getting him." No danger existed, he assured him, "for there is a great many others [slaves] in the army. He has faired much better than I have for the last three months and I am glad of it[.] he is a great use to me now and gets plenty to eat and I don't reckon he would do much at home if he was there." When writing home, John Crittenden frequently concluded his letters with the words "My love to the negroes."[4]

Alex McGowin of the 16th Alabama informed his parents: "Those who have servants send them out in the country and get whatever there is to be had. If we had a servant I expect we should have to pay for all that he made use of, both clothing and victuals, but I should make him clothe himself as he could make plenty to do it and more. While in camp any thing like a smart Negro can make 10 or 12 dollars a week by washing after doing his other work." Some brought in peaches and apples for sale. While the troops could not leave camp, blacks could go "where they please so long as they behave." In battle, blacks remained with the wagons and did not have to face "near so much danger as I." A Texan observed that the blacks in the army had been raised to despise Yankees, and they did so as much as the troops. "You can't make one of our black boys madder than by calling him a 'fool abolitionist'—if one darkey calls the other this, it is considered a fighting epithet & the wood flies."[5]

Louisianan Israel Gibbons, camped at Shelbyville, told of the near comical association that officers' body servants had with their owners' ranks:

A peculiar institution of our army here is the "colored wing"—the military Niggers—I mean the officers servants. They dress well, ride thousand dollar horses, smoke two-bit cigars, live on the fat of the land, get up five dollar dancing parties, put on airs over the country niggers, break the wretches' heart, and lay over the army and mankind in general. So far as ease, comfort and pleasure go, they seem to be the finest general in the army. They observe keenly the distinction of rank. A General's nigger won't associate with the Colonel's or Captain's nigger if he can help it; and they look upon the white foot soldiers as the wretchedest of mankind. Very often a tired and dusty volunteer, trudging along the road with his gun and knapsack, hears a clatter behind him, steps aside, and a dandy nigger gallops by without turning his head, stiff and dignified as a Major General.[6]

When Isham Thomas, a gunner in Stanford's Battery, heard about a runaway slave who was caught and brought back, he could not help but make a comparison between his life and "Old Tom's": "Foolish old Negro, he does not know when he is well off. If he knew what the soldiers has to go through he would be willing to remain at home where he has plenty to eat and good cloths and a comfortable cabin to shelter him from the pitiless storms of the wind, rain, and snow that the soldier has to endure." Blacks remained a vital part of the Army of Tennessee throughout 1864. Writing from Dalton in February 1864, Arch McLaurin noted: "I am in fine health now and getting along finely. We have a negro in our mess and I don't have anything to do. That is I have no cooking or washing to do."[7]

As Pillow conducted his conscript sweeps in early and mid-1863, blacks as a source of manpower did not escape his eye. By March 1863, he had offered all available slaves in three Alabama and six Tennessee counties, either through contracts with local planters or by threatening confiscation with impressment (it mattered not to him). "Our army [Army of Tennessee] has 2,000 veteran soldiers driving teams," he wrote. "We want to hire negro teamsters to relieve these soldiers and restore them to the ranks, thus strengthening the army." There were limitations—whites still had to drive all ordnance wagons and ambulances, but hundreds of commissary, baggage, and quartermaster wagons could be driven by blacks. As Wheeler withdrew from Middle Tennessee in the late summer, Brent instructed him to "bring with you all able-bodied negroes, who can be used as teamsters." The Union-controlled *Nashville Daily Union* insisted that blacks were being used in another capacity as well—in the ranks of Bragg's army. The report claimed that "hundreds and hundreds" served in Van Dorn's cavalry, a totally false assertion. The issue of conscripting blacks as soldiers had never come up for discussion—at least not yet.[8]

The Cleburne Document

On December 17, 1863, thirty-two officers of the Army of Tennessee, including Hardee, Stewart, Cleburne, Cheatham, Stevenson, Breckinridge, and Hindman, sent a petition to Richmond. Fourteen brigadiers and several colonels also signed. The gist of the document was that the draft age should be lowered to fifteen and raised as high as sixty. It also recommended that all able-bodied blacks and mulattoes, bond or free, should be conscripted to serve as "cooks, laborers, teamsters, and hospital attendants." It should be noted that many of the signatories had provisos, such as permanent consolidation of regiments. The "inspiration" behind the petition, according to Wiley Sword, was Hardee. Davis denied the initiative and responded that the Army of Tennessee had to be strengthened through returning absentees. Sword concluded that Hardee's document inspired Cleburne to write his famed proposal two weeks later urging that blacks be armed, trained, and placed in the ranks.[9]

No one can doubt that Cleburne's mentor was Hardee. The problem is that Hardee's proposal, at least as it regards the use of blacks, presented nothing new. Slaves serving in noncombatant roles had become routine by this time; indeed, the memorandum simply stated that which already existed. The controversial aspect of Hardee's proposal related to adjusting the draft ages. Even two of the signatories failed to endorse the adjusted ages. Mark Lowrey and Benjamin Hill signed under the proviso "I believe that old men and boys would be of more service to the country at home" and that teachers and ministers should remain exempt. Additionally, as Sword noted, Hardee sent a second proposal to Davis on the same day, suggesting essentially that the Army of Tennessee be reinforced by stripping troops from the coast and other departments. Thus, the *least* controversial aspect of the memorandum dealt with the issue of blacks. *If* Cleburne used Hardee's petition as the inspiration for his proposal, he read into Hardee's memorandum something that clearly was not there. Of course, we shall never know what Cleburne and Hardee discussed.[10]

Cleburne's proposal was not born in a vacuum. In early December 1863, an article appeared in the *Appeal* under the pen name "Calloden." In brief, the article suggested that blacks be armed, and when not needed on the battlefield, they would revert to being cooks and servants. The author of the proposal was in fact Cleburne's law partner, Thomas Hindman. The Arkansan drew up his proposal and actually got a congressman to present it to a House committee for legislation. No congressman would sponsor the bill, and it died in the House.[11]

In mid-December 1863, Cleburne penned his controversial proposal to arm slaves in exchange for their freedom. He stated his reasons: Lincoln was raising an army of 100,000 black soldiers (in fact 200,000), England and France might reconsider entering the war on the side of the Confederacy, the issue of emancipation in the North needed to be undercut, and the dwindling numbers of Southern white soldiers of conscript age needed to be replaced. Historically, it made sense to him, and he offered several examples where slave insurrections had been successful. Could blacks fight? Cleburne wrote that the slaves of Jamaica had revolted and held the mountains against their masters for 150 years. He himself was willing to train and lead a division of them. The proposal, to say the least, proved shocking. Why would blacks fight for their freedom, when they only had to wait for the Confederates to fall back and then could seek refuge with the Federals? To Cleburne, the issue was one of "common sense." The Federals had three sources of manpower: "motley" whites, slaves, and "immigrants fresh off the boat." Southerners had to make a decision as to which was more important — slavery or independence.[12]

Sword suggested a deeper motivation — Cleburne had an affinity with the plight of blacks. He based this assertion on a segment of Cleburne's recently discovered diary. In mid-October 1864, the Irishman made an entry about black Union soldiers captured after the Atlanta Campaign. "Our men were very bitter on the negroes and their [white] officers, hollering to the latter [in jest] to kiss their [black] brothers. A great many of the men think that negroes ought not to be taken prisoner, and in case of a fight I think they [blacks] will catch it. I told several [that] if the universally acknowledged principle that to a higher scale of intelligence was attached a heavier weight of responsibility be true [then] . . . whites, who employ, incite, and almost drive these poor creatures into their [Union] armies, are a thousand times more guilty than they [blacks]."[13]

Cleburne initially presented his proposal to his staff around the second week of December; they sat stunned. Buck warned of the extremely controversial nature of the proposal and that it might cost Cleburne a promotion to corps command, but Cleburne remained undeterred. Maj. Calhoun Benham, as Cleburne's modern biographer would write, "was positively appalled." When the division commander refused to back down, the major openly stated that he would like to see a copy to write a rebuttal. Ultimately, Hindman, all of Cleburne's brigadiers, and Brig. Gen. J. H. Kelly of the cavalry would endorse the proposal.[14]

Three days after Christmas, Cleburne discussed the proposal with Captain Key, his former hometown newspaper editor. "I had scarcely seated myself when he introduced a conversation upon the propriety of bringing into the military service, and at once beginning to drill, 300,000 negroes," Key wrote. Cleburne claimed that Hardee, Hindman, Govan, Lucius Polk, and Breckinridge all agreed with the proposal, although the last thought the idea premature. A stunned Key immediately said that slaves would have nothing to gain by fighting. To the contrary, the Irishman answered, they *and* their families would be granted their freedom. Would this not mean the death of slavery? Cleburne admitted that it probably would, but that independence was worth it. "The idea of abolishing the institution at first startles everyone," Key later wrote that day, "but when it is viewed as the means of giving us victory or closing the war, every person with whom I have conversed readily concurs that liberty and peace are the paramount questions and is willing to sacrifice everything to obtain them. All, however, believe the institution a wise one and sanctioned by God."[15]

Cleburne requested that Hardee summon the army's generals at 7:00 on the night of January 2, 1864, to the corps commander's Dalton headquarters. Present were Johnston, Hardee, Major Generals Walker, Stewart, Stevenson, Hindman, and Cleburne, and Brigadier Generals Anderson and Bate. Cheatham, who had been detained, was not present. Hardee introduced Cleburne, saying that he had prepared a paper "on an important subject." The Irishman proceeded to read the lengthy proposal and then opened the floor for discussion. Hindman, Cleburne's longtime friend, quickly supported it, but Anderson and Bate strongly objected. Walker exploded, blurting that "the propagation of such sentiments in the army will ruin [its] cause." He openly stated that he would write each officer for his opinion and send their responses to the War Department. Johnston denied this because the matter did not deal with military issues. Hardee then rose and changed the subject by discussing ways that blacks could be used other than by arming them. Cleburne withdrew his proposal, the issue was tabled, and all, except Walker, agreed to keep quiet on the subject. Walker would later explain to Bragg that the idea was at odds with "all the teachings of my youth and the mature sentiments of my manhood."[16]

The meeting adjourned, but Walker continued to seethe. He wrote his wife on January 7: "I have been going night and day for at least a week.

Matters of pressing importance have occupied me both day and night." He went to Cleburne and asked for a copy of the proposal, making it clear that he planned to send it to the president. Cleburne not only complied, but he also signed it, although he left off the other signatories. The night of the seventh, Walker sought out Hardee, who was preparing to leave for his wedding in Alabama; Hardee remained noncommittal. Walker later audaciously wrote the corps commander requesting a letter stating his views on the subject; Hardee never responded. Obsessed and unwilling to drop the subject, Walker next sent a circular letter to all the generals asking for their views. He made it clear that their answers would be forwarded to Richmond. Anderson, Bate, Stevenson, and Stewart gave, according to Walker, "just such answers as you would except Southern gen'ls to make."

Anderson believed the proposal "would shake our governments, both state and Confederate, to their very foundation." Stewart politely said that the idea was "at war with my social, moral and political principles." Stevenson, although totally against arming blacks, believed that they should be used in other ways. Hindman, on the other hand, gave a furious response, objecting to the lack of confidentiality that Walker had displayed. He had no right to question him, and he complained to Johnston. Cheatham, who had not been present, also refused to answer, although Bate whispered to Walker that the Tennessean had been willing to sign the proposal.[17]

Francis Shoup, the army chief of artillery, produced what might be considered a middle-of-the-road proposal: enlist slaves as soldiers. Many Southerners believed that blacks loved the Cause and would be willing to fight, even while remaining in servitude. Such a proposal, of course, raised the obvious question: Then why were blacks fleeing toward the Union army? Even Johnston had written: "We never have been able to keep the impressed Negroes with an army near the enemy. They desert." An anonymous writer, "Woodson," responded to Shoup's proposal in the press: "What if blacks become accustomed to killing white men?"[18]

Shortly after the conference, Cleburne candidly talked with Tennessee congressman A. S. Colyar about the meeting. On January 30, Colyar described the discussion in a letter to Col. Albert S. Marks:[19]

> While at Atlanta, I saw General Cleburne for the first time, and spent some time with him at his room. I found him to be apparently, and I suppose really, a very modest man. I was very surprised to hear him say that he considered slavery at an end. That we ought to put many of them in the service, but that we could not risk them and the consequences without first changing our relations with them. That no half-way measure would

do—that an entire change of our relations to the slaves, not by military law, but by the action of the States, was necessary. That as soon as this was done, the effect would be upon the North such that they could not keep their armies in the field; and certainly it would insure our recognition at once by the principal powers of Europe. That if we take this step now, we can mould the relations, for all time to come, between the white and colored races; and we can control the negroes, and that they will still be our laborers as much as they now are, and, to all intents and purposes, will be our servants at less cost than now. His great argument is, that if the Yankees succeed in abolishing slavery, equality and amalgamation will finally take place.

General Cleburne says he submitted his views in writing to a number of the officers of the army at a meeting some weeks ago. That his paper was signed and approved by most of the officers of his Division; that many officers at the meeting seemed favorably inclined to the views, and but one man—Major General Walker—took decided ground against him, and a few days afterward wrote him a note (which he showed me), asking a copy of the paper, to be forwarded to the Secretary of War. General Cleburne answered him, saying that he would take pleasure in furnishing a copy; he had no objection to the Secretary of War knowing his views; that he did furnish the copy, signing his own name, saying to General Walker that he had not consulted the other gentlemen, and did not feel authorized to give their names, as they signed the paper for the purposes of that meeting. General C. promised to send me a copy of this paper (23 pages).

I admire General Cleburne's boldness and the fearless manner in which he comes up to a question which he must know may overwhelm him in ruin; but I cannot agree with him in in the necessity for such a move. I have no doubt about the effect on European Powers; but I do not believe the negro could be used to much advantage after he was freed. (But General C. says, writing a man "free" does not make him so as the history of the Irish laborer shows.) We are fast approaching the crisis in this revolution when we may look for bold moves on the chess-board. No man need be surprised at anything. I am always hopeful.

Several conclusions emerge from the letter. First, the theory that Cleburne's proposal was born out of an affinity with blacks was patently untrue. Indeed, in 1861, Cleburne had written that he "never owned a Negro and cared nothing for them." His proposal was pragmatic and calculating, rooted in desperation, not morality. Second, his view that slavery was dead was not a political proclamation but simply based on what he had seen. Rosecrans had already freed thousands of slaves in Tennessee. Third, Cleburne's critics at the meeting, other than Walker, apparently played their cards close to their vests. The Irishman emerged from the meeting thinking that no general other than Walker showed hostility.

The opposition proved more courageous behind Cleburne's back. In a January 14 letter to Polk, Patton Anderson declared the proposal a "monstrous proposition" and "revolting to Southern sentiment, Southern pride, and Southern honor." "What are we to do?" he confided to the bishop. "If this thing is once openly proposed to the Army the total disintegration of that Army will follow in a fortnight." Mary Chesnut in Richmond knew of the paper by January 19, probably from her friend Breckinridge. Brig. Gen. Clement Stevens whispered the secret to Col. James Nisbet on the promise of confidentiality. Nisbet agreed with the memorandum, causing Stevens to bluntly state, "If slavery is to be abolished then I take no more interest in our fight." Bate declared the proposal "infamous" and "hideous and objectionable." On the tenth, Walker, with as many signatures as he could gather, forwarded a package with all of the appropriate papers by special messenger to Davis. In a second letter to the president, Walker wrote: "My excuse for sending the communication of Genl. Cleburne direct to you is that the Commanding Genl. of the Army of Tennessee declined for reasons satisfactory to himself to permit me to forward it through the regular official channel. My excuse for sending it at all is that I honestly believe that the propagation of such sentiments in our army will ruin our cause." As for Cleburne, he believed that Walker had done him an "unintentional service" by getting the proposal to the president. The only thing that could happen to him, he reasoned, was that he could be court-martialed and dismissed from the service, at which time he would again sign up as a private in his old regiment, the 15th Arkansas.[20]

Davis replied to Walker on January 23, stating that the best policy would be to avoid all publicity. The next day, the president wrote Johnston, praising Walker for notifying him and admonishing the army commander to instruct all officers present to maintain a discreet silence on the subject. Johnston, in turn, sent a copy of the president's letter to all of the generals. Cleburne dropped the issue and destroyed all but one copy of the proposal. In 1890, Buck's copy of the document was found and published in the *Official Records* in 1898. But for that, it has been written, this remarkable incident would have disappeared from the pages of history. (Colyar's letter was published in 1878.) Cleburne, Symonds concluded, "misread the society he called his own." It would cost him heavily. Most historians believe that the proposal struck such a nerve that it kept him from obtaining a corps command. In March, Bragg, declaring the signers "abolitionist men," thought that "they will bear watching." An elated Gist wrote, "I am delighted beyond expression to know that the traitors will meet with their just deserts at the hands of the 'powers that be.'"[21]

Lieutenant Colonel Walker heard the rumors and, on January 24, expressed to his wife: "Among Genl. Cleburne's notions is this, to fill up our ranks with negroes, not use them in subordinate positions, but actually arm them side by side with our brave soldiers in the field. Any man who could for a moment entertain such a thought is an abolitionist and I believe Genl. Cleburne at heart to be such, and if he was offered sufficient inducements would sign Lincoln's emancipation proclamation. So much for our leaders."[22]

The news also filtered into the ranks. Edward Brown of the 45th Alabama wrote his wife on January 12:

> Genl. Clayburn was the originator of a proposal to our Congress to arm and equip four Hundred thousand negro men as soon as possible that the condition that the negroes should have their freedom. He argues that the institution of slavery is gone away whether we are beaten or not & that we should now fight for a separate nationality. Their proposition I learn was signed by Clayburn's Brigadier & every Colonel in the division except the Col. of the 45th Ala. Regt. It was also endorsed by Major Generals Hindman and Breckinridge and by Lt. Gen. Hardee. When it reached Genl. Johnston he put his veto upon it & although it was promulgated under the garb of Secrecy it nevertheless got to be current in the army and was warmly discussed by all grades.
>
> I think the proposition has done harm since the natural conclusion to which the troops have come is that if the proposition was endorsed by those who are in position to best understand our real status, it shows that our case is almost a hopeless one, or at least that our Generals think so.[23]

Meanwhile, rumors about black soldiers in the Union ranks continued to stir. "Bring on your God damned nigger wool," pickets shouted during the Atlanta Campaign. In truth, Sherman, believing blacks to be inferior to whites as soldiers, kept them out of active campaigning. "I am told that they have a Brigade of negroes at Ringgold," wrote Alabamian John Crittenden. "If such is a fact our boys may get what they are wishing for sometime and that is a fight with a Negro Regt." Word finally leaked out about the Fort Pillow massacre on April 12, in which nearly half of the black garrison was gunned down, some while surrendering. A massacre had unquestionably occurred, but the question remained of whether it was done in hot or cold blood. After the fall of Atlanta, Rebels captured some black troops in the

Union garrison at Dalton. "Some of the soldiers [Rebels] were very anxious to kill them. But as they surrendered without fighting the men were not allowed to kill none only those who attempted to get away was shot by the guards," Georgian Nell Gillis wrote. "The Negroes had to obey the orders of the guards very strictly or they were shot immediately." Cleburne wrote in his diary on October 14: "Our men were very bitter on the negroes and the officers hollering to the latter to kiss their brothers. A great many of the men think that negroes ought not to be taken prisoners and in case of a fight I think they will catch it." The veil of white paternalistic love toward blacks had come down.[24]

In February 1865, both Davis and Lee agreed to arming a limited number of blacks. In terms of the historiography of the Army of Tennessee, the issue of slavery thus became another internal factor that led to collapse. While it did not have the catastrophic effect of the battlefield losses at Fort Donelson, Missionary Ridge, and the Atlanta Campaign, it did have the effect of lowering morale, raising the specter of sectionalism, and creating confusion as to the ultimate purpose and outcome of the war. It was enough.[25]

✻ 20 ✻

Home Sweet Home

"Oh Matilda how lonesome I feel, how memory carries me back to the happy Sabbath days we have passed together hardly knowing that were happy. I feel a long, long way from home and friends, but I feel that you are one that cares for me, and this is a great pleasure to be allowed to write to each other although I have never received but two from you since I left home. Matilda sometimes my hope almost fails me of ever seeing better days. . . . Sometimes I feel that if it were not for you and the children I would not care how soon my beloved Savior would call for me. But then I know that it is wrong to complain and I try to hold up the best way I can. Oh dearest and best of earthly friends pray to God earnestly that my spirits fail me not."

Thus wrote thirty-six-year-old Pvt. Grant Taylor to his "beloved wife," Matilda, on December 6, 1863. Not one of the eager volunteers of '61, Taylor had joined the 40th Alabama in the spring of 1862 to avoid the onus of being drafted. He farmed in northern Alabama, and his five children (the last born in May 1864) were constantly on his mind. "Kiss the dear children for me," he jotted on February 5, 1864. "I dreamed last night of hugging and kissing little Mary [three-year-old daughter]. I thought my mother was present and she [Mary] said, G[r]anny, my Pa came back again. Oh how I do want to see her but there is no chance now." One thing was for certain, he had no intention of reenlisting for the balance of the war "until I see there is no other chance."

Taylor fretted that the Yankees advancing from Meridian would eventually cut off their communications. His primary concern was the fact that death lurked everywhere. He was not obsessed with his own mortality—he remained a deeply religious man—but he worried for the welfare of his family and what would become of them. For weeks he languished in hospitals with pneumonia but eventually returned to his regiment to serve as a cook. He assured Matilda that he would "not make strenuous efforts to get out of the enemy's way." On June 16, he confided his intimate thoughts: "Home, Sweet home. Oh how sweet the very word sounds. Will I ever get there in peace. But I have this consolation if I never get to my earthy home. I have a home sweet home in heaven." He proved to be one of the lucky ones; Taylor returned to his Matilda at the end of the war and lived until 1908.[1]

The connection to home intersected with virtually every aspect of army life—recruitment, desertion, morale, and the perception of the war and why it was being fought. The breakdown of the home front ultimately proved to be a major blow to Confederate military fortunes.

Home offered the soldiers hope of a return to normalcy after the war. It allowed them to think beyond the immediacy of misery. While at Dalton, Mississippian George Lea wrote a friend: "Well Ivison you wish to know something about my best Girls. I guess you know about as much as I do about them, it has been so long since I heard from or seen them. I found some over here in Georgia that is pretty as red shoes. But Ivison I tell you what is the fact[.] I intend to marry the first furlough I get[.] I have waited long enough for the war to stop and it wont (that is I intend doing this [marrying] if I can find anyone to have me)."[2]

In his study of military and civilian morale in the West during the war, Bradley Clampitt concluded, contrary to popular thought, that home-front morale in occupied territory held up well. Example after example revealed the resilience of civilians and their ardent commitment to Confederate independence. Even Alabama unionism, according to one study, remained marginal. The theory that, after 1864, war-weariness began to wear on women and they were willing to sacrifice less was not substantiated in Clampitt's study. While some women, like some men, gave up hope, the majority continued to express support for the Confederacy.[3]

Clampitt also found that most civilians, even as late as the Atlanta Campaign, continued to look with disdain upon deserters. While most viewed desertion as dishonorable, some expressed sympathy. More important, the vast majority of soldiers remained at their posts, "considering deserting the army as an action that would bring shame not only upon themselves but their families." A Tennessee surgeon related to his wife that he wanted to be able to return home one day as a part of the list "who can return free from disgrace that would sink not only me but wife & children . . . beneath the best class of Tennesseans for all time to come."[4]

The Battle of Shiloh, at least from the perspective of Grant and thousands of Northerners, changed the perception of the war and of the role of civilians. Until the spring of 1862, Grant viewed the war as a police action against an aristocracy that lacked in-depth support from working yeomen. In today's vernacular, the Confederate government had not won the hearts and minds of Southerners. If a major battlefield victory or two could be won, "the rebellion against the Government would collapse suddenly and soon." Union policy, expressed in dozens of general orders, thus spared the property of civilians. Shiloh changed that perception. The surprise at Shiloh was, according to Woodworth, "not that the Confederates attacked but that they attacked as fiercely and effectively as they did." There was clear popular Southern support for the war. After Shiloh, Grant, realizing that this was a war of competing societies, reflected, "I gave up all idea of saving the Union except by complete conquest." This changed policy had a direct impact on civilians. While persons at home were to be protected, all property that could be used to support the Rebel armies would be consumed. Woodworth concluded that Grant changed his view "from ideas of a limited police action against a clique of insurgent politicians to an all-out war against a rebellious people."[5]

Civilians would pay the price. The plight of refugees fleeing the pending Battle of Stones River captured the attention of the soldiers. On December 28, 1862, a generals' meeting was held on the Nashville Pike two and a half miles from Murfreesboro. As they gathered, they noticed a long line of women, children, old folks, and blacks evacuating with horses, mules, oxen, and carts and wagons laden with furniture and household goods. Brigadier General Manigault, captivated by the moment, believed that a skilled artist could paint the scene of "a Battle Iminent."[6]

Sights of civilian property destruction and pilfering took a toll on army morale. In Tennessee, following the Battle of Stones River, some entire villages, such as LaVergne and Manchester, and parts of McMinnville were left in ruins. Everywhere were the sights of distraught refugees — women, children, blacks, and their animals fleeing Murfreesboro and later Chattanooga. "The woods and roadsides are lined with crying women and dirty babies," observed a Tennessean. In an address to the army, Bragg wrote of the "ruthless invader, where gentle women, feeble old age and helpless infants have been subjected to outrages without parallel in the warfare of civilized nations." A Yankee cavalryman, writing in April 1863, lamented what he saw: "It is really sad to see the beautiful country here so ruined. There are no fences left at all. There is no corn and hay for the cattle and horses, but there are no horses left anyhow and the planters have no food for themselves."[7]

Writing from North Georgia in March 1864, a member of the 3rd Tennessee lamented the state of his home:

I suppose they have finished poor old Giles [County] by this time and reduced it nearly to its primitive condition of wilderness. So far as enclosures and valuable property is concerned, the stock is nearly all taken or destroyed. The fences are broken down or burnt along and near ever thoroughfare. The able-bodied Negro men are forced into the Yankee army. The Negro women and children have followed them and are hanging around the outskirts of the Yankee camps, victims of exposure, disease, and debauchery. Such is the physical condition of our country and the moral condition seems to be even worse.[8]

Unfortunately, plundering was not limited to the Yankees. Polk issued an order prohibiting the theft of livestock, but the stealing continued. Following the Battle of Missionary Ridge, hundreds of refugees streamed south. "I cannot blame them. Our army treats the people nearly as bad as the Yankees do. They destroy everything to eat where they go. All that part of Tennessee and Georgia over which the army has passed is perfectly desolate."[9]

Heartbreaking letters from home created feelings of despair. Captain Key received terrible news following the loss of Atlanta. His four-year-old daughter Emma had taken calomel with disastrous results. Mercury poison had taken root in the bone, causing her teeth to fall out. The doctor had no choice but to remove a portion of her jaw, permanently disfiguring the child. "Oh, how this grieved my heart and distressed my good wife," the captain sadly wrote. Bad news continued to arrive; their Helena house was ransacked by black and white Union soldiers. They stole nearly everything of value, with the blacks yelling, "She's a Reb! She's a Reb!" Despite all that had befallen them, Key's wife remained defiant. "If they should take the last piece from my back," she wrote, "I'm not conquered. They may conquer the wood by fire, and rend my garments and scatter them to the four winds and all this; but I am not conquered. So like the old oak, the more the wind blows the firmer I stand."[10]

Mississippi artilleryman Charles Roberts also had concerns about raiding parties. In September 1864, he wrote his "Darling Wife": "If I had the money dear I would remove you to some place where is [sic] was not *probable* for Yankee's to annoy and disturb you, but it takes a fortune for a refugee to support life and I have not got it. It is terrible for me to think of, that my family [must] live in a section of country where at any time they are subject to the insult and depredation of an ungoverned band of marauding soldiers, for such only can be called the men composing [these] raiding parties — It is hard indeed for you to bear dearest and it is painful to me to know that you are subject to be [plundered] and insulted."[11]

Reports of atrocities, many by black soldiers, led to calls to raise the black flag. Malinda Taylor wrote her husband that "there was a Negro burnt to death in Eutaw the other day for taking a white lady of[f] her horse and doing what he pleased to her." Civilians saw themselves as victims, and revenge became a growing motivation. Captain Dent worried that his wife might catch smallpox. He himself had gone through a miserable bout of it. On June 21, 1864, he expressed his concern: "It seems to me that nearly every letter I receive Says something about some one being sick. . . . Do not grow too sad and desponding my Darling. Sorrow and Affliction will come Honey but let us meet it with the right spirit and it will be for good eventually."[12]

Some historians have argued that after mid-1863, the Northern armies inflicted "hard war," or "destructive war," which, although destructive of private property, was less destructive than the concept of total war. This unofficial Union policy deepened an already existing hatred. Pvt. G. H. Burns of the 34th Georgia wrote from Dalton of driving the "merciless foe" back so that the land might never be "polluted again by them." A Mississippian labeled some prisoners of Sherman's army as "cut-throat mercenaries."[13]

The desperate plight of civilians and the feelings of dual loyalty to country and home unquestionably affected morale and resulted in desertions. Alabamian John Crittenden confided to his wife, Bettie, that "hardly a day passes but what I hear of one or more of our company getting home. It renders me impatient. When we fall back again you may look for me. If I get half a chance I shall come home too." A Georgian in the Army of Tennessee expressed the frustration of many: "I have been in all the battles of the West, and wounded more than once, and my family, driven from their home, and stript of everything, are struggling in Georgia to get a shelter and something to eat. . . . Little sympathy is shown my wife and children — they are charged three prices for what scanty accommodation they get, and often are nigh starvation. We might as well be under Lincoln's despotism as to endure such treatement."[14]

In North Georgia, thousands of men were in the army, leaving an already sparse area short of labor for a crop. The study by Williams, Williams, and Carlson about how this affected nonslaveholding families, the so-called plain folk, is revealing. Hundreds of Georgia women wrote letters of desperation to the governor pleading for the return of their men. Typical was the heartbreaking missive of Susan Thurman, who pleaded for the return of her husband: All of his brothers and brothers-in-law had been killed, and their widows and children were destitute. As for her own sick husband, "he is a poor man with a wife and a hand full of little children [and] a widowed mother." Such requests were rarely granted. The shortages of manpower and food thus placed impossible demands upon the home front and in turn undermined the army.[15]

Even from afar, soldiers attempted to remain the heads of their families. A Mississippi cavalryman, writing during the Atlanta Campaign, longed to see his wife and his newborn child, Nellie, whom he had never seen. "Teach her to know my picture and call my name as soon as she begins to talk." He advised that his wife should wean the child as soon as possible. "If your system becomes enfeebled your milk may be an injury to her." He hoped that Nellie looked more like her mother, but above all else he desired her to be "good and intelligent."[16]

In 1862, British traveler W. C. Corsen journeyed throughout the South, including the western states of Louisiana, Mississippi, Alabama, and Georgia. He observed that civilians cared little for beef or poultry and that the standard dish was pork and hominy. "Give them plenty of Indian corn, salt pork, sweet potatoes and whiskey and, as a rule the rural Southerner asks for nothing, either for himself or for his negroes." Early on, however, the shortage of salt created problems. Everywhere Corsen went, he heard that "we have all the hogs we need, but so salt. Beef and mutton our people don't like, and won't take to it if they can avoid it."[17]

Georgia made attempts at indigent relief, but inflation, speculation, and incompetence complicated matters. The main problem, however, remained overproduction of cotton. Desperate women resorted to prostitution, a problem previously discussed, and on occasion violence. One study has documented a surprising number of anecdotal instances of female mobs throughout the state. One woman, armed with a navy revolver, led a dozen women on a raid in an Atlanta store. Augusta, Columbus, Milledgeville, and other cities encountered similar experiences with what one editor called "the baser sort."[18]

Speculators continued to wreak havoc on the poor. A wife from upstate Georgia wrote the governor, asking him to "assiste us in tellin the speculators how trifling they are treating the soldiers wives an that they are whiping our sodiers wors than the yankees." She claimed a month's wages would pay for only corn, and meat could not be obtained at any price. "Is this incouraging to a poor sodier who has to lye in ditches and bare all the hardships of a camp life?"[19]

Beyond facing physical survival, the saddest news came when the family circle was broken. Letters of consolation arrived from army relatives, company commanders, and colleagues. Following the Battle of Stones River, Alex McGowin of the 16th Alabama informed his parents of the loss of their son, his brother, twenty-three-year-old Joseph. "I write you at this time with feelings much mortified, and know too the sad news which this letter contains. Brother Joseph is no more in this world of pain and sorrow." Seven of the McGowin boys served in Company D, 16th Alabama; before war's end, five of them would be dead. A similar fate fell to Milton Walls of the 25th

Arkansas. On August 19, 1864, he sadly began by jotting, "Dear Ma and Pa." He continued: "How shall I prepare you for the sad and heartbreaking tidings? Our family, heretofore so fortunate during this struggle, must now mourn the loss of a loved one. Brother Jester is no more. He now 'sleeps the sleep that knows no waking,' beneath Georgia's blood-stained soil, a glorious martyr to the cause of liberty." Jester fell with a bullet to the chest while on the skirmish line. "All spoke of his piety — he died a Christian soldier. . . . We can meet him again — it is a glorious thought — our only consolation. He has only gone before, soon we shall follow him. Our family circle has been broken, may it be unbroken in heaven."[20]

Precisely what to do with slaves as the army fell back during the Atlanta Campaign became problematic. Some slaveholders in North Georgia took them along as they evacuated south, adding a tremendous burden to feed and clothe them. The local slave market had collapsed, so some attempted (unsuccessfully) to hire out their blacks. For civilians who remained at home, runaway slaves became an increasing problem. Acts of sabotage, such as cutting the bucket ropes of wells, occurred. Some blacks, probably from Bartow County in North Georgia, joined the 44th U.S. Colored Infantry, organizing at Dalton.[21]

Hebert's study of the 1864 Georgia Militia census revealed that 840 white males remained in Bartow County. While the number may sound surprisingly high, a closer examination revealed that 67 percent worked in three industries: the Western & Atlantic Railroad, the local ironworks, and the saltpeter mine. The majority of the balance had either occupational exemptions (ministers, millwrights, blacksmiths, etc.) or chronic ailments (15 percent). Deserters were not included in the census.[22]

Following the Battle of New Hope in May 1864, a Federal band, some 600–800 yards from the Rebel lines, struck up "The Star-Spangled Banner," which was followed by a great cheer from the Federals. A moment later, a Louisiana regimental band struck up a splendid rendition of "Dixie," followed by huzzahs from the Southerners. Not to be outdone, the Federal band replied with "Yankee Doodle," again followed by loud cheering from the bluecoats. In this contest of dueling bands, the Louisiana band played "The Bonnie Blue Flag," which was loudly cheered. Then, in the evening air, the Federal band replied with "Home Sweet Home." A member of the 40th Alabama remembered, "There was neither huzzah, nor cheer, but all around could be seen stern men with their faces blackened with the smoke of battle, wiping away with rough jacket sleeves, the tears that trickled down their faces."[23]

The home front represented one of several interconnected influences that shaped cohesion in the Army of Tennessee. Crises in households placed immense stresses upon the soldiers. The war did not last longer, because the collective voices of women increasingly held consequences. Social, political, and military fortunes became intertwined. The army affected the home front, and the home front influenced the army. On February 21, 1864, Breckinridge visited Richmond and took the opportunity to attend a play—a farce, as it turned out. As he returned to his quarters, Mary Chesnut commented on his melancholy mood. He answered merely, "Is this the same world?" The South would indeed never be the same.[24]

❖ 21 ❖

Struggle for Atlanta

Dalton to Resaca

Sherman was at last on the move. By May 4, 1864, Johnston knew that Thomas's Army of the Cumberland was massing at Ringgold, Georgia; Louis Schofield's Army of the Ohio (the 23rd Corps), at Cleveland, Tennessee; and James McPherson's Army of the Tennessee, in northern Alabama. Johnston suspected that Sherman intended to pin him down at Dalton and outflank him via Rome, Georgia, getting between him and Polk's small army in Alabama. One of Polk's soldiers in the 17th Alabama received a letter from a friend in the Army of Tennessee. "They [Confederate leadership] do not fear an attack at Dalton, but fear that the enemy are amassing their troops to flank us and force Genl Johnston to fall back and that is why Genl J. expresses so much anxiety about this place [Rome]," the soldier wrote his wife. By May 7, Union forces had driven in Rebel cavalry from Tunnel Hill (the tunnel was foolishly left intact), taking a position parallel to Rocky Face Ridge. "Until that day [May 7] I had regarded a battle in the broad valley [Crow Valley] in which Dalton stands as inevitable," Johnston would later write.[1]

Johnston urgently requested a part of Polk's army, and Bragg responded by directing the bishop-general to send W. W. Loring's Division. Davis, however, not consulting with Bragg, ordered Polk to report personally to Rome, bringing with him Loring's Division and "any other available force." The bishop, liberally interpreting the order, proceeded with virtually his entire army—two infantry divisions and a cavalry division, some 14,000 troops, and James Cantey's and Daniel Reynolds's brigades, together 5,300 troops, from Mobile. The traditional interpretation is that Davis never intended to send so large a force and the bishop's "self-willed twisting of orders," as Woodworth called it, angered the chief executive. William C. Davis gave a different interpretation. Due to Secretary of War Seddon's worsening physical health and the president's unwillingness to give Bragg a free hand, Davis increasingly took a direct role. He orchestrated the movement based on his "own perception of just how desperate the situation had become." Given the exchange of curt dispatches that subsequently occurred, the traditional view would appear more plausible.[2]

On May 8, the Rebels repulsed an attack by a division of the 4th Corps on the northern end of Rocky Face. The Confederates also stopped cold an advance by three divisions against Buzzard Roost Gap. "The Yankees advanced a double line of skirmishers against Bates's Division who are in the woods to our front," a Florida artilleryman wrote. "There was desultory fighting all day from 600 to 2000 yards ahead of us occasionally growing very warm." A more serious attack occurred at 2:00 by a division of the 20th Corps at Dug Gap, four miles southwest of Dalton. An Arkansas regiment, about 250 men, held the gap, and J. W. Grigsby's Kentucky cavalry brigade, about 1,000 strong, arrived at the last moment. The skirmish line was driven back to the gap, where the bluecoats made several unsuccessful assaults. Short of ammunition, the Kentuckians began pelting rocks and then boulders at the attackers. Late that afternoon, Cleburne arrived with Granbury's and Lowrey's brigades. The Federals sustained 357 casualties, the Rebels about 60. The assault, as matters developed, proved to be a diversion.[3]

Johnston's focus remained on Crow Valley at Dalton and Rome on his flank. The night of the eighth, he received a dispatch that McPherson's "corps" was nearing Villanow. From there, McPherson would veer off to Rome, or so Johnston suspected. He could, of course, take the road through Snake Creek Gap to Resaca, about twelve miles distant, but the army commander did not seem concerned. If Resaca were to be threatened, it most likely would be by cavalry. He thus sent Grigsby's exhausted Kentuckians south to that town. Guarding Resaca were two detached units from Walker's Division—the 66th Georgia and the 26th Georgia Battalion, 1,500 strong—and Brig. Gen. James Cantey's Brigade, 2,100 strong, which had opportunely arrived from Mobile the night of the seventh. A civilian guide mistakenly misled Grigsby's troopers, and they did not arrive until dawn on May 9. By that time, McPherson's five divisions, which had veered toward Resaca, had already emerged through Snake Creek Gap. In the dark, a long line of blue infantry fired into Grigsby's column, throwing it into confusion; a skirmish of several hours ensued. Although Johnston never admitted it before or after the war, he was in trouble.[4]

Fortunately for Johnston, McPherson stood down. He had another option, however, one for which Johnston was also not prepared. The Union column could continue south of Villanow and cross the Oostanaula River between Resaca and Rome, thus taking Resaca in reverse. Johnston belatedly realized the possibility on May 9. He ordered Cantey to begin fortifications south of the river, but of course it would take time. Johnston had had four months to inspect the roads south of Dalton, the gaps, and the Resaca defenses, yet Dug Gap and Snake Creek Gap had not been fortified and

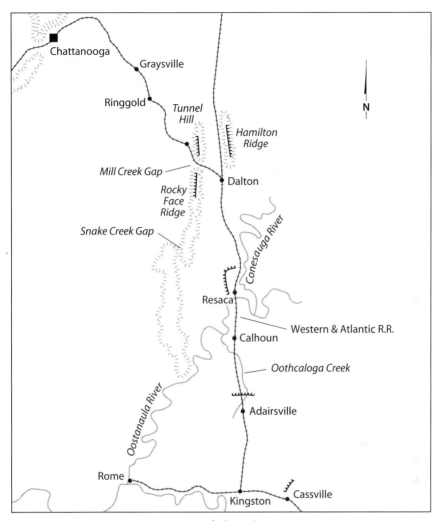

Map 5. North Georgia, 1864.
Adapted from "Dalton to Marietta" map in Hess, Kennesaw Mountain.

neither had the south bank of the Oostanaula River at Resaca nor Calhoun
Ferry or Lay's Ferry.[5]

On May 11, Johnston finally divined Sherman's intentions, and throughout the eleventh and twelfth he moved his army south to Resaca. The troops
formed in a hook-shaped defensive line, with Polk on the left, Hardee at the
center, and Hood in the curve on the right. Walker's Division was retained
south of the river at Calhoun. Precisely why Johnston placed his earthworks
on the north side of the river has long been questioned. The bridge would

be subjected to rifled artillery fire, and if a Missionary Ridge–type break occurred in the Rebel line, the army would have no place to escape. Would it not be better to entrench on the south bank and strike Sherman as he crossed? Newton took a stab at the issue, and his answer is as good as any. He pointed to the "modern mythical interpretation of Joseph Johnston as timorous and noncombative. The general persistently courted battle north of the Oostanaula River (in which he had already admitted to being in a strategic *cul de sac*) because he thought he could win." Castel believed that Johnston remained on the north bank and defended the town "until he had good reason otherwise," hoping that Sherman would "make a costly frontal assault or, better still, leave himself open to a devastating counterblow."[6]

By May 12, Loring's Division and Reynolds's Brigade from Mobile had arrived at Resaca. On the morning of the fourteenth, Sherman attacked, the brunt of the assault falling on Bate's and Hindman's divisions. Still hobbling on a crutch from his Shiloh wound, Bate would live to become both governor and senator of Tennessee. The Yankee attacks "were driven back in twenty minutes with much slaughter," he reported. Hindman likewise repulsed every assault. One of the last sorties fell on A. W. Reynolds's Brigade of Stevenson's Division. According to a correspondent for the *Atlanta Intelligencer*, the men of Brown's and Pettus's brigades rushed to the brigade's assistance, even though they were commanded by their officers to remain in position. Sherman accomplished nothing and sustained 1,600 casualties, so he brought up his artillery and opened what one Confederate recalled as "the most terrific artillery fire I was under in the war." Entire regiments fled the trenches. "The[ir] artillery has been playing the wilds with us," wrote one of Bate's infantrymen. Maj. Thomas Hotchkiss's artillery battalion occupied a crucial knoll between Hardee and Hood's connecting position. Thirty enemy guns blasted the position, with Semple's Battery losing twelve men and eight horses and having two Napoleon guns disabled.[7]

At 1:30 on May 15, the 20th Corps attacked Stevenson's Division. Although repulsed, the Federals captured Max Van den Corput's Georgia battery but were unable to haul away the guns. At 4:00, Johnston ordered an attack on the Union left, which had been reported in the air. The assault commenced as ordered, although a dispatch had been sent to army headquarters reporting "heavy movement of the enemy" in that sector. The attack was belatedly canceled, but not before Stewart's ill-fated division had already advanced. The Union flank was in fact not exposed but held by a division (Alpheus Williams's). Stewart's brigades encountered savage fire and reeled back with a loss of 1,000. "The Confederates have paid a stiff price for

Fighting at Resaca, May 15, 1864.
From Battlefields in Dixie Land and Chickamauga National Military Park
(Nashville: Nashville, Chattanooga & St. Louis Railway, 1928).

making an assault that had practically no chance of success and that would have been meaningless even had it succeeded," Castel evaluated.[8]

Confederate casualties at Resaca totaled about 3,000, including 500–600 captured. Col. James A. Williamson of the 2nd Arkansas Mounted Rifles had his leg amputated, and Col. S. S. Stanton of the 28th Tennessee fell dead while personally carrying his regiment's flag. Brigadier General Walthall sustained a slight wound and Brig. Gen. Jesse J. Finley a left broken arm. Johnston received intelligence that the Federals had crossed the Oostanaula River at Lay's Ferry and Walker's Division had been unable to dislodge the beachhead. Johnston abandoned Resaca on the night of the fifteenth.

Continued Retreat

The van of Johnston's army arrived at Adairsville on May 17. The general planned to give battle, but his maps had deceived him; the valley proved far too wide to deploy his army. He had little choice but to withdraw. That day, Red Jackson's 4,400-man cavalry division of Polk's army linked up. Johnston now planned a trap. He sent Hardee's Corps and the wagon train due south to Kingston, while Polk's and Hood's corps veered southeast down a little-used road to Cassville, where they deployed along Two Run

Creek north of Cassville. On May 19, Sherman took the bait. He had his main force, the Army of the Cumberland, follow Hardee. An attack on the unsuspecting Federal left appeared imminent, and Johnston even issued a cheering proclamation to the army. At the last moment, however, Hood's right stumbled into two Union cavalry divisions on the Canton Road east of Cassville. Stevenson's Division formed a line of battle, checking the blue horsemen. Hood aborted his attack and fell back two miles without informing Johnston. Hood and Johnston would argue long into the postwar years about the "Cassville Affair." Although Hood's reaction was prudent, he did not help his case with his totally unsubstantiated excuse, claiming that the Union cavalry was a mere reconnaissance and that he aborted the attack because there was no enemy to be found.[9]

Later that afternoon, Johnston withdrew his army to a ridge that ran roughly north-south, with Hardee on the left, Polk in the center, and Hood on the right. Francis Shoup, the chief of artillery, warned Johnston about an exposed salient occupied by James A. Hoskins's Mississippi battery that connected Polk's and Hood's corps. Late that afternoon, the Federal artillery predictably opened a fierce fire on the salient. That night, Polk and Hood became convinced that the section held by Samuel French's Division was untenable. In a conference with Johnston at 8:00 P.M., they argued that in the morning Polk could not hold forty-five minutes and Hood two hours. Johnston argued the issue for over two hours, but having received reports of Federal crossings below Kingston, he finally relented. He ordered a retreat across the Etowah River at midnight. As in all things Atlanta, a postwar dispute erupted. Hood and Polk's biographer's son William insisted that no recommendation was made for a retreat; indeed, the generals advocated for the offensive, an assertion Connelly labeled as "pure fabrication." Maj. Gen. Samuel French, who was also present, claimed that he always believed his position had been a strong one. Although Johnston had retreated from Dalton, Resaca, Calhoun, and Adairsville, Bradley Clampitt believed that Cassville was different. Not making a stand after reading a rousing proclamation resulted in "the first meaningful damage to the overall morale of the Army of Tennessee."[10]

Johnston crossed the Etowah by means of the railroad bridge, the ordinary road bridge, and two pontoons. He took a position at Allatoona Pass, hoping that Sherman would assault. Sherman instead had his eye on Dallas, fifteen miles south of the river and about sixteen miles west of Allatoona. Confederate cavalry detected Sherman's move from the outset. Rather than retreat, Johnston shifted Hardee's and Polk's corps west. Hardee arrived outside Dallas on May 23, and Polk deployed at Lost Mountain, in between

Battle of New Hope Church — "The Hell Hole" — May 25, 1864.
From Battlefields in Dixie Land and Chickamauga National Military Park
(Nashville: Nashville, Chattanooga & St. Louis Railway, 1928).

Hardee and Hood. A U.S. Army "staff ride" determined that Johnston missed an opportunity when he did not strike Sherman as he crossed to the low south bank of the Etowah. The terrain at that point would have offered his best chance in a pitched battle.[11]

Hood's Corps formed northeast of Dallas, with Hindman on the left, Stewart in the center, and Stevenson on the left. In the center, Stewart's men—all of Stovall's and Clayton's brigades and parts of Gibson's and Baker's brigades, backed by John Eldridge's artillery battalion, in all 4,000 men—deployed in front of the Dallas Road at the New Hope Church crossroads. At 4:00 P.M., with dark clouds in the sky, Joseph Hooker's three divisions, some 16,000 troops, came barreling down on them along a narrow front. The bluecoats were mowed down. A Mississippian wrote after the battle: "They were lying piled so thick that I could, had I chosen, walked over a large portion of the field on their mutilated bodies." According to J. L. Bostick, the battlefield "was visited by hundreds of officers, including Genls. Johnston, Polk, Hardee & all agreed that they had never seen dead Yankees piled more thickly on any battlefield. Along Granbury's front the dead lay in almost a perfect line of battle and such terrible wounds I never saw before. Some of the Yankees are pierced with twenty or thirty bullets and great numbers of them were shot in the head, their skulls being broken to pieces as if shot by artillery." Federal casualties totaled 1,732; Confederate, 448. Darkness and rain ended the slaughter. The battle would forever be saddled with the sobriquet "The Hell Hole."[12]

Sherman next determined to turn the Rebel right by going beyond Johnston's flank. Again, the move was detected almost immediately, and the Southerners shifted accordingly. On May 27, the Federals formed six lines deep in an attack on Cleburne's Division, deployed at Pickett's Mill along a low ridge bordered on the east by Little Pumpkin Vine Creek. It proved more murder than warfare, as the Federals dropped in windrows. Granbury's Texas brigade made a sudden sortie that captured 250. After the battle, an Alabamian recorded, "Such piles of dead men were seldom or never seen before on such a small space of ground." Union casualties tallied 1,600; Cleburne's, 500.[13]

The next day, May 28, Johnston received intelligence—false, as it turned out—that Sherman had withdrawn from Dallas. He ordered Hardee to reconnoiter. Jackson's cavalry division advanced on the flank at 3:45, but the troopers were quickly driven back. William Bate immediately canceled the planned advance of his division on Jackson's right, but the Kentucky and Florida brigades did not receive the order in time. It was Pickett's Mill in reverse. The regiments were "terribly cut up," wrote a Kentuckian. Word got out that Bate had reported a mere skirmish line in his front and received permission to make the charge. "The boys generally know what is in front, and could have told Gen. Bate better," a disgusted John Jackman noted. The order, however, had come from corps headquarters, and Bate was not to blame. The division sustained at least 1,000 casualties, perhaps as many as 1,500; the Federals, 379.[14]

When Sherman refused to make all-out assaults, Johnston, according to McMurry, became "demoralized" and lacked the "psychological strength" to deal with the changing trench warfare. "It was easier just to cancel the effort and renew the retreat," McMurry concluded. Johnston only thought in terms of "day to day operations," and while he made no serious mistakes, he never saw how his Fabian tactics were becoming a political and logistical disaster for the entire Confederacy. Had Johnston pursued Lee's Virginia tactics and inflicted similar losses on the Yankees, "the entire political-military equation of 1864 would have been changed." Perhaps, but offensive operations would have been costly and the results were not guaranteed.[15]

Johnston's only solution was to suggest cavalry raids in the Federal rear. "Our best mode of operating against it [enemy's progress] would be to use strong parties of cavalry to cut his railroad communications. Our own cavalry is so weak compared with that of the Federal army that I have been unable to do it." Symonds calls attention to the fact that twenty-four trains a day reached Chattanooga during June and July. "They crossed more than a dozen major bridges, the destruction of any one of which would have slowed the flow of supplies." Yet, even the destruction of Tunnel Hill, which should have been done, would only have slowed the inevitable. If geography could not stop the Federal army, limited cavalry raids surely would not. When the Nashville & Chattanooga was torn up by Federal cavalry near Decherd, the Confederates, even with their limited supplies, repaired it within hours. Small raids were nonetheless attempted. On Tuesday, May 24, Wheeler, with 4,000 troopers, struck the Union rear at Cass Station and brought off 70 wagons, 102 prisoners, and 300 horses and mules. The feeble raid proved a mere annoyance to Sherman.[16]

In early June, Johnston abandoned the New Hope Church–Pickett's Mill–Dallas line and established the ten-mile "first Kennesaw line" that ran northeast to southwest, with Lost Mountain on the left, Pine Mountain in the center, and Brush Mountain on the right. Pine Mountain extended from the main line and Hardee desired to withdraw Bate's Division from it. On June 14, Johnston, Polk, and Hardee went to the top of Pine Mountain for a reconnaissance. A Union battery spotted the cluster of officers and fired several shots. One of the balls passed directly through Polk, killing him instantly. Woodworth considered it a most unfortunate shot—for the Yankees. "Polk had damaged the Confederate cause consistently ever since joining the army, and he would have had opportunities to do much more damage in the weeks to come." Corps command temporarily went to W. W. Loring.[17]

Sustaining a punishing two-day artillery fire along the "second Kennesaw line," Johnston, in the midst of a heavy rain, pulled back two miles southeast to the "third Kennesaw line." Hood held the right, east of Kennesaw Mountain, Loring the center, which included Little Kennesaw, Big Kennesaw, and Pigeon Mountain, and Hardee the left. In Hardee's center, a high salient slightly extended beyond the line, which would become known as Cheatham's Hill. In little over a month, wrote historian Stephen Davis, Johnston had given up sixty miles of territory and six separate defensive positions.[18]

On the night of June 21–22, Johnston ordered Hood from the right to the left in order to block another suspected flanking movement. Wheeler's cavalry occupied Hood's old trenches. Two Federal corps took up positions on either side of the Sand Town Road and extended southwest down the road. In scouting up the road, the bluecoats took thirty prisoners of the 58th/60th North Carolina regiments of Carter Stevenson's Division. The alerted Federals quickly began throwing up breastworks and bringing up artillery. What now occurred was what Earl Hess termed "essentially a reconnaissance in force by two divisions [Hindman's and Stevenson's] that had just arrived on unknown ground." Unfortunately, a skirmish line was not advanced. At 5:00, the divisions assaulted. Cummings's Brigade, moving south of the road, encountered thick undergrowth, causing a Federal officer to remark that the men "approached reluctantly and in much disorder, resembling a mob more than they did soldiery." The resulting Battle of Kolb's Farm, as it became known, was what Stephen Davis termed "an easy Federal defensive victory." Hood lost 1,000 men (Castel claimed 1,500; Sherman, 215. Two-thirds of the Rebel casualties came from Stevenson's Division, which, Castel criticized, "again has demonstrated, as it did at Resaca, a lack of offensive punch." One wonders if more bodies were needed to uphold the division's honor. Hood's modern-day supporters feebly defended the corps commander's weak performance by saying that he accomplished what he was ordered to do—stop Sherman's flank maneuver. Hess countered that such a mission could have been accomplished by simply digging in. He criticized "Hood's faulty judgment about the best way to achieve the tactical goal set for him by Johnston."[19]

There is indeed evidence to suggest that Johnston saw the engagement at Kolb's Farm as a success—Hood had driven the Federals until he was stopped by artillery. Johnston did not criticize Hood, despite the fact that the Powder Springs Road, one of the army's main escape routes to the Chattahoochee River, was now threatened. Nonetheless, on June 20, Hardee wrote his wife: "I don't know what he will do under the circumstances. I found Hood with him when I arrived & I left him there. Hood, I think, is helping the General do the strategy, and from what I can see is doing most of it." Interestingly, at about the same time, Hood became "somewhat disappointed" in the treatment of his corps, believing that Hardee's Corps got the best positions.[20]

Hoping that Johnston had weakened his center to extend his line, Sherman now planned to strike the center. At 6:00 A.M., McPherson's Army of the Tennessee opened an intense fifteen-minute artillery barrage with fifty-one guns against Loring's Corps on Kennesaw. At 8:15, the skirmish line to Loring's left, south of the Burnt Hickory Road, held by the 63rd Georgia of Walker's Division, was overrun and about eighty men were killed, wounded, or captured. A serious attack was made on French's Division on Little Kennesaw and Pigeon Hill, causing the corps commander to think he was under a general assault, although it was easily repulsed. The main attack came against Cleburne's left and Vaughn's Brigade manning the Cheatham's Hill salient. Rebel pickets came darting in shouting, "Up boys; they are charging!" "Away went blankets and poles to the rear," recalled a Tennessean. As the Federal attack pivoted against Maney's left, the bluecoats came under the enfilade fire of Carter's and Strahl's brigades and Phelan's Alabama and Thomas J. Perry's Florida batteries to the south. Brigadier General Finley's Florida brigade was rushed forward, but it was not needed. Johnston had won the day with about 1,000 casualties to Sherman's 3,375.[21]

Sherman eventually outflanked the Kennesaw line, causing Johnston to withdraw to the more compact Smyrna line, which straddled the railroad. When it, too, was outflanked, Johnston withdrew on July 1 to his final defensive position north of the Chattahoochee River. The line, designed by Brigadier General Shoup, was an engineering masterpiece. It embraced a system of ten-foot-high spear-shaped forts with face walls ten feet thick to absorb artillery. The shoupades, as they were called, were placed at intervals of 60–175 yards and were connected by vertical eight-foot-high walls. One thousand blacks were collected to hurriedly construct the six-mile-long line. The troops unfortunately never understood the interconnected and enfilading system and tore down much of the construction to form traditional earthworks. Modern critics point to the fact that it would have to have been forty miles long to prevent Sherman from flanking it. Within two days, it was abandoned and the army escaped south of the river, as Union artillery "shelled the pontoon/bridges as we crossed." No hits were made, although "they threw their shells very close."[22]

Leading Atlanta historians have stood in line to criticize Johnston's performance north of the Chattahoochee. Stephen Davis points to the fact that at the end of June, Johnston had 62,700 present for duty as compared to Sherman's 106,000, or odds of 59 to 100. In Virginia, Lee faced odds of 47 to 100 and accomplished more. McMurry checked off one criticism after another: Johnston "could have moved west of Allatoona to threaten the Yankees' left flank." He failed to spot "either of the two wide gaps that yawned for several days in the Federal line at Dallas and New Hope." He even failed to "inflict serious damage on the railroad behind his own position." If Johnston's strategy was to encourage Sherman to launch a frontal assault, "perhaps he should not have fortified his positions so strongly." It was obvious by the end of May that Sherman was simply not going to make a massive frontal attack. McMurry also questioned Johnston's curious penchant for repeatedly fighting with a river to his back. Castel wrote bluntly that Johnston neither failed to check the Union army nor significantly reduced it. Indeed, his own losses were proportionately higher. His success in holding the New Hope Church line for a month was due more to weather and Sherman's supplies than to his military skill. Despite his excuses, which would extend into the postwar years, the "undeniable fact" remained that Johnston now had his back to

Atlanta. Hess concluded that Johnston's Fabian strategy "was, in short, a failed strategy, and it drained the patience of Johnston's superiors."[23]

Fateful Decision?

In late May, Hood dispatched a staff member, Henry P. Brewster, to present a letter to the president giving a current account of operations. Precisely what was said is not known, but Brewster subsequently went around Richmond and talked to anyone who would listen. He claimed that Johnston had "no plan," that he was "afraid to risk a battle," and that he had overridden the council of both Hood and Polk. He did so because "they do not hate Jeff Davis enough." Brewster should have been arrested for such an egregious undercutting of the army commander, but to the larger issue, he clearly represented Hood's negative and, it is difficult not to conclude, self-serving views.[24]

Johnston's constant retreats had indeed aroused the authorities in Richmond. Unless something was done quickly, the Army of Tennessee would be at the very gates of Atlanta. On June 24, Senator Wigfall arrived at Johnston's Marietta headquarters. The senator warned the army commander of the dissatisfaction in the War Department and that rumors were circulating that the president was going to remove the general and replace him with Hood. Johnston ticked off his litany of excuses: he was greatly outnumbered; the Federals fortified each position, making an attack impossible; and the only hope was for Forrest's cavalry to attack Sherman's supply line, even if it temporarily meant the loss of Mississippi. A week later, Senator Benjamin H. Hill of Georgia, an ally of the president, called upon Johnston. The senator got essentially the same response as Wigfall.[25]

Davis proved unyielding. Forrest was unavailable, Mississippi could not be abandoned, and Johnston had sufficient cavalry to perform the raid. The cabinet aligned against Johnston. Judah P. Benjamin, who had opposed Johnston's appointment from the outset, wrote that the general was "determined not to fight; it is of no use to reinforce him, he is not going to fight." Secretary of the Navy Stephen Mallory believed Johnston to be Benjamin's "favorite theme." Even Seddon, who had supported the general's assignment, now opposed him. The cabinet voted unanimously to relieve Johnston, to which Davis replied, "Gentlemen it is very easy to remove the Genl. but when he is removed his place must be filled and where will you find the man to fill it." Anticipating the worst, Davis asked Lee for his evaluation of Hardee and Hood. "Hood is a good fighter," Lee answered, "very industrious on the battlefield, careless off, & I have had no opportunity of judging his actions, while the whole responsibility rested upon him. I have a high opinion of his gallantry, earnestness & zeal. General Hardee has more experience in managing an army."[26]

Despite the unanimous verdict of the cabinet, Davis hesitated. He sent Bragg to Georgia to investigate, but some historians suspect that he already had his mind made up. Indeed, William C. Davis surmised that Bragg may even have been given the authority to replace Johnston, "but the timid general declined to take it." Bragg described his visit as a "casual visit"; surely no one believed it. Bragg, Johnston, and the corps commanders held a ten-hour conference on July 13. On July 15, Bragg wrote to Davis: "I have made General Johnston two visits, and have been received courteously and kindly. He has not sought my advice, and it was not volunteered. I cannot learn that he has anymore plan for the future than he had in the past." Bragg advised that Hardee should not receive command if it becomes necessary to relieve Johnston but that Hood would give "unlimited satisfaction." As for Hardee, he was openly miffed that Bragg did not confide in him as to the state of affairs; the two men detested each other.[27]

By July 16, Davis could no longer wait. He dispatched Johnston and asked for his future plans. The general answered: "As the enemy has double our number, we must be on the defensive. My plan of operations must, therefore, depend upon that of the enemy. It is mainly to watch for an opportunity to fight for advantage. We are trying to put Atlanta in condition to be held for a day or two by the Georgia militia, that our army movements may be freer and wider." Seddon later wrote that Johnston's "answer was deemed evasive and unsatisfactory, and then and not till then, under the belief that Genl. J. really meant to abandon Atlanta without decisive engagement did the President finally decide and authorize his removal."[28]

When Johnston submitted his stunningly vague document rather than a specific plan to defend the city as Davis had requested, the decision was made to fire him. Davis had once said of Johnston that there was not "a better fighter in the army, if he would only fight." The general received the order relieving him on the night of July 17—he could not have been surprised. Although a correct decision at the time, in retrospect it seems clear that the Federals (based on numbers and Union competence, Murray and Hsieh correctly surmised) could not have been stopped at this stage of the campaign.[29]

As for installing Hood as Johnston's replacement, there was not much of a choice. Nothing in his record suggested that Hardee was the man for the job; he had previously admitted as much to Davis. Cheatham was a fighter but had no experience at the corps level, much less general command. Beauregard was, of course, the better choice, but Davis's prejudice prevented his selection. Hood, on the other hand, seemed anxious for a fight, even though in reality he had shunned it in the past. Hadn't Hood positioned himself for army command by criticizing Johnston and meeting with Bragg? Earl Hess believed not, stating that the Texan was "genuinely surprised" and that army command proved "truly unexpected and unwanted." The traditional view, voiced by Stephen Davis and Castel, from my perspective appears more plausible.[30]

The impact of Johnston's removal on the army has been studied by Bradley Clampitt. He concluded that Johnston's departure was met with "near-universal discontent." The men in the army had "genuinely loved" the army commander as they had no other. That said, the soldiers' overall views changed to some extent in the weeks that followed. The troops reconciled "themselves to the situation relatively quickly."[31]

Other command changes occurred. For three weeks, Loring had led the old Army of Mississippi, but Stewart, who had no connection with the corps and was junior to both Loring and French, now received permanent command. Thirty-four officers in the corps, including French and eight brigadiers, unsuccessfully petitioned for Loring to be retained. Stevenson almost certainly seethed as well, being the senior major general in the army and having been passed over three times. Command of Hood's old corps went to thirty-one-year-old Lt. Gen. S. D. Lee, who had formerly commanded cavalry in Mississippi. A trooper described him thus: "Genl Lee is by no means presupposing and looks more like a country school master than a Maj. Gen. of Cavalry." Some thought that he had been promoted over more proven generals such as Cleburne and Cheatham. "The talk in camp was that President Davis was partial to him," wrote an artilleryman.[32]

Hood Attacks

With Sherman bearing down on Atlanta, Hood, on July 20, attempted to implement the plan proposed by the departing Johnston. With McPherson's and Schofield's armies east of Atlanta and approaching from Decatur, Hardee and Stewart would attack Thomas's army as it crossed Peachtree Creek from the north. Unfortunately, McPherson advanced from Decatur faster than anticipated, forcing Cheatham's Corps (S. D. Lee had not yet arrived) to shift south. The Tennessean "mishandled the movement," according to McMurry, shifting twice as far as necessary. In order to connect with Cheatham's left, Hardee was forced to shift eastward, with Stewart following, a move consuming three hours. Hardee has been blamed for sliding too far to the right and, in a sullen mood because he hadn't been tapped for army command, not communicating with Hood. According to Castel, Hardee's new position nonetheless proved ideal. He could now hurl his 15,000-man corps against

John Newton's 3,200-man Yankee division. "Not since Chickamauga have chance and circumstances so favored the Army of Tennessee," he wrote.[33]

Hood had five divisions and two in support to assault four Union divisions — 23,000 versus 20,000. At 4:00, Hardee's men attacked en echelon from the right. The thick undergrowth caused the two lines of Bate's Division to intermingle. Newton described the Rebel juggernaut as "immense brown and gray masses (not lines)." The attack was badly handled. Bate became separated and failed to get in the Union rear; Cleburne's reserve division was never brought forward; Maney's Division (Cheatham's old division) found the Yankees behind breastworks and took cover; and only three divisions (Walker's, Loring's, and Walthall's) became seriously engaged, with only two brigades from each of these divisions bearing the brunt of the engagement. The Battle of Peachtree Creek, as it became known, proved to be a failure for Hood, with the Southerners losing 2,500; the Federals, 2,000.[34]

Undeterred, Hood devised another plan. Realizing that McPherson's army faced north-south crossing the Georgia Railroad, the Texan ambitiously devised a wide flanking maneuver. Hardee's Corps would march south of Atlanta then turn back northeast on the night of July 21. About 1,500 of Wheeler's cavalry meanwhile would attack McPherson's wagon train at Decatur. Castel declared the tactic "worthy of Lee." The long dusty night march proved more grueling than Hood expected and hundreds of men fell behind. Realizing that Hardee would not be in position by the morning of the twenty-second, Hood modified the plan. The attack would now be made on the Union flank rather than the rear. Even so, Hardee would have a fifteen-mile march.[35]

On the morning of July 22, the Rebels trudged through thick underbrush, not knowing the exact position of McPherson's flank. Opportunely, the 16th Corps, on its way to tear up railroad track, happened to form a line perpendicular to the 17th Corps. The Union line thus formed a capital L, with a gap at the angle. Hardee's two right divisions, expecting to find no opposition, slammed into the 16th Corps. In the subsequent fighting, Walker was slain and the division knocked out of action. Cleburne's Division made some headway at the angle, and at 4:00, Hood ordered Cheatham's Corps out of the trenches east of Atlanta to join in the assault. The Confederates managed to break the 15th Corps line, capturing a dozen field guns, but they were eventually driven back by Union reinforcements. The Battle of Atlanta had cost Hood 5,300 casualties; Sherman, 3,500. Hood blamed the "partial success" on Hardee, for not getting to Decatur before attacking, an accusation Castel labeled "absurd." The reason for Hood's failure was "that he tried to do too much with too little and in too short a time." Rather than modifying the plan, thought Castel, Hood should have canceled the flank maneuver and aimed at the gap between the 16th and 17th Corps. This criticism presupposes that Hood knew about the existence of the gap prior to the attack.[36]

In late July, Hood received more troubling news. Sherman had unleashed three separate cavalry raids. The one under Kenner Garrand, a decoy as it turned out, was easily checked, but George Stoneman's column, estimated at 2,200, and Edward McCook's column, estimated at 3,000, caused alarm. McCook moved on Palmetto on July 28, destroying Hardee's baggage train; capturing 500 wagons, 1,600–2,000 mules (all sabered to death), and 422 prisoners; tearing up two and a half miles of track at Lovejoy's Station; and pulling down five miles of telegraph wire. As McCook returned, however, his men got trapped between Jackson's pursuing division and a detachment of Wheeler's cavalry at Brown's Mill near Newman. A remnant escaped as the Federals cut their way out, but 1,325 were either killed or captured. Stoneman's column headed toward Macon with the ultimate goal of freeing the 30,000 Federal prisoners at Andersonville. Unable to penetrate the Rebel defenses, McCook returned, but his column was intercepted by three brigades under Brig. Gen. Alfred Iverson at Sunshine Church on July 31. Some of the blue horsemen made their way out, but nearly 1,300 fell captive. Despite inferior arms, run-down animals, and a troubling lack of discipline, the Rebel cavalry still retained a punch. Connelly called the episode "Wheeler's finest hour."[37]

Sherman now sent the Army of the Tennessee to the west of Atlanta to strike the Macon & Western Railroad. Hood correctly determined Sherman's intent and planned to block the maneuver with S. D. Lee's and Stewart's corps, some 22,000 troops. The newly arrived Lee would march two of his three divisions out on the Lick Skillet Road and secure the crossroads near the Ezra Methodist Church. The next day, July 29, Stewart would proceed behind Lee and attack the Federal left flank. On the morning of the twenty-eighth, however, Lee discovered that the Federals had already occupied the crossroads. "Eager to prove himself," according to Hess, Lee "made a snap decision" and, without authorization, ordered an attack. Historians suspect that Lee thought that he could hit the Federals before they entrenched, but it was too late. Stewart later desperately joined in the battle at Lee's request. The result was a bloody one-sided Federal victory, with the Rebels losing 3,000 and the Federals losing 632.[38]

As in the Battle of Atlanta, Hood did not personally oversee operations, choosing to remain in Atlanta three miles distant. Castel defended the army chieftain — he was at his headquarters planning a battle for the twenty-ninth. The nation's top Atlanta scholars (Castel, McMurry, Stephen Davis, and

Hess) all blame Lee for his hasty decision to attack and his subsequent piece-meal assaults. Interestingly, Hood approved of the attack in his memoirs, leading to the conclusion that if he had been present, he would have given an approving nod; Castel concluded as much. The most recent book on the battle, written by Gary Ecelbarger, reversed traditional interpretation by exonerating Lee and blaming Hood. Had Hood dispatched Lee's divisions by at least 8:30 A.M., rather than after 10:00 A.M., Lee could have safely executed his orders. The "if only" argument could, of course, be argued for every battle in the West. Castel believed that, once again, Hood simply expected too much from his army and that even if the plan had been properly executed, it probably would not have succeeded.[39]

By August 3, Schofield's army, actually a corps, had moved from its former position northwest of Atlanta to the north fork of Utoy Creek. Supported by the 14th Corps, Schofield probed the West Point Railroad. On the sixth, he assaulted Rebel works, losing 300 men; the Southerners, 25. For the time being, Sherman was stalemated. Thus began the forty-day siege, or what Stephen Davis called the "semi-siege" of Atlanta, which accomplished little. By August 28, Sherman, leaving only one corps north of Atlanta, began what McMurry termed "a great wheel" south of the city. Realizing the threat to the Macon & Western Railroad, Hood moved Hardee's and Lee's corps to Rough and Ready and East Point, not realizing that the true target was Jonesboro. By the thirtieth, a reported two Federal corps, perhaps three, had crossed the Flint River and neared Jonesboro. Hood immediately ordered Hardee and Lee on a night march south to attack and drive the Yankees back. The subsequent assault on August 31 was, in McMurry's words, "a fiasco" and in Castel's, "farcical chaos." It was the most one-sided killing field in the western theater, with the Southerners losing 2,200 and Sherman losing 172, a staggering thirteen-to-one ratio. Among the wounded was Patton Anderson, who was shot in the mouth, resulting in a broken jaw. Castel suspected that the famed railroad scene in the movie *Gone with the Wind*, where a panoramic view revealed countless hundreds of wounded, "could only have come from the fighting at Jonesboro."[40]

McMurry defended Hood from accusations that he had foolishly attacked fortified positions. "Hood was not a blood thirsty butcher," he wrote. "At Peachtree Creek, Atlanta, and Jonesboro, it was his intention to attack unfortified positions, either by striking before works could be built or by marching his assaulting column around them." It was Lee, not Hood, who had ordered the attack at Ezra Church. Hood's mistake was in miscalculating "how far battle-weary men could march in a given time." Perhaps his best option would have been, following Utoy Creek, to construct a line of fortifications from East

Point to Jonesboro. "Such works would have covered the line off the Macon & Western and at least given Sherman pause. Their very existence might have dissuaded him from attempting the movement that led to Jonesboro."[41]

Hood became confused, not about Sherman's flank march, as some writers have suggested, but about Sherman's intent. Fearful that the railroad attack to the south was a feint and that Sherman would march back and attack Atlanta from the west, Hood ordered Lee's Corps back to the city, leaving Hardee's Corps at Jonesboro. In hindsight, the move, as McMurry wrote, "made the Rebels' situation even worse," but he had hardly any choice short of evacuating Atlanta on August 31. On the morning of September 1, news arrived of the Confederate defeat at Jonesboro the previous day. At that point, Hood did order an evacuation. Unfortunately, Sherman's target was not Atlanta but Jonesboro, and Hardee now had five Federal corps bearing down on him. The Federals attacked in the late afternoon, smashing Govan's salient and capturing 900 prisoners and the eight guns of Swett's and Key's batteries. Overwhelming Federal numbers, the only antidote to fortifications, had prevailed. Total Rebel casualties eclipsed 1,200. A patchwork defense line, coupled with Federal ineptitude, allowed Hardee to escape that night and march south to Lovejoy's Station. There the army regrouped. On the night of September 1, hearing the exploding ammunition in Atlanta twenty miles away, a Texan remarked that the army was indeed "in a bad fix."[42]

Did inept leadership lose Atlanta? Certainly, it played a role. Perhaps as Murray and Hsieh have suggested, Johnston had intended to break the cycle of constant bloody attacks that broke the will of the Confederates. If so, his defensive tactics did not work. A study by McMurry concluded that Johnston lost 15,450 killed, wounded, and missing in May and June, and that excluded deserters from early July. The Rebels, McMurry believed, undoubtedly sustained higher proportional losses than Sherman's army. Newton had the most complete estimate, but it is grounded in speculative math. His number of 14,213 casualties from May 7 to July 17 is nonetheless not far from McMurry's. Newton's estimate from July 18 to the end of the campaign equaled 17,615. The two numbers totaled a staggering 31,828 killed, wounded, and missing. In the end, however, the *Battles and Leaders* estimate may be the most accurate: 3,044 killed, 18,952 wounded, and 12,983 taken prisoner (which included captured deserters but not those who simply went home), for a total of 34,979, excluding those who died of disease or became permanently disabled through sickness. Hood's aggressive style clearly failed, but in his defense, once Johnston surrendered the North Georgia highland country, the Federal army could simply not be stopped.[43]

✳ 22 ✳

A Pathway to Victory
The Fog of War

"I do not believe we can decide it [the war] by fighting. I think it will be stopped some other way, and God grant it is soon for I believe both parties is tired of war." Thus wrote Mississippian William Honnell back in May 1863. Over a year later, in August 1864, Grant Taylor of the 40th Alabama, remarked similarly: "Oh how tired I am getting of this thing. But I do not see any chance or any effort being made to settle it except by fighting and I do not believe it will ever be done in that way." If the battlefield could not decide the outcome of hostilities, then was there "some other way"?[1]

The resilience of the troops in the Army of Tennessee proved remarkable. The Yankee armies nonetheless marched relentlessly ahead, consuming Kentucky, Arkansas, Tennessee, Mississippi, eastern Louisiana, and large portions of Alabama. The sheer raw manpower of the North appeared endless. In the Atlanta Campaign, Johnston would face not an army but what in modern terminology would be called an "army group." A Tennessee cavalryman began to raise questions. "There is no use in fighting unless we can accomplish something by it. I think we have one of the best armies in the world, but still if they outnumber us too far, we must not fight them, for when the army we have now is gone, I cannot see where the next one is to come from."[2]

The casualties sustained by the Army of Tennessee and its predecessors in 1861–63 could roughly be divided into three groups: Fort Donelson and Island No. 10, with slightly fewer than 25,000 casualties; Shiloh, Perryville, and Stones River, with slightly more than 25,000 casualties; and Chickamauga and Chattanooga, with slightly more than 25,000 casualties. Altogether, this was roughly 75,000 killed, wounded, and missing. True, many in the first group were among the 20,000 or so prisoners taken at Fort Donelson and Island No. 10 who were exchanged after nine months and placed back into the ranks. The attrition rate proved appallingly high, however, with many taking the oath of allegiance and others dying while languishing in Northern prison camps. Of the 14,000 prisoners exchanged in September and October 1862, 4,000 remained so sickly that they had to be discharged. Of the remaining 10,000, only 2,000 went to the Army of Tennessee, the balance going to the emerging Mississippi army.[3]

In his statistical study *Lost for the Cause*, Newton validates the remarkable strength the West mustered for the Atlanta Campaign. The Rebels fielded at least 63,941 troops present for duty in April 1864, including three regiments (26th Alabama, 55th Georgia, and 57th Georgia) that had been guarding the Andersonville prison but then went to Johnston. "The hardluck Army of Tennessee had been reinvigorated by a new commander [Johnston], reorganized almost from top to bottom, and reinforced heavily. If it had not completely put behind it the long shadows of two years of retreat and misfortune, its dogged persistence made it still a force that could not be discounted," Newton concluded. McMurry placed the June 1864 army strength at 69,946.[4]

To be sure, it would have been premature to wrap black crape around Johnston's headquarters at the beginning of the Atlanta Campaign. Many, if not most, of the soldiers in the Army of Tennessee believed that victory was achievable throughout the Atlanta Campaign and beyond. In March 1864, A. J. Neal "anticipate[d] brilliant successes this spring and after a few hard fights a glorious victory." R. N. Colville had "no fear of the result. I believe that we are certain to whip them as we fight, and if we once get them started back like we did at Chickamauga, Johns[t]on will follow them up and drive them out of Tenn. The whole army is in better health and spirits that I ever saw them." Thomas Warrick asserted that the Yankees "will Git the worse whippin tha hav had in A long tim."[5]

Morale remained high throughout the Atlanta Campaign even as the Rebels, in the eyes of modern historians, were losing. In the fog of war, the soldiers saw matters quite differently. "On the 22nd [July] we charged the enemy's works and carried them capturing 8 14 [twelve-pounder] guns and several stacks of colors," James Hall wrote after the Battle of Atlanta. G. W. Athey wrote similarly to his sister: "We captured a good many prisoners in the first fight [July 22] and drove the yankes from thaire frunt lines of breast works." Clampitt concluded that, "realistically or not," the soldiers continued to believe in Johnston's strategy, that the Federals would assault entrenched positions and that Sherman's supply line would be stretched to the breaking point.[6]

Despite continued high morale, the thought that the Army of Tennessee could militarily dominate the states north of the Ohio River in 1864 was simply not plausible. The *Memphis Appeal* published an article on October 14, 1863, entitled "How to Close the War." The editor based his premise on a Davis speech, in which the president claimed that a major defeat of Rosecrans's army "would effectively bring the war to a close." But even if every battle in the West was as big a victory as Chickamauga, the South would still run out of men before the North ran out of men—*if* the North was willing to take such huge losses. Besides, anyone set on another Northern invasion stood at odds with Johnston, who wrote in reference to Gettysburg on January 21, 1864: "I have never believed . . . that we had the means of invading the enemy's country." Davis encouraged Johnston to launch an offensive, but as historian William C. Davis humorously noted, "Joseph E. Johnston would never in his life lead an offensive on anyone or anything other than Jefferson Davis." What then was the pathway to victory?[7]

For diehards, there was no overarching victory plan other than to keep fighting; it was a war to the death. Flavel Barber, far from being in denial, wrote, "They have overrun Tennessee and Arkansas, driven us from the Mississippi River, and gained a foothold in Texas." He concluded that the "only tolerable alternative left us is resistance to the bitter end. We must fight, we can do nothing else, if necessary forever." Daniel Kelly came to a similar conclusion. He was "not willing to be driven back [into the Union] until the last man of us have perished."[8]

Even after the fall of Atlanta, some believed that the war could still be won militarily. After visiting the Army of Tennessee in September 1864, Davis stopped in Augusta and made a speech. "The only way to make spaniels civil is to whip them. And you can whip them. I have just returned from that army which we have had the saddest accounts—the Army of Tennessee, and I am able to bear to you the words of good cheer. That army has increased in strength since the fall of Atlanta. It has risen in tone, its march is onward, its face looking to the front." A naïvely but commonly held belief claimed that tens of thousands of men had yet to rally to the Confederate banner. "Let all the men from Ala., Miss., and South Carolina all turn out at once and come and stand by Johnston just 10 days and we will drive the last vistage of a enemy out of our land and have peace," J. B. Sanders of the 37th Mississippi defiantly wrote on July 13.[9]

Some still talked of foreign intervention, although by 1864 it seemed a pipe dream. If Great Britain and France had not become involved *before* Vicksburg and Gettysburg, what would interest them after those Southern defeats? Lieutenant General Hill explained "the belief then very prevalent, that England and France would recognize the Confederacy at its last extremity, when the Northern and Southern belligerents were both exhausted. France could not hope to retain her hold on Mexico. Besides, the English aristocracy, as is well known, were in full sympathy with the South." If intervention was no longer determinative, however, it would lose its value. More to the point, by 1864, England had become preoccupied with Europe. Davis did send Brig. Gen. William Preston, formerly of the Army of Tennessee, as an envoy to Mexico to deal with the puppet Maximilian government, installed by the French, but the president otherwise no longer engaged in foreign relations. "We have no friends abroad!" he was heard to say in March 1864. The *Appeal* concurred. On February 11, the paper noted that England had been "bullied by the Yankees" and that "we may well be satisfied that nothing has been further from its intentions during this war than the 'recognition of the Confederate State.'"[10]

Within the ranks of the Army of Tennessee, foreign affairs remained a topic of discussion, however. In the 10th South Carolina, Walker wrote his wife on March 20, 1864: "I think our chances for recognition are improving. I think Mexico will take the lead and be speedily followed by France and Great Britain. I don't think we may look for intervention, but we can for recognition, which will not have so much a physical or direct effect, but a moral one upon the enemy." The diary entry of a Tennessean spoke more realistically: "There are rumors of foreign recognition again but no one believes them. Our people have gained enough wisdom to cease building hope on any foundation except their armies, their efforts, and above all upon a just and merciful God." William Honnell remained of the opinion that France and England should "let us alone and let us settle it ourselves, for I am afraid France and England will try to subdue both parties, and keep us in war longer that it would [take] to settle it ourselves. If they will let us alone, it cannot last longer than winter."[11]

The financial ruin of the North seemed like another pathway. The *Albany (N.Y.) Argus* related in February that the war debt of the United States had grown so large that it now equaled the entire debt of Great Britain. The article appeared on the front page of the *Appeal*, along with similar articles that suggested that the United States was in economic shambles. Indeed, a headline in the *Appeal* of March 30 read, "Peace Coming Through Bankruptcy." "The financial system of the North seems to hang upon a thread," Walker wrote on March 13. "I think a Confederate victory will snap the thread, and bring ruin and distress upon the North." In truth, it was the Confederacy that faced financial ruin, with runaway inflation and near-starving conditions in some regions. Worthless currency presented a larger problem for the South. As early as August 3, 1863, Isaiah Harlan wrote his brother, "Confederate money is fast declining in value and will continue to do so until the war closes." Mississippian Walter Rorer believed that a combination of Northern dissention and French intervention remained the only path to victory — "I can at present see no other way to win the war."[12]

Could arming the slaves bring victory? Cleburne proposed this and he paid a price. Westerners expressed fury at the Federals "sending out an armed negro soldiery to conquer us," but viewing blacks as potential comrades in a common cause proved unbearable. By June 1864, Mississippian Charles Roberts admitted his ambiguities about the institution. He had become convinced that slaves were "more of a curse than a blessing," but "what would be the condition of society here [in] the South with negro labor abolished, we have to acknowledge that it is a necessary evil, so incorporated with the social system of the South, that without it neither you or I want to make the Confederacy our [home]." Historian George Rable concluded that the "will-o'-the-wisp dream of a military triumph with slavery intact still lived." Indeed, the "proslavery argument prevented many Confederates from realistically assessing their political future."[13]

Winning by Not Losing

Yet one more possible pathway to victory remained—to demoralize the Yankees by the war's length so that they would become war-weary and lose interest. In short, some saw not losing as winning; they could simply outlast the North. Historian Albert Castel not only recognized this as the South's best option but also believed that it could work. A victory for the Democratic Peace Party in the 1864 election would cause the North to sue for peace or at least stop the war. Once stopped, it could never be reignited. "In plain words, Southerners are counting on the Northern Democrats to bring about peace and Confederate independence. And Southerners believe that they can make this happen by denying military victory to the North in 1864." Castel concluded, "Paradoxically, the South's hope came from the North." McMurry concurred: "*Not* losing thus became the key to winning for the secessionists."[14]

William C. Davis, who emphatically disagreed with the thesis, noted that Johnston never saw denying Lincoln's reelection as a viable alternative. When Senator Benjamin Hill called upon Johnston and explained that the failure to repulse Sherman would ensure Lincoln's reelection, "the general only nodded and replied that he needed more cavalry. That nod is as close as Johnston got to taking any active part in attempting to affect the outcome of the election in November." In postwar years, Johnston wrote that had Davis subscribed to his defensive tactics, the war would have lasted longer, and in turn it would have enabled the Democrats to win the election. He expressed no such strategy during the campaign.[15]

There are problems with the "winning by not losing" thesis. First, it underestimates Northern resolve and assumes that the Northern will would break first, even though Southerners were disproportionately taking the losses. Second, it assumes that the Confederates could lose a string of battles and still see themselves winning in the long run. Third, and most significant, according to Stoker, the best method of protracting the war "was to sit on the strategic defensive." Did Southern soldiers have the temperament for such a strategy?[16]

If the "South could have won by not losing" thesis were truly viable, then the turning point would not have been Atlanta in 1864 but Vicksburg in 1863, when a serious two-front war was being waged. Mississippi and Tennessee were forever linked. The loss of Pemberton's 36,000 troops at Champion Hill, Big Black, and the capture of Vicksburg not only led to the Confederates' loss of Port Hudson and of control of the Mississippi River, but it also freed Grant's army for operations against the Army of Tennessee. The letters and diaries make it clear that the men of the Army of Tennessee did not grasp how inextricably their fate was linked to their sister army in Mississippi. Pemberton's army siphoned off manpower from the Army of Tennessee and protected the army's western flank. If Pemberton had won at Champion Hill, or if in losing he had abandoned Vicksburg and pulled his army out while he still could, then a linkage with Johnston's 26,000-man Army of Mississippi, though difficult, would not have been impossible. True, Vicksburg would then have been lost, Pemberton would have been fired, and Civil War panelists would today be insisting that Johnston's "Army of Relief" would actually have relieved the city. As it was, the South lost both the army *and* the city, and Pemberton still became the most hated man in the Confederacy. True, 8,000 or so (all I have been able to document) of Pemberton's exchanged troops ended up in the Army of Tennessee. It is nonetheless fair to say that probably half, if not more, of the Vicksburg army's men simply melted away or crossed back to the Trans-Mississippi, where if they fought again it would be in a theater that made no difference. The point is that a 52,000-man combined army in Mississippi in late 1863 (larger than the Army of Tennessee at that time) could have made a crucial difference. A stalemated Mississippi would have denied Grant his subsequent command in Virginia; big doors swing on small hinges. As matters stood, the full weight of the Union army in the West bore down on the Army of Tennessee.[17]

Gen. U. S. Grant, Stoker points out, believed that a protracted war was the South's best strategy. "I think his policy [strategy] was the best one that could have been pursued by the whole South—protract the war which was all that was necessary to enable them to gain recognition in the end." Grant concluded that "the North was already growing weary." Stoker believed, however, that Grant failed to grasp what was happening within the Confederate high command. "His [Grant's] attributing to Johnston a conscious decision to pursue a strategy of protraction was too generous; there was no such determination. Johnston had adopted his approach out of weakness and inclination, nothing else." Stoker conceded that intentional protraction was the strategy that *should* have been tried, but Davis "did not coordinate the political and military efforts of the South in order to deny sufficient Union military success, before the presidential election. Davis's action in Georgia clearly shows this."[18]

Whether or not breaking the Northern will provided a viable strategy, the men in the Army of Tennessee *believed* it to be so. A Tennessean emphatically wrote that in the North, "a doubt has begun to spring up, more from seeing our resolution than from any other cause. Some Northern papers are beginning to speak out and to declare their belief that the South can never be subjugated and they attribute it to the false policy of the president. They profess to believe that the Union could have been restored if conciliatory measures had been employed but they seem to despair of the Union now." T. B. Kelly concluded that "in all probability this spring and summer [1864] will prove in vain for the North longer to dispute our rights." By April 2, he was not so certain. "The Copperhead newspapers and orators of the North have all turned loose with the bitterest invective against Abe Lincoln. . . . I think at present, with the army and the treasury, he is too powerful for his opponents." The next day, he wrote, "We watch and wait for the coming election." Lt. Francis P. Fleming concurred, writing: "In no case have they gained a success. I trust that they will soon see the madness of their undertaking to subjugate us."[19]

More and more, the men began to take an interest in the Northern election. J. T. Kern was convinced that "they can't carry the war successfully & a presidential election." Writing on April 5, Flavel Barber expressed: "The Northern opposition to the administration is daily assuming a more embittered form, but Lincoln holds the reins with a bold hand and seems utterly unscrupulous as to the means employed to crush out any spirit of insubordination. We watch and wait for the coming election." A Texas cavalry officer noted: "The Chicago Convention (Copperhead) has been postponed until 27th August. I suppose their object is to be enabled to make nominations & adopt a platform to suit the times. If Grant and Sherman both fail they will have an out & out peace man, if both succeed a war man, if only one succeeds then they will be non-committal—so I think." In September, he would write: "I have seen [George] McClellans letters of acceptance [for Democratic nominee]. He *is* in favor of reconstruction peaceably if possible. If peaceable means fail he is for war. I would much prefer Lincoln to

McClellan." On September 4, William Ball of the 33rd Mississippi offered his evaluation: "If McClellan be elected I think the war will end though even that is not certain." A Lincoln reelection nonetheless assured continuation of the war.[20]

Captain Dent saw the fall of Atlanta as a game changer. "If Lincoln is re-elected the war will go on. If McClellan is elected then there is no certainty that we will have peace and the yankees will be so much inspirited by the fall of Atlanta." Atlanta, of course, did fall, and Lincoln was reelected by a wide margin in the electoral college. With the most viable pathway to victory off the table, where then was the hope? "It seems that Old Abe is re-elected and there is some probability of another four years war—isn't it horrible to think of it? The Northern vote is but a ratification of all his former acts and means of carrying on the war, and we cannot expect anything better for the future. If God is on our side we will triumph nevertheless, but the future presents a gloomy picture for the homes and fire-sides of the South." Thus wrote Captain Miller on November 15. Two days later, Captain Key described the confusion within the ranks. "There was a rumor in town [Florence, Alabama] to the effect that Lincoln has issued a draft for one million Northern soldiers. If that be true the war will be waged with renewed vigor and more bloody than ever this year has been. How the South will be able to contend with such overwhelming numbers we cannot imagine, for she now has almost all her available force in the field. . . . Many Southern men have preferred the election of Lincoln to McClellan, but we have thought it a strange course of reasoning to desire the South's bitterest enemy to rule the nation with which we are at war."[21]

The reelection of Lincoln failed to deter most Confederates. "Well, let her rip, I say. It is better to fight always than to give it up," believed a Louisianan. He later wrote: "Well, I suppose we are in for four more years [of fighting]. Damn the day, fight it out, I say, as long as there is a man [remaining] to fight with. I am devilish tired of Jeff Davis and his crew, but I am not in favor of stopping the war until we are independent." Others expressed similar views. Mississippian John Marshall was to the point: "I can never let a Yankee boast of whipping us to me I will shoot him whenever he does it. . . . Let it be as it may."[22]

Talk of a political settlement (emancipation for independence) did not emerge until early 1865, when Confederate officials met with Union delegates at Hampton Roads, Virginia. The talks quickly collapsed. Lincoln would discuss only reunion and made it clear that no armistice would be considered until the Rebels laid down their arms. Captain Key concluded that "the terms that Lincoln laid down . . . are so dishonorable that it has had the happy result of cementing our people for a more energetic prospection of the war."[23]

Even with all of the viable pathways to victory off the table, save that of divine intervention, the letters and diaries all spoke of continuing the war. "We have come too far to think of retracing our steps now even if we desired," a Texan concluded. He wrote of the "thousands of brave men whose lives have been sacrificed." There had simply been too much blood spilled, too many lives sacrificed on the altar of their nation, not to play out the war to its inevitable conclusion. The Yankees felt the same way.[24]

✳ 23 ✳

Conquered

North Georgia Campaign

The Atlanta Campaign thoroughly drained the army; for most men, morale plummeted. "Genl Hood has been completely 'outgeneraled' by Sherman. Genl Johnston would have done much better with this Army than Hood has," an Arkansan wrote. John Marshall of the 41st Mississippi was "almost willing to give the thing up and quit." Lt. R. N. Colville wrote bluntly: "Our troops are very much demoralized. They do not have the confidence in Hood that they had in Johnston." William Berryhill of the 43rd Mississippi remarked on September 9: "Gen. Johnston never lost anything on his retreats and the whole army wishes that he was our General still." Charles Roberts believed that "the fall of Atlanta has killed Hood as a general." Morale nonetheless remained complicated and mixed. James Hall believed that the troops were "much less demoralized that you would suppose." Captain Dent likewise wrote, "I do not think it [surrender of Atlanta] renders our cause hopeless." Rumors and a partisan press fanned optimism.[1]

The fall of Atlanta and private letters from Generals Hardee and French telling of eroding morale prompted the chief executive to visit the army for the third time. Davis arrived at Palmetto, Georgia, at 3:30 P.M. on September 25. The next morning, he reviewed the army. There were a few embarrassing shouts of "Give us Johnston," but for the most part, the men gave a polite welcome. "Though scarcely a man left the bivouac, who had not determined to treat him [Davis] coldly, his calm, pale and frosty looks created a deep sympathy in behalf of the born Executive, and when General S. R. Gist proposed 'Three cheers for the President' a wild united shout was given," J. A. Tillman described to his mother. That night, the band of the 20th Louisiana serenaded the president.[2]

Davis held extensive conferences the next day, first with Lee and Stewart and then separately with Hardee. By now, Hood and Hardee detested each other. In a document memorializing the meeting, the corps commander wrote: "I told him [Davis] that things had reached a point when it was necessary to relieve either Hood or myself, that I did not ask him to relieve Hood, but insisted on his relieving me. I told him that if he wished to know what the

Army wished, I would tell him that they wanted a change of commanders. He then discussed the matter, but did not say what he would do. I told him Johnston had a wonderful hold on the affections of the Army, that the men were devoted to him. He discussed Johnston and satisfied me that he would not send him back." Davis reassigned Hardee to the Department of South Carolina, Georgia, and Florida, with headquarters in Charleston. Cheatham, the senior division commander, received corps command. Hardee attempted to depart quietly, but word leaked out, and his old Arkansas brigade flocked to his headquarters. He emerged and "for a long time he mingled with them . . . exhorting them to continue to be good soldiers and faithful patriots. Then, bidding them an affectionate farewell, he quietly withdrew to his quarters," recalled a soldier. The men gave a loud cheer and then slowly drifted back to their quarters. Davis also revived the old Military Division of the West under the nominal command of Beauregard.[3]

Although badly reduced, the army remained strong enough to be dangerous. The September 10 return showed 38,129 present for duty, excluding Wheeler's cavalry in Alabama. The officer corps had been shattered, with Polk and Walker dead and three major generals and fourteen brigadiers wounded, four of the latter (A. J. Vaughn, Lucius Polk, W. F. Tucker, and Matthew Ector) requiring amputations. Three other brigadiers received extensive sick leaves. Some restructuring was done after the battles around Atlanta, including dissolving Walker's Division and reassigning the brigades to other divisions. Marcus J. Wright's Brigade in Cheatham's Division was also dissolved and the regiments redistributed.[4]

Reequipping the troops proved more problematic. It became necessary to phase out four artillery battalions with forty-two guns, retaining their horses but sending the guns and men to the fortifications at Macon. A Floridian admitted, "We are very scarce of blankets and pieces of carpets are highly prized, the way most lost their blankets were being broken down on the march to save themselves from capture, they would throw away any blankets in preference to clothes and many blankets were literally torn to pieces by shells and mine [sic] balls." Captain Dent believed the principal problem remained "the want of something to eat. We are only drawing beef now and very poor at that, get no bacon and have no grease[.] we have flour but can't use it." Hood requested 5,000 pairs of shoes and 300 more wagons, 80 to come from the defunct artillery reserve.[5]

As early as September 6, Hood proposed marching north of the Chattahoochee River and striking the Western & Atlanta Railroad, Sherman's sole supply line. After destroying the railroad, he would then march west, hoping that Sherman would follow. If Sherman marched toward Augusta, Macon, or Columbus, the Army of Tennessee would be in his rear. Historians have supported the strategy. To remain on the defensive would have been "impractical both politically and strategically," thought Sword. Even Connelly believed that Hood "had no choice." Anne Bailey labeled the maneuver as "the only alternative in a desperate situation." McMurry thought the plan "as sound as anything the Confederates could have devised."[6]

The North Georgia Campaign began on September 29–30, when Hood crossed the Chattahoochee River on pontoons west of Palmetto. John Marshall took an opportunity to write his wife: "We are now fixing to march. I have no idea where we are going but you will not hear from me again soon if ever. . . . We may move in direction of Corrinth [sic] Miss. We think we will aim north. . . . I may never see you again though I still have hopes." Writing on October 1, Lt. George Warren, a Missourian in Francis Cockrill's Brigade, believed that the men were "in very good spirits."[7]

Stewart's Corps captured Big Shanty and Ackworth on October 3, taking 425 prisoners. Samuel French's Division went north to take Allatoona, but he hit a brick wall. The Federal garrison fought viciously, repulsing French with 900 casualties. Hood crossed the Coosa River near Rome on the tenth. He soon abandoned his plan to operate south of the Oostanaula River, and on the twelfth, Stewart struck the Western & Atlantic north of Resaca. The small garrison refused to surrender and Hood did not waste his time, continuing to strike the railroad all the way to Tunnel Hill. The garrisons at Tilton, Dalton, and Mill Creek Gap capitulated with about 1,000 prisoners.[8]

Cleburne, writing in his diary on October 13, told of the excitement. The men would lift up 100 yards of track at a time and then pitch the section over, breaking loose the ties and rails. "The shouting of the long lines of lifters, the ringing of pick and ax heads against the iron pins fastening the rails to the wood, the interminable lines of fire as the cross-ties were given to the flames, the thousand columns of smoke" all proved to be a sight not to be forgotten.[9]

On October 15–16, the army bivouacked at a place Hood termed the "crossroads," nine miles south of La Fayette in the Chattooga Valley. Sherman, in pursuit with 40,000 men, approached from Snake Creek Gap. This was the moment to offer battle and Hood knew it, yet he declined. He surmised that the troops remained dispirited and that the army was simply in no condition for an offensive. This conclusion flew in the face of Manigault's report. The morale issue aside, Hood made the right decision. To go into a pitched battle meant that the army would again be butting against breastworks, yet he could not afford to yield the offensive. Connelly admitted that a retreat "may have been necessary."[10]

After pursuing Hood for another day, Sherman called off the chase.

"I could not guess his movements as I could those of Johnston, who was a sensible man and only did sensible things. . . . He [Hood] could turn and twist like a fox and wear out my army in pursuit," Sherman wrote. He instead turned Tennessee over to George Thomas with the 4th and 23rd Corps, some 23,000 troops. Another 15,000-man corps (A. J. Smith's) would be coming from Missouri to join the Nashville garrison. The Federals would eventually assemble over 60,000 men in Tennessee. With his remaining army, some 62,000 men, Sherman planned his "March to the Sea," from Atlanta (from which he evacuated all civilians) to Augusta. "Sherman had determined to bring the war home to the South in a devastating and unforgettable manner," concluded McDonough. Sherman and Hood thus marched in opposite directions.[11]

The Southern troops saw the North Georgia Campaign as a victory, and morale soared with rumors of a Tennessee offensive. Alabamian Edward Brown wrote his wife on October 19: "Hood has shown himself to be a man of no ordinary skill. The whole army is decidedly won over by Hood. Much doubt of his ability obtained at the beginning of this campaign, but it has all disappeared. He is today the most popular Genl. that has yet commanded this army." Brigadier General Clayton believed that the "spirit of our men is improving daily. The Tennesseans are perfectly jubilant at the prospect of going again into their state." J. W. Ward of the 24th Mississippi agreed: "The morale of the army is good all seem to want to go to Tenn." When John Crittenden returned to his regiment, he found the men in high spirits. "They think that they have ruined Sherman's Railroad. It is told in your country that our army is demoralized but such is not the case. I never saw less straggling in my life." Wiley Donothan of the 24th Texas wrote his sister on October 18, "Our prospects were never brighter for a great change has been wrought within the last two weeks."[12]

Tennessee Campaign

The army arrived at Gadsden, Alabama, on October 20. The next day, Thomas Roane, the surgeon of the 51st Tennessee, wrote his wife: "We are doing the finest marching I ever saw from 15 to 20 miles a day with ease over rough roads, although many of the men are barefoot & their feet raw and blistered. We have a large train of Supply Wagons to haul meal & bacon & drive our beeves along ahead of us. We have here [Gadsden] 7000 beef cattle & Eat from 250 to 300 a day. We have also a Pontoon train of 80 boats which are fitted as wagons like the body of a wagon. . . . So you see we are prepared for traveling."[13]

Beauregard finally caught up with Hood on the twenty-first. Hood proposed to strike Sherman's communications by crossing the Tennessee River at Guntersville, Alabama, tearing up the railroad track to Stevenson, and destroying the vital bridge at Bridgeport. The plan was virtually identical to the one proposed by Davis back at Palmetto. What the president had not approved, but what Hood clearly had in mind, was a subsequent offensive into Middle Tennessee. Sherman, he believed, would be forced to follow. Thus was born Hood's Tennessee Campaign. McMurry consider it "a wild dream," although "it is difficult to imagine a viable alternative." Woodworth concurred, stating, "The plan skirted on the far edges of reality, but under the circumstances it might have been as good as anything else he could have done—provided he moved very fast and made no mistakes." Stephen Sears raised the question, "What, really, were Hood's choices in the failing western theater in 1864?" Symonds nonetheless considered the campaign "foolish," and William C. Davis dismissed it as "a wildly impractical idea, reminiscent of some of Beauregard's schemes." Beauregard did in fact embrace the idea, but it must be clear what he understood: Hood would take care of Georgia *first*, by striking at Stevenson-Bridgeport. As for a campaign in Tennessee, Beauregard saw possibilities, although he expressed concerns about logistics, of which "General Hood was disposed to be oblivious." Beauregard did insist that Wheeler's cavalry remain in Georgia to harass Sherman. Hood would retain Jackson's cavalry division, and Forrest's cavalry in Mississippi would link up.[14]

Shoes and clothing remained in short supply. Edward Brown described the situation: "A large number are barefoot and many are without jacket or blanket, but we are expecting supplies hourly. . . . Shoes and clothing ought by all means to be issued before we march any farther. Many of the men have marched from Dalton here barefoot while some have made sandals of green cowhides. These sandals do tolerably well for a short time but they soon get too hard and become unpleasant to the feet." Large shipments of clothing and shoes soon arrived, but they had to be hauled by wagon from the depot at Jacksonville, Alabama. If the observation of Lt. Hamilton Branch was accurate, most of the men departed Gadsden without blankets.[15]

The army proceeded toward the Tennessee River, but rather than turning north and crossing at Guntersville, as Beauregard had been told it would, Hood, on October 23, turned northwest toward Decatur, fifty miles west of Guntersville, where he arrived on the twenty-seventh. He remained at Decatur two days, skirmishing with the reinforced garrison. Not wishing to tangle with the Federals, he continued west toward Tuscumbia, where the army arrived on October 30. The nine-day march had proved grueling, with horrid weather and scant rations. "The troops are suffering now for something to eat for this country has nothing in it to feed an army. They [troops] have been living on bread for several days," William Berryhill related to his wife. Everywhere in northern Alabama the men saw desolation. "As I passed down the once beautiful valley of the Tennessee, I saw nothing except wrecks of palaces and devastated plantations," noticed Captain Key. A large portion of Tuscumbia had been burned and the streets appeared "weather-worn and dilapidated."[16]

Hood failed to inform the president of his change of plans until November 6, twenty days after the maneuver was in progress, something McMurry labeled "an inexcusable neglect." Hood eagerly wrote, "General Beauregard *agrees with me* as to my plans of operation." It was a half-truth. What Beauregard had approved was a strike *first* on Stevenson-Bridgeport in order to draw Sherman back. Beauregard did *not* approve the de facto abandonment of Georgia. With the campaign in motion, President Davis did not call Hood back, although he wrote, "I consider this movement into Tennessee ill-advised." William C. Davis correctly wrote that the president "neither planned nor approved the operation." Even Hood acknowledged that President Davis believed that "the Army should have been equal to battle by the time it had reached the Alabama line, and was averse to my going into Tennessee." As for Beauregard, he angrily rebuked Hood for leaving him out of the loop. According to T. Harry Williams, Beauregard was "infuriated by his subordinate's refusal to take him into his confidence." With the campaign already in motion, the theater commander acquiesced to the plan. After the war, Beauregard wrote that he had never embraced Hood's Tennessee plan, thought it would fail, and openly accepted it because he believed that Davis favored it. Williams rejected this postwar account.[17]

Hood expected his new depot at Tuscumbia to be well stocked when he arrived, but he found no stockpiles. Supplies were coming from Selma—which had replaced Atlanta as the new central base—by rail to Meridian, Mississippi, along the Mobile & Ohio route to Corinth. Rations and ordnance would then be transferred to the Memphis & Charleston Railroad. Unfortunately, fifteen miles of that line (between Cherokee Station and Tuscumbia) were inoperable. Removing the railroad iron from west of Tuscumbia to get the Memphis & Charleston operational proved to be no small task. Meanwhile, all supplies had to be shipped over the break in wagons over dirt roads that had turned into quagmires. The rail line would not become operational until November 21. Hood had no choice but to sit for three weeks, consuming the twenty-day supply received at Gadsden. Frank Vandiver thus proposed that logistics lost the campaign from the outset. The only hope that Hood had was to move before Federal forces could concentrate. The "fateful delay at Tuscumbia allowed the enemy ample time to prepare for his coming."[18]

There were other logistical issues. Getting the supply train to Tuscumbia proved merciless on the animals; fully 1,500 horses and mules were lost between Palmetto and Tuscumbia. Maj. E. H. Ewing, army chief of transportation, warned that as many more would be lost if Hood continued his pace into Tennessee. The general ordered that all usable mules hauling baggage wagons be given to the ordnance and commissary trains. Run-down mules would then haul the baggage to Aberdeen, Mississippi. Some 300 horses were also needed for the artillery. Not having any, Hood used 240 newly arrived mules from Alabama. Ewing sent 450 broken-down animals to the depot at Selma, where Hood ordered authorities to begin accumulating mule shoes, wagon covers, nails, and of course, more horses and mules.[19]

The army's pontoon train—83 boats, 150 wagons, and 400 mules—soon arrived. Florence, on the other side of the river from Tuscumbia, was occupied by about 1,000 enemy cavalry. The railroad bridge spanning the Tennessee River had been out of commission for two and a half years. On the night of October 30, three brigades loaded into the pontoons, twenty men to a boat; the infantry quickly seized the town. The engineers proceeded to construct a 1,000-yard-long pontoon bridge, using the bridge piers as anchors. To Federal engineers, it may have appeared routine, but this proved to be the first time in the war that the western Confederates had accomplished such a feat. Brigades crossed in fours, with a band playing at the head of each column. All did not go well. Heavy rains caused the pontoon bridge to break on November 9, resulting in the loss of some of the boats. Replacements had to come from Corinth. It would be late on the twelfth before the bridge reopened, with Cheatham's Corps crossing the next day. However, when a herd of cattle crossed on November 13, the steers bunched together, snapping the bridge again and dumping two mules and forty-five cattle into the river.[20]

As the army idled away at Florence-Tuscumbia, Hood began pointing fingers. He claimed that he was not moving because Forrest had not yet arrived, for which he blamed Beauregard. From the outset, however, the plan had been to meet Forrest in Tennessee. "Everyone seemed ready to shift the responsibility for future operations on someone else—Hood blamed Forrest, and by extension Beauregard, for the delays, and Beauregard distanced himself from the whole operation," Bailey wrote. In a meeting of the generals on November 1, French questioned carrying so much artillery into Tennessee with the army so short of horses. Hood answered that once in Tennessee, more men would join, and horses, shoes, and supplies would be available. If he truly believed that, however, then he should have crossed the army at Guntersville. The general, Bailey concluded, was "out of touch with reality."[21]

Meanwhile, serious friction developed between Beauregard and Hood. The theater commander requested a detailed plan of Hood's future operations. Initially dismissive of the request, Hood eventually answered, "It is not possible for me to furnish any plan of my operations for the future, as so much must depend upon the movements of the enemy." Casually passing Stewart's Corps one day, Beauregard asked to review it the next day. Hood, believing that he had been bypassed, erupted. All orders relating to the army must go through him, he sharply reminded the theater commander. Additionally, he questioned the advisability of having reviews with Union spies about. Beauregard answered that it was a misunderstanding; he thought that Stewart would have notified him about this "informal review." As far as spies, Hood must have had a low opinion of the enemy if he thought they did not already know everything. Then, just to prove that he could do it, he ordered not only Stewart's Corps on review, but Cheatham's and Lee's as well. It was a power struggle with the hapless troops used as pawns.[22]

As the army prepared to embark into Tennessee, its spirit unquestionably remained high and not just among the Tennesseans. "I never was so hopeful for our immediate success than now," thought Irvine Walker. Hamilton Branch wrote his mother on November 21, "We expect to have a hard time and to have some fighting to do, but we intend with God's help to ruin Thomas' Army." Edward Brown admitted that "the men are generally in good spirits and confident of success," although he privately entertained doubts.[23]

Hood's overarching strategic plan was to go to Nashville, march into Kentucky, threaten Cincinnati, and recruit the army along the way. If Sherman returned to give battle, Hood planned to occupy a position around Richmond, Kentucky. If victorious, he would then send troops to reinforce Lee in Virginia or march through the mountain gaps to attack Grant in the rear at Petersburg before Sherman could unite. Precisely why Hood thought that he could recruit any more men in Kentucky than the insignificant numbers Bragg had raised in 1862 is not known, beyond the vague notion that the state was "more aroused and embittered against the Federals than at any period in the war."[24]

Forrest's cavalry spearheaded the march north on a snow-blowing, bitterly cold November 19. On the twenty-first, the infantry advanced in three columns: Cheatham's Corps to Waynesboro, Stewart's Corps to Lawrenceburg, and Lee's Corps on a country road (the Butler Creek Road) between them. John Schofield's and Stanley's corps (23,000 infantry) and Maj. Gen. James H. Wilson's cavalry (7,000) were known to be in and around Pulaski. By late November 23, the Confederate columns had begun converging on Waynesboro. Fearful that Forrest's cavalry would get to Columbia and over-whelm the small Union garrison, Schofield's forces began withdrawing. In the "race for Columbia," as Eric Jacobson called it, the Federals easily won. Connelly claimed that the so-called race "was more fiction than reality." Hood had no desire to cut Schofield off at Columbia. Connelly's argument convinced McMurry, who wrote that Hood's "objective was probably Nashville, not the force at Pulaski."[25]

On November 27, the army deployed south of Columbia. In a meeting with his corps commanders and Forrest that night, Hood explained his plan to pin down Schofield with two divisions, while most of the army swung around "through the woods" and crossed the Duck River to the left. Engineers worked throughout the night to prepare Davis Ford and lay a pontoon bridge. Once across, the troops would march thirteen miles northwest to Spring Hill and block the main road to Nashville. Forrest arrived at Spring Hill on the twenty-ninth and engaged in sporadic skirmishing with Wilson's cavalry. Hood advanced Cleburne's Division and ordered the Irishman to cross McCutcheon Creek and seize the Columbia-Franklin Turnpike. Once at the pike, Cleburne would turn south and block Schofield's force from Columbia. Cleburne drove back Luther Bradley's Federal brigade and, disobeying his orders, turned north toward the town. He later admitted that he "disobeyed the spirit of my orders" by attacking Bradley and veering parallel, rather than perpendicular, to the pike. Cleburne "walked into a trap," wrote Connelly, coming under the massed artillery fire of twenty guns; the Rebels reeled back to the creek bed. John C. Brown's (formerly Cheatham's) Division arrived and the corps commander planned a renewed attack. Bate's Division belatedly formed on Cleburne's left, but due to the lateness of the hour and the arrival of another enemy brigade, the attack was canceled. Symonds, Cleburne's biographer, did not give the division commander a pass: "Perhaps he ought to have renewed the advance on the turnpike after disposing of Bradley instead of waiting for Brown's attack, which never came." Hood angrily asked Cheatham, "General, why in the name of God have you not attacked the enemy and taken possession of the pike?" The Tennessean answered that he was awaiting the arrival of Stewart's Corps.[26]

Hood, perhaps miffed at Cleburne for his failure to seize the pike, did not appear alarmed. The events of the day were "not of great significance" and he would defeat Schofield's force in the morning. He did instruct Forrest that night to block the pike to the north. Brig. Gen. Sullivan "Sul" Ross's

700-man Texas cavalry brigade temporarily blocked the road but was driven back. That evening, Ross watched as Schofield marched past Spring Hill. Whether or not he related this information to Forrest is not known. In the morning, Hood found the enemy gone and the town deserted. At one point on the night of November 29, Hood had 19,000 infantry arrayed against David Stanley's 6,000-man division. In focusing on the southern outskirts of Spring Hill, however, the Federals had simply walked out to the west. Sword labeled it "one of the greatest overreactions in the history of the Army of Tennessee." The myth of Spring Hill, McMurry nonetheless argued, has been greatly exaggerated. Even if the pike had been blocked, the Federals could simply have marched farther west and still gotten to Franklin. Indeed, in an emergency, the Yankees could have bypassed Franklin altogether.[27]

On November 30, Hood dogged Schofield all the way to Franklin, where the bluecoats, not having a pontoon bridge, dug in on the south side of the Harpeth River. As Hood observed the Federal position from Winstead Hill in midafternoon, he stunned officers by ordering a frontal assault. Forrest's suggestion that the Federals could be flanked by crossing upriver was dismissed. Historians have speculated about his reasons, but a common theme that emerged was that he was seething with anger from the Spring Hill fiasco.[28]

Stephen Hood offered a fresh and convincing interpretation of why Forrest's flanking proposal was rejected. The plan called for Forrest's 4,500 cavalry plus 2,000 infantry to flank Schofield to the right at Hughes's Ford and then cut the highway to Brentwood. Stephen Hood points to the fact that the column would have been struck in flank by Wilson's 5,000 well-armed troopers posted just two miles upriver at McGavock's Ford and Thomas Wood's 4,000-man infantry division. Assuming that Hood rejected the proposal based on this information nonetheless raises the question: Why didn't Hood flank with Forrest's cavalry and Stewart's entire corps, with perhaps S. D. Lee's reserve division, while Cheatham pinned down Schofield (two of Lee's divisions had not yet come up), in a plan similar to what Hood had attempted at Columbia? There were alternatives to a near-suicidal frontal assault.[29]

The attack commenced at 4:00 P.M., the battle flags of eighteen brigades flapping in the November breeze and bands playing "Dixie" and "The Bonnie Blue Flag." So perfect and disciplined was the advance that even the enemy looked on with amazement. Hundreds were unable to clear the abatis. "Nothing could be heard above the din of musketry and the roar of cannon," a Tennessean recalled. "Whenever the dense smoke, in some degree was cleared away by the flash and blaze from the guns, great masses of our infantry could be seen struggling to get over these ingeniously wrought obstructions, who were being slain by hundreds and piled in almost countless numbers." The Rebels made it to the outer ditch of the Federal works, where the dead were piled seven deep. "It was fatal to leave the ditch and attempt to escape to the rear. Every man who attempted it — and a number did — was at once shot down." The center of the Federal line was temporarily breached, but Union reinforcements plugged the gap. Fighting continued in the dark before the assault sputtered out. Casualties proved ghastly — about 7,000 dead, wounded, and missing, including eleven generals (among the slain, the irreplaceable Cleburne) and fifty-five regimental commanders.[30]

On a gloomy December 2, with the Federal army having crossed the river during the night, the Confederate army moved toward Nashville; morale remained remarkably high. Once there, the Southerners began throwing up five miles of earthworks extending from the Hillsboro Pike to the Nashville & Chattanooga Railroad, with Cheatham on the right, Lee in the center, and Stewart on the left. Deducting cavalry, Hood could not have had more than 20,000 men. Astonishingly, he dispatched two of Forrest's divisions and Bate's 1,600-man division to operate against the 8,000-man Murfreesboro garrison. Bucking the historical trend, Stephen Hood praised the move, claiming that it protected Hood's supply route and retreat route, and if the Federals sent a relief column, he could attack it. Matters, nonetheless, did not go well. Lieutenant Branch wrote of the engagement on the seventh, when the Federals advanced: "Bates men, seeing the [enemy] skirmish line advancing, ran like a scared dog. Forrest, seeing this galloped up in the midst of them and failing to rally them cursed them and knocked several of them down." Hood eventually left only Thomas Smith's Brigade of Bate's Division and one of Forrest's divisions as an observation corps.[31]

Suffering began to take a toll. The mercury plunged to ten degrees on December 8. The next day, Captain Key entered in his diary, "The sleet obliterates our fire and keeps us wet, and if we go under our little fly we suffer with cold so our teeth chatter." On the tenth, he added, "Our artillery carriages are frozen to the ground, and ice half an inch thick coats my brass guns." That same day, a South Carolinian wrote: "The most bitter day of the winter so far. . . . Ground frozen and covered with sleet, snow and ice. Much suffering, many men nearly barefooted, rations short." Irvine Walker admitted that his only goal was "to keep the blood from freezing in my veins. I really suffered from cold, and if I, who am so comfortably clad, with thick warm clothes suffered, what must have been that of hundreds who are in the Army around me, but thinly clad and many barefooted? I only wish I had Gen. Hood to spend the day with me, and I think he would be more anxious to put the Army into Winter Quarters." Some 3,500 men required shoes. Soon the truth became known about recruiting. Since being in Tennessee, only 164 had volunteered; more than that had deserted. Hundreds of Tennesseans fled to avoid service. Of the 296 dismounted cavalry who had been placed in Johnson's Division as infantry, all but forty-two deserted.[32]

Hood had few options when he marched to Nashville. He could have avoided the city and marched into Kentucky, but such a move would have invited a flank attack. McDonough concluded, "In fairness to Hood, acceptable alternatives did not exist." It was proposed at the time, and supported by some historians since, that Edmund Kirby Smith could have raided into Missouri and threatened St. Louis, thereby forcing A. J. Smith's 15,000-man corps to remain in Missouri. Such a move had already been attempted in Sterling Price's fall 1864 Missouri raid, which ended in disaster. Nothing was going to stop A. J. Smith's transfer. And the transfer of troops from across the Mississippi River to reinforce Hood was nothing more than a pipe dream. John Walker's 4,000-man Texas division had previously deserted en masse rather than cross the river. Hood had gone out on a limb and no one would be standing by his side.[33]

On December 15, George Thomas made his move. At midmorning, enemy artillery opened a heavy barrage. At 10:00, the bluecoats, in division strength, attacked Cheatham's right near the Nolensville Pike. Captain Key wrote, "When a colored brigade, led by white officers, was within 200 yards of our line, our batteries opened on them and they were routed in ten minutes." The attack on the right turned out to be a feint. Simultaneously, Thomas unleashed an assault on the Confederate left along the Hillsboro Pike. By 4:30, Stewart's Corps had collapsed and was streaming back toward the Granny White Pike, losing 800–1,000 prisoners and 16 guns in the process. A disgusted Mississippi gunner expressed, "The infantry ran like cowards and the miserable wretches who were to have supported us refused to fight and ran like a herd of stampeded cattle." A stunned staff officer wrote with trepidation: "The men seemed utterly lethargic and without interest in the battle. I never witnessed such want of enthusiasm, and began to fear for tomorrow, hoping that Gen'l Hood would retreat during the night."[34]

The army withdrew two miles south to a new and more compact line, with Cheatham on the left, resting on Shy's Hill, Stewart's battered corps in the center, and S. D. Lee on the left, anchored on Overton Hill. Cheatham did not like his position, but engineers had laid it out and he had to make do. The next morning, Thomas again assaulted, feinting on the right and, at 4:00, unleashing a huge 40,000-man strike force. Yankee artillery blasted the summit of Shy's Hill from three directions. The Federals overran the hill and Cheatham's men were routed. Cheatham himself rode his horse pell-mell, shouting, "Take care of yourselves, boys, the best you can, I am going to make that pass in the ridge or die in the attempt." The panic spread to Stewart's Corps as the army appeared to melt. Only Lee's skilled defense on Overton Hill saved the army. The Federals counted 4,462 prisoners and 53 guns in the two-day battle. From Christmas Day through the twenty-eighth, the army crossed the Tennessee River near Florence. "There could be no gainsaying the fact that the campaign had miserably failed," concluded McDonough.[35]

Conclusion

The shattered Army of Tennessee sloshed back to Mississippi, with Cheatham's Corps arriving at Corinth on January 1, 1865. Stewart's and Lee's corps camped overnight at Burnsville and Rienzi, respectively. "I have never seen such suffering," Irvine Walker admitted to his wife. "Hundreds of bare-footed men, many sick and even wounded could be seen hobbling along with the Army. Half of my Regt. [10th South Carolina] is non-effective from want of shoes and the destination is heart rendering. Nearly all are in rags, and some almost without even rags." Officially, 18,730 infantry and artillery arrived, as well as Forrest's cavalry with 2,306, for a total of 21,036. Precisely how many casualties had been sustained throughout the campaign has been debated, but they exceeded 16,000. Once at Tupelo, Hood furloughed the West Tennessee troops of Cheatham's Corps and some smaller outfits, in all 3,500 men. A January 10 inspection noted: "Great numbers are going home every day, many never more to return, I fear. Nine-tenths of the men and line officers are barefooted and naked."[36]

The men expressed demoralization in their letters. "Genl Hood's army is . . . the worst whipped army you ever saw," L. B. Welch wrote. G. W. Peddy believed that "Hood is a complete failure." W. H. Reynolds admitted that the army was "badly whipped and it seems as though they are not going to get over it Soon, especially if Gen. Hood continues in command." Charles Roberts heard a rumor that Hood would be relieved and Gen. A. P. Hill given command. He supported the change but believed that "nothing short of Genl Johnston will satisfy the bulk of the army. It is astonishing with what tenacity they retain implicit faith in Genl. Johnston." A Mississippian recorded, "All are ragged, dirty, and covered with vermin, some not having sufficient clothing to hide their bodies." The men were "fully convinced that the Confederacy is gone."[37]

The Tennessee Campaign had indeed been a disaster. The Battle of Nashville was the only time in the war that an army had been effectively destroyed.

In the end, Hood was an anachronism. At another time, his aggressiveness might have succeeded, but by 1864, the war had drastically changed; 1862 tactics no longer prevailed. Added to this was Hood's own ineptitude, which impaled his army at Franklin and Nashville, where battles did not even have to be fought. Davis was forced to remove Hood and return Johnston to command. The Army of Tennessee was scattered, but a 5,000-man remnant made its way to North Carolina, where, along with other Confederate forces, it fought in the Battle of Bentonville in March 1865. The Rebels suffered a defeat, sustaining 2,600 casualties, about half of those from the Army of Tennessee. The army formally surrendered at the Bennett farm in Durham on April 26, seventeen days after Robert E. Lee's surrender.[38]

✻✻

EPILOGUE

Following the Battle of Nashville, Lincoln related a story to his cabinet: There was once a bullying man by the name of Slocum who owned a bull-dog by the name of Bill. Both man and dog terrorized the small Illinois community in which they lived. One day, a man decided to dispose of the dog. He chucked a morsel of meal in the road, charged with gunpowder inside, and attached it to a slow match. Bill ate the bait in one gulp and walked blissfully along until he suddenly exploded, leaving fragments scattered along the dusty road. Viewing the remains, Slocum lamented, "Bill was a good dog, but as a dog I guess his usefulness is over." Lincoln then offered the moral of the story: The Army of Tennessee had been a good army that had generated much fear. "But as an army, I reckon, its usefulness is over."[1]

The Army of Tennessee had indeed been conquered, but nagging questions remained. Was Connelly correct in his assumption? That is, could the epitaph of the Army of Tennessee have read "Died of Inept Leadership"? To put it another way, could effective leadership at the top have counteracted most of the army's handicaps? If, for example, Lee or a "second Lee" had commanded the army, would the outcome have been different? Not necessarily. Lee depended on his corps and divisions commanders to properly implement his plans. While he, at times, suffered incompetent and insubordinate generals, it paled in comparison to the backstabbing encountered by Bragg. When offered the western army command, Lee claimed that even he would not receive cooperation.[2]

There were other factors that Lee could not have overcome. The de facto absence of border state Kentucky hurt the Army of Tennessee more than the loss of border state Maryland detracted from the Army of Northern Virginia. If Lee had commanded in the West, would it have encouraged more Kentuckians into the Rebel ranks? Possibly, but it might conversely have also driven a far greater number into the Northern ranks. That is precisely what occurred when Bragg and Edmund Kirby Smith seemed poised to reach the banks of the Ohio River; it only produced more Northern recruits. To offset the manpower disparity in the West, the Confederacy needed Kentucky to supply as many men as Tennessee. In terms of the percentage of whites who fought for the South, Kentucky ranked dead last.[3]

Nor would Lee have resolved the great unsolvable political/tactical problem of geography, notably the problem of the Mississippi, Tennessee, and Cumberland Rivers. The James River at Richmond was hardly the Mississippi River at Memphis. Politically, the rivers could not simply be abandoned, but the static defenses of Polk, Pemberton, and Davis proved disastrous. The other geographical problem was that Mississippi and Tennessee were inextricably linked. Even if a hypothetical Lee had won in Tennessee, an incompetent Pemberton would still have lost at Vicksburg, thus freeing the Union Army of the Tennessee for further operations and endangering the flank of the Army of Tennessee.

Additionally, Lee in the West likely would not have altered Davis's damaging administrative policies, such as territorial defense, with which neither Albert Sidney Johnston nor Bragg agreed; an unstated but obvious preference for Mississippi over Tennessee, with which Joseph E. Johnston disagreed; and the lack of unified command during the Kentucky Campaign, with which Bragg, once again, totally disagreed. The point is that with more effective political policies, perhaps Lee in the West would not have been necessary.[4]

A Lee in the West could possibly have delayed, but not ultimately postponed, a declining western cavalry corps. He could have replaced Wheeler, which would have been a positive step, but professionally trained cavalry talent was not plentiful. Nor could he have modernized any faster a far-outmatched artillery corps, which was not streamlined for a full ten months after the long arm modernized in the Army of Northern Virginia. Combat efficiency thus favored the North. Nor could a more skilled army commander have changed the foundational base of the western officer corps. The Fort Donelson "army" was almost totally led by amateurs. Of four brigadiers and twenty-six colonels, only two (Buckner and Bushrod Johnson) were West Pointers. It was slightly better at Shiloh — eleven of fifteen generals had graduated from West Point. At the field level, however, only four of forty-three infantry colonels were West Pointers and one a Virginia Military Institute graduate. At a time when the troops were still green and undisciplined, a more professional and skilled officer corps would have made a difference. Andrew Haughton also faults western leadership for their lack of tactical creativity. They could have expanded their sharpshooter companies and developed more compact formations, and their offensive maneuvers became "predictable."[5]

The western army had to rely essentially on a weak rail-based system to supply and transport troops, whereas the Northern armies in the West had, at least to some extent, a more reliable river-based system. Rapidly shifting troops from Tennessee to Mississippi could simply not be done. The state of Virginia had over 2,800 railroad cars at the beginning of the war, as compared to Tennessee's approximately 1,100. A more effective army commander might have been able to save more equipment from destruction, but the overall fact of a weak logistical system was simply the reality of the West.[6]

The argument has been made that the sheer size of the western theater favored the Southerners, since it offered possibilities for maneuvering, a luxury Lee lacked due to his proximity to Richmond. Besides, the North had to defend long lines of communication from raids and, in Lee's case, the North Carolina coast had to be defended. With far less manpower, however, the western Confederates also had to protect their rail lines from raids, and a division-size force was kept penned down to garrison Mobile. At their peak in January 1863, the Rebels had no more than 123,000 men in the western theater to protect an operational zone of 175,000 square miles. Additionally, as Johnston discovered while at Dalton, not all sectors in the theater offered realistic maneuvering possibilities, such as East Tennessee, where sufficient supplies could simply not be sustained. There was not a single north-south rail line in northern Alabama beyond Blue Mountain, near the Georgia border. Indeed, the three most prominent towns in North Alabama — Decatur, Florence, and Huntsville — numbered only 600, 1,400, and 3,600, respectively. There was no living off the land in northern Alabama.[7]

In light of the numerous defeats, what bound the loyalties of Army of Tennessee soldiers? A web of connections — religion, the brotherhood, generalship, the home front — and degrees of commitment to secession, nationalism, and slavery allied officers, enlisted men, and families. The subject is nonetheless complex. Loyalty was not simply raising the hand and taking an oath of reenlistment. The brotherhood had its limitations; comradeship was generally confined to companies and regiments, and unresolvable tensions were sometimes created. Religion intersected with patriotism and shielded men from the stresses of war, but it also raised serious issues. Believing that victory was connected with piety and divine favor, how were the troops to maintain hope in light of huge territorial losses? Loyalty was also fluid, waxing and waning throughout the war. In the end, loyalties were placed within the context of a system of coercion and the fear of social dishonor in one's failure to perform one's duty.

Nor can the ultimate collapse of the Army of Tennessee be viewed in a vacuum of internal factors. Defeat was also influenced by the North's policy of exhaustion. While revised numbers reveal that Union strength at the

Battle of Stones River had an impact, this stands as an anomaly. More often than not, the Army of Tennessee had near parity of strength and, in some cases (Chickamauga, the first day at Fort Donelson, and Shiloh), superiority in numbers. What made the difference was skilled Union leadership and the resilience of Federal soldiers who quickly rebounded after their initial routs at Shiloh, Perryville, and Chickamauga. The superb Union charge up Missionary Ridge, without orders, revealed the fighting prowess of western Federals. Whether the western Rebels were superior to the bluecoats in the Army of the Potomac, as they claimed, can be debated, but the fact that Army of Tennessee soldiers had their hands full is undeniable. To be sure, Federal leadership made mistakes. Forming a beachhead at Pittsburg Landing made the initial Confederate victory at Shiloh possible. The failure of Buell's army to advance directly to Chattanooga after the fall of Fort Donelson, rather than reinforcing Grant's army, proved costly. Likewise, Buell's decision to follow Bragg into Kentucky, rather than to send at least a portion of his army to Chattanooga, was flawed. Nonetheless, the Federal "bench," which included Grant, Sheridan, Sherman, Thomas, Wilder, Minty, and others (Castel would certainly add Rosecrans to the list), simply proved deeper than the Confederate bench.[8]

Glatthaar concluded his history of the Army of Northern Virginia by stating that the Confederate constitution had created a government but "Lee's army built a nation." Lee's army fostered nationalism, embodied the revolution, and had soldiers and civilians alike believing that it was unconquerable. "As long as Lee's army existed, the rebellion survived." None of these conclusions could, of course, be reached about the Army of Tennessee, but in many ways defeat—how people react to it and how they are changed by it—makes for a more fascinating story than success. What keeps soldiers fighting and the home front supporting them, even in the midst of social and military collapse—that is the story of the Army of Tennessee. It is a complicated narrative and one not grounded entirely in generalship. It is a story of intertwining influences that cumulatively led to an army being conquered.[9]

NOTES

ABBREVIATIONS

ADAH	Alabama Department of Archives and History, Montgomery
AHS	Atlanta Historical Society, Atlanta, Georgia
AU	Auburn University, Auburn, Alabama
CCNBP	Chickamauga-Chattanooga National Battlefield Park, Fort Oglethorpe, Georgia
DU	Duke University, Durham, North Carolina
EU	Emory University, Atlanta, Georgia
FHS	Filson Historical Society, Louisville, Kentucky
FLSA	Florida State Archives, Tallahassee
GDAH	Georgia Department of Archives and History, Morrow
GLC	Gilder Lehrman Collection, Institute of American History, New York, New York
GPL	Grenada Public Library, Grenada, Mississippi
GRPL	Greenwood Public Library, Greenwood, Mississippi
LC	Library of Congress, Manuscripts Division, Washington, D.C.
LSU	Louisiana State University, Baton Rouge
MC	Museum of the Confederacy, Richmond, Virginia
MDAH	Mississippi Department of Archives and History, Jackson
MSU	Mississippi State University, Starkville
MVC	Mississippi Valley Collection, University of Memphis, Memphis
NARG	National Archives Record Group 109, Washington, D.C.
OR	*The War of the Rebellion: A Compilation of the Official Records of the Union and Confederate Armies*. 128 vols. Washington, D.C.: Government Printing Office, 1880-1901. Unless otherwise indicated, all references are to Series 1. *OR* citations take the following form: volume(part number where applicable):page number.
PC	Private Collection
PP	Pamplin Park (Wiley Sword Collection), Petersburg, Virginia
SHC	Southern Historical Collection, Chapel Hill, North Carolina
SNBP	Shiloh National Battlefield Park, Shiloh, Tennessee
SOR	Hewitt, Janet B., ed. *Supplement to the Official Records of the Union and Confederate Armies*. 128 vols. Wilmington, N.C.: Broadfoot, 1994-2001.

SRNBP	Stones River National Battlefield Park, Murfreesboro, Tennessee
TSLA	Tennessee State Library and Archives, Nashville
TU	Tulane University, New Orleans, Louisiana
UALA	University of Alabama, Tuscaloosa
UFLA	University of Florida, Gainesville
UMISS	University of Mississippi, Oxford
US	University of the South, Sewanee, Tennessee
USAMHI	United States Army Military History Institute, Carlisle Barracks, Pennsylvania
USMISS	University of Southern Mississippi, Hattiesburg
UT	University of Tennessee, Knoxville
UTX	University of Texas, Austin
VMI	Virginia Military Institute, Lexington
WRHS	Western Reserve Historical Society, Cleveland, Ohio

PREFACE

1. Glatthaar, *General Lee's Army*, 472, 468.

2. For a more detailed examination of the McMurry thesis see *Fourth Battle of Winchester*, 63–79, and "From the West," 18–21. For a rebuttal, see Gallagher, "War Was Won," 18–21.

CHAPTER 1

1. Robert H. White, *Messages of the Governors*, 5:285; Civil War Centennial Commission, *Tennesseans in the Civil War*, 1:309; Hughes and Stonesipher, *Pillow*, 8–104, 157, 162, 319–29, 324–25; William C. Davis, *Jefferson Davis*, 342; Marcus J. Wright, *Tennesseans in the Civil War*, 24; Patricia L. Faust, *Historical Times Encyclopedia*, 15.

2. Losson, *Tennessee's Forgotten Warriors*, 27, 38; Robert McBride, *Biographical Dictionary*, 1:259, 687; Patricia L. Faust, *Historical Times Encyclopedia*, 850; Connelly, *Army of the Heartland*, 37.

3. Ellsworth, *West Point*, 334, 351, 390, 411; Patricia L. Faust, *Historical Times Encyclopedia*, 224, 397, 457, 719; Allardice, *Confederate Colonels*, 409 (Wright); McMurry, *Virginia Military Institute*, 246–47; "Wright," Genealogy Trails, accessed April 6, 2016, geneologytrails.com/ten/carroll/biowright.html. Lucius M. Walker, although from Tennessee, was living in Arkansas at the commencement of the war. Cadmus M. Wilcox, though not born in Tennessee, grew up in Tipton County. He soon received a Confederate commission. See Myers E. Brown, *Images of America*, 28. Several other native-born Tennesseans lived in other states at the beginning of the war.

4. West, *Tennessee Encyclopedia*, 885; *Memphis Avalanche*, April 16, 1861; Hamer, *Centennial History*, 136; *OR*, 4:248–50; "Cunningham," TNGenWeb Project, accessed July 10, 2017, tngenweb.org/warren/tag/cunningham; "Avent," TNGenWeb Project, accessed July 10, 2017, http://www.aventfamily.org/TNG/getperson.php?personID=I1899 &tree=avefam; Schroeder-Lein, *Confederate Hospitals*, 186.

5. Allardice, *Confederate Colonels*; McMurry (*Two Great Rebel Armies*, 98–105) con-

cluded that the dominance of Virginia Military Institute and Citadel alumni, along with West Pointers, gave the Army of Northern Virginia a "reservoir of trained manpower" that the Army of Tennessee lacked. This meant better training, tighter discipline, and a deeper bench from which to draw officers as casualties occurred.

6. *OR*, 52(2):90, 103, 111, 112, 123; and ser. 4, 1:358–59; *Nashville Union & American*, May 19, 31, 1861; *Memphis Appeal*, March 29, April 14, 18, 1861.

7. Hall to wife, June 11, 1861, Hall Letters, SHC; *Memphis Appeal*, June 18, 1861; Owens to wife, June 20, 1861, in Mitchell, "Letters of a Confederate Surgeon," 4:341–43; John F. Goodner letter, June 18, 1861, https://camptrousdale2.wordpress.com/1861/06/18/john-f-goodner-letter-6-18-1861/.

8. Law diary, May 4, 1861, in Law, "Diary of J. G. Law," 379; Buchanan to brother, December 15, 1861, Buchanan Letters, SHC.

9. Russell, *My Diary*, 295–325.

10. Polk to wife, June 18, 1861, Polk Letters, PC.

11. *Tennessee Baptist*, November 16, 1861; *Nashville Patriot*, November 13, 1861; Jackman diary, January 3, 1862, in William C. Davis, *Diary*, 23–24. See also Schroeder-Lein, *Confederate Hospitals*, 42–43; Scarborough Diary, September 14, 15, 19, 1861, SNBP; Davis Yandell to father, October 9, 1861, Yandell Papers, FHS; *Clarksville Chronicle*, November 8, 1861; Clark and Riley, "Medical Department," 55–82; E. T. Broughton to wife, July 3, August 2, 9, 1861, in "E. T. Broughton Letters," accessed January 3, 2017, www.battleofraymond.org; and *Memphis Appeal*, July 3, August 2, 9, 1861.

12. McMurry, *Two Great Rebel Armies*, 104–5.

13. McMurry, 14–18; "Consolidated Report of Strength and Transportation, March 1863," Bragg Papers, WRHS.

14. *Nashville Patriot*, May 18, 1861; Weitz, *More Damning Than Slaughter*, 68.

15. *OR*, ser. 2, 3:388–89; Weitz, *More Damning Than Slaughter*, xviii, 20–21.

16. Timothy B. Smith, *Shiloh*, 32–33.

17. Weitz, *More Damning Than Slaughter*, 67, 186; Smith to Miss Katie, January 17, 1863, Smith Letters, ADAH; *Chattanooga Daily Rebel*, May 13, 1863; Harwell, *Kate*, 210.

18. Connelly and Jones, *Politics of Command*, 88–91, 92–93, 100; Archer Jones, *Confederate Strategy*, 51; McMurry, *Two Great Rebel Armies*, 58–68.

19. Groce, *Mountain Rebels*, 88; Hebert, *Long Civil War*, 70–74.

20. Searcy to mother, August 31, 1862, James Searcy Letters, Searcy Family Papers, ADAH; Sparkman Diary, October 20, 1863, CCNBP.

21. Groce, *Mountain Rebels*, 75–76, 80–81, 85–86, 95–96.

22. Weitz, *Higher Duty*, 11–13, 15, 16, 18, 69–70, 118, 119.

23. Brewer to sister, October 2, 1863, in James Brewer Letters, accessed February 5, 2017, www.msgw.org/confederate/brewerletters.htm; Rennolds Diary, November 8, 1863, UT.

24. Connelly, *Army of the Heartland*, 3; Connelly, "Robert E. Lee," 118–19. For Albert Castel's response to Connelly, see "Historian and the General," 66–67. Earl Hess (*Civil War in the West*, 317–19) argued for the primacy of the Mississippi Valley, while Donald Stoker (*Grand Design*, 129) insisted that the "real war" was in Tennessee.

25. McMurry, *Two Great Rebel Armies*, 15–16.

26. Hess, *Civil War in the West*, 11–12; *OR*, 4:187, 192; and 52(2):215; Woodworth, *This Great Struggle*, 59.

27. Castel, *Victors in Blue*, 40; Beringer et al., *Why the South Lost*, 122. In no other instance have western historians been more singularly united. Nathaniel Hughes characterized Polk's invasion as "a political disaster of the first order." McMurry considered the move "a major disaster for the Southern cause." Benjamin Cooling believed the seizure of the town "changed the course of the war." The maneuver, according to Steven Woodworth, earned Polk the number two spot on the list of the worst Confederate generals. Steven Newton disagreed with Woodworth—he gave Polk the number one spot. See Girardi, "Leonidas Polk," 12; Hughes, *Battle of Belmont*, 4; McMurry, *Fourth Battle of Winchester*, 95; Cooling, *Forts Henry and Donelson*, 11; and "Who Were the Worst," 15, 16, 20.

28. *Mobile Advertiser & Register*, February 8, 1862 (spoke French); Polk, *Leonidas Polk*, 2:76–78; Timothy B. Smith, *Grant Invades Tennessee*, 10, 13, 17; J. B. Jones, *Rebel War Clerk's Diary*, 1:106, 112.

29. Roman, *Beauregard*, 1:236–37; *OR*, 10(2):352; Johnston, "Jefferson Davis," 474; Timothy B. Smith, *Grant Invades Tennessee*, 8. Pemberton's works at Grenada, Mississippi, according to Johnston, proved "so extensive" and the "practicality of defending it" so questionable that it was fortunate that they were never tested.

30. Daniel and Bock, *Island No. 10*, 34–160; Woodworth, *Decision in the Heartland*, 72.

CHAPTER 2

1. Garey diary, January 27, 1862, in Welker, *Keystone Rebel*, 66.

2. Roland, *Albert Sidney Johnston*, 6–257; Hess, *Civil War in the West*, 13; Timothy B. Smith, *Grant Invades Tennessee*, 11. Historians have given mixed reviews of Johnston. Albert Castel saw him as having many of the attributes of Lee. McMurry did not see him as "necessarily a great military leader who would have won the war for the Confederacy." Kenneth Noe believed it was "difficult to imagine Johnston ever becoming a great general," but he conceded that he could have evolved. Connelly, his greatest critic, saw Johnston as totally overrated, a poor administrator, naïve, and an inept strategist. See Castel, "Savior of the South," 40; Bresnahan, *Revisioning the Civil War*, 50, 51; and McMurry, *Two Great Rebel Armies*, 120–21. Grady McWhiney attended only a single meeting of the Civil War Historians of the Western Theater before his death in 2006. At that time, however, he adamantly defended Johnston along the same lines as Castel.

3. Freehling, *South vs. the South*, 68–69, 72–73; Daniel, *Days of Glory*, 9; *OR*, 7:258–59.

4. Connelly, *Army of the Heartland*, 66–67; Roland, "Albert Sidney Johnston," 15; Woodworth, *Decision in the Heartland*, 8.

5. Freehling, *South vs. the South*, 69–73; Murray and Hsieh, *Savage War*, 136.

6. Timothy B. Smith, *Grant Invades Tennessee*, 151–52, 137 (interior lines), 108–28, 138–41 (raid to Florence); Smith, email to Daniel, September 17, 2017; Hess, *Civil War in the West*, 34–36; Woodworth, *This Great Struggle*, 84; Freehling, *South vs. the South*,

66–67. The Confederates were at work on another fort (Fort Heiman) opposite Henry, but it was incomplete at the time of the battle.

7. Connelly, *Army of the Heartland*, 63; Beauregard, "Campaign of Shiloh," 570–71; Roland, "P. G. T. Beauregard," 48.

8. Hess, *Civil War in the West*, 39; Daniel, *Shiloh*, 24; Timothy B. Smith, *Grant Invades Tennessee*, 148–49; Stoker, *Grand Design*, 115. Bragg is usually credited with influencing Davis's decision to concentrate, but others, including Beauregard, made the same argument.

9. Woodworth, *This Great Struggle*, 85; Cooling, *Fort Donelson's Legacy*, 12; Roland, *Albert Sidney Johnston*, 290–91; Freehling, *South vs. the South*, 76. Castel and Woodworth shared their views with me in private conversations.

10. Bresnahan, *Revisioning the Civil War*, 49 (McMurry); Roland, *Jefferson Davis's Greatest General*, 37; *OR*, 7:259.

11. Connelly, *Army of the Heartland*, 113; Roland, *Albert Sidney Johnston*, 293.

12. Beringer et al., *Why the South Lost*, 123; Woodworth, *This Great Struggle*, 88; Connelly, *Army of the Heartland*, 123; Timothy B. Smith, *Grant Invades Tennessee*, 322, 325–26; "Who Were the Worst," 12, 15, 16.

13. Timothy B. Smith, *Grant Invades Tennessee*, 397; *OR*, 7:260; 17(1):441, 449; 24(3):624; and ser. 2, 3:388–89.

14. Daniel, "Assaults of the Demagogues," 329; *Richmond Examiner*, February 20, 1862.

15. Daniel, "Assaults of the Demagogues," 330–31; *Richmond Dispatch*, March 11, 1862; Howard Jones, *Union in Peril*, 104–5.

16. Daniel, *Shiloh*, 45–47. Roland (*Jefferson Davis's Greatest General*, 48–49) partially defended Johnston's decision to remain with Hardee's wing rather than proceed to Corinth, claiming that the corps commander remained skittish about the move.

17. Cox, "R. L. Davis Letters," 40; Johnston, *Johnston*, 539, 543. See also Folmar, *From That Terrible Field*, 52; and Woods, *Livaudais*, 19.

18. As quoted in Haughton, *Training, Tactics, and Leadership*, 63.

19. Daniel, *Shiloh*, 117–18; *OR*, 10(2):394; *New Orleans Crescent*, April 9 (Griffin letter), 17 (five crackers), 1862; Lyman to wife, April 3, 1862, Lyman Letters, Yale University, New Haven, Connecticut.

20. Rosser to wife, April 5, 1862, Rosser Diary, PC; Samuel Latta to wife, April 10, 1862, Latta Letters, TSLA; Timothy B. Smith, *Shiloh*, 74–75.

21. Beringer et al., *Why the South Lost*, 123. Several historians have attempted to explain the mystifying Confederate formation and how it related to Johnston's master plan. See, for example, Roland, *Albert Sidney Johnston*, 321, 323; and Haughton, *Training, Tactics, and Leadership*, 64–65.

22. Timothy B. Smith, *Shiloh*, 84, 89; Daniel, *Shiloh*, 149–50; Lundberg, "'I Must Save This Army,'" 21; *OR*, 10(1):386 ("Alpine avalanche"). Supporting Johnston's decision to lead from the front were Roland (*Albert Sidney Johnston*, 345) and Woodworth (*Jefferson Davis*, 99). Opposing the decision were Connelly (*Army of the Heartland*, 160) and Smith (104–5). For Beauregard's criticism, see "Campaign of Shiloh," 589.

23. Cunningham, *Shiloh*, 220, 225.

24. Allen, "Brief Analysis," SNBP; Allen, "Hornet's Nest Update," SNBP; Dosch, "Hornet's Nest at Shiloh," 175–89; Timothy B. Smith, *Shiloh*, 200–208.

25. Mary Gorton McBride, *Randall Lee Gibson*, 57, 59, 79–83.

26. Daniel, *Cannoneers in Gray*, 29–32; Timothy B. Smith, *Shiloh*, 209–13; Grimsley and Woodworth, *Shiloh*, 103–4.

27. Daniel, *Cannoneers in Gray*, 367n125. Roland (*Albert Sidney Johnston*, 334–35) wrote that the plan was for Breckinridge "to feel his way up the river and turn the flank of the enemy." Instead, his three brigades were committed "near the right flank of Bragg's sector." Timothy B. Smith ("Anatomy of an Icon," 74) concluded that the Confederates had already split into two concentrations, neither of which was against the Confederate center. "The reality is that the center had so few troops in it that the strength of the Hornet's Nest was less because of the inherent power of the Union line and more the result of the lack of numbers against it."

28. Roman, *Military Operations*, 1:286–89; Johnston, *Johnston*, 593; Timothy B. Smith, *Shiloh*, 183 (Breckinridge description); Jordan, "Notes," 601; Allen, "Shiloh!," 51; Connelly, *Army of the Heartland*, 160. Jordan admitted, "Assuming the authority of my position, I gave the orders in the name of General Johnston."

29. Allen, "Shiloh!," 51, 52–53; Taylor to parents, April 11, 1862, Hughes Collection, SHC; Mecklin Diary, April 6, 1862, MDAH.

30. John Lundberg ("'I Must Save This Army,'" 24–25) concluded that Johnston was improving as a commander and he might have become as great as Lee or Jackson. Castel ("Savior of the West," 38–40) believed that Johnston "might well have developed into a military leader superior to any of his successors in the West." Roland (*Jefferson Davis's Greatest General*, 87) concluded that Johnston "might have done for the Western Theater what Lee did for the Eastern Theater." For negative evaluations, see Bresnahan, *Revisioning the Civil War*, 54–55 (comments by Craig Symonds, Keith Poulter, and John Simons). Newton (interview in "Overrated Generals") concluded, "'If only Johnston had lived' is a mantra I recall reading quite widely and I give a lot of credit to historians like Thomas L. Connelly for dissecting his doubtful contributions to the Confederate cause." Stoker (*Grand Design*, 128) believed that Johnston never "demonstrated any particular brilliance as a commander."

31. Grimsley and Woodworth, *Shiloh*, 107–11; Timothy B. Smith, *Shiloh*, 226–32.

32. Timothy B. Smith, *Shiloh*, 231–33. Referring to a possible final assault on Grant's last line, George Rable stated: "Speculating that the battle would have turned out differently assumes that the battle plan will be executed flawlessly. That's like expecting to watch a football game without penalties or turnovers. It might happen, but it's extremely rare." Ed Bearss believed that a night attack would have failed. See Bresnahan, *Revisioning the Civil War*, 52, 53. Castel (*Victors in Blue*, 81) concurred.

33. Connelly, *Army of the Heartland*, 171–72; McWhiney, "General Beauregard's 'Complete Victory,'" 115–20. Connelly (*Autumn of Glory*, 168) criticized Beauregard for not "merely halting the action, but in not retreating to Corinth." If Beauregard had

made such a move, there would have been vehement accusations that his heart was not in the battle from the outset. Besides, Beauregard believed that Monday's battle would be a mop-up operation. T. Harry Williams (*Beauregard*, 142), Beauregard's biographer and apologist, would defend the decision. "Today [1953] Beauregard's decision seems as right as it did to him on the evening of that hard-fought Sunday."

34. Jordan and Pryor, *Campaigns*, 136–37.

35. Daniel, *Shiloh*, 290–91, 296–97.

36. Pugh to parents, April 10, 11, 1862, Pugh Letters, LSU; "H. R." to father, April 11, 1862, "H. R." Letter, USAMHI.

37. Archer Jones, *Civil War Command*, 53. Castel (*Victors in Blue*, 82) concluded that the Confederates lost Shiloh simply because "they lacked the strength."

38. Murray and Hsieh, *Savage War*, 158–59; Woodworth, *Nothing but Victory*, 200.

39. Daniel, *Shiloh*, 316–17; Castel, *Victors in Blue*, 81–82. McMurry believed that even if the Confederates had won on the first day at Shiloh it would have made no difference. There were still enough Federals nearby that the Rebels could not "undo all the damage they had suffered in January and February in Kentucky and West Tennessee." See Bresnahan, *Revisioning the Civil War*, 57.

40. Livaudais diary, April 11, 1862, in Woods, *Livaudais*, 33–37; Magee Diary, April 7, 1862, DU; Joseph Lyman to wife, April 19, 1862, Lyman Letters, Yale University, New Haven, Connecticut; Harwell, *Kate*, 15; George Dobson to wife, April 10, 1862, Dobson Letters, Corinth Civil War Interpretive Center, Corinth, Mississippi; *Highland (Ohio) Weekly News*, June 19, 1862; *OR*, 10(2):405; *Memphis Appeal*, April 10, 1862; *Selma Daily Register*, April 21, 1862; Rufus Catlin to cousin, May 24, 1862, Catlin Letters, LC.

41. Snead, "With Price," 726; *OR*, 10(2):523; Harwell, *Kate*, 30; *Montgomery Weekly Mail*, May 31, 1862; Timothy B. Smith, *Corinth*, 15; *Camden (S.C.) Confederate*, April 25, May 2, 1862; Irvine Walker to wife, April 26, 29, 1862, in William Lee White and Runion, *Great Things*, 5, 7; Tower, *Carolinian Goes to War*, 15.

42. William Lee White and Runion, *Great Things*, 10; *OR*, 10(1):776.

43. William Paxton to wife, March 27, 1862, in Paxton, "Dear Rebecca," 185; James Searcy to wife, May 8, 1862, James Searcy Letters, Searcy Family Papers, ADAH; Rogers to wife, April 18, 1862, in Rogers, "Diary and Letters," 286; Bergeron, *Grisamore*, 51; *Savannah Republican*, May 29, 1862.

44. *OR*, 10(1):776; Roman, *Beauregard*, 1:383.

45. *Richmond Dispatch*, May 30, 1862; *Memphis Appeal*, May 25, 29, 1862; "Medical Director's Consolidated Report of Sick and Wounded, January–May 1862," Jones Collection, TU; *OR*, 10(1):792.

46. Woodworth, *This Great Struggle*, 118; Eicher, *Dixie Betrayed*, 106.

47. Garey diary, May 10, 1862, in Welker, *Keystone Rebel*, 95.

48. Knighton to father, April 20, 1862, Knighton Letters, LSU; Mecklin Diary, April 19, 1862, MDAH; John Cato to wife, April 20, 1862, in Skellie, *Lest We Forget*, 1:290; Erasmus Stirman to wife, May 16, 1862, Stirman Letters, University of Arkansas, Fayetteville; Garey diary, April 20, 1862, in Welker, *Keystone Rebel*, 89; *OR*, 10(2):779–80.

49. Hall to parents, April 27, 1862, Hall Letters, SHC; Stewart to wife, April 12, 1862, Stewart Letters, USAMHI; Knighton to wife, April 25, 1862, Knighton Letters, LSU; Mecklin to parents, April 1862, Mecklin Letters, MDAH.

50. Timothy B. Smith, *Corinth*, 85-86; *OR*, 10(1):777, 793, 869, 871-73.

51. *Evening Argus*, June 7, 1862; *Highland (Ohio) Weekly News*, June 5, 1862.

CHAPTER 3

1. Jackman diary, June 8, 1862, in William C. Davis, *Diary*, 45 ("small dirty looking"); *OR*, 10(1):774-86.

2. Welsh, *Medical Histories*, 19; T. Harry Williams, *Beauregard*, 158; William C. Davis, *Jefferson Davis*, 408; Carlisle quoted in McDonough, *War in Kentucky*, 26; S. H. Dent to wife, June 22, 1862, Dent Letters, AU ("I am glad"); Miller to Cellie, July 27, 1862, in McMurry, *Uncompromising Secessionist*, 79.

3. Davidson to sister, July 24, 1862, Davidson Letters, SHC.

4. *OR*, 10(1):791; Roberts to wife, June 8, 1862, Roberts Letters, UMISS; Daniel, *Soldiering*, 128.

5. Haughton, *Training, Tactics, and Leadership*, 80-83; "Leigh," letter to the editor, *Memphis Appeal*, July 11, 1862; Knox Miller to "Dear Friend," July 7, 27, 1862, in McMurry, *Uncompromising Secessionist*, 79; "Consolidated Report of Sick and Wounded, July-November 1862," Jones Papers, TU.

6. "Weekly Return of the 1st Brigade, 1st Division, 1st Corps, Army of the Mississippi," June 2, 10, 1862; and "Weekly Returns of 2d Brigade, 1st Division, 1st Corps, Army of the Mississippi," July 5, 1862, Weekly Returns, MDAH; Daniel, *Soldiering*, 108.

7. Daniel, *Soldiering*, 110; Davis to wife, July 11, 1862, in Skellie, *Lest We Forget*, 1:337; Urquhart, "Bragg's Advance and Retreat," 609; McWhiney, *Braxton Bragg*, 265. Hess (*Braxton Bragg*, 44-46) discovered a source that described in detail the events of this much written about episode. He concluded that Bragg countermanded the execution.

8. Magee Diary, June 10, 1862, DU; Polignac Diary, June 11, 1862, USAMHI; Andrews, *South Reports*, 232; Hess, *Banners to the Breeze*, 19 (Lockett quote); Preston to Johnston, June 14, 1862, Johnston Letters, folder 20, TU.

9. McDonough, *War in Kentucky*, 33-34, 35-36; Daniel, *Days of Glory*, 85-86.

10. *OR*, 16(2):681, 696, 727 (McCown), 734 (Smith's strength); McWhiney, *Braxton Bragg*, 267-68.

11. Lawrence W. Hewitt, "Braxton Bragg," 74; McWhiney, *Braxton Bragg*, 267-68, 271; Archer Jones, *Civil War Command*, 89; Connelly, *Army of the Heartland*, 197; Hess, *Banners to the Breeze*, 20-21; Woodworth, *This Great Struggle*, 167-68; McDonough, *War in Kentucky*, 27, 74. It was McWhiney who first suggested that McCown's movement was "apparently" a test of the railroad system for a larger maneuver. Other historians picked up on the idea. Hewitt rightly concluded that Bragg did "not deserve all of the credit for moving to Chattanooga."

12. Longacre, *Cavalry of the Heartland*, 106-8; Daniel, *Days of Glory*, 102-3.

13. Lawrence W. Hewitt, "Braxton Bragg," 75–76; Noe, *Perryville*, 36.

14. Lockett, "Defense of Vicksburg," 482; *OR*, 17(1):441, 449; and 16(2):888–89; Connelly, *Army of the Heartland*, 196–97.

15. Lawrence W. Hewitt, "Braxton Bragg," 77–78; Woodworth, *Jefferson Davis*, 138; Glatthaar, "Edmund Kirby Smith," 220. Hess (*Banners to the Breeze*, 24) concluded that Smith had no intentions of uniting with Bragg. Noe (*Perryville*, 33) wrote similarly: "Any resulting glory would be his and not Bragg's; it would be Manassas all over again, only better." McMurry thought that Smith was "determined to stay out of Bragg's command." Bresnahan, *Revisioning the Civil War*, 100.

16. Bresnahan, *Revisioning the Civil War*, 100–103. McMurry wrote that, due to logistics, the Southerners "would have to get in and get out quickly."

17. Trask journal, August 29, 1862, in Hafendorfer, *Civil War Journal*, 46; *OR*, 16(1):530, 292; Murray and Hsieh, *Savage War*, 213 ("ragged, greasy, and dirty").

18. Lawrence W. Hewitt, "Braxton Bragg," 79; Daniel, *Days of Glory*, 119–20.

19. McDonough, *War in Kentucky*, 145–46; Symonds, *Stonewall of the West*, 90–92.

20. McDonough, *War in Kentucky*, 129–46; Noe, *Perryville*, 69–70.

21. Connelly, *Army of the Heartland*, 228, 231–34; Lawrence W. Hewitt, "Braxton Bragg," 79; McWhiney, *Braxton Bragg*, 291–94. Smith later defended himself by stating that Bragg's order to march to Bardstown was garbled. The message he received, or so he claimed, was to "prepare to move to Bardstown." See Noe, *Perryville*, 73. While historians criticized Bragg for fighting at Munfordville, Hess (*Braxton Bragg*, 63) saw a troubling larger picture. "It was becoming more apparent that the Confederates had embarked upon a risky venture with minimal manpower, and a lack of coordination, not to mention the absence of a secure line of supply linking Bragg and Kirby Smith with their home base."

22. Daniel, *Days of Glory*, 126; Seitz, *Braxton Bragg*, 207 (2,500); Connelly, *Army of the Heartland*, 235, 236; McWhiney, *Braxton Bragg*, 296 (50,000); Ramage, *Rebel Raider*, 123 (estimate of Kentucky recruits); Noe, *Perryville*, 102–4. McDonough (*War in Kentucky*, 182–85) believed that if Bragg had immediately departed Munfordville, he could have captured Louisville, but he concedes the difficulties. Bragg's belief that unification with Smith was more imperative than the prize of Louisville was correct.

23. Noe, *Perryville*, 104–6; Brent Diary, October 1, 1862, Bragg Papers, WRHS.

24. McWhiney, *Braxton Bragg*, 302–3; Noe, *Perryville*, 124–25.

25. Connelly, *Army of the Heartland*, 247–48. Hess (*Braxton Bragg*, 70) agreed with Connelly.

26. McWhiney, *Braxton Bragg*, 305–6. Herman Hattaway, Archer Jones, McDonough, and Woodworth agreed with McWhiney. See McDonough, *War in Kentucky*, 230–31. Noe (*Perryville*, 128) and I align with Connelly. Noe commented that, at the time, Bragg was actually not upset about Polk's retreat. His anger came only as he searched for a scapegoat for failure.

27. Connelly, *Army of the Heartland*, 254–55, 257. My best approximation of Confederate strength at this time is 44,700. See *OR*, 16(2):734, 752, 896; and Ramage, *Rebel Raider*, 124.

28. For criticism of Polk's decision, see Connelly, *Army of the Heartland*, 260–61; McWhiney, *Braxton Bragg*, 306–7; and Hess, *Braxton Bragg*, 70. For support of Polk, see McDonough, *War in Kentucky*, 232; and Noe, *Perryville*, 158. I agree with McDonough and Noe.

29. Noe, *Perryville*, 196–286; Daniel, *Days of Glory*, 151–54.

30. Castel, *Victors in Blue*, 151–52; Stoker, *Grand Design*, 204–5; Brent Diary, October 14, 1862, Bragg Papers, WRHS.

31. *Richmond Dispatch*, October 18, 1862.

32. J. B. Jones, *Rebel War Clerk's Diary*, 1:172–74; Younger, *Inside the Confederate Government*, 28; *Richmond Dispatch*, October 21, 1862.

33. Hess, *Civil War in the West*, 104 (Gilmer quote); Johnston to wife, October 27, 1862, Johnston Papers, TU; Davis to Edmund Kirby Smith, October 29, 1862, in Rowland, *Jefferson Davis, Constitutionalist*, 8:468.

34. Seitz, *Braxton Bragg*, 206 ("dogs of detraction"); McWhiney, *Braxton Bragg*, 325; Andrews, *South Reports*, 253; *Richmond Dispatch*, October 23, 1862; *Charleston Daily Mercury*, October 25, November 18, 1862.

35. *OR*, 16(2):982–83; Bragg Diary, October 27, 1862, SHC; J. B. Jones, *Rebel War Clerk's Diary*, 1:176; *Charleston Daily Mercury*, November 4, 5, 1862.

36. Davis to Smith, October 29, 1862, in Rowland, *Jefferson Davis, Constitutionalist*, 8:468; William C. Davis, *Jefferson Davis*, 473–75; Daniel, *Battle of Stones River*, 6; McWhiney, *Braxton Bragg*, 328; Archer Jones, *Civil War Command*, 92.

37. Rowland, *Jefferson Davis, Constitutionalist*, 8:468; Parks, *Kirby Smith*, 243, 245.

38. Parks, *Polk*, 79–80; William C. Davis, *Jefferson Davis*, 473.

39. Hughes, *Hardee*, 134–35.

40. Symonds, "No Margin for Error," 8; McMurry, *Two Great Rebel Armies*, 127.

41. Johnston, "Jefferson Davis," 473; Glatthaar, "Davis, Johnston," 122; Connelly and Jones, *Politics of Command*, 113; *OR*, 20(2):493; Symonds, "No Margin for Error," 9.

42. Connelly and Jones, *Politics of Command*, 110, 112, 113, 116, 118.

43. Stoker, *Grand Design*, 234–35; Daniel, *Battle of Stones River*, 2, 25–26, 227–28; Johnston, "Jefferson Davis," 473, 482; Archer Jones, *Confederate Strategy*, 112.

44. Symonds, *Johnston*, 187–88, 191; Connelly and Jones, *Politics of Command*, 109–11.

45. Stoker, *Grand Design*, 205; Brown to wife, October 24, 1862, Brown Letters, ADAH.

CHAPTER 4

1. Coffman, *Old Army*, 88–89; McWhiney, *Braxton Bragg*, 259–60; Hess, *Braxton Bragg*, 6; Taylor as quoted in McDonough, *War in Kentucky*, 6; Noe, *Perryville*, 18.

2. Murray and Hsieh, *Savage War*, 10, 54; Elliott, *Doctor Quintard*, 69; Hess, *Braxton Bragg*, xiii ("a very stern"); Hughes, *Liddell's Record*, 106; Gallagher, *Fighting for the Confederacy*, 307; Jacob Goodson to mother, September 28, 1863, Goodson Letters, CCNBP. Castel (*Decision in the West*, 28; and "Historian and the General," 67–68) believed that the army high command never gelled due to "Bragg's abrasive personality

and chronic incompetency." McWhiney, the general's biographer, found his subject so repugnant that he gave up after one volume of an intended two-volume work. Connelly was brutal in his attacks. See McMurry, *Two Great Rebel Armies*, 127. In a list of the ten worst generals in the war compiled by six historians, only John Floyd edged out Bragg for the number one spot. Symonds placed him at the top of the list. "Who Were the Worst," 15, 16, 20, 23, 24. McMurry has facetiously told me that if William Rosecrans, commanding the Army of the Cumberland, ever presented his sword to Bragg, he would have had to call a staff meeting—"he wouldn't know what to do!"

3. Mackall to wife, September 29, 1863, in Mackall, *Son's Recollections*, 178–79.

4. McDonough, *War in Kentucky*, 4; Clark and Riley, "Medical Department," 67; Hess, *Braxton Bragg*, xii, xv, 77–78, 199.

5. Urquhart, "Bragg's Advance and Retreat," 609; Wheeler to Bragg, July 1864, Bragg Letters, DU; McWhiney, *Braxton Bragg*, 332, 381. McWhiney also pronounced Adams and Liddell to be "pro-Bragg," but after Stones River both were highly critical. I have not been able to find information one way or the other on George Maney, Joseph Palmer, Bushrod Johnson, or S. A. M. Wood. Even long after the war, Urquhart continued to see Patrick Cleburne and John C. Brown as supporters, but both clearly turned on him.

6. James I. Robertson, "Braxton Bragg," 72, 84; Ellis Memoirs, LSU; Robert Myers to wife, September 21, 1863, Myers Letters, MC; McWhiney, "Needed but Misused," 245–46.

7. Stoker, *Grand Design*, 120–21; "Who Were the Worst," 23; Archer Jones, *Civil War Command*, 233–34.

8. Hess, *Braxton Bragg*, 41, 72, 89, 96, 97, 147, 194, 213. Hess made the "half a Lee" comment in a speech at the Gettysburg Forum on June 10, 2017. Murray and Hsieh (*Savage War*, 547) state that Bragg was "racist, vicious, incompetent." I won't argue the racist part, but he was definitely not vicious and incompetent.

9. Hess, *Braxton Bragg*, 72, 276, 279.

10. William C. Davis, *Jefferson Davis*, 376; Bonds, "Leonidas Polk," 46; Robins, *Bishop of the Old South*, 146–48; Woodworth, *This Great Struggle*, 59.

11. McWhiney, "Bishop as General," 7. On the "Worst Ten Generals" list, Polk ranked fifth. Woodworth placed him second, and Newton concurred: "Polk consistently helped seize defeat out of victory and disaster out of defeat." Connelly saw him as "stubborn," "childish," and "quarrelsome." McMurry, *Two Great Rebel Armies*, 114–15. Hess (*Braxton Bragg*, 165) concluded, "Polk was a poor corps commander ill-suited for his important position within the Army of Tennessee." Polk's surviving family members, according to McMurry, insist that his first name was pronounced with an accent on the second syllable.

12. John Bragg to sister, October 12, 1863, as quoted in Hess, *Braxton Bragg*, 196.

13. James Bates to mother, September 12, 1863, in Lowe, *Texas Cavalry Officer's*, 271–72. When Nathaniel Hughes researched his biography of Hardee in the early 1960s, he found a direct descendant by placing an ad in the Augusta newspaper. He discovered that the family pronounced their last name with an emphasis on the second syllable.

Connelly criticized Hardee for his "love of intrigue." Powell evaluated him as "competent but not much more than that." Woodworth described him as "lackluster" and "one who never accomplished anything striking." Newton fired the loudest salvo: "Finally, I give you William J. Hardee, as nearly as I can tell the most thorough going mediocrity and back-stabbing subordinate ever to be nicknamed 'Old Reliable.'" He searched in vain "for something—*anything*—to justify the near awe with which writers generally treat him." Thomas E. Schott weakly defended the "love of intrigue" accusation by saying essentially that in the Army of Tennessee everyone was doing it. McMurry, *Two Great Rebel Armies*, 134; Powell, *Chickamauga Campaign*, 1:47; Woodworth, *No Band of Brothers*, 85; "Overrated Generals," 19; Schott, "Lieutenant General," 162, 163.

14. Hughes, *Liddell's Record*, 122; *Chattanooga Daily Rebel*, December 17, 1862; Hughes, *Hardee*, 187; French Diary, February 1, 1863, TSLA; Irving Buck to sister, in Buck, *Dear Irvie, Dear Lucy*, 150; Beatty Diary, April 10, 1863, SHC (women staying at headquarters); Fremantle, *Three Months*, 141 (women staying at headquarters); Webster Memoir, TSLA; *Fayetteville (Tenn.) Observer*, February 26, 1863 (engagement to Alice); ? to Mrs. A. G. McWhorter, April 5, 1863, in Fitch, *Annals*, 576 ("difficult to find"); Shapiro, "Star of the Collection," 2–27; Hafendorfer, *Civil War Journal*, 103. Symonds (*Stonewall of the West*, 126) labeled Hardee "an outrageous flirt."

15. Warner, *Generals in Gray*, 136; Hill, "Chickamauga," 638.

16. Powell, *Chickamauga Campaign*, 1:54; Welsh, *Medical Histories*, 100–110; Bridges, *Lee's Maverick General*, 149–50.

17. Bridges, *Lee's Maverick General*, 148, 149–50; Woodworth, *Davis and Lee*, 178, 234–36; Hill, "Chickamauga," 639.

18. *OR*, 17(2):628, 655, 668, 673; and 31(3):716; Patricia L. Faust, *Historical Times Encyclopedia*, 761, 352.

19. Allardice and Hewitt, *Kentuckians in Gray*, 124–29; Warner, *Generals in Gray*, 325–26, 70; Allardice, *Confederate Colonels*, 205 (Hunt); Tower, *Carolinian Goes to War*, ii, ix; Bishop, *Civil War Generals*, 164; Welsh, *Medical Histories*, 53, 175 (Polk); *OR*, 20(2):449; Manigault to Bragg, November 30, 1862, and Brent Diary, December 14, 1862, Bragg Papers, WRHS.

20. *Southern Confederacy*, November 15, 1862 (Wood recovering); J. B. Jones, *Rebel War Clerk's Diary*, 1:177; Welsh, *Medical Histories*, 35, 226; *OR*, 20(2):417; Duke, *Reminiscences*, 317.

21. *OR*, 20(2):508–9; McWhiney, *Braxton Bragg*, 343; Hughes, *Liddell's Record*, 103; Cash and Howorth, *My Dear Nellie*, 130.

22. Welsh, *Medical Histories*, 55; Elliott, *Isham G. Harris*, 129, 134–35; Gillum, *Sixteenth Volunteer Tennessee*, 2:143–48.

23. *OR*, 20(2):497 (Wright), 417 (Bate), 508; Welsh, *Medical Histories*, 15 (Bate), 98 (Helm); Wright Diary, December 29, 1862, January 15, 1863, SHC.

24. Elliott, *Soldier of Tennessee*, 84–85; *OR*, 23(2):856, 860; *Chattanooga Daily Rebel*, June 11, 1863. See also *Chattanooga Daily Rebel*, June 11, July 8, 1863; and Bishop, *Civil War Generals*, 197–98.

25. Bishop, *Civil War Generals*, 75–76; Welsh, *Medical Histories*, 55, 228.

26. Anderson to wife, January 11, 1863, in Rabb, *J. Patton Anderson*, 84, 84; Tower, *Carolinian Goes to War*, 78–79.

27. Neal and Kremm, *Lion of the South*, 162; Walker to wife, August 16, 1863, in William Lee White and Runion, *Great Things*, 63; Tower, *Carolinian Goes to War*, 78; Walthall to parents, September 15, 1863, Walthall Letters, UMISS.

28. Anderson, *Parson's Texas Cavalry Brigade*, 168; Rennolds Diary, May 28, April 10, 1863, UT; James Mitchell to wife, May 10, 1863, Mitchell Letters, ADAH; Davidson to wife, January 23, 1863, Davidson Letters, AHS; Fremantle, *Three Months*, 152–53.

29. Taylor Diary, April 29, 1863, SNBP; Fowler, *Mountaineers in Gray*, 70–75; *OR*, 10(2):781.

30. Statistics based on Allardice, *Confederate Colonels*.

31. *OR*, 20(1):676–81; Fremantle, *Three Months*, 160.

32. Orders Received, NARG; Rennolds Diary, April 13, 1863, UT; Davis to wife, June 23, 1863, Davis Letters, ADAH; John Davidson to wife, February 28, 1863, Davidson Letters, AHS.

33. Spence to wife, December 24, 1862, in Christ, *Being Shot At*, 54; Batchelor to wife, December 1, 1862, in Rugeley, *Batchelor-Turner Letters*, 36; Fowler, *Mountaineers in Gray*, 87; John Harris to wife, June 13, 1863, Harris Letters, LSU.

34. McMurry, *Two Great Rebel Armies*, 98–105; Murray and Hsieh, *Savage War*, 9, 10, 54.

CHAPTER 5

1. *OR*, 17(2):679; McWhiney, *Braxton Bragg*, 342.

2. Johnson, "Confederate Staff Work," 132, 135; Hess, *Braxton Bragg*, 140 (horses); *OR*, 20(1):671; Myers Diary, September 21, 1863, CCNBP. Bragg's August 1862 staff roster was published in the *New York Times*, August 15, 1862. For the original Pensacola staff, see *OR*, 6:725.

3. Gow, "Chiefs of Staff," 347–50; McWhiney, *Braxton Bragg*, 279; Warner, *Generals in Gray*, 77–78; Welsh, *Medical Histories*, 77; *OR*, 16(2):780; and 20(2):403, 411.

4. McWhiney, *Braxton Bragg*, 342; *OR*, 20(2):403; Gow, "Chiefs of Staff," 349–50; Brent Diary, October 2, 1862; and Stout, "Reminiscences," Bragg Papers, WRHS; Gow, "Military Administration," 190, 191, 192–93; *Savannah Republican*, December 26, 1863.

5. Allardice, *Confederate Colonels*, 74; Gow, "Chiefs of Staff," 347; Brent Diary, October 1, 1862, Bragg Papers, WRHS.

6. *Savannah Republican*, December 26, 1863; Blakey, Lainhart, and Stephens, *Rose Cottage Chronicles*, 177, 183, 241.

7. Gow, "Military Administration," 194; Mackall, *Son's Recollections*, 178–79; Brent Diary, September 15, 17, 1863, Bragg Papers, WRHS; William G. Robertson ("Chickamauga Campaign: The Fall," 14) concluded that Mackall "attempted to bring order to a rather chaotic army staff by rationalizing staff positions and organizing paper flow." His efforts only partially succeeded, "because of Bragg's tendency to do much of the staff's work himself."

8. Blakey, Lainhart, and Stephens, *Rose Cottage Chronicles*, 229, 241; Hughes, *Liddell's Record*, 134.

9. Garner Biographical Sketch, USMISS; *OR*, 20(2):411; "Kinloch Falconer Biography," PP. See also Hess, *Braxton Bragg*, 141.

10. Warner, *Generals in Gray*, 279; Welsh, *Medical Histories*, 198; *OR*, 17(2):679; and ser. 2, 5:3; Krick, *Staff Officers in Gray*, 316; Sheppard, *By the Noble Daring*, 14; Crist, *Papers*, 9:406n2.

11. Walter Biographical Sketch, 03399-2, SHC; Allardice, *Confederate Colonels*, 267 (McKinstrey), 220–21 (Jones); *OR*, 31(2):717 (gather in absentees). McKinstrey was once called on the carpet by Bragg for harshly interrogating prisoners.

12. Krick, *Staff Officers in Gray*, 3. At Stones River, Brent actively performed reconnaissance missions. See *OR*, 20(1):667, 760.

13. Crist, *Papers*, 9:31; *OR*, 23(1):621; Urquhart, "Bragg's Advance and Retreat," 604–5; *Memphis Appeal*, March 19, 1880; *New Orleans Democrat*, March 18, 1880; *Daily Public Ledger*, July 7, 1900; "David Urquhart," *New Orleans Picayune*, July 8, 1900; *Evening Star*, July 7, 1900.

14. "Johnston," www.findagrave.com/memorial/22633859/josiah-stoddard-johnston; William C. Davis, *Breckinridge*, 361–62; Johnston to William Preston Johnston, June 17, 1863, Johnston Letters, folder 21, TU.

15. McWhiney, *Braxton Bragg*, 183–84; Russell, *My Diary*, 188; Conner Biographical Sketch, LSU; Hughes, *Yale's Confederates*, 68, 44. Neither Ellis nor Conner graduated from Yale.

16. Starr, *Colonel Grenfell's Wars*, 95–97; Fremantle, *Three Months*, 149–50.

17. *OR*, 20(1):671. See also Elliott, *Isham G. Harris*, 131.

18. "Death of Col. Hypolite Oladowski," *Columbus Daily Enquirer*, August 17, 1878; "Colonel Hypolite Oladowski," *New Orleans Star & Catholic Register*, August 25, 1878; *OR*, 6:892; Dawson, *Reminiscences of Confederate Service*, 104–5.

19. *OR*, 10(1):794–97; "McLean," accessed September 24, 2018, https://www.findagrave.com/memorial/10605823/eugene-eckel-mclean.

20. "O'Bannon," accessed December 1, 2016, http://angelfire.com/mi/robynn/index pagessix.html; *OR*, 17(2):669–70, 6:892; McWhiney, *Braxton Bragg*, 342; *New Orleans Times Picayune*, September 12, 1878; *Chattanooga Daily Rebel*, January 30, 1863; Clark and Riley, "Medical Department," 72 (McMicken); Crist, *Papers*, 10:146.

21. "Death of Major W. W. Walker," *New York Times*, November 5, 1884; "Death of Col. Giles M. Hillyer," *Weekly Clarion*, June 11, 1871; "Death of a Prominent Man," *Daily Phoenix*, May 9, 1871; *Chattanooga Daily Rebel*, August 25, 1863; Crist, *Papers*, 10:148; Hess, *Braxton Bragg*, 142 ("He has instructions").

22. James H. Hallonquist, Military Service Files, NARG; *Richmond Dispatch*, October 18, 1861; Bragg to David Powell, March 25, 1862, Bragg Papers, WRHS; "1887 Annual Reunion," 78, United States Military Academy, West Point, New York; *Anderson (S.C.) Intelligencer*, December 7, 1865; *News & Herald*, September 10, 1878.

23. Kundahl, *Confederate Engineer*, 193–95, 197, 200, 146, 263.

24. Schroeder-Lein, *Confederate Hospitals*, 189-90; "The Late Dr. A. J. Foard," *Nashville Republican Banner*, May 16, 1868.

25. Patricia L. Faust, *Historical Times Encyclopedia*, 361; *Chattanooga Daily Rebel*, January 30, 1861; Welsh, *Medical Histories*, 100.

26. Krick, *Staff Officers in Gray*, 7 (staff criticism), 66, 100, 112, 152, 198, 203, 214, 242, 283, 292, 297. William G. Robertson ("Chickamauga Campaign: The Fall," 14) bluntly characterized Bragg's staff as "plodding nonentities of no more than average competence."

27. Robertson concluded that the army staff was not "a positive influence of great consequence," in part due to Bragg himself. "Seemingly incapable of delegating tasks, however mundane toothers, Bragg made little use of his staff." William G. Robertson, "Chickamauga Campaign: The Fall," 14.

CHAPTER 6

1. Brent Diary, November 2, 1862, Bragg Papers, WRHS; Walker to wife, November 28, 1862, Walker Letters, MSU; *Chattanooga Daily Rebel*, October 24, 1862; Crittenden to wife, October 25, 1862, Crittenden Letters, AU.

2. Crittenden to wife, October 25, 1862, Crittenden Letters, AU; Arliskas, *Cadet Gray*, 41; Dent to wife, October 25, 1862, Dent Letters, AU; *Columbus Weekly Enquirer*, November 4, 1862; Marshall to wife, October 28, 1862, Marshall Letters, MSU.

3. *OR*, 20(2):385, 386, 392-93, 412; William C. Davis, *Diary*, 64; Brent Diary, November 6, 1862, Bragg Papers, WRHS; *Knoxville Daily Register*, December 16, 1862.

4. *OR*, 20(2):386, 411, 392; Brent Diary, November 4, 1862, Bragg Papers, WRHS; *Chattanooga Daily Rebel*, December 18, 1863; Walker to wife, November 27, 1862, in William Lee White and Runion, *Great Things*, 34.

5. *OR*, 16(2):916, 938; and 20(2):988 (Federal strength); Elliott, *Isham G. Harris*, 121. Connelly (*Autumn of Glory*, 13-15, 23) asserted that Bragg made the decision for a Middle Tennessee invasion while he was in Kentucky. He based his conclusion on the fact that Bragg sent Forrest into Middle Tennessee while the army was in Kentucky. In truth, Bragg had stripped Forrest of his command (except for a couple of companies) and sent him back into Tennessee to recruit a new command. Longacre, *Cavalry of the Heartland*, 129-30; Dyer, *"Fightin' Joe" Wheeler*, 56.

6. William C. Davis, *Orphan Brigade*, 130-33; Jackman diary, September 12, October 3, 1862, in William C. Davis, *Diary*, 57, 60.

7. *OR*, 16(2):1002; Rosecrans quoted in Varney, "Men Grant Didn't Trust," 157.

8. Brent Diary, November 4, 1862, Bragg Papers, WRHS.

9. *OR*, 20(2):421; Holmes diary, November 11, 1862, in Dennis, *Kemper County Rebel*, 15; John F. Nugent to mother, November 18, 1862, Nugent Letters, GLC; John Crittenden to wife, November 26, 1862, Crittenden Letters, AU; Clarkson Diary, November 1, 1862, SRNBP.

10. *OR*, 16(2):979; Parks, *Kirby Smith*, 245, 247; Brent Diary, November 11, December 1, 1862, Bragg Papers, WRHS.

11. *OR*, 20(2):422–23, 426, 446; Brent Diary, November 17, 18, 20, 28, December 5, 6, 1862, Bragg Papers, WRHS; *Chattanooga Daily Rebel*, December 14, 1862.

12. Ramage, *Rebel Raider*, 128–31; William C. Davis, *Orphan Brigade*, 144–46; Duke, *History of Morgan's Cavalry*, 309–16; S. H. Dent to wife, December 11, 1862, Dent Letters, AU.

13. Johnston, *Military Operations*, 150; *Chattanooga Daily Rebel*, November 25, December 4, 9, 14, 1862.

14. *Chattanooga Daily Rebel*, December 17, 1862; William C. Davis, *Jefferson Davis*, 480–82; Bradley and Jones, *Murfreesboro*, 61. Oaklands is today open to the public, and visitors may still visit "the Davis room."

15. Polk to wife, December 17, 1862, in Polk, *Leonidas Polk*, 2:177; Jackman diary, December 13, 1862, in William C. Davis, *Diary*, 65; Anderson, *Parson's Texas Cavalry Brigade*, 123; Hall to sister, December 14, 1862, Hall Letters, ADAH. See also Reuben Searcy to father, December 12, 1862, Reuben Searcy Letters, Searcy Family Papers, ADAH; Thomas Warrick to wife, December 15, 1862, Warrick Letters, ADAH; *Mobile Advertiser & Register*, December 18, 1862; and Crittenden to wife, December 15, 1862, Crittenden Letters, AU.

16. *OR*, 17(2):743, 755, 769, 773, 775; Connelly, *Autumn of Glory*, 40–41; Archer Jones, *Civil War Command*, 116; Archer Jones, *Confederate Strategy*, 126–27. McMurry (*Two Great Rebel Armies*, 63) makes the traditional argument: "The division had left too soon to be of help in Tennessee and arrived too late to be of assistance in Mississippi." This argument is of course made in hindsight. In early December, Pemberton had a force of 21,000 in North Mississippi and 6,000 at Vicksburg to confront an army estimated at 60,000.

17. Stoker, *Grand Design*, 229.

18. Bearss, "Forrest's West Tennessee Campaign," 48–49; Ramage, *Rebel Raider*, 137–45.

19. Rogers Memorandum Book, December 25, 1862, SHC; Bush Diary, December 25, 1862, CCNBP; Reuben Searcy to mother, December 25, 1862, Reuben Searcy Letters, Searcy Family Papers, ADAH; Walker to wife, December 27, 1862, in William Lee White and Runion, *Great Things*, 39.

20. Castel, *Victors in Blue*, 166; Wheeler to Brent, December 26, 1862, and Brent Diary, December 26, 1862, Bragg Papers, WRHS; *OR*, 20(2):462.

21. *OR*, 20(2):226–27, 958, 960, 965; Wheeler after-action reports, Bragg Papers, WRHS; McMurry, *Uncompromising Secessionist*, 116, 118; Kniffen, "Battle of Stone's River," 614; *Montgomery Weekly Advertiser*, January 6, 1863.

22. McWhiney, *Braxton Bragg*, 347–48; Connelly, *Autumn of Glory*, 24, 47, 49; *OR*, 20(2):398; Hess, *Braxton Bragg*, 106; Varney, *General Grant*, 141.

23. Daniel, *Battle of Stones River*, 48–49. Hess (*Banners to the Breeze*, 11) defended Bragg's deployment. If Rosecrans had attempted to turn Bragg's right by way of Jefferson, it would have indeed neutralized McFadden's Hill—but he didn't.

24. Urquhart, "Bragg's Advance and Retreat," 665; Brent Diary, December 30, 1862,

Bragg Papers, WRHS; McWhiney, *Braxton Bragg*, 363-64. Hess (*Banners to the Breeze*, 194) also raised questions about the right-wheel maneuver.

25. Lanny K. Smith, *Stone's River Campaign*, 1:9; Haughton, *Training, Tactics, and Leadership*, 163; Castel, "Mars and Reverend Longstreet," 126-29. Rosecrans took McCook's postbattle strength and used it to calculate his prebattle strength. He also failed to count Walker's brigade and he underestimated Van Cleve's division by at least 2,000 and the artillery by 500.

26. *OR*, 20(1):926, 927, 933-34, 944, 950-51, 955; *SOR*, 3:650; Gammage, *Camp*, 63; P. R. Jones, "Recollections," 341-42; Stroud, *Ector's Texas Brigade*, 76-77; Henry Watson to parents, January 23, 1863, Watson Letters, SRNBP; Worley, *War Memories*, 38-40; James Douglas to Sallie, January 29, 1863, in Douglas, *Douglas' Texas Battery*, 37; John Templeton to parents, January 9, 1863, in "War Time Letters," 24.

27. *OR*, 20(1):853, 875, 877, 889, 890-93; Symonds, *Stonewall of the West*, 110; Lewis, "Battle of Stones River," 23.

28. Daniel, *Battle of Stones River*, 95.

29. Losson, *Tennessee's Forgotten Warriors*, 90-91; *Savannah Morning News*, January 29, 1863.

30. Hess, *Banners to the Breeze*, 206-7.

31. Castel, *Victors in Blue*, 168; Hess, *Banners to the Breeze*, 219; Skellie, *Lest We Forget*, 1:441. Hess concluded that Bragg ordered the attack "probably because he increasingly came to view this assault as his last chance to salvage a victory from the heavy fighting of December 31." I concur.

32. Labouisse to father, January 10, 1863, Labouisse Letters, box 1, folder 7, TU.

33. Hess, *Banner to the Breeze*, 219-20.

34. Daniel, *Battle of Stones River*, 181-82; Parks, *Polk*, 299.

35. *Southern Confederacy*, January 13, 1863; William C. Davis, *Breckinridge*, 344-45; *OR*, 20(1):759, 803, 808, 813; Rice Graves report, Breckinridge Papers, New York Historical Society, New York; Chalaron, "Memories of Rice Graves," 9; Hannibal Paine to sister, January 10, 1863, Paine Letters, TSLA. Connelly (*Autumn of Glory*, 64) concluded that "command disagreements" doomed the assault. With the artillery fire massed against Breckinridge, however, it is difficult to envision how any plan would have succeeded.

36. Hess, *Braxton Bragg*, 111-12; Castel, *Victors in Blue*, 169-71.

37. Carter to wife, January 4, 15, 1863, Carter Letters, DU; Street to wife, January 3, 1863, Street Letters, SHC; Fayette McDonald to sister, January 9, 1863, accessed January 18, 2016, www.articlelibrary.info/Reference/civilwar_civilwar_sourcebook.htm (site discontinued); William Rogers to parents, January 22, 1863, Rogers Letters, FLSA; Crittenden to wife, January 14, 1863, Crittenden Letters, AU.

38. Hammer to wife, January 10, 1863, Hammer Letters, West Tennessee Historical Society, Memphis; Carter to wife, January 6, 1863, Carter Letters, DU; Charles George to wife, January 24, 1863, George Letters, AU; Patton to mother, January 13, 1863, Patton Letters, SHC; Buck to sister, January 13, 1863, in Buck, *Dear Irvie, Dear Lucy*, 124.

See also *Nashville Daily Courier*, January 30, 1863. See also McDonald Diary, January 4, 1863, UFLA.

39. Bell to wife, January 11, 1863, Bell Letters, DU; Walker to wife, January 8, 15, 29, 1863, in William Lee White and Runion, *Great Things*, 40, 44, 47; "C," letter to the editor, *Memphis Appeal*, January 20, 1863; Batchelor to wife, January 10, 1863, to father, January 25, 1863, in Rugeley, *Batchelor-Turner Letters*, 45; Alexander to sister, February 26, 1863, Alexander Letters, SHC.

40. Reese to wife, January 10, 1863, thomaslegioncherokee.tripod.com/reese.html; Warrick to wife, January 11, 1863, Warrick Letters, ADAH; Bell to wife, January 11, 1863, Bell Letters, DU. See also John W. Caldwell to wife, January 7, 1863, Caldwell Letters, SRNBP; and *OR*, 20(1):674-75, 676.

41. J. B. Jones, *Rebel War Clark's Diary*, 1:232; *Richmond Dispatch*, January 2, 3, 1863; *Richmond Enquirer*, January 7, 1863; *Mobile Advertiser & Register*, January 10, 1863 (press back out).

42. *Richmond Dispatch*, January 5, 6, 1863; J. B. Jones, *Rebel War Clerk's Diary*, 1:232; Scarborough, *Diary*, 2:532; William Preston Johnston to Jefferson Davis, January 6, 1863, Johnston Papers, TU.

43. *Richmond Examiner*, January 6, 1863; *Richmond Dispatch*, January 6, 7, 1863; Johnston to William Preston, January 9, to wife, January 6, 1863, Johnston Papers, folders 2, 1, 5, TU.

44. *Southern Literary Messenger*, January 1863, 57; *Richmond Enquirer*, January 23, 1863; William Preston Johnston to wife, February 8, 1863, Johnston Papers, TU.

45. "Proceedings of the First Congress, Third Session," 209-10; Pugh to Bragg, March 5, 1863, Bragg Papers, WRHS; Eicher, *Dixie Betrayed*, 161; Estill, "Diary," 299.

46. Pugh to Bragg, March 5, 1863, Bragg Papers, WRHS; Jewitt, *Rise and Fall*, 163-64.

47. Younger, *Inside the Confederate Government*, 83; *Charleston Daily Mercury*, September 19, 1863; *Richmond Whig*, August 26, 1863.

48. Sale to Bragg, March 5, 1863, in Seitz, *Braxton Bragg*, 284-85.

49. Younger, *Inside the Confederate Government*, 43; Johnston to Thomas Jordan, March 28, 1863, Johnston Papers, folder 11, TU; *Charleston Daily Mercury*, March 13, 1863; Gale to Polk, March 27, 1863, Gale Papers, SHC.

50. *Richmond Enquirer*, March 31, 1863.

51. Tennessee Delegation to Davis, March 8, 1863, Henry Papers, TSLA; Jefferson Davis, *Rise and Fall*, 2:38; Foote, *War of the Rebellion*, 313-14. I disagree with Connelly's assessment (*Autumn of Glory*, 87) that Bragg's support in Congress rebounded in March.

52. Younger, *Inside the Confederate Government*, 46, 50, 71-72.

CHAPTER 7

1. Holmes diary, January 6, 7, 1863, in Dennis, *Kemper County Rebel*, 41; Elliott, *Doctor Quintard*, 62; *OR*, 23(2):617-18, 52(2):403; *Chattanooga Daily Rebel*, January 30, 1863; Hay, *Cleburne and His Command*, 132; *Richmond Enquirer*, April 15, 1863.

2. Bragg to Davis, January 8, 1863, Bragg to Samuel Cooper, January 15, 1863, and

Davis to Bragg, January 15, 1863, in Crist, *Papers*, 9:18, 21, 26; Connelly, *Autumn of Glory*, 71; Kolakowski, *Stones River*, 107; *OR*, 20(1):657, 662(2):498; and 52(2):404, 407; Isham Harris to Davis, January 15, 1863, in Rowland, *Jefferson Davis, Constitutionalist*, 5:418; Willie Bryant to mother, January 30, 1863, in Blakey, Lainhart, and Stephens, *Rose Cottage Chronicles*, 197; Robert Vance to brother, January 28, 1863, Vance Letters, North Carolina State Archives, Raleigh. Castel (*Victors in Blue*, 169) believed that Bragg withdrew to a "much stronger position" after Murfreesboro.

3. Brent Diary, January 10, 1863, Bragg Papers, WRHS. The January 7 issue of the *Rebel* has not survived. Since the January 6, 8, 9, and 10 editions are extant but the article in question does not appear, this leaves only the seventh as a possibility. See Urquhart, "Bragg's Advance and Retreat," 608.

4. *OR*, 20(1):699; Brent Diary, January 17, 1863, Bragg Papers, WRHS; McWhiney, *Braxton Bragg*, 377–78; Woodworth, *Jefferson Davis*, 195.

5. Brent Diary, January 12, 1863, Bragg Papers, WRHS; *OR* 20(1):683; O'Hara quoted in Hughes and Ware, *O'Hara*, 128; Hess, *Braxton Bragg*, 124–26.

6. *OR*, 20(1):682; William C. Davis, *Breckinridge*, 327–28, 349; Connelly, *Autumn of Glory*, 73–74. See also *Memphis Appeal*, February 17, 1863.

7. Gibson to "Dear Will," March 9, 1863, Johnston Letters, TU; Ehlinger, *Kentucky's Last Cavalier*, 146; O'Hara to Breckinridge, January 24, 1863, quoted in Hughes and Ware, *O'Hara*, 129; *Charleston Daily Mercury*, June 10, 1863; Allardice, *Confederate Colonels*, 375; Hughes and Stonesipher, *Pillow*, 259–69. For additional information on the Trabue incident, see Hess, *Braxton Bragg*, 130–31.

8. *OR*, 20(1):684; Urquhart, "Bragg's Advance and Retreat," 609; Fremantle, *Three Months*, 154 (Bragg's praise of Cleburne); *Mobile Advertiser & Register*, January 14, 16, 18, 1863. The other pro-Bragg generals on Urquhart's list were Wheeler, Withers, Anderson, Brown, Jackson, Bate, and Walthall. A July 1864 letter from Wheeler also placed Stewart on the list of supporters. Wheeler to Bragg, July 1864, Bragg Letters, DU. McWhiney (*Braxton Bragg*, 331n72, 377n16, 380, 381) would expand the list to include Wright, Chalmers, and Preston Smith.

9. Brent Diary, January 12, 1863, Bragg Papers, WRHS; Bragg to Davis, January 17, 1863, in Crist, *Papers*, 9:28.

10. *OR*, 52(2):407; Bragg to Benjamin Ewell, January 14, 1863, quoted in Hess, *Braxton Bragg*, 116; Bragg to Davis, January 17, 1863, in Crist, *Papers*, 9:28.

11. O'Hara quoted in Hughes and Ware, *O'Hara*, 128–29.

12. *OR*, 20(1):698, 701; *Chattanooga Daily Rebel*, January 27, 1863; Connelly, *Autumn of Glory*, 76. For Polk's February 4 letter to Davis, see Polk, *Leonidas Polk*, 2:206–7.

13. *OR*, 20(1):698; Losson, *Tennessee's Forgotten Warriors*, 94; Joseph E. Johnston to Davis, February 3, 1863, in Crist, *Papers*, 9:48–49; Withers, letter to the editor, *Mobile Advertiser & Register*, January 18, 1863; Anderson to wife, January 8, 11, 1863, quoted in Rabb, *J. Patton Anderson*, 83–84; Tower, *Carolinian Goes to War*, 158. On September 8, 1863, Kate Cummings recorded, "Mrs. Anderson, who is well acquainted with General Bragg, says her husband has every confidence in him, and thinks he is one of our greatest generals." Harwell, *Kate*, 139.

14. Polk, *Leonidas Polk*, 2:205–6.

15. *Augusta Constitutionalist* quoted in *Memphis Appeal*, February 17, 1863; Davis to Johnston, January 21, 1863, in Crist, *Papers*, 9:35, 48, 50; *Southern Confederacy*, January 16, 1863; *OR*, 23(2):613–14, 24(3):670, 52(2):418.

16. Connelly, *Autumn of Glory*, 69; Johnston to Wigfall, January 26, 1863, in Girand Wright, *Southern Girl*, 121; *OR*, 17(2):827, 20(2):487–88. On January 12, Johnston estimated that Pemberton had 42,000 to contest Grant's 58,000 and Nathaniel Banks's 25,000, the latter at Baton Rouge.

17. *OR* 23(2):632–33; Johnston to Davis, February 4, 1863, in Crist, *Papers*, 9:49.

18. *OR*, 23(2):632–33, 52(2):426; Johnston to Davis, February 3, 1863, in Crist, *Papers*, 9:49.

19. *Chattanooga Daily Rebel*, February 24, 28, 1863; *Atlanta Intelligencer*, February 21, 1863; Bragg to Mackall, February 14, 1863, Mackall Letters, SHC; Gale to wife, February 21, 1863, Gale Papers, SHC; Urquhart, "Bragg's Advance and Retreat," 608–9.

20. Johnston to wife, February 3, 12, 1863, in Crist, *Papers*, 9:49, 60; Symonds, *Johnston*, 19–99; *OR*, 23(2):658–59. Woodworth (*Jefferson Davis*, 197) argues that it had less to do with his "disappointed vanity" than the fact that he always considered the Army of Northern Virginia "rightfully his."

21. Connelly, *Autumn of Glory*, 123; Bragg to William Mackall, February 14, 1863, Mackall Letters, SHC.

22. *OR*, 23(2):653–54, 713, 722; Gideon Pillow to William Clare, March 9, 1863, Bragg Papers, WRHS; *Chattanooga Daily Rebel*, January 17, 1863; Symonds, *Stonewall of the West*, 122.

23. Bragg to Mackall, February 14, 1863, in Mackall, *Son's Recollections*, 194; William C. Davis, *Breckinridge*, 350–52, 357–60; Connelly, *Autumn of Glory*, 82–83; Alexander F. Stevenson, *Battle of Stone's River*, 132; John A. Buckner and Theodore O'Hara reports, Breckinridge Papers, New York Historical Society, New York; *Nashville Union*, April 28, 1863; Thomas Osborne to mother, March 24, 1863, in "Letters of Thomas D. Osborne," 3, CCNBP. The Northern press was well aware of the Bragg-Breckinridge dispute. See, for example, the *Chicago Times* article reprinted in the *Memphis Appeal* on April 6, 1863. The *Southern Confederacy* of May 22, 1863, considered Bragg's after-action report unfortunate. If Breckinridge was such a bad general, then Bragg should have immediately requested a court-martial. Simply to make "grave insinuations" was "in bad taste." Hess (*Braxton Bragg*, 130) contends that although Breckinridge bore much of the blame for the attack, Bragg "exaggerated his case against him."

24. Allardice and Hewitt, *Kentuckians in Gray*, 219; Mary Gorton McBride, *Randall Lee Gibson*, 94–95.

25. Losson, *Tennessee's Forgotten Warriors*, 95–96; Charles Roberts to wife, February 13, 1863, Roberts Letters, UMISS; *Chattanooga Daily Rebel*, March 22, 1863 (Cheatham cheered); Johnston Diary, March 15, 1863, Bragg Papers, WRHS (Cheatham cheered); Connelly, *Autumn of Glory*, 84–85.

26. *OR*, 23(2):196-97; *Chattanooga Daily Rebel*, March 17, 1863; *Savannah Republican*, March 4, 1863; Leonidas Polk to wife, February 16, 1863, Leonidas Polk Letter, Vol. 3, WPA Civil War Letterbook, 38-39, TSLA. Numbers for both armies are based on men present for duty on March 31.

27. Johnston to Davis, March 2, 1863, in Crist, *Papers*, 9:86-87; Johnston to Wigfall, March 4, 1863, Wigfall Papers, LC; Johnston to Bragg, March 8, 1863, Johnston Papers, DU; *OR*, 23(2):658-59.

28. *OR*, 23(2):660, 724 (exchange bases), 760 (subsistence raid); *Chattanooga Daily Rebel*, February 13, 14, 28, 1863.

29. *OR*, 23(2):656, 659, 662, 684-85, 705, 726-27; Johnston to Wigfall, March 4, 8, 1863, Wigfall Papers, LC.

30. *OR*, 23(2):661, 674, 681, 684, 685; Hess, *Braxton Bragg*, 126.

31. Johnston Diary, March 18, 1863, FHS; Brent Diary, March 16, 1863, Bragg Papers, WRHS; Thomas Bigbee to wife, March 24, 1863, Bigbee Letters, AU; Johnston, "Jefferson Davis," 476-77; *OR*, 23(2):708-9; Hess, *Banners to the Breeze*, 228. Symonds (*Joseph E. Johnston*, 200) noted that Johnston only technically assumed command.

32. Johnston Diary, March 19, 1863, FHS; *Chattanooga Daily Rebel*, March 15, 25, 1863; Coleman Diary, March 19, 1863, SHC; Beatty Diary, March 18, 1863, SHC; Semple to wife, March 20, 1863, Semple Letters, ADAH; John Scott to "Miss Phil," March 30, 1863, Scott Letters, AU.

33. *OR*, 23(2):757; John T. Biggs to sister, April 5, 1863, Biggs Letters, SHC; William D. Rogers to parents, April 17, 1863, Rogers Letters, SRNBP; Lindsley, *Military Annals of Tennessee*, 205, 223; *Winchester (Tenn.) Daily Bulletin*, April 26, 1863.

34. William C. Davis, *Orphan Brigade*, 164; *Chattanooga Daily Rebel*, March 25, 1863; Johnston Diary, March 19, 1863, FHS; McMurry, *Twentieth Tennessee*, 250, 325; Garrett, *Diary*, 51-52; Thomas Osborne to mother, March 24, 1863, in "Letters of Thomas D. Osborne," 3, CCNBP; William C. Davis, *Jefferson Davis*, 499.

35. *Macon Telegraph*, April 7, 9, May 22, 1863; Welsh, *Medical Histories*, 120; Johnston to Davis, April 10, 1863, in Crist, *Papers*, 9:137; Coleman Diary, April 18, 1863, SHC; Brent Diary, April 1, 2, 7, 13, 14, 1863, Bragg Papers, WRHS.

36. *Mobile Advertiser & Register*, April 19, 1863; Beatty Diary, April 10, 1863, SHC; Buck to sister, April 11, 1863, in Buck, *Dear Irvie, Dear Lucy*, 139.

37. Polk to wife, April 11, 1863, in Polk, *Leonidas Polk*, 2:212-13; William B. Richmond to Alexander Polk, April 1, 1863, Richmond Letters, University of Notre Dame, South Bend, Indiana.

38. *OR*, 16(1):1097-107, 1109; Wooley, "An Apology for the Campaigns in Kentucky and Middle Tennessee," and Wooley to Mrs. Polk, September 22, 1868, Polk Papers, US; Samuel J. Martin, *General Braxton Bragg*, 258. Connelly (*Autumn of Glory*, 88) states that Bragg's attack on Polk and Hardee came at a time when "the Army's morale [was] already depleted." If he is referring to troops' morale, it is not borne out in the letters and diaries.

39. Polk to wife, April 16, 1863, in Polk, *Leonidas Polk*, 2:213; Joshua Callaway to

wife, April 16, 1863, in Hallock, *Callaway*, 83. See also Rogers Memorandum Book, April 16, 1863, SHC; Fielder diary, April 16, 1863, in Franklin, *Civil War Diaries*, 113; Mayer Diary, April 16, 1863, SRNBP; Holmes diary, April 16, 1863, in Dennis, *Kemper County Rebel*, 86–87; Newton Davis to wife, April 16, 1863, Davis Letters, ADAH; *OR*, 23(2):751; and Isaac Alexander to sister, April 18, 1863, Alexander Letters, SHC.

40. *OR*, 16(1):1097–107.

41. *OR*, 52(2):817–19.

CHAPTER 8

1. *OR*, 20(2):487, 23(2):57 (seventy-five days); Brent Diary, January 22, 1863, Bragg Papers, WRHS; Castel, *Victors in Blue*, 205; *Memphis Appeal*, February 6, 1863.

2. Longacre, *Soldier to the Last*, 7, 13, 14–15; *Southern Confederacy*, January 24, 1863; *Augusta Constitutionalist*, January 21, 1863; Fremantle, *Three Months*, 159; Powell, *Failure in the Saddle*, xx–xxi ("a very small man"). The *Constitutionalist* article has so much detail that it had to have come from a Wheeler staff member with the general's assistance. Longacre (*Cavalry of the Heartland*, 197) wrote that Elisha Burford, Wheeler's adjutant, served in the role of publicist, even giving him the name "War Child."

3. *Atlanta Daily Register*, November 18, 1863; "Dixie" article in *Fayetteville (Tenn.) Observer*, March 13, 1863; "Overrated Generals," 18; Longacre, *Cavalry of the Heartland*, 217; Connelly, *Autumn of Glory*, 27; Brent Diary, September 3, 1863, Bragg Papers, WRHS; Wills, *Confederacy's Greatest Cavalryman*, 302 ("I ain't"); Powell, *Failure in the Saddle*, xx; Woodworth, *Jefferson Davis*, 225; Welsh, *Medical Histories*, 232; *SOR*, 20(1):9. McMurry (*Two Great Rebel Armies*, 7) found neither Wheeler nor Morgan to be rivals of Jeb Stuart. Castel (*Decision in the West*, 111) gave Wheeler generally high marks, although he admitted that he lacked "the panache of Stuart and the genius of Forrest." Only Longacre (*Soldier to the Last*, 50) unequivocally supported the promotion — it "made much sense."

4. *OR*, 20(2):503; and 23(2):622, 625, 637–38; Duke, *History of Morgan's Cavalry*, 249.

5. Wills, *Confederacy's Greatest Cavalryman*, 98–102; Longacre, *Soldier to the Last*, 90–93; Hurst, *Nathan Bedford Forrest*, 113–14.

6. Gustave Cook to wife, February 17, 1863, Cook Letters, GLC; *Chattanooga Daily Rebel*, February 13, 22, 1863; "FABIUS," in *Atlanta Daily Register*, November 18, 1863, remarked, "It is frequently charged that Gen. Wheeler is a pet of Gen. Bragg's."

7. *Augusta Constitutionalist*, December 19, 1863.

8. Ramage, *Rebel Raider*, 147–48; *OR*, 23(2):656; Jerry W. Smith, *French's War Journal*, 69; *Nashville Union*, February 24, 1863. Ramage concluded that Morgan was increasingly diverted and "depended upon Mattie for security and comfort from depression," thus losing his "creativity and motivation."

9. Wheeler Circular, January 22, 1863, GLC.

10. *OR*, 23(1):125, 135(2):663; Allardice, *Confederate Colonels*, 330; Fitch, *Annals*, 423–24; Sheridan, *Memoirs*, 1:138–39; Bragg to Wheeler, March 9, 1863, Letter Book, Bragg Papers, WRHS; *Montgomery Daily Mail*, April 2, 1863. A March 22, 1863, article

in the *Chattanooga Daily Rebel* refers to sixty-three men of the 4th Alabama Cavalry being captured at Unionville. This clearly was a reference to the March 4 affair.

11. Bragg to Wheeler, March 9, 1863 (three separate letters), and Bragg to Wharton, April 4, 1863, Letter Book, Bragg Papers, WRHS; *OR*, 23(2):660.

12. Powell, *Failure in the Saddle*, 316–17.

13. Ramage, *Rebel Raider*, 152–53; Brent Diary, March 22, 1863, Bragg Papers, WRHS; *Nashville Union*, April 5, 1863.

14. Ramage, *Rebel Raider*, 155–56; Longacre, *Cavalry of the Heartland*, 218–19; *OR*, 23(1):204–14; Duke, *History of Morgan's Cavalry*, 382–89; Ed Porter Thompson, *Orphan Brigade*, 205.

15. *OR*, 23(2):824; Ramage, *Rebel Raider*, 156–57.

16. *Mobile Advertiser & Register*, April 29, 1863; Rennolds Diary, July 2, 1863, UT; Tower, *Carolinian Goes to War*, 74; Bunting, letters to the editor, *Tri-Weekly Telegraph*, January 6, March 11, 1863, in Cutrer, *Our Trust*, 110, 128; Frank Batchelor to wife, January 10, 1863, in Rugeley, *Batchelor-Turner Letters*, 44.

17. Duke, *History of Morgan's Cavalry*, 401; Robert Bunting, letter to the editor, *Tri-Weekly Telegraph*, May 12, 1863, in Cutrer, *Our Trust*, 158; MacMurphey Diary, May 14, 16, 1863, CCNBP.

18. *Mobile Advertiser & Register*, April 22, May 31, 1863; *OR*, 23(2):613, 733, 758; West Walker to wife, March 26, June 22, July 31, 1863, Walker Letters, SRNBP. The *Richmond Examiner* of January 27, 1863, ran an editorial expressing a similar concern—there was simply too much cavalry in the Confederacy. Two conscript cavalry companies were dismounted and placed in Smith's Brigade. See Rogers Memorandum Book, January 25, 1863, SHC.

19. *Shelbyville (Tenn.) Banner*, February 15, 1863, as quoted in *Memphis Appeal*, February 24, 1863; *Chattanooga Daily Rebel*, February 27, 1863 (Shelbyville ball); Smith, *French's War Journal*, 68, 69, 71, 85; *Mobile Advertiser & Register*, April 29, 1863; Dodson, *Campaigns of Wheeler*, 80–85.

20. Fremantle, *Three Months*, 161–63.

21. *OR*, 23(2):762; Hypolite Oladowski to T. M. Jones, August 6, 1863, Letters Sent, chap. 4, NARG; Inspection Report, CCNBP.

22. Castel, *Victors in Blue*, 205–6; Powell, "Incubator of Innovation," 99–105; Daniel, *Days of Glory*, 241–42; Schillar, "Two Tales of Tennessee," 82–83.

23. *OR*, 23(2):733, 17(2):832; Woodworth, *Jefferson Davis*, 207; *Savannah Republican*, March 13, 1863.

24. *Mobile Advertiser & Register*, March 8, 1863; *Savannah Republican*, March 5, 1863.

25. *OR*, 23(1):116–17, 122–24, 221, 222, 224; and (2):667; Hartje, *Van Dorn*, 279–81, 285–89; Crabb, *All Afire to Fight*, 146, 152; *Mobile Advertiser & Register*, May 14, 1863; Hale, *Third Texas Cavalry*, 165–67; Griscom, *Fighting with Ross' Texas*, 59–60; Welcher and Liggett, *Coburn's Brigade*, 58–64, 66–68; *Memphis Appeal*, March 21, 1863; Lowe, *Texas Cavalry Officer's*, 236; *Memphis Appeal*, March 21, May 9, 1863.

26. Connelly, *Autumn of Glory*, 122–24; Woodworth, *Six Armies in Tennessee*, 28–29;

Powell, *Failure in the Saddle*, xxix–xxx; Welsh, *Medical Histories*, 232; Cutrer, *Our Trust*, 160.

27. Carter, *Tarnished Cavalier*, 178–79; Longacre, *Cavalry of the Heartland*, 207–8.

28. Longacre, *Cavalry of the Heartland*, 181–92; John McCreight to wife, May 10, 1863, in Fleming, *Ninth Tennessee*, 154. The amazing details of the true story were related to Carter in 1967 by Kimmel's son, Col. Manning M. Kimmel Jr. His father revealed the story to him in 1913.

29. Wills, *Confederacy's Greatest Cavalryman*, 122–27.

CHAPTER 9

1. *OR*, 20(2):385, 386, 392–93, 412; William C. Davis, *Diary*, 64; Brent Diary, November 6, 1862, Bragg Papers, WRHS; *Knoxville Daily Register*, December 16, 1862.

2. *OR*, 20(2):489, 501, 503; and ser. 4, 2:280.

3. *OR*, 23(2):749; and ser. 4, 2:563–64.

4. Alex McGowin to parents, January 11, 1863, McGowin Letters, SRNBP; *Charleston Courier* as quoted in *Winchester (Tenn.) Daily Bulletin*, February 25, 1863; Crittenden to wife, February 1, 1863, Crittenden Letters, AU; Mitchell, "Civil War Letters," 55; Walker to wife, February 22, 1863, in William Lee White and Runion, *Great Things*, 48. See also James Mitchell to father, March 21, 1863, Mitchell Letters, ADAH; and Carruth to "Dear Friend," February 1, 1863, in Skellie, *Lest We Forget*, 2:478.

5. *OR*, 20(2):494; and 23(2):618, 623, 629, 636; Ives to sister, January 14, 1863, in Cabaniss, *Civil War Journal*, 32. See also Michael Royster to wife, January 27, 1863, Royster Letters, UFLA; and Bragg to William Mackall, February 14, 1863, Bragg Papers, SHC.

6. Jones to wife, January 20, February 7, 1863, Jones Letters, ADAH.

7. Orders Received, entry P11013, NARG.

8. *OR*, 23(1):496, 501, 503; 23(2):618, 622, 642, 654, 749; 52(2):426; and ser. 4, 2:361, 387, 431, 433, 434, 435, (3):445; Frank Batchelor to wife, December 1, 1862, in Rugeley, *Batchelor-Turner Letters*, 36 ("We expected"); Hughes and Stonesipher, *Pillow*, 260–63; Fremantle, *Three Months*, 144 ("Union hole"); *Memphis Appeal*, February 13, 1863; Weitz, *More Damning Than Slaughter*, 150–51. The claim of nineteen conscripts in the army was either an exaggeration or outright incorrect. The Talladega, Alabama, office alone furnished the army with 200 soldiers in early February 1863. See *OR*, ser. 4, 3:436.

9. *OR*, ser. 4, 2:371; *Nashville Union*, January 27, 1863; *Mobile Advertiser & Register*, May 10, 1863.

10. *Fayetteville (Tenn.) Observer*, April 30, 1863; Fielder diary, January 28, 1863, in Franklin, *Civil War Diaries*, 104; Ambrose Doss to wife, February 19, 1863, Doss Letters, SRNBP; Crittenden to wife, February 20, 1863, Crittenden Letters, AU.

11. *OR* 23(2):758; Mitchell to father, March 21, 1863, Mitchell Letters, ADAH; *Chattanooga Daily Rebel*, February 17, March 18, 1863; *Nashville Union*, April 15, 1863.

12. *Chattanooga Daily Rebel*, February 28, 1863; *Macon Telegraph*, April 28, 1863 (Stones River wounded exchanged); *OR* 20(1):503, 23(2):749; Dillon Diary, April 5–12,

1863, UMISS. Some of the returning prisoners were in such poor health that they had to be discharged. Gustavus W. Dyer, *Veterans Questionnaires*, 1:185; *Nashville Union*, April 9, 1863 (400 exchanged prisoners).

13. *OR*, ser. 4, 3:100–102; Holmes diary, March 3, 1863, in Dennis, *Kemper County Rebel*, 62, 70; Fowler, *Mountaineers in Gray*, 102; Cathey and Waddey, *"Forward My Brave Boys!,"* 257–420.

14. "Consolidated Report of Strength and Transportation, March 1863," Bragg Papers, WRHS; *OR*, 23(2):778; A. M. Clayton to mother, January 18, 1863, accessed August 1, 2016, natedsanders.com/Letters-From-The-39th-Alabama-Infantry, ; Holmes diary, April 20, 1863, in Dennis, *Kemper County Rebel*, 89.

15. Treadwell to wife, April 29, 1863, Treadwell Letters, ADAH; Crittenden to wife, April 15, 1863, Crittenden Letters, AU.

16. *OR*, ser. 4, 2:741–43.

17. *OR*, ser. 4, 2:670–71, 695–96.

18. Weitz, *More Damning Than Slaughter*, 80–81.

19. Weitz, *Higher Duty*, 98–99, 116, 130–31.

20. *Nashville Union*, January 22, 1863; Fleming, *Ninth Tennessee*, 188–293; Fowler, *Mountaineers in Gray*, 108–9; Hardy, *Fifty-Eighth North Carolina*, 56.

21. A. T. Gray to father, March 14, 1863, Gray Letters, SRNBP.

22. *Chattanooga Daily Rebel*, January 23, 1863; Treadwell to wife, April 5, 9, 1863, Treadwell Letters, ADAH; *New York Times*, May 1, 1863.

23. Parrott to wife, April 12, 1863, www.articlelibrary.info/Reference/civilwar_civil war_civil_war.sourcebook.htm (site discontinued); Gilliland to wife, May 17, 1863, Gilliland Letters, MVC; Warrick to wife, May 4, 1863, Warrick Letters, ADAH.

24. Boles to wife, April 17, 1863, www.tennessee-scv.org/camp155/Dr.Bradley.civil war.

25. Weitz, *More Damning Than Slaughter*, 135.

26. Weitz, 173; McGowin to brother, July 13, 1863, McGowin Letters, SRNBP; *OR*, 23(2):564; "Tri-Monthly Report of Wheeler's Cavalry, July 10, 1863," accessed October 1, 2016, www.horsesoldier.com/products/documents-and-paper-goods/959 (site discontinued); *OR*, 23(1):610.

27. D. D. Griffin to wife, July 6, 1863, in Albertson, *Letters Home to Minnesota*, n.p.

28. *OR*, 23(2):591; Beatty, *Citizen Soldier*, 294–95; Allen to ?, Allen Letters, sec. A, box 2, DU.

29. Cort to "Dear Friend," April 24, 1863, in Cort and Tomlinson, *"Dear Friends,"* n.p.; Bartholomew to sister, May 6, 1863, Bartholomew Letters, SRNBP.

30. McDonald to wife, July 7, 1863, accessed January 18, 2016, www.articlelibrary .info/Reference/civilwar_civilwar_sourcebook.htm (site discontinue); Jamison to wife, July 28, 1863, Jamison Letters, TSLA; Caldwell to father, July 14, 1863, Caldwell Letter, Vol. 4, WPA Civil War Letterbook, 58–59, TSLA; Crittenden to wife, July 9, 1863, Crittenden Letters, AU.

31. Wilson to wife, September 3, 1863, Wilson Letters, CCNBP; A. P. Adamson to

sister, August 30, 1863, in Abell and Gecik, *Sojourns of a Patriot*, 183; Brindley to sister, September 3, 1863, as quoted in Haughton, *Training, Tactics, and Leadership*, 122; Groce, *Mountain Rebels*, 106-7; *OR*, 30(1):232 (750 deserters).

32. George Lea to wife, August 18, 1863, in Skellie, *Lest We Forget*, 2:552, 555; Patton to wife, September 10, 1863, Patton Letters, SHC.

33. Floyd to Mary, October 8, 1863, in Givens, *Tennesseans in the Civil War*, 142; Bigbee to wife, November 1, 1863, Bigbee Letters, AU.

34. Holt to wife, September 8, 1862, in Partin, "Alabama Confederate Soldier's Report," 34.

35. Crittenden to wife, December 20, 1862, Crittenden Letters, AU.

36. Lowry and Laska, *Confederate Death Sentences*, 27, 40, 50; *Memphis Appeal*, January 5, 1863; Ed Porter Thompson, *Orphan Brigade*, 201-2; Ridley, "Camp Scenes around Dalton," 68; William C. Davis, *Orphan Brigade*, 147-48; Kirwan, *Johnny Green*, 59-61; *Rebel Banner*, December 27, 1862.

37. Norman to wife, December 25-26, 1862, Norman Letter, SRNBP. See also Crittenden to wife, December 26, 1862, Crittenden Letters, AU.

38. John Hurley to sister, May 22, 1863, Hurley Letters, VMI; Lowry and Laska, *Confederate Death Sentences*, 50-52; Coleman Diary, February 13, 1863, SHC; Rogers Memorandum Book, February 19, 1863, SHC. An example of leniency is that of three deserters from the 16th Tennessee, who were sentenced to sit astride an eight-foot-high wooded horse at two-hour increments for several days—painful to be sure, but not a death sentence. Gillum, *Sixteenth Volunteer Tennessee*, 2:159.

39. "Three Deserters," 128; John Reese to wife, March 26, 1863, Reese Letters, DU; Mussina Diary, January 7, 1863, EU. See also R. H. Richards to wife, March 19, 1863, accessed August 3, 2016, www-scv.org/ . . . /cwrc//Richards.html; Elliott, *Doctor Quintard*, 73-75; Rennolds Diary, June 12, 1863, UT; and Fremantle, *Three Months*, 158.

40. Joshua Callaway to wife, September 17, 1863, in Hallock, *Civil War Letters*, 132-33.

41. Augustus C. Abernathy to father, June 7, 1863, http://freepages.geneology.roots web.ancestry.com/~bandy/kestletter.html.

42. Sheppard, *By the Noble Daring*, 173-74 (McLeod); Warrick to wife, April 11, 1864, Warrick Letters, ADAH; Smith diary, March 22, 1864, in Garrett, *Diary*, 57; Walker to wife, April 10, 1864, in William Lee White and Runion, *Great Things*, 110; Christian M. Epperson to wife, May 8, 1864, Epperson Letters, LC.

43. Davenport Diary, May 4, 1864, TSLA; Brown Diary, May 4, 1864, GRPL; Daniel Kelly to wife, May 6, 1864, Kelly Letters, EU; Mitchell "Letters of a Confederate Surgeon," 5:167; *Our Southern Home*, August 10, 1899; Ridley, *Battles and Sketches*, 283-86; William Stephens to wife, May 7, 1864, Stephens Letters, EU; Lindsley, *Military Annals of Tennessee*, 478; Ferrell, *Holding the Line*, 182; Hardy, *Fifty-Eighth North Carolina*, 106-7; Benedict Semmes to wife, May 4, 1864, Semmes Letters, SHC; *Memphis Appeal*, May 6, 1864; Joseph Searcy to parents, May 14, 1864, James Searcy Letters, Searcy Family Papers, ADAH.

44. Sparkman Diary, December 31, 1863, CCNBP; Weitz, *Higher Duty*, 67, 71;

Weitz, *More Damning Than Slaughter*, 246, 262; *OR* 32(1):12–13; Dawes, "Confederate Strength," 281.

45. Clampitt, *Confederate Heartland*, 26–27; Brown to wife, February 5, 1864, Brown Letters, ADAH; Sparkman Diary, March 10, 1864, CCNBP.

46. Sheppard, *By the Noble Daring*, 169–70; *OR*, 31(3):855, 32(2):558; Taylor to wife, December 28, 1863, in Bloomquist and Taylor, *This Civil War*, 209–10; Dawes, "Confederate Strength," 281. See also *Chronicle & Sentinel*, January 1, 1863.

47. Rabb to wife, February 18, 1864, Rabb Letters, EU; Brown to wife, January 8, March 20, 1864, Brown Letters, ADAH.

48. Charles Roberts to wife, March 7, 1864, Roberts Letters, UMISS; Cate, *Two Soldiers*, 34–36.

49. Pickett, "Re-Enlistments by the Confederates," 171; "Re-Enlistments in the Army," 351–52; "More About Re-Enlistments," 399–400; Hughes, *Civil War Memoir*, 158–59; *Memphis Appeal*, January 20, April 20, 1864; Walker to wife, January 24, February 7, 1864, in William Lee White and Runion, *Great Things*, 96–97; Brown to wife, February 12, 1864, Brown Letters, ADAH.

50. Lea to cousin, January 25, 1864, in Skellie, *Lest We Forget*, 2:626; Lynn to wife, February 1, 1864, Lynn Letters, SHC; Letterman to parents, April 3, 1864, in Wommack, *Call Forth*, 371; *Memphis Appeal*, January 19, 20, 26, 27, February 12, April 6, 20, 1864; Irvine Walker to wife, January 31, 1864, in William Lee White and Runion, *Great Things*, 96–97.

51. Patton to mother, January 23, 1864, Patton Letters, SHC; Crittenden to wife, February 21, 1864, Crittenden Letters, AU; Taylor to wife, February 5, 1864, in Bloomquist and Taylor, *This Civil War*, 221; Barber diary, January 20, 1864, in Ferrell, *Holding the Line*, 156; Thomas Newberry to father, January 21, 1864, in Mitchell, "Civil War Letters," 76; Hundley to wife, February 11, 1864, Hundley Letters, UALA.

52. Stewart's Corps, Army of Tennessee, September 20, 1864, collection 172, box 20, folder 8, TU.

CHAPTER 10

1. Flora, "'I Consider the Regiment,'" 134.

2. Tower, *Carolinian Goes to War*, 72; George W. Higgins to wife, March 1, 1863, in Bender, "Letters," n.p.; Holmes diary, January 8, 11, 1863, in Dennis, *Kemper County Rebel*, 42; *Chattanooga Daily Rebel*, January 23, 1863; *Memphis Appeal*, February 2, 1863; Rogers Memorandum Book, January 14, 1863, SHC; Dent to wife, January 14, 1863, Dent Letters, AU; John H. Hudson to wife, January 12, 1863, John H. Hudson Letters, accessed January 1, 2016, brendahardesty.com/Jan.-html; Newton Davis to wife, January 18, 22, 1863, Davis Letters, ADAH; Coleman Diary, January 27, 1863, SHC; Thomas Warrick to wife, April 8, 1863, Warrick Letters, ADAH; Crittenden to wife, January 14, 1863, to father, January 15, 1863, and to J. S. Bryant, January 29, 1863, Crittenden Letters, AU; Rennolds Diary, January 13, 15, 1863, UT; *Mobile Advertiser & Register*, February 27, 1863; Bush Diary, January 6, 10, 12, 14, 15, 27, 1863, CCNBP.

3. Bigbee to wife, February 3, 1863, Bigbee Letters, AU; "H. W.," 19th South Caro-

lina, letter to the editor, *Abbeville (S.C.) Press*, March 9, 1863; *Chattanooga Daily Rebel*, February 6, 12, 1863; Johnston Diary, February 28, 1863, FHS; Hannibal Paine to sister, February 4, 1863, Paine Letters, TSLA; Taylor to parents, February 12, 1863, Taylor Letters, Vol. 2, WPA Civil War Letterbook, 262, TSLA.

4. "M. H. S." letter to the editor, *Selma Morning Register*, January 27, 1863; Bell to wife, January 11, 1863, Bell Letters, DU; Roberts to wife, January 30, 1863, Roberts Letters, UMISS.

5. Sparkman Diary, January 14, 1863, CCNBP; Mussina Diary, January 7, 1863, EU (men staying in blankets); Rennolds Diary, January 25, February 22, 1863, UT; Coleman Diary, February 18, 1863, SHC; *Chattanooga Daily Rebel*, February 10, 1863; Edwards to mother, February 11, 1863, as quoted in Wommack, *Call Forth*, 263; Grammer Diary, January 27, 1863, MDAH (uprooted tree).

6. Crittenden to wife, February 16, 20, 1863, Crittenden Letters, AU; Smith diary, February 27, 1863, in Garrett, *Confederate Diary*, 49; Charles Ally diary, July 24, 1863, accessed August 16, 2016, www.articlelibrary.info/Reference/civilwar_civilwar_source book.htm (site discontinued).

7. "Claude" article in *Mobile Advertiser & Register*, February 18, 1863 (condition of roads); Anderson to wife, January 11, 1863, in Uhler, "Civil War Letters," 159; John Routt to wife, January 11, 1863, Routt Letters, Vol. 2, WPA Civil War Letterbook, 97-98, TSLA; Charles Roberts to wife, January 7, 1863, Roberts Letters, UMISS; John Davidson to wife, January 13, 1863, Davidson Letters, AHS; Michael Royster to wife, January 27, 1863, Royster Letters, UFLA; John Burk to wife, January 30, 1863, Burk Letters, SRNBP; *Selma Morning Register*, January 27, 1863, as quoted in Sheppard, *By the Noble Daring*, 109.

8. Lacey to cousin, January 30, 1863, Lacey Letter, PP; Ives to father, January 26, 1863, in Cabaniss, *Civil War Journal*, 37; Roberts to wife, February 12, 1863, Roberts Letters, UMISS; Irvine Walker to wife, January 29, 1863, in William Lee White and Runion, *Great Things*, 47; Johnston Diary, February 14, 1863, FHS; Hezekiah Rabb to wife, February 13, 1863, Rabb Letters, EU; Rogers Memorandum Book, February 17, 1863, SHC (Northwest Conspiracy); Crittenden to father, January 15, to wife, February 20, 1863, Crittenden Letters, AU; Magee Diary, February 21, 24, 1863, DU; Polk to wife, February 20, 1863, Polk Letter, Vol. 3, WPA Civil War Letterbook, 38-39, TSLA; *Southern Confederacy*, February 28, 1863.

9. Roberts to wife, January 7, 1863, Roberts Letters, UMISS; Davidson to wife, February 9, 1863, Davidson Letters, AHS; Pittman to wife, February 21, 1863, Pittman Letters, USMISS; Spears to wife, February 12, 1863, in Flora, "'I Consider the Regiment,'" 154. See also John T. Scott to "Miss Phil," January 29, 1863, Scott Letters, AU.

10. *Chattanooga Daily Rebel*, February 27, 1863; Callaway to wife, February 22, 1863, in Hallock, *Civil War Letters*, 71.

11. Holmes diary, March 3, 4, 1863, in Dennis, *Kemper County Rebel*, 62; William Jones, *Christ in Camp*, 573; Fielder diary, March 8, 1863, in Franklin, *Civil War Diaries*, 109; Rogers Memorandum Book, March 7, 1863, SHC; Brent Diary, March 14, 1863,

Bragg Papers, WRHS; *Southern Confederacy*, June 1, 1863; *Chattanooga Daily Rebel*, March 14, 1863 (high water levels).

12. Jones Diary, March 5, 1863, GPL; Semple to wife, March 6, 1863, Semple Letters, ADAH; Callaway to wife, March 9, 15, 17, 1863, in Hallock, *Civil War Letters*, 72, 74, 75; Bigbee to wife, March 31, 1863, Bigbee Letters, AU; Riggs to sister, April 18, 22, 1863, Riggs Letters, ADAH; Morgan to wife, April 26, 1863, blogs.baylor.edu/1862/04/09 /camp_corinth_april_9_1862.

13. Buck to sister, March 11, 1863, in Buck, *Dear Irvie, Dear Lucy*, 135–36; Joseph Sams to wife, March 17, 1863, Sams Letters, SHC; Brent Diary, March 23, 1863, Bragg Papers, WRHS (meat ration reduced); Isaac Thomas to wife, March 11, 1863, Thomas Letters and Diaries, GRPL; *Fayetteville (Tenn.) Observer*, March 19, 1983.

14. Crittenden to wife, March 20, 1863, Crittenden Letters, AU; Holmes diary, March 26, 1863, in Dennis, *Kemper County Rebel*, 73; Rennolds Diary, March 31, 1863, UT; *Abbeville (S.C.) Press*, March 27, 1863 (Lumsden's Battery); Reynolds to cousin, March 21, 1863, in Skellie, *Lest We Forget*, 2:638.

15. Coleman Diary, March 13, 1863, SHC; Rogers Memorandum Book, March 16, 1863, SHC; S. H. Dent to wife, March 17, 1863, Dent Letters, AU; Spence to wife, March 22, 1863, in Christ, *Being Shot At*, 55; Jones Diary, March 16, 1863, GPL; Irwin to family, March 23, 1863, Irwin Letters, TSLA.

16. Mayer Diary, March 27, 28, 1863, SRNBP; Beatty Diary, March 29–31, 1863, SHC; Moorman, "Moorman Memorandum," 69; Bigbee to father, March 31, 1863, and to wife, March 31, 1863, Bigbee Letters, AU; Rogers Memorandum Book, March 30, 31, 1863, SHC; Fielder diary, March 30, 1863, in Franklin, *Civil War Diaries*, 111; *Chattanooga Daily Rebel*, April 1, 1863.

17. *Southern Confederacy*, April 4, 1863.

18. Sparkman Diary, March 31, 1863, CCNBP.

19. Coleman Diary, April 1, 1863, SHC; Lumsden Diary, April 1, 1863, ADAH; Godwin to "Miss Bettie," April 5, 1863, Godwin Letters, CCNBP.

20. *Chattanooga Daily Rebel*, April 1, 1863; Joshua Callaway to wife, April 5, 7, 1863, in Hallock, *Civil War Letters*, 79, 82; S. H. Dent to wife, April 8, 1863, Dent Letters, AU; Alex Spence to parents, April 11, 12, 1863, in Christ, *Being Shot At*, 67; Thomas Patton to mother, April 18, 1863, Patton Letters, SHC; William Rogers to brother, April 17, 1863, Rogers Letters, SRNBP; John Davidson to wife, April 22, 1863, Davidson Letters, AHS; Coleman Diary, April 27, 1863, SHC; Holmes diary, April 18, 1863, in Dennis, *Kemper County Rebel*, 88; Jamison to wife, April 11, 1863, Jamison Letters, TSLA; Jim H. Buford to sister, April 12, 1863, Buford Letters, Brown Collection, UMISS; Parrott to wife, April 12, 1863, www.rootwebancestry.com/~tnoverto/docs/CivilWarLetters (site discontinued); *Columbus Weekly Enquirer*, April 21, 1863 ("ripe for the fight"); George W. Higgins to wife, April 5, 1863, in "Letters of George Washington Higgins," CCNBP; Marshall to wife, April 17, 1863, Marshall Letters, MSU.

21. Beatty Diary, May 5, 1863, SHC; H. M. Lynn to wife, January 18, 1863, Lynn Letters, SHC; John McCreight to sister, May 10, 1863, in Fleming, *Ninth Tennessee*,

154; Joshua Callaway to wife, May 10, 1863, in Hallock, *Civil War Letters*, 91; Mitchell to father, May 24, 1863, Mitchell Letters, ADAH; Thompson to wife, May 16, 1863, Thompson Letters, TSLA.

22. Joshua Callaway to wife, May 10, 14, 1863, in Hallock, *Civil War Letters*, 88, 90; John Biggs to sister, April 5, 1863, Biggs Letters, SHC; William C. Davis, *Orphan Brigade*, 168–69; *Fayetteville (Tenn.) Observer*, March 19, 1863.

23. Crittenden to wife, May 1, 1863, Crittenden Letters, AU; Callaway to wife, May 24, 1863, in Hallock, *Civil War Letters*, 89, 91; S. H. Dent to wife, March 18 (bathing), April 8, May 1, 1863, Dent Letters, AU; Jones Diary, March 22, 1863, GPL; *Mobile Advertiser & Register*, May 24, 1863; Irvine Walker to wife, May 17, 1863, in William Lee White and Runion, *Great Things*, 56; Douglas to wife, April 21, 1863, in Douglas, *Douglas' Texas Battery*, 65; Bush Diary, February 24, 18623, CCNBP; Kennedy to sister, June 20, 1863, Kennedy Letters, University of Southwestern Louisiana, Lafayette; *Montgomery Weekly Advertiser*, April 12, 1863.

24. Rennolds Diary, January 20, 1863, UT; "M. H. S." in *Selma Morning Register*, January 27, 1863; Saunders, letter to the editor, April 12, 1863, *Montgomery Weekly Advertiser*, April 22, 1863; Holmes diary, March 21, 1863, in Dennis, *Kemper County Rebel*, 70; Brannock to wife, January 24, 1863, Brannock Letters, Virginia Historical Society, Richmond.

25. Davis to wife, April 4, 14, 1863, Davis Letters, ADAH; Rennolds Diary, March 21, 23, 1863, UT; Rogers to parents, April 17, 1863, Rogers Letters, FLSA; Holmes diary, March 27, 1863, in Dennis, *Kemper County Rebel*, 74; Joshua Callaway to wife, March 19, 1863, in Hallock, *Civil War Letters*, 76; Dillon Diary, April 13, 1863, UMISS (cockfighting).

26. *Tri-Weekly Telegraph*, May 1, 1863; MacMurphey Diary, April 4, 1863, CCNBP; Dodd Diary, April 4, 1863, CCNBP.

27. Daniel Diary, March 20, 1863, USAMHI; Hay, *Cleburne and His Command*, 126; Joshua Callaway to wife, April 16, May 14, 1863, in Hallock, *Civil War Letters*, 83; *Mobile Advertiser & Register*, April 8, 1863. Captain Coleman mentioned fishing in the Duck River and catching "a good many trout." Coleman Diary, April 25, 1863, SHC.

28. Puckett to wife, February 10, 1863, Puckett Letters, UTX.

29. Jamison to wife, April 16, 1863, Jamison Letters, CCNBP; Callaway to wife, May 1, 1863, in Hallock, *Civil War Letters*, 85.

30. *Mobile Advertiser & Register*, May 30, 1863; Warrick to wife, March 22, 1863, Warrick Letters, ADAH; Callaway to wife, May 10, 1863, in Hallock, *Civil War Letters*, 88.

31. Thomas Warrick to wife, December 24, 1863, Warrick Letters, ADAH; Holmes diary, March 19, 20, 1863, in Dennis, *Kemper County Rebel*, 68–69; Joshua Callaway to wife, March 17, 1863, in Hallock, *Civil War Letters*, 75; Scurlock to brother, March 8, 1863, www.rootsweb.com.ancestry.com (site discontinued); Dillon Diary, April 16, 1863, UMISS; *Mobile Advertiser & Register*, February 28, 1863.

32. Tripp to wife, April 30, 1863, www.articlelibrary.info/Reference/civilwar_civil_war_sourcebook.htm (site discontinued); Rogers Memorandum Book, April 29, 31, May 1, 1863, SHC; Fielder diary, May 5, 7, 8, 1863, in Franklin, *Civil War Diaries*, 116;

Holmes diary, April 24, 1863, in Dennis, *Kemper County Rebel*, 91; Rennolds Diary, May 5, 1863, UT; Newberry to father, June 27, 1863, in Mitchell, "Civil War Letters," 73.

33. Johnston Diary, May 15, 1863, Bragg Papers, WRHS (target practice); Hughes, *Pride*, 94; Jones Diary, April 27–May 11, 1863, GPL; Douglas to wife, April 21, May 10, 1863, in Douglas, *Douglas' Texas Battery*, 65–66; Tower, *Carolinian Goes to War*, 73.

34. Rennolds Diary, April 27, 1863, UT; Rogers to parents, April 10, 1863, Rogers Letters, FLSA; *Mobile Advertiser & Register*, April 29, 1863; Robert Jamison to wife, April 21, 1863, Jamison Letters, TSLA.

35. Haughton, *Tactics, Training, and Leadership*, 116–17.

36. Rogers Memorandum Book, March 5, 1863, SHC; Coleman Diary, March 16, 1863, SHC; J. W. Ward to father, March 28, 1863, Ward Letters, EU.

37. Peterson, *Confederate Combat Commander*, 115.

38. Rennolds Diary, April 11, May 4, 1863, UT; Rogers Memorandum Book, April 6, 11, 1863, SHC; Oldham Diary, May 15, 1863, UT; Thomas Osborne to mother, April 10, 1863, in "Letters of Thomas D. Osborne," 6, CCNBP.

39. *Southern Confederacy*, May 31, 1863. See also R. B. Brown to James, April 15, 1863, Brown Letters, SHC. For similar optimistic comments, see Joseph O'Brien to sister, May 27, 1863, O'Brien Letters, CCNBP; and R. B. Pittman to wife, May 10, 1863, Pittman Letters, USMISS.

CHAPTER 11

1. Drew Gilpin Faust, *Southern Stories*, 95, 106, 97.

2. Beringer et al., *Why the South Lost*, 269–70, 276; Phillips, *Diehard Rebels*, 26, 28.

3. Routt to wife, January 11, 1863, Routt Letters, Vol. 3, WPA Civil War Letterbook, 97–99, TSLA; Hudson to wife, January 12, 1863, brendahardesty.com/HudsonLetters.html; Ward to sister, January 12, 1863, Ward Letters, GLC.

4. Ward to sister, July 11, 1862, Ward Letters, GLC.

5. *Richmond Dispatch*, March 27, 1863; Holmes diary, March 27, 1863, in Dennis, *Kemper County Rebel*, 73–74; Sparkman Diary, March 27, 1863, CCNBP; J. E. Scott to wife, January 18, 1863, Scott Letters, TSLA.

6. Coleman Diary, March 8, 1863, SHC; Smith diary, January 21, 1863, in Garrett, *Confederate Diary*, 46; *Columbus Daily Sun*, April 21, 1863; Prim, "Born Again," 251; Mitchell to father, January 18, 1863, Mitchell Letters, ADAH; Webb to wife, March 2, 1863, www.tngenweb.org/humphreys/thomas-martin-webb-letters. See also A. B. Flint to John Clark, February 24, 1863, Flint Letters, University of Arkansas, Fayetteville.

7. Roberts to wife, March 9, 1863, Roberts Letters, UMISS.

8. *Fayetteville (Tenn.) Observer*, June 4, 1863.

9. Prim, "Born Again," 252, 253; Newton Davis to wife, April 12, 1863, Davis Letters, ADAH; Callaway to wife, March 15, 1863, in Hallock, *Civil War Letters*, 74; *Chattanooga Daily Rebel*, March 27, 1863; Coleman Diary, March 8, 1863, SHC.

10. Cutrer, *Our Trust*, 162; Rennolds Diary, April 25, 1863, UT; Andrew J. Harris to mother, May 4, 1863, in Birchfield, "Civil War Letters," n.p.; Magee Diary, May 10, 1863, DU; Davidson to wife, May 10, 1863, Davidson Letters, AHS; Rogers Memoran-

dum Book, May 10, 1863, SHC; Coleman Diary, May 10, 1863, SHC; Michael Royster to wife, May 17, 1863, as quoted in Sheppard, *By the Noble Daring*, 67; Estes Diary, May 19, 1863, MC; Thomas Bigbee to wife, May 31, 1863, Bigbee Letters, AU; John Harris to mother, May 30, 1863, Harris Letters, LSU. See also Fred Davis to wife, June 12, 1863, and R. B. Pittman to wife, June 15, 1863, in Skellie, *Lest We Forget*, 2:506, 507; and Brannock to wife, May 19, 1863, Brannock Letters, Virginia Historical Society, Richmond.

11. Drew Gilpin Faust, *Southern Stories*, 24, 27-28, 100-101; Rable, *God's Almost Chosen People*, 99-100, 279, 24-25; Woodworth, *While God*, 16.

12. Bennett, *Narrative*, 280-81; Patton to wife, May 3, 1863, Patton Letters, SHC; Roberts to wife, May 3, 1863, Roberts Letters, UMISS; Rennolds Diary, May 3, 1863, UT; William Jones, *Christ in Camp*, 546, 547.

13. Bunting, letter to the editor, *Tri-Weekly Telegraph*, May 12, 1863, in Cutrer, *Our Trust*, 161; *Southern Presbyterian*, August 27, 1863, in Elliott, *Doctor Quintard*, 66.

14. Grammer Diary, May 1, 1863, MDAH; Bradford to mother, May 16, 1863, www .articlelibrary.info/Reference/civilwar_civil_war_sourcebook.htm (site discontinued); Royster to wife, March 17, 1863, Royster Letters, UFLA; Carruth to wife, June 19, 1863, in Skellie, *Lest We Forget*, 2:513.

15. McCreight to wife, May 10, 1863, in Fleming, *Ninth Tennessee*, 155. See also Rogers Memorandum Book, May 10, 1863, SRNBP; and Magee Diary, May 10, 1863, DU.

16. Fremantle, *Three Months*, 154; Fielder diary, May 1, 3, 1863, in Franklin, *Civil War Diaries*, 116; R. B. Pittman to wife, June 15, 1863, Pittman Letters, USMISS.

17. William Jones, *Christ in Camp*, 543, 575; Rennolds Diary, April 26, 1863, UT; Daniel Diary, May 10, 1863, USAMHI; Grammer Diary, May 3, 1863, MDAH; John McCreight to sister, May 10, 1863, in Fleming, *Ninth Tennessee*, 156.

18. William Jones, *Christ in Camp*, 546; Roberts to wife, May 3, 1863, Roberts Letters, UMISS; Holt to wife, July 19, 1863, in Partin, "Alabama Confederate Soldier's Report," 34; Polk, *Leonidas Polk*, 2:215; Glatthaar, *General Lee's Army*, 237-38, 240. For thoughts on death, see Partin, "Sustaining Faith," 436.

19. Rennolds Diary, April 19, May 6, 1863, UT.

20. Fitzgerald, *John B. McFerrin*, 271-73; Fielder diary, March 22, May 22, 1863, in Franklin, *Civil War Diaries*, 110, 119.

21. Nichols-Belt, *Onward Christian Soldiers*, 43-52; Elliott Diary, May 31, 1863, GDAH; Elliott, *Doctor Quintard*, 69; Coleman Diary, May 16, 1863, SHC; Fremantle, *Three Months*, 154. For more of Elliott's sermons, see Drew Gilpin Faust, *Confederate Nationalism*, 23-24.

22. *Macon Telegraph*, June 3, 1863.

23. Bennett, *Narrative*, 281; Warner, *Generals in Gray*, 195; Patton to mother, May 3, 1863, Patton Letters, SHC (Lowrey); George W. Higgins to wife, May 23, 1863, in "Letters of George Washington Higgins," CCNBP.

24. Elliott, *Doctor Quintard*, 70-71; Elliott Diary, June 2, 1863, GDAH; Fremantle, *Three Months*, 162. Bragg's baptism was mentioned in the *Chattanooga Daily Rebel* of July 2, 1863, which noted that Polk was present.

25. Pittman to wife, May 14, June 15, 1863, in Skellie, *Lest We Forget*, 2:507.

26. *Biblical Recorder*, August 19, 1863; William Jones, *Christ in Camp*, 577; Kelly to "Miss Honnell," September 12, 1863, Kelly Letters, EU; Godwin to "Miss Bettie," September 18, 1863, Godwin Letters, CCNBP; Carruth to "Dear Friend," June 19, 1863, as quoted in Skellie, *Lest We Forget*, 2:513. Jason Phillips (*Diehard Rebels*, 9, 28) concluded that the "diehards" were particularly moved by the revivals: "For devout Christians, the cause of victory was transparent: God delivered Chickamauga to the Rebels because they rededicated themselves to them."

27. *Confederate Union*, February 16, 1864.

28. Adamson to sister, March 6, 1864, in Abell and Gecik, *Sojourns of a Patriot*, 212; Ferrell, *Holding the Line*, 171, 173, 175; Sheppard, *By the Noble Daring*, 176 (Inglis). See also Washington Ives to father, April 3, 1863, in Cabaniss, *Civil War Journal*, 63.

29. Crittenden to wife, April 4, 1863, Crittenden Letters, AU; Weaver to sister, May 3, 1864, Weaver Letters, EU.

30. Gay, *Life in Dixie*, 80–85; Edward Brown to wife, April 27, 1863, Brown Letters, ADAH; Woodworth, *While God*, 214.

31. Daniel, *Soldiering*, 122.

32. Phillips, *Diehard Rebels*, 29; McPherson, *For Cause and Comrades*, 76; Woodworth, *While God*, 241.

33. Brown to wife, May 1, 1864, Brown Letters, ADAH.

CHAPTER 12

1. *OR*, 23(1):267, 276–77; *Chattanooga Daily Rebel*, April 29, May 2, 1863; Bradley, *Tullahoma*, 43–44; John Davidson to wife, May 10, 1863, Davidson Letters, AHS.

2. *OR*, 23(2):790, 791, 796–97; *Chattanooga Daily Rebel*, May 13, 1863; Absolom H. Harrison to wife, undated but probably April 1862, http://www.civilwarhome.com /letters.htm; Stausel to wife, April 27, 1863, Stausel Letters, UALA. Bradley (*Tullahoma*, 42) suggested that Bragg should have established a secondary line at the Elk River between the Allisonia Bridge and the Bethpage Bridge two miles upriver.

3. Hughes, *Liddell's Record*, 122; Irving Buck to sister, May 19, 1863, in Buck, *Dear Irvie, Dear Lucy*, 150; Hughes, *Hardee*, 155, 314; Coleman Diary, May 23–24, 1863, SHC.

4. *OR*, 23(2):791; Fremantle, *Three Months*, 145; Stout, "Reminiscences," Bragg Papers, WRHS; Beatty Diary, May 1, 1863, SHC.

5. Johnston, "Jefferson Davis," 478; William C. Davis, *Jefferson Davis*, 502.

6. Johnston, "Jefferson Davis," 477, 481–82; Johnston to Mackall, June 7, 1863, Mackall Letters, SHC; Elliott, *Doctor Quintard*, 63. William C. Davis (*Jefferson Davis*, 503) insisted that the president had ample reason to replace Bragg, but the only alternative would have been Beauregard. "Davis's animosity toward this one general continued to influence, perhaps even direct, the course of war in the West. Davis's unhappy and largely unwilling adherence to Joseph E. Johnston would be his greatest mistake of 1863, and one of his greatest in the war."

7. *OR*, 23(2):847, 848, 849; Johnston Diary, May 24, 1863, FHS.

8. William C. Davis, *Breckinridge*, 365; Ed Porter Thompson, *Orphan Brigade*, 206–7; Jackman diary, May 24, 1863, in William C. Davis, *Diary*, 74–75; William C. Davis, *Orphan Brigade*, 173.

9. Johnston Diary, April 21, May 19, 1863, FHS; *Macon Telegraph*, April 28, 1863; Collins, *Unwritten History*, 131; Norman D. Brown, *One of Cleburne's Command*, 42–43, 45n3; *Rome (Ga.) Tri-Weekly Courier*, May 15, 1863. The 9th Alabama Battalion of Clayton's Brigade, which later arrived from Mobile, I estimate at 400. In estimating Breckinridge's strength, I have deducted an estimated 400 from the 20th Tennessee. Johnston claimed that he received only 2,500 effective cavalry in Jackson's Division, but the present-for-duty strength was 900 more. For strength estimates, see *OR*, 23(2):733, 846, 873; and 52(2):472.

10. Elliott, *Soldier of Tennessee*, 83–86.

11. Connelly, *Autumn of Glory*, 110; *OR*, 23(2):378–79, 873. In calculating Federal figures, I used only the strength of Rosecrans's movable army, the army that Bragg would potentially have point of contact with on the battlefield.

12. Johnston Diary, May 12, 1863, FHS; *Chattanooga Daily Rebel*, May 13, 1863.

13. Hallock, *Braxton Bragg*, 16 ("better than"), 25 (June 29); Hughes, *Liddell's Record*, 128; *OR*, 23(1):623 (Hardee to Polk); Elliott, *Doctor Quintard*, 76.

14. Hallock, *Braxton Bragg*, 15 (Rosecrans: 82,000, Bragg: 55,000); Kolakowski, *Stones River and Tullahoma*, 108–9 (Bragg: 43,000); Kniffen, "Maneuvering Bragg," 635–36 (Rosecrans: 50,617, Bragg: 46,665); Powell, *Chickamauga Campaign*, 1:52 (Rosecrans: 65,000, Bragg: 50,000); Brewer, "Tullahoma Campaign" (Rosecrans: 70,000, Bragg: 45,000). For Bragg's infantry and artillery strength, I used the June 10 return in *OR*, 23(2):873. To this I added the present-for-duty strength of Clayton's and Churchill's brigades. For the cavalry total I used the July 10 return, which took into account Morgan's departure for Kentucky. See *OR*, 23(1):586. Giving allowances for Wheeler's casualties sustained between June 24 and July 9, I place his strength at the beginning of the campaign at about 5,300. For Rosecrans's strength I added 6,700 infantry of Granger's reserve corps. A trimonthly report from July 10, 1863, of Wharton's and Martin's brigades listed 3,172 and 1,546 present, respectively. Tri-Monthly Return, July 10, 1863, www.horsesoldier.com/products/documents-and-paper-goods/959/.

15. *OR*, 23(2):862.

16. Brewer, "Tullahoma Campaign," 61–62, 68; Alford, "Tullahoma Campaign," 20.

17. *Mobile Advertiser & Register*, June 30, 1863.

18. Longacre, *Soldier to the Last*, 103 (criticism); Connelly, *Autumn of Glory*, 102 (criticism); Woodworth, "Braxton Bragg," 160–61 (criticism); Dodson, *Campaigns of Wheeler*, 85–86; Powell and Friedrichs, *Maps of Chickamauga*, 4. Wheeler had undoubtedly encouraged the raid, but the decision was Bragg's. Brent unfortunately took a leave of absence due to illness, and his vital diary is silent on the events at army headquarters.

19. Bradley, *Tullahoma*, 41; *OR*, 23(1):459, 602–3, 612; Johnston Diary, May 16, 1863, FHS; Roth, "Tullahoma Campaign," 51; Elliott, *Soldier of Tennessee*, 91–92; Furqueron, "Fight or a Footrace," 85; *Chattanooga Daily Rebel*, July 3, 1863. See also *Columbus*

Weekly Enquirer, July 7, 1863; *Chattanooga Daily Rebel*, July 26, 1863; Connelly, *Autumn of Glory*, 119; and Brewer, "Tullahoma Campaign," 61–62. Hardee simply advised Stewart to keep an eye on the column reportedly headed toward Manchester and, if heavily pressed at Beech Grove, to fall back on Wartrace. Woodworth (*Six Armies in Tennessee*, 23) was slightly critical of Stewart, stating that "his inexperience showed."

20. Woodworth, *Six Armies in Tennessee*, 26.

21. Bradley, "Tullahoma Campaign," 40, 41–42, 55; *OR*, 23(1):587–89, 594–95, 599.

22. Hughes, *Liddell's Record*, 127.

23. Woodworth, "Braxton Bragg," 163–66; *OR*, 23(1):618, (2):760–61.

24. Hess (*Braxton Bragg*, 146–47) uses Bragg's plan as evidence that the general was clearly not indecisive, and he blames Hardee and Polk for their failure to support it. I believe that Bragg's plan was not as clearly developed as Woodworth and Hess claim nor did it factor in potential problems.

25. *OR*, 23(1):583, 618; and (2):886.

26. *OR*, 23(1):536, 537, 558–59; *Memphis Appeal*, June 30, 1863; Dubose, *General Joseph Wheeler*, 175–76; Knox Miller to Cellie, July 10, 1863, in McMurry, *Uncompromising Secessionist*, 141–42; Rex Miller, *Wheeler's Favorites*, 8.

27. *Chattanooga Daily Rebel*, July 3, 1863.

28. Poulter, "But Then Again," 36–38, 82–83; Bradley, "Tullahoma," 50; *OR*, 23(1):461, 621; *Chattanooga Daily Rebel*, June 28, 1863 (advance of Buckner's troops). *Atlas to Accompany the Official Records*, plate 35.1, shows the crossings of the Elk as follows: Morris Ferry, Jones Ford, Bethpage Bridge, Gossage Ford, Allisonia Bridge, Island Ford (or Rock Creek Ford), Hinton's Mill (or Winchester Springs), and Lee's Ford.

29. Fielder diary, June 29, 1863, in Franklin, *Civil War Diaries*, 125; Beatty Diary, June 29, 1863, SHC; James Mitchell to father, June 30, 1863, Mitchell Letters, ADAH; *OR*, 23(1):621.

30. *OR*, 23(1):621–22.

31. *OR*, 23(1):622–23, (2):893–94; Woodworth, *Six Armies in Tennessee*, 40.

32. Hess, *Braxton Bragg*, 147–48.

33. *OR*, 23(1):624–27; Beatty Diary, June 30, 1863, SHC; *Columbus Weekly Enquirer*, July 14, 1863; *Savannah Republican*, July 5, 8, 1863.

34. *OR*, 23(1):424, 425, 592, 610, 614.

35. Magee Diary, July 9, 1863, DU; Bostick to sister, July 19, 1863, in Wills, *Old Enough to Die*, 92; McLaurin to sister, July 22, 1863, in Skellie, *Lest We Forget*, 2:537; Harlan to brother, July 13, 1863, Harlan Letters, CCNBP; Joshua Callaway to wife, July 11, 1863, in Hallock, *Civil War Letters*, 110; A. M. Glazner to T. M. Shuford, August 17, 1863, Glazner Letters, CCNBP; Elliott, *Doctor Quintard*, 76. See also Jackman diary, July 8, 1863, in William C. Davis, *Diary*, 79; Bunting, letter to the editor, [unidentified newspaper], July 30, 1863, in Cutrer, *Our Trust*, 179; Dillon Diary, July 11, 1863, UMISS; Fielder diary, July 21, 1863, in Franklin, *Civil War Diaries*, 130; R. D. Jamison to wife, July 28, 1863, Jamison Letters, TSLA; and Beatty Diary, June 30, 1863, SHC.

CHAPTER 13

1. *OR*, 30 (4):520, 522, 525, 526, 529; Brent Diary, August 21, 1863, Bragg Papers, WRHS; Woodworth, *Six Armies in Tennessee*, 56.

2. Brent Diary, August 21, 1863, Bragg Papers, WRHS; *OR*, 30(4):518.

3. Brent Diary, August 24, 1863, Bragg Papers, WRHS; *OR*, 30(4):434, 532-35, 540; Elliott, *Soldier of Tennessee*, 114; William G. Robertson, "Chickamauga Campaign: The Fall," 23.

4. Woodworth, "'In Their Dreams,'" 51. Woodworth concluded that the linkup of Burnside's and Rosecrans's armies was so severe a threat "that Bragg simply could not afford to permit it. He had to play Rosecrans strong to the northeast of Chattanooga even at the expense of leaving a weak side to the southwest of town, where a Federal passage of the mountains and river would be less disastrous." See also Woodworth, *This Great Struggle*, 232. Woodworth was correct in his conclusion, but I fault Bragg for taking no offensive action in that sector.

5. Brent Diary, August 25-27, 1863, Bragg Papers, WRHS; Connelly, *Autumn of Glory*, 168; William G. Robertson, "Chickamauga Campaign: The Fall," 19.

6. Polk to wife, August 27, 1863, Polk Papers, US; *Chattanooga Daily Rebel* Chickamauga article, as quoted in *Memphis Appeal*, September 2, 1863; Brent Diary, August 28, 1863, Bragg Papers, WRHS; *OR*, 30(4):561.

7. *OR*, 30(4):554; Brent Diary, August 28, 1863, Bragg Papers, WRHS.

8. Irving Buck to Lucy, August 29, 1863, in Buck, *Dear Irvie, Dear Lucy*, 179; *OR*, 30(4):563-64; Tower, *Carolinian Goes to War*, 92; Hill, "Chickamauga," 641.

9. Brent Diary, August 29, 1863, Bragg Papers, WRHS; "Memo Furnished by Col. B. J. Hill, August 29, 1863," Bragg Papers, WRHS; and *OR*, 30(2):27. Fortunately all of the cars of the East Tennessee & Georgia Railroad were safely removed to Dalton. See *Atlanta Intelligencer*, September 10, 1863.

10. Brent Diary, August 29, 1863, Bragg Papers, WRHS; *OR*, 30(4):564; *Chattanooga Daily Rebel* as quoted in *Memphis Appeal*, September 2, 1863.

11. *OR*, 30(4):567, 570, 571; Hess, *Knoxville Campaign*, 14; Brent Diary, August 30, 1863, Bragg Papers, WRHS; *Richmond Examiner*, September 14, 1863; Powell, *Chickamauga Campaign*, 1:82; William G. Robertson, "Chickamauga Campaign: The Fall," 21.

12. Shook, "Timely Information," 310; *OR*, 30(2):137, 27, 579, 574; Brent Diary, August 31, September 1, 1863, Bragg Papers, WRHS. Hill, in his official report, indicated that the civilian event occurred on the thirtieth and that this is what prompted Bragg to withdraw Buckner from Loudon. Bragg, however, wrote that the incident occurred "on the last of August." The incident in question was almost certainly the jarring news mentioned by both Mackall and Brent. William G. Robertson ("Chicamauga Campaign, McLemore's Cove," 23) claims the 2:00 A.M. dispatch was the one written by Thomas Mauldin three hours earlier. He may well be correct, but that would mean a sixteen-hour ride in darkness in three hours—a remarkable feat.

13. *OR*, 30(2):27, 27(4):564; Bunting article of August 11, 1863, in Cutrer, *Our Trust*, 183; Mackall to Bragg, August 28, 1863, Letter Book, Bragg Papers, WRHS.

14. Brent Diary, September 1, 2, 1863, Bragg Papers, WRHS; *OR*, 30(4):580. For

criticism of Wheeler, see Powell, *Failure in the Saddle*, 40–44; Longacre, *Cavalry of the Heartland*, 236; and Connelly, *Autumn of Glory*, 169–70. Interestingly, both Hazen and Minty expressed concern about a raid in their rear by Forrest by crossing the river by way of Harrison. See Wyeth, *Forrest*, 222. I posed the question of Forrest's failure to David Powell. His response: "Union accounts do show encounters with small parties of Rebels on the north bank, but nothing larger. Forrest seems to have sent small groups of scouts and spies, but he did not attempt to force the Union screen with larger effort. None of these scouts seem to have brought back information solid enough for Bragg to realize that Minty and Wilder were not backed by the full XXI Corps. What is in the *OR* has Forrest misreading the situation." Powell, email to Daniel, June 20, 2015.

15. *OR*, 30(4):583; Hughes, *Liddell's Record*, 135–36; Brent Diary, September 4, 1863, Bragg Papers, WRHS.

16. *OR*, 30(4):540, 561; Hughes, *Liddell's Record*, 133; Powell, *Chickamauga Campaign*, 1:84.

17. *OR*, 30(4):594, 597, 601.

18. Wyeth, *Forrest*, 225.

19. *OR*, 30(4):601–2, 614–15; and 30(1):485, 887–88. The harshest criticism of Wheeler comes from Powell, *Chickamauga Campaign*, 1:88–90.

20. *OR*, 30(2):137; 30(4):621–22; and 30(3):459, 463; "Richmond Notes," September 7, 1863, Polk Papers, US; Oldham Diary, September 7, 1863, UT. Connelly (*Autumn of Glory*, 173) questioned whether leaving Buckner's Corps in the city would have been an option, but Peter Cozzens dismissed the idea and supported Bragg's decision to evacuate.

21. Connelly, *Autumn of Glory*, 144, 174–85.

22. Bridges, *Lee's Maverick General*, 203; Hess, *Braxton Bragg*, 157. For other evaluations, see Mendoza, "Censure," 78–81; and Woodworth, "'In Their Dreams,'" 65–66.

23. Clark, *Railroads in the Civil War*.

CHAPTER 14

1. Powell, *Failure in the Saddle*, 134–36.

2. Powell, 137; Daniel, "Jay's Mill," 54–55. I have based the times on Powell and Friedrichs, *Maps of Chickamauga*, 56.

3. Daniel, "Jay's Mill," 57; *Huntsville Daily Confederate*, September 25, 1863.

4. *OR*, 32(2):240, 251–52, 263, 273–74; Powell and Friedrichs, *Maps of Chickamauga*, 62–67.

5. William G. Robertson, "Chickamauga—Day One," 23–24; Losson, *Tennessee's Forgotten Warriors*, 102–3.

6. Dillon Diary, September 19, 1863, UMISS; Mendoza, *Chickamauga*, 76, 78–79; Losson, *Tennessee's Forgotten Warriors*, 104–7; *OR*, 30(2):89, 94–95, 101–3, 118, 361; Powell and Friedrichs, *Maps of Chickamauga*, 70–77. William G. Robertson ("Chickamauga—Day One," 40) nonetheless faulted Cheatham for his failure to press Union brigades as they arrived piecemeal.

7. *OR*, 30(2):400, 404, 405; Elliott, *Soldier of Tennessee*, 123–24; Powell, *Chickamauga Campaign*, 1:414–19.

8. Woodworth, *Deep Steady Thunder*, 47, 49–50.

9. Mendoza, *Chickamauga*, 94–97; Woodworth, *Chickamauga*, 28–34; Powell, *Chickamauga Campaign*, 1:544.

10. Hughes, *Liddell's Record*, 143–44; Powell, *Chickamauga Campaign*, 1:612–13.

11. Connelly, *Autumn of Glory*, 205–6; Powell, email to Daniel, June 6, 2016; Woodworth, *Six Armies in Tennessee*, 100–101.

12. *Memphis Appeal*, September 22, 23, 1863.

13. Woodworth, *Six Armies in Tennessee*, 103; Polk, *Leonidas Polk*, 2:255–56; Powell, *Chickamauga Campaign*, 2:29, 32; Mendoza, "Perfect Tornado," 104–5. Hess (*Braxton Bragg*, 162) wrote that Bragg "displayed distrust of Hill during the subordinate's short tenure with the Army of Tennessee."

14. William G. Robertson, "Bull of the Woods," 120–22.

15. The confused events of that night have been written about in a half dozen accounts. For the most detailed, see Powell, *Chickamauga Campaign*, 2:33–38; and Connelly, *Autumn of Glory*, 211–16. See also Bridges, *Lee's Maverick General*, 206–16; and William G. Robertson, "Chickamauga—Day Two," 6–7. The Pollock Lee story has long been dismissed by historians.

16. Mendoza, *Chickamauga*, 104–9.

17. William G. Robertson, *Staff Ride*, 173 (weather); William G. Robertson, "Chickamauga—Day Two," 20; William C. Davis, *Breckinridge*, 373; Russell K. Brown, *To the Manner Born*, 174–75; Mendoza, *Chickamauga*, 123; Powell and Friedrichs, *Maps of Chickamauga*, 164.

18. *OR*, 30(2):198–99, 203–5; William C. Davis, *Orphan Brigade*, 190–91; Woodworth, *Chickamauga*, 52–53; Woodworth, *Deep Steady Thunder*, 70; Mendoza, *Chickamauga*, 122.

19. William G. Robertson, "Chickamauga—Day Two," 23; Connelly, *Autumn of Glory*, 222; Powell, email to Daniel, June 3, 2016.

20. Powell, *Chickamauga Campaign*, 2:223–26.

21. Haughton, *Training, Tactics, and Leadership*, 128; Mendoza, *Chickamauga*, 128.

22. Daniel, *Days of Glory*, 330; Powell and Friedrichs, *Maps of Chickamauga*, 192–93; Woodworth, *Chickamauga*, 70–71; Powell, *Chickamauga Campaign*, 2:256 ("Go ahead").

23. Joshua Callaway to wife, September 24, 1863, in Hallock, *Civil War Letters*, 136; *OR*, 30(2):431; Tower, *Carolinian Goes to War*, 98–99, 102.

24. Powell, *Chickamauga Campaign*, 2:308–9, 445–46.

25. Daniel, *Cannoneers in Gray*, 108; Powell, *Failure in the Saddle*, 156–57.

26. Woodworth, *Deep Steady Thunder*, 91–93; Powell and Friedrichs, *Maps of Chickamauga*, 220–21.

27. William G. Robertson, "Chickamauga—Day Two," 44; Hallock, *Braxton Bragg*, 80.

28. William G. Robertson, "Chickamauga—Day Two," 47; *OR*, 30(2):304–5.

29. Powell, *Chickamauga Campaign*, 2:695–96; Connelly, *Autumn of Glory*, 225.

30. Woodworth, *Six Armies in Tennessee*, 132; Hallock, *Braxton Bragg*, 80–82; William G. Robertson, "Chickamauga—Day Two," 49; Connelly, *Autumn of Glory*, 229. For postwar accounts see Longstreet, *From Manassas to Appomattox*, 458; and Hill, "Chickamauga," 662.

31. William G. Robertson, "Chickamauga—Day Two," 49; Livermore, *Numbers and Losses*, 106.

32. Anderson, *Parson's Texas Cavalry Brigade*, 122; Ives to parents, September 27, 1863, in Cabaniss, *Civil War Journal*, 44; Callaway to wife, September 24, 1863, in Hallock, *Civil War Letters*, 138.

33. Castel, *Winning and Losing*, 72; Andrews, *South Reports*, 352–55; Woodworth, *This Great Struggle*, 238; Bresnahan, *Revisioning the Civil War*, 156, 158; Murray and Hsieh, *Savage War*, 345–46. Historians have overwhelmingly concluded that Chickamauga was a hollow victory for Bragg and that even a rapid pursuit would probably have not led to a decisive victory.

34. *OR*, 30(2):54; Bragg to Davis, September 25, 1863, in Crist, *Papers*, 9:404–5; Polk to Bragg, September 28, 1863, in Polk, *Leonidas Polk*, 2:292–94.

35. *OR*, 30(2):67–68, 30(4):705–6, 52(2):549; Longstreet, *From Manassas to Appomattox*, 464; Mackall to wife, October 9, 1863, in Mackall, *Son's Recollections*, 182. Historians have long recognized Longstreet's grasping desire to replace Bragg. See Connelly, *Autumn of Glory*, 238; Woodworth, *Six Armies in Tennessee*, 51; and Symonds, "War and Politics," 162–64.

36. Brent Diary, September 26, 1863, Bragg Papers, WRHS; Polk to Davis, September 27, 1863, in Crist, *Papers*, 9:410; Hess, *Braxton Bragg*, 173.

37. Urquhart, "Bragg's Advance and Retreat," 608; Brent Diary, September 29, 1863, Bragg Papers, WRHS; *OR*, 30(2):55; Symonds, "War and Politics," 162.

38. *Memphis Appeal*, October 19, 1863; William C. Davis, *Jefferson Davis*, 318; *OR*, 30(4):727, 742–43; and 52(2):534–35; William Mackall to wife, October 9, 1863, in Mackall, *Son's Recollections*, 182; Bridges, *Lee's Maverick General*, 240.

39. As quoted in Hallock, *Braxton Bragg*, 92.

40. Woodward, *Mary Chesnut's Civil War*, 482; *OR*, 30(4):728.

41. *OR*, 30(2):66; Bridges, *Lee's Maverick General*, 234–37; Symonds, "War and Politics," 164–65; William C. Davis, *Breckinridge*, 382.

42. William C. Davis, *Breckinridge*, 381; Connelly, *Autumn of Glory*, 240; Losson, *Tennessee's Forgotten Warriors*, 113; Robert Myers to brother, October 14, 1863, Myers Letter, CCNBP.

43. Brent Diary, October 8, 1863, Bragg Papers, WRHS; Mackall to wife, October 5, 1863, in Mackall, *Son's Recollections*, 182.

44. Hughes, *Liddell's Record*, 151–52.

45. *OR*, 52(2):538; Brent Diary, October 5, 1863, Bragg Papers, WRHS; William C. Davis, *Jefferson Davis*, 518–19; Mackall to wife, October 9, 1863, in Mackall, *Son's Recollections*, 183.

46. Beasley, "Annals," 237; Johnston to wife, October 1863, Johnston Letters, TU; Cooper, *Jefferson Davis*, 491; *Memphis Appeal*, October 18, 1863; William C. Davis,

Jefferson Davis, 318; *OR*, 30(4):727, 742–43; and 52(2):534; Mackall to wife, October 9, 1863, in Mackall, *Son's Recollections*, 182.

47. *Memphis Appeal*, October 19, 1863; Neal to father, October 12, 1863, Neal Letters, EU; Watson Diary, October 10, 1863, CCNBP; Anderson, *Parson's Texas Cavalry Brigade*, 123; Bullock to wife, October 11, 1863, Bullock Letters, GDAH; Jackman diary, November 10, 1863, in William C. Davis, *Diary*, 91.

48. Mackall to wife, October 10, 1863, in Mackall, *Son's Recollections*, 183; *Mobile Advertiser & Register*, November 24, 1863.

49. Buck, *Cleburne and His Command*, 155–56; Longstreet, *From Manassas to Appomattox*, 465; Mackall to wife, October 10, 1863, in Mackall, *Son's Recollections*, 183–84; Symonds, "War and Politics," 168; Woodworth, *Jefferson Davis*, 242; Crist, *Papers*, 10: 530. Woodworth blamed the horrid state of affairs on Davis, who allowed "Polk and his band of malcontents to undermine Bragg." Hess (*Braxton Bragg*, 212) concurred: "Insisting on keeping Bragg in place while not punishing the dissidents, Davis created an insurmountable difficulty for Bragg."

50. *OR*, 30(4):735, 745; Brent Diary, October 10, 1863, Bragg Papers, WRHS; Woodworth, *Jefferson Davis*, 242. In 1872, Davis wrote that he retained Bragg because the conference convinced him that there was no better selection. Hallock, *Braxton Bragg*, 99. Symonds (*Stonewall of the West*, 241) was perhaps too defensive of Cleburne when he wrote that the Irishman did not openly express his views. Woodworth (*Jefferson Davis*, 241) offered the best rationale for the meeting: "Apparently Davis reasoned that the reported hostility to Bragg was greatly exaggerated and that even if some of the generals had been engaging in loose talk here and there, they would surely profess loyalty to Bragg in his presence and the president's."

51. Connelly, *Autumn of Glory*, 249; Mackall to wife, October 12, 1863, in Mackall, *Son's Recollections*, 184–85; *OR*, 30(2):148.

52. *OR*, 30(2):149; Bridges, *Lee's Maverick General*, 240, 242–52; William C. Davis, *Jefferson Davis*, 521. William C. Davis believed that Hill became the victim of a "shabby vendetta" by Bragg.

53. Andrews, *South Reports*, 360–61; *OR*, 30(4):744; Cooper, *Jefferson Davis*, 491; Parks, *Polk*, 351.

54. Brent Diary, October 21, 1863, Bragg Papers, WRHS; *OR*, 31(3):651.

55. *Richmond Dispatch*, October 7, 12, 20, November 3, 1863; *Memphis Appeal*, October 8, 1863.

CHAPTER 15

1. Lanny K. Smith, *Stone's River Campaign*, 2:614; *Chicago Times*, January 16, 1863; Harwell, *Kate*, 84; "Lexington" article in *Southern Confederacy*, January 28, 1863; "General Summary of the Hospitals in the District of Chattanooga February 1863," Stout Papers, box 2, G425, UTX; Schroeder-Lein, *Confederate Hospitals*, 64; *Chattanooga Daily Rebel*, January 1, 4, 14 (Thornton), 1863; Gustavus W. Dyer, *Veterans Questionnaire*, 1:164–65 (Acuff); "General Hospitals of the Army of Tennessee Under S. H.

Stout, February 28, 1863," and "Buildings and Outhouses Occupied as Hospitals in the District of Tennessee, March 1863," Bragg Papers, WRHS.

2. Lea to father, March 31, 1863, as quoted in Skellie, *Lest We Forget*, 2:475; Gunter to wife, January 6, 1863, as quoted in Stephen Davis, *What the Yankees Did*, 24–25.

3. "Weekly Report of Sick Shipped from Depot Hospital of Shelbyville for Weeks Ending May 6, 23, 1863," Stout Papers, UTX; "Medical Director's Consolidated Report of Sick and Wounded, January 1–May 31, 1863," Jones Collection, TU; Hardee to Breckinridge, February 18, 1863, Hardee Papers, ADAH.

4. Crittenden to wife, January 14, 1863, and to father, April 23, 1863, Crittenden Letters, AU; Charles Roberts to wife, January 7, 1863, Roberts Letters, UMISS; Michael Royster to wife, April 13, 1863, Royster Letters, UFLA; *Columbus Daily Sun*, April 15, 1863; Sheppard, *By the Noble Daring*, 110; Sparkman Diary, April 28–20, 1863, CCNBP; Pridmore to wife, January 18–20, 1863, Pridmore Letters, MSU.

5. "Medical Director's Consolidated Report of Sick and Wounded, January 1–May 31, 1863," Jones Collection, TU; Davidson to wife, May 10, 1863, Davidson Letters, AHS; Sparkman Diary, April 30, 1863, CCNBP. The sick received at the Atlanta Fairground Hospitals 1 and 2 between January and May 1863 had their illnesses diagnosed in the following percentages: "Diarrhea—30.72, dibility—19.78, rheumatism—9.28, fevers—6.72, pneumonia—4.04, bronchitis—3.66, and typhoid—31.4." See Welsh, *Two Confederate Hospitals*, 129–31.

6. *OR*, 20(2):455; *Memphis Appeal*, July 27, 1863; Clark and Riley, "Medical Department," 69–70.

7. "All Hospitals, Army of Tennessee, Patients, Property, Personal Reports, February 1863–August 1863," and "Consolidated Weekly Report Ending July 7, 1863," Stout Papers, UTX. Federal officers praised the ventilation of Dr. Samuel H. Stout's hospitals, but there was criticism of one hospital "on a hill," clearly a reference to the Academy Hospital, which lacked doors and windows. Clark and Riley, "Medical Department," 70; *Medical and Surgical History*, 1(2):281.

8. Harwell, *Kate*, 109–10.

9. "General Summary of Hospitals in Districts of Tennessee for Month of June 1863," Stout Papers, UTX; Challie Brown to Samuel Stout, August 21, 1863, Stout Papers, UTX; Harwell, *Kate*, 127; Samuel Stout to Edward Flewellen, March 6, 1863, Stout Papers, UTX; Freemon, "The Medical Support System," 45.

10. Welsh, *Two Confederate Hospitals*, 129–31.

11. Schroeder-Lein, *Confederate Hospitals*, 25, 78, 81–82, 189–90; "Dr. Edward A. Flewellen," 443.

12. Schroeder-Lein, *Confederate Hospitals*, 186–95; Rogers to father, March 20, 1863, Rogers Letters, TSLA; "Proceedings of the Army Medical Board at Shelbyville May 1863," Stout Papers, UTX.

13. M. B. McMicklin to Flewellen, April 23, 1863, Stout Papers, UTX; "Consolidated Report of Strength and Transportation, March 1863," Bragg Papers, WRHS; *OR*, 20(1):228–29; Roberts, "Field and Temporary Hospitals," 258, 260.

14. Schroeder-Lein, *Confederate Hospitals*, 122–24, 193–94; Clark and Riley, "Medical Department," 70–71; *Medical and Surgical History*, 1(2):281.

15. "Consolidated Weekly Report of Bragg's Hospitals, September 30, 1863," Stout Papers, UTX; *Montgomery Weekly Advertiser*, May 25, 1863; Harwell, *Kate*, 152, 156.

16. Schroeder-Lein, *Confederate Hospitals*, 124; Harwell, *Kate*, 138–39.

17. *OR* 30(1):225 (2,500 wounded); Schroeder-Lein, *Confederate Hospitals*, 125; *Medical and Surgical History*, 1:274, 276–77, 281; *Atlanta Intelligencer*, September 27, 1863.

18. *OR*, 30(1):225; Clark and Riley, "Medical Department," 71; Elliott, *Doctor Quintard*, 79; *Atlanta Intelligencer*, October 1, 1863; Stout to Moore, October 13, 1863, box 1, folder 20, Stout Papers, UTX.

19. Tower, *Carolinian Goes to War*, 102; Harwell, *Kate*, 150–53.

20. *Confederate States Medical and Surgical Journal*, 1:75–77.

21. Clark and Riley, "Medical Department," 72; C. Miller Report, September 26, 1863, Stout Papers, UTX; Frank M. Dennis Report, October 22, 1863, Stout Papers, SHC; Powell, *Chickamauga Campaign*, 2:203–4.

22. Clark and Riley, "Medical Department," 72; Stout to Moore, October 10, 1863, box 1, folder 20, Stout Papers, EU; *Atlanta Intelligencer*, September 22, 24, 26, 1863. For other problems transporting the wounded, see H. I. Warmuth Report, October 30, 1863; W. J. Sneed Report, November 29, 1863; and J. E. Negle Report, November 30, 1863, all in Stout Papers, UTX.

23. Frank M. Dennis Report, October 22, 1863; W. M. Baird Report, November 30, 1863 (cattle); and Stout to Edward Flewellen, November 1, 1863, all in Stout Papers, UTX; *Atlanta Intelligencer*, September 24, 1863.

24. Clark and Riley, "Medical Department," 72; "Dr. Edward A. Flewellen," 443.

25. *Atlanta Intelligencer*, September 26, 1863.

26. *Atlanta Intelligencer*, October 1, 1863; Flewellen to Samuel Cooper, October 30, 1863, Army of Tennessee Medical Director, Letters Sent, NARG.

27. Livingston to sisters, October 25, 1863, Livingston Letters, MC.

28. Stout to Moore, October 10, 1863, box 1, folder 20, Stout Papers, EU; "Monthly Report of Bragg's Hospitals for the Month Ending September 30, 1863," Stout Papers, UTX; *Atlanta Intelligencer*, September 27, 1863.

29. Duncan, *Medical Department*, 303, 305.

30. Iobst, *Civil War Macon*, 108–11.

31. Harwell, *Kate*, 166–67, 169.

32. *OR*, 30(4):733; Watson Diary, September 30, 1863, CCNBP; Bullock to wife, October 7, 1863, Bullock Letters, GDAH.

33. *OR*, 30(1):259; Duncan, *Medical Department*, 279.

34. Schroeder-Lein, *Confederate Hospitals*, 279.

35. *Richmond Sentinel*, January 11, 1864; Circular, Medical Purveyor's Office, July 2, 1864, Stout Papers, UTX.

36. Tower, *Carolinian Goes to War*, 168, 184.

37. Erskine to S. D. Lee, August 13, 1864, Erskine Letter, PP.

38. Harwell, *Kate*, 198–99.

39. "Tabular Statement of Medical Officers on Duty and Number of Beds Occupied and Unoccupied, March 1864," and "Consolidated Hospital Report, Army of Tennessee, July 1, 1864," Stout Papers, UTX; "Hospitals Arrangements of the Army," *Memphis Appeal*, March 29, 1864; Breeden, "Medical History," 31–59.

40. Welsh, *Two Confederate Hospitals*, 129–31; Freemon, "Medical Support System," 46.

41. *Albany (Ga.) Patriot*, September 22, July 7, 1864.

42. Harwell, *Kate*, 231–32.

CHAPTER 16

1. *OR*, 20(2):503.

2. *Chattanooga Daily Rebel*, December 20, 1862.

3. Stephen Davis, *What the Yankees Did*, 44; *OR*, 23(2):769–70, 772–73, 647; Wilson, *Confederate Industry*, 101.

4. *OR*, 23(2):759, 764; J. W. Henderson to wife, June 7, 1863, Henderson Letters, UMISS. My estimates are roughly based upon 2,276 wagons averaging four mules each, 10,000 cavalry, 2,500 artillery horses, and 1,000 horses for escorts, staff, and field officers. The number of railcars needed is based upon 250 bushels of corn per car, standard for railroad use in the West. William Dillon (Dillon Diary, April 29, 1863, UMISS) noted that a dozen wagons from his brigade went on a forty-mile foraging expedition that took three days.

5. *OR*, 23(2):764. The one-ton figure is based on the average load for Confederate wagons during the Vicksburg Campaign. See *OR*, 34(3):983.

6. See 1861 Nashville & Chattanooga Railroad reports; D. W. Cole to Joseph Brown, December 29, 1862; and John Bransfield to A. C. Myers, February 17, 1863, all in www .csa-railroads.com (website by David L. Bright).

7. *OR*, 16(2):839, 20(2):421, 23(2):583 (removal of track); M. Levy to Hypolite Oladowski, December 20, 1862, and Moore & Marsh contract, January 24, 1863, in www .csa-railroads.com (website by David L. Bright); *Montgomery Weekly Mail*, December 30, 1862.

8. *OR*, 23(2):601; and ser. 4, 2:486. The Confederate rail freight is based on the measurement of seven and a half tons per car. Corn is estimated at 250 bushels per car, pork at 8,333 pounds per car, and steers at 13 per car. See *OR*, 24(3):836, 52(2):621 (corn); and NA/RR, March 19, 1864 (thirteen animals per car), www.csa-railroads.com (website by David L. Bright).

9. Stephen Davis, *What the Yankees Did*, 44–46; Report of the Joint Committee of the Legislature of the State of Georgia on Transportation, April 11, 1863, www.csa -railroads.com (website by David L. Bright).

10. *OR*, 23(2):648, 680, 657–58.

11. *OR*, 23(2):674, 816–17, 775–76.

12. *OR*, 23(2):724, 816–17, 775–76.

13. Taylor, "Rebel Beef," 17–21, 24, 25.

14. Taylor, 680, 688–89, 724, 858, 706 ("knaves or fools"); *Nashville Union & American*, December 29, 1861; "Death of Col. Giles M. Hillyer," *Weekly Clarion*, June 15, 1871; "Death of a Prominent Man," *Daily Phoenix*, May 9, 1871.

15. *OR*, 23(2):626.

16. Holmes diary, March 21, 23, 1863, in Dennis, *Kemper County Rebel*, 70, 71; Jones Diary, March 5, 1863, GPL; "Mentor" article in *Columbus Weekly Enquirer*, April 21, 1863; Settles to sister, April 4, 1863, Settles Letters, Brown Collection, UMISS; Isham Thomas to wife, March 11, 1863, Thomas Letters and Diaries, GPL; *Chattanooga Daily Rebel*, April 1, 1863 (fruit crop); Thomas Patton to wife, April 18, 1863, Patton Letters, SHC (fruit crop); Hurley to sister, May 22, 1863, Hurley Letters, VMI; Rogers to brother, April 17, 1863, Rogers Letters, SRNBP; Crittenden to wife, May 3, 1863, Crittenden Letters, AU (process); "Bayonet" article in *Mobile Advertiser & Register*, May 10, 1863 (prices). See also William Gilliland to wife, May 30, 1863, Gilliland Letters, MVC.

17. Davidson to wife, February 8, 23, 1863, Davidson Letters, AHS; Estes to family, February 1, 1863, as quoted in Hardy, *Fifty-Eighth North Carolina*, 49; McDonald to sister, January 9, 1863, accessed January 18, 2016, www.articlelibrary.info/Reference /civilwar_civilwar_sourcebook.htm (site discontinued); Puckett to wife, February 10, 1863, Puckett Letters, UTX; Georgia letter in *Southern Confederacy*, February 28, 1863; Charles Roberts to wife, February 12, 1863, Roberts Letters, UMISS; *Chattanooga Daily Rebel*, February 28, 1863 (no hunting allowed); Preston Diary, 16, ADAH (chitterlings).

18. Thomas Warrick to wife, August 2, 1863, Warrick Letters, ADAH; Glazner to wife, August 16, 1863, Glazner Letters, CCNBP; *OR*, 30(4):548, 25(2):730.

19. *Atlanta Intelligencer*, December 18, 1863; various vouchers in Bragg Papers, WRHS; *Columbus Weekly Enquirer*, July 7, 1863.

20. Stephen Davis, *What the Yankees Did*, 40–42.

21. Thomas, *Confederate Arsenals*, 1:50–51, 56.

22. *OR*, 23(2):758; Oladowski to Wright, May 19, September 2, 1863; Oladowski to Gorgas, July 23, 1863; "Ammunition Expended in Polk's Corps at Chickamauga," October 29, 1863; and Oladowski to W. D. Humphreys, March 14, 1863, all in Letters Sent, Ordnance Officer, NARG; Wright to Oladowski, January 28, June 29, 1863, in Moses Wright, Military Service Files, NARG; *Atlanta Intelligencer*, October 6, 1863; "Statement of Artillery Ammunition on Hand, Army of Tennessee," April 30, 1863, Bragg Papers, WRHS.

23. Thomas, *Confederate Arsenals*, 1:57, 73.

24. "Inspection of Polk's Artillery, February 1, 1863," and "Inspection of Polk's Artillery, May 9, 1863," Inspection Reports, NARG; *OR*, 23(2):763.

25. *OR*, 23(2):763, 758.

26. As quoted in Thomas, *Confederate Arsenals*, 1:52.

27. *OR*, 23(2):647, 702, 706, 762; Stephen Davis, *What the Yankees Did*, 41; Rennolds Diary, April 22, 23, 1863, UT.

28. Stephen Davis, *What the Yankees Did*, 41; Knopp, *Made in the C. S. A.*, 16, 81.

29. *OR*, 20(1):678–81, 233–42; and 23(2):762; Wright to Oladowski, February 13, 1863, in Moses Wright, Military Service Files, NARG.

30. "List of Batteries Receiving Leeds & Company Guns," April 29, 1863; Oladowski to Josiah Gorgas, March 9, 1863; Oladowski to W. A. Taylor, June 1, 1863; and Oladowski to Wright, July 23, 1863, all in Letters Sent, Ordnance Officer, NARG; *OR*, 23(2):967–69; "Report of Guns Engaged, Ammunition Expended, etc. in the Army of Tennessee, commanded by General B. Bragg C. S. A., at the Battle of Chickamauga, September 18, 19, 20, 1863," Inspection Reports, NARG; *Memphis Appeal*, March 27, 1863; Fremantle, *Three Months*, 176.

31. Oladowski to Gorgas, July 25, 1863, Letters Sent, Ordnance Officer, NARG; *OR*, 23(2):763.

32. *OR*, 23(2):764–65.

33. "N" article in *Savannah Republican*, June 11, 1863; *OR*, 23(2):759, 30(4):717; Fremantle, *Three Months*, 163; Hurley to sister, April 28, 1863, Hurley Letters, VMI.

34. *OR*, 23(2):759, 768; *Columbus Weekly Sun*, January 13, 1863.

35. *Columbus Weekly Sun*, September 23, December 16, 1862; *Augusta Constitutionalist*, September 23, 1863; *Mobile Advertiser & Register*, December 4, 1862.

36. *OR*, 23(2):765–66.

37. Fremantle, *Three Months*, 155–56.

38. Goff, *Confederate Supply*, 241–51.

39. *OR*, 52(2):621.

40. Athey to mother, November 12, 1863, Athey Letters, ADAH; Weaver to father, November 18, 1863, Weaver Letters, ADAH.

41. *Wilmington Journal*, November 26, 1863.

42. J. R. Throckmorton to M. B. McMicken, November 17, 18, 19, 1863; W. W. Mackall to Joseph Brown, December 27, 1863; and E. B. Walker to F. W. Sims, December 7, 1863, all in www.csa-railroads.com (website by David L. Blight).

43. Lash, *Iron Horse*, 120; *OR*, 32(2):548, 775; and 52(2):602, 607; Lawton to Jefferson Davis, February 11, 1864, in www.csa-railroads.com (website by David L. Blight).

44. J. M. Hottel to James Burton, March 2, 1864; J. P. Horbach to McMicken, March 9, 1864; Horbach to Irvine, March 17, 1864; and James Kerry to Thomas Clark, March 19, 1864, all in www.csa-railroads.com (website by David L. Blight); Lash, *Iron Horse*, 121, 128–29; Patton to wife, January 27, 1864, Patton Letters, SHC. In February 1864, Polk sent fifteen slaves to drive 1,000 beeves from Mississippi to the Army of Tennessee.

45. *Memphis Appeal*, May 22, 1864; Cummings to Johnston, January 1, 1864, in Crist, *Papers*, 10:149.

46. "Quarterly Return of Quartermaster Stores Received and Issued at Dalton in Quarter Ending March 31, 1864," Record Book, NARG.

47. *OR*, 32(2):510, 603, 612.

48. Trask journal, May 16, 1864, in Hafendorfer, *Civil War Journal*, 142; Douglas to wife, June 10, 1863, in Douglas, *Douglas' Texas Battery*, 108; Hall to children, July 8,

1864, Hall Letters, ADAH; Foster to father, July 13, 1864, Foster Letter, MDAH. See also William Offield to wife, August 23, 1864, in Aiken, "Letters," 124; Betts, "Civil War Letters," 26; and Z. T. Armistead to brother, May 31, 1864, Armistead Letters, GDAH.

49. Oladowski to Wright, December 20, 1863; Oladowski to Gorgas, December 25, 1863; and Wright to Gorgas, March 18, 1864, all in Letters Sent, Ordnance Officer, NARG.

50. Oladowski to Wright, February 8, 1864, Letters Sent, Ordnance Officer, NARG; Record of Receipts, NARG; Daniel, *Cannoneers in Gray*, 140–41.

51. Wright to Oladowski, December 27, 1863, in Thomas, *Confederate Arsenals*, 1:69; "Monthly Inspection of Hood's Corps, March 7, 1864," Weekly Returns, MDAH; *OR*, 32(2):788; "Captain John Claiborne Inspection Report, April 13, 1864," Claiborne, LC.

52. *OR*, 38 (4):782, 864.

53. "Consolidated Monthly Report of Ordnance and Ordnance Stores on Hand in Use of the Troopers of Wheeler's Corps, July 31, 1864," compiled by Ken K. Knapp, Wheeler Papers, CCNBP.

54. "Consolidated Report of the Guns Engaged at Missionary Ridge, November 24–25, 1863," Bragg Papers, WRHS; Wright to Gorgas, February 12, 1864, Letters Sent, Ordnance Officer, NARG.

55. *OR*, 31(3):826–27; Mebane's Battery Requisition, December 31, 1863, Robert Cobb, Military Service Files, NARG; "List of Articles Required in the Artillery of Cheatham's Division, November 30, 1863," Melancthon Smith, Military Service Files, NARG; Oladowski to Gorgas, February 5, 1864, and Oladowski to Rains, February 1864, Letters Sent, Ordnance Officer, NARG; Felix Robertson to Oladowski, February 7, 1864, Felix H. Robertson, Military Service Files, NARG; W. C. Duxbury Report, April 25, 1864, Ordnance Department Correspondence, MDAH.

CHAPTER 17

1. Hallock, *Braxton Bragg*, 127–29.

2. *OR*, 30(4):705–6, 709–10; and 52(2):548, 554; Gallagher, *Fighting for the Confederacy*, 47; Grant, "Chattanooga," 683–87; *Mobile Advertiser & Register*, October 6, 1863.

3. Connelly, *Autumn of Glory*, 142–44.

4. As quoted in Wills, *Confederacy's Greatest Cavalryman*, 142–43; *OR*, 30(2):526.

5. Longacre, *Cavalry of the Heartland*, 244; Brent Diary, October 30, 1863, Bragg Papers, WRHS; Powell, *Failure in the Saddle*, 219–20; *OR*, 30(2):723, 30(4):724.

6. Wyeth, *Forrest*, 248–49.

7. Longacre, *Cavalry of the Heartland*, 246; Longacre, *Soldier to the Last*, 119–20; *Chattanooga Daily Rebel*, October 6, 14, 21, 1863; McDonough, *Chattanooga*, 69; *OR*, 30(2):665–66, 673, 676; and 30(4):719; Frank Batchelor to wife, October 18, 1863, in Rugeley, *Batchelor-Turner Letters*, 71; Dubose, *General Joseph Wheeler*, 209–10. The Northern press placed the damage at fifty clothing and ammunition wagons, forty wagons of medical stores, 50 fifty sutler's wagons, and 300 mules.

8. As quoted in McDonough, *Chattanooga*, 72.

9. Cooling, *Fort Donelson's Legacy*, 309–11; McDonough, *Chattanooga*, 72.

10. *OR*, 30(4):58; Daniel, *Soldiering*, 58; Daniel, *Cannoneers in Gray*, 114-15; Watson Diary, October 23, 1863, CCNBP; Ives to father, November 12, 1863, Ives Letters, CCNBP; *Mobile Advertiser & Register*, October 24, 1863; Ambrose Doss to wife, November 13, 1863, Doss Letters, SRNBP; Sword, *Southern Invincibility*, 223.

11. Grant, "Chattanooga," 687-91; *OR*, 52(2):558; Mendoza, "Perfect Storm," 5, 14-15, 16. Mendoza concluded that Longstreet "had failed to secure the pivotal left flank of the Confederate army," resulting in a corps command "fractured with internal rivalries and bitterness."

12. *OR*, 30(4):721, 32(2):656, 52(2):557; Hughes, *Liddell's Record*, 157. Edward Franks ("Braxton Bragg, James Longstreet," 34-40) suggests that there was a difference of only 1,000 troops in the transfers. He uses "aggregate" numbers, however, while I use "present for duty." He also adds two brigades that Bragg expected from Mobile but that did not arrive in time for the Battle of Missionary Ridge. Thus, while my numbers are markedly different, he makes his point—historians have overestimated the net numerical loss to Bragg's army.

13. Connelly, *Autumn of Glory*, 267; McDonough, *Chattanooga*, 164; William C. Davis, *Breckinridge*, 385; Hess, *Braxton Bragg*, 200; Livermore, *Numbers and Losses*, 106-7. One must be careful in using the return of October 10, 1863 (*OR*, 31[2]:656), because Moore's Brigade and eight companies of Buckner's Division, together 3,223, are not included. Connelly often used "effective" numbers to downplay Confederate strength.

14. *OR*, 31(3):685-86, 52(2):546; Connelly, *Autumn of Glory*, 2150-52; Woodworth, *Jefferson Davis*, 244-45; Rennolds Diary, November 11, 13, 1863, UT; Oldham Diary, December 7, 1863, UT; Dillon Diary, November 9, 1863, UMISS; *Chattanooga Daily Rebel* as quoted in *Mobile Advertiser & Register*, December 5, 1863.

15. Hughes, *Liddell's Record*, 149.

16. *OR*, 31(3):738; and 31(2):656, 745-46; Sword, *Mountains Touched with Fire*, 170. Castel (*Victors in Blue*, 242) wrote: "Bragg, of course, knew that Sherman had reinforced Grant. But displaying his abundant talent for jumping to the wrong conclusion, he decided that Grant intended to send Sherman to rescue Burnside at Knoxville." The low number in Buckner's Division is due to the fact that Bragg removed eight regiments at the reorganization. See Livermore, *Numbers and Losses*, 107n4.

17. Tower, *Carolinian Goes to War*, 130-31; Hoffman, *Confederate Collapse*, 35, 58, 68.

18. Tower, *Carolinian Goes to War*, 132-33.

19. *Richmond Dispatch*, November 28, 1863; Sword, *Mountains Touched with Fire*, 385.

20. Castel, *Victors in Blue*, 244; Sword, *Mountains Touched with Fire*, 213-14.

21. Sword, *Mountains Touched with Fire*, 219-26; Walter Hebert, *Fighting Joe Hooker*, 265. See also Woodworth, *Six Armies in Tennessee*, 188-89.

22. Hughes, *Hardee*, 171-72; William C. Davis, *Breckinridge*, 394-96; Lundberg, "Baptizing," 74. Woodworth (*Six Armies in Tennessee*, 190) concluded that Bragg had little choice but to hold the line. Connelly's suggestion (*Autumn of Glory*, 273) to stay and fight was, of course, made in hindsight.

23. Symonds, *Stonewall of the West*, 161; Woodworth, *Six Armies in Tennessee*, 190–91; Daniel, *Cannoneers in Gray*, 119–20.

24. Lundberg, "Baptizing," 76–81.

25. Tower, *Carolinian Goes to War*, 137; Hughes, *Civil War Memoir*, 139.

26. Sheppard, *By the Noble Daring*, 162 ("Oh, what a purity"); Rennolds Diary, November 28, 1863, UT; Daniel, *Cannoneers in Gray*, 123; *Mobile Advertiser & Register*, December 8, 1863.

27. Hoffman, *Confederate Collapse*, 55, 70–71.

28. *Huntsville Daily Confederate*, November 28, 1863; William Bass report in Skellie, *Lest We Forget*, 2:606; Chunn to wife, December 1, 1863, Chunn Letters, DU; Hall to father, December 2, 1863, Hall Letters, ADAH; Beatty Diary, October 25, 1863, SHC.

29. *OR*, 31(2):99–100; Daniel, *Cannoneers in Gray*, 131.

30. *Mobile Advertiser & Register*, December 3, 1863; Symonds, *Stonewall of the West*, 171–76.

31. William C. Davis, *Breckinridge*, 395–96; Hess, *Braxton Bragg*, 203.

32. *OR*, 31(2):681, 666; Hallock, *Braxton Bragg*, 148; Hess, *Braxton Bragg*, 203; Cate, *Two Soldiers*, 8–9.

33. *Richmond Whig*, November 27, 1863; William C. Davis, *Jefferson Davis*, 529.

34. William Mackall to wife, November 27, 1863, in Mackall, *Son's Recollections*, 196–97; Neal to sister, December 6, 1863, Neal Letters, EU; Rennolds Diary, December 3, 1863, UT; Daniel Diary, December 2, 1863, USAMHI; James Hall to father, January 31, 1864, Hall Letters, SHC; Carter to wife, December 3, 1863, Carter Letters, DU.

35. *Memphis Appeal*, December 3, 1863; *OR*, 31(3):774–76; Hallock, *Braxton Bragg*, 155–56; Hess, *Braxton Bragg*, 214, 215; William C. Davis, *Jefferson Davis*, 532; Hughes, *Liddell's Record*, 160.

36. William C. Davis, *Jefferson Davis*, 528; Thomas B. Roy sketch, Hardee Papers, ADAH; Hall to father, December 6, 1863, Hall Letters, ADAH; Wyman to mother, December 11, 1863, Wyman Letters, ADAH; *OR*, 31(3):801; Thomas Bigbee to wife, December 7, 1863, Bigbee Letters, AU. Hughes (*Hardee*, 183) conceded that Hardee "lacked the strategic ability and daring of Bragg" and was "inferior to Johnston as a strategist and as an inspiring leader."

37. Hughes, *Hardee*, 186–87.

38. *OR*, 31(3):776.

39. Ives to mother, December 6, 1863, in Cabaniss, *Civil War Journal*, 54; Lea to father, December 5, 1863, in Skellie, *Lest We Forget*, 2:618; Wyman to mother, December 11, 1863, Wyman Letters, ADAH; Stephens to wife, December 24, 1863, Stephens Letters, EU; Mason to "Miss Kenny," December 3, 1863, Mason Letters, EU; Cotton to wife, December 14, 1863, in Griffith, *Yours Till Death*, 98; Ledbetter to wife, December 25, 1863, Ledbetter Letters, GDAH.

40. *OR*, 32(2):141.

41. Crittenden to father, February 21, 1864, Crittenden Letters, AU; Roberts, "In Winter Quarters," 274–75; Cate, *Two Soldiers*, 11; Barber diary, January 13, 1864, in Ferrell, *Holding the Line*, 154–55; Hughes, *Civil War Memoir*, 157.

42. Brown Diary, December 8, 1863, GRPL; Andrew Edge to wife, December 8, 1863, Edge Letters, EU; Washington Ives to mother, December 6, 1863, in Cabaniss, *Civil War Journal*, 54.

43. Connelly, *Autumn of Glory*, 289–90; Allardice, *Confederate Colonels*, 210; *OR*, 31(3):573–74, 783; Johnston, *Military Operations*, 269.

44. *OR*, 31(3):781, 783, 804, 826–28, 860; and (2):657–64; *Memphis Appeal*, January 1, 1864; Arch McLaurin to sister, December 7, 1863, in Skellie, *Lest We Forget*, 2:620; Williams diary, February 28, 1863, in Wynne and Taylor, *This War So Horrible*, 35; Andrew Edge to wife, December 8, 1863, Edge Letters, EU; Watkins, *"Co. Aytch,"* 111; Grammer Diary, December 10, 1863, MDAH.

45. *OR*, 32(2):860, 857. A soldier in Cheatham's Division nonetheless wrote in that he had not seen a single case of suffering due to a shortage of shoes or clothing. "Dalton is not Valley Forge," he insisted. *Columbus Weekly Enquirer*, January 1, 1864.

46. Rennolds Diary, December 24, 25, 1863, UT; Farris to wife, December 26, 1863, Farris Letters, EU; Edward Brown to wife, December 23, 25, 1863, Brown Letters, ADAH; William C. Davis, *Diary*, 102; Dallas Wood to sister, December 25, 1863, as quoted in Sheppard, *By the Noble Daring*, 168.

47. Sparkman Diary, December 16, 25, 1863, CCNBP; *Mobile Advertiser & Register*, December 8, 1863.

48. *OR*, 32(3):643.

49. Miller to wife, January 2, 1864, in McMurry, *Uncompromising Secessionist*, 164–65; *OR*, 31(1):641–44; *Memphis Appeal*, January 5, 1864. On December 20, 1863, Wheeler wrote Bragg: "Gen'l W[harton] is still hard at work to get command of the cavalry of this army. He is aided by his friends in Richmond." As quoted in Longacre, *Cavalry of the Heartland*, 254.

CHAPTER 18

1. J. B. Jones, *Rebel War Clerk's Diary*, 2:106, 110; *Richmond Dispatch*, December 1–3, 1863.

2. William C. Davis, *Jefferson Davis*, 528; J. B. Jones, *Rebel War Clerk's Diary*, 2:110; *Mobile Advertiser & Register*, December 10, 1863; Younger, *Inside the Confederate Government*, 124.

3. William C. Davis, *Jefferson Davis*, 528–30.

4. Davis, 509–11.

5. Symonds, *Johnston*, 225–26, 248; Strode, *Confederate President*, 510; William C. Davis, *Jefferson Davis*, 530; Stoker, *Grand Design*, 355–56; Connelly, *Autumn of Glory*, 284–85; McMurry, *Atlanta 1864*, 7, 11; *OR*, 31(3):800–801; Johnston, *Military Operations*, 268–69; Rable, *Confederate Republic*, 238. Dick Ewell and A. P. Hill in Lee's army were both in frail condition at the time and not even considered. Welsh, *Medical Histories*, 65, 100. McMurry believed that Johnston's selection "can be explained only on the grounds that no better alternative existed." But William C. Davis (563) believed that, a Davis prejudice notwithstanding, Beauregard was the better choice. Woodworth ("Reassessment," 7–8) suggested a third alternative—Edmund Kirby Smith. He de-

clared Beauregard to be the "daring choice," Hardee the "cautious choice," and Smith the "good, well-balanced choice."

6. Connelly, *Autumn of Glory*, 286–88; McMurry, "Enemy at Richmond," 27; Glatthaar, *General Lee's Army*, 46; Gallagher, *Fighting for the Confederacy*, 82–83.

7. McMurry, "Enemy at Richmond," 19; Gallagher, *Fighting for the Confederacy*, 82. The Huff House still stands today.

8. *OR*, 31(3):873–74; McMurry, *Atlanta 1864*, 39.

9. Johnston, *Military Operations*, 272; Russell K. Brown, *To the Manner Born*, 192–93; Hughes, *Hardee*, 188–89; Patton to mother, January 23, 1863, Patton Letters, SHC.

10. *Memphis Appeal*, April 29, May 19 (hat), 1864; George Lea to H. M. Lea, March 6, 1864, in Skellie, *Lest We Forget*, 2:634; Cate, *Two Soldiers*, 30; Hall to father, January 31, 1864, Hall Letters, ADAH; *OR*, 32(2):608.

11. *OR*, 31(3):877–78, 32(2):521; Cate, *Two Soldiers*, 29, 64; Sheppard, *By the Noble Daring*, 168; Hoffman, *Confederate Collapse*, 22–23; *Mobile Advertiser & Register*, December 3, 1863, February 2, 1864.

12. McMurry, *John Bell Hood*, 82–83, 87, 88; Woodward, *Mary Chesnut's Civil War*, 534; Stephen M. Hood, *John Bell Hood: The Rise*, 287–88; Stephen M. Hood, *Lost Papers*, 19–38; Peddy to wife, March 6, 1864, in Cuttino, *Saddle Bag and Spinning Wheel*, 224.

13. McMurry, *John Bell Hood*, 93, 94–95, 99; Hundley to wife, March 3, 6, 1864, Hundley Letters, UALA.

14. McMurry, "Enemy at Richmond," 21; Symonds, *Johnston*, 253.

15. Russell K. Brown, *Our Connection with Savannah*, 81–82.

16. Allardice, *Confederate Colonels*, 141; Symonds, *Johnston*, 252.

17. Welsh, *Medical Histories*, 23; Cutrer, *Our Trust*, 251; Knox to Cellie, March 27, 1864, in McMurry, *Uncompromising Secessionist*, 186–87, 52–53; *OR*, 52(2):606.

18. As quoted in William C. Davis, *Jefferson Davis*, 546–47.

19. Johnston, *Military Operations*, 291–97; Connelly, *Autumn of Glory*, 298.

20. Johnston, *Military Operations*, 295–303; Connelly, *Autumn of Glory*, 299; *OR*, 32(3):637–41. Connelly is quick to point out that in October 1863, when Bragg commanded the army, he turned down a similar plan to outflank Chattanooga.

21. Glatthaar, "Davis, Johnston," 106; McMurry, "Enemy at Richmond," 25–26.

22. *OR*, 32(3):685–86, 696; Daniel, *Cannoneers in Gray*, 140–41.

23. *OR*, 23(3):592, 636, 671, 686, 688, 742; Cate, *Two Soldiers*, 73.

24. *OR*, 32(3):753, 772–74, 794, 100–101, 424.

25. *OR*, 32(3):839–40; Connelly, *Autumn of Glory*, 310; Allardice, *Confederate Colonels*, 141.

26. *OR*, 32(2):839–41.

27. McMurry, "Enemy at Richmond," 28–29.

28. Hood to Bragg, April 3, 1864, Bragg Papers, WRHS; *OR*, 32(2):781. Many western theater authors, including Castel, Sword, and Woodworth, have all denounced Hood's correspondence. McMurry takes a softer view. Sam Hood surprisingly concluded that the April 13 letter, when read in full, "reveals rather unremarkable tone and wording."

Perhaps Symonds comes closer to the truth when he wrote that the general became "trapped by his compulsion for promotion." Connelly *Autumn of Glory*, 322–24; Castel, *Decision in the West*, 356; Woodworth, *Jefferson Davis*, 284; McMurry, *John Bell Hood*, 96–97; Stephen M. Hood, *John Bell Hood: The Rise*, 21–24; Symonds, *Johnston*, 264.

29. Kundahl, *Confederate Engineer*, 161, 293n35; "Report of Inspection," PC; Wynne and Taylor, *This War So Terrible*, 34, 36, 40, 49; Jenkins, "Dalton," 19; *SOR*, 73(2):608, 620, 613; *OR*, 32(2):697; and (3):666, 714, 772–73; Newton Davis to wife, March 11, 1864, Davis Letters, ADAH; John Palmer to wife, March 26, 1864, Palmer Letters, DU; Lewis Sleep to "Fab," April 24, 1864, in Skellie, *Lest We Forget*, 2:647.

30. Brown to wife, January 23, 1864, Brown Letters, ADAH.

31. Roberts to wife, February 11, 1864, Roberts Letters, UMISS.

32. *Memphis Appeal*, January 21, 1864; Livingston to sister, December 26, 1863, in Loski, "Anything for Success," 79; Washington Ives to father, January 5, 1864, in Cabaniss, *Civil War Journal*, 59; *Rome (Ga.) Tri-Weekly Courier*, February 4, 1864; Daniel, *Cannoneers in Gray*, 137–38.

33. Brown to wife, December 23, 1863, January 23, 1864, Brown Letters, ADAH.

34. Wiley, "Billy Yank," 18; Benedict Semmes to wife, March 16, 1864, Semmes Letters, SHC; McKittrick to wife, April 24, 1864, in Lewis, "Confederate Officer's Letters," 492. For Johnston's updated ration issuance, see *OR*, 32(2):608.

35. *OR*, 32(2):600, 645, 697; "Monthly Inspection of Hood's Corps, March 7, 1864," Weekly Returns, MDAH; Daniel, *Soldiering*, 33; Chapman, "Reminiscences," 107–8; http://freepages.geneology.rootsweb.ancestry.com/~bandy/kestletters.html.

36. *OR*, 32(2):530–35; Crittenden to wife, March 7, 1863, Crittenden Letters, AU; Patton to mother, January 23, 1864, Patton Letters, SHC; Brown to wife, January 23, 1864, Brown Letters, ADAH.

37. Wiley, *Life of Johnny Reb*, 53; Cate, *Two Soldiers*, 20–21; Edward Brown to wife, January 8, 1864, Brown Letters, ADAH.

38. Sheppard, *By the Noble Daring*, 169–70 (Inglis); *OR*, 31(3):855, 32(3):558; Grant Taylor to wife, December 28, 1863, in Bloomquist and Taylor, *This Civil War*, 209–10; Dawes, "Confederate Strength," 281; Hezekiah Rabb to wife, February 18, 1864, Rabb Letters, EU; Edward Brown to wife, January 8, March 20, 1864, Brown Letters, ADAH.

39. *OR*, 32(2):631, 28(2):782; Tower, *Carolinian Goes to War*, 164, 176.

40. Hensley to brother, February 14, 1864, Hensley Letters, DU; *Rome (Ga.) Tri-Weekly Courier*, February 20, 1864.

41. Losson, *Tennessee's Forgotten Warriors*, 133, 135; Charles Roberts to wife, February 15, 1864, Roberts Letters, UMISS.

42. Madaus and Needham, *Battle Flags*, 63–65, 91.

43. Polk, *Leonidas Polk*, 2:334–35.

44. *OR*, 32(3):751–52, 79; and (2):621; Castel, *Decision in the West*, 52–53.

45. *OR*, 32(1):476–83; Davis to wife, February 22, 1864, Davis Letters, ADAH; Patton to mother, March 2, 1864, Patton Letters, SHC; Williams diary, February 25, 1864, in Wynne and Taylor, *This War So Horrible*, 32; Reynolds to sister, February 29, 1864, in 26th North Carolina Regiment website, 26nc.org: history.

46. Gallagher, *Confederate War*, 72, 73, 86, 89, 140.

47. Fremantle, *Three Months*, 167; *Mobile Advertiser & Register*, October 10, 1863.

48. Blackford, *Letters*, 226.

49. Huger to wife, November 7, 1863, in Tate, *Col. Frank Huger*, 75; Mendoza, *Confederate Struggle for Command*, 76. See also Sword, *Southern Invincibility*, 215; and Daniel, *Soldiering*, 20–21.

50. Pickett, "Re-Enlistments," 171; "Re-Enlistments in the Army," 351–52; "More About Re-Enlistments," 399–400; Hughes, *Civil War Memoir*, 158–59; *Memphis Appeal*, April 20, 1864.

51. *Memphis Appeal*, January 20, 1864. See also Irvine Walker to wife, January 24, 31, February 7, 1864, in William Lee White and Runion, *Great Things*, 96, 97; Edward Brown to wife, February 12, 1864, Brown Letters, ADAH; George Lea to cousin, January 25, 1864, in Skellie, *Lest We Forget*, 2:626; H. M. Lynn to wife, February 1, 1864, Lynn Letters, SHC; Morgan Letterman to parents, April 3, 1863, in Wommack, *Call Forth*, 371; *Memphis Appeal*, January 19, 20, 26, 27, February 12, April 6, 20, 1864; and *Macon Telegraph*, February 1, 11, 1864.

52. Madaus and Needham, *Battle Flags*, 63–65, 91.

53. Phillips, *Diehard Rebels*, 6, 80, 97.

54. Porter Diary, April 7, 1864, EU; Crittenden to wife, April 9, 1864, Crittenden Letters, AU; Harper to wife, April 7, 1864, Harper Letters, SHC; Kern to mother, April 2, 1864, Kern Letters, SHC. See also Sheppard, *By the Noble Daring*, 175; Benjamin Sheppard to wife, March 31, 1864, Cheatham Papers, TSLA; Cate, *Two Soldiers*, 66; and J. P. Graves to sister, April 25, 1864, J. P. Graves Letters, PP.

55. Glatthaar, *General Lee's Army*, 46; Riggs to uncle, March 19, 1864, Riggs Letters, ADAH; Phillips, *Diehard Rebels*, 97–98 (Brannock and Hampton quotes).

CHAPTER 19

1. McPherson, *For Cause and Comrades*, 19–20; Drew Gilpin Faust, *Confederate Nationalism*, 58–61; Beringer et al., *Why the South Lost*, 69, 72; Genovese, "Yeoman Farmers," 331–42; Rable, *Confederate Republic*, 12–13.

2. Bunting, letter to the editor, *Tri-Weekly Telegraph*, February 2, 1863, in Cutrer, *Our Trust*, 126; *Chattanooga Daily Rebel*, January 21, 1863.

3. Richmond to Mrs. Rayner, May 9, 1863, Polk Papers, US.

4. Freehling, *South vs. the South*, 193; Frank Batchelor to wife, December 17, 1863, in Rugeley, *Batchelor-Turner Letters*, 38; Lea to father, November 15, 1862, in Skellie, *Lest We Forget*, 1:421; Crittenden to wife, March 30, 1864, Crittenden Letters, AU.

5. McGowin to parents, January 11, 1863, McGowin Letters, SRNBP.

6. *Mobile Advertiser & Register*, April 19, 1863.

7. Thomas to wife, March 11, 1863, Thomas Letters and Diaries, GRPL; McLaurin to sister, February 9, 1864, in Skellie, *Lest We Forget*, 2:629.

8. *OR*, ser. 4, 2:421; 23(2):698, 921; and 30(4):505.

9. Sword, "'Our Fireside in Ruins,'" 232, 241–43.

10. Sword, 243.

11. Levine, *Confederate Emancipation*, 26, 38.

12. *OR*, 52(2):586-92; Dubose, *Wheeler*, 257; Freehling, *South vs. the South*, 190-91.

13. Sword, "'Our Fireside in Ruins,'" 236.

14. Symonds, *Stonewall of the West*, 184-85.

15. Key diary, December 28, 1863, in Cate, *Two Soldiers*, 18-19.

16. Connelly, *Army of the Heartland*, 319; Russell K. Brown, *To the Manner Born*, 196-97.

17. Russell K. Brown, *To the Manner Born*, 199-200.

18. Levine, *Confederate Emancipation*, 65, 82, 85, 87.

19. "General Cleburne's Views," 51-52.

20. "General Cleburne's Views," 200-201; Buck, *Cleburne and His Command*, 213; Symonds, *Johnston*, 190-91; Levine, *Confederate Emancipation*, 28; *OR*, 52(2):598-99.

21. Connelly, *Army of the Heartland*, 319-20; Symonds, *Stonewall of the West*, 190-92; Mallock, "Cleburne's Proposal," 71.

22. Walker to wife, January 24, 1864, in William Lee White and Runion, *Great Things*, 95.

23. Brown to wife, January 12, 1864, Brown Letters, ADAH.

24. Crittenden to wife, March 29, 1864, Crittenden Letters, AU; Clampitt, *Confederate Heartland*, 36; Gillis to wife, October 22, 1864, Gillis Letters, EU; Cleburne diary, October 14, 1864, in Lee White, "Long Lost Diary," 17.

25. Levine, *Confederate Emancipation*, 148.

CHAPTER 20

1. Bloomquist and Taylor, *This Civil War*, viii, ix, 204, 221, 224, 232.

2. Lea to Ivison, January 25, 1864, in Skellie, *Lest We Forget*, 2:626. See also Augustus Adamson to sister, March 5, 1864, in Abell and Gecik, *Sojourns of a Patriot*, 212.

3. Clampitt, *Confederate Heartland*, 12-17, 19.

4. Clampitt, 41-42.

5. Woodworth, *Nothing but Victory*, 200.

6. Tower, *Carolinian Goes to War*, 54-55.

7. Jackman diary, January 6, 1863, in William C. Davis, *Diary*, 71; Tower, *Carolinian Goes to War*, 54-55; G. W. James to brother, May 5, 1863, James Letters, TSLA; Oldham Diary, August 23, 1863, UT; Gallagher, *Confederate War*, 161 (cavalryman).

8. Ferrell, *Holding the Line*, 167.

9. Rennolds Diary, June 21, 1863, UT; *Chattanooga Daily Rebel*, November 19, 1862; William Lee White and Runion, *Great Things*, 13; Edward Brown to wife, December 15, 1863, Brown Letters, ADAH. See also *OR*, 20(2):396.

10. Cate, *Two Soldiers*, 155-57.

11. Roberts to wife, September 6, 1864, Roberts Letters, UMISS.

12. Phillips, *Diehard Rebels*, 64-65; Dent to wife, April 4, June 21, 1864, Dent Letters, AU.

13. Noe, *Reluctant Rebels*, 92–96.

14. Crittenden to wife, December 16, 1863, Crittenden Letters, AU; David Williams, Williams, and Carlson, *Plain Folk*, 89 ("I have been").

15. David Williams, Williams, and Carlson, *Plain Folks*, 76–78.

16. William Nugent to wife, June 9, 1864, in Cash and Howorth, *My Dear Nellie*, 180–81.

17. Corsan, *Two Months*, 33.

18. David Williams, *Georgia's Civil War*, 116–17, 119, 121, 122–29; McCurry, *Confederate Reckoning*, 178.

19. Weitz, *Higher Duty*, 112–13. See also Williams, *Georgia's Civil War*, 89–96.

20. McGowin to parents, January 7, 1863, McGowin Letters, SRNBP; Walls to parents, August 19, 1864, Walls Letters, USAMHI.

21. Hebert, *Long Civil War*, 121, 148–49.

22. Hebert, 119.

23. Louis R. Smith and Quist, *Cush*, 100–101.

24. Drew Gilpin Faust, *Southern Stories*, 136–37; McCurry, *Confederate Reckoning*, 135, 180, 203; Glatthaar, *General Lee's Army*, xiv.

CHAPTER 21

1. *OR*, 38 (4):660; Castel, *Decision in the West*, 126–27; Thomas Burnett to wife, April 30, 1864, in Illene D. Thompson and Thompson, *Seventeenth Alabama*, 78; Johnston, "Opposing Sherman's Advance," 262; Jenkins, "Dalton," 9, 21. Robert Jenkins conjectures that Johnston contemplated falling back behind the Oostanaula River to "protect the Rome to Calhoun line."

2. Woodworth, *Jefferson Davis*, 275; William C. Davis, *Jefferson Davis*, 555; *OR*, 38(4):733, 735, 737, 740. Castel (*Decision in the West*, 127) claimed that Davis was "annoyed" by Polk's action. The president acquiesced only to defeat Sherman and launch an offensive.

3. A. J. Neal to father, May 10, 1864, Neal Letters, EU; Breckinridge, "Atlanta Campaign," 278–79; Symonds, *Stonewall of the West*, 203; Jenkins, "Dalton," 25–26.

4. Jenkins, "Dalton," 27, 41, 50; Castel, *Decision in the West*, 136–38; McMurry, *Atlanta 1864*, 64–66; Breckinridge, "Atlanta Campaign," 280; Newton, "Joseph Johnston," 57–66. Although historians have near-universally condemned Johnston for his failure to protect Snake Creek Gap, Newton defended the general. He believed that Johnston knew about and appreciated the importance of the gap, he was not caught off guard, the so-called strategic pipeline was sound, and Resaca remained well protected. The general's decision to defend the bridge rather than the gap was "a conscious decision." The argument, however, should not be framed as either defending the gap or the bridge—*both* had to be held. The place to defend Resaca was the gap, McMurry insisted.

5. *OR*, 38(4):684.

6. Newton, "Joseph Johnston," 66; Castel, *Decision in the West*, 153. Elliott (*Soldier of Tennessee*, 177) labeled Johnston's position as "precarious."

7. Castel, *Decision in the West*, 173–78; Jackman diary, May 4, 1864, in William C.

Davis, *Diary*, 124; Hardy, *Fifty-Eighth North Carolina*, 115; Daniel, *Cannoneers in Gray*, 152.

8. Castel, *Decision in the West*, 173–78.

9. McMurry, *Atlanta 1864*, 80–81; Connelly, *Autumn of Glory*, 346–48; Shanahan, "Atlanta Campaign," 31.

10. Connelly, *Autumn of Glory*, 33; Clampitt, *Confederate Heartland*, 60; McMurry, *Atlanta 1864*, 82. McMurry believed that "Johnston would not have remained at Cassville on May 20." Separate research by McMurry and me concluded that there was a substantial loss of Confederate morale as Johnston retreated. Newton criticized the McMurry-Daniel methodology because it did not take into account that infantry divisions greatly varied. Most complainers, he concluded, came from certain divisions, such as Walker's, which he dismissed as a "second-rate division." Complaints were not generally spread throughout the army. "A sheaf of complainers from Cheatham's, Cleburne's, or Stewart's divisions would be news indeed." See Newton, "Formidable Only in Flight?," 52–54. Accepting the challenge, I found anti-Johnston correspondence in the following: letters by James Hall, Newton Davis, S. H. Dent, and Irvine Walker, all in Hindman's Division; letters by A. J. Neal and Hugh Black, in Bate's Division; diaries by Robert Patrick, Hirman Williams, and W. J. Trask, in Stewart's Division; and letters by W. H. Berryhill, in Loring's Division. Several anti-Bragg letters by members of the cavalry have also been found.

11. McMurry, *Atlanta 1864*, 88.

12. Castel, *Decision in the West*, 224–26; Blount, *New Hope Church*, 127; Bostick to wife, May 31, 1864, in Wills, *Old Enough to Die*, 113.

13. Castel, *Decision in the West*, 233–41; McMurry, *Atlanta 1864*, 90–91 ("Such piles"); Shanahan, "Atlanta Campaign," 41–42.

14. Shanahan, "Atlanta Campaign," 43–45; Jackman diary, May 28, 1864, in Davis, *Diary*, 132–33.

15. McMurry, *Atlanta 1864*, 94–96; McMurry, "Policy So Disastrous," 243–48.

16. Symonds, *Johnston*, 311; *OR*, 38(3):946–47; Longacre, *Cavalry of the Heartland*, 275; McMurry, *Uncompromising Secessionist*, 206–7.

17. Hess, *Kennesaw Mountain*, 5–10; Woodworth, *Decision in the Heartland*, 109.

18. Stephen Davis, *Long and Bloody Task*, 69.

19. Davis, 70–71; Hess, *Kennesaw Mountain*, 35–40, 44–45; Castel, *Decision in the West*, 295.

20. Hughes, *Hardee*, 211; Hess, *Kennesaw Mountain*, 44.

21. Shanahan, "Atlanta Campaign," 55–60; Hess, *Kennesaw Mountain*, 109–12, 131–35, 149–56; "Battle of Kennesaw Mountain," 109–14; McMurry, *Atlanta 1864*, 108–10.

22. Scaife, "Chattahoochee River Line," 42–58.

23. Stephen Davis, *Atlanta Will Fall*, 90; McMurry, *Atlanta 1864*, 111–12; Castel, *Decision in the West*, 344; Hess, *Kennesaw Mountain*, 214.

24. Symonds, *Johnston*, 295–96; Connelly, *Autumn of Glory*, 371; McMurry, *John Bell Hood*, 110, 114.

25. McMurry, *Atlanta 1864*, 131–32.

26. Castel, *Decision in the West*, 446–47; William C. Davis, *Jefferson Davis*, 560; Younger, *Inside the Confederate Government*, 151, 154; Stephen Davis, "Reappraisal of the Generalship," 63–65; Stephen Davis, *Long and Bloody Task*, 99.

27. *OR*, 39(2):712–14; Hess, *Braxton Bragg*, 231.

28. Stephen Davis, *Long and Bloody Task*, 100.

29. Stephen Davis, *Atlanta Will Fall*, 117; McMurry, *Atlanta 1864*, 138–39; Stoker, *Grand Design*, 162; Castel, *Decision in the West*, 358; William C. Davis, *Jefferson Davis*, 563. Noe believed "that Johnston at some point would have abandoned Atlanta and moved south." Symonds believed that Johnston "did not intend to fight for Atlanta but relieving him proved a truly desperate act" at a time when the situation "was serious yet not irretrievable." Bresnahan, *Revisioning the Civil War*, 186, 187. Connelly (*Autumn of Glory*, 421) thought the removal, though justified, proved to be a "costly error" due to timing. The sharpest criticism of Johnston came from William C. Davis. "While critics then and later would severely castigate him [Jefferson Davis] for removing Johnston, they did so chiefly because of Johnston's exalted reputation rather than his actual performance, which had been lack luster since First Manassas. He rarely risked anything, gained little, and habitually avoided responsibility. As a subordinate he was constantly uncommunicative, slow to follow instructions, and frequently insolent." Murray and Hsieh (*Savage War*, 511) nonetheless believed that Johnston should have been retained. He would have held Atlanta longer than Hood, "thus exacerbating political dissention in the North." Such a conclusion, from my perspective, is simply peering too deeply into a crystal ball.

30. McMurry believed that Hood was the best selection under the circumstances, although he admitted that Beauregard would have been better. William C. Davis was to the point: "By replacing Johnston with Hood, Davis only compounded one mistake with another, and capped then both by keeping his best man [Beauregard] in a post that suffocated his abilities." Stephen Davis nonetheless considered Hood's selection "logical." Castel believed that Hardee was never given serious consideration since Bragg detested him and desired revenge. Woodworth did not see anything in Hardee's record that suggested that he was the man for the job. McMurry, *Atlanta 1864*, 140; William C. Davis, *Jefferson Davis*, 561–64; Castel, *Decision in the West*, 357; Hess, *Battle of Peachtree Creek*, 15, 23; Stephen Davis, *Long and Bloody Task*, 101, 132–33.

31. Clampitt (*Confederate Heartland*, 184n16, 185nn17–19), Daniel (*Soldiering*, 195n45), and Sword (*Southern Invincibility*, 390n94) list ten soldiers who eventually came around and supported Hood.

32. McMurry, *Atlanta 1864*, 118, 143–44; Ecelbarger, *Slaughter at the Chapel*, 42–43; James Bates to mother, September 12, 1863, in Lowe, *Texas Cavalry Officer's*, 271.

33. Castel, *Decision in the West*, 373, 375–76; McMurry, *Atlanta 1864*, 147, 150; Connelly, *Autumn of Glory*, 442–43. Woodworth (*Jefferson Davis*, 286) wrote that Hardee "sulked, delayed, and generally told Hood as little as he could of what was happening at the front."

34. McMurry, *Atlanta 1864*, 151–52; Waters, "Partial Atlanta Reports," 218; Daniel, *Days of Glory*, 413–14 (Newton); Jenkins, *Battle of Peachtree Creek*, 143–45.

35. McMurry, *Atlanta 1864*, 153–55; Castel, *Decision in the West*, 379; Woodworth, *Jefferson Davis*, 287.

36. Castel, *Decision in the West*, 393–414; Stephen Davis, *Atlanta Will Fall*, 139. Stephen Davis believed that the battle revealed Hood's "inability both to rise above the fog of war and to override its friction."

37. *OR*, 38(2):761–62, 768, 776, 783, 925; and 38(3):951, 953; Evans, *Sherman's Horsemen*, 195–376. McCook initially reported 500 wagons destroyed at Palmetto but later raised the number to a ridiculously high 1,160. Based upon the number of prisoners and mules captured, the initial number seems more plausible.

38. Castel, *Decision in the West*, 425–32; McMurry, *Atlanta 1864*, 156–57; Stephen Davis, *Atlanta Will Fall*, 153; Hess, *Battle of Ezra Church*, 56. Historians have generally accepted that Hood was attempting to emulate Robert E. Lee's flanking maneuvers. See, for example, Connelly, *Autumn of Glory*, 453.

39. Castel, *Decision in the West*, 435, 436; Ecelbarger, *Slaughter at the Chapel*, 201–2, 204–5; Hess, *Ezra Church*, 172–73. Hess was sharply critical of Lee, saying that he exercised "far too much latitude." Had Hood been present, Hess believed that the attack might not have occurred, but I concur with Castel on that point.

40. Stephen Davis, *Atlanta Will Fall*, 183–85; Castel, *Decision in the West*, 502–3; McMurry, *Atlanta 1864*, 160–61, 163, 164, 170–73; Shanahan, "Atlanta Campaign," 77; Castel, *Winning and Losing*, 83. McDonough (*Sherman*, 544) placed Southern casualties at 2,500 — "perhaps more." McMurry, Stephen Davis, Castel, and Connelly have all come to Hood's defense for his maneuvers on March 29–30. He was not "befuddled" or "outgeneraled" but "managed his response as well as he could under the limitations of intelligence at hand." See Stephen Davis, *Atlanta Will Fall*, 190. Hughes (*Hardee*, 242) blamed Hardee for the disaster of August 31. He judged him attributable for a wide frontal assault, lack of coordination, and poor timing.

41. McMurry, *Atlanta 1864*, 188–89. Ed Bearss dismissed Hood as "too reckless"; see Bresnahan, *Revisioning the Civil War*, 187.

42. McMurry, *Atlanta 1864*, 174; Stephen Davis, *Atlanta Will Fall*, 179; Bonds, *War Like the Thunderbolt*, 274–76.

43. Murray and Hsieh, *Savage War*, 421–22; McMurry, "Policy So Disastrous," 237–38; Newton, "Formidable Only in Flight?," 44–46; "The Opposing Forces in the Atlanta Campaign." See also Stephen Davis, *Long Bloody Task*, 1031–35. Newton placed Federal losses at 37,634.

CHAPTER 22

1. Honnell to wife, May 19, 1863, Honnell Letters, EU; Taylor to wife, August 4, 1864, Bloomquist and Taylor, *This Civil War*, 271.

2. Hammer to wife, April 11, 1863, Hammer Letters, West Tennessee Historical Society, Memphis.

3. *OR*, 16(2):888–89, 17(1):449.

4. Newton, *Lost for the Cause*, 151, 271; McMurry, "Policy So Disastrous," 235.

5. Gallagher, *Confederate War*, 36, 39 (Neal); Clampitt, *Confederate Heartland*, 40 (Colville and Warrick).

6. Daniel, *Soldiering in the Army of Tennessee*, 149; Clampitt, *Confederate Heartland*, 72.

7. Andrews, *South Reports*, 422–34n10; William C. Davis, "Turning Point That Wasn't," 131.

8. Barber diary, December 31, 1863, in Ferrell, *Holding the Line*, 151; Kelly to friend, January 23, 1864, Kelly Letters, EU.

9. Sword, *Embrace an Angry Wind*, 57; Sanders to wife, July 13, 1864, Sanders Letters, MDAH.

10. Hill, "Chickamauga," 639; Howard Jones, *Union in Peril*, 226–29; William C. Davis, *Jefferson Davis*, 545–46; *Memphis Appeal*, February 11, 1864.

11. Walker to wife, March 20, 1864, in William Lee White and Runion, *Great Things*, 105; Barber diary, March 18, 1864, in Ferrell, *Holding the Line*, 167; Honnell to friend, July 17, 1864, Honnell Letters, EU. See also Phillips, *Diehard Rebels*, 133.

12. *Memphis Appeal*, February 11, 1864; Walker to wife, March 13, 1864, in William Lee White and Runion, *Great Things*, 104; Harlan to brother, August 3, 1863, Harlan Letters, CCNBP; Jenkins, *Gates of Atlanta*, 145–46 (Rorer).

13. Roberts to wife, June 23, 1864, Roberts Letters, UMISS; Rable, *Confederate Republic*, 289–90.

14. Castel, *Decision in the West*, 27; Castel, "Atlanta Campaign," 17.

15. William C. Davis, "Turning Point That Wasn't," 131; Johnston, *Military Operations*, 363. See also Daniel, "South Almost Won," 44–51.

16. Stoker, *Grand Design*, 176.

17. McMurry, *Fourth Battle of Winchester*, 67, 84–88.

18. Stoker, *Grand Design*, 376–77.

19. Barber diary, February 3, April 2, 5, 1864, in Ferrell, *Holding the Line*, 159, 171, 174; Kelly to Miss L. A. Honnell, April 1864, Honnell Letters, EU; Fleming to aunt, May 4, 1864, in Williamson, "Francis P. Fleming," 150.

20. Kern to mother, April 2, 1864, Kern Letters, SHC; Barber diary, April 5, 1864, in Ferrell, *Holding the Line*, 174; J. L. Bates to "Will," July 3, 1864, and to mother, September 22, 1864, in Lowe, *Texas Cavalry Officer's*, 303, 318; Ball to wife, September 4, 1864, www.civilwarvoices.com.

21. Dent to wife, September 10, 1864, Dent Letters, AU; Miller to wife, November 15, 1864, in McMurry, *Uncompromising Secessionist*, 259; Key diary, November 17, 1864, in Cate, *Two Soldiers*, 151.

22. As quoted in Clampitt, *Confederate Heartland*, 102–3; Sword, *Southern Invincibility*, 298.

23. Rable, *Confederate Republic*, 292; Phillips, *Diehard Rebels*, 155.

24. Lowe, *Texas Cavalry Officer's*, 321. In his book *Atlanta 1864*, McMurry devotes appendix 4 to a comparison of my thesis with Castel's. He declared that Castel was correct by claiming that the South could have won in 1864 by not losing. He states that I was correct in thinking that there were sufficient Union victories in 1864 to sustain Northern

morale, even if Atlanta had not fallen before the election. He also concurred with my thesis that Lincoln most likely would have carried his home state of Illinois regardless of the events in Georgia, thus assuring reelection in the electoral college.

CHAPTER 23

1. Alex Spence to parents, September 6, 1864, in Christ, *Being Shot At*, 102; Marshall to wife, September 3, 1864, Marshall Letters, MSU; Colville to father, September 7, 1864, Colville Letters, Kennesaw Mountain National Battlefield Park, Kennesaw, Georgia; Berryhill to wife, September 9, 1864, in Mary M. Jones and Martin, *Gentle Rebel*, 91; Roberts to wife, September 6, 1864, Roberts Letters, UMISS; Hall to father, September 4, 1864, Hall Letters, ADAH; Dent to wife, September 13, 1864, Dent Letters, AU; Phillips, *Diehard Rebels*, 134–35, 141, 145–46. Hood claimed to have only 26,000 infantry on September 11, but his own records reveal otherwise. See *OR*, 39(2):829.

2. John Bell Hood, *Advance and Retreat*, 253; *OR*, 39(2):836; Tillman to mother, September 26, 1864, in Bobbie Swearinggen Smith, *Palmetto Boy*, 109. See also Daniel, *Soldiering*, 26. We now know, through the research of Stephen Davis, that Lee had gently lobbied Davis to replace Hood with Beauregard. The president remained unmoved. See Stephen Davis, "P. G. T. Beauregard," 36–41.

3. John Bell Hood, *Advance and Retreat*, 254; Hughes, *Hardee*, 247–48; Hughes, *Civil War Memoir*, 267–68; William C. Davis, *Jefferson Davis*, 566; Anne J. Bailey (*Chessboard of War*, 21) concluded that Beauregard was "eager to increase his authority and anxious to leave Virginia." McMurry (*John Bell Hood*, 158) suspected that the Beauregard appointment was "intended to silence his [Davis's] critics (who were still bemoaning the removal of Johnston) than to provide a real change in the western structure."

4. *OR*, 39(2):828–29; Russell K. Brown, *To the Manner Born*, 283–84; Losson, *Tennessee's Forgotten Warriors*, 197. Officer casualties taken from Welsh, *Medical Histories*.

5. Key diary, September 12, 1864, in Cate, *Two Soldiers*, 133; Washington Ives to sister, September 17, 1864, in Cabaniss, *Civil War Journal*, 73; Dent to wife, September 13, 1864, Dent Letters, AU; *OR*, 39(2):875, 38(3):684.

6. McMurry, *John Bell Hood*, 156–58; Sword, *Embrace an Angry Wind*, 45–46; Connelly, *Autumn of Glory*, 447.

7. Marshall to wife, September 29, 1864, Marshall Letters, MSU; Gottschalk, "Surrender or Fight?," 121 (Warren quote).

8. Sword, *Embrace an Angry Wind*, 54–57; McMurry, *John Bell Hood*, 160–61.

9. Lee White, "Long Lost Diary," 16–17.

10. John Bell Hood, *Advance and Retreat*, 263; Scaife, *Hood's Campaign for Tennessee*, 15 (Manigault); McMurry, *John Bell Hood*, 161; Connelly, *Autumn of Glory*, 483.

11. Scaife, *Hood's Campaign for Tennessee*, 15–16; McDonough, *Sherman*, 557, 559, 561, 562.

12. Brown to wife, October 19, 1864, Brown Letters, ADAH; Stephen M. Hood, *John Bell Hood: The Rise*, 74 (Clayton quote); Ward to father, October 18, 1864, Ward Letters, EU; Crittenden to wife, October 22, 1864, Crittenden Letters, AU; Lundberg, *Granbury's Texas Brigade*, 203 (Donothan quote).

13. Roane to wife, October 21, 1864, Roane Letters, MVC.

14. McMurry, *John Bell Hood*, 161–62; Woodworth, *Jefferson Davis*, 294; "Who Were the Worst," 13 (Symonds), 23 (Sears); William C. Davis, *Jefferson Davis*, 575. Stephen M. Hood (*John Bell Hood: The Rise*, 74, 81, 84) is critical of historians who fail to understand the general's goal, namely "to help Robert E. Lee and force a retrograde movement by Sherman." He is particularly critical of Sword. I read the evidence differently. Sword (*Embrace an Angry Wind*, 62–65) never criticized the concept of a campaign, only the consequences of failure and poor logistical planning. This is similar to McMurry's criticism; see *Two Great Rebel Armies*, 130–31.

15. Brown to wife, October 19, 1864, Brown Letters, ADAH; Hamilton Branch to mother, November 12, 1864; Joslyn, *Charlotte's Boys*, 285.

16. Anne J. Bailey, *Chessboard of War*, 43; Scaife, *Hood's Campaign for Tennessee*, 17; Berryhill to wife, October 29, 1864, in Mary M. Jones and Martin, *Gentle Rebel*, 105; Key diary, October 31, November 3, 1864, in Cate, *Two Soldiers*, 145–46. Hood claimed that he did not cross at Guntersville because Forrest was at Jackson, Tennessee, and could not cross the Tennessee River at the present high gauge. He therefore deflected west to join up with Forrest *before* crossing. John Bell Hood, *Advance and Retreat*, 270.

17. John Bell Hood, *Advance and Retreat*, 272–73; McMurry, *John Bell Hood*, 162; Woodworth, *Jefferson Davis*, 295; William C. Davis, *Jefferson Davis*, 575; T. Harry Williams, *Beauregard*, 244–45; Anne J. Bailey, *Chessboard of War*, 41. Stephen Hood's (*John Bell Hood: The Rise*, 82) statement that "Hood's superiors, military and political, knew of and gave their blessings to his northward movement" leaves much unsaid.

18. Vandiver, "General Hood," 148, 150–51. Beauregard's postwar criticism that Hood should have crossed the Tennessee River at Guntersville was, of course, ridiculous. At that point, the army had no base and the men were living on bread rations. Some rations got through before the twenty-first. Stephen Hood's claim (*John Bell Hood: The Rise*, 91) that Sword was "the first major author to slam Hood's lack of logistical ability" is incorrect. Vandiver, McMurry (*John Bell Hood*, 165, 167), and Woodworth (*Jefferson Davis*, 295) all criticized Hood's administration and logistical abilities before Sword did.

19. *OR*, 39(3):828, 888–89, 797–98.

20. *OR*, 39(1):808, 811, 874, 890; and 39(3):745, 870; Lanning Diary, October 31, 1864, EU; M. A. Traynham to wife, November 19, 1864, Traynham Letters, EU; Norman D. Brown, *One of Cleburne's Command*, 144; William Berryhill to wife, November 13, 1864, in Mary M. Jones and Martin, *Gentle Rebel*, 110–11; Williams diary, October 30, 1864, in Wynne and Taylor, *This War So Horrible*, 119; John Marshall to wife, November 1, 1864, Marshall Letters, MSU; Key diary, November 13, 1864, in Cate, *Two Soldiers*, 149.

21. Anne J. Bailey, *Chessboard of War*, 45.

22. *OR*, 39(1):798–801, 808; and 39(3):879, 880, 904, 914.

23. Walker to wife, November 18, 1864, in William Lee White and Runion, *Great Things*, 144; Branch to mother, November 21, 1864, in Joslyn, *Charlotte's Boys*, 288; Brown to wife, November 10, 1864, Brown Letters, ADAH. See also James Orr to sister,

November 9, 1864, in Anderson, *Parson's Texas Cavalry Brigade*, 148; and Stephen M. Hood, *John Bell Hood: The Rise*, 75, 77–83.

24. John Bell Hood, *Advance and Retreat*, 267–68.

25. Jacobson and Rupp, *For Cause, for Country*, 48, 55, 57, 61, 68; Connelly, *Autumn of Glory*, 490–91; McMurry, *John Bell Hood*, 170. Sword (*Embrace an Angry Wind*, 92) believed that Hood was, indeed, in a race for Columbia. *OR* (45[1]:657, 1243) clearly shows that Hood was trying to get between Schofield and Nashville.

26. Symonds, *Stonewall of the West*, 250–54; Connelly, *Autumn of Glory*, 495; Losson, *Tennessee's Forgotten Warriors*, 204; Cheatham, "Lost Opportunity," 526. The conflicting orders and miscommunications of this day are, to say the least, involved and beyond the scope of this work. I would recommend reading Jacobson and Rupp's book, *For Cause, for Country*, for the specifics.

27. Sword, *Embrace an Angry Wind*, 136, 138–39; Jacobson and Rupp, *For Cause, for Country*, 162–63; McMurry, *John Bell Hood*, 173. McMurry (174) blamed Hood and S. D. Lee for the Spring Hill debacle; Stephen Hood (*John Bell Hood: The Rise*, 113–15) blamed Lee and Forrest. Jacobson and Rupp (171–74) blamed Cheatham; Woodworth (*Jefferson Davis*, 299) and Anne J. Bailey (*Chessboard of War*, 86) blamed Hood. Connelly (*Autumn of Glory*, 494–502) blamed everybody.

28. McMurry, *John Bell Hood*, 174–75; Sword, *Embrace an Angry Wind*, 156, 177; Woodworth, *Jefferson Davis*, 299; Connelly, *Autumn of Glory*, 504.

29. Stephen M. Hood, *John Bell Hood: The Rise*, 147–48.

30. Hood, 175–76; Logsdon, *Eyewitnesses*, 43, 53; Sword, *Embrace an Angry Wind*, 269. The lost generals included Adams, Cleburne, Granbury, Strahl, and Gist. Sword bases his casualty estimate on Union sources—1,750 killed, 3,800 wounded, and 702 missing, totaling 6,252.

31. Stephen M. Hood, *John Bell Hood: The Rise*, 184–86; Branch to mother, December 12, 1864, in Joslyn, *Charlotte's Boys*, 293; *OR*, 45(1):755.

32. Key diary, December 9, 10, 1864, in Cate, *Two Soldiers*, 165–66; Tillman diary, December 11, 1864, in Bobbie Swearinggen Smith, *Palmetto Boy*, 129; Walker to wife, December 14, 1864, in William Lee White and Runion, *Great Things*, 149; Sword, *Embrace an Angry Wind*, 304–5; *OR*, 45(2):685.

33. McDonough, *Nashville*, 136; Anne J. Bailey, *Chessboard of War*, 134, 137; Stephen M. Hood, *John Bell Hood: The Rise*, 189–93. Bailey wrote: "What Hood planned to do after he invested the city is hard to determine. He does not seem to have had any long-term strategy in mind, for it appears he only intended to react to circumstances."

34. Sword, *Embrace an Angry Wind*, 330–44; Key diary, December 15, 1864, in Cate, *Two Soldiers*, 167–68; Noyes, "Eggleston," 356.

35. Sword, *Embrace an Angry Wind*, 394–403; Russell B. Bailey, "Reminiscences," 71 (Cheatham quote); *OR*, 45(1):40; McDonough, *Nashville*, 181.

36. Walker to wife, January 6, 1865, in William Lee White and Runion, *Great Things*, 152; *OR*, ser. 4, 3:989; and ser. 1, 47(3):780, 774; and 45(2):775; Stephen M. Hood, *John Bell Hood: The Rise*, 200–204, 310 (Forrest's cavalry); John Bell Hood, *Advance*

and Retreat, 309. Stephen Hood placed Confederate casualties during the campaign at 11,823. He arrives at this figure on the basis of the November 6 return plus Forrest's cavalry of 5,000, together 32,859. He then subtracts 21,036, the number at the conclusion of the campaign. The problem is that Hood begins with "effectives" and concludes with "present for duty," thus minimizing the starting number and maximizing the ending number. The starting present-for-duty figure was 37,861. Subtracting the concluding present-for-duty number would leave a difference of 16,825 as the actual loss. See *OR*, 45(1):678–79, 664, 752; and Stephen M. Hood, *John Bell Hood: The Rise*, 200–204. Jacobson and Rupp (*For Cause, for Country*, 428) use a different methodology but come out just short of 16,000, very close to my number.

37. McMurry, *John Bell Hood*, 182–83; Roberts to wife, January 7, 1865, Roberts Letters, UMISS; Sword, *Southern Invincibility*, 305–36; Brian Craig Miller, *John Bell Hood*, 163.

38. For criticism of Hood's leadership, see "Who Were the Worst," 13 (Symonds); McMurry, *John Bell Hood*, 190–91, 199; Bresnahan, *Revisioning the Civil War*, 201 (Noe); Sword, *Embrace an Angry Wind*, 439–40; and Murray and Hsieh, *Savage War*, 456, 459–60. Stephen Hood (*John Bell Hood: The Rise*, 208–26, 287–88, 267–78) attempted to place the general in a more positive light. The problem was not Hood, he asserted, but the fact that control of the narrative has been dominated by a few historians who either told untruths or simply repeated materials from other authors without examination.

EPILOGUE

1. Brian Craig Miller, *John Bell Hood*, 167.

2. Castel, *Victors in Blue*, 4.

3. Freehling, *South vs. the South*, 69.

4. For Davis's influence in the West, both positive and negative, see Woodworth, *Jefferson Davis*, 313–16.

5. Haughton, *Training, Tactics, and Leadership*, 184–85.

6. Hess, *Civil War in the West*, 319. The approximation of railroad equipment is based on www.csa-railroads.com (website by David L. Bright). I used one-third of the estimated Louisville & Nashville rolling stock as the number that remained in Tennessee, and I did not count the Memphis & Charleston as a Tennessee road, although it of course began in Chattanooga and ended in Memphis. Its length, however, ran through northern Mississippi and Alabama.

7. Castel, "Historian and the General," 66; *OR*, ser. 4, 2:380.

8. Murray and Hsieh (*Savage War*, 533, 547) pronounced Bragg "the worst in the war at every level, a major contributing factor to Union victories in the West and eventually the war." They further denounce him as a "vicious incompetent." I am inclined to lean more toward Earl Hess's interpretation, which removes Bragg from the realm of caricature and views him as a flawed but complicated personality.

9. Glatthaar, *General Lee's Army*, 464–65.

BIBLIOGRAPHY

PRIMARY SOURCES

Manuscripts

Alabama Department of Archives and History, Montgomery
    W. C. Athey Letters
    J. D. Barnes, "Incidents of the Great Battle," Ketchum's Battery File
    Edward Norphlet Brown Letters
    Newton Davis Letters
    John Hall Letters
    William J. Hardee Papers
    George D. Johnson Letters
    William Wiley Jones Letters
    Charles Lumsden Diary
    James B. Mitchell Letters
    William E. Preston Diary [Memoir]
    James R. Riggs Letters
    Searcy Family Papers (James, Reuben, and Jasper Letters)
    Henry Semple Letters
    J. Morgan Smith Letters
    E. W. Treadwell Letters
    Thomas Warrick Letters
    Daniel Weaver Letters
    B. L. Wyman Letters
Atlanta Historical Society, Atlanta, Georgia
    John Davidson Letters
Auburn University, Auburn, Alabama
    Thomas Bigbee Letters
    John Crittenden Letters
    S. H. Dent Letters
    Charles George Letters
    John T. Scott Letters
Chickamauga-Chattanooga National Battlefield Park, Fort Oglethorpe, Georgia
    Squire Helm Bush Diary (6th Kentucky File)
    Ephraim S. Dodd Diary (8th Texas Cavalry File)
    M. Glazner Letters (18th Alabama File)

George Godwin Letters (51st Tennessee File)

Jacob Goodson Letters (44th Alabama File)

Inspection Report of the 8th Texas Rangers, March 30, 1863 (8th Texas Cavalry
File)

Isaiah Harlan Letters (10th Texas File)

Washington Ives Letters (4th Florida File)

R. D. Jamison Letters (45th Tennessee File)

Milton P. Jernigan Reminiscences (Braxton Bragg File)

"Letters of George Washington Higgins" (45th Mississippi File)

"Letters of Thomas D. Osborne" (6th Kentucky File)

G. I. MacMurphey Diary (8th Texas Cavalry File)

Robert P. Myers Diary (Braxton Bragg File)

Joseph O'Brien Letters (1st Tennessee File)

John Sparkman Diary (48th Tennessee File)

Robert G. Stone Diary (15th Georgia File)

Theodore Trimmer Letters, compiled by William R. Morales (41st Alabama File)

Robert Watson Diary (7th Florida File)

Joseph Wheeler Papers

Claudius C. Wilson Letters (30th Georgia File)

Corinth Civil War Interpretive Center, Corinth, Mississippi

George Dobson Letters (10th Mississippi File)

Duke University, Durham, North Carolina

Dwight Allen Letters

Alfred W. Bell Letters

Braxton Bragg Letters

Frank Carter Letters

M. M. Chunn Letters

Neal Hensley Letters

Joseph E. Johnston Papers

Robert Looney After-Action Report, H. H. Price Papers

John Magee Diary

John S. Palmer Letters

John W. Reese Letters

Emory University, Atlanta, Georgia

Andrew Edge Letters

John Farris Letters

Nell Gillis Letters

William Honnell Letters

Daniel L. Kelly Letters

James Lanning Diary

J. B. Mason Letters, Confederate Miscellany

E. Mussina Diary

Andrew J. Neal Letters
W. P. Porter Diary
Hezekiah Rabb Letters
William A. Stephens Letters
S. H. Stout Papers
M. A. Traynham Letters
J. W. Ward Letters
Jacob Weaver Letters
Filson Historical Society, Louisville, Kentucky
Stoddard Johnston Diary
David Yandell Papers
Florida State Archives, Tallahassee
William Rogers Letters
Georgia Department of Archives and History, Morrow
Z. T. Armistead Letters
Robert Bullock Letters
Steven Elliott Diary
R. B. Ledbetter Letters
Gilder Lehrman Collection, Institute of American History, New York, New York
Gustave Cook Letters
Alfred Jones Letters
John F. Nugent Letters
Edward Ward Letters
Joseph Wheeler Circular
Greenwood Public Library, Greenwood, Mississippi
W. A. Brown Diary
Isham W. Thomas Letters and Diaries, Thomas-Gattas Papers
Grenada Public Library, Grenada, Mississippi
George W. Jones Diary
Kennesaw Mountain National Battlefield Park, Kennesaw, Georgia
R. N. Colville Letters
Library of Congress, Manuscripts Division, Washington, D.C.
Braxton Bragg Letters
Rufus Catlin Letters
John F. C. Claiborne Letters
Christian M. Epperson Letters
Louis Wigfall Papers
Louisiana State University, Baton Rouge
Lemuel Parker Conner Biographical Sketch, Lemuel C. Conner Papers
John Ellis Memoirs
John Harris Letters
Josiah Knighton Letters

Richard Pugh Letters

Thomas Chinn Robertson Letter

Mississippi Department of Archives and History, Jackson

Otis T. Baker Diary

James Foster Letter, Yerger Family Papers

George A. Grammer Diary

"Headquarters Army of Mississippi, In the Field, Marietta, June 24, 1864,"
Confederate Records, box 391, vol. 112, RG 9

Augustus Mecklin Diary and Letters

Ordnance Department Correspondence, vol. 3

J. B. Sanders Letters

Weekly Returns, Army of the Mississippi

Yerger Family Papers

Mississippi State University, Starkville

John H. Marshall Letters, Misc. Manuscripts, box 22

F. Pridmore Letters, Misc. Manuscripts, box 4, folder 6

Emmett Ross Letters, Emmett Ross Papers, box 1, folder 32

John J. Walker Letters, Rice Family Papers, box 2, folder 24

Mississippi Valley Collection, University of Memphis, Memphis

William G. Gilliland Letters

Thomas Roane Letters

Murray State University, Murray, Kentucky

W. J. Stubblefield Diary

Museum of the Confederacy, Richmond, Virginia

William Estes Diary

Theodore Livingston Letters

Robert P. Myers Letters

National Archives Record Group, Washington, D.C.

Army of Tennessee Medical Director, Letters Sent, chap. 6, vol. 749, RG 109

General Orders, chap. 2, vol. 53, RG 109

Inspection Reports and Related Records Received by the Inspector General's
Branch of the Adjutant General, RG 109

Letters Sent, chap. 4, vol. 143, RG 109

Letters Sent, Ordnance Officer, Army of Tennessee, chap. 4, vols. 141, 143, RG 109

Military Service Files, RG 109

Orders Received by Brig. Gen. Brown's Brigade, Army of Tennessee 1863–64,
chap. 8, vol. 341, RG 109

Record Book of A. L. Landis, Quartermaster of the Army of Tennessee, 1863–64,
chap. 5, vol. 226, RG 109

Record of Receipts and Deliveries at the Atlanta Arsenal, December 1863–
June 1864, chap. 4, vol. 18,

New York Historical Society, New York

John C. Breckinridge Papers

North Carolina State Archives, Raleigh
  Robert Vance Letters
Pamplin Park (Wiley Sword Collection), Petersburg, Virginia
  J. H. Erskine Letter no. 859
  "Kinloch Falconer Biography"
  W. R. Lacey Letter no. 125
  John W. Wiggins Letter no. 1816
Private Collections
  Marshall Polk Letters
  "Report of Inspection of Roads from Dalton to Resaca by W. D. Pickett,
        December 10 1863," in possession of Doug Schantz
  James Rosser Diary, in possession of Gloria Parker
Shiloh National Battlefield Park, Shiloh, Tennessee
  Stacey Allen, "Brief Analysis of Donald H. Dosch's 'The Hornet's Nest'"
  Stacey Allen, "Hornet's Nest Update," Misc. File
  T. C. Buck Letters (Stanford's Mississippi Battery File)
  D. W. Reed Letters (4th Tennessee File)
  Lemuel Scarborough Diary (13th Tennessee File)
  T. A. Taylor Diary (4th Tennessee File)
Southern Historical Collection, Chapel Hill, North Carolina
  Isaac Alexander Letters
  C. O. Bailey Letters
  Taylor Beatty Diary
  John T. Biggs Letters
  Braxton Bragg Papers
  Thomas Bragg Diary
  R. B. Brown Letters
  Matthew Buchanan Letters, Buchanan-McClellan Papers
  Daniel Coleman Diary
  Thomas Davidson Letters
  Joseph S. Espey Letters
  William Dudley Gale Papers, Leonidas Polk Papers
  James Hall Letters
  George F. Harper Letters
  Clyde Hughes Collection
  J. T. Kern Letters
  H. M. Lynn Letters
  William W. Mackall Letters
  Thomas Patton Letters
  William Rogers Memorandum Book
  Joseph Sams Letters
  Benedict Joseph Semmes Letters
  S. H. Stout Papers

J. K. Street Letters

Harvey Washington Walter Biographical Sketch

Marcus J. Wright Diary

Stones River National Battlefield Park, Murfreesboro, Tennessee

Azra Bartholomew Letters (21st Michigan File)

John Burk Letters (10th Texas Cavalry Dismounted File)

John W. Caldwell Letters (9th Kentucky File)

John Clarkson Diary (10th South Carolina File)

Ambrose Doss Letters (19th Alabama File)

A. T. Gray Letters (31st Tennessee File)

Simon Mayer Diary (10th Mississippi File)

William L. McGaughy Letters (16th Alabama File)

Alex McGowin Letters (16th Alabama File)

A. J. Murphey Letters (8th Tennessee File)

E. P. Norman Letter (28th Alabama File)

H. F. Nuckols Letters (4th Kentucky File)

William Rogers Letters (1st Florida File)

West Walker Letters (4th Tennessee Cavalry File)

Henry Watson Letters (10th Texas Cavalry Dismounted File)

J. A. Williamson Letters (2nd Arkansas Mounted Rifles Dismounted File)

Tennessee State Library and Archives, Nashville

B. F. Cheatham Papers

Thomas Davenport Diary

Virginia French Diary

Gustavus A. Henry Papers

Robert Irwin Letters

G. W. James Letters

Robert Jamison Letters

Samuel Latta Letters

Hannibal Paine Letters

J. A. Rogers Letters, Confederate Collection

J. E. Scott Letters

William Thompson Letters

Rowena Webster Memoir, Jill Garrett Collection, MF 1196

WPA Civil War Letterbook

Vol. 2 (R. H. Taylor Letters)

Vol. 3 (John M. Routt Letters, Leonidas Polk Letter)

Vol. 4 (Anthony W. Caldwell Letter)

Tulane University, New Orleans, Louisiana

William Preston Johnston Letters, LaRC, Collection 1

Joseph Jones Collection, LaRC, Collection 172

John Labouisse Letters, LaRC, Collection 614

Stewart's Corps, Army of Tennessee, September 20, 1864, LaRC, Collection 172

United States Military Academy, West Point, New York
  "1887 Annual Reunion of the Association of Graduates"
United States Army Military History Institute, Carlisle Barracks, Pennsylvania
  Rufus Daniel Diary
  "H. R." Letter, *Civil War Times Illustrated* Collection
  Camille Polignac Diary, *Civil War Times Illustrated* Collection
  Charles Stewart Letters, *Civil War Times Illustrated* Collection
  Milton Walls Letters
University of Alabama, Tuscaloosa
  V. M. Elmore Letters
  Daniel R. Hundley Letters
  Martin L. Stausel Letters
University of Arkansas, Fayetteville
  A. B. Flint Letters
  Erasmus Stirman Letters
University of Florida, Gainesville
  J. L. Hammer Letters
  Augustus D. McDonald Diary
  Michael O. Royster Letters
University of Mississippi, Oxford
  Juanita Brown Collection
    J. H. Buford Letters
    T. B. Settles Letters
  William S. Dillon Diary
  J. W. Henderson Letters
  Charles Roberts Letters
  E. C. Walthall Letters
University of Notre Dame, South Bend, Indiana
  William B. Richmond Letters
University of Southern Mississippi, Hattiesburg
  George C. Garner Biographical Sketch, Collection M61
  R. B. Pittman Letters
University of Southwestern Louisiana, Lafayette
  Robert C. Kennedy Letters, Givens-Hopkins Collection
University of Tennessee, Martin
  Van Buren Oldham Diary
  Edwin Rennolds Diary
University of Texas, Austin
  Joel H. Puckett Letters
  S. H. Stout Papers
University of the South, Sewanee, Tennessee
  Leonidas Polk Papers

Virginia Historical Society, Richmond
  James M. Brannock Letters
Virginia Military Institute, Lexington
  John R. Hurley Letters
Western Reserve Historical Society, Cleveland, Ohio
  Braxton Bragg Papers
    George Brent Diary
    J. Stoddard Johnston Diary
    Letter Book, Headquarters, Army of Tennessee, January 1–August 20, 1863
    S. H. Stout, "Reminiscences"
West Tennessee Historical Society, Memphis
  J. L. Hammer Letters
Yale University, New Haven, Connecticut
  Joseph Lyman Letters

Newspapers

Abbeville (S.C.) Press
Albany (Ga.) Patriot
Anderson (S.C.) Intelligencer
Atlanta Daily Register
Atlanta Intelligencer
Augusta Constitutionalist
Biblical Recorder
Camden (S.C.) Confederate
Charleston Daily Mercury
Chattanooga Daily Rebel
Chicago Times
Chronicle & Sentinel (Augusta, Ga.)
Clarksville Chronicle
Cleveland Daily Banner
Columbus Daily Enquirer
Columbus Daily Sun
Columbus Weekly Enquirer
Columbus Weekly Sun
Confederate Union (Milledgeville, Ga.)
Daily Gazette (Nashville)
Daily Phoenix (Columbia, S.C.)
Daily Public Ledger (Maysville, Ky.)
Edgefield (S.C.) Advertiser
Evening Argus (Ohio)
Evening Star (Washington, D.C.)
Fayetteville (Tenn.) Observer
Gillipolis (Ohio) Journal

Highland (Ohio) Weekly News
Huntsville Daily Confederate
Knoxville Daily Register
Macon Telegraph
Memphis Appeal
Memphis Avalanche
Mobile Advertiser & Register
Montgomery Daily Mail
Montgomery Weekly Advertiser
Montgomery Weekly Mail
Nashville Daily Courier
Nashville Patriot
Nashville Republican Banner
Nashville Union
Nashville Union & American
New Orleans Crescent
New Orleans Democrat
New Orleans Picayune
New Orleans Star & Catholic Register
New Orleans Times Picayune
News & Herald (Winnsboro, S.C.)
New York Herald
New York Times
Ottowa (Ohio) Free Trader
Our Southern Home
Rebel Banner
Richmond Dispatch

Richmond Enquirer
Richmond Examiner
Richmond Sentinel
Richmond Whig
Rockbridge (Ill.) Register
Rome (Ga.) Tri-Weekly Courier
Savannah Morning News
Savannah Republican
Savannah Southern Banner
Selma Daily Register

Selma Morning Register
Shelbyville (Tenn.) Banner
Southern Confederacy (Atlanta)
Southern Literary Messenger
Tennessee Baptist
Tri-Weekly Telegraph (Houston)
Weekly Clarion
Wilmington Journal
Winchester (Tenn.) Daily Bulletin

Official Documents

Atlas to Accompany the Official Records of the Union and Confederate Armies.
Washington, D.C.: Government Printing Office, 1891–95.

Dyer, Gustavus W., comp. *Tennessee Civil War Veterans Questionnaires.* 5 vols.
Greenville, S.C.: Southern Historical Press, 1985.

Hewitt, Janet B., et al., eds. *Supplement to the Official Records of the Union and
Confederate Armies.* 128 vols. Wilmington, N.C.: Broadfoot, 1994–2001.

McBride, Robert. *Biographical Dictionary of the Tennessee General Assembly.* 2 vols.
Nashville: Tennessee State Library and Archives, 1975.

The Medical and Surgical History of the War of the Rebellion, 1861–1865. 5 vols.
Washington, D.C.: Government Printing Office, 1870.

"Proceedings of the First Congress, January–March 1863." *Southern Historical Society
Papers*, 48:1–329. 1941. Reprint, Wilmington, N.C.: Broadfoot, 1992.

"Proceedings of the First Congress, Third Session, January 29–March 19, 1863."
Southern Historical Society Papers, 47:113–229. 1941. Reprint, Wilmington, N.C.:
Broadfoot, 1992.

Rowland, Dunbar, ed. *Jefferson Davis, Constitutionalist: His Letters, Papers, and
Speeches.* 10 vols. Jackson: Mississippi Department of Archives and History, 1923.

White, Robert H., ed. *Messages of the Governors of Tennessee.* 9 vols. Nashville:
Tennessee Historical Commission, 1952–90.

U.S. War Department. *The War of the Rebellion: A Compilation of the Official Records
of the Union and Confederate Armies.* 128 vols. Washington, D.C.: Government
Printing Office, 1880–1901.

Published Primary Sources

Abell, Richard B., and Fay A. Gecik, eds. *Sojourns of a Patriot: The Field and Prison
Papers of an Unreconstructed Confederate.* Murfreesboro, Tenn.: Southern Heritage
Press, 1998.

Aiken, Linda Taylor, ed. "Letters of the Offield Brothers, Confederate Soldiers from
Upper East Tennessee." *East Tennessee Historical Society* 46 (1974): 116–25.

Albertson, Joan W., comp. *Letters Home to Minnesota: 2nd Minnesota Volunteers.*
Spokane, Wash.: P. D. Enterprises, 1993.

Anderson, John Q., ed. *Campaigning with Parson's Texas Cavalry Brigade, CSA.* Hillsboro, Tex.: Hill Junior College Press, 1967.

Bailey, Russell B., ed. "Reminiscences of the Civil War by T. J. Walker." *Confederate Chronicles of Tennessee* 1 (1986): 37–74.

"Battle of Kennesaw Mountain." In *The Annals of the Army of Tennessee and Early Western History Including a Chronological Summary of Battles and Engagements in the Western Armies of the Confederacy*, 109–14. Nashville: A. D. Haynes, 1878.

Beasley, James E. "The Annals of the Army of Tennessee." In *The Annals of the Army of Tennessee Including a Chronological Summary of Battles and Engagements in the Western Armies of the Confederacy*, edited by Edwin L. Drake, 237. Nashville: A. D. Haynes, 1878.

Beatty, John. *The Citizen Soldier.* Cincinnati: Wilstach, Baldwin, 1879.

Beauregard, P. G. T. "The Campaign of Shiloh." In *Battles and Leaders of the Civil War*, edited by Richard U. Johnson and Clarence C. Buel, 1:569–93. New York: Thomas Yoseloff, 1956.

Bender, Jane Mariue, ed. "Letters of George Washington Higgins." Printed by the author, n.d.

Bennett, William. *A Narrative of the Great Revival Which Prevailed in the Southern Armies.* 1877. Reprint, Harrisonburg, Va.: Sprinkle Publications, 1989.

Bergeron, Arthur W., Jr. *The Civil War Reminiscences of Major Silas T. Grisamore C. S. A.* Baton Rouge: Louisiana State University Press, 1993.

Betts, Vicki, ed. "The Civil War Letters of Elbridge Littlejohn." *Chronicles of Smith County, Texas* 18 (Summer 1979): 22–50.

Birchfield, Steven A., comp. *Civil War Letters.* N.p., n.d.

Blackford, Charles M., ed. *Letters from Lee's Army or Memoirs of Life In and Out of the Army in Virginia during the War Between the States.* New York: Charles Scribner's Sons, 1947.

Blakey, Arch F., Ann S. Lainhart, and Winston B. Stephens Jr. *Rose Cottage Chronicles: Civil War Letters of the Bryant-Stephens Families.* Gainesville: University of Florida Press, 2012.

Bloomquist, Ann K., and Robert A. Taylor, eds. *This Civil War: The Civil War Letters of Grant and Malinda Taylor.* Macon, Ga.: Mercer University Press, 2000.

Breckinridge, W. C. P. "The Opening of the Atlanta Campaign." In *Battles and Leaders of the Civil War*, edited by Robert U. Johnson and Clarence C. Buel, 4:277–81. New York: Thomas Yoseloff, 1956.

Brown, Norman D., ed. *One of Cleburne's Command: The Civil War Reminiscences and Diary of Capt. Samuel T. Foster, Granbury's Texas Brigade, CSA.* Austin: University of Texas Press, 1980.

Cabaniss, Jim R., comp. *Civil War Journal and Letters of Washington Ives 4th Fla. C. S. A.* Printed by the author, 1987.

Cash, William L., and Lucy S. Howorth, eds. *My Dear Nellie: The Civil War Letters of William L. Nugent to Eleanor Smith Nugent.* Jackson: University of Mississippi Press, 1977.

Cate, Wirt A., ed. *Two Soldiers: The Campaign Diaries of Thomas J. Key, C. S. A. and Robert J. Campbell, U.S.A.* Chapel Hill: University of North Carolina Press, 1938.

Chalaron, J. A. "Memories of Rice Graves, C. S. A." *Daviess County Historical Quarterly* 3 (1985): 3–13.

Chapman, Sallie. "Reminiscences — Mother of the Confederacy." *Confederate Veteran* 2 (April 1894): 107–8.

"Chat with Col. W. C. McLemore." *Confederate Veteran* 8 (June 1900): 262.

Cheatham, Benjamin F. "The Lost Opportunity at Spring Hill, Tenn. — General Cheatham's Reply to Hood." *Southern Historical Society Papers* 9 (1881): 524–41.

Christ, Mark K., ed. *Getting Used to Being Shot At: The Spence Family Civil War Letters*. Fayetteville: University of Arkansas Press, 2002.

Clark, Sam L., and H. D. Riley, eds. "Outline and Organization of the Medical Department of the Confederate Army and Department of Tennessee by Samuel H. Stout." *Tennessee Historical Quarterly* 16 (Spring 1967): 55–82.

Collins, R. M. *Chapters from the Unwritten History of the War Between the States*. St. Louis: Nixon-Jones, 1893.

Confederate States Medical and Surgical Journal. 2 vols. Richmond: Ayres and Wade, 1864–65.

Cort, Charles E., and Helyn Tomlinson. *"Dear Friends": The Civil War Letters and Diaries of Charles Edwin Cort*. Printed by the authors, 2011.

Cox, Brent. "R. L. Davis Letters." *Sons of the South* 3 (April 1986): 34–40.

Crist, Lynda B., ed. *The Papers of Jefferson Davis*. 12 vols. Baton Rouge: Louisiana State University Press, 1971–2008.

Cutrer, Thomas W. *Our Trust Is in the God of Battles: The Civil War Letters of Robert Franklin Bunting, Chaplain, Terry's Texas Rangers, C. S. A.* Knoxville: University of Tennessee Press, 2006.

———. "We Are Stern and Resolved: The Civil War Letters of John Wesley Rabb, Terry's Texas Rangers." *Southwestern Historical Quarterly* 91 (October 1987): 185–226.

Cuttino, George Peddy, ed. *Saddle Bag and Spinning Wheel: Being the Civil War Letters of George W. Peddy, M.D., Surgeon, 56th Georgia Volunteer Regiment, C.S.A. and his Wife Kate Featherston Peddy*. Macon, Ga.: Mercer University Press, 1981.

Davis, Jefferson. *Rise and Fall of the Confederate Government*. 2 vols. New York: Thomas Yoseloff, 1958.

Davis, William C., ed. *Diary of a Confederate Soldier: John S. Jackman of the Orphan Brigade*. Columbia: University of South Carolina Press, 1990.

Dawes, E. C. "The Confederate Strength in the Atlanta Campaign." In *Battles and Leaders of the Civil War*, edited by Robert U. Johnson and Clarence C. Buel, 4:281–83. New York: Thomas Yoseloff, 1956.

Dawson, Francis. *Reminiscences of Confederate Service*. Baton Rouge: University of Louisiana Press, 1993.

Dennis, Frank A., ed. *Kemper County Rebel: The Civil War Diary of Robert Masten Holmes, C. S. A.* Jackson: University and College Press of Mississippi, 1973.

Douglas, Lucia R., ed. *Douglas' Texas Battery, C. S. A.* Waco, Tex.: Smith County Historical Society, 1966.

"Dr. Edward A. Flewellen." *Confederate Veteran* 14 (October 1906): 443.

Duke, Basil W. *The Civil War Reminiscences of General Basil W. Duke, C. S. A.* Garden City, N.Y.: Doubleday, Page, 1911.

———. *A History of Morgan's Cavalry.* Cincinnati: Miami, 1867.

Duncan, Louis C. *The Medical Department of the United States Army.* Gaithersburg, Md.: Olde Soldiers Books, 1987.

Estill, Mary S., ed. "Diary of a Confederate Congressman, 1862–1863." *Southwest Historical Quarterly* 38 (April 1935): 270–301.

Ferrell, Robert H., ed. *Holding the Line: The Third Tennessee Infantry, 1861–1865 by Flavel C. Barber.* Kent, Ohio: Kent State University Press, 1994.

Fitch, John. *Annals of the Army of the Cumberland.* 1864. Reprint, Mechanicsburg, Pa.: Stackpole Books, 2003.

Flood, F. W. "Captures by Eighth Confederate Cavalry." *Confederate Veteran* 13 (1905): 458–59.

Flora, Samuel R., ed. "'I Consider the Regiment My Home': The Orphan Brigade Life and Letters of Capt. Edward Ford Spears, 1861–1865." *Register of the Kentucky Historical Society* 94 (Spring 1996): 134–73.

Folmar, John F., ed. *From That Terrible Field: Civil War Letters of John M. Williams, Twenty-First Alabama Infantry.* University, Ala.: University of Alabama Press, 1981.

Foote, H. S. *War of the Rebellion: Or Scvilia and Rvbdis.* New York: Harper & Brother, 1886.

Franklin, Ann Y., comp. *The Civil War Diaries of Capt. Alfred Tyler Fielder 12th Tennessee Regiment Infantry, Company B 1861–1865.* Louisville: Printed by the author, 1996.

Fremantle, Arthur James L. *Three Months in the Southern States, April–June 1863.* New York: J. Bradburn, 1864.

French, Samuel G. *Two Wars: An Autobiography.* Nashville: Confederate Veteran, 1901.

Gallagher, Gary W., ed. *Fighting for the Confederacy: The Personal Recollections of General Edward Porter Alexander.* Chapel Hill: University of North Carolina Press, 1989.

Gammage, Washington L. *The Camp, the Bivouac, and the Battlefield, Being a History of the Fourth Arkansas Regiment, from Its Organization Down to the Present Date [. . .].* Little Rock: Arkansas Southern Press, 1955.

Garrett, Jill K., ed. *Confederate Diary of Robert D. Smith.* Columbia, Tenn.: Captain James Madison Sparkman Chapter UDC, 1975.

Gay, Mary A. *Life in Dixie during the War.* Atlanta: Charles P. Byrd, 1897.

"General Cleburne's Views on Slavery." *Annals of the Army of Tennessee and Early Western History* 1 (May 1878): 50–52.

George, Henry. *History of the 3d, 7th, 8th and 12th Kentucky*. Louisville: C. T. Dearing, 1911.

Givens, Howard L., comp. *Tennesseans in the Civil War: Confederate Narratives*. Jackson, Tenn.: Main Street, 2006.

Grant, Ulysses, S. "Chattanooga." In *Battles and Leaders of the Civil War*, edited by Robert U. Johnson and Clarence C. Buel, 3:679–711. New York: Thomas Yoseloff, 1956.

Griffith, Lucille, ed. *Yours till Death: Civil War Letters of John W. Cotton*. Tuscaloosa: University of Alabama Press, 1951.

Griscom, George L. *Fighting with Ross' Texas Cavalry Brigade C. S. A.: The Diary of George L. Griscom, Adjutant, 9th Texas Cavalry Regiment*. Hillsboro, Tex.: Hill Junior College Press, 1976.

Hafendorfer, Kenneth A., ed. *Civil War Journal of William L. Trask: Confederate Sailor and Soldier*. Louisville: KH Press, 2003.

Hallock, Judith Lee, ed. *The Civil War Letters of Joshua K. Callaway*. Athens: University of Georgia Press, 1997.

Harwell, Richard B., ed. *Kate: The Journal of a Confederate Nurse*. Baton Rouge: Louisiana State University Press, 1959.

Hay, Thomas R., ed. *Cleburne and His Command by Irving A. Buck*. Jackson, Tenn.: McCowat-Mercer, 1957.

Hill, Daniel H. "Chickamauga — The Great Battle of the West." In *Battles and Leaders of the Civil War*, edited by Robert U. Johnson and Clarence C. Buel, 3:638–62. New York: Thomas Yoseloff, 1956.

Hoffman, John. *The Confederate Collapse of the Battle of Missionary Ridge: The Reports of James Patton Anderson and His Brigade Commanders*. Dayton, Ohio: Morningside, 1985.

Holmes, Henry Mackall. *Diary of Henry McCall Holmes Army of Tennessee, Assistant Surgeon Florida Troops with Related Letters, Documents, Etc*. State College, Miss., 1968.

Hood, John Bell. *Advance and Retreat: Personal Experiences in the United States & Confederate States Armies*. Bloomington: Indiana University Press, 1959.

Hughes, Nathaniel C., ed. *The Civil War Memoir of Philip Daingerfield Stephenson, D. D.: Private, Company K, 13th Arkansas Volunteer Infantry, Louder, Pierce No. 4, 5th Company, Washington Artillery, CSA*. Conway, Ark.: UCA Press, 1995.

———. *Liddell's Record: St. John Richardson Liddell; Brigadier General, CSA Staff Officer and Brigade Commander Army of Tennessee*. Dayton, Ohio: Morningside, 1985.

Jewitt, Clayton B., ed. *Rise and Fall of the Confederacy: The Memoir of Senator Williamson S. Oldham, CSA*. Columbia: University of Missouri Press, 2006.

Johnson, Robert U., and Clarence C. Buel, ed. *Battles and Leaders of the Civil War*. 4 vols. New York: Thomas Yoseloff, 1956.

Johnston, Joseph E. "Jefferson Davis and the Mississippi Campaign." In *Battles and*

Leaders of the Civil War, edited by Robert U. Johnson and Clarence C. Buel, 3:472–82. New York: Thomas Yoseloff, 1956.

———. *Narrative of Military Operations during the Civil War.* 1874. Reprint, New York: Da Capo, 1990.

———. "Opposing Sherman's Advance to Atlanta." In *Battles and Leaders of the Civil War*, edited by Robert U. Johnson and Clarence C. Buel, 4:260–77. New York: Thomas Yoseloff, 1956.

Johnston, William Preston. *The Life of Gen. Albert Sidney Johnston, Embracing His Services in the Armies of the United States, the Republic of Texas, and the Confederate States.* New York: D. Appleton, 1879.

Jones, J. B. *Rebel War Clerk's Diary of the Confederate States Capital.* 2 vols. Philadelphia: J. P. Lippincott, 1866.

Jones, Mary M., and Leslie J. Martin, eds. *The Gentle Rebel: The Civil War Letters of William Harvey Berryhill.* Yazoo City, Miss.: Sassafras, 1982.

Jones, P. R. "Recollections of the Battle of Murfreesboro." *Confederate Veteran* 31 (September 1923): 341–42.

Jones, William. *Christ in Camp or Religion in Lee's Army.* Harrisonburg, Va.: Sprinkle Publications, 1986.

Jordan, Thomas. "Notes of a Confederate Staff Officer at Shiloh." In *Battles and Leaders of the Civil War*, edited by Robert U. Johnson and Clarence C. Buel, 2:594–603. New York: Thomas Yoseloff, 1956.

Jordan, Thomas, and Roger Pryor. *The Campaigns of Lieut.-Gen. N. B. Forrest, and Forrest's Cavalry.* New Orleans: Blelock, 1868.

Joslyn, Maurice Phillips, ed. *Charlotte's Boys: Civil War Letters of the Branch Family of Savannah.* Berryhill, Va.: Rockbridge, 1996.

Kirwan, A. K. *Johnny Green of the Orphan Brigade: The Journal of a Confederate Soldier.* Lexington: University of Kentucky Press, 1956.

Kniffen, G. C. "The Battle of Stone's River." In *Battles and Leaders of the Civil War*, edited by Robert U. Johnson and Clarence C. Buel, 3:613–32. New York: Thomas Yoseloff, 1956.

———. "Maneuvering Bragg Out of Tennessee." In *Battles and Leaders of the Civil War*, edited by Robert U. Johnson and Clarence C. Buel, 3:635–37. New York: Thomas Yoseloff, 1956.

Law, J. G. "Diary of J. G. Law." *Southern Historical Society Papers* 10 (July 1882): 378–81; 11 (January 1883): 175–81; (April–May 1883): 297–303; (October 1883): 460–65; 12 (January–February 1884): 22–28; (May 1884): 215–19; (July–September 1884): 390–95; (October–December 1884): 538–43.

Lewis, Davis W. "A Confederate Officer's Letters on Sherman's March to Atlanta." *Georgia Historical Quarterly* 51 (December 1967): 491–94.

Lindsley, John B., ed. *Military Annals of Tennessee, Confederate.* Nashville: J. M. Lindsey, 1886.

Lockett, Samuel H. "The Defense of Vicksburg." In *Battles and Leaders of the Civil*

War, edited by Robert U. Johnson and Clarence C. Buel, 3:482–92. New York: Thomas Yoseloff, 1956.

Longstreet, James. *From Manassas to Appomattox: Memoirs of the Civil War in America*. 1896. Reprint, Bloomington: Indiana University Press, 1960.

Loski, John M., ed. "I Am in for Anything for Success." *North & South*, April 2003, 76–86.

Lowe, Richard., ed. *A Texas Cavalry Officer's Civil War: The Diary and Letters of James C. Bates*. Baton Rouge: Louisiana State University Press, 1999.

Mackall, William W. *A Son's Recollections of His Father*. New York: E. P. Dutton, 1930.

Martin, William. "A Defense of General Bragg's Conduct at Chickamauga." *Southern Historical Society Papers* 11 (April 1883): 201–6.

McCardle, Linda S., ed. *A Just and Holy Cause: The Civil War Letters of Marcus Bethune Ely and Martha Frances Ely*. Macon, Ga.: Mercer University Press, 2016.

McKee, E. L. "Events of Camp Life in the Army." *Confederate Veteran* 11 (March 1903): 113.

McMurray, W. J. *History of the Twentieth Tennessee Regiment Volunteer Infantry, C. S. A.* Nashville: Publication Committee, 1904.

McMurry, Richard M., ed. *An Uncompromising Secessionist: The Civil War of George Knox Miller, Eighth (Wade's) Confederate Cavalry*. Tuscaloosa: University of Alabama Press, 2007.

Meadows, J. A. "The Fourth Tennessee Infantry." *Confederate Veteran* 14 (July 1906): 312.

Mitchell, Enoch L., ed. "The Civil War Letters of Thomas Jefferson Newberry." *Journal of Mississippi History* 10 (January 1948): 44–80.

———. "Letters of a Confederate Surgeon in the Army of Tennessee to His Wife." *Tennessee Historical Quarterly* 4 (December 1945): 341–53; 5 (March 1946): 61–81; (June 1946): 142–81.

Moorman, Hiram Clark. "The Moorman Memorandum." *Confederate Chronicles of Tennessee* 3 (1989): 53–87.

"More About Re-Enlistments at Dalton." *Confederate Veteran* 10 (April 1902): 399–400.

Morton, John W. *The Artillery of Nathan Bedford Forrest: "The Wizard of the Saddle."* Nashville: Publishing House for the M. E. Church, South, 1909.

Noyes, Edward, ed. "Excerpts of the Civil War Diary of E. T. Eggleston." *Tennessee Historical Quarterly* 17 (December 1958): 336–58.

"The Opposing Forces in the Atlanta Campaign." In *Battles and Leaders of the Civil War*, edited by Robert U. Johnson and Clarence C. Buel, 4:292. New York: Thomas Yoseloff, 1956.

Otey, W. M. Mercer. "Organizing a Signal Corps." *Confederate Veteran* 7 (December 1899): 549–51.

Partin, Robert. "An Alabama Confederate Soldier's Report to His Wife." *Alabama Review* 31 (January 1950): 22–35.

————. "A Confederate Sergeant's Report to His Wife during the Campaign from Tullahoma to Dalton." *Tennessee Historical Quarterly* 12 (December 1953): 291–308.

Paxton, William E. "Dear Rebecca: The Civil War Letters of William Edward Paxton, 1861–1863." *Louisiana History* 20 (Spring 1979): 169–96.

Pickett, William D. "Re-Enlistments by the Confederates." *Confederate Veteran* 10 (April 1902): 171.

————. "Reminiscences of Murfreesboro." *Confederate Veteran* 16 (September 1908): 7–8.

Polk, William K. *Leonidas Polk: Bishop and General.* 2 vols. New York: Longmans, Green, 1915.

"Re-Enlistments in the Army." *Confederate Veteran* 10 (August 1902): 351–52.

Ridley, B. L. *Battles and Sketches of the Army of Tennessee.* Mexico: Missouri Printing, 1906.

————. "Camp Scenes around Dalton." *Confederate Veteran* 10 (February 1902): 68.

Roberts, Deering J. "Field and Temporary Hospitals." In *Photographic History of the Civil War*, edited by Francis T. Miller, 7:256–72. New York: Thomas Yoseloff, 1956.

Roberts, Frank S. "In Winter Quarters at Dalton, Ga., 1863–1864." *Confederate Veteran* 26 (June 1918): 274–75.

Rogers, William P. "The Diary and Letters of William P. Rogers." *Southwestern Historical Quarterly* 32 (1929): 259–99.

Roman, Alfred. *The Military Operations of General Beauregard in the War between the States, 1861–1865: Including a Brief Personal Sketch of His Services in the War with Mexico, 1846–48.* 2 vols. New York: Harper & Row, 1883.

Rugeley, H. J. H., ed. *Batchelor-Turner Letters: 1861–1864; Written by Two of Terry's Texas Rangers.* Austin: University of Texas Press, 1961.

Russell, William H. *My Diary North & South.* Boston: T. G. H. P. Burnham, 1862.

Scarborough, William K., ed. *The Diary of Edwin Ruffin.* 2 vols. Baton Rouge: Louisiana State University Press, 1976.

Sheridan, Philip H. *The Personal Memoirs of P. H. Sheridan.* 2 vols. 1888. Reprint, New York: Da Capo, 1992.

Shook, Robert D. "Timely Information to Gen. Bragg." *Confederate Veteran* 18 (July 1910): 310.

Skellie, Ron, ed. *Lest We Forget: The Immortal Seventh Mississippi.* 2 vols. Birmingham, Ala.: Banner Digital, 2012.

Smith, Bobbie Swearinggen. *A Palmetto Boy: Civil War–Era Diaries and Letters of James Adams Tillman.* Columbia: University of South Carolina Press, 2010.

Smith, Jerry W., ed. *Virginia French's War Journal 1862–1865.* Manchester, Tenn.: Beaver, 2007.

Smith, Louis R., and Andrew Quist, eds. *Cush: A Civil War Memoir.* Livingston, Ala.: Livingston Press, 1999.

Snead, Thomas L. "With Price East of the Mississippi." In *Battles and Leaders of the*

Civil War, edited by Robert U. Johnson and Clarence C. Buel, 2:717–34. New York: Thomas Yoseloff, 1956.

Stevenson, Alexander F. *The Battle of Stone's River Near Murfreesboro, Tenn. December 30, 1862, to January 3, 1863*. Dayton, Ohio: Morningside, 1983.

Stevenson, William G. *Thirteen Months in the Rebel Army*. New York: Barnes, 1864.

Sword, Wiley, ed. "Wiley Sword's Civil War Letters Series, J. P. Graves Letters." *Blue & Gray* 24 (Winter 2008): 29–30.

Tate, Thomas K., ed. *Col. Frank Huger, C. S. A.: The Civil War Letters of a Confederate Artillery Officer*. Jefferson, N.C.: McFarland, 2011.

Terry, James G. "Record of the Alabama State Artillery from Its Organization in May 1861 to the Surrender in April 1865 and from Its Re-organization Jan'y 1872 to Jan'y 1875." *Alabama Historical Quarterly* 20 (Summer 1958): 141–47.

Thompson, Ed Porter. *History of the Orphan Brigade*. Louisville: L. N. Thompson, 1898.

"Three Deserters Shot at Shelbyville." *Confederate Veteran* 16 (March 1908): 128.

Tower, R. Lockwood, ed. *A Carolinian Goes to War: The Civil War Narrative of Arthur Middleton Manigault; Brigadier General, C. S. A.* Columbia: University of South Carolina, 1983.

Uhler, Margaret A., ed. "Civil War Letters of Major General James Patton Anderson." *Florida Historical Quarterly* 56 (October 1977): 154–66.

Urquhart, David. "Bragg's Advance and Retreat." In *Battles and Leaders of the Civil War*, edited by Robert U. Underwood and Clarence C. Buel, 3:600–609. New York: Thomas Yoseloff, 1956.

Vaughn, A. J. *Personal Record of the Thirteenth Regiment, Tennessee Infantry*. Memphis: S. C. Toof, 1897.

Warner, Ezra J. *Generals in Gray: Lives of the Confederate Commanders*. Baton Rouge: Louisiana State University Press, 1959.

"War Time Letters of the Sixties." *Confederate Veteran* 12 (January 1904): 24.

Waters, Zack C., ed. "The Partial Atlanta Reports of Confederate Maj. Gen. William B. Bates." In *The Campaign for Atlanta and Sherman's March to the Sea*, edited by Theodore P. Savas and David A. Woodbury, 197–219. Campbell, Calif.: Savas Woodbury, 1994.

Watkins, Sam R. *"Co. Aytch": A Side Show of the Big War*. 1882. Reprint, New York: A Touchstone Book, 1962.

Welker, David A., ed. *A Keystone Rebel: The Civil War Diary of Joseph Garey, Hudson's Battery Mississippi Volunteers*. Gettysburg, Pa.: Thomas Publications, 1996.

White, Lee. "The Long Lost Diary of Major General Patrick R. Cleburne." In *The Tennessee Campaign of 1864*, edited by Steven E. Woodworth and Charles D. Grear, 7–22. Carbondale: Southern Illinois University Press, 2016.

White, William Lee, and Charles D. Runion, eds. *Great Things Are Expected of Us: The Letters of Colonel C. Irvine Walker, 10th South Carolina Infantry, C. S. A.* Knoxville: University of Tennessee Press, 2009.

Williamson, Edward C., ed. "Francis P. Fleming in the War for Southern Independence: Letters from the Front, Part II." *Florida Historical Quarterly* 28 (1949): 144–55.

Wills, Ridley, II. *Old Enough to Die.* Franklin, Tenn.: Hillsboro Press, 1996.

Woods, Earl C., ed. *The Shiloh Diary of Edmond Enoul Livaudais.* New Orleans: Archdiocese of New Orleans, 1992.

Woodward, C. Van, ed. *Mary Chesnut's Civil War by Mary Boykin Chesnut.* New Haven, Conn.: Yale University Press, 1981.

Worley, Ted R., ed. *The War Memories of Captain John W. Lavender C. S. A.: They Never Came Back; The Story of Co. F Fourth Arks. Infantry, C. S. A. Originally Known as the Montgomery Hunters, as Told by Their Commanding Officer.* Pine Bluff, Ark.: W. M. Hackett and D. R. Perdue, 1956.

Worsham, W. J. *Old Nineteenth Tennessee Regiment C. S. A.: June 1861–April 1865.* Knoxville, Tenn.: Press of Paragon, 1902.

Wright, Girand. *A Southern Girl in '62 — The War Time Memoirs of a Confederate Senator's Daughter.* New York: Doubleday, Page, 1905.

Wyeth, John Allen. *Life of General Nathan Bedford Forrest.* New York: Harper & Brothers, 1899.

Wynne, Lewis N., and Robert A. Taylor, eds. *This War So Horrible: The Civil War Diary of Hiram Smith Williams.* Tuscaloosa: University of Alabama Press, 1993.

Younger, Edward, ed. *Inside the Confederate Government: The Diary of Robert Garlick Kill Kean.* New York: Oxford University Press, 1967.

SECONDARY SOURCES
Books and Articles

Allardice, Bruce. *Confederate Colonels: A Biographical Register.* Columbia: University of Missouri Press, 2008.

Allardice, Bruce, and Lawrence Lee Hewitt. *Kentuckians in Gray: Confederate Generals and Field Officers of the Bluegrass State.* Lexington: University Press of Kentucky, 2008.

Allen, Stacey D. "Shiloh! The Campaign and First Day's Battle." *Blue & Gray* 14 (February 1977): 6–64.

Andrews, J. Cutler. *The South Reports the Civil War.* Pittsburgh, Pa.: University of Pittsburgh Press, 1985.

Arliskas, Thomas M. *Cadet Gray and Butternut Brown.* Gettysburg, Pa.: Thomas Publications, 2006.

Bailey, Anne J. *The Chessboard of War: Sherman and Hood in the Autumn Campaigns of 1864.* Lincoln: University of Nebraska Press, 2000.

Bearss, Ed. "Forrest's West Tennessee Campaign of 1862 and the Battle of Parker's Crossroads." *Blue & Gray*, Fall 2003, 7–22, 43–50.

Beringer, Richard E., Herman Hattaway, Archer Jones, and William N. Still Jr. *Why the South Lost the War.* Athens: University of Georgia Press, 1986.

Bishop, Randy. *Civil War Generals of Tennessee.* Gretna, La.: Pelican, 2013.

Blount, Jr., Russell W. *The Battles of New Hope Church*. Gretna, La.: Pelican, 2010.

Bonds, Russell S. "Leonidas Polk: Southern Civil War General." *Civil War Times Illustrated* 45 (May 2006): 46–58.

———. *War Like the Thunderbolt: The Battle and Burning of Atlanta*. Yardley, Pa.: Westholme, 2009.

Bradley, Michael R. *Tullahoma: The 1863 Campaign for the Control of Middle Tennessee*. Shippensburg, Pa.: Burd Street, 2000.

Bradley, Michael R., and Shirley F. Jones. *Murfreesboro in the Civil War*. Charleston, S.C.: History Press, 2012.

Breeden, James O. "A Medical History of the Latter Stages of the Atlanta Campaign." *Journal of Southern History* 35 (February 1969): 31–59.

Bresnahan, James C., ed. *Revisioning the Civil War: Historians on Counter-Factual Scenarios*. Jefferson, N.C.: MacFarland, 2005.

Bridges, Hal. *Lee's Maverick General*. 1961. Reprint, Lincoln: University of Nebraska Press, 1991.

Brown, Myers E. *Images of America: Tennessee Confederates*. Charleston, S.C.: Arcadia, 2011.

Brown, Russell K. *Our Connection with Savannah: A History of the 1st Battalion Georgia Sharpshooters*. Macon, Ga.: Mercer University Press, 2004.

———. *To the Manner Born: The Life of General William H. T. Walker*. Macon, Ga.: Mercer University Press, 2005.

Carter, Arthur B. *Tarnished Cavalier: Major General Earl Van Dorn, C. S. A.* Knoxville: University of Tennessee Press, 1999.

Castel, Albert. "The Atlanta Campaign and the Presidential Election of 1864: How the South Almost Won by Not Losing." In *Winning and Losing in the Civil War: Essays and Stories*, 15–32. Columbia: University of South Carolina Press, 1996.

———. *Decision in the West: The Atlanta Campaign of 1864*. Lawrence: University of Kansas Press, 1992.

———. "The Historian and the General: Thomas L. Connelly Versus Robert E. Lee." In *Winning and Losing in the Civil War: Essays and Stories*, 63–78. Columbia: University of South Carolina Press, 1996.

———. "Mars and Reverend Longstreet: Or, Attacking and Dying in the Civil War." In *Winning and Losing in the Civil War: Essays and Stories*, 119–32. Columbia: University of South Carolina Press, 1996.

———. "Savior of the South?" *Civil War Times Illustrated* 36 (March 1997): 38–40.

———. *Victors in Blue: How Union Generals Fought the Confederates, Battled Each Other, and Won the Civil War*. Lawrence: University of Kansas, 2011.

———. *Winning and Losing in the Civil War: Essays and Stories*. Columbia: University of South Carolina Press, 1996.

Cathey, M. Todd, and Gary W. Waddey. *"Forward My Brave Boys!": A History of the 11th Tennessee Volunteer Infantry, CSA*. Macon, Ga.: Mercer University Press, 2016.

Civil War Centennial Commission. *Tennesseans in the Civil War*. 2 vols. Nashville: Civil War Centennial Commission, 1964.

Clampitt, Bradley R. *The Confederate Heartland: Military and Civilian Morale in the Western Confederacy*. Baton Rouge: Louisiana State University Press, 2011.

Clark, John E. *Railroads in the Civil War: The Impact of Management on Victory and Defeat*. Baton Rouge: Louisiana State University Press, 2001.

Coffman, Edward M. *The Old Army: A Portrait of the American Army in Peacetime, 1784–1898*. New York: Oxford University Press, 1986.

Connelly, Thomas L. *Army of the Heartland: The Army of Tennessee, 1861–1862*. Baton Rouge: Louisiana State University Press, 1976.

———. *Autumn of Glory: The Army of Tennessee, 1861–1865*. Baton Rouge: Louisiana State University Press, 1971.

———. "Robert E. Lee and the Western Confederacy: A Criticism of Lee's Strategic Ability." *Civil War History* 15 (June 1969): 116–32.

Connelly, Thomas L., and Archer Jones. *The Politics of Command: Factions and Ideas in Confederate Strategy*. Baton Rouge: Louisiana State University Press, 1973.

Cooling, Benjamin Franklin. *Fort Donelson's Legacy: War and Society in Kentucky and Tennessee, 1862–1863*. Knoxville: University of Tennessee Press, 1997.

———. *Forts Henry and Donelson: The Key to the Confederate Heartland*. Knoxville: University of Tennessee Press, 1987.

Cooper, William J., Jr. *Jefferson Davis, American*. New York: Knopf, 2000.

Cozzens, Peter. *No Better Place to Die: The Battle of Stones River*. Urbana: University of Illinois Press, 1990.

———. *This Terrible Sound: The Battle of Chickamauga*. Urbana: University of Illinois Press, 1992.

Crabb, Martha L. *All Afire to Fight: The Untold Story of the Civil War's Ninth Texas Cavalry*. New York: Avon Books, 2000.

Cullum, George W. *Biographical Register of the Officers and Graduates of the U.S. Military Academy*. 3 vols. Boston: Houghton, Mifflin, 1891–1910.

Cunningham, O. Edward. *Shiloh and the Western Campaign of 1862*. Edited by Gary D. Joiner and Timothy B. Smith. El Dorado Hills, Calif.: Savas Beatie, 2007.

Daiss, Timothy. *In the Saddle: Exploits of the 5th Georgia Cavalry*. Atglen, Pa.: Schiffer Military History, 1999.

Daniel, Larry J. " 'The Assaults of the Demagogues in Congress': General Albert Sidney Johnston and the Politics of Command." *Civil War History* 37 (December 1991): 328–35.

———. *Battle of Stones River: The Forgotten Conflict between the Confederate Army of Tennessee and the Union Army of the Cumberland*. Baton Rouge: Louisiana State University Press, 2012.

———. *Cannoneers in Gray: The Field Artillery of the Army of Tennessee*. Rev. ed. Tuscaloosa: University of Alabama Press, 2005.

———. *Days of Glory: The Army of the Cumberland, 1861–1865*. Baton Rouge: Louisiana State University Press, 2004.

———. "Jay's Mill: The Opening Action at Chickamauga." *North & South* 9 (June 2006): 50–59.

————. *Shiloh: The Battle That Changed the Civil War.* New York: Simon & Schuster, 1997.

————. *Soldiering in the Army of Tennessee: A Portrait of Life in a Confederate Army.* Chapel Hill: University of North Carolina Press, 1991.

————. "The South Almost Won by Not Losing: A Rebuttal." *North & South* 3 (February 1998): 44–51.

Daniel, Larry J., and Lynn N. Bock. *Island No. 10: Struggle for the Mississippi Valley.* Tuscaloosa: University of Alabama Press, 1996.

Davis, Stephen. *Atlanta Will Fall: Sherman, Joe Johnston and Yankee Heavy Battalions.* Wilmington, DE: Scholarly Resources, 2001.

————. *A Long and Bloody Task.* El Dorado Hills, Calif.: Savas Beatie, 2016.

————. "A Reappraisal of the Generalship of General John Bell Hood in the Battles for Atlanta." In *The Campaigns for Atlanta and Sherman's March to the Sea*, edited by Theodore P. Savas and David A. Woodbury, 49–95. Campbell, Calif.: Savas Woodbury, 1994.

————. *What the Yankees Did to Us: Sherman's Bombardment and Wrecking of Atlanta.* 2012. Reprint, Macon, Ga.: Mercer University Press, 2014.

————. "Would P. G. T. Beauregard Lead the A of T?" *Civil War Times* 56 (April 2007): 36–51.

Davis, William C. *Breckinridge: Statesman, Soldier, Symbol.* Baton Rouge: Louisiana State University Press, 1974.

————. *Jefferson Davis: The Man and His Hour.* New York: Harper Collins, 1991.

————. *The Orphan Brigade: The Kentucky Confederates Who Couldn't Go Home.* Garden City, N.Y.: Doubleday, 1980.

————. "The Turning Point That Wasn't: The Confederates and the Election of 1864." In *The Cause Lost: Myths and Realities of the Confederacy*, 127–47. Lawrence: University of Kansas Press, 1998.

"Did the Confederacy Have a Strategy?" *North & South* 13 (July 2011): 54–63.

Dodson, William Carey, ed. *Campaigns of Wheeler and His Cavalry, 1862–1865.* Atlanta: Hudgins, 1899.

Dosch, Donald. "The Hornet's Nest at Shiloh." *Tennessee Historical Quarterly* 37 (1978): 175–89.

Dubose, John W. *General Joseph Wheeler and the Army of Tennessee.* New York: Neale, 1912.

Dyer, John P. *"Fightin' Joe" Wheeler.* Baton Rouge: Louisiana State University Press, 1941.

Ecelbarger, Gary. *Slaughter at the Chapel: The Battle of Ezra Church 1864.* Norman: University of Oklahoma Press, 2016.

Ehlinger, Peter J. *Kentucky's Last Cavalier: General William Preston, 1816–1887.* Lexington: Kentucky Historical Society, 2004.

Eicher, David C. *Dixie Betrayed: How the South Really Lost the Civil War.* New York: Little, Brown, 2006.

Elliott, Sam Davis, ed. *Doctor Quintard, Chaplain C. S. A. and Second Bishop of*

Tennessee: The Memoir and Civil War Diary of Charles Todd Quintard. Baton Rouge: Louisiana State University Press, 2003.

———. *Isham G. Harris of Tennessee: Confederate Governor and United States Senator*. Knoxville: University of Tennessee Press, 2010.

———. *Soldier of Tennessee: General Alexander P. Stewart and the Civil War in the West*. Baton Rouge: Louisiana State University Press, 1999.

Ellsworth, Elliot, Jr. *West Point in the Confederacy*. New York: G. A. Baker, 1941.

Engle, Stephen D. *Struggle for the Heartland: The Campaign from Fort Henry to Corinth*. Lincoln: University of Nebraska Press, 2001.

Evans, Davis. *Sherman's Horsemen: Union Cavalry Operations in the Atlanta Campaign*. Bloomington: Indiana University Press, 1996.

Faust, Drew Gilpin. *The Creation of Confederate Nationalism: Ideology and Identity in the Civil War South*. Baton Rouge: Louisiana State University Press, 1958.

———. *Southern Stories: Slaveholders in Peace and War*. Columbia: University of Missouri Press, 1992.

Faust, Patricia L., ed. *Historical Times Encyclopedia of the Civil War*. New York: Harper & Row, 1986.

Fitzgerald, D. P. *John B. McFerrin: A Biography*. Nashville: Publishing House of the M. E. Church, South, 1888.

Fleming, James R. *The Confederate Ninth Tennessee Infantry*. Gretna, La.: Pelican, 2006.

Fowler, John D. *Mountaineers in Gray: The Nineteenth Tennessee Volunteer Infantry Regiment, C. S. A.* Knoxville: University of Tennessee Press, 2004.

Franks, Edward L. "Braxton Bragg, James Longstreet, and the Chattanooga Campaign." In *Leadership and Command in the American Civil War*, edited by Steven E. Woodworth, 29–65. Campbell, Calif.: Savas Woodbury, 1995.

Freehling, William W. *The South vs. the South*. Oxford, N.Y.: Oxford University Press, 2001.

Freemon, Frank R. "The Medical Support System of the Confederate Army of Tennessee During the Georgia Campaign, May–September 1864." *Tennessee Historical Quarterly* 52 (Spring 1993): 44–55.

Fullerton, Dan C. *Armies in Gray: The Organizational History of the Confederate States Army in the Civil War*. Baton Rouge: Louisiana State University Press, 2017.

Furqueron, James P. "A Fight or a Footrace? The Tullahoma Campaign." *North & South* 11 (January 1998): 28–38, 82–89.

Gallagher, Gary W. *The Confederate War: How Popular Will, Nationalism, and Military Strategy Could Not Stave Off Defeat*. New York: Oxford University Press, 1997.

———. "The War Was Won in the East." *Civil War Times* 50 (February 2011): 18–21.

Genovese, Eugene D. "Yeoman Farmers in a Slave Holders' Democracy." *Agricultural History* 49 (1975): 331–42.

Gillum, Jamie. *The History of the Sixteenth Volunteer Tennessee Regiment in the American Civil War*. 3 vols. Spring Hill, Tenn.: Printed by the author, 2011–13.

Girardi, Robert I. "Leonidas Polk and the Fate of Kentucky in 1861." In *Confederate Generals of the Western Theater: Essays on America's Civil War*, edited by Lawrence L. Hewitt and Arthur W. Bergeron Jr., 3:1–19. Knoxville: University of Tennessee Press, 2011.

Glatthaar, Joseph T. "Davis, Johnston, and Confederate Failure in the West." In *Partners in Command: The Relationships between Leaders in the Civil War*, 95–133. New York: Free Press, 1994.

———. "Edmund Kirby Smith." In *Leaders of the Lost Cause: New Perspectives on the Confederate High Command*, edited by Gary W. Gallagher and Joseph T. Glatthaar, 205–47. Mechanicsburg, Pa.: Stackpole Books, 2004.

———. *General Lee's Army: From Victory to Collapse.* New York: Free Press, 1908.

Goff, Richard D. *Confederate Supply.* Durham, N.C.: Duke University Press, 1969.

Gottschalk, Phil. "Is It Surrender or Fight? The Battle of Allatoona Pass." In *The Campaign for Atlanta*, edited by Theodore P. Savas and Davis W. Woodbury, 117–55. Campbell, Calif.: Savas Woodbury, 1994.

Gow, June I. "Chiefs of Staff in the Army of Tennessee under Braxton Bragg." *Tennessee Historical Quarterly* 27 (Winter 1968): 341–60.

———. "Military Administration in the Confederate Army of Tennessee." *Journal of Southern History* 40 (May 1974): 183–98.

Grimsley, Mark, and Steven E. Woodworth. *Shiloh: A Battlefield Guide.* Lincoln: University of Nebraska Press, 2006.

Groce, W. Todd. *Mountain Rebels: East Tennessee Confederates and the Civil War, 1860–1870.* Knoxville: University of Tennessee Press, 1999.

Hafendorfer, Kenneth A. *Mill Springs: Campaign and Battle of Mill Springs, Kentucky.* Louisville: KH Press, 2001.

Hale, Douglas. *The Third Texas Cavalry in the Civil War.* Norman: University of Oklahoma Press, 1993.

Hall, Richard. *Patriots in Disguise: Women Warriors in the Civil War.* New York: Paragon House, 1993.

Hallock, Judith. *Braxton Bragg and Confederate Defeat.* Tuscaloosa: University of Alabama Press, 1991.

Hamer, Phillip M. *The Centennial History of the Tennessee State Medical Association 1830–1930.* Nashville: Tennessee State Medical Association, 1930.

Hardy, Michael C. *The Fifty-Eighth North Carolina Troops: Tar Heels in the Army of Tennessee.* Jefferson, N.C.: McFarland, 2010.

Hartje, Robert G. *Van Dorn: The Life and Times of a Confederate General.* Nashville: Vanderbilt University Press, 1967.

Haughton, Andrew. *Training, Tactics, and Leadership in the Confederate Army of Tennessee.* London: Frank Cass, 2000.

Hebert, Keith S. *The Long Civil War in the North Georgia Mountains: Confederate Nationalism, Sectionalism, and White Supremacy in Bartow County, Georgia.* Knoxville: University of Tennessee Press, 2017.

Hebert, Walter H. *Fighting Joe Hooker.* Indianapolis, Ind.: Bobbs-Merrill, 1944.

Henry, J. Milton. "The Revolution in Tennessee, February 1861 to June 1861."
   Tennessee Historical Quarterly 18 (June 1959): 99–119.

Hess, Earl J. *Banners to the Breeze: The Kentucky Campaign, Corinth, and Stones
   River*. Lincoln: University of Nebraska Press, 2000.

———. *The Battle of Ezra Church and the Struggle for Atlanta*. Chapel Hill:
   University of North Carolina Press, 2015.

———. *The Battle of Peachtree Creek: Hood's First Sortie Effort to Save Atlanta*.
   Chapel Hill: University of North Carolina Press, 2017.

———. "Braxton Bragg and the Stones River Campaign." Speech given at the 150th
   Stones River Anniversary, Murfreesboro, Tenn. October 27, 2012.

———. *Braxton Bragg: The Most Hated Man of the Confederacy*. Chapel Hill:
   University of North Carolina Press, 2016.

———. *The Civil War in the West: Victory and Defeat from the Appalachians to the
   Mississippi*. Chapel Hill: University of North Carolina Press, 2012.

———. *Kennesaw Mountain: Sherman, Johnston, and the Atlanta Campaign*. Chapel
   Hill: University of North Carolina Press, 2013.

———. *The Knoxville Campaign: Burnside and Longstreet in East Tennessee*.
   Knoxville: University of Tennessee Press, 2012.

Hewitt, Lawrence W. "Braxton Bragg and the Confederate Invasion of Kentucky
   in 1862." In *Confederate Generals in the Western Theater*, edited by Lawrence W.
   Hewitt and Arthur W. Bergeron Jr., 1:71–86. Knoxville: University of Tennessee
   Press, 2010.

Hood, Stephen M. *John Bell Hood: The Rise, Fall, and Resurrection of a Confederate
   General*. El Dorado Hills, Calif. Savas Beatie, 2013.

———. *The Lost Papers of Confederate General John Bell Hood*. El Dorado Hills,
   Calif.: Savas Beatie, 2015.

Hughes, Nathaniel C., Jr. *The Battle of Belmont*. Chapel Hill: University of North
   Carolina Press, 1991.

———. *Bentonville: The Final Battle of Sherman & Johnston*. Chapel Hill: University
   of North Carolina Press, 1996.

———. *General William J. Hardee: Old Reliable*. 1965. Reprint, Wilmington, N.C.:
   Broadfoot, 1987.

———. *The Pride of the Confederate Artillery: The Washington Artillery in the Army of
   Tennessee*. Baton Rouge: Louisiana State University Press, 1997.

———. *Yale's Confederates: A Biographical Dictionary*. Knoxville: University of
   Tennessee Press, 2008.

Hughes, Nathaniel C., Jr., and Roy P. Stonesipher Jr. *The Life and Wars of Gideon J.
   Pillow*. Chapel Hill: University of North Carolina Press, 1993.

Hughes, Nathaniel C., Jr., and Thomas Clayton Ware. *Theodore O'Hara: Poet-Soldier
   of the Old South*. Knoxville: University of Tennessee Press, 1993.

Hurst, Jack. *Nathan Bedford Forrest: A Biography*. New York: Vintage Books, 1994.

Iobst, Richard W. *Civil War Macon: The History of a Confederate City*. Macon, Ga.:
   Mercer University Press, 1999.

Jacobson, Eric A. "Hood's Tennessee Campaign: From the Fall of Atlanta to the
Battle of Franklin—September 2 to November 30, 1864." *Blue & Gray* 30 (2014):
6–9, 19–26, 42–50.

Jacobson, Eric A., and Richard A. Rupp. *For Cause, for Country: A Study of the Affair
at Spring Hill and the Battle of Franklin*. Franklin, Tenn.: O'More, 2007.

Jenkins, Robert D., Sr. *The Battle of Peachtree Creek: Hood's First Sortie 20 July 1864*.
Macon, Ga.: Mercer University Press, 2013.

———. "Dalton." *Blue & Gray* 32 (2015): 6–9, 19–27, 41–50.

———. *To the Gates of Atlanta: From Kennesaw Mountain to Peachtree Creek*. Macon,
Ga.: Mercer University Press, 1991.

Jones, Archer. *Civil War Command and Strategy: The Process of Victory and Defeat*.
New York: Free Press, 1992.

———. *Confederate Strategy from Shiloh to Vicksburg*. 1961. Reprint, Baton Rouge:
Louisiana State University Press, 1991.

Jones, Howard. *Union in Peril: The Crisis over British Intervention in the Civil War*.
Chapel Hill: University of North Carolina Press, 1992.

Jones, R. Steven. *The Right Hand of Command: Use and Disuse of Personal Staffs in
the Civil War*. Mechanicsburg, Pa: Stackpole Books, 2000.

Knopp, Ken R. *Made in the C. S. A.: Saddle Makers of the Confederacy*. Printed by the
author, 2003.

Kolakowski, Christopher L. *The Stones River and Tullahoma Campaigns*. Charleston,
S.C.: History Press, 2011.

Krick, Robert K. "'Snarl and Sneer and Quarrel': Joseph E. Johnston and an
Obsession with Rank." In *Leaders of the Lost Cause: New Perspectives on the
Confederate High Command*, edited by Gary W. Gallagher and Joseph T. Glatthaar,
165–203. Mechanicsburg, Pa.: Stackpole Books, 2004.

———. *Staff Officers in Gray: A Biographical Register of the Staff Officers in the Army
of Northern Virginia*. Chapel Hill: University of North Carolina Press, 2003.

Kundahl, George G. *Confederate Engineer: Training and Campaigning with John
Morris Wampler*. Knoxville: University of Tennessee Press, 2000.

Lash, Jeffrey N. *Destroyer of the Iron Horse: General Joseph E. Johnston and
Confederate Rail Transport, 1861–1865*. Kent, Ohio: Kent State University Press,
1991.

Levine, Bruce. *Confederate Emancipation: Southern Plans to Free and Arm Slaves
during the Civil War*. New York: Oxford University Press, 2006.

Lewis, Jim. "The Battle of Stones River." *Blue & Gray* 28 (2012): 6–8, 19–26, 43–48.

Livermore, Thomas L. *Numbers and Losses in the Civil War of America*. New York:
Houghton, Mifflin and Company, 1900.

Logsdon, David R., ed. *Eyewitnesses to the Battle of Franklin*. Nashville: Kettle Mills,
2000.

Longacre, Edward G. *Cavalry of the Heartland: The Mounted Forces of the Army of
Tennessee*. Yardley, Pa.: Westholme, 2009.

———. *A Soldier to the Last: Maj. Gen. Joseph Wheeler in Blue and Gray.* Washington, D.C.: Potomac Books, 2007.

Losson, Christopher. *Tennessee's Forgotten Warriors.* Knoxville: University of Tennessee Press, 1989.

Lowry, Thomas P., and Lewis Laska. *Confederate Death Sentences.* Printed by the authors, 2008.

Lundberg, John R. "Baptizing the Hills and Valleys: Cleburne's Defense of Tunnel Hill." In *The Chattanooga Campaign,* edited by Steven E. Woodworth and Charles D. Greer, 70–83. Carbondale: Southern Illinois University Press, 2012.

———. *Granbury's Texas Brigade: Diehard Western Confederates.* Baton Rouge: Louisiana State University Press, 2012.

———. "'I Must Save This Army': Albert Sidney Johnston and the Shiloh Campaign." In *The Shiloh Campaign,* edited by Steven E. Woodworth, 8–28. Carbondale: Southern Illinois University Press, 2009.

Madaus, Howard D., and Robert D. Needham. *The Battle Flags of the Confederate Army of Tennessee.* Milwaukee, Wis.: Friends of the Museum, 1976.

Mallock, Daniel. "Cleburne's Proposal." *North & South* 11 (December 2008): 64–72.

Martin, Samuel J. *General Braxton Bragg, C. S. A.* Jefferson, N.C.: MacFarland, 2011.

Matthews, Gary R. "Beleagured Loyalties: Kentucky Unionism." In *Sister States, Enemy States: The Civil War in Kentucky and Tennessee,* edited by Kent T. Dollar, Larry H. Whitaker, and W. Calvin Dickinson, 9–24. Lexington: University Press of Kentucky, 2009.

McBride, Mary Gorton. *Randall Lee Gibson of Louisiana: Confederate General and New South Reformer.* Baton Rouge: Louisiana State University Press, 2007.

McCurry, Stephanie. *Confederate Reckoning: Power and Politics in the Civil War South.* Cambridge, Mass.: Harvard University Press, 2010.

McDonough, James L. *Chattanooga: A Death Grip on the Confederacy.* Knoxville: University of Tennessee Press, 1984.

———. *Nashville: The Western Confederacy's Final Gamble.* Knoxville: University of Tennessee Press, 2004.

———. *War in Kentucky: From Shiloh to Perryville.* Knoxville: University of Tennessee Press, 1994.

———. *William Tecumseh Sherman: In the Service of My Country.* New York: W. W. Norton, 2016.

McMurry, Richard M. *Atlanta 1864: Last Chance for the Confederacy.* Lincoln: University of Nebraska Press, 2000.

———. "The Atlanta Campaign and the Election of 1864." In *Atlanta 1864: Last Chance for the Confederacy,* 204–8. Lincoln: University of Nebraska Press, 2000.

———. "The Enemy at Richmond: Joseph E. Johnston and the Confederate Government." *Civil War History* 27 (1961): 5–31.

———. *The Fourth Battle of Winchester: Toward a New Civil War Paradigm.* Kent, Ohio: Kent State University Press, 2002.

————. "From the West Where the War Was Decided." *Civil War Times* 50 (February 2011): 18–21.

————. *John Bell Hood and the War for Southern Independence*. Lexington: University of Kentucky Press, 1982.

————. "A Policy So Disastrous: Joseph E. Johnston's Atlanta Campaign." In *The Campaign for Atlanta and Sherman's March to the Sea*, edited by Theodore P. Savas and David A. Woodbury, 223–48. Campbell, Calif.: Savas Woodbury, 1994.

————. *Two Great Rebel Armies: An Essay in Confederate Military History*. Chapel Hill: University of North Carolina Press, 1989.

————. *Virginia Military Institute Alumni in the Civil War*. Lynchburg, Va.: H. E. Howard, 1969.

McNeil, William J. "A Survey of Confederate Soldier Morale during Sherman's Campaign through Georgia and the Carolinas." *Georgia Historical Quarterly* 55 (Spring 1971): 1–25.

McPherson, James M. *The Battle Cry of Freedom: The Civil War Era*. New York: Ballentine Books, 1989.

————. *Drawn with the Sword: Reflections on the American Civil War*. New York: Oxford University Press, 1996.

————. *For Cause and Comrades: Why Men Fought in the Civil War*. New York: Oxford University Press, 1997.

McWhiney, Grady. "A Bishop as General." In *Confederate Crackers and Cavaliers*, 1–23. Abilene, Tex.: McWhiney Foundation Press, 2002.

————. *Braxton Bragg and Confederate Defeat*. New York: Columbia University Press, 1969.

————. "General Beauregard's 'Complete Victory' at Shiloh." In *The Shiloh Campaign*, edited by Steven E. Woodworth, 110–22. Carbondale: Southern Illinois University Press, 2009.

————. "Needed but Misused." In *Confederate Crackers and Cavaliers*, 245–61. Abilene, Tex.: McWhiney Foundation Press, 2002.

McWhiney, Grady, and Perry D. Jamieson. *Civil War Military Tactics and the Southern Heritage*. Tuscaloosa: University of Alabama Press, 1982.

Mendoza, Alexander. "The Censure of D. H. Hill: Daniel Harvey Hill and the Chickamauga Campaign." In *The Chickamauga Campaign*, edited by Steven E. Woodworth, 68–83. Carbondale: Southern Illinois University Press, 2010.

————. *Chickamauga 1863: Rebel Breakthrough*. Santa Barbara, Calif.: Praeger, 2013.

————. *Confederate Struggle for Command: General James Longstreet and the First Corps in the West*. College Station: Texas A&M University Press, 2008.

————. "A Perfect Tornado of Ineffectiveness: The First Corps and the Loss of Lookout Mountain." In *The Chattanooga Campaign*, edited by Steven E. Woodworth and Charles D. Grear, 15–21. Carbondale: Southern Illinois University Press, 2012.

Miller, Brian Craig. *John Bell Hood and the Fight for Civil War Memory*. Knoxville: University of Tennessee Press, 2010.

Miller, Rex. *Wheeler's Favorites: A Regimental History of the 51st Alabama Cavalry Regiment*. New York: Patrex, 1991.

Mitchell, Enoch L., ed. "Letters of a Confederate Surgeon in the Army of Tennessee to His Wife." *Tennessee Historical Quarterly* 4 (December 1945): 341–53; 5 (March 1946): 61–81; 5 (June 1946): 142–81.

Murray, Williamson, and Wayne Wei-Siang Hsieh. *A Savage War: A Military History of the Civil War*. Princeton, N.J.: Princeton University Press, 2016.

Neal, Diane, and Thomas W. Kremm. *Lion of the South: General Thomas C. Hindman*. Macon, Ga.: Mercer University Press, 1993.

Newton, Steven H. "Formidable Only in Flight? Casualties, Attrition, and Morale in Georgia." *North & South* 3 (April 2000): 43–56.

———. "Joseph Johnston and Snake Creek Gap." *North & South* 4 (March 2001): 56–67.

———. *Lost for the Cause: The Confederate Army in 1864*. Mason City, Iowa: Savas, 2000.

Nichols-Belt, Traci. *Onward Southern Soldiers: Religion and the Army of Tennessee in the Civil War*. Charleston, S.C.: History Press, 2011.

Noe, Kenneth W. *Perryville: This Grand Havoc of Battle*. Lexington: University Press of Kentucky, 2001.

———. *Reluctant Rebels: The Confederates Who Joined the Army after 1861*. Chapel Hill: University of North Carolina Press, 2010.

"Overrated Generals." *North & South* 11 (December 2009): 14–22.

Parks, Joseph H. *General Edmund Kirby Smith, C. S. A.* Baton Rouge: Louisiana State University Press, 1954.

———. *General Leonidas Polk, C. S. A.: The Fighting Bishop*. Baton Rouge: Louisiana State University Press, 1962.

Partin, Robert. "The Sustaining Faith of an Alabama Soldier." *Civil War History* 6 (December 1960): 425–38.

Pate, James P., ed. *When This Evil War Is Over: The Civil War Correspondence of the Frances Family*. Tuscaloosa: University of Alabama Press, 2006.

Peterson, Lawrence K. *Confederate Combat Commander: The Remarkable Life of Brigadier General Alfred Jefferson Vaughan, Jr.* Knoxville: University of Tennessee Press, 2013.

Phillips, Jason. *Diehard Rebels: The Confederate Culture of Invincibility*. Athens: University of Georgia Press, 2007.

Poulter, Keith. "But Then Again . . . ." *North & South* 1 (January 1998): 36–38, 82–83.

Powell, David A. *The Chickamauga Campaign*. 3 vols. El Dorado Hills, Calif.: Savas Beatie, 2014–16.

———. *Failure in the Saddle: Nathan Bedford Forrest, Joseph Wheeler, and the Confederate Cavalry in the Chickamauga Campaign*. El Dorado Hills, Calif.: Savas Beatie, 2010.

———. "Incubator of Innovation: The Army of the Cumberland and the Spirit of

1863." In *Gateway to the Confederacy: New Perspectives on the Chickamauga and Chattanooga Campaigns, 1862–1863*, edited by Evan C. Jones and Wiley Sword, 94–128. Baton Rouge: Louisiana State University Press, 2014.

Powell, David A., and David A. Friedrichs. *The Maps of Chickamauga*. El Dorado Hills, Calif.: Savas Beattie, 2009.

Prim, G. Clinton. "Born Again in the Trenches: Revivals in the Army of Tennessee." *Tennessee Historical Quarterly* 43 (Fall 1984): 250–72.

Rabb, James W. *J. Patton Anderson, Confederate General: A Biography*. Jefferson, N.C.: McFarland, 2004.

Rable, George. *The Confederate Republic: A Revolution against Politics*. Chapel Hill: University of North Carolina Press, 1994.

———. *God's Almost Chosen People: A Religious History of the American Civil War*. Chapel Hill: University of North Carolina Press, 2010.

Ramage, James A. *Rebel Raider: The Life of General John Hunt Morgan*. Lexington: University of Kentucky Press, 1986.

Robins, Glenn. *The Bishop of the Old South*. Macon, Ga.: Mercer University Press, 2006.

Robertson, James I., Jr. "Braxton Bragg: The Lonely Patriot." In *Leaders of the Lost Cause: New Perspectives on the Confederate High Command*, edited by Gary W. Gallagher and Joseph T. Glatthaar, 71–100. Mechanicsburg, Pa.: Stackpole Books, 2004.

Robertson, William G. "Battle of Chickamauga—Day One." *Blue & Gray*, Spring 2008, 6–8, 19–26, 40–52.

———. "Battle of Chickamauga—Day Two." *Blue & Gray*, Summer 2008, 6–9, 19–31, 40–50.

———. "Bull of the Woods? James Longstreet at Chickamauga." In *The Chickamauga Campaign*, edited by Steven E. Woodworth, 116–39. Carbondale: Southern Illinois Press, 2010.

———. "The Chickamauga Campaign: The Fall of Chattanooga." *Blue & Gray*, Fall 2006, 6–9, 12–15, 19–26, 43–50.

———. "The Chickamauga Campaign, McLemore's Cove: Rosencrans Gamble, Braggs' Lost Opportunity." *Blue & Gray*, Spring 2007, 6–26, 42–50.

———. *The Staff Ride*. Washington, D.C.: U.S. Army Center of Military History, 2014.

Roland, Charles P. *Albert Sidney Johnston: Soldier of Three Republics*. Austin: University of Texas Press, 1964.

———. "Albert Sidney Johnston and the Defense of the Confederate West." In *Confederate Generals in the Western Theater: Classic Essays on America's Civil War*, edited by Lawrence L. Hewitt and Arthur W. Bergeron, 1:13–23. Knoxville: University of Tennessee Press, 2010.

———. *Jefferson Davis's Greatest General: Albert Sidney Johnston*. Abilene, Tex.: McWhiney Foundation Press, 2010.

———. "P. G. T. Beauregard." In *Leaders of the Lost Cause: New Perspectives on the*

Confederate High Command, edited by Gary W. Gallagher and Joseph T. Glatthaar, 43–69. Mechanicsburg, Pa.: Stackpole Books, 2004.

Roth, Dave. "The Tullahoma Campaign." *Blue & Gray* 27 (2010): 51–65.

Scaife, William R. "The Chattahoochee River Line: An American Maginot." *North & South*, November 1997, 42–58.

———. *Hood's Campaign for Tennessee*. Atlanta: Printed by the author, 1986.

Schillar, Laurence D. "Two Tales of Tennessee: The Ups and Downs of Cavalry Command." *North & South* 4 (April 2001): 78–86.

Schott, Thomas E. "Lieutenant General William J. Hardee, the Historians, and the Atlanta Campaign." In *Confederate Generals in the Western Theater: Essays on America's Civil War*, edited by Lawrence L. Hewitt and Arthur J. Bergeron Jr., 2:159–84. Knoxville: University of Tennessee Press, 2010–11.

Schroeder-Lein, Glenna R. *Confederate Hospitals on the Move: Samuel H. Stout and the Army of Tennessee*. Columbia: University of South Carolina Press, 1994.

Seitz, Don Carlos. *Braxton Bragg, General of the Confederacy*. Columbia, S.C.: State, 1924.

Shanahan, Edward P. *Atlanta Campaign Staff Ride Briefing Book*. Atlanta: Camp Creek Business Center, 1995.

Shapiro, Norman M. "The Star of the Collection." *The Huntsville Historical Review* 24 (Winter–Spring 1997): 2–27.

Sheppard, Jonathan C. *By the Noble Daring of Her Sons: The Florida Brigade of the Army of Tennessee*. Tuscaloosa: University of Alabama Press, 2012.

Smith, Lanny K. *The Stone's River Campaign, 26 December 1862–January 1863*. 2 vols. Printed by the author, 2008–10.

Smith, Timothy B. "'Anatomy of an Icon': Shiloh's Hornet's Nest in Civil War Memory." In *The Shiloh Campaign*, edited by Steven E. Woodworth, 55–76. Carbondale: Southern Illinois University Press, 2009.

———. *Corinth 1862: Siege, Battle, Occupation*. Lawrence: University Press of Kansas, 2012.

———. *Grant Invades Tennessee: The 1862 Battles for Forts Henry and Donelson*. Lawrence: University of Kansas Press, 2016.

———. *Shiloh: Conquer or Perish*. Lawrence: University Press of Kansas, 2014.

Starr, Stephen Z. *Colonel Grenfell's War: The Life of a Soldier of Fortune*. Baton Rouge: Louisiana State University Press, 1971.

Stoker, Donald. *The Grand Design: Strategy and the U.S. Civil War*. New York: Oxford University Press, 2010.

———. "The Myth of the Confederate 'Offensive-Defensive' Strategy." *North & South* 13 (September 2011): 48–54.

Strode, Hudson. *Jefferson Davis, Confederate President*. New York: Harcourt, Brace, 1959.

Stroud, David V. *Ector's Texas Brigade and the Army of Tennessee, 1862–1865*. Longview, Tex.: Ranger, 2004.

Sword, Wiley. *Embrace an Angry Wind: The Confederate Last Hurrah; Spring Hill, Franklin, and Nashville.* New York: Harper Collins, 1992.

———. *Mountains Touched with Fire: Chattanooga Besieged, 1863.* New York: St. Martin's, 1995.

———. "'Our Fireside in Ruins': Consequences of the 1863 Chattanooga Campaign." In *Gateway to the Confederacy: New Perspectives on the Chickamauga and Chattanooga Campaign, 1862–1863,* edited by Evan C. Jones and Wiley Sword, 227–53. Baton Rouge: Louisiana State University Press, 2014.

———. *Shiloh: Bloody April.* 1974. Reprint, Dayton, Ohio: Morningside, 2001.

———. *Southern Invincibility: A History of the Confederate Heart.* New York: St. Martin's Griffin, 1999.

Symonds, Craig L. *Joseph E. Johnston: A Civil War Biography.* New York: W. W. Norton, 1992.

———. "No Margin for Error: Civil War in the Confederate Command." In *The Art of Command in the Civil War,* edited by Steven E. Woodworth, 1–16. Lincoln: University of Nebraska Press, 1998.

———. *Stonewall of the West: Patrick Cleburne and the Civil War.* Lawrence: University of Kansas Press, 1997.

———. "War and Politics: Jefferson Davis Visits the Army of Tennessee." In *Gateway to the Confederacy: New Perspectives on the Chickamauga and Chattanooga Campaigns, 1862–1863,* edited by Evan C. Jones and Wiley Sword, 159–71. Baton Rouge: Louisiana State University Press, 2014.

Taylor, Robert A. "Rebel Beef: Florida Cattle and the Confederate Army." *Florida Historical Quarterly* 67 (July 1988): 15–31.

Thomas, Dean S. *Confederate Arsenals, Laboratories and Ordnance Depots.* 3 vols. Gettysburg, Pa.: Thomas Publications, 2014.

Thompson, Illene D., and Wilbur E. Thompson. *The Seventeenth Alabama Infantry: A Regimental History and Roster.* Westminster, Md.: Heritage Books, 2009.

Vandiver, Frank E. "General Hood as Logistician." In *Military Analysis of the Civil War: An Anthology by the Editors of Military Affairs,* 141–51. Millwood, N.Y.: K & O, 1977.

Varney, Frank P. *General Grant and the Rewriting of History.* El Dorado Hills, Calif.: Savas Beatie, 2013.

Weber, Jennifer L. *Copperheads: The Rise and Fall of Lincoln's Opponents in the North.* New York: Oxford University Press, 2006.

Weitz, Mark A. *A Higher Duty: Desertion among Georgia Troops during the Civil War.* Lincoln: University of Nebraska Press, 2000.

———. *More Damning Than Slaughter: Desertion in the Confederate Army.* Lincoln: University of Nebraska Press, 2005.

Welcher, Frank J., and Larry G. Ligget. *Coburn's Brigade: 85th Indiana, 33rd Indiana, 19th Michigan, and 22nd Wisconsin in the Western Theater.* Carmel, Ind.: Guild Press of Indiana, 1999.

Welsh, Jack D. *Medical Histories of Confederate Generals*. Kent, Ohio: Kent State University Press, 1995.

———. *Two Confederate Hospitals and Their Patients: Atlanta to Opelika*. Macon, Ga.: Mercer University Press, 2005.

West, Carol Van, ed. *The Tennessee Encyclopedia of History and Culture*. Nashville: Rutledge Hill, 1998.

"Who Were the Worst Ten Generals?" *North & South* 7 (May 2004): 12–25.

Wiley, Bell I. "Billy Yank and Johnny Reb in the Campaign for Atlanta." *Civil War Times Illustrated* 3 (1974): 18–22.

———. *The Life of Johnny Reb*. Indianapolis: Bobbs-Merrill, 1962.

William, David. *Georgia's Civil War: Conflict on the Home Front*. Macon, Ga.: Mercer University Press, 2017.

Williams, David, Teresa Crisp Williams, and David Carlson. *Plain Folk in a Rich Man's War: Class Dissent in Confederate Georgia*. Gainesville: University Press of Florida, 2002.

Williams, T. Harry. *P. G. T. Beauregard: Napoleon in Gray*. 1955. Reprint, Baton Rouge: Louisiana State University Press, 2011.

Wills, Brian S. *The Confederacy's Greatest Cavalryman: Nathan Bedford Forrest*. Lawrence: University Press of Kansas, 1992.

Wilson, Harold S. *Confederate Industry: Manufacturers and Quartermasters in the Civil War*. Jackson: University Press of Mississippi, 2002.

Wommack, Bob. *Call Forth the Mighty Men*. Bessemer, Ala.: Colonial, 1987.

Wood, W. J. *Civil War Generalship: The Art of Command*. New York: Da Capo, 1997.

Woodworth, Steven E. "Braxton Bragg and the Tullahoma Campaign." In *The Art of Command*, edited by Steven E. Woodworth, 157–82. Lincoln: University of Nebraska Press, 1999.

———. *Chickamauga: A Battlefield Guide with a Section on Chattanooga*. Lincoln: University of Nebraska Press, 1999.

———. *Davis and Lee at War*. Lawrence: University of Kansas Press, 1995.

———. *Decision in the Heartland: The Civil War in the West*. Lincoln: University of Nebraska Press, 2011.

———. *A Deep Steady Thunder*. Abilene, Tex.: McWhiney Foundation Press, 1998.

———. "'In Their Dreams': Braxton Bragg, Thomas C. Hindman, and the Abortive Attack in McLemore's Cove." In *The Chickamauga Campaign*, edited by Steven E. Woodworth, 50–67. Carbondale: Southern Illinois University Press, 2010.

———. *Jefferson Davis and His Generals: The Failure of Confederate Command in the West*. Lawrence: University of Kansas Press, 1990.

———. *No Band of Brothers: Problems of the Rebel High Command*. Columbia: University of Missouri Press, 1999.

———. *Nothing But Victory: The Army of the Tennessee, 1861–1865*. New York: Knopf, 2005.

———. "A Reassessment of Confederate Command Options during the Winter of 1863–64." In *The Campaign for Atlanta and Sherman's March to the Sea*, edited

by Theodore P. Savas and David A. Woodbury, 1–20. Campbell, Calif.: Savas
Woodbury, 1994.

———. *Six Armies in Tennessee: The Chickamauga and Chattanooga Campaigns*.
Lincoln: University of Nebraska Press, 1998.

———. *This Great Struggle: America's Civil War*. New York: Rowman & Littlefield,
2011.

———. "When Merit Is Not Enough: Albert Sidney Johnston and Confederate
Defeat in the West, 1862." In *Civil War Generals in Defeat*, edited by Steven E.
Woodworth, 9–27. Lawrence: University Press of Kansas, 1990.

———. *While God Is Marching On: The Religious World of Civil War Soldiers*.
Lawrence: University Press of Kansas, 2001.

Wright, Marcus J. *Tennesseans in the Civil War*. New York: Ambrose Lee, 1908.

Dissertations and Thesis

Alford, Julian D. "The Tullahoma Campaign: The Beginning of the End for the
Confederacy." Master's diss., USMC Command and Staff College, 2002.

Brewer, Richard. "The Tullahoma Campaign: Operational Insights." Master's thesis,
U.S. Army Command and General Staff College, 1991.

Johnson, Robert Lewis. "Confederate Staff Work at Chickamauga: An Analysis of the
Staff of the Army of Tennessee." Master's diss., U.S. Army Command and General
Staff College, 1992.

McMurry, Richard M. "The Atlanta Campaign: December 23, 1863 to July 18, 1864."
PhD diss., Emory University, 1967.

Varney, Francis Phillip. "The Men Grant Didn't Trust: Memoir, Memory, and the
American Civil War." PhD diss., Cornell University, 2007.

INDEX

sertions in, 33, 120–28; discipline breakdown in, 257–58; drunkenness in, 133, 245, 258; furloughs given, 116, 129–30, 260; nationalism in, 263–65; officer dissention in, 90–97, 192–99; ordnance in, 3, 110, 218–22, 226–28; punishments in, 34, 125–29; Provisional Army, 1; and reenlistments, 131; reorganized, 38, 72, 233, 313; revivals in, 146–52; sectionalism in, 5–11; sickness in, 4–5, 28, 201–3, 212; strength of, 71, 97, 104, 115–16, 161–62, 172, 234; training, 143–45; use of slaves in, 266–67

Army of the Cumberland, xii, 74, 77, 84, 165, 192, 215, 237

Army of the Mississippi, 33, 38, 43, 62, 72

Army of the Ohio, 19, 20, 51, 192

Army of the West, 28

Athey, G. W., 304

Athey, W. C., 224

Atkins, John, 19

Atlanta: Arsenal, 218–20; Commissary Depot, 213–16; hospitals in, 201, 203, 212; Quartermaster Depot, 222–23; siege of, 301

Atlanta Campaign, 156, 210–12, 285–302

Augustine, Numa, 23

Avent, Benjamin W., 2

Bagby, George, 45, 85–87

Bailey, Anne, 314, 318–19

Baille, Melville, 34

Baker, Alpheus, 252

Baldwin, William, 244

Ball, William, 310

Banks, A. B., 217

Barber, Flavel, 132, 155, 305, 309

Bardstown Council, 41

Barr, James, 235

Barrct, W. Overton, 220

Bartholomew, Azra, 124

Batchelor, Frank, 60, 83

Bate, William, 50, 56, 57, 164, 184, 252, 271–72, 292

Beard, William K., 65

Beatty Samuel, 81, 82

Beatty, Taylor, 99, 159, 170, 238

Beauregard, Armand, 197

Beauregard, P. G. T., 14, 17, 20, 45, 59, 62, 64, 66, 69, 102, 137, 247; arrives in West, 12; commands Army of the Mississippi, 28–29, 32; commands Military Division of the West, 313, 315–16, 318–19; increasing influence of, 19; meets J. E. Johnston, 16; relieved of command, 33; at Shiloh, 21–23; withdraws from Corinth, 30–32

Beckworth, John J., 242

Bell, Alfred W., 83, 134

Benham, Calhoun, 144, 270

Benjamin, Judah P., 248, 296

Bennett, W. T., 150

Berryhill, William, 312, 317

Bigbee, Thomas, 125, 133, 136, 138

Blackford, Charles M., 263

Blakemore, George, 34

Blythe, Andrew, 7

Boles, T. H., 122

Bostick, J. L., 291

Bostick, T. H., 170

Botts, William H., 141

Bowen, John S., 24

Bradley, Luther, 320

Bradley, Michael, 168

Bragg, Braxton, 7, 14–15, 36, 55, 57, 60–61, 84, 93–103, 107, 110–11, 143, 158, 160–61, 172–77, 181, 250, 275; assumes army command, 32–33; and John C. Breckinridge, 195–99; at Chickamauga, 187–92; confronts his generals, 89–93; deteriorating health of, 159, 162; enlisted men's views of, 82–83, 170, 241; and Forrest, 104, 230; initiates strict disci-

302; and J. E. Johnston, 294; at Kolb's Farm, 293; and North Georgia Campaign, 313–15; at Peachtree Creek, 298–99; and Tennessee Campaign, 316–25

Hood, Stephen, 321

Hooker, Joseph, 192, 240

Hoover's Gap, 89, 98, 158, 163–66

Hsieh, Wayne Wei-Siang, 27, 297, 302

Hudson, John, 146

Huffmaster, Isaiah, 60

Huger, Frank, 263

Hulbert, Stephen A., 23

Hundley, Daniel, 132, 252

Hunt, Thomas, 55

Hurley, John R., 217, 222

Inglis, John, 130, 155

Irwin, Robert, 137

Island No. 10, 13, 27, 30, 37

Ives, Joseph Christmas, 244

Ives, Washington, 130, 232, 242

Jackman, John, 75, 292

Jackson, Andrew, III, 2

Jackson, Henry R., 252

Jackson, John K., 24, 50, 236, 241

Jackson, William H., 110–12, 160

Jacobson, Eric, 320

James, J. A., 243

Jamison, Robert, 124, 139, 142

Jenkins, Robert D., 211

Jenkins, Micah, 232

Johnson, Bushrod, 1, 2, 123, 156, 195

Johnson, Richard, 165, 184

Johnson, Robert W., 86

Johnston, Albert Sidney, 7, 15, 19, 25, 35, 37, 66, 67, 87; meets Beauregard, 16; Fort Donelson mistakes, 17; criticism of, 18; at Shiloh, 21–24

Johnston, Joseph E., 12, 14, 67, 70, 74, 76, 85, 86, 87–88, 92, 93–100, 108, 111, 129–30, 159–60, 172, 240, 298, 305, 307; appointed Army of Tennessee commander, 247–48; appointed western theater commander, 87; arrives in Dalton, 250; in Atlanta Campaign, 285–98; background of, 46, 249; and Cleburne's proposal, 271–72; instills discipline, 258–61; and western strategy, 253–54

Johnston, Josiah Stoddard, 66, 86, 161

Johnston, William Preston, 20, 25, 32, 35, 36, 44, 66, 85, 87, 98–99, 196

Jones, Archer, 51, 76

Jones, George, 136, 141, 247

Jones, John, 44, 45, 84

Jones, O. H., 207

Jones, Samuel, 49

Jones, William P., 65, 117, 194

Jordan, Thomas, 23, 62, 64, 65

Kean, Robert, 44, 86, 87, 88

Kelly, Daniel, 154, 305

Kelly, J. H., 271

Kelly, T. B., 309

Kennedy, Robert, 141

Kentucky, fails to support South, 14–15, 37, 326–27

Kentucky Campaign, 8, 36–43, 91, 94, 159

Kentucky units
2nd Cavalry, 109
6th Infantry, 126, 133
9th Infantry, 108, 119, 160

Kern, J. T., 265, 309

Kershaw, Joseph, 190

Key, Thomas, 130, 240, 250, 255, 260, 271, 280, 310, 317, 322–23

Kimmell, Manning M., 111

King, John, 182

Knighton, Josiah, 30

Kolb's Farm, battle of, 293

24th Infantry, 315
Douglas's Battery, 143
Thomas, George, 66, 165, 166, 175, 234, 315, 323
Thomas, Isham, 136, 268
Thompson, Edwin Porter, 87
Thompson, Elijah, J.,127
Thompson, Jacob, 25
Thompson, William, 140
Thompson Station, engagement at, 112
Thornton, P. F., 200
Thurman, Susan, 281
Tillman, J. A., 312
Trabue, Robert P., 91
Trapier, James, 55
Trask, William L., 38, 226
Treadwell, E. W., 120, 122
Tucker, W. F., 107, 313
Tullahoma Campaign, 162–71
Turchin, John, 168

Urquhart, David, 23, 24, 50, 66, 91, 92, 94, 161, 241

Van Cleve, Horatio, 183
Van Deveer, Ferdinand, 182
Vandiver, Frank, 317
Van Dorn, Earl, 27, 37, 43, 98, 103, 111–14, 147, 217
Van Dorn's army, 28, 36, 37
Vaughn, A. J., 80, 144
Vicksburg, Miss., surrender of, 170–71
Virginia units
54th Infantry, 128, 227
63rd Infantry, 227

Wade, William B., 245
Wagner, George D., 177
Walker, Irvine, 58, 77, 83, 116, 128, 131, 151–52, 170, 275
Walker, John J., 68–69, 215, 217
Walker, LeRoy, 3, 69

Walker, Lucius M., 56
Walker, Marshal, 15
Walker, W. H. T., 50, 178, 188, 195, 234, 250, 271–72, 274, 306
Wallace, Lew, 24
Walls, Milton, 282
Walter, Harvey W., 65, 198
Walthall, Edwin C., 50, 56, 58, 96, 178
Ward, Edward, 146
Ward, J. W., 315
Warren, George, 314
Warrick, Thomas, 83, 122, 128, 144, 151, 304
Watson, Clement, 34
Watson, Robert, 196, 231
Weaver, Daniel, 224
Weaver, Jacob, 156
Webb, James D., 20
Webb, Thomas, 110, 147
Webster, Rowena, 54
Weitz, Mark, 5, 10, 121
Welch, L. B., 324
Western & Atlantic Railroad, 223–26, 313
western theater, 11
Wharton, John A., 56, 77, 81, 105, 111–12, 133, 170, 172, 179, 245, 253
Wheeler, Joseph E., 9, 50, 67, 78, 98, 106–7, 111–12, 164, 167–68, 172, 214, 253; in Atlanta Campaign, 300; background of, 103; as Bragg's protégé, 104; at Chickamauga, 191; criticism of, 105,179, 245
Whitfield, John, 111
Whiting, Jasper S., 63
Wigfall, Louis, 86, 94, 97, 248, 251, 296
Wilder, John T., 42, 111, 164, 190
Wiley, William B., 60
Williams, J. Mimmick, 113
Williams, T. Harry, 317
Williamson, James A., 60, 288
Williamson, Sue, 54
Wilson, Claudius C., 124